In memory of my parents,
Carl and Fredericka Teiwes

POLITICS AND PURGES IN CHINA

"A classic of its genre just got better. Teiwes's timely revision ensures that *Politics and Purges* will remain an essential part of every Sinologist's reference collection."

Richard Baum,
University of California, Los Angeles

"*Politics and Purges* provides a major contribution to our understanding of the pre-Cultural Revolution politics in China and its re-publication is a most welcome event. It is all the more welcome because of the lucid new introduction that provides a masterful reassessment of Teiwes's own earlier views and those of other recent scholarship. The main conclusion still stands that politics in the period 1949–1965 should be understood in terms of a dominant Mao rather than 'two-line' struggle or the various western permutations of this Chinese formulation.

"The new introduction reveals even more strongly a politics at 'Mao's Court' in which senior leaders try to second guess Mao, adjust their preferences to his desires, and try to exploit his ambiguities to advance bureaucratic and political interests. This new introduction offers an admirable model for how the new sources and interviews with Chinese scholars and participants can bring Chinese politics to life by helping us to understand better the motivations of individual players in the political process. Taken together, the original book and the new introduction are a powerful *tour de force* that will ensure that this remains the standard work covering the period."

Tony Saich,
University of Leiden

Politics/Asia

Studies on Contemporary China

THE POLITICAL ECONOMY OF CHINA'S SPECIAL ECONOMIC ZONES
George T. Crane

WORLDS APART
RECENT CHINESE WRITING AND ITS AUDIENCES
Howard Goldblatt, editor

CHINESE URBAN REFORM
WHAT MODEL NOW?
R. Yin-Wang Kwok, William L. Parish, and Anthony Gar-on Yeh with Xu Xuequang, editors

REBELLION AND FACTIONALISM IN A CHINESE PROVINCE
ZHEJIANG, 1966–1976
Keith Forster

POLITICS AT MAO'S COURT
GAO GANG AND PARTY FACTIONALISM IN THE EARLY 1950s
Fredrick C. Teiwes

MOLDING THE MEDIUM
THE CHINESE COMMUNIST PARTY AND THE LIBERATION DAILY
Patricia Stranahan

THE MAKING OF A SINO-MARXIST WORLD VIEW
PERCEPTIONS AND INTERPRETATIONS OF WORLD HISTORY IN THE PEOPLE'S REPUBLIC OF CHINA
Dorothea A.L. Martin

POLITICS OF DISILLUSIONMENT
THE CHINESE COMMUNIST PARTY UNDER DENG XIAOPING, 1978–1989
Hsi-sheng Ch'i

CONQUERING RESOURCES
THE GROWTH AND DECLINE OF THE PLA'S SCIENCE AND TECHNOLOGY COMMISSION FOR NATIONAL DEFENSE
Benjamin C. Ostrov

THE PARADOX OF POWER IN A PEOPLE'S REPUBLIC OF CHINA MIDDLE SCHOOL
Martin Schoenhals

CHINA'S ECONOMIC DILEMMAS IN THE 1990s
THE PROBLEMS OF REFORMS, MODERNIZATION, AND INDEPENDENCE
Edited by the Joint Economic Committee, Congress of the United States

CHINA IN THE ERA OF DENG XIAOPING
A DECADE OF REFORM
Michael Ying-mao Kau and Susan H. Marsh, editors

DOMESTIC LAW REFORMS IN POST-MAO CHINA
Pittman B. Potter, editor

POLITICS AND PURGES IN CHINA
RECTIFICATION AND THE DECLINE OF PARTY NORMS, 1950–1965
Frederick C. Teiwes

MORNING SUN
INTERVIEWS WITH POST-MAO CHINESE WRITERS
Laifong Leung

CHINESE FIRMS AND THE STATE IN TRANSITION
PROPERTY RIGHTS AND AGENCY PROBLEMS IN THE REFORM ERA
Keun Lee

THE MARKET MECHANISM AND ECONOMIC REFORMS IN CHINA
William A. Byrd

CHINA, THE UNITED STATES, AND THE SOVIET UNION
TRIPOLARITY AND POLICY-MAKING IN THE COLD WAR
Robert S. Ross, editor

AMERICAN STUDIES OF CONTEMPORARY CHINA
David Shambaugh, editor

Studies on Contemporary China

POLITICS AND PURGES IN CHINA

RECTIFICATION AND THE DECLINE OF PARTY NORMS, 1950-1965

SECOND EDITION

FREDERICK C. TEIWES

An East Gate Book

Routledge
Taylor & Francis Group
LONDON AND NEW YORK

An East Gate Book

First published 1993 by M.E. Sharpe

Published 2015 by Routledge

2 Park Square, Milton Park, Abingdon, Oxon OX14 4RN
711 Third Avenue, New York, NY 10017, USA

Routledge is an imprint of the Taylor & Francis Group, an informa business

Library of Congress Cataloging-in-Publication Data

Teiwes, Frederick C.
Politics and purges in China : rectification and the decline of party norms, 1950–1965 /
Frederick C. Teiwes.—2nd ed.
p. cm.
Includes bibliographical references and index.
ISBN 1-56324-226-5 —ISBN 1-56324-227-3 (pbk.)
1. China—Politics and government—1945–
2. Chung-kuo kung ch'an tang—Purges.
DS777.55.T335 1993
951.05—dc20
93-1545
CIP

ISBN 13: 9781563242274 (pbk)
ISBN 13: 9781563242267 (hbk)

Contents

Preface to the Second Edition

After the limited run first edition of *Politics and Purges in China* quickly sold out, Douglas Merwin of M.E. Sharpe and I discussed on various occasions the possibility of a paperback edition with the aim of bringing the book to a larger audience. While I was disappointed that commercial and technical considerations prevented this from happening, as is so often the case this disappointment turned out to be a blessing in disguise. With the passage of time a rich vein of new material has become available which allows both a reevaluation of the arguments of *Politics and Purges* and a deeper understanding of the processes behind the events examined in the book. I am grateful to Doug for reviving the project at a time when new insights are possible, and I have attempted both to reexamine and extend the earlier analyses of the pre-Cultural Revolution period in the lengthy introduction to this second edition.

Of all the people contributing to the new section of this volume, one stands out. Warren Sun not only provided the tireless wide ranging services normally thought of as research assistance, he also repeatedly engaged me on points of interpretation, made fruitful suggestions on where the original draft manuscript could be expanded and deepened, and in countless ways helped me refine my understanding of the events and processes under study. I am deeply appreciative of his help.

A number of other people assisted in various ways. Lucien Bianco, Anita Chan, Timothy Cheek, Bruce Dickson, Keith Forster, David Goodman, Carol Hamrin, Nancy Hearst, Bruce Jacobs, Roderick MacFarquhar, Mary Mazur, Tony Saich, Susan Shirk, K. K. Shum, Dorothy Solinger and Graham Young provided comments on the draft and/or generously shared their own research findings or sources. Thanks are due them all.

As will quickly become apparent to readers of the new portion of this edition, an enormous debt is owed to numerous Chinese scholars who provided important data on and much insight into the political history of the People's Republic. As in other recent research, I have been profoundly impressed with their generosity, care and candor in discussing difficult intellectual issues under sometimes problematic circumstances. It is difficult to express the depth of my gratitude to these men and women who necessarily must remain anonymous.

Significant support was provided by the University of Sydney's Department of Government and its staff. Lyn Fisher, as so often in the past, gave efficient and prompt research assistance, Kathy Dempsey both indexed the new introduction to this edition and adjusted the original index to the present format, and Roz Conyngham, Wilma Sharp (from the University though not the Department) and especially Isobel Horton prepared the manuscript. At M.E. Sharpe, in addition to Doug Merwin's support for the project, Aud Thiessen and Angela Pilioura addressed the complex technical questions involved in producing the new edition.

I gratefully acknowledge the financial support of the Australian Research Council, the University of Sydney's overseas travel grant program, and the Ian Potter Foundation. In particular, the generous funding of the Australian Research Council provided the resources without which the substantial new research going into this edition would not have been possible.

Finally, no acknowledgment of support would be complete without a mention of my family. As always, Kathi, Inge and Jack sustained my spirits throughout, while recognition of the love and nurture of my father and mother has been especially deeply felt as this project was completed. It is to their memory that this volume is dedicated.

Frederick C. Teiwes
Sydney
January 1992

Preface to the First Edition

This study has evolved from a doctoral dissertation undertaken at Columbia University in the mid-1960s to the version finally emerging in the late 1970s and presented here. Over this period many people have provided help and support in various ways, for which I am deeply appreciative.

Four individuals require special mention. A. Doak Barnett, my mentor, drew me to the study of Chinese politics, saw the potential for a larger study in a graduate research paper, and provided warm encouragement and guidance as my dissertation supervisor. Michel Oksenberg, first as a fellow graduate student, then as second reader of the thesis, provided a constant flow of trenchant criticism which forced me to refine my ideas and tighten my arguments. Roderick MacFarquhar was not only extremely generous with his comments on the manuscript and particularly with his personal research materials, but in addition his book, *The Origins of the Cultural Revolution,* contributed inestimably to my understanding of the 1956–57 period both in terms of new information and challenging interpretations. Indeed, my own account of the period can be viewed in part as a friendly dialogue with *Origins.* Finally, Richard Baum shared a first encounter with the 1962–65 period over a decade ago in our collaboration on *Ssu-Ch'ing: The Socialist Education Movement,* a collaboration valuable both in terms of research vistas opened up and intellectual stimulation as we both grappled with what remains an obscure period. Since then, on the basis of new evidence, we have both arrived at differing reinterpretations of the Socialist Education Movement and, as with MacFarquhar's book, my version owes much to the research and insights of Baum's *Prelude to Revolution.*

In addition, I am particularly grateful to Gordon Bennett and David Denny for repeated close criticism of portions of the manuscript. Comments and/or research data which have strengthened the study were also contributed by Parris Chang, John Fincher, Thomas Fingar, Lois Hager, Alex Ikonnikov, Ellis Joffe, Con

Kiriloff, Donald Klein, Hong Yung Lee, Kenneth Lieberthal, Robert F. Miller, Peter Moody, Pierre Ryckmans, Mark Selden, Richard Sorich, Wang Gungwu and Michael Yahuda. I thank them all for their help.

Research assistance was provided by many people, most significantly by Kam Chak-yee and Wong Yuk-lam in Hong Kong in 1967, and by Lam Lai-sing in Canberra from 1974 to 1976. Others who provided research aid at various times are Florence Deeley, Lau Yee-fui, Tanaka Kyoko, Teng Hua and Ka-che Yip. Assistance in preparing earlier drafts of the manuscript was provided by Shari Heinrich, Marcia Milnes and Sandra Donnelly. The version which appears on the following pages was jointly produced by Sylvia Krietsch and Wilma Sharp.

Mary Ann O'Loughlin toiled with good humor to produce the bibliography and index. During the dissertation phase, Shari Heinrich provided invaluable editorial assistance in helping shape an unruly monster into a passable product. In recent years, when I was on the verge of despair over finding a publisher for a study of this length, Mervyn Adams Seldon was a repeated source of encouragement and advice. Finally, I am grateful to Douglas Merwin for taking the initiative which resulted in the study appearing in its present form.

Financial assistance is thankfully acknowledged from the following sources: the Fulbright-Hays Fellowship Program, Columbia University's East Asian Institute and Research Institute on Communist Affairs, the China Program of Cornell University, the Contemporary China Centre of The Australian National University, and the Department of Government and University Research Committee of the University of Sydney. In addition, the unique services and facilities of the Universities Service Centre, Hong Kong, made possible a fruitful year of research in 1966–67.

The following institutions have given me permission to reprint material:

1. The Contemporary China Institute, School of Oriental and African Studies, to quote from "The Purge of Provincial Leaders 1957–1958," *The China Quarterly,* No. 27 (1966); and "The Origins of Rectification: Inner-Party Purges and Education before Liberation," *The China Quarterly,* No. 65 (1976).

2. The Regents of the University of California to quote from *Ssu-Ch'ing: The Socialist Education Movement of 1962–1966,* Center for Chinese Studies, Berkeley, China Research Monographs No. 2, 1968; and "Liu Shao-ch'i and the Cadre Question," *Asian Survey,* April 1968.

3. The Contemporary China Centre, The Australian National University, to quote from *Elite Discipline in China: Coercive and Persuasive Approaches to Rectification, 1950–1953,* Contemporary China Papers No. 12, 1978.

Finally, special thanks to Kathi and Inge for providing much joy during the hectic struggle to complete the long, arduous task.

Frederick C. Teiwes
Sydney
December 1978

Abbreviations

Organizations and Policies

APC	Agricultural Producers' Cooperative
CCP	Chinese Communist Party
CDL	China Democratic League
CPPCC	Chinese People's Political Consultative Conference
FFYP	First Five Year Plan
GAC	Government Administrative Council
GMD	Guomindang
GPD	General Political Department
MAC	Military Affairs Committee
NPC	National People's Congress
PLA	People's Liberation Army
PLMPA	Poor and Lower Middle Peasant Association
PRC	People's Republic of China
SPC	State Planning Commission

Publications and Publishing Agencies

AJCA	*The Australian Journal of Chinese Affairs*
CB	*Current Background*
CJRB	*Changjiang ribao* [Yangtze Daily]
CLG	*Chinese Law and Government*
CNA	*China News Analysis*
CNS	*China News Summary*
CQ	*The China Quarterly*
DBRB	*Dongbei ribao* [Northeast Daily]

DGB	*Dagong bao* [Impartial Daily]
DZRB	*Dazhong ribao* [Masses Daily]
ECMM	*Extracts from China Mainland Magazines*
FBIS	*Foreign Broadcast Information Service: Communist China*
GMRB	*Guangming ribao* [Guangming Daily]
GRRB	*Gongren ribao* [Workers' Daily]
HF	*The Hundred Flowers*
HQ	*Hongqi* [Red Flag]
JFJB	*Jiefangjun bao* [Liberation Army Daily]
JFRB	*Jiefang ribao* [Liberation Daily]
JPRS	*Joint Publications Research Service*
MMT	*Miscellany of Mao Tse-tung Thought*
MP	*Mao Papers: Anthology and Bibliography*
MU	*Mao Tse-tung Unrehearsed, Talks and Letters: 1956–71*
NCNA	New China News Agency
NFCPRS	*News from Chinese Provincial Radio Stations*
NFRB	*Nanfang ribao* [Southern Daily]
PDA	*Communist China 1955–1959: Policy Documents with Analysis*
RMRB	*Renmin ribao* [People's Daily]
RMSC	*Renmin shouce* [People's Handbook]
SC	*Ssu-Ch'ing: The Socialist Education Movement of 1962–1966*
SCMM	*Selections from China Mainland Magazines*
SCMM-S	*Selections from China Mainland Magazines—Supplement*
SCMP	*Survey of China Mainland Press*
SCMP-S	*Survey of China Mainland Press—Supplement*
SSSC	*Shishi shouce* [Current Events Handbook]
SW	*Selected Works of Mao Tse-tung*
SXWS	*Mao Zedong sixiang wansui* [Long Live Mao Zedong's Thought]
URS	*Union Research Service*
WHB	*Wenhui bao* [Wenhui Daily]
XHBYK	*Xinhua banyuekan* [New China Semi-Monthly]
XHRB	*Xinhua ribao* [New China Daily]
XHYB	*Xinhua yuebao* [New China Monthly]
XX	*Xuexi* [Study]
YCWB	*Yangcheng wanbao* [Yangcheng Evening Paper]
ZGQN	*Zhongguo qingnian* [Chinese Youth]
ZGQNB	*Zhongguo qingnian bao* [Chinese Youth Daily]
ZZXX	*Zhengzhi xuexi* [Political Study]

Introduction to the Second Edition

Politics and Purges in China was basically written during the lifetime of Mao Zedong, with the final editing and conclusion finished just after the epochal Third Plenum of December 1978.[1] In the intervening period much has changed in the People's Republic of China (PRC) as a result of the reform policies growing out of the Third Plenum. Besides the multifaceted impact on the lives of the Chinese people, the post-1978 changes have also involved a significant enhancement of the quantity and quality of available sources which have allowed scholars, both foreign and Chinese, far greater access to detailed information on Chinese politics and given them reason to reconsider their earlier analyses and conceptualizations of political processes in the PRC. While the new edition of *Politics and Purges* presents the same text as the 1979 version, this new introduction offers some reflections on the interpretations and arguments of the book which have been stimulated by the materials that have become available over the past dozen plus years.

Politics and Purges can be read at three levels—as an analysis of rectification campaigns and high level elite purges during the 1950–65 period, including an attempt to delineate and explain patterns and variations; as a broader examination of the norms shaping inner Party life generally and their decline in the pre-Cultural Revolution period; and as a major reinterpretation of key developments in and the nature of elite conflict at the Politburo level from 1949 to 1965. In all of these senses, but most particularly as a general reinterpretation of pre-1966 PRC politics, the book provided detailed evidence to undermine the influential "two-line struggle" model of Chinese politics in favor of a dominant Mao interpretation, thus supporting my earlier more thematic statement of this approach.[2] From the perspective of more than a decade later, I believe that both new data and subsequent developments broadly support the arguments of the book at all three levels, and none more so than its rejection of "two line struggle." This, of course, does not mean that there are no errors of fact or interpretation in *Politics and Purges*; indeed, in one case—that of the purge of Gao Gang and Rao Shushi (see below)—they were of major importance. At the same time, the new data and perspectives of the post-1978 period provide the basis for some adjustments of interpretation in other cases and new insights into the texture of Chinese elite politics, i.e., the political culture of the top leadership generally, as well as a richer understanding of particular events. I shall explore these new departures in the belief that fundamentally they supplement rather than contradict *Politics and Purges*.

As indicated, there has been no attempt to revise the first edition despite the flood of new information. This is not simply because the magnitude of the effort required to evaluate and incorporate the new data comprehensively into a revised version is beyond my current research agenda, but it is also due to the belief on the basis of a general reading of the new material that the broad analysis is unlikely to be altered by more intensive research. For the purposes of this introduction, however, such intensive investigations have been made into a number of key issues emerging from the book. In addition to the results of these investigations discussed below, relevant further argumentation and evidence can be obtained by reading *Politics and Purges* in conjunction with my two subsequent books, *Leadership, Legitimacy, and Conflict in China* (1984) and *Politics at Mao's Court* (1990).[3] The former is a collection of essays which in broad thematic terms deal with some of the key issues that were, in a sense, left dangling by *Politics and Purges*: What was the basis of Mao's dominance of elite politics, what dilemmas did this dominance pose for other Chinese Communist Party (CCP) leaders as they confronted the contradictions between normative Party rules and "prudential rules," i.e., the requirements of political survival, what were the dynamics of leadership conflict in the last decade of Mao's rule, and how were elite conflict and Party norms manifested in the politics of the initial post-Mao and early reform periods? *Politics at Mao's Court*, by contrast, is a detailed reinterpretation of the one case where *Politics and Purges* got the story significantly wrong. It reexamines the Gao Gang-Rao Shushi case of 1953–54 using a wide array of new documentary sources as well as extensive interviews with Chinese scholars and officials, and corrects the errors of Chapter 5 of this book which, nevertheless, still contains much useful information and not a few valid analyses. Of equal importance, *Politics at Mao's Court* is a case *par excellence* of the above mentioned enhanced insight into the texture of elite politics made possible by post-1978 sources.

The remainder of this new introduction discusses the light shed on specific analyses of *Politics and Purges* by the sources of the reform era. After a brief consideration of the general issue of Mao's dominance, I elaborate the changes necessary in the analysis of the Gao-Rao case, and then examine a number of other important developments from the Hundred Flowers experiment to the eve of the Cultural Revolution where modifications are required, or where particularly contentious interpretations of *Politics and Purges* have been bolstered by new data. The discussion then turns to an examination of a number of key questions concerning the CCP's normative regime and the texture of elite politics before the Cultural Revolution. In this context special attention is given to the issue of how significant official norms were for the participants in Chinese politics and especially to the recurrent tension between the norms and the requirements of political practice. Related to this, I conclude with an examination of a number of textural features of leadership politics which are not only distinctive of the Chinese system but are also ambiguously related to the CCP's formal norms.

Politics, Purges and Rectification, 1949–1965: Confirmation and Reevaluation

When *Politics and Purges* was written it went directly against the grain of both the official CCP view of elite politics and the predominant trend in Western scholarship. This, of course, was the "two-line struggle" interpretation—usually translated into social science terminology in the West—which posited an ongoing and often sharp conflict between Chairman Mao Zedong and various powerful colleagues in the Party hierarchy over general ideological orientation and a wide range of specific policy issues. In many such interpretations, moreover, this involved a finely balanced contest with Mao sometimes in retreat before a victorious coalition of opponents. In contrast, the story told in *Politics and Purges*, on the basis of detailed investigation into some of the critical events of the 1949–65 period, portrayed a Mao who dominated his colleagues. This did not mean that the Chairman was totally "in command" since, like all politicians, he had to respond to events and circumstances beyond his control, and because some of his major projects led to unanticipated and counterproductive results which on occasion left him confused as to the desirable course of action. But what it did mean was that in any elite debate, when Mao chose to assert himself, he got his way. The Chairman was the pivot of leadership politics, and the nature of conflict had much more to do with winning Mao over to one's favored position than with opposing him. Opposing Mao in the policy sense—once Mao's position was clear—was rare; opposing Mao in the political sense was unheard of.

Since 1978 official CCP history has adopted a view remarkably close to that argued in *Politics and Purges*. "Two line struggle" has been rejected, and many of the specific propositions of the book have been tacitly or explicitly endorsed. But while it is possible to draw pleasure from such confirmation, it of course cannot be considered conclusive since Party history in the reform era is still official history and therefore subject to various restrictions and motivated—at least in part—by the objective of sustaining a particular point of view. Nevertheless, it is clear to all serious scholars that the historiography and materials of the reform period have been far more reliable and balanced than what was available during Mao's reign both before and during the Cultural Revolution. More important than the official rejection of "two line struggle" is the vast amount of new documentary evidence which provides detailed support for the general picture. In addition, I am particularly impressed with the information and interpretations given by Chinese scholars during interviews and discussions.[4] In my experience, these scholars, who in not a few cases have been willing to deal with sensitive subjects in unorthodox ways, have lent overwhelming backing to the dominant Mao thesis. If anything, I am led to conclude that *Politics and Purges* slightly understated the degree to which Mao dominated his colleagues. This, however, still leaves my interpretation in conflict with much recent scholarship in the West. While "two line struggle" has been jettisoned as an explicit mode of analysis, there is still a strong tendency to interpret pre-Cultural Revolution politics in terms of opposition to Mao rather than as adjustments to the Chairman which, in my view, the evidence increasingly demonstrates was the case.

Gao Gang and Rao Shushi

Ironically, the dominance of Mao is particularly borne out in the case where *Politics and Purges* was wide of the mark—the purge of Politburo member and State Planning Commission (SPC) head Gao Gang and Party organization department chief Rao Shushi for factional activities designed to split the Party. This becomes apparent through an examination of the differences between the interpretation published in 1979 and my present understanding as detailed in *Politics at Mao's Court* and further supported by new sources which have subsequently become available, most notably the recollections of one of the central figures of the affair, Bo Yibo.5 The major conclusions of the earlier analysis reproduced in Chapter 5 below were: (1) despite charges that Gao established an "independent kingdom" in the Northeast, regionalism was not a major factor in his purge as his Northeast region had not been beyond the effective control of the central authorities; (2) while Gao had good relations with the Soviet leadership and particularly Stalin, those relations were not a major aspect of his activities or a precipitating factor in his fall; (3) policy issues played a secondary role at best in the efforts of Gao and Rao who did not put forward a coherent policy program; (4) the main factional appeal used by Gao Gang—an attempt to fan the resentment of army leaders against those with "white area" or underground careers during the revolutionary period, especially Liu Shaoqi and Zhou Enlai—was poorly conceived and had limited impact; (5) the key circumstantial factor in the situation was Mao's poor health which led Gao to begin maneuvers for a possible succession struggle aimed at Liu and Zhou; and (6) overall, the effort of Gao and Rao was marked by inept politics and was easily beaten back with only minimal damage to Party unity.

The new materials available since 1979 necessitate the following observations concerning the above conclusions. The first two conclusions substantially hold. Regionalism and the Soviet factor, while playing a tangential role in the affair, were by no means central to the purge. The third conclusion on the comparatively minor role of policy also retains some validity, but Gao and Rao openly raised policy issues as a significant part of their activities. Moreover, the general policy debates of the period were an essential factor shaping the attitudes of key figures in the drama, none more so than those of Mao. The fourth and sixth conclusions must be substantially revised; the effort to manipulate tensions between "red" and "white" area cadres was far more potent than originally believed, and Gao made considerably more headway than previously seemed likely—even though the activities of Gao and Rao can in many respects still be considered inept. Finally, Mao's health, although somewhat poor in this period and relevant to the unfolding events, was not a precipitating cause of Gao's activities.[6] Instead, what set Gao in motion was several personal discussions with Mao during late 1952-early 1953 in which the Chairman indicated dissatisfaction with Liu Shaoqi and Zhou Enlai.[7] Rightly or wrongly, Gao interpreted these conversations as providing an opportunity to displace Liu and himself become Mao's successor.

The last factor—Mao's conversations with Gao and other clear if indirect expressions of dissatisfaction with Liu and Zhou—are crucial not only for launching the entire affair but for demonstrating the dynamic of elite politics that prevailed throughout: other leaders consistently reacted to Mao's positions or perceived preferences, hung on his often ambiguous words, and anticipated his moves and objectives. The centrality of Mao's position was clearly reflected in the precipitating case of the new tax policies formulated by one of Liu's closest "factional" associates, Minister of Finance Bo Yibo, and endorsed by Premier Zhou Enlai.[8] This issue, which was erroneously treated as having no relationship to the Gao-Rao affair in *Politics and Purges*, emerged during the period of Mao's private conservations with Gao Gang. The hastily constructed new tax system, which sought to solve the problem of securing adequate state revenues at a time when ownership was shifting to the state sector, was promulgated on December 31, 1952, and immediately caused a political storm. In part, this was due to the practical consequences of the new regulations which increased the tax burden of state enterprises and also decreased their profits, the latter development producing considerable conflict with local leaders who depended on state sector profits for their revenue. But the greater vulnerability was the result of local protests coming to the attention of Mao who focussed on two rather different aspects of the situation. In a mid-January 1953 letter to Zhou, Bo and others Mao complained that the new tax system had not been discussed by the Party Center and that he only became aware of it through the newspapers. The Chairman's displeasure had an immediate impact—Zhou responded the same night, while Bo quickly called a meeting of the government's Financial and Economic Committee in a state of "half serious concern and half bewilderment." In particular, Bo regarded Mao's comment that he only read of the matter in the newspapers a grave matter. While Mao apparently had not been consulted because the issue had been regarded as a concrete government question not requiring his attention, once raised by the Chairman it set off alarm bells at the highest levels.[9]

The second vulnerable point was an ideological one raised shortly thereafter when, during a briefing of the Politburo by representatives of Bo's Finance Ministry and other central departments in February, Mao sharply criticized the tax system's key principle of "equality between public and private enterprises" as a "right opportunist" mistake violating the overall course of Party policy laid down by the Central Committee in early 1949.[10] The Chairman's sensitivity on this point must be seen in the context of discussions which had been underway since the latter part of 1952 on the formulation of a "general line for the transition to socialism." In this situation where Mao sought ways to push forward the development of the socialist system, a program placing the bourgeoisie and the state on equal footing for tax purposes was seen by the Chairman as raising serious political questions which he now placed on center stage for much of the remainder of the year. This concern, moreover, dovetailed with his dissatisfaction over a number of past cases involving Liu Shaoqi such as the famous 1949 Tianjin talks where Liu downplayed socialist objectives to sooth capitalist fears at the time of communist takeover. Although Mao had actually concurred in some of these instances, they now seemingly grated given the new emphasis on the transition to socialism with the result that his discontent became known within the top elite and, to some greater or lesser degree, was conveyed to Gao Gang in their private talks.[11]

The joining of the tax issue to Mao's more generalized concerns about the transition to socialism created a degree of uncertainty within the leadership in which the Gao-Rao affair took shape. Even more than Mao's letter complaining about not being informed about the new system, the Chairman's sharp handling of the ideological issue left Bo Yibo in a state of shock. But while the matter was widely viewed within the leadership as a serious mistake on Bo's part, it does not appear to have produced extreme tension before the middle of the year. Gao Gang, however, fortified by his conversations with Mao seemingly saw the situation as one where Liu and Zhou had lost Mao's trust which therefore presented an opportunity to change the leadership pecking order and himself become the CCP's main leader under the Chairman. In this he was encouraged not only by the tax issue and Mao's other discontents with Liu and Zhou, but by his own substantially enhanced status since arriving in the capital in late 1952. In addition to his posting as head of the SPC, administrative reorganizations in the first half of 1953 gave Gao broad authority over many of the key sectors of the economy while at the same time reducing Zhou's role and thus reflecting Mao's displeasure with the Premier and the alleged "dispersionism" of his government apparatus. This development, which clearly indicated Mao's high evaluation of Gao, not only fed Gao's own assessment of his expanding power but added further uncertainties within the leadership as a whole. While the possible significance of Gao's enhanced position was unclear, the fact of Mao's regard for him and that he of all the regional leaders transferred to Beijing in 1952–53 was destined to play the most influential role—a perception reflected in the saying that "five horses have entered the capital led by one horse"—was widely known. In the context of Mao's dissatisfaction with Liu and Zhou it could only create tension, however suppressed for the moment.[12]

The uncertainty gave way to conflict at the National Conference on Financial and Economic Work from mid-June to mid-August. Apart from factional appeals behind the scenes (see below), the key development was the treatment of the tax issue at the conference—a process which largely reflected Mao's actions and perceived preferences. While initially the conference had been planned as a routine gathering, under the circumstances created by the new tax system it changed into a major meeting under the direction of Zhou Enlai. Nevertheless, the meeting seemingly proceeded in a fairly normal manner for four weeks until, on the evening of July 11, Mao directed that a leadership small group meeting be convened and that Bo make a self-examination before it. While this, in Bo's recollection, was designed to bring out into the open harsh criticism which Gao and others had been making in group meetings, it also clearly reflected Mao's view that Bo's errors were serious and must be struggled against. When the leadership group meeting convened on July 13 it was, as Bo remembered, a "turning point"; the atmosphere suddenly turned tense and Bo was subjected to eight criticism sessions over the next two weeks with Gao Gang taking a prominent role in depicting Bo's errors as a question of political line, and using the criticism of Bo to attack indirectly Liu Shaoqi. Bo was then required to undertake a second self-criticism which, after nervously requesting a delay, he gave on August 1. This effort, however, was considered insufficient and not passed leaving Bo full of doubts and the meeting in a state of disarray.[13]

While Mao's ideological concerns had set the stage for Bo's ordeal, the Chairman now moved to lower the tension of the meeting. Briefed by Zhou on a daily basis of developments at the conference which he rarely attended, Mao seemingly became concerned at the damage being done to Party unity and took a number of steps to repair the situation. Realizing that the overheated atmosphere made it difficult for Zhou, who was also vulnerable on the tax issue, to bring the conference to a quick conclusion, Mao suggested calling for outside help and arranged for Chen Yun, who was formally on sick leave, and Deng Xiaoping to address the conference. In their speeches Chen and Deng criticized Bo for the errors Mao had pointed out, but at the same time they moved to lessen his predicament by declaring the issues involved were not those of opposing lines. This same approach was adopted in Zhou's conference summary on August 11 which had been personally checked by Mao who deleted the most serious charges, and by the Chairman's own August 12 speech. In the same period Mao worked to cool things down further by counselling various leaders on the need for Party unity, rebutting specific accusations raised by Gao and Rao against Bo and Liu, declaring Liu selfless and honest, and (unsuccessfully) suggesting to Gao that he see Liu personally to sort out their differences. Particularly revealing was an incident at the August 9 Politburo meeting convened to discuss Zhou's summary which Mao notified Bo to attend, and when Gao critically interrupted Bo's effort to explain himself the Chairman in turn interrupted Gao with a rebuke which resulted in Gao shrinking back. The net result of Mao's actions was to defuse, but not resolve, the situation.[14]

The reason the matter was not settled definitively was that the ambiguity of Mao's position left key leaders uncertain of his intentions, a pattern which would be repeated on many occasions in the future. While the Chairman had rescued Bo Yibo, the criticism of his errors in both Zhou's summary and Mao's concluding speech remained very harsh with the result that Bo felt obliged to request his dismissal.[15] Moreover, Mao's rebuke of August 9 not withstanding, the Chairman apparently did not confront Gao over his general performance at the conference. On the contrary, Zhou Enlai's summary expressed agreement with Gao's characterization of Bo as dishonest, and while Gao ignored Mao's suggestion of seeking out Liu, Liu for his part deemed it necessary to twice go to Gao and conduct self-criticism before him. In these circumstances, Gao concluded progress had been made in undermining Liu and Zhou, and stepped up his activities. He now sought to win support for his elevation over Liu and Zhou from military cadres, and especially a number of key CCP leaders including Lin Biao, Peng Dehuai, Deng Xiaoping and Chen Yun, both during a "holiday" trip to East and Central-South China after the financial and economic conference and in Beijing. In lobbying for support Gao used a number of appeals including the promise of high positions in a Gao administration and by creating resentment among leaders with military and base area backgrounds against those like Liu and Zhou with substantial "white area" experience. In this effort he not only argued that underground cadres had a disproportionate share of power in the existing arrangements, but that they also formed a faction that was seeking unfairly to increase its representation on the new Politburo to be chosen at the Eighth Party Congress which was planned for the near future.[16] Here, significantly, Gao tried to draw on Mao's prestige by claiming that the Chairman was the representative of "red" or base area cadres while Liu was the representative of the "white areas." But undoubtedly Gao's strongest weapon was the "rumor" that Liu was no longer trusted by Mao, an assertion which surely had some credibility in the minds of other leaders given the developments of the spring and summer.[17]

The potency of these appeals was shown by the fact that a significant although indeterminate number of high ranking leaders offered varying degrees of support to Gao. Most important was the backing, albeit fairly passive, given by Lin Biao and Peng Dehuai who tellingly later sought to excuse themselves by claiming that Gao had duped them into believing that Mao had actually lost confidence in Liu.[18] The importance of perceptions of the Chairman's intentions was even more strikingly reflected in the cases of the two key leaders who did not offer backing to Gao Gang—Chen Yun and Deng Xiaoping. These leaders were apparently approached by Gao about September but only reported his activities to Mao about November after a delay of perhaps two months.[19] As an authoritative oral source put it, they had to be extremely careful in dealing with the issue since Gao might indeed represent Mao. Yet these leaders were perhaps better placed than any others to divine the Chairman's meaning. Initially, their hesitancy to back Gao arguably was related to their roles—at Mao's behest—in easing the predicament of Bo Yibo and by extension of Liu and Zhou; thus while they were well aware of Mao's dissatisfaction with Liu and Zhou they also had reason to believe that the Chairman was not prepared to take serious action against them. Moreover, when they did decide to act, it most likely came after the National Conference on Organization Work which concluded in late October. During the course of this conference Mao had become increasingly hostile to the activities of Gao's "ally," Rao Shushi, who attacked another long-term associate of Liu, deputy organization department director An Ziwen, with the assitance of Gao's subordinates in the Northeast. When Mao determined to bring these activities to a halt, as in August he dispatched Deng Xiaoping to the conference to drive the message home. Seemingly, it was the Chairman's more clear-cut position which emboldened Chen and Deng to go to Mao and reveal Gao's approaches to them.[20]

Once informed of Gao's lobbying activities, Mao apparently determined that his commitment to Party unity outweighed any ideological or personal partiality to Gao Gang, or any discontent with Liu Shaoqi or Zhou Enlai. He subsequently spread the message to other still confused leaders, sending Chen Yun to talk to Lin Biao and Deng Xiaoping to Peng Dehuai. Meanwhile Zhou Enlai and Mao himself held discussions with still other leaders so that by sometime in December virtually all support for Gao had evaporated.[21] Then, at a December Politburo meeting, Mao apparently stage-managed a situation where Gao was induced to oppose Mao's proposal that Liu Shaoqi take over while the Chairman went on holiday, an attitude which was seen as evidence of Gao's sinister designs. When Mao finally—for the first time—directly challenged Gao's activities on December 24, 1953, the "conspiracy" collapsed like a house of cards.[22]

The centrality of Mao's position in politics at the top revealed in the preceding developments did not mean that other leaders were simply reactive to the Chairman, however. These leaders had a range of responsibilities and policy preferences throughout this period and could not simply sit back and wait for Mao. They promoted their agendas and sought to nudge the Chairman toward their solutions—a game played with consummate skill throughout the Gao-Rao affair by Chen Yun in gaining Mao's backing on a number of policy issues such as bureaucratic control of the socialist transformation of the bourgeoisie and the moderation of policy toward commercial capitalists.[23] If Mao was clearly opposed to the policy preferences of another leader or group of leaders, then the prudent choice was to retreat[24]; throughout 1953 officials on different sides of various issues ranging from Bo Yibo on tax policy to Gao Gang objecting to a peaceful approach to the transformation of bourgeoisie put aside their views once the Chairman declared his position.[25] As suggested, where the Chairman had no known position or his precise preferences were unclear, there was room for initiative, but in many instances uncertainty led to temporizing and inaction. Either way, the pattern of following Mao's cues and tailoring goals and strategies to his perceived preferences was not limited to the policy and political issues of the Gao-Rao period; it can also be clearly seen in subsequent major developments throughout the pre-Cultural Revolution years.

The Hundred Flowers

A key question which could not be decided on the basis of information available when *Politics and Purges* was written and has continued to be the subject of scholarly contention is the degree of Politburo conflict over Party rectification and the Hundred Flowers movement in 1957. I argued in *Politics and Purges* that while some degree of debate in top Party bodies was likely given the innovative nature of the proposed rectification—especially criticism from non-Party bourgeois intellectuals—the existing evidence suggested that any differences were substantially contained and did not break out into polarized conflict as claimed by the dominant scholarly interpretation. This evidence, I further argued, did not present any convincing documentation that the two "opponents" of Mao's rectification singled out by Western scholarship—Liu Shaoqi and Peng Zhen—had actually argued against the Chairman's position within the Politburo although this could not be ruled out. The analysis also emphasized ambiguities in Mao's known position, and noted apparent changes in his attitude toward the role of intellectuals over the 1956–57 period. In this view shifts in Party policy followed the changes in the Chairman's perceptions.[26]

While definitive evidence is still lacking in the absence of detailed documentation on Politburo discussions,[27] this broad analysis is sustained by new information which has become available since 1978. At the most general level, one of the PRC's most authoritative Party historians told me that he had no knowledge of top leadership differences over the Hundred Flowers and expressed the opinion that "everyone followed Mao." While such an assessment is perhaps painted with too broad a brush, in my view it is barely conceivable that a major conflict within the Politburo would not be known to my source. This analysis was further supported by other well placed oral sources. Most impressive were those with access to detailed central documents from the period who strongly denied divisions within the core leadership. In their opinion, different views existed at lower levels, particularly at what was described as the deputy department head level,[28] but not in the "Central Committee." The reasons for this, they argued, was that Central Committee officials understood the complete rationale of the Hundred Flowers, while outsiders did not have this understanding and consequently worried about the effects of the unprecedented policy. Taken together, these several oral sources provide powerful backing for my low conflict argument. In addition, it is noteworthy that no post-1979 documentary source I am aware of acknowledges differences between Mao and his ranking colleagues on this issue. Of course, as with the failure of Cultural Revolution sources to cite such differences, the absence of documentation cannot prove the case but it does provide additional support for the interpretation.[29]

There is, however, one major new documentary source, a substantial number of Mao's unpublished speeches from February to April 1957 when the Chairman, to use his own term, "lobbied" for the Hundred Flowers policy.[30] These speeches confirm and provide richer detail on what was already known in 1979—the ambiguity of Mao's position and his perception of "opposition" within the Party as a whole. In particular, in these speeches the Chairman repeatedly harped on the failure of up to 90 percent of Party officials to support the policy and criticized the restrictive view published in the Central Committee's newspaper, *Renmin ribao* [People's Daily], by Chen Qitong and three other army literary critics in early January 1957. In this same period Mao extended his dissatisfaction with *Renmin ribao* and its editorial staff headed by Deng Tuo to include the paper's failure to publicize his February speech on "Contradictions." Although the Chairman worked himself up to considerable anger over the latter matter in particular, the new documentation as a whole provides yet more backing for the original interpretation of *Politics and Purges* while at the same time providing new insights into the Mao-centered political process.

In broad terms, Mao's lobbying efforts of spring 1957 were clearly designed to win over a Party membership that was confused and fearful over where the Hundred Flowers might lead, as well as uncomprehending as to why the victors of the Chinese revolution should be subjected to criticism from suspect bourgeois intellectuals. Mao's tone is generally understanding to the point of acknowledging, on one occasion, that the concerns raised were "quite logical," and his advice to officials was to lay aside their fears. When discussing the (usually) nine out of ten high ranking officials assertedly against the policy, Mao's description does not suggest opposition to him or even a focused rejection of the policy across the board, but rather a situation of considerable doubt and lack of understanding. As the Chairman put it in his "Contradictions" speech in late February, ". . . among high level cadres nine out of ten do not approve or [only] half approved, or do not understand well. [Those] who really understand, really think this policy is correct, are a minority, so there is a real need to work [at this], to work at persuading [people]."[31] Apart from this modulated view of "opposition," these speeches strongly imply, as asserted by oral sources, that any resistance did not come from the Center. Throughout spring 1957 Mao consistently depicted the Hundred Flowers as the "Center's" policy, never implying any division within the core leadership, and in mid-March he flatly asserted that "We [at the Center] have a unanimous opinion."[32] The overall picture from Mao's own statements in this period, then, is of a Party understandably confused, suspicious of the new policy, but led by a unified top leadership.

While the precise attitudes and reactions of leaders at the very top remain unknown, these new documents depict a familiar picture of lower ranking officials, including some with significant positions at the Center, attempting to figure out Mao's meaning, guide him in the direction of their policy preferences, and hesitating to act in the face of uncertainty over his precise position. Apart from perplexity caused by the inherent novelty of the Hundred Flowers experiment, confusion was further created by the ambivalences in Mao's position which is even more clearly revealed by his spring speeches than from previously available sources. Thus while the Chairman's overall determination to promote blooming and contending comes through, negative comments about intellectuals, endorsement of the need to criticize them, assertions of the existence of only two schools—the proletarian and the bourgeois, and reaffirmations of Party leadership undoubtedly added to the uncertainty.[33] Indeed, on various occasions Mao's talks were interrupted by officials wishing, as Mao observed, "to fathom what is the Center's policy at the bottom," and seeking guidance from the Chairman, a directive or the convening of a meeting that would sort things out. In some instances the concerned officials clearly sought to draw Mao toward their views, as in a March 10 exchange where an official of *Renmin ribao*, perhaps chief editor Deng Tuo, suggested that the danger of confusion from the Hundred Flowers policy argued for its delimitation. Here, as elsewhere, the overoptimistic Mao waved aside the request, effectively gave no clear guidance, and told people not to worry and consider the matter for themselves. None of this relieved anxieties, nor had the effect of maximizing momentum behind the very policies Mao favored.[34]

The specific cases preoccupying the Chairman in spring 1957 further reinforce this picture. Throughout this period Mao cited the early January article of Chen Qitong *et al.* as a dogmatist attack on the Hundred Flowers. Yet the full range of Mao's remarks indicate a more complex picture. First, as argued in *Politics and Purges*, when the article by Chen's group initially appeared, it came at a time of comparative restriction in the official attitude toward dissent in society as reflected in the late 1956 *Renmin ribao* editorial, "More on the Historical Experience of the Dictatorship of the Proletariat," an editorial fully endorsed by the Chairman at the time and even as late as mid-March although by then linked to a call for its flexible application.[35] Moreover, according to Mao, when the Chen group submitted its article, rather than acting at the behest of higher levels, they did it "without waiting for orders" and "didn't even [bother] to check it with the [central] propaganda department."[36] Again, the picture is one of deep concern, even panic at the lower levels rather than resistance organized from above. In this instance, moreover, given the recent authoritative editorial Chen and associates may have been convinced that they were supporting the Party's policy. Mao, in any case, later observed that others might plausibly have thought that their article represented the Center's opinion.[37]

Whatever the early January perceptions of the Chen group or the *Renmin ribao* editors who accepted their article, the evidence suggests Mao took a while to focus on its negative aspects. At the late January 1957 conference of provincial secretaries, Mao, by his later admission, only made a few less than totally clear side comments on the case. On that occasion, in a context where Mao's own more general remarks still had a decidedly restrictive side,[38] he praised Chen *et al.* as loyal and devoted to the Party while at the same time calling for a policy of blooming and, according to his subsequent recollection, adding the rider that their article could not serve as a guide. Subsequently the Chairman would complain mildly that reports summarizing the conference for lower levels by those who attended distorted his views by portraying him as approving the article and by omitting his qualifications.[39]

While this was arguably a case of conscious tailoring of Mao's words to suit the preferences of the officials concerned, the Chairman's lack of clarity left ample scope for such an interpretation. Moreover, even as Mao turned to a more vigorous advocacy of the Hundred Flowers in mid-February, he still muddied the waters concerning the Chen Qitong group by declaring that the standpoint of their article was good, it was OK for *Renmin ribao* to publish it, and its main "dogmatist" failings were that it was dull, oversimplified, and unconvincing. Given Mao's ambiguous record on this score, it would not be surprising if leading members of *Renmin ribao* were nonplused when the Chairman accused them of a grovelling and unclear attitude toward the article over the next few weeks when, for the first time, he declared his view that the article was wrong.[40]

If the *Renmin ribao* leadership had reason to feel uncomfortable over Mao's changing views on the Chen Qitong question, they soon received more serious expressions of his dissatisfaction with their performance. By early April he linked the Chen Qitong issue to what he saw as a deliberate policy of *Renmin ribao* not to propagate his ideas on contradictions and thus sabotage the whole Hundred Flowers effort, a belief which culminated in a particularly nasty incident when Mao furiously berated editor Deng Tuo in the Chairman's personal quarters on April 10. The responsible officials of *Renmin ribao*, however, had been faced with a complex situation where Party regulations banned publicity on and quotations from Mao's speeches before any text was published, and official procedures required a process of revision and approval of such speeches. In this case Mao himself declared his intention not to publish the late February "Contradictions" speech without revision shortly after its delivery and expressed mock horror at the consequences of issuing an unamended version. The revision process was all the more difficult given that the speech was so disorganized, unclear and plain contradictory that three complete rewritings were required before it was publicly presentable. Although the Party's daily had drawn up a plan to publicize Mao's speeches, it delayed given uncertainty as to how to proceed—an uncertainty contributed to by Mao's March 10 refusal to give specific guidelines on the Hundred Flowers policy more generally when so requested by his propagandists. This, together with the fact that as late as March 20 the Chairman spoke of launching rectification in 1958, could reasonably have led the responsible officials to conclude that a deliberate pace was not at variance with Mao's projected schedule, and that the complexities of the situation argued for caution.

While one can readily infer that the officials involved were anxious concerning the more radical implications of Mao's ideas, their hesitancy to act is most economically explained by the absence of clear orders from either the "Party Center" or from the Chairman himself.[41]

Indeed, the official of the Party Center responsible for newspaper work who was also one of Mao's leading secretaries, Hu Qiaomu, assumed some responsibility for the performance of *Renmin ribao* at the April 10 meeting in Mao's quarters by indicating that he was unsure how to handle Mao's speeches and had temporarily put the draft articles concerning them on the back burner.[42] That a figure who played such a key role in Mao's personal office, a figure sensitive to the Chairman's many moods, was also unclear concerning the proper course of action, further points to uncertainty over what Mao actually wanted as the key factor explaining the course of events. In any case, both *Renmin ribao* and the propaganda apparatus now began to publicize the Hundred Flowers heavily. While it is possible, as was done in *Politics and Purges*, to detect restrictive sentiments in some media statements throughout April and May,[43] overall the performance of the propaganda apparatus surely gave effective support to Mao's policies. For how else but through sustained organizational pressure can the large scale blooming and contending of the hitherto suspicious bourgeois intellectuals which emerged in May be explained?

In sum, the new data reviewed above suggest that in 1957 as in 1953 officials treated Mao gingerly, attempted to nudge him in their preferred direction, and, while undoubtedly using the uncertainties of the situation to press their own views, fundamentally carried out the Chairman's program once it was clearly set. The detailed evidence concerning the *Renmin ribao*, however, applies specifically to sub-Politburo officials, while the precise views of those at the very top remain obscure. Nevertheless, the overall picture remains that of *Politics and Purges*—Party officials, including his leadership colleagues, largely followed Mao without offering systematic opposition to his policies regardless of reservations they may have harbored.[44] Where the response to Mao's initiatives in spring 1957 lacked vigor, it was in large part due to the ambiguities of and uncertainty over the Chairman's own position.

Chen Yun during the Great Leap Forward

The general pattern of Mao dominance was revealed even more dramatically during the Great Leap Forward. In two key instances concerning the rectification-purge process during this period, however, some modification of my 1979 interpretations is in order. In the first case, the downgrading of Chen Yun in 1958, the broad point remains valid that this was the first post-1949 occasion when the authority of a Politburo member was emasculated as a result of differences relating to current policy, but new information suggests a rather different process from what was, in contrast to all other cases examined in *Politics and Purges*, originally argued solely on the basis of contextual evidence. In the earlier analysis Chen's declining influence was depicted as a case of applying informal sanctions against him for policy advocacy that was inimicable to the Great Leap program. Chen, in other words, was being pushed out of a position of real influence, but the actual process was rather low key, lacking both formal punishment and internal criticism. In several respects this view requires revision.

First, it is now clear that the circumstances surrounding Chen Yun's reduced role were less gentle than those suggested in *Politics and Purges*. As shall be discussed at greater length later in this introduction, at the Nanning conference in January 1958 Mao launched a scathing attack on not only Chen but also Premier Zhou Enlai, an onslaught which also slated two additional Politburo members and leading economic officials, Minister of Finance Li Xiannian and State Economic Commission head Bo Yibo.[45] The attack was notable not only for the severity of its criticism of these Politburo members, but also for the fact that it was not directed against expressed dissent from current policy but instead at the allegedly "rightist conservative" policies of "opposing reckless advance" *(fan maojin)* that these four leaders had promoted in 1956 to deal with imbalances created by an overheated economy—although at that time with Mao's concurrence.[46] Under the intense pressure created by Mao's onslaught it was not only impossible to articulate 1956-type views which contrasted so sharply to the emerging Great Leap Forward line, but Chen, Zhou, Li and Bo were required to make self-criticisms at the Second Session of the Eighth Party Congress in May 1958.[47] Yet these leaders fared quite differently during the leap forward: Li and Bo played major policy roles under Mao's direct control of the economy; Zhou, although perhaps suffering a slight loss of status,[48] continued to perform his key administrative function; but Chen, although still active on ceremonial occasions, seemingly had little operational role in the economic sphere he had dominated during the first eight years of the PRC. How can these differences be explained?

Li Xiannian and Bo Yibo, although key figures in the *fan maojin* program, seemingly fully accepted Mao's criticisms of "anti-reckless advance" soon after he began them in September 1957. Indeed, even before he suffered Mao's attack by name at Nanning, in December 1957 Bo condemned the policies he helped shape eighteen months earlier. At the May Congress session both Bo and Li offered apparently fulsome self-criticisms of their 1956 "transgressions," and following the meeting threw themselves enthusiastically into the work of guiding the Great Leap. Mao was impressed, as shown in his favorable comments on their respective June 1958 reports on the economy. In particular, the Chairman seemed pleased with Bo's claim that Britain could be overtaken in two to three years' time rather than the fifteen or seven years previously projected.[49] In contrast, no reference in Party history sources to similar praise of Zhou in 1958 by Mao has been located.

Zhou's complex attitude, however, is perhaps best indicated by his self-criticism to the May Party Congress. In the period between the March 1958 Chengdu conference when Mao again lambasted those responsible for *fan maojin* and May, Zhou and the others had to prepare their self-examinations.

From the account of his secretary, this process caused the Premier considerable distress. While Zhou, on the basis of a personal conversation with Mao, apparently accepted the view that the basic cause of his errors was that his thought had not kept up with the Chairman's, the actual drafting of the self-criticism was a painful experience which revealed "contradictions in his heart." A possibly revealing incident during the process occurred when Chen Yun rang Zhou, perhaps reminding him of the reasons for "anti-reckless advance," and afterwards, seemingly given pause, the Premier lapsed into five or six minutes of silence. In the event, however, whatever his reservations, Zhou produced an excessive self-criticism at the Congress in the same style he had shown during the Yan'an rectification. He not only assumed the main responsibility for the errors committed which he characterized as mistakes of guiding principle *(fangzhen)*, endorsed Mao's view that such mistakes had been used by the non-Party "rightists" in 1957 to launch a serious class struggle against the CCP, and equated *fan maojin* with government work breaking away from Party leadership, but he also devoted a special section of his speech to "learning from Chairman Mao." In this lavish praise, which prefigured Lin Biao's notorious January 1962 paean to the Chairman, Zhou held that experience showed Mao represented the truth, good results were inseparable from Mao's correct leadership, and on the contrary mistakes and losses occurred when the Party became divorced from his leadership and directives—something demonstrated by the Premier's own case.[50]

Chen Yun's self-criticism, however, displayed a cooler tone. While Chen too accepted responsibility for the "completely mistaken" *fan maojin* policies, the main thrust seemed to be on his insufficient understanding and excessively negative assessments of the economic situation in 1956 and, some acknowledgement of Mao's timely rectification of the situation and his setting the economy on its current victorious course notwithstanding, it apparently lacked a discourse on the need to study the Chairman.[51] This more modulated position may provide a clue to Chen's apparent loss of function, but it is only part of a larger story. When other leaders set about carrying out the Great Leap with their varying degrees of enthusiasm, Chen seemingly lapsed into comparative inactivity. Chen's distinctive behavior was summed up in an understated manner over twenty years later by Deng Xiaoping: "Neither Comrade Liu Shaoqi nor Comrade Zhou Enlai nor I for that matter objected to [the Great Leap], and Comrade Chen Yun didn't say anything either."[52] Of course Liu in particular did more than not object, he became a major force in driving the venture forward.[53] But in "not saying anything" Chen both ceased any contrary policy advocacy and no longer played a major implementing role—he didn't oppose but, on the whole, neither did he participate actively.[54] The central question for our purposes is whether he was pushed aside by an annoyed Mao or stepped aside of his own volition, and the answer is by no means entirely clear-cut.

According to one authoritative oral source, Chen's role in 1958 reflected a career long *modus operandi*: when Mao was unwilling to listen to his ideas

Chen's practice was to stop talking or go into hospital.[55] Other sources place greater emphasis on the other side of the equation, i.e., because of Chen's different ideas Mao pushed him aside as an effective actor.[56] On balance, the evidence gathered from oral sources in particular suggests that at least to some degree Chen Yun's reduced role in 1958 was a matter of his own choice, that he was unwilling to play an active role *à la* Bo Yibo or Li Xiannian in carrying out an economic strategy he believed to be deeply flawed. However, the comment of one such source who was a significant participant in the high level politics of the leap, someone with a close personal knowledge of Chen from an earlier period, that it was impossible for him to say whether Chen was pushed or stepped aside undoubtedly reflects a larger truth. Not only were both elements present, but there were important limits with respect to both the "pushing" and "stepping" aspects of the situation—limits which reflected the complex relationship between the Chairman and one of his key subordinates.

For Mao's part, his harsh criticism and Chen's apparent reluctance to shoulder major duties notwithstanding, he did not push Chen too far off the political stage. This was reflected not only in the fact that Chen's formal rank remained unchanged and he continued to appear in public, but also in his June 1958 appointment to head a new financial and economic small group of the Party Center. Although other key members of the group—Li Fuchun, Li Xiannian, Bo Yibo and Tan Zhenlin—were active proponents of the leap, it is clear that the group as such, while in theory providing overall supervision of economic policy, in fact like Chen himself had little real function.[57] This had two apparent advantages. First, it provided a non-operational organ including the regime's most respected economic specialist that Mao could consult, or as quickly became the case, choose to ignore. Second, it provided a role, however empty in practice, for one of the CCP's most senior officials commensurate with this status. In a system so sensitive to status, such an arrangement allowed the Chairman to honor Chen's historical contributions and position without inhibiting Mao from taking direct personal control of economic policy for the first time in the history of the PRC.[58] Meanwhile, on Chen's side, his role as group head, while not intrinsically significant, was indicative of the fact that while he had "stepped aside" he had not entirely "stepped off" the political stage. Although apparently largely keeping silent as Great Leap expectations reached their most absurd heights in summer and early fall 1958, Chen maintained his presence within the leadership and was positioned for a more active role should Mao change his mind. In the event, such a change on the Chairman's part came sooner than Chen probably imagined likely.

Oral sources assert that Mao was the first to point out the shortcomings of the Great Leap and the need for policy adjustments.[59] By the time of the first Zhengzhou conference in November 1958 he began to address the excesses of the leap forward, now attacking economists as "leftists" who got by on false pretences. Moreover, at Zhengzhou Mao dropped a favorable reference to Chen Yun as more knowledgeable than himself about the economy.[60] But given that the Chairman remained fundamentally committed to the broad thrust of the Great Leap, Chen had to proceed with great caution and began to speak up about the time of the November–December Wuchang Central Committee plenum. In one of his first moves just before the plenum he drafted a proposal not to publish the wildly ambitious grain and steel targets, but Mao's secretary, Hu Qiaomu, in an apparent effort to shield Chen, failed to pass on Chen's opinion to the Chairman. Mao, however, now seemed inclined to give Chen some room to air his views and criticized Hu for his temerity in pigeonholing the opinion of a Party Vice Chairman. Later in December, moreover, Chen gave a speech in Hangzhou where Mao was also staying which raised some "serious mistakes and shortcomings" and called for more attention to the quality of output as opposed to the current obsession with quantity. That Mao was not particularly displeased is perhaps suggested by the invitation Chen received to the Chairman's birthday party a few days later, an occasion that Chen used to air his concerns directly to Mao. While the Chairman did not accept Chen's views, he left the door ajar with the comment that they should let practice judge the matter. Mao later claimed that at this time he began to share some of Chen's opinions, but this seemingly was not articulated forcefully to others. As a result, while Chen was able to voice his opinions more openly over the next few months, "No one listened to him." What seemingly had happened was familiar—a shift in the Chairman's position had opened up possibilities for a concerned leader to try and shape policy in a preferred direction. Contrary to the erroneous view in the original edition of *Politics and Purges*, rather than lapse into virtual silence by 1959, Chen had taken up the challenge of trying to curb the excesses of the leap. But in the context of a continuing, if somewhat toned down, leap forward, the opportunity created was strictly limited.[61]

With Mao's perceptions of economic problems deepening during the first half of 1959, Chen's role—while still limited—grew accordingly. At the Shanghai Central Committee plenum in early April, the Chairman praised Chen for his contrary opinions on the 1958 food and steel targets, observing that "the truth is sometimes grasped by a minority even to the point of being in the hands of one person."[62] After the plenum, moreover, Mao berated several economic policy makers by telling them they knew nothing about the economy and should seek out Chen to find out if their targets for steel were practical. As a result Chen was formally entrusted with investigating the steel situation, his views were now listened to, and the steel target was reduced.[63] Finally, in July during the early part of the Lushan meetings, several of Mao's secretaries approached the Chairman with the suggestion that Chen be placed in charge of economic work. The Chairman responded positively, not only stating that Chen's economic thought was correct, but observing that "only when the country is in chaos do you long for a good general." When the Peng Dehuai affair erupted at the conference, however, the situation changed drastically. Even though Chen was not involved or even present at Lushan, following the meeting he not only was not given control of the economy, but the central financial and economic small group that he headed was abolished.[64]

To summarize, the new information available since 1979 provides a much richer and more complex understanding of the downgrading—and subsequent partial revival—of Chen Yun during the Great Leap than was possible originally. It shows a process that had harder edges than seemed the case earlier, yet at the same time one where the reduction of Chen's role was to a substantial extent a product of his own will. The new data also provide further evidence of a leadership in awe of Mao, falling into line behind his demands, and at most gently seeking to guide him to preferred outcomes when the opportunity arose. In contrast to 1953, however, even so astute a leader as Chen Yun had only limited success in moving the Chairman. Yet this limited success did help moderate policy for a time and, while not restored to a major role, Chen was left in a position where his talents could be used on another day. Chen Yun's cautious, sensitive handling of Mao was clearly preferable to Peng Dehuai's approach which triggered the explosion at Lushan.

The Crisis at Lushan

The second key development from the Great Leap period needing some reexamination is precisely the events at the Lushan meetings which culminated in the dismissal of Minister of Defense Peng Dehuai. Here the basic picture presented in 1979 of events leading up to and unfolding at Lushan has been confirmed by voluminous PRC sources including Peng's "self-statement," various memoir accounts of Lushan, Party history analyses, and interviews with Chinese scholars, as well as by new Western scholarship.[65] That is, in the entire period since late 1958 Mao began to confront the shortcomings of the leap and, as seen in the above discussion of Chen Yun's role, was prepared to make significant modifications to the policies but not the concept of the Great Leap. Moreover, when the Lushan conference convened, Mao seemed ready to continue this development until he received Peng's far-reaching critique of the leap and drastically altered his attitude. But the question of Peng's intent in writing his critical "letter of opinion," and thus the larger political meaning of Lushan, has remained contentious. Was Peng, and others like Zhang Wentian who also criticized the leap forward, engaging in "an all-out attack on [Mao's] policies"[66] and indeed on the Chairman himself, as various analysts have asserted, or was he seeking to persuade Mao to alter his course as argued in *Politics and Purges*? The new data greatly strengthen my original interpretation although, as suggested earlier, not without some qualification.[67]

The unanimous view of the Party historians consulted is that although Peng Dehuai, Zhang Wentian and others in the alleged "anti-Party clique" represented a broad strand of opinion within the leadership, their aim was not to confront Mao but to deepen the trend of correcting the excesses of the leap which the Chairman himself had set in motion. There were, as I shall discuss in a later section, concerns with Mao's "undemocratic" tendencies which had been in particularly strong evidence during the Great Leap, but the main story was the familiar one of divining the Chairman's intentions and making use of the opportunities they presented to advance one's policy preferences. That Mao's desire to correct the "left" was widely perceived during the "first stage" of the Lushan conference is amply demonstrated by the range of officials revealed by post-1979 sources to have adopted this perspective. This included not only government administrators like Zhou Enlai who now had scope to express his presumably moderate inclinations, but also such Great Leap radicals as Shanghai leader Ke Qingshi who brought materials critical of leftist phenomena to Lushan, and Mao's long time secretary and troubleshooter, Chen Boda, who both openly aired concern in group meetings and joined in private criticisms of the leap with the Chairman's other secretaries Hu Qiaomu, Tian Jiaying, Li Rui and Wu Lengxi. That these leaders of different ideological tendencies, work responsibilities and Party rank—but who all had a high degree of personal access to Mao—were on the same track indicates that an anti-left posture was seen as important to retaining or regaining the Chairman's favor.[68]

But while the main direction was relatively clear as Party leaders gathered at Lushan, as argued in *Politics and Purges* there was considerable ambiguity as to the precise policy implications of this direction and particularly of how far Mao was prepared to go in correcting left errors. This was inherent in the Chairman's attitude since late 1958 that the Great Leap concept was correct and errors were limited to concrete work problems, a view typified by his statement on the eve of Lushan that although problems were "quite a few," "our achievements are great . . . and the future is bright." As we have seen, in this general context many had earlier chosen to ignore Chen Yun's moderating suggestions, and Chen, apparently mistakenly,[69] even felt it necessary to make a self-criticism in spring 1959. Others like Wang Jiaxiang, who expressed doubts about the adequacy of the measures to correct the people's communes adopted in December 1958, experienced Mao's displeasure, while still others stifled their critical opinions given the uncertainty of the situation notwithstanding Mao's more cautious bent. Thus when the Lushan meetings began, even allowing for the critical comments being made, considerable restraint was evident. As Peng Dehuai observed, people were not airing opinions freely, a situation undoubtedly due to fear of offending Mao.[70]

In this situation Peng could later interpret his actions at Lushan as designed to overcome such hesitancy and foster the process of correcting the left trend by gaining Mao's backing, for problems "could be easily resolved" if the Chairman endorsed correct policies. Such a calculation, of course, was based on the principle that Mao was unchallengeable—a principle that informed his actions and those of others in his "clique" throughout the Lushan meetings. Rather than having a plan to confront Mao, Peng did not even want to go to Lushan, preferring instead to remain in Beijing overseeing military affairs, and only went when, among others, the Chairman himself rang up and urged him to attend.

Similarly, Peng's greatest ally at Lushan, Vice Minister of Foreign Affairs and alternate Politburo member Zhang Wentian, was also somewhat reluctant to go, but was persuaded to attend by Foreign Minister Chen Yi who argued that it would not produce problems since Mao had raised no objections to the critical remarks concerning the leap both Chen and Zhang had raised at a June foreign affairs conference. Thus both Peng Dehuai and Zhang Wentian—their deep concern over the economic situation and subsequent boldness notwithstanding—manifested caution about even attending the conference.[71] Once present, other signs of prudence were in evidence. Despite some indiscretions,[72] Peng later claimed he felt uneasy about raising difficult questions at group discussions as it could produce "confusion." Moreover, in several talks with Hunan First Secretary Zhou Xiaozhou, a secretary of Mao's in the 1930s who would soon be labelled a leading member of Peng's "clique," the two men sought not simply to reinforce each other's critical opinion of the leap, but also apparently to urge one another to raise their concerns with the Chairman. In the event, it was only after Zhou Xiaozhou did see Mao and reported back that the Chairman was sincere that Peng reluctantly decided to approach Mao himself. But while he was wary that his impetuous nature might result in giving offence to the Chairman, Peng had already concluded that at worst Mao would sack him as Minister of Defense with the effect of promoting his close colleague Chief of Staff Huang Kecheng to the post.[73]

Moved by these factors, Peng went to the Chairman's quarters only to find Mao asleep. This led to Peng's fateful decision to write his "letter of opinion," a private letter that could not be regarded as an open attack on Mao. Once written, the letter was circulated on Mao's instruction by the Central Committee's General Office—not by Peng as claimed in *Politics and Purges*. Thus Peng's private communication was turned into an inner Party document. Peng seemed concerned that the very fact of making the letter public could mean trouble and asked the General Office to take it back, thereby indicating that he saw even the possible perception that he was criticizing Mao as politically dangerous. Moreover, once Mao did launch his attack on Peng, the old marshal, like many other participants at Lushan, was astonished by the ferocity of the Chairman's reaction. Peng could not see how a letter meant only for Mao's eyes could be interpreted by the Chairman as a political attack, and he bitterly asked himself why after thirty years of close collaboration Mao could not have privately talked with him if he had made such a grave mistake. Peng's anger, as well as the circumstances of his letter, strongly suggest that he did not conceive of it as an attack on the Chairman.[74]

Yet we are left with the curious nature of the letter itself; part the polite memorial to the throne depicted by *Politics and Purges* which, as the editors of Peng's "self-statement" assert, "seems diplomatic and mild,"[75] yet which on reflection clearly contained some barbed commentary on the contemporary situation.[76] The answer to this paradox seems to lie in Peng's provocative nature.

Peng had a history of not simply speaking his mind, but also of provoking people to get them to do what he wanted. He had spoken crudely to the Comintern's military representative, Otto Braun, during the fifth encirclement campaign in 1934 in an effort to secure a change in tactics,[77] and now he attempted to use a more measured variation of the same approach on Mao. After writing his letter Peng told Zhang Wentian that he believed Mao's pre-Lushan measures to modify the Great Leap had not gone far enough, and he deliberately included a few stings *(ci)* in the letter to induce Mao to go further.[78] Thus the letter was not quite the polite memorial previously argued, nor does it appear to have been an effort to shift the blame to Liu Shaoqi as speculatively suggested in *Politics and Purges*.[79] Rather, the aim was to provoke Mao through a private communication, not to challenge him politically, but in hopes of producing the desired policy change. It was disastrous psychology, and produced fateful results for China in retarding the process of redressing the excesses of the Great Leap as well as for Peng personally.

That Peng's letter was not meant as a political attack, as well as the importance of anticipating Mao's attitude, is further suggested by the reactions of other leaders following the circulation of the letter. These reactions were varied. At first many participants at the conference not only agreed with the letter's policy advocacy, but significantly saw no major political problem with it. For example, Zhou Enlai, normally a sensitive observer of the Chairman, commented that there was nothing to worry about. Others close to Mao, however, sensed that a delicate situation had arisen. Thus Li Rui, one of Mao's secretaries, felt that Peng had shown a lot of daring that was virtually unique in writing the letter even though he too did not anticipate any serious consequences. Hu Qiaomu was even more wary, observing privately that the letter might cause trouble. Still others of demonstrated leftist inclination such as Ke Qingshi and Sichuan leader Li Jingquan began to criticize the letter whether because they felt its policy implications went further than they could accept, that in their view it genuinely did slight the Chairman, or in anticipation of Mao's displeasure with Peng. In any case, these initial reactions suggest that the letter was far from universally perceived as an attack on Mao, but that some at Lushan had an inkling that the Chairman might respond badly.[80]

One of the most revealing responses was that of Zhang Wentian. Zhang shared Peng's dim view of the consequences of the leap forward, and they had exchanged views privately before and during the conference. In the new, more uncertain situation created by Peng's letter, Zhang determined to support Peng's views by giving a speech that would argue the case more rigorously than Peng had. As he prepared his speech he was warned by Hu Qiaomu that it was not a wise thing to do, but he decided to go ahead even though he recognized that it could potentially cause severe repercussions. As he subsequently argued to his wife who questioned his involvement where, as a foreign affairs official, he had no direct responsibility, in view of the dire plight of the masses he had an obligation to speak up regardless of the consequences. In the event, his speech on July 21 was an ordeal for Zhang given frequent hostile interjections. Yet even at this stage he could not have known the full implications of what he had done, implications which began to become clear when Mao addressed the meeting on July 23. Once Mao had spoken and Zhang faced demands that he confess to seeking to overthrow Mao, Zhang commented on the absurdity of the accusation to his secretary by observing, in a manner similar to Peng Dehuai's rationale for acting in the first place, that such an aim was simply impossible and only the Chairman could rectify the excesses of the Great Leap.[81]

The emotional, intemperate nature of Mao's outburst on the 23rd was apparent when *Politics and Purges* was written, but post-1979 sources give a much clearer picture of its impact. The immediate impact was to astonish the audience: it was not only Peng who was taken aback by Mao's ferocity. Perhaps most revealing was the fact that four of the Chairman's secretaries, including Chen Boda who would soon change his colors to adopt a posture sharply critical of Peng, returned from the meeting to sit in stunned silence with no one speaking for half a day. Yet given Mao's track record of harsh attacks that were not followed by severe punishment—as had been demonstrated the previous year concerning Zhou Enlai and Chen Yun—many leaders apparently still believed the situation could be repaired and sought to play down the transgressions of Peng and Zhang over the following days. Thus Bo Yibo and An Ziwen, two officials who had clashed with Peng in the past and were specially summoned to Lushan following Peng's letter, limited their criticisms of Peng to historical questions, while other leaders as varied as revolutionary military commander in chief, Zhu De, and the leftist agricultural boss, Tan Zhenlin, sought to lighten Peng's sins. On the 26th, however, Mao declared that people and not just the issues had to be dealt with, and it quickly became clear that he was demanding Peng's head regardless of the widespread desire to cool matters down. As so often before, and as would be the case again in the future, now that Mao's attitude was completely unambiguous the resistance of his colleagues collapsed and attention focused on intensified criticism of Peng, Zhang and others now implicated in his "clique."[82]

Thus once Mao had placed his authority on the line the leadership closed ranks behind him; the implications of this for inner Party democracy will be examined later in this introduction. This did not mean that individuals did not object to what had happened, but their objections were limited to private expressions of sorrow rather than resulting in any attempt to curb the Chairman. The sympathy that existed was now channeled into persuading Peng, whose options had been reduced to stubbornly holding his ground in the face of massive attack, engaging in self-criticism, or, apparently, suicide, to make the necessary demeaning self-examination.[83] Peng finally accepted pleas to "consider the interests of the whole situation" and undertook the required self-criticism in consideration of Party unity and Mao's prestige, but he remained bitter over the fact that "for the first time in my life, I have spoken out against my very heart!"[84] Despite significant elite reservations over Mao's actions as well as his policies, the most his leadership colleagues were willing to do was to try and find a way to ease Peng's dilemma while protecting the Chairman's prestige and giving him the outcome he wanted.

Conflict without Opposition, 1960–65

If any period before the Cultural Revolution seemingly fits the "two line struggle" model of elite conflict, it is 1960–65 following the collapse of the Great Leap Forward. Indeed, scholarly interpretations of this type focus on these years when official policy reversed the Great Leap strategy that had been advocated so strongly by Mao (but also by many other leaders including, not least, Liu Shaoqi), Mao's involvement in daily affairs markedly decreased as he withdrew to the "second line"of leadership,[85] and the new policies which saved the day were largely the handiwork of others on the "first line" such as Liu and Deng Xiaoping—the chief "capitalist roaders" of the Cultural Revolution—and, in 1961–62, Chen Yun who returned from inactivity to play a critical role in overall economic policy. Once the crisis was past, and Chen Yun among others was preemptorily cast aside by Mao in the latter part of 1962, different tendencies coexisted uneasily in CCP programs until the onset of the Cultural Revolution. Clearly Mao was in the forefront of efforts, however partial and lacking in coherence, to place class struggle at the top of the CCP's agenda, while his colleagues on the "first line" were often preoccupied with the more prosaic tasks of sustaining economic production and running a complex bureaucratic machinery. Given these circumstances, it is understandable that many scholars fashioned their own versions of the official CCP line in explaining the politics of the period from the Great Leap to the Cultural Revolution as one of significant opposition to and fluctuating fortunes of the Chairman.

New sources available since 1979, however, support the contrary interpretation advanced in *Politics and Purges*. First, a fragile and limited consensus emerged by 1961 on the measures required to deal with the post-Great Leap crisis, with Mao remaining a crucial figure in endorsing this approach even while he often kept his distance from the actual policy making process.[86] The Chairman, moreover, was fully able to get his way once he reasserted his own substantially idiosyncratic concerns on policy and personnel matters starting with the August 1962 Beidaihe conference, but he proved unable to frame a clear, unambiguous program for other leaders to implement, thus leaving them uncertain as to his actual intent. Furthermore, as the case of the Socialist Education Movement dramatically demonstrates, Mao frequently shifted positions, siding with the changing policy prescriptions of his colleagues at different times rather than follow a consistent line on major issues. Finally, over this period the Chairman gradually lost confidence in many of his key colleagues but this was not the result of any concerted opposition on their part—in the words of one senior Party historian, it would have been unreal to confront Mao. As before the key element of elite politics was the effort of all parties to win Mao over to their preferred positions and to interpret successfully the Chairman's elusive wishes. Yet the new evidence also allows a more nuanced view of the critical relationship between Mao and his loyal but uncertain colleagues than was possible when *Politics and Purges* was written.

Mao's continuing dominance of his colleagues and their willing acceptance of this situation is indicated by numerous events over the 1960–65 period. A clear example is the gingerly treatment of the Chairman by his top associates at the time of what should have been his greatest weakness during the crisis years of 1961–62. When Mao made a self-criticism in mid-1961 in an effort to promote inner Party democracy and an effective response to the crisis, he asked that his statement be circulated throughout the Party but this was not done.[87] Rather than being the result of actions by lower level officials as asserted in the 1979 edition, oral sources reveal it was none other than Liu Shaoqi who baulked at its circulation out of fear of the consequences. This can be read in several ways. Liu undoubtedly was concerned for the stability of the system if its central figure were openly revealed to have feet of clay. Yet Liu was arguably also acting out of prudence—prudence which warned that such an act, notwithstanding the Chairman's own request, could be read as anti-Mao by his enemies or by Mao himself at some future date. Whatever Liu's actual reasoning, his suppression of the self-criticism clearly does not indicate someone trying to undermine the Chairman politically. Similarly, an authoritative Party historian related, in the same period Peng Zhen undertook many talks to cadre meetings in Beijing to counter sharp dissatisfaction with Mao on the part of ordinary officials, arguing that the victory of the CCP was due to Mao, and "if we don't support him who can we support?" Thus at a time of presumptive vulnerability, a time when there was serious disaffection with the Chairman's leadership at lower levels of the Party in view of the national economic disaster, Mao's leading comrades rallied around in an effort to protect his prestige, as well as out of prudence concerning their own careers.

Another sign of Mao's pivotal role was his ability to dictate terms to both ranking leaders and entire bureaucratic organizations. A case in point was his strong criticism and abrupt shunting aside of Chen Yun in 1962 for alleged "rightism" in formulating economic policies just as these policies helped rescue the regime from its self- (and Mao-) made crisis.[88] At the same juncture Mao not only dismissed or downgraded other officials who had contributed to national survival such as agricultural specialist Deng Zihui, his displeasure also extended to abolishing Deng's Central Committee rural work department—a word from the Chairman and a significant bureaucratic unit was disbanded.[89] Two years later a similar instance occurred involving a much more powerful institution, the SPC, whose leadership included several active Politburo members. By mid-1964 Mao was displeased with the efforts of the SPC to draw up a new five-year plan, felt that work was too slow and gave insufficient attention to defense preparations, and demanded changes which were dutifully implemented in 1965. Mao's authority was vividly revealed not only by the massive shift in resources which resulted from his intervention, but also by his blistering rejection of the initial response to his prodding and the setting up of a new body to take over as China's main economic policy organ. When the SPC prepared a September 1964 document in response to Mao's concerns, and after the document was approved by Liu Shaoqi, Zhou Enlai and Deng Xiaoping in the belief that it would satisfy the Chairman, Mao astounded the planners by declaring "You just want to practise the Three People's Principles." SPC head Li Fuchun, for his part, rushed home and ordered his secretary to prepare a self-criticism. Shortly thereafter a so-called small planning commission *(xiao jiwei)* displaced the existing SPC leaders as the overlords of the economy with a group of officials of considerably lower rank led by Yu Qiuli. Mao's displeasure had swept aside significant members of the Politburo who had been in charge of the successful process of economic recovery and reduced the role of arguably the regime's most potent economic bureaucracy.[90]

In all of these cases and many others in the immediate pre-Cultural Revolution years Mao demonstrated the capacity to intervene decisively. Yet even while the evidence of *Politics and Purges* demonstrating that the Chairman's mercurial policy preferences rather than sustained high level resistance explain pronounced swings in official programs has been further strengthened, the issue of "opposition" remains. Fortunately, the materials of the past decade help to unravel further the paradox of clashing ideological and policy perspectives without political opposition by shedding light on the attitudes of both Mao and his leading comrades. Perhaps the most satisfactory summary of the overall situation was put by one Chinese scholar in informal conversation who remarked that "there was no opposition but Mao may have believed there was—and that's another matter." For Mao's part, the Chairman sensed—accurately—the divergence of outlook between himself and his colleagues on the "first line," but at the same time confused this with questions of personal loyalty and fears that his own power was ebbing which resulted in distorted interpretations of events and people. From the perspective of other top leaders, as throughout the history of the PRC there was no inclination to take Mao on politically—both collective loyalty to the founder of the regime and individual prudence ruled out any such ideas. However, in the context of 1962–65 when the Chairman emitted many contradictory signals,[91] a form of limited passive resistance was possible to a greater degree than perhaps suggested by *Politics and Purges*. The outstanding case in point was Deng Xiaoping who apparently ignored Mao-inspired ideological movements to a considerable extent and focused on developing production while reducing his activities more generally, a posture which was retrospectively termed "passive sabotage" by Hu Qiaomu.[92] But it is also important to emphasize that despite the assertions of various Party historians of the basic unanimity of the "first line," in fact there were some significant differences if not necessarily those posited in *Politics and Purges*.[93]

Ironically, given both their linking as "capitalist roaders" and Mao's efforts to protect Deng—but not Liu—during the Cultural Revolution, in this period Liu Shaoqi picked up various of Mao's ideological themes and adopted a relatively "left" posture while, as suggested, Deng Xiaoping largely avoided radical programs. Nonetheless, in a larger sense the "first line" did collectively face the Chairman aware of his various discontents yet charged with running the country and thus risking exacerbating those discontents. How did they protect themselves from this dilemma? According to several senior Party historians, the "first line" leaders, once they had reached a collective view, took their major decisions to Mao and only proceeded if he gave his approval—in this way believing there would be no problem.[94] As can be seen from several major developments in 1962–65, this was a grave miscalculation given Mao's increasingly erratic, even paranoid, perceptions.

A crucial case illustrating the complex leadership pattern was the 7,000 cadres conference convened in January 1962 to deal with the deteriorating economic situation—the instance when, Mao was later to claim, he first became aware that there was something seriously amiss with his "first line" colleagues. As already indicated, this was a time of considerable disaffection among lower level cadres who were represented among the 7,000; Mao himself recognized this and decreed that the conference go into a second "let off steam" phase. Nevertheless, as in other instances during this crisis, the Chairman's colleagues moved remarkably cautiously. A striking example of this was the knowing submission of false financial figures to the conference by Bo Yibo and Li Fuchun; even at this late date officials hesitated to exhibit full candor while Mao still retained illusions that the economy was in better shape than it actually was and continued to affirm the Great Leap despite sanctioning many practical policy adjustments. Also revealing was the reluctance of Chen Yun to take a prominent role at the conference. Although invited by Mao to speak to the meeting, Chen declined on the grounds that he was unclear about some matters. This, in the view of one senior Party historian, was a wise decision as the time was not yet right for more thorough going policy changes; only as the full seriousness of the situation became apparent in subsequent months did Chen assume overall responsibility for economic policy at the urging of Liu Shaoqi and with the approval of Mao.[95]

Finally, fullsome praise of the Chairman was expressed at the conference. Post-Mao historiography, probably accurately, makes a great deal of Lin Biao's lavish adulation of Mao on this occasion as fostering the cult of personality, but at least Deng Xiaoping was apparently not too far behind. Lin ascribed the difficulties of the previous few years to the failure to follow the directives, warnings and thoughts of Chairman Mao. Things would get markedly better, he argued, if only the Party listened to Mao's words and realized his spirit. The Chairman's views were correct and in accord with reality; he was always ahead of everyone else in this regard. Blame for the existing situation was ascribed to "some comrades" who pulled his thought to the left, who didn't pay sufficient respect to or obstructed his opinions. Deng, speaking a few days later and arguably under some pressure after Lin's remarks, linked the Party's positive features to the Chairman and its recent shortcomings to "not a few comrades" insufficiently studying and failing to understand truly his exhortations. Strikingly, Deng declared that "to follow Chairman Mao's road is to follow the right road," and called on all assembled to "read the Quotations from the Works of Chairman Mao" which had been published by Lin's army newspaper over the past half year. Generally speaking, while Lin Biao's praise of Mao may have been extreme, ranking leaders seemingly all showed respect towards the Chairman. Perhaps a more important difference is that other leaders like Deng linked their praise of Mao to a serious discussion of the problems facing the regime, while the gist of Lin's message was that things weren't nearly as bad as they seemed, the previous years had seen a significant "spiritual income" for the Party, and what was needed was a little faith. Significantly in terms of Mao's state of mind, even though he shared the view of the majority that serious problems had to be dealt with, Lin Biao's words of all those articulated at the conference most gratified the Chairman; he commented privately at the time that the standard of Lin's speech was very high, a level other leaders could not match.[96]

If Mao's reaction to Lin's speech was revealing of both his state of mind and the delicate situation facing his leading comrades, even more significant was Liu Shaoqi's report and his speech to the conference. The report was the main document of the conference which had been produced by an elaborate drafting process involving the conference participants. Moreover, it not only received Mao's approval, but the Chairman also asked Liu to deliver a more pithy oral statement which Liu duly made after prior discussion of its content with Mao. In these efforts Liu articulated what was, in effect, a systematic critique of the leap and outlined the various measures being taken to save the situation. Liu did not introduce policies which Mao rejected; in his own speech to the conference Mao endorsed the whole set of policies which would be attacked as revisionist during the Cultural Revolution. Nor did Liu seek to undercut Mao's position; he rather assumed primary responsibility for past mistakes as the leading comrade on the "first line." Some of his statements, particularly in the oral presentation, had far-reaching implications, e.g., that peasants in some areas believed 70 percent of the disasters facing China were man-made, many of Peng Dehuai's Lushan views had proven correct, and the leap, i.e., whether it was correct or not, could be reconsidered after five or ten years, but Mao's own conclusions that "during the last few years we made many stupid mistakes," the Great Leap policies were not as persuasive as the First Five Year Plan, and "it is not enough to have the general line" were also sweeping. And despite his bolder statements, Liu was careful to affirm the correctness of the Party's line, claim that achievements outweighed mistakes, and assert that most errors had already been overcome.[97]

Notwithstanding Mao's similar views as to what was necessary in policy terms and the Chairman's explicit approval of Liu's report, various well-placed oral sources are convinced that the 7,000 cadres conference was a watershed in his attitudes toward Liu. While Mao himself might say similar things ("it is not enough to have the general line"), for another leader to raise even cautiously questions about the adequacy of the political and theoretical line with which the Chairman was so closely identified evidently appeared to Mao to smack of disloyalty. In particular, Liu's "new formulations" in his oral remarks even though Mao had been briefed on the gist of the speech seemingly left the Chairman very unhappy much as Peng Dehuai's stings had done at Lushan. But while it is unlikely that Liu was seeking to provoke Mao as Peng had intended, he nevertheless demonstrated considerable political boldness of a type that the Chairman had admired in the revolutionary period.[98] Indeed, according to a well informed oral source, Zhou Enlai observed Liu's behavior with a mixture of admiration and surprise, commenting that he didn't expect Liu to be so determined in adjusting the economy since anyone who challenged the leap forward was likely to be jailed.[99] Mao, however, perhaps chastened by the serious economic situation and lower level disaffection, did not explode as at Lushan and gave no obvious sign of disapproval. The new materials available since 1978 do not undermine the argument of *Politics and Purges* that in the *policy* sense it was more the further retreat from February 1962 which angered the Chairman, but they clearly indicate the *emotional* impact of the January conference on Mao. From that time the Chairman apparently began to harbor unspoken resentment, and he would return to the "rightist deviation" of 1962 with Liu's 7,000 cadres conference speech as its prime manifestation when explaining his loss of confidence in Liu at the outset of the Cultural Revolution.[100]

A second major source of Mao's evolving distrust of Liu concerns the Socialist Education Movement. Here too new information on Mao's state of mind and Liu's own leadership traits become crucial to a better understanding than was possible when *Politics and Purges* was written although important uncertainties remain. In the policy sense, the basic 1979 analysis of the movement holds with some modification. In 1963–64 changes in orientation occurred in response to shifting circumstances and leadership perceptions, Liu's posture towards the movement was largely "leftist" although it now seems problematic that he was involved in any major conflict with Peng Zhen over its implementation,[101] and Mao endorsed each major shift of direction proposed by others up to the start of 1965 when the Chairman imposed his own idiosyncratic stamp on the campaign by raising the issue of "capitalist roaders" within the Party. A fascinating if ironic aspect of these developments is that of all the Party leaders on the "first line,"[102] Liu Shaoqi was in some ways most in tune with Mao's concerns. A number of senior Party historians emphasised that from the fall 1962 Tenth Plenum Liu began to follow Mao on the issue of class struggle, a position reflected in the movement's Second Ten Points directive of September 1963 which fell under Liu's overall authority and raised for the first time the slogan of class struggle as the key link.[103] In a more concrete sense, Liu's leftism was most dramatically reflected in his September 1964 Revised Second Ten Points which endorsed, with Mao's approval, a deep purge of rural cadres.

What explains Liu's "left" orientation? Party historians offer various factors —his position as the leader of the "first line" with ultimate responsibility for putting Mao's wishes into practice, the fact that the Chairman's policies were invariably endorsed by Party conclaves as at the Tenth Plenum and had to be carried out as a matter of discipline, but also due to certain personal proclivities. In the view of one specialist on Liu Shaoqi, Liu had a tendency to sway from one ideological position to another, particularly after criticism such as Mao handed out in abundance in fall 1962, and to seek one-sidedly theoretical justification for the Chairman's new views. All of this meant, various divergent perspectives notwithstanding, that Liu pursued Mao's emphasis on class struggle particularly in the context of socialist education during the very period he fell out of favor with his leader.

Why, then, did Mao turn on Liu and make him the number one enemy in the Cultural Revolution? Policy differences, as in Mao's rejection of Liu's Revised Second Ten Points in late 1964-early 1965,[104] obviously played a role, but undoubtedly there were larger dynamics at work. Part of the answer, as argued by some Party historians, is simply that as the main responsible person of the "first line" Liu had to suffer the brunt of Mao's more general disaffection with his colleagues. Other scholars, however, point to the Chairman's perception—albeit a faulty perception—that his power was slipping away to Liu in particular. According to an authoritative oral source, Mao had been struck by what he saw as a more wholehearted bureaucratic response to Liu's commands than to his own. The issue was the dispatch of cadres to the countryside to participate in socialist education work. In 1963 Mao called for officials to go to the villages in a very general way but very few high-ranking cadres actually went. At a summer 1964 conference Liu sought to remedy this situation by emphasizing and making obligatory the need to respond to Mao's call. As a result of Liu's strict directive Party and government departments made the necessary arrangements and large numbers of officials were dispatched to the countryside. In my source's opinion, however, rather than being gratified at Liu's actions to effect his wishes, Mao harbored resentment that Liu could achieve results where he could not and worried that he was in the shadows while Liu had real political clout.[105] While necessarily speculative, this analysis gains support from Mao's moody comment in November 1964 at the height of Liu's radical approach to socialist education. Mao observed that it would be better for Liu to be in command to avoid succession problems, that he should be the Chairman and Emperor Qinshihuang, for "even though I curse a lot it's no use, I'm ineffective, you [Liu] are formidable *(lihai)*. . . ."[106] There was an air of dissatisfaction in these words where the concern with power was palpable, and it was soon followed by the critical break with Liu.

December 1964 not only saw a sudden shift in Mao's position on the Socialist Education Movement virtually "from out of the blue" as one senior Party historian put it, it also was the occasion of a remarkable petulant outburst by the Chairman. Shortly after Mao's comments on Liu's formidability and his own uselessness, Deng Xiaoping suggested that it was not necessary for Mao to come to a scheduled work conference, assertedly in view of the Chairman's health and out of respect and certainly because Mao rarely attended such meetings. Deng's purported intentions notwithstanding, Mao reportedly was very displeased with his suggestion. Subsequently when the conference was convened to discuss socialist education, Mao advanced his novel notion of "powerholders" and in the process seemingly turned the emphasis away from ordinary cadres and rural class enemies which Liu—and the Chairman—had previously stressed and towards the alleged powerholders on the capitalist road in the Party. Liu made some effort to clarify his views but he did not directly oppose Mao's formulation. Only *after* Mao concluded speaking did he state that some people thought there was a mixing of different types of contradictions and the situation was very complex. Mao's outburst, however, occurred not on this occasion but at the next meeting when the Chairman, holding the state constitution in one hand and the Party constitution in the other, declared that one person (Deng Xiaoping) violated his rights by trying to prevent him from attending the conference, while another (Liu Shaoqi) interrupted him and wouldn't let him speak. As the conference went on into January, Mao continued his criticism of Liu and as on so many earlier occasions his policy preferences were adopted. Moreover, at a Party life meeting *(shenghuohui)* of the Politburo held following the conference Liu was required to engage in self-criticism. This extraordinary expression of irrationality on Mao's part, similar in content although vastly different in form to his reaction to the speeches of Liu and Lin Biao at the 7,000 cadres conference, suggests a Chairman more preoccupied with perceived personal slights and a sense of his own vulnerability than policy issues *per se*. It also demonstrated that once again his leading comrades had failed to anticipate Mao's desires, a project which had become increasingly difficult given the Chairman's erratic behavior since Lushan.[107]

The developments at the turn of 1964–65 have also contributed to an alteration of my earlier view concerning the timing and nature of Mao's decision to purge Liu Shaoqi. In *Politics and Purges* I took Mao's statement to Edgar Snow that he decided in January 1965 that Liu had to go as simply indicating the start of an unfolding process that remained fluid and open to change well into 1966. Now, however, to a significant degree on the basis of discussions with a leading Party historian, I have revised my view and believe that Mao was determined to get rid of Liu politically from the time he indicated and soon set out on a deliberate, if obscure, course to achieve that objective. To this end the Chairman secretly organized or at least abetted the attack on historian Wu Han which became public in late 1965, and then used that affair to undercut Peng Zhen and the Beijing municipal apparatus which he regarded as a crucial underpinning of Liu's power.[108] Subsequently, while it is possible to view Mao's initial entrusting of the Cultural Revolution to Liu's stewardship in mid-1966 as a test of his long time comrade's reliability, in the opinion of my main source it was a test Liu was bound to fail. Liu's attempt to channel the movement into non-threatening directions resulted in his denunciation for "suppressing the masses," but in the unlikely event he had chosen a hands off attitude my source argued that Liu would have been vulnerable to charges of suborning anarchy. Moreover, once Liu was under attack events unfolded inexorably. Liu was denied access to Mao, his personal staff was withdrawn, and he was subjected to physical mistreatment within the confines of Zhongnanhai with little intervention by Mao to ameliorate the lot of his old comrade. In contrast to the picture of the Chairman reassessing his designated successor for well over a year after January 1965, this interpretation argues a pitiless determination to destroy Liu politically throughout this period.[109]

In sum, while Mao's motives must be a matter of speculation, the new evidence available since 1979 not only confirms the Chairman's unchallenged dominance throughout the 1949–65 period but also provides a richer picture of an elite politics marked by adjusting to his desires, seeking his support for one's policy preferences, and making use of ambiguities in his attitudes to advance bureaucratic and political interests. Mao's unquestioned power and the efforts of other leaders to use or accommodate that power were apparent as early as 1953 in the Gao-Rao case and as late as the Socialist Education Movement in the mid-1960s. The frequent ambiguity of the Chairman's position created not only opportunities but also significant difficulties for his leading comrades throughout, but these difficulties became more severe with the passage of time and they were linked to the erosion of Party norms.

Party Norms with Chinese Characteristics

If the official conclusions of the post-1978 period have upheld the arguments of *Politics and Purges* concerning the dominance of Mao, they have even more explicitly supported the book's basic theme of the decline of the normative structure protecting inner Party democracy and safeguarding the CCP from unregulated factional struggle. To a striking degree the 1981 Resolution on Questions in History since the Founding of the PRC replicated my analysis of an initial post-1949 period during which Party organizational norms were largely observed followed by a period of Mao "gradually undermining democratic centralism in Party life."[110] While this official position, as well as a wealth of new material, affirms the fundamental argument of *Politics and Purges*, the detailed evidence suggests the need for some modification of the broad picture and a reconsideration of some key questions concerning the norms of inner Party behavior. Is the distinction between a period when the norms were followed and a period where they began to erode as clear-cut as implied? To what degree, in fact, were the norms a significant independent factor in elite politics? And what broader textural features of elite political culture formed the context in which CCP organizational norms functioned?

Inevitably there are gaps between reality and various official claims now made concerning Party norms—e.g., the Yan'an tradition of persuasive rectification as totally antithetical to the ruthless methods of the Cultural Revolution, the distinction between the good, democratic Mao of the early and mid-1950s and the erratic, arbitrary Chairman of the post-1957 period, and the picture of an elite with a deep commitment to inner Party democracy. Against these assertions various analysts have claimed that the Yan'an rectification was a precursor of the Cultural Revolution[111] and no golden age of Party democracy existed in the early post-1949 period.[112] More broadly, it has been argued that, in effect, the normative rules were largely pious statements of intent which never really functioned as claimed, and rather than shaping a system that regulated conflict these rules were observed only when everyone was in basic agreement.[113] And an even more fundamental challenge to the view of a norm-influenced polity are general characterizations of Chinese politics under Mao as marked by vicious, life and death struggles, an essentially conflict ridden milieu where there was no substitute for victory, permanent losers abounded, compromise was not promoted as a value, and victors remained insecure in the face of widespread impulses for revenge.[114] Such politics could not be further removed from the "democratic" and consensual practices officially said to prevail during at least the 1949–57 period.

Politics and Purges actually stood somewhere between the two perspectives outlined above, although clearly closer to the current official interpretation. Throughout the book the emphasis was on the fragility of the norms; indeed, the very theme of decline underlined that fragility. This analysis quite correctly pointed to the key factor of Mao's dominance as always being a potential threat to the norms of collective leadership and minority rights, a threat which became a particularly pronounced reality from late 1957. The book also pointed to other sources of fragility such as the internal contradictions and ambiguities of the norms, e.g., the demand for disciplined implementation of the policy line which naturally inhibited critical discussions and sat uncomfortably beside the formal right to retain dissenting opinions, and the even more fundamental conflict between organizational rules and revolutionary values. Given the course of the Cultural Revolution, the latter tension was nowhere expressed more poignantly than by Liu Shaoqi in 1939 when he declared that majority rule must be pushed aside in cases when a mistaken line had captured the majority.[115] Subsequently, in *Leadership, Legitimacy, and Conflict* I discussed the fragility of the norms in terms of a systematic comparison of normative rules with prudential rules, the requirements of political survival in both the Maoist and post-Mao periods.[116] It is important to emphasize, however, that while the conflict between various formal democratic rights and the political imperative of obeying Mao was crucial to elite calculations, the norms themselves involved important prudential elements. That is, the norms were important not simply as values leaders *should* adhere to, but as a framework providing predictability in inner Party life that served to safeguard the most immediate interests of the vast majority of leading and ordinary cadres alike.

While the evidence of the post-1978 period sustains the view of Party norms as a real and important aspect of elite politics, it also calls for some modification of the general and particular analyses advanced in *Politics and Purges*. At the most general level, the 1979 edition probably placed too much emphasis on the letter of the norms when, for CCP leaders, a much looser appreciation was more to the point. Thus while in a formalistic sense collective leadership implied that Mao had only one vote, in fact it referred to a consultative style whereby Mao took on board the opinions of his colleagues before reaching a decision. Importantly, such a loose understanding seemingly was perfectly acceptable as inner Party "democracy" to the Chairman's colleagues. More broadly, it is most likely the case that both a culturally derived sense of just behavior and a belief that rights accrue to major contributors to the revolution had more to do with normative expectations than did Party regulations. In terms of the role of these looser norms, I now believe that CCP leaders under Mao gave less though still significant weight to them than seemed the case a decade ago. This, in turn, is related to the judgment that Mao's imperial behavior was considerably more in evidence at an earlier period than previously believed—a judgment most clearly supported by the Gao Gang affair. These considerations will be explored by examining the evolution of the norms after 1949, but first a brief discussion of the basic rectification model is in order.

While the original Yan'an rectification of the early 1940s has been repeatedly hailed as a reform oriented, educational movement, the reality was clearly more complex. *Politics and Purges* dealt with the coercive aspects of the campaign, although arguably it did not attach sufficient weight to these aspects.[117] Yet perhaps more important for my purposes here than the underexamined blatantly coercive elements including arrests and torture is the need to emphasize some essential aspects of rectification. As argued in *Politics and Purges* and reaffirmed in post-Mao sources, the rectification approach combines "persuasion" with often intense pressure—the pressure which as Mao observed made cadres "break out into a cold sweat" before achieving a higher understanding of the correct line. Thus even though rectification was to avoid the "ruthless struggles and merciless blows" of inner Party life in earlier days, it most decidedly was not designed to spare sensibilities when exposing officials' mistakes. Indeed, despite the rejection of past excesses, the initial rectification encompassed the struggle culture of earlier periods and engendered—albeit without official sanction—an attitude that when dealing with errors the more severe the criticism the better.[118] Given such an orientation, it is not surprising that rectification subsequently was to cause unease among many cadres even to the point that the word "rectification" struck fear into their hearts.[119] Moreover, at the leadership level, it was inevitable that individual leaders would feel badly done by criticism they received in the Yan'an movement. Undoubtedly the most celebrated case concerns the extensive criticism endured by Peng Dehuai at the 1945 North China rectification meeting for alleged military and political mistakes. Peng clearly felt such criticism had been unfair, and he alluded to it on such subsequent occasions as in 1953 in the context of the Gao-Rao affair and again at Lushan in 1959. In this case, moreover, a main critic of Peng in 1945 and a target of Gao Gang in 1953, Bo Yibo, came to regret his role, agreeing that the criticism had been too harsh.[120]

Nevertheless, it is striking that the highest CCP leaders who have been through the process themselves have largely perceived the rectification tradition as being *relatively* benign. In Peng's case, according to Bo Yibo's recollection of a 1953 conversation, the old marshal could accept the validity of the inner Party criticism he had received whatever his resentments concerning its excesses and particular issues. For his own part, having just passed through harsh criticism during the Gao-Rao affair, Bo was also able to accept the process particularly in view of Mao's efforts to lessen its severity, correct unsuitable criticism and recognize his merits.[121] In other words, whatever specific injustices were perceived, Yan'an style rectification was widely accepted within the leadership as having a valid reform function tied to the Party's overriding revolutionary objective and as being lenient in comparison to the CCP's past. Thus when the 1957 rectification was launched the Yan'an campaign was cited, however inaccurately in historical detail, to reassure Party members that the new campaign would be conducted in the manner of a "gentle breeze and mild rain." Similarly, as we shall see, even on the eve of the Cultural Revolution there were widespread expectations that rectification norms would hold and most cadres and leaders would escape serious consequences. And the reform period rectification of the 1980s also repeatedly recalled the Yan'an experience as proof of the educational thrust of the drive and to distinguish it clearly from the chaotic and vicious Cultural Revolution approach.[122]

None of this is to deny an important element of underlying commonality between Yan'an and the Cultural Revolution—once a correct line had been laid down officials fundamentally had no choice but to accept it and admit their own past mistakes. Again the example of Liu Shaoqi is particularly poignant. Liu was not only one of the key architects of the Yan'an movement, during it he even engaged in an extreme Cultural Revolution style negation of other leaders.[123] Yet in the Cultural Revolution itself Liu not only became the preeminent target, but he was unable to defend himself given the accepted understanding which had also marked the Yan'an movement that whoever was under attack had no right to speak except in self-criticism.[124] Nevertheless, in the eyes of the elite which personally experienced both campaigns a fundamental difference did exist, and in fact the Yan'an criticism was conducted within significant limits for the most part, quasi-objective criteria were used in the assignment of fault, the great bulk of leaders retained positions within the higher echelons of the CCP, and Party unity was a genuine overriding objective of the exercise. What the surviving elite has failed to recognize adequately was the vulnerability of the rectification approach and organizational norms generally to the various contradictions noted above, and most particularly to the overwhelming dominance of Mao.

Gao Gang and the "Golden Age" of Party Norms

The previous discussion of the Gao Gang-Rao Shushi affair not only demonstrated Mao's dominance, it also raised questions concerning the degree of commitment of the leadership to Party norms. In their efforts to anticipate Mao's wishes and avoid his wrath, key leaders either clearly violated official norms or laid low in circumstances where a firm commitment to the norms would have argued for bolder action. Factional activity, the pursuit of power and position by informal groups outside of normal Party channels and largely unrelated to any principled stand on ideology or policy, was unambiguously banned by CCP organizational principles as well as by the looser conception of Party unity, yet such activity was a key feature of the Gao-Rao case. Not only did Gao, based on his apparent misreading of the Chairman,[125] engage in behind the scenes maneuvers designed to alter fundamentally the leadership lineup under Mao, but as we have seen a significant number of high ranking officials secretly backed his cause. This reflected additional considerations to the all important perception that Liu Shaoqi was in trouble with Mao while Gao Gang had found his favor. In particular, it related to the way in which the *norm* of opposing factionalism related to the *interests* of various groupings or "factions" within the CCP.[126]

The desirability of avoiding conflict among the various armies, organizations and personal networks of the revolutionary period in the interests of larger Party unity conveniently dovetailed with the power interests of the various factions. The groupings which had formed all sought recognition of their particular contributions to the revolution and a share of the fruits of victory. These desires were satisfied by a generally equitable share out of official positions after the establishment of the PRC. The norm banning factional conflict, then, not only served to bolster Party unity, it also acted to protect the stake of different groups in a satisfactory *status quo*. In 1953, however, with both the Eighth Party Congress and a new state structure projected for the near future,[127] a new balancing act would be required. As noted earlier Gao—assertedly falsely—claimed that Liu and his "white area" followers were planning to upset the factional balance by increasing *their* representation on the Politburo. Gao pointed to a draft Politburo list drawn up by Liu's old associate, deputy organization chief An Ziwen, which Gao asserted had originated with Liu and discriminated against military cadres, specifically Lin Biao who had allegedly been left off the list while the much lower ranking "white area" figure Bo Yibo had been included. This seemingly angered various generals who now supported Gao and participated in secret activities clearly forbidden by official principles. Given the added factor of Mao's perceived disenchantment with Liu, the ban on factional activity was substantially breached in large part due to the belief that group interests were under threat. Significantly, when Mao moved to redress Gao's factionalism he not only reaffirmed the ban and preached Party unity, he again carried out a skillful balancing in the new Party and state appointments to provide political support for the norms.[128]

At the very top, however, the response to Gao's effort to build factional support was marked more by circumspection than open support. As discussed earlier, those who reportedly gave a sympathetic hearing to Gao—most notably Lin Biao and Peng Dehuai—seemed passive in their backing. Even more suggestive were the responses of Chen Yun and Deng Xiaoping who, apparently uncertain of Mao's true aims, deflected Gao's advances but waited about two months before reporting to the Chairman on his flagrant violation of organizational norms. Deng's caution is further reflected in his 1980 remark that he entered "formal negotiations" *(zhengshi tanpan)* with Gao, an action supporting an authoritative oral source's conclusion that Deng (and Chen) had to be very careful since they could not be sure that Gao did not have Mao's backing. Although three decades later Deng attempted to explain his and Chen's reporting to Mao in terms of their concern for Party unity and upholding principle, their delay until the Chaiman's attitude was clearer strongly suggests their personal political futures were a more critical factor in their actions. Nevertheless, it would be rash to conclude that Party norms played no role in their actions, or in their preferences for the outcome of the affair. For Gao Gang's effort threatened to upset not only the Party unity which had contributed so mightily to the victory of 1949, but also the relative predictability of existing arrangements which placed them in key positions. Again, calculations of political interest worked to reinforce the norms, albeit after a period of uncertainty when the two factors stood in potential conflict. In any case, whatever the inherently unknowable degree of attachment to the norms on the part of Chen, Deng and others, it was clearly less than that implied by the notion of a golden age of inner Party democracy.[129]

But in another sense the distinction between the pre- and post-1957 periods is confirmed since, at least on a benign reading of the Chairman's intentions,[130] during the Gao-Rao affair Mao did not directly violate the norms in the loose sense they applied to him as he did so blatantly in attacking Peng Dehuai in 1959. Indeed, taken at face value Mao's actions from the latter part of the summer 1953 financial and economic conference served to reinforce Party norms. Not only did he reaffirm and privately lobby for Party unity, he seemingly eventually decided that adherence to the norms and a stable leadership was more important than any personal or policy preferences for Gao Gang. Moreover, when the Chairman initially moved to cool down inner Party conflict in early August, he took the step of himself engaging in self-criticism. Mao acknowledged that he shared some responsibility for Bo Yibo's errors concerning

Xiannian and Bo Yibo) as responsible, and particularly his assertion that those guilty of the error stood "only 50 meters from the rightists" sent shock waves through the assembled participants. The use of the dreaded rightist label meant no one dared to speak out for fear of being so classified. By raising what had been a policy question to a political-ideological one the Chairman created a situation where any real debate was impossible.[139]

Yet the situation at and following Nanning was more complicated than this account of Mao simply striking fear into the hearts of his leading comrades would suggest. First, related to our larger concern and the comparative lack of attention to the question of inner Party democracy after 1949, there is little evidence—in contrast to events in 1959—of whether top leaders saw the Chairman's actions as a major break of the norms. Although there are indications that Zhang Wentian—who was not at Nanning—was unhappy with Mao's attack on "anti-reckless advance," oral sources generally claim no knowledge of the attitudes of other leaders towards the Chairman's actions. In part, this seems due to the fact that quite apart from the element of fear a significant consensus had quickly formed behind Mao. Whether because of a genuine desire for the rapid development of their backward country or the habit of accepting Mao's perceived superior wisdom, with the obvious exception of Chen Yun there were no signs of even tacit opposition at the very top. Thus oral sources that are well aware of the strong pressures at Nanning and subsequently conclude that "generally speaking there was still collective leadership in 1958." From this perspective, because of the broad consensus[140] within the leadership and the ratification of decisions by Party conferences, even though Mao now completely stopped attending Politburo meetings the process was "democratic" and Chen Yun was simply an isolated minority figure. Even Zhang Wentian was initially part of the consensus. According to a source specializing in Zhang's career, in February 1958 Zhang wrote a letter to Mao after conducting a local survey to express his enthusiasm and delight at the excellent situation. In the draft of the letter, however, Zhang also noted some shortcomings, but in the final version deleted these as not appropriate to raise at that time given his limited knowledge of the whole picture. Thus even the strongest proponent of inner Party democracy within the leadership restricted his expression on policy out of both enthusiasm for the new program and prudence in the face of an aroused Mao.[141]

This situation where the question of inner Party democracy was not confronted continued throughout 1958 as the fervor for the Great Leap built to even greater heights. In addition, the fact that as with Bo Yibo in 1953 and Deng Zihui in 1955 Mao did not severely punish Zhou and Chen, and that the May 1958 Second Session of the Eighth Party Congress was treated as a rectification meeting with the benign overtones that implied,[142] further served to reduce the salience of "democracy" as an issue. So too did the fact that when problems became apparent in the latter part of the year the Chairman took the lead in addressing them, even as others—again including Zhang Wentian[143]—held back in expressing their own criticisms. Yet as further evidence of faults in the Great Leap strategy mounted, not only economic policy but also the question of "democratic" expression became increasingly important. This question would be raised in various ways—first at the spring 1959 Shanghai meeting, and then at Lushan.

Significantly, the key actors in placing inner Party democracy on the agenda at Shanghai were Zhang Wentian and Mao himself. As in so many other aspects of elite politics the Chairman was the catalyst. Aware by this time of not only the seriousness of economic problems but also of the need to encourage critics to speak out if these problems were to be adequately dealt with, Mao now called on Party members to emulate Hai Rui, the Ming dynasty official who criticized the emperor and lost his position as a result, and dare to speak out and even be prepared for beheading. Ironically, in view of subsequent developments, the Chairman personally gave Peng Dehuai a copy of the Hai Rui biography. At the same time, however, Mao privately confessed during the conference that while he wanted Hai Ruis to appear he feared he might not be able to bear criticism if it was offered. He also noted that even "[Liu] Shaoqi doesn't dare to speak to me frankly," and that although he had notionally been on the "second line" he was not completely confident of others and thus returned to the "first line" to attend to detail. While Mao clearly was ambivalent, by raising the Hai Rui analogy he provided room for Zhang to air his concerns about inner Party democracy. Although my oral source specializing in Zhang does not believe it was intended as a criticism of Mao, Zhang now spoke out at a group meeting and extended the Chairman's call for candid speaking. While agreeing with Mao's appeal for daring, Zhang went on to say that this was not enough, that it was necessary for the leadership to create a democratic atmosphere, an environment which encouraged lower levels to disclose different views without fear of the consequences. By calling for more than acts of individual heroism Zhang now publicly raised the crucial question of the necessary conditions for democratic life within the CCP.[144]

When the Lushan meeting convened three months later the issue of Party democracy was even more salient to various CCP leaders. Peng Dehuai criticized the tendency of first secretaries to monopolize power, a comment ostensibly aimed at regional leaders as everyone avoided direct criticism of Mao. Indeed, given Mao's Shanghai posture, early in the conference in private conversation with the Chairman Zhou Xiaozhou expressed his concern that people were not speaking out at Lushan, that many didn't dare to talk about shortcomings, and he received a sympathetic hearing. But even at this stage before the increased tension caused by Peng's letter, not to mention Mao's outburst of July 23, various leaders spoke privately of the problems created by the Chairman's increasingly willful leadership style. Again Zhang Wentian was most acute in his assessment of the situation. Speaking to his secretary Zhang complained that the Party had become arrogant and had lost its perspective, things were becoming like Stalin's later period, collective leadership was no longer tenable, and although he was a Politburo member he didn't know what was going on. In another more celebrated conversation with Peng Dehuai, Zhang again raised the Stalin analogy but, ironically, Peng sought to defend Mao by arguing he was different from Stalin and far superior in his recognition of non-antagonistic contradictions, although Peng went on to complain that the Chairman only criticized others and would never admit his own mistakes. As the situation became more tense once Peng's letter was circulated, the democracy issue became even more acute and Zhang Wentian, not without foreboding, gave a systematic, theoretically based analysis of the great importance of inner Party democracy in a July 21 speech. Thus considerable concern had been expressed both publicly and privately within the leadership before and after Peng's letter, but the biggest test of leadership commitment to democratic norms came with Mao's withering attack of the 23rd.[145]

As we have seen, in the shock and confusion following Mao's attack various leaders sought to cushion the blow and hoped the Chairman's anger would soon pass. Undoubtedly a variety of motives were involved including personal closeness[146] and, in a status conscious Party, respect for Peng's historic contributions to the revolution. Another factor which undoubtedly came into play was the policy concerns of those who shared Peng's attitude toward the Great Leap and correctly feared the necessary remedial measures could not be taken if a major campaign was launched against the old marshal. Yet clearly a sense that the CCP's loosely constructed rules had been broken was also deeply felt at Lushan. Deng Xiaoping's 1980 observation that "it was normal for [Peng] as a member of the [Politburo] to write to the Chairman"[147] was more than an *ex post facto* judgment; at the time there were considerable, albeit private, laments concerning the damage done to inner Party democracy. It was the night of the 23rd, once they had recovered from the initial shock, that Mao's secretaries began to talk in earnest about Mao as the later Stalin. The next day Zhang Wentian spoke of the tense situation which made speaking up difficult and identified inner Party democracy as the key issue. And a week later one of the Chairman's secretaries, Tian Jiaying, complained about the inappropriateness of subjecting Peng, a Politburo member, to criticism in small group meetings when the Politburo had not discussed the case, and sadly observed that if Mao acted in this dictatorial manner his reputation in his later years would suffer.[148] Thus democratic norms were at issue—at least for part of the elite. Yet perhaps more telling for these people than the letter of the Party rules was a more traditionally based sense that Peng had only been acting as an upright official should—speaking out for the good of the realm regardless of the consequences. This view is supported not only by the currency of the Hai Rui example which Mao himself had introduced, but also by the fact that the individuals concerned felt there was no option but to accept Mao's actions much as Hai Rui had to accept the emperor's edict.[149]

Perhaps the strongest indication of the importance of the norms is evidence that even those who differed with Peng on policy questions were distressed by his fate, although the details in this regard seem to be somewhat different from what was advanced in *Politics and Purges*. In the first edition reference was made to the alleged defence of Peng's right to speak out shortly after the meetings by the leftist leader of Sichuan, Li Jingquan.[150] This information, based on Cultural Revolution sources, is hotly contested by a participant in the Lushan events who declared such a view on Li's part as "impossible" given that Li, along with Ke Qingshi, stood out for the ferocity of his attacks on Peng. But another Great Leap leftist, chief agricultural policy maker Tan Zhenlin, did show concern for Peng and implicitly for the norms in a July 26 speech. While Tan declared he would engage in principled struggle against Peng's letter to the end, he lauded Peng as a good comrade who was loyal to the Party and country with many contributions to the revolution. Moreover, he praised the writing of the letter as a brave act, as a very good thing. Yet despite his attitude, which was reportedly representative of the feelings of many others, Tan was forced to withdraw his remarks two days later as the pressure grew.[151] This crumbling of the will to stand up for the norms was evident in the ineffectual actions of other leaders. Zhu De, undoubtedly the most sympathetic of all on a personal basis, could only try to assist Peng by making his criticism as mild as possible under the circumstances, an effort which only resulted in Zhu also coming under harsh criticism at both Lushan and the Military Affairs Committee meeting convened immediately following. And when Foreign Minister Chen Yi, who had not been present at Lushan, questioned Bo Yibo on what happened and expressed disappointment with the undemocratic way of handling Peng's views, Bo agreed but quickly added that they could only exchange these opinions in private.[152]

The rich vein of new post-1978 evidence thus strongly supports the argument of *Politics and Purges* that the norms of inner Party democracy were an important leadership concern at Lushan, but at the same time a concern which was rudely shoved aside by a determined Chairman. Yet this evidence provides a more subtle picture of the leadership's attitude to the norms over the entire period from Nanning to Lushan. While undoubtedly a feeling that inner Party democracy was desirable existed before Nanning, it was not a high salience issue given Mao's generally consultative leadership style up to that point—notwithstanding several major deviations. The events at Nanning clearly increased the salience of the question, but it remained comparatively low given the broad leadership consensus on and enthusiasm for the Great Leap. But as problems with the leap became more prominent, and as Mao himself realized the need for more democratic expression, the significance of inner Party democracy became even more apparent for many leaders. When Mao reacted harshly to Peng Dehuai at Lushan, far more harshly than he had reacted to any other leader in the entire period of his leadership going back to revolutionary days, the significance of the norms was brought home with startling force to the leadership but they were powerless to resist in the face of Mao's authority. A new benchmark had been created in elite politics. If Nanning had been the start of "abnormal inner Party life," then Lushan raised abnormality to a new level. Not only as before was the question of inner Party democracy raised publicly only in ways which largely excluded the Chairman from criticism, but there is little evidence to indicate that after Lushan top leaders even discussed Mao's violations of democratic norms privately among themselves however they may have felt individually.[153]

Party Norms under Arbitrary Rule, 1960–66

Politics and Purges argued that following the Lushan watershed Party norms were significantly but far from totally swept aside in this new period of increased "abnormality." Mao himself reaffirmed organizational principles on various occasions in the 1959–65 period, but this aspect of the Chairman's activities was probably overstated in 1979. With the benefit of new data the sheer arbitrariness of so much of Mao's behavior stands in even sharper relief than a decade ago. Examples of this arbitrary behavior have already been discussed—Mao's disbanding of the Central Committee's rural work department in 1962, his criticism of the SPC in 1964 for practicing the ideology of the Guomindang (GMD), and his irrational outburst at the end of 1964 that he was being denied his right to speak. Perhaps the most bizarre example, and one with severe consequences for the leader involved, concerned Vice Premier Xi Zhongxun at the crucial Tenth Plenum of 1962, the occasion when Mao issued his famous slogan to "never forget class struggle." While other leaders such as Chen Yun were sharply rebuked by the Chairman at this time for their perceived policy mistakes, Xi's "crime" was his approval of an historical novel about the old Northwest revolutionary base area where Gao Gang had been active. Although Gao's name had not been used, it was clear which character represented him. The appearance of this novel, which fortuitously coincided with Peng Dehuai's efforts to secure a reexamination of his case, was viewed by Kang Sheng and others as an attempt to "reverse the verdict" on Gao as well. They managed to convince Mao of this position, and when he read out a note from Kang at the plenum that "using a novel to attack the Party is a remarkable invention," these words suddenly became a quotation from Chairman Mao. Xi's fate was sealed, he lost his posts, was dispatched to the basic levels, and apparently was treated harshly even during the pre-Cultural Revolution years.[154]

But if Mao's regard for the norms in the years from Lushan to the Cultural Revolution now seems even more cavalier than that pictured in *Politics and Purges*, in some respects the degree to which his colleagues still placed faith in these principles during the period of their decline might have been greater than believed earlier. To be sure, a palpable awareness of Mao's growing unpredictability permeated the leadership. Yet within the heightened prudential constraints caused by this situation, most key leaders apparently observed the norms. According to a senior Party historian, the leaders on the "first line" consistently applied "democratic centralism" in these years. Even the most questionable practices such as Deng Xiaoping's reported "passive sabotage" seemingly amounted to ignoring certain of Mao's preoccupations in the ideological sphere and leaving them to other leaders to implement rather than acting against the Chairman's orders.[155] Contrary to the analysis of the first edition, the famous Changguanlou incident of 1961 reinforces the general point. This meeting of Beijing muncipal leaders near the Beijing zoo was convened in late 1961 by Peng Zhen to examine CCP documents including Mao's speeches since 1958 in order to analyze the reasons for the Great Leap debacle. *Politics and Purges* followed the Cultural Revolution version of this event—i.e., Peng clearly violated organizational norms by keeping it secret from higher Party authorities, thus reflecting the prudential requirement of avoiding Mao's anticipated ire.[156] According to another well placed oral source, however, this version is a gross distortion. In fact, these activities, although not formally reported to the Party Center, were not secret either and simply represented Peng's gathering of reference material as part of his preparations for the January 1962 7,000 cadres conference. This was an acceptable procedure before a major conference, and the focus on leftist errors was consistent with Mao's own contemporary emphasis on the need for investigation and criticism of the leap's shortcomings. The incident was used in the Cultural Revolution to frame Peng, but, according to my source, it in no way violated Party rules.[157] Indeed, the central secretariat, where Peng also sat second only to Deng Xiaoping, had concluded its own review of Party documents and sent its report to Mao.[158]

While the new evidence of the past decade suggests Mao's observance of Party norms after Lushan was even more chequered than it seemed in 1979, this evidence also allows a deeper understanding of Mao's sporadic efforts to uphold the norms and the reaction of his leading colleagues to those efforts. In the view of an authoritative oral source Mao generally accepted the collective proposals of the "first line" in the years leading up to the Cultural Revolution, his dramatic initiatives and lapses notwithstanding. In addition, when Mao did insist on his own way it was generally endorsed by some formal Party body producing a veneer of legality. More specifically, particularly in the crisis period of 1961–62 the Chairman made a special effort to promote collective leadership and free expression, and even, as we have seen, to practice self-criticism. Two instances stand out—a May–June 1961 central work conference and the January 1962 7,000 cadres conference. As in 1959, Mao now recognized the need for greater inner Party democracy to help overcome the economic mess but his attitude was ambivalent and his associates treaded with caution.

The 1961 work conference was convened to summarize the experience of the Great Leap and overcome its mistakes—particularly its leftist errors in agriculture. At this conference Mao not only addressed defects in inner Party life, this was also the occasion that the Chairman made his self-criticism which Liu refused to transmit to lower levels. Unfortunately little is known of Mao's self-criticism except that he said the Central Committee and especially he himself should bear the principal responsibility for the mistakes of the past few years. In the conference's discussion of the shortcomings of inner Party democracy, however, the focus was on the consequences of Lushan rather than the rights or wrongs of the meetings themselves and the issue was apparently deflected to the lower levels where, it was said, first secretaries were monopolizing control to the detriment of collective leadership. While some progress was made, on the democracy question as on other issues the progress in correcting the left trend was not thorough. Especially revealing was Mao's reaction to the efforts of "some people" to explain the persistence of leftism. According to their analysis, which is both the view of *Politics and Purges* and consistent with the Chairman's January 1961 observations,[159] the shock of Lushan and particularly the campaign against right opportunism launched following the meetings had a wide impact which prevented effective measures to deal with left mistakes and caused the suppression of inner Party democracy. Mao, showing the ambivalence which had become so typical of his opinions at critical junctures, baulked at accepting the full implications of this view. Instead he held that the struggle against right opportunism at Lushan had been necessary and the only mistake had been to transmit the results of that struggle to the county and lower levels which indeed had the effect of disrupting their efforts to correct leftism.[160]

Mao's ambivalence, and the reluctance of his comrades to press the sensitive democracy issue too far, were even more apparent at the 7,000 cadres conference. By the latter stages of the conference democratic centralism had become a central item on the conference agenda, and it was addressed by various leaders from Mao and Liu down. Mao's role in pushing the question was clearly critical. He not only decided on the second or "release anger" stage of the conference where plain talking became more pronounced, but he also encouraged the leaders of the conference group sessions to make sure the anger was well and truly released. Moreover, Mao again engaged in self-criticism, one which seemingly went somewhat further than his 1961 effort. Now Mao not only again assumed responsibility for the errors of the recent past, but affirmed that he too was bound by majority decisions—albeit with a peculiar definition of a majority as everyone else having a view contrary to his own. And perhaps particularly telling was the fact that Liu Shaoqi's report, which had been bold in dealing with economic questions, did not include a section on inner Party democracy in its first two drafts. Only after the Chairman intervened to emphasize the importance of democracy was such a section included, and it was carefully phrased to point away once more from Mao and toward regional leaders and lower level cadres.[161]

Yet as we have seen Mao's emphasis on democracy did not persuade an unprepared Chen Yun to offer his views nor prevent Li Fuchun and Bo Yibo from placing before the conference a report they knew was false.[162] And it did not prevent a "self-critical" Chairman from feeling that Lin Biao's unvarnished praise was on a higher level than the efforts of his other colleagues who tried to balance the pressing policy needs of the moment with the need to avoid offending Mao. The caution of his colleagues notwithstanding, they could not have been fully aware of Mao's internal confusion on the issue. According to a senior Party historian who was present on the occasion, the general effect of Mao's efforts was very beneficial and people felt at ease. Mao's major speech on democratic centralism seemed positive, and even today, "if one reads it word for word," it appears all right. But, in his current view, Mao's self-criticism was superficial, it didn't really address either the nature of his own errors or the fundamental shortcomings of the leap forward. And, although it wasn't apparent to my source at the time, he now sees an element of rebuke in response to Liu's speech, a surfacing of concern with domestic revisionism in the Chairman's interpretation that if there was no democratic centralism in the Party then there could be no socialist economy, and if there was no socialist economy then China would degenerate into a Yugoslav style bourgeois dictatorship. But if this hint was not appreciated at the time, various of the Chairman's particular sensitivities were. As a result, when Liu observed that many of Peng Dehuai's views at Lushan were correct and there was nothing wrong in writing a letter to Mao—a proposition that reportedly angered Mao, he nevertheless hastened to add that Peng could not be rehabilitated because of his illicit links to foreign countries, i.e., the Soviet Union, and his having formed an anti-Party clique—charges that were false. Soon, however, Peng would seek a reconsideration of his case which would culminate in a puzzling encounter with the Chairman in 1965 after additional blows to Party norms.[163]

While further occasional statements in support of the norms were made by Mao in the period leading up to the Cultural Revolution, nothing remotely matched his emphasis on democracy in 1961–62. Instead, as oral sources have indicated, the Chairman's attacks on various colleagues in fall 1962 and late 1964 produced even greater caution in dealing with Mao than previously.[164] The predicament this created for such leaders, a predicament which produced not only caution but also some indications, however modest, of continuing respect for the norms, was richly illustrated by Peng Dehuai's case. In mid-1962 Peng presented his 80,000 character letter to the Center requesting a reexamination of his case. In so doing he was apparently first of all registering a protest over the conclusion presented by Liu at the 7,000 cadres conference, yet arguably Peng was also expressing some faith or more likely hope in Party procedures which at the conference specifically sanctioned "verdict reversals" and in Mao's capacity to forgive. It is now clear from the testimony of a senior Party historian that this letter set in motion the events leading to Peng's September 1965 audience with Mao when the Chairman, now endorsing a new posting for Peng in the Southwest, by Peng's account went so far as to observe that "perhaps the truth is on your side." What had happened in the intervening three years, according to my source, is that following Peng's request a committee to examine his case had been established under Marshal He Long at the fall 1962 Tenth Plenum in a context where Mao both reaffirmed that Peng should not be rehabilitated and criticized the "wind of verdict reversals." He Long's appointment was significant for two reasons: first, he had been a sharp critic of Peng at Lushan; second, only someone of He's rank as a marshal had sufficient status to investigate Peng. The committee conducted prolonged but inconclusive investigations into the various charges, above all concerning Peng's "illicit" ties with foreign countries. As a result, in the absence of solid evidence the committee reached no conclusion, neither condemning nor clearing Peng Dehuai. This clearly showed both prudence given Mao's declared attitude, but also some commitment to procedures—and especially, it would seem, respect for Peng's historic status—in that no bogus verdict was concocted. Moreover, some leaders believed that even if Peng could not be absolved he should be given some work, and in these circumstances Mao apparently felt obliged to make a gesture toward Peng resulting in his new appointment. Yet in fact the Chairman's anger with the old marshal had hardly abated and by the next month he was again attacking Peng at a Party work conference. In this instance, then, we see Peng's willingness to test Party procedures, other leaders implementing those procedures honestly, albeit gingerly, in an area of sensitivity for the Chairman, Mao feeling it necessary to acknowledge leadership sentiment arising from the investigation, but the Chairman ultimately refusing to alter his hostility toward Peng Dehuai.[165]

Peng Dehuai, of course, was also linked to another strange development of late 1965 which became the immediate forerunner of the Cultural Revolution—the criticism of Wu Han's play about the upright Ming official Hai Rui who Mao now decided was an allegorical representation of Peng. The basic analysis of the Wu Han affair given in *Politics and Purges*[166] has been amply confirmed by post-1978 materials: the publication of Yao Wenyuan's critical article in November 1965, after months of secret preparation with Mao's blessing, left the "first line" leaders surprised and confused; Peng Zhen's actions in defending Wu Han reflected both a defense of Party norms in the sense that Wu Han had no culpable organizational links to Peng Dehuai and anger that bureaucratic procedures had apparently been violated by the publication of the article in Shanghai without clearing it with the Center; and Mao's position remained elusive right up to March 1966 so that Peng could reasonably assume that, even if he didn't have the Chairman's explicit blessing, there was at least enough room for him to try and persuade Mao of his own view. The new information, moreover, allows some clarification of key aspects of these developments. First, Peng Zhen, while clearly trying to advance his own preferences, proved remarkably sensitive to Mao's wishes once they were expressed; at the same time the Chairman's opaqueness throughout this period is even more apparent. Peng's initial reaction to Yao's article was based on his ignorance of its origins; once informed in late November by Zhou Enlai and army Chief of Staff Luo Ruiqing that it had Mao's blessing he quickly convened a large meeting to organize propagation of the article. While this together with subsequent measured criticism of Wu Han could be seen as—and in fact it undoubtedly was—a maneuver to help Wu "pass the test," it was also consistent with Mao's known attitudes concerning the historian whose protection the Chairman had called for in 1964 in the context of the ideological criticism then underway. Moreover, in a February 8 audience, Peng subtly endorsed Mao's December linking of Hai Rui and Peng Dehuai while at the same time seeking to protect Wu, and the Chairman responded that Wu could remain a vice mayor after undergoing criticism. On this occasion, moreover, Mao accepted without comment Peng's February Outline which treated the errors of Wu and others as academic matters, nor did he raise contrary opinions to other leaders who visited him in this period. The uncertainty of the Chairman's position at this late date is indicated by the fact that, contrary to Cultural Revolution assertions cited in the first edition, another member of the group responsible for the Outline, the radical Kang Sheng, voiced no dissent from its conclusions. Kang, too, apparently was still in the dark, and only began to distance himself from the report in March as Mao's attitude became clear.[167]

Another aspect of the story, one perhaps not given sufficient emphasis in *Politics and Purges*, concerns the elite's continuing guarded faith in Party traditions and Mao's self restraint. This is seen most dramatically in the reaction of Wu Han and his family to unfolding events. While Wu's reaction to Yao's article clearly had its ups and downs, swinging from scorn to concern mixed with confidence to worry that some powerful figure might be behind it all,[168] his wife expressed at the time the view that "after criticism, everything will be all right" *(pipan, pipan, jiu haole)*.[169] What this remark reflected was not a sense that the criticism of Wu Han was appropriate—it was grossly unfair and perceived as such, but rather that as long as the criticism and self-criticism ritual was conformed to normal political life would be restored. This further indicated a widespread elite expectation that things would not get out of control, that the traditional methods with their convenient limitations on criticism and the predictability of a favorable result as long as the game was played appropriately would still be applied. Yet it was also more than a "game"; Wu Han and many other imminent victims of the Cultural Revolution lived very willingly within Party procedures, accepted them and cooperated in observing them however much they resented error in particular cases.[170] Only as 1966 wore on did such officials and the leadership more broadly become aware that more than specific errors were involved, that a deeply disturbed Chairman was now willfully, if not fully consciously,[171] distorting the process itself.[172]

The attachment to Party principles in this instance, as in earlier cases, undoubtedly had as much or more to do with self interest as with normative obligation, but the norms clearly were important to the elite in both respects. This, in turn, is one of many considerations which strongly indicate that pre-Cultural Revolution elite politics is not adequately or accurately characterized as a vicious, revenge filled, life and death struggle. As the preceeding discussion has amply illustrated, the Party's loosely structured norms were a significant feature of CCP politics even if they were easily violated by Mao and even if elite support for them was at least as much based on prudential as principled impulses. Moreover, expectations of limits on inner Party conflict existed even in the most problematic periods before full scale Cultural Revolution.

Conclusion: Party Norms and Political Practice—The Texture of Elite Politics

The foregoing argument is essentially two-edged. On the one hand, the norms were a significant feature of pre-Cultural Revolution Party life. On the other, they coexisted with practices and impulses of the leadership political culture—what I call the texture of elite politics—which in various ways were in tension with the norms yet in others contributed to a pattern of elite interaction broadly supportative of CCP organizational principles. These practices and impulses, and their complex relationship to Party norms, were a constant of the 1949–65 period notwithstanding the dramatic swings of Party politics, and they can be seen in the rich new evidence available concerning the various cases analyzed above. The elite political culture they reflect derives from both traditional hierarchical relationships and the specific traditions of the CCP's revolution, a potent amalgam which produced a mode of politics contrary to not only Western practice but also to the way many Western analysts have interpreted Chinese politics.

The most fundamental textural feature of elite politics is indicated by the title of my revised analysis of the Gao-Rao case—*Politics at Mao's Court.* Here the imagery is of the imperial palace, of the emperor surrounded by anxious courtiers seeking to gain or retain his favor, to obtain his backing for their various projects and political interests. Some indication of the evidence supporting this image has already been given, but the significance of the phenomena for official norms justifies further comment. As previously noted, at the time of the Gao-Rao affair Chen Yun proved the past master of this brand of court politics, winning Mao's approval for such objectives as bureaucratic control of the socialist transformation of the bourgeoisie and the moderation of policy toward commercial capitalists. Later, however, when Mao became more involved in economic policy the task was difficult even for someone as skilled as Chen Yun. During the Great Leap Forward Chen could only pick his opportunities to articulate his preferences to limited effect in accord with Mao's changing assessments, and basically keep quiet when the Chairman was not in a mood to listen. While in one sense convincing the leader of one's position is part and parcel of democratic politics universally, in the Chinese case the absolute discretion on Mao's part reflected a far more authoritarian reality. Even more telling, of course, was the reluctance to approach Mao on the absolutely vital question of the leadership lineup at the highest level. The impulse to keep one's distance even in the relatively "democratic" period of the early 1950s while the Chairman was perceived to be ruminating on the fate of his most senior colleagues, as in the behavior of Chen Yun and Deng Xiaoping during the Gao Gang affair when the fate of Liu Shaoqi and Zhou Enlai was perceived to be in the balance, reflects both an acceptance of Mao's power to alter the most critical power relationships and a fear of being dragged down by a false step. There was simply no recourse to the Chairman's disfavor, a situation in profound tension with even the prevailing modest interpretations of the rights of other Party leaders.

The reasons for this situation bear analysis. The primary reason, as argued in *Leadership, Legitimacy, and Conflict*, was the charismatic legitimacy conferred on Mao by the victory of 1949.[173] For CCP leaders Mao's great contributions in achieving the revolutionary goals they had devoted their lives to outweighed all his excesses. Chen Yun probably put this attitude best in 1981 when he observed, "When Comrade Mao Zedong committed mistakes many old cadres suffered but everyone still had faith in him [and] could not forget his achievements."[174] The resultant impulse to obedience was reinforced by both the authoritarian traditions of the international Communist movement and China's "feudal" past, both of which created pressure for ideological conformity and veneration of the top leader.[175] This, of course, was reflected in a more widespread tendency to one man leadership at all levels which permeated the entire Party structure. According to the post-Mao critique of this tendency, such attitudes as "obeying the [P]arty's leadership meant listening to a certain person's words," "say[ing] yes to whatever [one's] 'superior' says without reserve," and attributing "all our victories and achievements to individuals" was rife among CCP cadres. Moreover, with regard to the Chairman himself, many cadres particularly from rural areas adopted a deeply reverential attitude of "loyalty to the monarch."[176] For all these reasons a political culture of submissiveness existed at both high and low levels within the CCP. While the formal quasi-democratic norms corresponded to real leadership values and expectations, ultimately they were less powerful than the need to have someone "in charge" (*zhuchi*), a need naturally growing out of the search for dynamic leadership of the perilous revolutionary enterprise yet fully compatible with and influenced by traditional culture.

Other features of elite political culture, however, had a much more ambiguous relationship to Party norms. A prime case in point concerns the unusually acute CCP sensitivity to status—status largely derived from seniority in and contributions to the pre-1949 Chinese revolution. In the Gao-Rao affair this was manifested in many ways. Thus because of his great military victories during the revolution, Lin Biao was both a key target for Gao to win over to his cause and someone widely recognized as worthy of Politburo membership despite persistent ill health which prevented him from playing an active political or administrative role. Also, Deng Xiaoping claimed to have rejected Gao's approach on the grounds that Liu Shaoqi's status *(diwei)* had been fixed by history. Moreover, when an angry Mao wanted to denounce Rao Shushi openly at the fall 1953 organization conference, Zhou Enlai successfully counselled the Chairman against this course on the grounds that washing the top level leadership's dirty linen in front of mere provincial level figures wouldn't do.[177] Such sensitivity to status was compatible with leadership stability and Party unity—as long as the requisite interests of various leaders and groups was observed. As argued earlier, the pragmatic concern with maintaining a broadly accepted "factional" balance reinforced the official norm banning overt factional activity. At the same time, however, even false rumors such as those allegedly spread by Gao Gang that the balance of factions was being challenged by Liu's group could ironically stimulate clearly illegitimate factional maneuvers. And while status might have shielded ranking leaders from *threatening* criticism in the absence of Mao's dissatisfaction,[178] the systematic exclusion of broader Party audiences from high level differences did little to encourage an atmosphere of "democratic" discussion within the organization as a whole.[179]

Status consciousness also served to reduce responsibility, and therefore the effective functioning of the system, in a number of ways. Although perhaps a unique case given both his continuous ill health and Mao's unusually high regard for him, Lin Biao's career demonstrates several paradoxical consequences of status considerations. While at the time of the Gao-Rao case Lin—although on sick leave—did have a major posting as head of the Central-South region, subsequently until Lushan he only held positions of high prestige but no operational authority as a Politburo member, vice premier and, from 1958, Party vice chairman. This, of course, was in large part due to Lin's ill health, but according to a well informed oral source it also reflected the difficulty of finding a position appropriate to Lin's status. With Peng Dehuai Minister of Defence, it would have been inappropriate for Lin who had roughly equal status[180] to serve under Peng in the area of his expertise, the military. Thus, in the view of this source, the convenient solution was to give Lin the title of vice premier but he had nothing to do. Had Lin actually been healthy and this logic applied, the regime would have foregone a major talent for the sake of respecting status.

But Lin *was* ill, at least to some degree,[181] and subsequent developments showed how great political influence and administrative clout could be exercized by someone of questionable capabilities. Although Lin initially did not attend the Lushan meetings presumably because of ill health, he was summoned by Mao after Peng Dehuai's letter and played a major role in attacking Peng—a role which undoubtedly gained in effectiveness because of Lin's reputation as a great general. After Lushan Mao appointed Lin to replace Peng as Minister of Defense despite the view of Marshal Luo Ronghuan that Lin was too ill to do the job effectively, and henceforth Lin presided over military affairs. According to oral sources, while from 1959 to the Cultural Revolution Chief of Staff Luo Ruiqing administered the army, ultimate authority (subject to Mao) rested clearly with Lin. Thus, in a way strongly replicating the relationship between Mao and the "first line," Lin was able to intervene decisively but at the same time remain aloof from and even uninterested in daily affairs. It was clearly not a recipe for collective leadership, but rather a highly authoritarian and curiously inefficient superior-subordinate setup.[182]

More generally, the use of sick leave or other leave by high ranking leaders also has ambiguous implications for the norms.[183] Even where real illnesses are at issue as apparently was the case with Lin Biao, the ability of powerful politicians to retreat from official duties for substantial periods suggests a weakening of accountability. In at least some instances, moreover, sick leave appears to have been as much a political tactic as a medical imperative. Arguably a case in point was Chen Yun's sick leave in early 1962 which allowed him to delay his return to an active leadership role to a more propitious moment.[184] Even more striking was the assertedly bogus sick leave of Kang Sheng from 1949 to 1955. Kang, having been passed over in favor of Rao Shushi in 1949 as the leading Party official in East China, a position that would have befitted his Politburo status, reportedly falsely declared himself ill and only reemerged as an active force with Rao's fall.[185] Other forms of leave could also be used by top level figures. For example, in December 1951 Liu Shaoqi apparently went on holiday rather than attend the trade union congress which fell under his direct responsibility because his position on the role of trade unions had been overturned by Mao in the previous months. Hugely embarrassed, Liu decided to leave Beijing rather than attend the meeting which would endorse the rejection of his views.[186] Thus various forms of leave, whether for illness, holiday or to tend to regular work rather than attend conferences,[187] were convenient devices available to high status leaders for prudential reasons of political advantage—or even simply the indulgence of hurt pride. While diplomatic illnesses are hardly unknown elsewhere, the Chinese case including long self-imposed periods in the shadows followed, Mao willing, by the restoration of one's power is particularly striking. The practice probably contributed to elite stability by providing a mechanism for leaders to avoid conflict, but in none of the cases above did the officials in question vigorously participate in collective policy debate as ostensibly dictated by the principles of inner Party democracy. Yet paradoxically, given the larger authoritarian leadership culture, the ability to stand aside and then return at strategic junctures facilitated the process of policy adjustment provided the Chairman was receptive.

The deliberate opting out from collective decision making by the use of official leave perhaps reflects broader phenomena of elite interaction indicative not of collegiality but of the relative isolation of various top leaders from one another. While any judgment must be tentative, the Gao-Rao case in particular suggests considerable distance among at least some leaders at the top with close links limited to people working in the same functional area or from the same revolutionary "faction." While in one sense this is hardly remarkable and would be mirrored by similar tendencies in any political system, the suggestion of separate circles in the Chinese case seems particularly pronounced and is clearly in tension with the formal emphasis on collective leadership.

The most striking example to emerge from the events of 1953 is that Gao and Rao themselves, despite official charges of having engaged in a conspiracy, apparently never engaged in face to face consultation concerning their political maneuvers. Rather, Rao seems to have concluded that Gao was gaining Mao's favor and independently carried out supportative activities accordingly, while Gao observed Rao's actions and left it at that. This, of course, had the advantage for Rao in that he observed the explicit ban on overt factional plotting, but it also reflected the distance between the two men given their different revolutionary experiences and functional responsibilities. Perhaps most telling in this regard was the incredulity with which many cadres greeted the official version of a Gao-Rao plot—an incredulity based on the belief that their separate revolutionary careers made intimate relations implausible.[188] The larger implication of this instance, however, is that the genuine free exchange of views for legitimate purposes according to the CCP's organizational norms would be significantly inhibited by the tendency for leaders to keep to their own circles.[189]

If the various status related features of elite political culture did little to promote vigorous democratic life, as indicated above it could—and normally did—contribute to a comparatively stable leadership politics as sought by the CCP's normative regime. As radical and dramatic as various policy shifts were in the pre-Cultural Revolution period, the name of the game was essentially conservative. The objective was to hold one's position or gradually rise as openings naturally arose, not to leapfrog over the bodies of politically disgraced colleagues. Moreover, where "bodies" did exist as in the case of Peng Dehuai after Lushan, it is significant that only figures of requisite historical status such as Lin Biao moved into the breach. The degree of meaningful collegiality which actually existed outside of well established personal networks or work related contacts may have been limited, but the balanced sharing of positions among different groups served to defuse potential tensions. Structurally, the system of life tenure with no well-defined exit pattern meant that although the loss of position could signal very hard times, in fact only serious political trouble would result in dismissal from official posts. Rectification may have been a ritual to a degree, but the reform emphasis did serve to keep purging under considerable constraints especially before the Great Leap, and particularly at the higher levels. Indeed, the Politburo elected in 1945 was substantially in place 20 years later on the eve of the Cultural Revolution.[190] The general pattern was not a vicious life and death struggle among different factions before 1966; at most a cautious wariness of other groups, a phenomenon not unknown in far different political systems, served to inhibit the genuine impulse to collective discussion which existed despite everything. The real threat, however, came not from the dynamics of elite competition but from the supreme leader. Each major breach of organizational norms can be traced to Mao's actions—whether seemingly inadvertent as in the Gao-Rao case, due to explosive pique as with Peng Dehuai, or as a result of a deliberate if confused plan as in the launching of the Cultural Revolution.

The inner Party democracy which did exist in 1949–65 might paradoxically be termed "feudal democracy." That is, the CCP's various quasi-democratic practices existed at the discretion of the "emperor," a discretion which was always somewhat erratic but decidedly more so after 1957. These practices also coexisted with other textural features of elite political life emphasizing status considerations and cautious politics which, while not antithetical to Party norms, often stood in some tension with them. Status often translated into a certain lack of responsibility, while caution above all meant not pressing either one's views or the very right to have a voice in the face of an aroused Mao. At the same time another aspect of the CCP's normative culture—the pursuit of ideological correctness which allowed for, albeit in the name of rectification, considerable inner Party struggle—also impinged on both the conflict moderation and "democratic" aspects of Party principles. But all these complicating considerations notwithstanding, elite attachment to the norms, as indicated most dramatically at Lushan, was real if secondary to loyalty to the leader and the requirements of political survival at his court. Understandably then, once the Chairman had passed away it was no surprise that restoring traditional principles became a heartfelt initiative of Mao's former leadership colleagues with major ramifications for reform era politics.[191]

POLITICS AND PURGES IN CHINA

Introduction to the First Edition

The history of post-1949 Chinese politics has normally been written in terms of debate and conflict over social and economic questions. However, another set of issues has also been of enormous importance to the leaders of the People's Republic of China—the organizational norms defining acceptable behavior within the elite. What rights do Chinese Communist Party leaders have in the policy making process? What principles bind Party officials in the implementation of policy? What types of behavior are beyond the pale? How is inner elite conflict ideally handled? What norms guide the administration of discipline? When are purges justified? This study focuses on these questions for the period from the founding of the PRC to the start of the Cultural Revolution.

Rectification, the distinctive approach to elite discipline developed by the CCP leadership under Mao Zedong in the early 1940s, occupies a key position in the Party's organizational norms. It embodies several principles which quickly became basic Party doctrine: the vast majority of officials are "basically good" and their mistakes can be corrected, discipline must aim at achieving reform and utilizing the talents of such officials for the CCP's cause, and disciplinary methods on the whole should be lenient and limit purges to exceptional cases. In the revolutionary period, this approach built on existing leadership unity to extend and deepen the commitment of the CCP elite to Maoist programs and methods, thus playing an important role in the Party's eventual success. Quite naturally, Chinese leaders subsequently applied rectification methods to major problems and conflicts which arose after the nationwide seizure of power.

Rectification principles are firmly linked to other key organizational understandings. Given a basic commitment to the CCP's cause, leaders can participate in a relatively open policy making process marked by collective decisions and rights for minorities. In the conduct of policy debate, the participants must openly advocate positions addressed solely to the merits of the issues at hand; no disciplinary action should be taken against the expression of views—however erroneous—provided it is done within legitimate Party forums. But sanctions are called for in cases of factional activity where groups of leaders seek personal advantage by banding together outside normal Party channels. In general, discipline will focus on shortcomings in policy implementation as indicated by the explicit concern of rectification with "work style"—the manner of performing duties and dealing with people. Moreover, the administration of discipline should be essentially an inner elite affair. Although the "masses" might be drawn into the process from time to time, ultimate authority rests firmly with the Party and any popular role is subject to strict control. While these understandings form a coherent set of organizational norms, it is a fragile one subject to multiple strains. Post-1949 Chinese politics can be seen in terms of the erosion of these organizational principles after an initial period of smooth functioning in the early and mid-1950s. The following analysis traces this process up to the Cultural Revolution when the norms were almost totally shattered.

At the center of this drama was Mao Zedong. Mao, with some but not total justification (see Chapter 3), has been credited with creating the rectification approach in contrast to the "ruthless struggles and merciless blows" employed by the pre-Mao leaderships of the CCP. In emphasizing this contrast the emerging Maoist leadership of the 1940s pictured itself as tolerant of former opponents and eager to create an atmosphere in which diverse elements could contribute to the revolutionary cause without fear of arbitrary purges and excessive punishment. Yet by the late 1950s important differences appeared within the leadership over organizational practices, differences which placed the traditional approach under challenge. As with conflict over economic and social policies, these differences should not be seen as reflecting a "two line struggle" between Mao and his supposed opponents in the Party machine.[1] The pattern of conflict was far more complex, with Mao himself a crucial variable who frequently changed his position. Indeed, Mao was at once the foremost proponent of long established organizational norms and the political force whose actions cut the ground from beneath those norms. Ironically, Mao's concern for maintaining the values of the Chinese revolution destroyed the organizational guidelines which had served the revolution so well.

Aims and Targets of Rectification

The conduct of rectification, and with it the whole structure of CCP organizational norms, has been affected by changing patterns of problems, goals and target groups. Rectification movements have sought to achieve a number of related yet often contradictory objectives: the consolidation of CCP leadership over society, the ascendancy of a particular group within that leadership, bureaucratic control in a goal oriented organization where the goals frequently change, vigorous implementation of new Party policies, improved cadre "work style," the elimination of behavior judged deviant by the Party leadership, and the internalization of values and outlooks promoted by the regime—i.e., genuine attitudinal change.

The target of the rectification process is a broadly defined political elite composed of millions of individuals. It ranges from members of the Party's top policy making organ, the Politburo, to the lowest officials outside the Party. This elite includes all members of the CCP, with or without office, and all cadres in the official and quasi-official organizations of the PRC: the Party apparatus, the state bureaucracy, the People's Liberation Army (PLA), state and joint state-private economic enterprises, educational institutions, rural production units, urban residential organizations, "mass organizations" such as trade unions and women's bodies, and the so-called "democratic parties" left over from preliberation days.

Analysis must delineate which segments of this elite are the primary targets of a given movement. Does a campaign reach leaders with a role in shaping policy or only those with responsibility for implementing policy? How does the impact of a movement vary with administrative levels, geographic regions, and functional specialties? Are Party and non-Party cadres, or rural and urban officials treated differently? The answers to these questions will be related to the types of deviant behavior under attack, the methods used and the degree of their severity, as well as with the relationship of campaign objectives to contemporaneous Party programs and the general political context.

Several broad variables shape both the focus and methods of a rectification campaign. One critical factor is the degree of leadership cohesion. Analytically, the cases examined in this study[a] fall into two categories. Most rectification movements were responses to problems arising outside the top Party leadership; in such instances relative unity or different degrees of division existed over the nature of the problems and the appropriate response. But in two cases—the purge of Gao Gang and the dismissal Peng Dehuai—rectification efforts originated in leadership conflict at the highest level and were only subsequently extended to similar questions within the ranks of lower level cadres. Generally, in both situations the greater the divisions within the leadership the more likely rectification would depart from established norms and employ harsh purge methods.

---

[a] This book deals with nationwide rectification campaigns centering on Party and government cadres. It generally excludes rectification efforts implemented on a sub-national level, nationwide campaigns in a single functional area, and Party reform measures undertaken as a subordinate part of other political movements or on a fixed basis as the annual overhaul of rural communes. Of the cases examined here, only the study campaigns carried out in conjunction with the 1954–55 purge of Gao Gang (see Chapter 5) fell short of a full scale rectification movement. See Zhao Han, ed., *Tantan Zhongguo gongchandang de zhengfeng yundong* [Talks on the CCP's Rectification Campaigns], (Beijing: Zhongguo qingnian chubanshe, 1957), which excludes mention of the Gao affair. Nevertheless, it is included here for its intrinsic importance as a purge at the very apex of the CCP.

A second major variable is the short term phase characterizing the political system. Post-1949 China has been marked by a political rhythm of periods of intense mass movements seeking social, economic and/or political breakthroughs —mobilization phases—and periods of relaxation devoted to correcting imbalances which appeared during upheavals—consolidation phases.[b] Normally, a mild rectification approach has prevailed during consolidation phases while more severe sanctions have been employed during mobilization periods. Thirdly, the nature of administrative arrangements at a given time, especially the degree of centralization or decentralization, will have an important bearing on the aims and targets of rectification.

The aims and instrumentalities of rectification have also varied with the distinctive overall objectives of each major period since 1949. In 1950–53, a period of basic leadership consensus, programs concentrated on the consolidation of power and economic recovery leading to planned economic construction and socialist transformation. From 1954 to early 1956 construction and transformation on the Soviet model were the dominant concerns of a still united leadership; the marginal impact of the Gao Gang affair stood as testimony to that essential unity. With institutional transformation largely completed, emphasis turned even more sharply to economic development in 1956–57. Soon, however, the inadequacies of the Soviet model in Chinese conditions became increasingly apparent and initial steps were taken to develop uniquely Chinese innovations. In this process significant leadership differences emerged over both economic policy and the conduct of rectification, but these differences were contained by established Party norms. The need to find an appropriate developmental strategy led, in late 1957, to the radical Great Leap Forward. From that time until 1962 Chinese politics was dominated successively by the crash implementation of the Great Leap, efforts to modify the experiment and major conflict over its course, and total retreat from the strategy. New leadership divisions intensified and organizational norms were repeatedly violated. Finally, from late 1962 to early 1966 efforts focused on both economic recovery from the disasters of the Great Leap period and ideological revitalization to offset the costs of the retreat. Throughout this period the leadership groped for new directions, uncertain as to how to reconcile its various tasks. Differences—but not polarization—again emerged over rectification as well as social and economic policies. Such differences, combined with the inability to reconcile ideological and economic objectives, set the stage for the Cultural Revolution.

While the focus of rectification efforts has shifted according to the above factors, many problems repeatedly requiring rectification are inherent in certain salient features of the political system. The revolutionary heritage and goals of the CCP demand ideological zeal, close ties to the masses of Chinese people, and

[b] In actual practice phases are frequently mixed, having aspects of both consolidation and mobilization. Moreover, in the 1960s the alternation of phases began to break down.

strict discipline from members of the elite. This creates constant tension with poorly educated officials lacking a clear grasp of the ideological and policy goals of the Party, others who fall into routinized bureaucratic patterns of behavior, and those who assume attitudes of superiority towards ordinary people and use their positions to seek special privileges. In these and other matters the gap between Party ideals and elite reality has been a persistent source of concern leading to rectification efforts as early as 1950 and as late as fall 1965.

The commitment both to social transformation required by Marxist-Leninist ideology and to modernization has led policy makers and officials in charge of policy implementation to strive for socialist objectives and rapid economic development with insufficient regard for material obstacles and popular attitudes. During the mass campaigns of the 1950s this caused unrealistic assessments of possibilities, gross exaggerations of accomplishments, and harsh measures to drive the population in pursuit of elusive goals. Moreover, the realignment of social classes which accompanies rapid change in a revolutionary society is not a smooth process: a major problem has been the lingering prestige and influence of former elite classes among a wide range of officials. This was particularly significant just after liberation in the early 1950s, and signs of its revival appeared in the 1960s following the dislocations of the Great Leap Forward.

While remnants of the old elite may impede social change, their skills are often needed for technological and economic development. Furthermore, efforts to build a modern state create tension between the highly politicized revolutionary virtues idealized by Mao and apolitical technical skills. This can be seen in aggressive efforts by professionals to maximize authority within their spheres of competence at the expense of the Party apparatus. The clash of these efforts with the "totalitarian"[c] impulse to establish firm control overall spheres of activity was reflected throughout the 1950s and 1960s in fluctuations between Party control and professional autonomy.

The sheer size and complexity of China and its bureaucracies also create constant friction between necessary flexibility in policy implementation and centralized control. While rigid policy implementation creates economic losses and social tensions, legitimate adaptation of policy to local conditions is often distorted into promotion of parochial interests. Similarly, as in all large bureaucracies, individual administrative departments neglect overall interests and engage in bureaucratic infighting to increase their own authority and resources. The difficulty of obtaining efficient communication in a complex organization is a major aspect of these problems, and of the previously noted tendency towards exaggeration in mass campaigns. Moreover, an organization the size of the Party

[c] While the "totalitarian model" as applied to the Chinese political system has many shortcomings, the concept is nevertheless useful in highlighting policy centralization, single party dominance, state penetration and control of society, and ideologically prescribed social change.

and state bureaucracies is of necessity staffed by a heterogeneous elite, a situation which inevitably gives rise to conflict. Not only have recurrent conflicts of interest arisen between Party members and officials outside the CCP, but also differences in social origins, revolutionary and post-revolutionary experiences, and functional responsibilities have caused tensions. While Maoist ideology sees considerable virtue in conflict, their disruptive consequences have required frequent efforts to contain such disputes. In addition, other bureaucratic phenomena such as overlapping organizations, bloated staffs and red tape, though repeatedly denounced, periodically reappear as vexing problems.

Despite the organizational principle that policy advocacy as such is not culpable behavior, the insistence common to Communist parties everywhere that there is only one correct policy line for a given period generates still another set of problems. If contrary views continue to be articulated after a policy is laid down, the result may be to undermine implementation of official decisions. Moreover, if policy debate is particularly bitter, the victors will be tempted to attack and punish those offering alternative policies. While criticism of proponents of "incorrect" policies has been a repeated feature of post-1949 Chinese politics, in the early and mid-1950s such criticism was relatively restrained and largely outside the rectification process. From the late 1950s, however, as the policy consensus eroded disciplinary sanctions were increasingly used against advocates of rejected points of view.

Finally, the absence of an institutionalized process for the transfer of supreme leadership is always a potential source of instability. The organizational norms which guided the CCP in the pre-Cultural Revolution period were closely linked to a stable leadership headed by Mao. When Mao's health apparently came into question in 1953–54, leadership conflict broke out at the apex of the CCP resulting in the purge of Gao Gang. In the immediate pre-Cultural Revolution years Mao's questionable health and maneuvering for the succession were undoubtedly important factors in the tensions of the period. In a succession situation, the danger will always exist that rectification will be transformed from a method of resolving problems to a weapon for seizing power.

Rectification Campaigns and Purges

Thus far we have emphasized the persuasive orientation of rectification. This orientation is apparent in the Chinese Communist term for "rectification," *zhengfeng,* a contraction of *zhengdun,* to "correct" or "put in order," and *zuofeng,* "work style" or "spirit." The literal meanings of these terms accurately reflect the reform and reindoctrination emphasis of rectification found in official discussions:

> In order to realize unity of thought and unity of organization, Chairman Mao created the method of the "rectification campaign." . . . Through the rectification campaign, the entire Party membership . . . studies certain selected docu-

> ments, makes contact with reality, carries out systematic criticism and self-criticism, and on the basis of carrying out study puts into effect necessary organizational procedures. This enables us effectively to solve problems met in the course of Party building, and to reach the goals of reforming and raising the ideological level of Party members and putting in order Party organization. Concerning ... rectification, Chairman Mao has pointed out two principles: "First, 'learn from past mistakes in order to avoid future ones'; second, 'cure the illness in order to save the patient.' The meaning of 'learning from past mistakes in order to avoid future ones' is that we must expose past mistakes without reservation ... to enable our future work to be more careful and better done. But the aim of our exposing mistakes and criticizing shortcomings is like a doctor curing an illness entirely for the purpose of saving the patient and not in order to use the patient to examine his death.... We must welcome one who has committed mistakes, no matter how serious his mistakes may be, as long as he is not afraid to see the doctor and does not persist in his mistakes until they reach the stage of incurability and is sincere and truly willing to reform, so as to help him cure his illness and become a good comrade."[2]

Clearly the stress is on education rather than coercion, redemption rather than punishment.

In actual practice, however, rectification campaigns have utilized various coercive sanctions including the purge. There is no single term in CCP usage to express the concept of "purge," nor is there a body of official doctrine concerning this method of elite discipline. However, the three most commonly used terms for "purge," *qingchu*, *qingxi* and *suqing*, all convey the sense of "weed out," "get rid of," "liquidate" and "eradicate." In contrast to rectification, the tone is one of retribution and punishment. While there is no explicit Chinese Communist statement delineating which disciplinary punishments constitute a purge, the basic measures seem to be expulsion from the Party and expulsion from the ranks of cadres. These sanctions can be employed in movements specially organized to weed out undesirable elements from Party and other organizations,[3] but they have more commonly been used in conjunction with rectification and other political movements or simply as part of regular disciplinary checkups.

In addition, there are a number of disciplinary measures somewhere between the educational emphasis of rectification and the punitive stress of the purge. For example, the sanction of dismissal from official posts bears some of the connotations of "purge," but also holds out the possibility of return to active political life if willingness to reform is demonstrated. Such measures, as well as more informal devices which reduce or eliminate the power of erring officials, are aptly described by Donald Klein's phrase, "semi-purge."[4]

Despite their different emphases, the rectification campaign and the purge are related concepts. While rectification assumes willingness to reform, it recognizes some officials will resist persuasive methods. As a result, rectification campaigns also make substantial use of coercive disciplinary measures. In cases where cadres persist in deviant behavior despite repeated educational efforts, the most severe disciplinary measure of expulsion is invoked. Thus the purge is regarded as an extreme action taken only when rectification fails. Conversely, in Party doctrine, disciplinary punishment has a persuasive role both by providing inducements to reform and as a lesson for rank and file cadres.[5] Therefore, purges of major figures are frequently accompanied by intensive propaganda and educational efforts, and dismissed officials are often given new positions after repenting. Even when severe criminal sanctions are applied, attention is given to the possibility that purged cadres will reform themselves and play a useful role in society.[6] In sum, rectification campaigns nearly always involve a degree of purging, while purges have educational as well as disciplinary functions.

Although rectification normally involves purging and other disciplinary measures, specific campaigns vary greatly in terms of the relative leniency or harshness of the methods actually involved. Indeed, individual movements can be placed on a persuasive-coercive continuum (see Chapter 2) reflecting the severity of methods and sanctions employed. The subsequent analysis, after tracing relevant developments before liberation, then examines in detail each of the major rectification efforts from 1950 to 1965 with major attention to these questions. The tendency of rectification campaigns since the late 1950s to cluster at the coercive end of the continuum is eloquent testimony to the decline of Party norms in the pre-Cultural Revolution period.

PART I

Doctrine, Methods and Historical Development

1
Rectification Doctrine

The theoretical underpinnings of rectification were laid in Yan'an during the late 1930s and early 1940s as part of the creation of a coherent set of Party organizational norms. This doctrine underwent remarkably little development in the 1950–65 period despite a profound evolution in Mao's overall thought. The theoretical refinement that did take place was mostly confined to Mao's 1957 writings—especially his essay "On the Correct Handling of Contradictions among the People" which elaborated the concept of "non-antagonistic contradictions." This development, although accompanied by a major departure in rectification methods, did not break with past doctrine. It was essentially an effort to extend well established principles to a new situation following "the victory of socialist transformation" (see Chapter 6). A far more significant impact on the rectification process grew out of Mao's increasing preoccupation with protracted class struggle from 1959 onwards, but this did not directly alter formal rectification theory.[a]

Cultural Revolution sources have claimed that this relatively unchanging body of theory in fact contained two conflicting tendencies, one associated with Mao and another with his chosen heir, Liu Shaoqi. This has led some scholars to see important divergencies in the writings of Mao and Liu on organizational matters. Mao is pictured as making obedience conditional on correct policies, emphasizing dramatic displays of emotion in resolving tensions, and being intent upon bringing extra Party forces into the rectification process. In contrast, Liu is viewed as the advocate of rigid discipline, rationalizing conflict and repressing undue emotion, and maintaining a strict demarcation between inner Party rectifi-

[a] Disagreements over the conduct of the Socialist Education Movement (1962–65) did, however, involve different theoretical formulations concerning the targets of that particular campaign. See Chapter 11.

cation and mass activities.[1] This analysis rejects such an interpretation. While differences did appear between Mao and Liu on rectification in the pre-Cultural Revolution period, they did not consistently argue opposing positions. Moreover, their writings of the Yan'an period which formulated rectification doctrine were fundamentally complementary; any differences were matters of nuance or the degree of attention each gave to specific problems. To the extent Mao and Liu differed over specific rectification campaigns in the following two and a half decades, it was in large measure due to the difficulty of applying the ambiguities of the doctrine to new circumstances rather than to any long standing differences in emphasis.

Contradictions and Proletarian Consciousness

Rectification doctrine is firmly linked to the larger body of CCP ideology. Party theoretical writings, particularly those of Mao, place enormous emphasis on the existence and implications of "contradictions" *(maodun)*.[2] In the dialectical perspective, the world "teems with contradictions" and neither history nor society can be properly understood without an analysis of the relation of contradictory forces. The Party as an active force in history is required to define the principal contradiction of each historical period and align with its progressive aspect in a struggle to overcome and transform the reactionary aspect. Moreover, the contradictions of society are reflected within the Party itself and struggle is a necessary feature of Party life. According to Mao, "If there were no contradictions in the Party and no ideological struggles to resolve them, the Party's life would come to an end."[3] The nature and form of contradictions both in society and the Party, however, are in perpetual flux, and therefore pose major problems for analysis and handling.

As elaborated by Mao in 1957, there are two kinds of contradictions, "antagonistic" *(duikangxing)* and "non-antagonistic" *(feiduikangxing)*. Rectification techniques are particularly designed for handling non-antagonistic contradictions, while purges are suited to antagonistic contradictions. An antagonistic contradiction is one "between ourselves and the enemy," i.e., in the post-1949 period, between those who support socialism as defined by the CCP and those who relentlessly oppose it. Such a contradiction is irreconcilable; one antagonistic force must prevail over the other. In contrast to contradictions "between ourselves and the enemy," contradictions "among the people" are generally non-antagonistic. While the composition of the "people" is always subject to change, since the establishment of the PRC it has consisted of all classes, strata and social groups which approve and support socialist transformation and construction. Among these classes, strata and groups, and between them and the Party, exist conflicting interests, but these contradictions are subordinate to the common interest of the people as a whole. Such contradictions can be reconciled, adjustments can be made to accommodate the different needs of various groups without undue strain on the people's unity.[4]

It is important to note that what distinguishes antagonistic from non-antagonistic contradictions, and thus the suitability of rectification or purge methods, is not "objective" considerations of class but rather the "subjective" attitudes of the groups concerned. Although class contradictions, especially those between the bourgeoisie and proletariat, are frequently antagonistic, this need not be the case in all situations.[b] An enemy is defined by his hostility to the Party and not by his class status, even though in many cases there may be an identifiable link between the two.

But while theory delineates the types of contradictions which require the use of rectification or purge techniques, it provides no clear guidelines for identifying these contradictions in practice. The slippery task of determining the nature of any specific contradiction, already made difficult by the subjective criteria which must be applied, is further complicated by the fact that the contradiction itself is subject to constant flux. In everyday life as well as periods of major historic change antagonistic contradictions may be transformed into non-antagonistic ones and vice versa. Mao spoke of both possibilities in "On the Correct Handling of Contradictions among the People":

> The contradiction between exploiter and exploited, which exists between the national bourgeoisie and the working class, is an antagonistic one. But, in the concrete conditions existing in China, such an antagonistic contradiction, if properly handled, can be transformed into a non-antagonistic one and resolved in a peaceful way. But *if it is not properly handled, if, say, we do not follow a policy of uniting, criticizing and educating the national bourgeoisie, or if the national bourgeoisie does not accept this policy,* then the contradiction between the working class and the national bourgeoisie can turn into an antagonistic contradiction as between ourselves and the enemy.[5]

Thus the possibility of change in the nature of a contradiction, whether for good or ill, depends on two factors—the willingness of the people concerned to accept transformation and the proper or improper handling of the situation by the Party. As we shall see, both considerations stand at the heart of the rectification process.

---

[b] Mao's great stress in the 1960s on antagonistic class struggle raises the question of whether he changed his mind on this point. While his new emphasis on protracted, bitter class struggle did alter the implications of the notion that class contradictions could be non-antagonistic, the doctrine itself continued to receive official sanction through the reprinting without alteration of "Correct Handling of Contradictions" even during the Cultural Revolution. Moreover, in the immediate pre-Cultural Revolution period there were statements that antagonistic contradictions between the working class and bourgeoisie would nevertheless still be handled as a contradiction among the people. See Zhou Enlai's 1964 government work report in *Main Documents of the First Session of the Third National People's Congress of the People's Republic of China* (Beijing: Foreign Languages Press, 1965), p. 32.

Cultivating Proletarian Consciousness

Rectification is not designed simply to correct deviant thoughts and attitudes. Above all it seeks to develop "proletarian consciousness" *(wuchanjieji yishi),* to raise systematically the level of each person's knowledge of and commitment to proletarian values. Thus rectification involves education and training, what Liu Shaoqi termed "cultivation" *(xiuyang),* in pursuit of a fundamental transformation. This concept, while originally applied to Party members, can easily be extended to non-Party cadres as well.

In CCP theory proletarian consciousness is not simply a reflection of the attitudes of a particular class. It is a state infused with moral fervor involving the utmost dedication in striving for highly valued yet elusive goals. Liu passionately stated this view with reference to Party members:

> When contradictions arise between the interest of the Party and the individual, we can, without the slightest hesitation or feeling of compulsion, submit to Party interests and sacrifice the individual. To sacrifice the individual for the sake of the Party, for the sake of class, for national liberation, or the liberation of mankind, even to sacrifice one's own life, without the slightest hesitation, with a feeling of happiness—this is the highest expression of Communist morality, the highest expression of principle by the Party member, a pure and honest expression of the Party member's proletarian consciousness.[6]

True proletarian consciousness is not an easy state to attain. Seeking that state may be compared to travelling down a long, tortuous road beset by dangers on all sides. As an individual starts such a journey he is subject to a wide variety of evil influences left over from traditional and bourgeois societies which still persist in the ideological realm after basic changes in production relations. Even Party members of pure proletarian origin or veteran cadres who have gone through years of revolutionary struggle are threatened by particularistic pressures and selfish temptations. Often these pressures can only be overcome through an emotionally and psychologically exacting process. As Mao put it in 1942:

> It is necessary to destroy these [petty bourgeois influences] and sweep them away, but it is not easy. . . . The first step . . . is to give the patient a powerful stimulus: yell at him, "You're sick!" so the patient will have a fright and break out in an overall sweat; then he can actually be started on the road to recovery.[7]

Indeed, the need for such traumatic methods is understandable since what is asked of the individual is nothing less than he transform his world outlook, that he overturn his entire identity *(fanshen)* by shaking off all pernicious influences of the past. But at the same time the need for emotional trauma raises problems in implementing Party reform, particularly in view of the danger of excessive struggle. It is a delicate task to determine when emotional intensity is required and when it is counterproductive to the aims of rectification.

Despite awareness of the difficulties involved, rectification doctrine is optimistic about the potentialities of the process. Official statements have repeatedly held that 90 to 95 percent of cadres are good or comparatively good and capable of being reformed by proper rectification techniques. While proletarian consciousness is subject to backsliding, repeated education will assure that these cadres return to the path of righteousness.

The basis of this optimistic view is firmly rooted in the assumption that the vast majority of individual cadres and Party members want to be transformed or at least are willing to accept transformation. This can be seen in one of Mao's most characteristic concepts: "unity-criticism-unity" *(tuanjie-piping-tuanjie).* Starting with a desire for unity, the application of criticism results in the attainment of unity on a new basis.[8] That is, most cadres subjectively desire to serve the people despite their shortcomings; the Party, as the repository of truth, reveals the nature and source of their mistakes through criticism; and as a result unity is achieved on a higher, more conscious level and shortcomings are overcome. While proper educational methods are a key factor in this process, the matter rests ultimately with an exercise of individual will. Even cadres among the 5 to 10 percent who are judged unworthy, provided they sincerely desire to change their ways, can be saved.[9] The Party only rejects those who despite patient, persistent education steadfastly refuse to accept transformation. Thus rectification may be seen as a morality play in which the sinner, beset by temptation on all sides, can by means of a moral choice obtain salvation. It was one of Mao's deepest convictions that, faced with such a choice, only a very few will reject the grace offered by the Party.

Rectification Doctrine and Party Organizational Norms

While the willingness to accept the Party's offer of grace is essential for ideological reform, successful rectification also requires that Party leaders skillfully manage the reform process itself. Rectification, then, must be seen in the context of the CCP's general approach to the management of complex organizations. Since struggle within the Party and other official organizations is deemed both inevitable and desirable, the task of the leadership is to see that it assumes proper forms and is channeled into productive ends. This task is closely linked to the larger framework of CCP organizational norms.

Discipline and Democracy

To be acceptable, struggle must be "principled," i.e., it must involve basic ideological differences. Its aim must be to assure the victory of positive proletarian views over reactionary bourgeois ideology. But what are the implications of this for Party discipline? In theory, organizational discipline is contingent upon the ideological correctness of Party policies. Liu Shaoqi[c] stated this clearly in 1939:

> The content and essence of Party unity is ideological unity created by Marxism. This ideological unity is absolutely basic. Without it the Party's cohesion cannot be assured and is bound to break down. Therefore, if there are ideological differences or differences of principle within the Party, then struggle should be launched to regain unity. If there are a few Party members who persist in their mistaken ideas and principles and will not give them up, in the end they must be expelled (like the Trotskyites and rightists). If those insisting on these mistaken ideas and principles are a majority in the Party, then in the end there may be no choice but to split with them and establish a separate organization (just as Lenin left the Social Democratic Party and set up a separate Communist Party).[10]

The need for organizational splitting, however, only applies where the Party leadership follows an incorrect policy line. In the current situation where a "correct" leadership unified around Mao had assumed control of the CCP, Liu advocated strict Leninist discipline. Party members were to obey majority decisions and higher level orders even when they were convinced such decisions were wrong in principle. While Liu allowed that the existing leadership could make mistakes, these were merely passing shortcomings which would inevitably be corrected.[11] At the same time, Mao also hammered home the need for obedience. He repeatedly spoke of the need to observe organizational discipline, to march in step, and directly attacked the tendency of minorities to refuse to submit to the majority.[12] Like Liu, Mao held that the Party also needed democracy, "but it needs centralization even more."[13] Although flexibility was allowed in applying higher orders,[d] both men clearly felt an effective organization requires a disciplined chain of command where the authority of higher levels is accepted without question.

Disciplined policy implementation, then, is a natural by-product of an ultimately correct Party leadership. But if the leadership is ultimately correct, this is

[c] During the Cultural Revolution Liu was repeatedly accused of promoting blind obedience to orders from above, thus creating an ideologically unprincipled "slavish mentality" within the Party. The following demonstrates that his advocacy of discipline was not absolute. More importantly, a full reading of the writings of Mao and Liu during the Yan'an period indicates that, if anything, Mao placed even greater emphasis than Liu on the need for discipline. Cf. Stuart R. Schram, "The Party in Chinese Communist Ideology," *CQ*, No. 38 (1969), p. 8.

[d] The need to apply central directives flexibly to suit local conditions is a basic tenet of CCP administrative doctrine. While there is considerable ambiguity concerning precisely what is legitimate flexible application, there is no right to refuse to implement higher level orders as a matter of principle. See Liu's July 1941 essay, "On the Intra-Party Struggle," in Boyd Compton, trans., *Mao's China: Party Reform Documents, 1942–44* (Seattle: University of Washington Press, 1966), pp. 221–22.

due in large measure to an open, democratic decision making process. Within appropriate Party bodies, CCP leaders have clear rights to argue their views vigorously without fear of retribution for winding up on the losing side. Moreover even if one is in the minority, as long as he implements the majority decision he is free to continue to hold his opinion and again advocate it at future Party meetings. Indeed, dissenters have a duty to press their case since their views might prove correct and eventually win over the majority.[14] These measures, by encouraging a free flow of ideas and opinions, have in fact worked to strengthen the policy process by facilitating decisions based on adequate information and the correction of errors in due course. Furthermore, these norms have clear implications for Party rectification. If advocacy of alternative policy views is legitimate, then rectification could not be aimed at "erroneous" policy views *per se.* Instead it would focus on "deviations" in "work style" and policy implementation as is emphasized by rectification doctrine. Indeed, such assurances are necessary to guarantee the vigorous debate required for sound policy.

Of course, matters are not so simple. An inevitable tension exists between the right to "reserve opinions" *(baoliu yijian)*—i.e., to continue to hold to dissenting views after a decision—and the need for strict discipline in implementing Party policies. The need to bolster implementation by asserting the correctness of official policies augurs ill for those attempting to persuade their comrades of the desirability of a different course. Moreover, the notion that the leadership is ultimately correct is in basic conflict with the principle of minority rights. According to Liu Shaoqi:

> If lines of reasoning have been worked out but still no final unanimity has been reached, it becomes quite clear who is running counter to the interests of the struggle of the Party and proletariat, and the problem can easily be solved by making organizational decisions against those comrades who persist in their errors.[15]

Thus while the norms concerning minority rights contribute to an open policy process, contradictions exist which pose major obstacles to realizing such rights and openness.

Inner Party democracy, furthermore, does not mean the absence of restrictions on acceptable types of conflict. Rectification doctrine forbids "unprincipled struggle" *(wuyuanze douzheng)* reflecting the narrow interests of individuals and groups devoid of ideological substance. Here such matters as individual position and prestige, personal likes and dislikes, and conflicting departmental interests become objects of contention. Particularly dangerous is "factional struggle" *(paibie douzheng)* where a group of Party members bands together to seek power within a given unit or area, or even within the CCP as a whole. Factions simply use policy issues to further their schemes for aggrandizement; they are hypocritical and have no principled position on anything.[16] But as with other matters, no clear criteria exist to determine when a group of leaders is engaging in factional activities, and when they are simply exercising their right to express dissenting views. In politics policy advocacy and the pursuit of power are hardly separable. The critical variable in pre-Cultural Revolution China was the relative cohesion of the top leadership. While leadership cohesion was strong there was little incentive for factional politics; correspondingly, new policies could be introduced with only marginal effect on the power structure. But as that cohesion weakened the tensions and uncertainty surrounding policy advocacy necessarily increased.

Uncertainty over motives is linked to important ambiguities concerning acceptable modes of expressing policy disagreements. Factions plot behind the backs of those they oppose; they exchange views and make plans secretly outside of official Party bodies.[17] While such practices are clearly unacceptable, informal discussions of policy matters are an inevitable and necessary part of leadership activities. Yet critical views expressed in such an informal manner are clearly vulnerable to charges of conspiracy, especially when divisive issues are before the leadership. On the other hand, to speak only in official councils can also be dangerous. If a strong dissenting view is stated in such bodies without prior warning, it may be taken as a "sneak attack" on one's colleagues. Thus a considerable gray area exists in CCP organizational norms concerning the exercise of the right of minorities to dissent.

Minority rights are clearly within the framework of the minority obeying the majority. But what, then, is the role of individual leaders? The norms which emerged in the 1940s, consistent with the letter of Leninism, assert the principle of collective leadership. Decisions should be made according to the wishes of the collective rather than the inuividual Party secretary; in this fashion policy reflects more comprehensive and better balanced views. In principle, Mao too was bound by majority decisions; as Liu put it, "Comrade Mao [Zedong] is the leader of the whole Party yet he also obeys the Party." Yet in virtually the same breath Liu observed that ". . . Mao [Zedong has] handled things well and represented the truth so we obey [him]."[18] Such statements, together with contemporary exaltation of Mao as "savior of the Chinese people," clearly qualified the norm of collective leadership. Still, as shall be seen in subsequent chapters, it does appear that this norm did apply to Mao at least flexibly, and that he was willing to accept and indeed promoted the notion of a certain responsibility on his part to adhere to majority views contrary to his own. Nevertheless, Mao did not speak as a mere first among equals and his prestige undoubtedly allowed him to persuade a majority to support him on matters he felt most deeply about. But while this might have been sufficient to sustain the norm of collective leadership as long as an overall policy consensus existed, the vitality of the principle would clearly be in question if Mao's views fundamentally differed from those of significant numbers of his comrades.

The Parameters of Struggle

In dealing with the rights and duties of CCP members and leaders, Party organizational norms also lay down guidelines for handling improper behavior within the elite. In the early 1940s Mao and Liu addressed themselves to such questions as the appropriate methods for and desirable limits on "inner Party struggle" *(dangnei douzheng)*. One crucial question concerned the proper role of the masses in internal Party reform. In general terms, both men took positions which emphasized the separate, leading role of the Party but did not bar some mass participation in Party rectification.[e] Liu was particularly clear concerning the separateness of the Party: "The vanguard of the proletariat should differentiate itself not only from all other classes but also from the masses of its own class."[19] Meanwhile, Mao emphasized the Party's functions of "leading" and "acting for" the masses. On the question of rectification, neither Mao nor Liu was especially clear on what type of role people outside the Party could play. Liu asserted self-cultivation could not be divorced from the masses and responsible officials had to conduct self-criticism before the people, while Mao sanctioned the participation of non-Party people in the investigation of cadres.[20] Nevertheless, both leaders demonstrated concern that dissidents would circumvent proper procedures and attempt to mobilize support outside the Party. As Mao put it:

> Many Party members do not offer criticism within the Party but on the outside. This is because the political meaning of Party organization has not yet been established in the average Party member's mind. As a consequence, he does not understand the importance of organization . . . and can see no reason to distinguish between criticism within and criticism without. This could lead the Party down the road to destruction.[21]

Thus the CCP's leading spokesmen were concerned with limiting the role of extra Party forces in rectification and emphasizing Party leadership of the process, but they were not precise in dealing with this complex question. While some mass participation in Party discipline was allowed, the parameters remained clouded with uncertainty.

In exercising its leadership over the rectification process, Mao and Liu argued, the Party is responsible both for seeing that struggle is adequately devel-

---

[e] Cultural Revolution sources have pictured Liu as the advocate of "closed door" rectification designed to prevent mass participation in Party reform. In fact, not only were the views of Mao and Liu in the early 1940s similar in their emphasis on the need to control such mass participation, but Liu subsequently played a leading role in several of the most dramatic instances of popular intrusion into the rectification process (see Chapters 3 and 11).

oped, that problems are not swept under the rug, and for preventing excesses.[f] One dangerous tendency is to gloss over real differences in ideology during inner Party struggle. This deviation, "liberalism" *(ziyouzhuyi),* is frequently manifested in the failure to criticize someone because of a desire to maintain cordial personal relationships, e.g., with old friends, fellow villagers, fellow students, and old colleagues and subordinates. Another factor stifling criticism is fear of retaliation by the person criticized. As a result discontent is channeled into irresponsible, behind the back criticism outside the framework of regular Party procedures, causing disunity behind a screen of false organizational harmony.[22]

While attacking the avoidance of conflict, Mao and Liu also criticized several tendencies leading to unnecessary struggle. One was the failure to distinguish between enemies and comrades. Mao raised this question in criticizing the disciplinary methods of earlier CCP leaders:

> Hitherto, two phrases have appeared constantly in our essays and speeches, one is "struggle ruthlessly," and the other is "attack mercilessly." It is entirely necessary to use such means in dealing with the enemy and with opposition thought, but it is a mistake to use them in dealing with our comrades . . .[23]

Another tendency was to raise minor questions to the level of principle. Liu argued that problems of a "purely practical nature" involving routine administration do not, in theory, concern questions of principle. On such matters differences of opinion are natural and acceptable; these conflicts do not require ideological struggle to assure that the "correct" view prevails. Instead, such problems should be settled by compromise to avoid prolonged conflict.[24]

Allowing questions of a purely practical nature and differences among comrades to escalate into bitter disputes often leads to "mechanical struggle" *(jixie douzheng).* In this form of struggle the goal of ideological reform is cast aside; rectifying mistakes degenerates into attacks on individuals. Personal grievances and factional differences come to the fore and instead of strengthening Party unity such struggles deepen already existing rifts. In these circumstances, Liu observed, extreme methods become common as ". . . some comrades think . . . the sharper the criticism, the more severe and rude the method and attitude of criticism, the better. . . ."[25] "Mechanical struggle," moreover, relies heavily on organizational measures, including criminal sanctions, while ignoring persuasive methods. The only "education" involved is that of making an example of a person who has committed errors in order to coerce others into line. Shortcom-

[f] Liu was charged during the Cultural Revolution with advocating "inner Party peace" in an effort to inhibit genuine ideological struggle within the organization. While Liu, as the chief exponent of the doctrine of "inner Party struggle," did lay down rules to curb excessive conflict within the Party, these guidelines did not rule out all struggle indiscriminately and in fact dovetailed with Mao's Yan'an efforts to create a more lenient disciplinary process.

ings are grossly exaggerated and no defense is allowed. Even the act of confession becomes an empty ritual:

> ... certain comrades confess too many errors. As a means of escaping attack, nothing can equal a full confession. *Although the error is confessed, in actuality, the comrade himself still has no understanding. . . .*[26]

Thus excesses in inner Party struggle undermine the goals of rectification. Morale is jeopardized by harsh sanctions, true reform becomes impossible, and Party unity is weakened rather than raised to a higher level.

The preceding suggests some of the difficulties involved in channeling organizational tensions toward desired objectives. On the one hand, the popular desire to maintain harmony—frequently due to the persistence of traditional ties—accentuates the need to induce conflict within official organizations. On the other hand, repeated efforts to promote struggle can create an environment conducive to conflicts over narrow ends which only intensify existing divisions without providing the desired ideological unity. Such efforts thus produce tensions which spill over the boundaries of "principled" struggle but are particularly hard to control because they have been initiated in the name of "principle." And attempts to suppress the resulting excesses make it more difficult to foster a spirit of struggle.

Moreover, the various distinctions defining which types of struggle are proper do not offer clear guidance for the implementation of rectification. As Liu noted, ". . . comrades still ask, what is principle? What problems are purely of a practical nature and do not involve principle?"[27] In reality, this demarcation is highly ambiguous. If enough details of routine administration are compromised then basic Party policies may be compromised as well. In addition, the view of a world in constant flux further complicates efforts to maintain such distinctions. Since day to day administrative questions may become questions of principle as conditions change, the boundaries of the categories are subject to repeated alteration. Moreover, how can principled struggle over ideology be reconciled with "reserving opinions" on policy? Even when it is clear that struggle is justified uncertainty may appear concerning the methods to be adopted. How severe should the struggle be in a given case? At what point are educational methods no longer sufficient and organizational measures including purges called for? Concrete answers to such questions are not found in CCP writings on rectification.

Thus the guidelines for rectification, and Party organizational norms generally, contain large areas of ambiguity. The overall thrust of the norms is clear; they support a coherent system marked by relative openness in decision making, strict obedience in policy implementation, and leniency in elite discipline. But applying the norms to specific circumstances is a task fraught with difficulty. Despite the responsibility in theory of each Party member to initiate "principled" struggle on his own, rectification doctrine assumes the existence of a unified and "ever correct" Party Center to regulate debate within the elite, identify objects of struggle, and determine appropriate methods of discipline. Without the authoritative voice of the organization struggle would surely degenerate into anarchy as individuals and groups tried to apply vague criteria according to their own lights.

In the final analysis, rectification theory is highly optimistic on two scores. First, although recognizing the persistence of unhealthy ideological trends in the Party and society, it postulates a basic unity of interests among the leadership, cadres and people, and a willingness to be saved on the part of an overwhelming majority of each group. Second, the theory places great faith in the effectiveness of educational methods and the capacity of CCP leaders to manage the rectification process. Such sanguine assumptions drastically overestimate both the malleability of Chinese society and the ability of the central leadership to withstand the inevitable conflicts of politics. Rectification doctrine—and the larger structure of CCP organizational norms—provide the foundation of a viable system for managing elite behavior. But this system, far from being universally valid, is itself dependent upon transient political circumstances.

2
The Rectification Process: Methods, Sanctions and Effectiveness

Together with rectification doctrine, a variety of techniques and sanctions gave the Party reform process its distinctive cast in the entire period from the early 1940s to the Cultural Revolution. In this chapter we first highlight the nature of Chinese rectification by contrasting it with Stalinist terror. Next, we discuss the crucial role of small group methods during rectification movements. We then elaborate the various informal and formal disciplinary sanctions involved in the process, including their impact on the careers of high ranking officials. Finally, an assessment is made of the effectiveness of rectification by examining factors enhancing and limiting this approach to elite discipline. In this assessment we evaluate persuasive and coercive measures and develop a persuasive-coercive continuum for analyzing different rectification movements.

The Absence of Terror

Besides the "ruthless struggles" of pre-Mao CCP leaders, the rectification approach was developed with another "negative example" in mind: the Stalinist Great Purge of the 1930s.[a] As is well known, the Stalinist purge and CCP rectification differ significantly. Stalin's methods involved a far higher purge rate, harsher sanctions including frequent use of capital punishment, secret police administration, and a cynical disregard for reform and education.[1] But

[a] No open criticism of Soviet methods was articulated during the initial rectification effort of the early 1940s. In the 1950s, however, Mao on several occasions indicated disapproval of Stalin's harsh approach to discipline; e.g., see his 1957 comments in *HF*, p. 270.

one of the most notable contrasts with the Stalinist period, the lack of "terror," has not been sufficiently emphasized.

Dallin and Breslauer, authors of the most systematic study of terror in Communist systems, merely conclude that terror has manifested "significant distinctive features" and "has been far more restricted in China than it had been at a comparable stage in Soviet Russia or Eastern Europe." Yet, as Dallin and Breslauer themselves point out, coercion and terror are not identical. The essence of terror is its unpredictability and arbitrariness in striking someone regardless of whether he obeys the state's commands. Flouting commands may court danger, but even enthusiastic compliance is no guarantee of safety. This was clearly the situation in Stalin's day when, in Ilya Ehrenburg's words, "the fate of man was not like a game of chess but like a lottery." Although a rationale existed for determining categories of victims, there was arbitrariness in the choice of individual victims.[2]

The rectification process has occasionally produced phenomena associated with Stalinist terror: escalating denunciations, breakdown of trust between people, and intense anxiety. Nevertheless, the basic approach in dealing with individuals has been selective and surgical rather than arbitrary.[b] Rectification movements prior to the Cultural Revolution were generally under strict Party control with targets carefully chosen, models of deviant behavior widely propagated, and sanctions meted out according to the seriousness of offenses. The emphasis on persuasion required a demonstrable link between those punished and the deviations criticized. Compared to Stalin's expansive suspicion, the assumption that hard core political opponents are only a small portion of the community in China has encouraged a discriminating approach.

The process has by no means been infallible, and the innocent have suffered from distortions and excesses. There have been cases, as in the 1951–52 attacks on former Nationalist administrative personnel (see Chapter 4), in which individuals suffered as much for their group association as for their own acts. Nor has the Chinese approach guaranteed predictability. Behavior seemingly necessitated by a given set of policies has come under attack following a change of line. However, once the orientation of a campaign became clear, a cadre could assess his vulnerability on the basis of past actions and mitigate discipline by appropriate acts of contrition. The failure to tolerate such calculation and manipulation made the Cultural Revolution into the only CCP campaign to

[b] Here the discussion is limited to control of the elite as distinct from control of the general population. While the latter case is less clearcut since entire groups—e.g., landlords, bourgeois intellectuals, urban capitalists—have come under sweeping attack, the generalization of an absence of terror also applies. Even in dealing with such suspect groups the CCP has differentiated between individuals according to behavioral criteria when meting out sanctions.

approximate "terror." In the pre-1966 period, however, even relatively coercive movements were marked by a substantial degree of predictability.[c]

The Rectification Process: Small Group Methods, Disciplinary Sanctions and Leadership Career Patterns

The core of the rectification process in China is the small group *(xiaozu).*[3] Organizing members of work and residential units into small groups for discussion purposes has been a basic feature of life in post-1949 China, particularly in urban areas. The use of small groups of ten to fifteen persons for political activities has been most developed in the Party, state bureaucracy and educational institutions. Small group activity has normally followed the rhythm of post-1949 development, intensifying in content and frequency during mobilization phases, relaxing and becoming more routine during consolidation phases. The tempo has increased during rectification movements, but has varied considerably according to the policy objectives and political climate of the moment.

The use of small groups greatly facilitates Party control. Although there may be some group choice, group leaders are officially designated by and responsible to higher authority. They are briefed on official policy and taught how to conduct group meetings. If the system functions well the leadership can communicate its objectives and expectations in intimate circumstances. Moreover, small group discussions provide information about the participants which the leader may record and pass on to higher levels. As a result, bureaucratic control is enhanced since individual cadres may be punished or rewarded on the basis of what is revealed in the group meetings.[4]

The potency of the small group lies in its ability to link "study" *(xuexi)* of documents on current policy or basic theory and "criticism and self-criticism" *(piping ziwopiping)* in group discussion. In discussions, passivity is ruled out and some participation ensured by requiring all to express an opinion. Involvement is increased by relating the discussion of policies and theories to the performance of the unit and its members. Here criticism and self-criticism, the systematic

---

[c] Particularly striking is the evidence of predictability in hostile memoir accounts. E.g., Robert Loh as told to Humphrey Evans, *Escape from Red China* (New York: Coward-McCann, 1962), cites various examples of sanctions unrelated to actual behavior. Nevertheless, the overall thrust of Loh's book demonstrates how even someone with a questionable background can avoid heavy sanctions and indeed gain important positions within established institutions by consciously adjusting actions to current Party policy.

In contrast, during the Cultural Revolution with the absence of tight organizational control and clear definitions of "anti-Mao" acts, virtually all save a handful of Party leaders were fair game for Red Guard attacks. Moreover, no strategy of action could assure political survival under these circumstances. See Chen Yi's Cultural Revolution lament that "everybody is in a panic and nobody knows when misfortune will befall him"; "Collection of Chen Yi's Speeches" (Red Guard pamphlet), in *SCMM,* No. 636.

examination of the faults of each member of the group, comes into play. Thus dry discussions of problems and shortcomings in Party directives are enlivened by criticisms of others and confessions of one's own defects.

Under such circumstances, the pressures for behavioral and attitudinal conformity can be immense. Assuming most of the group accepts the official position, a number of factors contribute to group pressures. First, a form of collective responsibility exists because members know they will be judged according to how successfully problem cases are handled. For example, when a group must approve the confessions of its members before forwarding them to higher bodies, there is an incentive to be more demanding. Secondly, individuals who are not major targets of criticism may feel the need to change their ways to avoid such criticism in the future. Finally, the threat of ostracism exerts tremendous pressure to conform to group norms, whether the norms are spontaneous or a calculated response to political cues.

Disciplinary Sanctions

The pressures of the small group are enhanced by a wide range of informal and formal sanctions. Any bureaucratic or production unit can initiate informal sanctions against its members. Formal disciplinary punishments *(jilü chufen)* are imposed by the Party, government administrative organs, or police and legal organs. Party cadres are subject to all three types of discipline and legal punishment.[d] While all sanctions may be meted out at any time, their frequency tends to increase during rectification campaigns and other political movements.[5]

Bureaucratic and production units have a variety of informal sanctions at their disposal.[e] The mildest of these sanctions are included in regular methods of small group education and reform. Criticism and self-criticism can be applied as the mild informal sanction of "education through criticism" *(piping jiaoyu)*. Somewhat more severe is the requirement for a cadre to make a "self-examination"

[d] "Administrative discipline" by government organs against cadres in their employ is not to be confused with the "administrative" punishment meted out by the public security apparatus which is treated as a form of legal punishment in this study. In our usage legal punishment consists of (1) "administrative" sanctions ranging from formal warnings, modest fines and short periods of detention to indefinite periods of "rehabilitation through labor" in labor camps, i.e., sanctions administered by the police alone under the Security Administration Punishment Act of 1957; and (2) criminal sanctions ranging from "supervised labor" to capital punishment which legally must be imposed through the court system. While the following discussion is in the present tense, it is based on information available for the pre-Cultural Revolution period. Nevertheless, many of the same sanctions appear to have been operative since 1966. For example, Party disciplinary measures stipulated in the 1956 CCP Constitution were also included in the 1969, 1973 and 1977 Constitutions.

[e] The CCP has been inconsistent on this point. For example, official sources have occasionally referred to education through criticism as a formal disciplinary measure *(chufen)*, but Party and state disciplinary regulations treat it as an informal device to be used before formal measures are applied.

(jiantao) or "confession" *(tanbai)* before his unit, often in specially convened "criticism meetings" *(pipinghui* or *pipanhui).* These two sanctions are frequently imposed when education through criticism has failed and involve more intensive criticism from a cadre's co-workers. Normally, if these measures lead to reform, a cadre is exempted from formal disciplinary action *(mianyu chufen).*[6]

A much more severe informal measure is "struggle" *(douzheng)* which is generally accompanied by formal sanctions. This is frequently a central feature of rectification campaigns, occurring in the climactic stages of a movement. It focuses on a limited number of cadres who have been singled out as representative of the most serious evils. Struggle is conducted in small groups and, in its most severe form, in large scale "struggle meetings" *(douzhenghui)* which may last for days. Struggle targets are subjected to carefully organized torrents of abuse while forced to stand mute with bowed heads. Public humiliation is sometimes coupled with physical intimidation such as hitting and kicking. At its worst, struggle can be an unnerving and terrifying experience, and suicide is not uncommon.[7]

In addition, there are the obvious sanctions inherent in the power over careers held by leaders of bureaucratic and production units. The lowest of these sanctions is the subtle one of one the job harassment. Often the regular personnel device of transfer *(diaodong* or *tiaopei)* is used to remove troublesome or disruptive cadres while avoiding formal disciplinary procedures. In cases where a cadre's political background is questionable but formal action seems too harsh, transfer to a less sensitive post offers a prudent solution. For example, a former cadre interviewed in Hong Kong said that after he came under political suspicion he was quietly sent to another locale. Apparently his unit leader was unwilling to take formal action because he was popular with his co-workers. The use of such job reassignments is a significant sanction since a cadre can be dispatched to a far less desirable job or location and forced to pull up whatever roots he had established in his original unit.[8] Similarly, the periodic "downward transfer of cadres" *(xiafang ganbu)* to lower administrative levels can operate as a formidable informal sanction.[f]

---

[f] *Xiafang* first appeared in the early 1940s as the "to the villages" campaign, but it did not become a widely used technique in post-1949 China until 1957. This process has multiple goals including retrenching excess higher level personnel, eliminating bureaucratic phenomena, and strengthening basic level leadership as well as educating and disciplining those sent down. Downward transfer differs from the "simplification of organs and retrenchment of personnel" *(zhengdun jigou jinshu bianzhi, zhengdun bianzhi jingjian jigou* or *jinshu jigou he bianzhi)* which was used in the early and mid-1950s by having both broader aims and a substantially larger scope. For example, simplification and retrenchment in the first half of 1954 dispatched 150,000 cadres to lower posts while the first year of *xiafang* resulted in the downward transfer of 1.3 million cadres. John Wilson Lewis, *Leadership in Communist China* (Ithaca: Cornell University Press, 1963), pp. 220–32; Rensselaer W. Lee III, "The *Hsia Fang* System: Marxism and Modernisation," *CQ,* No. 28 (1966), pp. 43–49; and *RMRB,* April 17, 1955, in *SCMP,* No. 1042.

All personnel serving in government organs are subject to administrative disciplinary measures *(xingzheng chufen)* which supplement informal sanctions. Party members generally receive coordinated Party discipline as well. However, when administrative punishment is administered for work errors due to low cultural level or inexperience, no Party discipline is considered necessary.[9]

The administrative measures are[10]: warning *(jinggao);* registration of a demerit *(jiguo)* or a major demerit *(jidaguo);* demotion in grade *(jiangji);* suspension of duties in order to confess *(dingzhi fanxing)*[11]; demotion in office *(jiangzhi);* dismissal from office *(chezhi);* probationary expulsion *(kaichu liuyong chakan);* expulsion from the ranks of cadres *(qingxi chudui* or *qingchu chudui)*[12]; and [permanent] expulsion from the ranks of cadres *(kaichu, kaichu ganbu* or *kaichu duiji).*

The relatively light penalties of warning and the registration of demerits deal with minor violations of state discipline. Even these sanctions are serious because, along with all other informal and formal disciplinary measures, they are entered in cadres' dossiers and affect future career prospects. Demotion in grade, also for minor violations, means a reduction in civil service ranking and salary, but the cadre retains his original office. More serious violations may result in periods of suspension during which cadres write confessions, often under a form of house arrest within their unit. This can continue for weeks or months before a satisfactory confession is made and the cadres are allowed to return to their former posts or to other posts.

Demotions to lower ranking posts are also invoked for major violations of state discipline. Dismissal from office[g] for someone holding more than one positions generally pertains to his primary position, but in serious circumstances can apply to concurrent posts as well. Probationary expulsion for very serious violations is accompanied by trivial assignments, reduced wages, and continuing examinations of behavior. Those who repent may be reassigned to responsible work, usually of lesser importance than their former duties. Those who do not show evidence of reform are expelled. The two forms of expulsion differ in that *qingxi* or *qingchu chudui* allows for possible readmittance after repentance, while *kaichu* is intended to be permanent. In either case, expulsion is harsh since it means the end of the relatively good wages and living conditions of official life and relegation to the status of an ordinary laborer or peasant.[13]

Apart from or beyond discipline by state administrative units, a number of Party disciplinary measures *(dangji chufen)* are available in cases involving Party members. One sanction, although technically not a disciplinary measure, is "exhortation to withdraw from the Party" *(quangao chudang).* It is applied to Party members who fall short of membership standards due to erroneous political

[g] Dismissal from posts *(chezhi)* should be distinguished from removal from office *(mianzhi).* The former is a disciplinary measure while the latter is an administrative device which carries no implication of punishment.

views or failure to observe strict discipline and an austere living style.[14] Such "voluntary" withdrawal implies less disgrace than expulsion, but it is still a severe measure since loss of Party membership removes a cadre from the most powerful segment of the elite and otherwise damages his career.

Formal Party disciplinary measures are[15]: warning *(jinggao);* serious warning *(yanzhong jinggao)*; registration of a demerit *(jiguo)* or a major demerit *(jidaguo)*[16]; dismissal from posts within the Party *(chexiao dangnei zhiwu);* probation within the Party *(liudang chakan)*; expulsion from the Party *(qingxi chudang* or *qingchu chudang)*[17]; and [permanent] expulsion from the Party *(kaichu dangji).*[h]

Party warnings and demerits are a blot on an official's record which may inhibit advancement. Dismissal from posts in the Party bureaucracy applies to leadership positions only. If a cadre holds more than one leading position, he may be deprived of one or all posts depending on the circumstances. A Party member stripped of his Party posts still retains membership rights and may be assigned to lesser positions. Probation is generally set for a specific period varying from several months to several years and involves the loss of Party posts and such membership rights as voting in Party meetings. At the end of the probationary period, a member who has shown good behavior may have his rights restored but he is unlikely to regain his former positions.[18] Expulsion, with or without the possibility of readmission, is the most severe Party sanction. It is usually accompanied by the loss of any significant government posts, and frequently of purely formal positions in representative bodies. Although expelled Party members may serve in minor government posts, it is only in exceptional cases that they ever again play important roles.[19]

Administrative and Party sanctions may apply to violations of discipline and policy, the misuse of official power, immoral behavior (particularly in sexual matters), and poor work style generally. They are also used for minor violations of state law committed while performing official duties. Serious violations of law, however, require legal sanctions as well as Party and/or administrative measures.[i]

For Party members, criminal sanctions must be preceded by expulsion from

---

[h] Under the 1945 CCP Constitution disciplinary measures could also be taken collectively against entire Party committees or branches. These measures were: censure *(zhize);* partially reorganizing leading organs *(bufen gaizu qi lingdao jiguou);* dismissing leading organs and appointing new leading organs *(chezhi qi lingdao jiguan bing zhiding qi lingdao jiguan);* dissolving an entire organization *(jiesan zhengge zuzhi);* and carrying out a new registration of Party members *(jinxing dangyuan de zhongxin dengji).* These collective measures were dropped from the 1956 Party Constitution. See *Gongchandang dangzhang* [Constitution of the CCP], June 11, 1945 (n.p.: n.pub.), p. 23.

[i] The police and court system not only administer such sanctions, but they have also taken a leading role in implementing purge movements, e.g., the *sufan* campaign of 1955–57 (see above, n.3, Introduction). In such cases, however, overall responsibility has been placed clearly in the hands of the Party organization.

the Party, while government regulations require automatic removal from office of state personnel receiving criminal punishment from the courts.[20] As the various legal punishments have already been studied in detail elsewhere they will not be treated comprehensively here.[21] The full range of legal sanctions from fines, confiscation of property and deprivation of political rights to various forms of forced labor, long term or life imprisonment and the death penalty have long been used against Party members. But, in as far as can be determined, capital punishment has been used only in a tiny fraction of cases, at least until very recently.[j]

Finally, there is the quasi-legal sanction, frequently used in major campaigns, of classifying a cadre or Party member as an enemy of the state, a politically ostracized element. Such classification *(dai maozi,* literally "to put on the cap") as a landlord, rich peasant, counterrevolutionary, bad element or rightist involves the loss of political rights and continuous police surveillance, and is generally accompanied by struggle and formal disciplinary measures.[22]

Although the coercive aspects of discipline are recognized,[23] the principles behind the application of informal and formal sanctions reflect the education and reform emphasis of rectification doctrine. These principles stress (1) the seriousness of the circumstances of the case—mainly the extent to which an act may influence other cadres or the public; (2) past behavior—a good record, especially if linked to good class status, will soften disciplinary action, while a politically questionable history will lead to harsher penalties; and (3) willingness to reform—the extent of confessing past errors, the sincerity of self-examination, and often informing on others.[24]

The ambiguity of these guidelines allows ample scope for subjective judgment reflecting prevailing political winds in the administration of elite discipline. Flexible criteria thus contribute to great variation in the severity of measures actually employed during rectification campaigns.

Leadership Career Patterns: The "Semi-Purge" of High Officials

How are the CCP's disciplinary guidelines applied to high ranking leaders? Career data reveal that the reform emphasis of rectification doctrine has in fact been adopted in cases involving powerful central and regional figures. In addition to situations where criticism short of formal disciplinary sanctions is deemed

[j] There are indications that the death penalty has been used more frequently in the campaign against the "gang of four" than before October 1976. The evidence as of late 1978 has been insufficient to judge whether its use has extended beyond those who have committed various acts of violence. There is as yet no evidence of its application to former leading officials.

sufficient,[k] this can involve various forms of the "semi-purge" where leading officials suffer actual career setbacks.

In the mildest form of "semi-purge," formal disciplinary measures have been applied to high ranking cadres without seriously damaging their careers. This is illustrated by a case during the Three Anti Campaign involving serious bureaucratic behavior on the part of Wuhan Party and government leaders. As punishment for their errors in 1952 Party First Secretary Zhang Pinghua was demoted to deputy secretary, while Mayor Wu Defeng was dismissed from office *(chezhi)*. In neither instance, however, did this result in a severe career setback. Zhang remained an active figure in Wuhan and by 1954 again was first secretary. Subsequently he gained alternate Central Committee status and held important Party posts in Hubei and Hunan, becoming first secretary of Hunan in 1959. Wu, within seven months of his dismissal, was appointed secretary-general of the important Political and Legal Affairs Committee of the Central-South regional administrative apparatus and in 1954 became deputy director of the State Council staff office dealing with political and legal affairs. He subsequently held additional key posts in this sphere including the vice presidency of the Supreme People's Court and CCP Central Control Committee membership.[25]

In the Wuhan case, the career impact of the actions taken were highly marginal and temporary at best. Whether some subtle limits were placed on possible future advancement is impossible to say, but there is little to indicate that such was the case. This example strongly suggests that the use of formal sanctions is genuinely regarded as a method of "learning from past mistakes in order to avoid future ones" where high ranking officials are concerned.

The reform aspect in handling leadership cases is even more strikingly illustrated by instances of leading officials suffering severe career setbacks but resuming responsible duties after a period in the political wilderness. One such pattern involves assuming a post of markedly reduced importance compared to one's previous position. Huang Kecheng is a good example. Huang was PLA chief of staff, vice minister of defense, and a Central Committee secretary when he became involved in the Peng Dehuai affair in 1959 (see Chapter 9). At that time he was relieved of his PLA and defense posts *(mianzhi)* and completely disappeared from public view. Although spared public disgrace, Huang was severely criticized in secret Party documents and apparently had been cast into

[k] While self-criticisms by high officials are often *pro forma* exercises to encourage active self-examinations by ordinary cadres, in some instances it is clear that serious problems are involved. For example, during the 1951–52 Three Anti Campaign (see Chapter 4), the governor and two vice governors of Jiangxi province made a joint self-criticism of their concealing information from higher authorities. Nevertheless, these officials were not dismissed and continued to serve as three of the most important leaders of Jiangxi for over a decade. *CJRB*, February 9, 1952; and Frederick C. Teiwes, *Provincial Party Personnel in Mainland China 1956–1966* (New York: Occasional Papers of the East Asian Institute, Columbia University, 1967), pp. 26, 34–35.

political oblivion. Yet in late 1965 he reappeared as a vice governor of Shanxi.[26] While quite a comedown for Huang, his case does typify the CCP practice of giving useful work to errant officials even in serious cases.

Formerly disgraced leaders who regain positions equal to their previous standing are especially interesting. Pan Fusheng is a striking example. Pan, an alternate Central Committee member, was first secretary of Henan in the mid-1950s. By 1958, however, he had been dismissed from his posts *(chezhi)* and publicly denounced for forming an "anti-Party faction" (see Chapter 8). After an absence of five years, Pan reappeared in late 1962 as head of the All China Federation of Supply and Marketing Cooperatives. In 1966 Pan again became a provincial first secretary, this time in Heilongjiang, thus completing the full cycle.[27] An even more surprising case is that of Li Shinong, a Party secretary in Anhui expelled from the Party *(qingchu chudang)* in 1958 who resumed the same position by 1963.[28] Li's case indicates that the provision for a non-permanent form of expulsion from the Party is a device actually used in politically significant instances.

Undoubtedly political comebacks such as those of Huang, Pan and Li do not simply reflect recognition of their sincere repentance. More complex factors such as changing perceptions of needs and shifts in the political balance of power are surely involved. Indeed, one of the largest rehabilitations of disgraced officials in post-1949 China—the 1961–62 "reversal of verdicts" (see Chapter 10)—explicitly involved an admission of error by the Party Center rather than the reform of the rehabilitated. This development in fact reflected a weakening of rectification norms as the administration of elite discipline from the late 1950s became increasingly linked to changes in overall policy lines. Nevertheless, the practice of restoring power to previously denounced officials, a rare phenomenon in Communist systems,[1] obviously owes much to the rectification ethos.

Factors Influencing the Effectiveness of Rectification

The effectiveness of sanctions and techniques employed during rectification movements vary with circumstances. Before examining this variation in specific campaigns of the pre-Cultural Revolution period in subsequent chapters, we shall first draw upon theoretical literature, as well as empirical studies of CCP methods, to analyze factors which affect the efficiency of the rectification process.

The difficulty in gauging the success of rectification measures derives in part from the multiple and frequently conflicting goals of the process. While rectification attempts both to root out deviant cadre behavior and raise rank and file morale, the intense pressure directed against shortcomings can be profoundly depressing to

[1] While this has been most prominent in the PRC, it has not been unique to China. Rehabilitations were a significant feature of East European politics following the death of Stalin as shown by the cases of Gomulka in Poland and Nagy in Hungary. These developments, however, were clearly part of the political struggle accompanying policy changes in the post-Stalin period and did not reflect any established approach to elite discipline.

morale. Similarly, the process seeks officials who both vigorously implement current Party policies and avoid errors which offend popular sensibilities—a balance of activeness and circumspection which is often difficult to maintain.[29]

People with varying socio-economic or political backgrounds (not to mention different personality types) will respond to rectification appeals and techniques differently. For example, studies indicate that youths of middle school and university age are much more likely than their more cautious elders to respond enthusiastically to pressure for attitudinal change—i.e., in Robert Lifton's phrase, to be "zealous converts." [30] Class differences may also have an effect. Although influenced by ideologies most liable to produce opposition to Party objectives, idealistic intellectuals appear more prone to whole hearted conversion than pragmatic and phlegmatic workers and peasants.[31] In general, members of a group accorded high prestige are more likely to respond to official appeals than members of low prestige groups.[32]

There is the added complication that certain groups may be more responsive to some rectification objectives than others. Old Party cadres well versed in democratic centralism might energetically carry out new policies linked to rectification but ignore injunctions to correct petty abuses as not applicable to them, while non-Party administrators especially vulnerable to such movements may cease deviant behavior but tread cautiously regarding new directives.[33] Finally, group reactions will vary from campaign to campaign according to how each group's interests are affected by the movements in question.

Coercive, Persuasive and Tangible Appeals

The appeals used to implement rectification vary greatly. This variation is only partially reflected in the ingenious phrase coined by Schein and associates—"coercive persuasion." For the process not only involves changing proportions of coercive and persuasive appeals, it also encompasses obtaining compliance and change through the allocation of rewards—i.e., tangible appeals in the broadest sense.[m]

[m] While this analysis does not regard the tripartite categorization of "appeals" (also variously labelled "powers," "controls," "rewards" or "sanctions") as comprehensive and does not accept all theoretical propositions concerning these "appeals," it basically adopts the categories of "coercive," "persuasive," (also termed "symbolic" or "normative") and "utilitarian" or "remunerative" (i.e., "tangible") appeals as articulated in Amitai Etzioni, *The Active Society: A Theory of Societal and Political Processes* (New York: The Free Press, 1968), pp. 370–73; and G. William Skinner and Edwin A. Winckler, "Compliance Succession in Rural Communist China: A Cyclical Theory," in Amitai Etzioni, ed., *Complex Organizations, A Sociological Reader*, 2nd ed. (New York: Holt, Rinehart and Winston, 1969), pp. 411–12. It should be noted that the discussion of "tangible rewards" does not imply the degree of measurement, precision and rationality suggested by Etzioni and Skinner and Winckler. It simply means that in some rectification situations there has been a valid expectation that approved behavior will secure such concrete rewards as jobs, promotions and Party membership, while deviant behavior will result in the denial or loss of such rewards.

In particular, Party control over all career options provides powerful tangible backing to both coercion and persuasion. Not only does the possibility of losing official positions inhibit deviant behavior, but concern with one's future place in society enhances susceptibility to official arguments.[34] Moreover, the rectification process provides strong incentives through the recruitment of new cadres and Party members. "Activists" *(jijifenzi)* who take the lead in criticizing errors during rectification become prime targets for recruitment, although generally some evidence of political enthusiasm before the movement is equally important.[35] Upward mobility is provided for those already in official positions by the need to fill posts left vacant by dismissals and purges in the course of a campaign. Thus the career opportunities generated further the aims of rectification both by stimulating participation in the process and by replacing unsuitable cadres with vigorous new blood. This suggests, however, that the availability of desirable posts becomes an important limiting factor. More broadly, the ability of the state to provide material rewards for major social groups will influence the receptivity of cadres drawn from those groups to the objectives of rectification.[36]

Turning to "coercive persuasion," it is clear that the two elements of coercion and persuasion cannot be easily separated. While rational and emotive arguments are used to secure a change of viewpoint, this takes place in the context of some form of external pressure. The subjects of the process, in the words of Schein, "[are] coerced into allowing themselves to be persuaded."[37] But if coercion and persuasion cannot be separated, it is possible to distinguish different mixes of the two appeals in various rectification movements. The distinguishing features of a relatively persuasive approach are heavy reliance on rational argument (although not to the exclusion of emotive symbols) in a calm setting with infrequent use of sanctions of any kind. A heavily coercive approach, on the other hand, involves extensive use of a wide range of criminal, administrative, Party and informal sanctions[n] in a highly charged, threatening atmosphere. The range of possible approaches is illustrated by the persuasive-coercive continuum represented in Figure 1. Each rectification campaign can be placed on this continuum according to the types and frequency of sanctions employed.

Coercion and persuasion both seek three kinds of compliance: negative behavioral compliance—abstaining from proscribed acts; positive behavioral compliance—carrying out designated activities; and attitudinal compliance—bringing beliefs into line with official doctrine.

Coercion is widely regarded as particularly suited for securing negative be-

[n] Only criminal punishments and some of the more severe informal sanctions fit the precise definition of coercion as "physical sanctions or forceful deprivation of basic needs" (Skinner and Winckler, "Compliance Succession," p. 412). Administrative, Party and many informal measures could more precisely be viewed as tangible sanctions in that they take away or threaten jobs and wages, but in terms of "coercive persuasion" they may be treated as coercive devices.

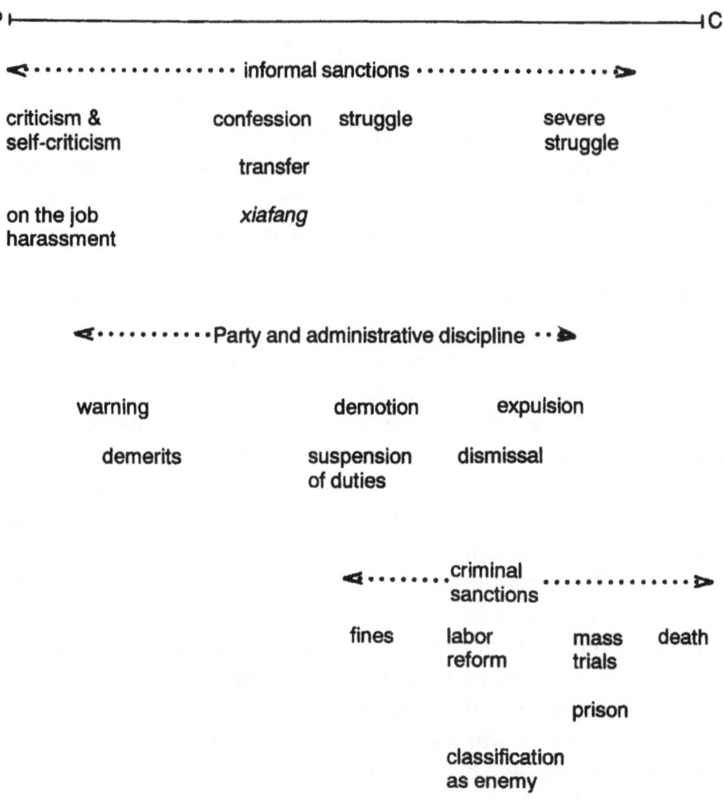

Figure 1. **Persuasive and Coercive Measures to Obtain Compliance**

havioral compliance. Even here, however, there are limits to its effectiveness. Coercion, particularly in heavy doses, generates alienation from and hostility towards those who exercise it. While in some circumstances coercion inhibits undesirable behavior and crushes opposition, in others it stimulates evasion and resistance. Coercive appeals are also of limited effectiveness in securing positive behavioral compliance. Generally quite large scale undertakings can be sustained at a high level of activity for short periods, but over longer periods disaffection, paralysis and fatalism undermine continued performance. Therefore, timing—knowing when to ease the pressure—becomes a key to the successful use of coercion. Similarly, it is important to apply only the proper degree of coercion. Experimental psychology has demonstrated that anxiety induced by threats can improve individual task performance up to a certain threshold but beyond that threshold performance drops significantly. The important point is to manipulate pressure to induce moderate stress which heightens motivation but to avoid extreme stress which destroys it.[38]

The impact of coercion on attitudinal compliance follows a similar pattern. Generally, resentment and hostility engendered by prolonged coercion undermine receptivity to official values. Coercion can, however, play a positive role at a key stage in the process of attitudinal change. Here the distinction developed by Schein between "unfreezing"—creating a willingness to abandon prior beliefs, and "changing"—the formation of a new set of beliefs, is important. During the "unfreezing" stage coercive pressures, often including quite severe ones, are vital for success; the anxiety, humiliation and exhaustion thus created is needed to motivate the subject to discard officially disapproved attitudes. As we have seen, Mao reached much the same conclusion when he declared it necessary to "give the patient a fright" before actual reform could be started.[39]

Even at this stage, however, the possibility of making people psychotic or, as has frequently happened during intense campaigns, driving them to suicide indicates the need to ease pressures before things get out of hand. Moreover, the "changing" stage requires a non-hostile atmosphere where the emphasis has shifted to persuasion if new ideas are to be successfully internalized. Only when the individual perceives the solicitude of the authorities for his well being and some autonomy in analyzing the situation is he likely to adopt officially approved beliefs. Thus rectification and thought reform have often been marked by a shift from "assault" to "leniency." As with positive behavioral compliance, timing is crucial if coercion is to be effective in securing attitudinal compliance.[40]

In contrast to coercion, persuasion is widely regarded as best suited for securing attitudinal compliance. If persuasion creates a consensus on values, however, in an important sense it will also be more successful than coercion in obtaining both positive and negative behavioral compliance. If widespread agreement exists on norms of behavior, it follows that desirable behavior will be facilitated and deviant behavior discouraged. The net result will most likely be less deviance than if alienation producing coercion were the main guarantor of order.[o] Nevertheless, there will still be individuals and groups outside the consensus prone to anti-social acts. With these people persuasive methods are unlikely to work and coercion will be more effective for achieving negative behavioral compliance. In terms of rectification, this suggests persuasion will be better suited for remedying relatively minor shortcomings of large numbers of cadres who basically accept the official value system. While harsh methods might also curb such deviations, it would be at considerable cost in terms of alienation and disruption. But in cases of serious violations by a few, coercion will be more efficient in rooting out dangerous behavior.[p] If serious violations are widespread

---

[o] Similarly, the distribution of ample tangible rewards throughout society can provide potent support for public order.

[p] Coercion may also be more effective than persuasion in securing positive behavioral compliance when the acts involved conflict with deeply held values or demand extreme sacrifices for causes which do not have widespread popular support.

coercion may also be necessary despite the danger of counterproductive side effects.

The degree to which persuasion can predominate over coercion in attempts to achieve compliance is closely linked to the extent of attitudinal change required. If the aim is the learning of new but non-controversial concepts, then little "unfreezing" and hence little coercion is needed. On the other hand, if new beliefs are incompatible with deeply held values, considerable coercive pressure —or "giving the patient a fright" in Mao's terms—will be required for "unfreezing" although there will be a point at which it becomes self defeating. Irrespective of the use of coercion, however, the effectiveness of persuasion *per se* depends on a number of rational and emotive considerations. The process of forming new beliefs—the "changing stage"—is largely a cognitive process. Once "unfreezing" has occurred, people seek information on which to base their new outlook. If this outlook is to correspond to the wishes of the authorities, they must be able to control information so that only what affirms desired opinions reaches those undergoing change. The Party's monopoly of mass communications greatly facilitates such information control by allowing constant repetition of approved ideas, barring all but orthodox interpretations of events, and censoring facts challenging the official line.

Nevertheless, the denial of disconfirming evidence will be impossible if there is a substantial discrepancy between official policy and readily observable social phenomena—e.g., claims of the correctness of Great Leap Forward policies during the economic crisis of 1961–62. It is therefore crucial that beliefs being promoted be compatible with the experience of those undergoing persuasion. Moreover, for persuasion to be successful beliefs must be logically coherent, they should provide a convincing interpretation of what is known. One of the strengths of CCP ideology is that its view of foreign aggression and internal exploitation offers a credible explanation for much of Chinese political and social history. But where there are glaring inconsistencies official assertions produce doubt and confusion rather than genuine acceptance. Finally, it has been demonstrated that an individual's acceptance of ideas is directly related to the clarity with which he perceives them. Thus when a clear picture of desired attitudes is presented, people motivated to change can easily grasp them. But where signals are ambiguous or subject to sudden alteration even someone eager for change will have difficulty in forming a new belief system.[41]

In addition to the above cognitive considerations, the success of persuasion also depends on emotive factors. Rectification is largely concerned with values rather than fact and therefore involves intensely emotional matters. Even when persuasive measures are carried out in a calm atmosphere, without orchestrated tension, an emotional content may be present. Such content may enhance the effectiveness of persuasion when the new values promoted are analogous to existing values. For example, rectification efforts to further the collective ethic and self-sacrifice draw on strong feelings that people should behave in this manner. Emotional support is further provided if a reference group advocates official values. The Party's image of invincibility also creates a powerful attraction to the organization and its views. Conversely, if the authorities appear weak and unsure of themselves there will be less inclination to accept their assertions. Further, where official ideology attacks deeply held values, as in the case of filial piety, strong emotional forces will be arrayed against persuasion. The need for "unfreezing" and coercion is then created.[42]

In sum, effective rectification requires skillful use of all appeals—coercive, persuasive and tangible. In general, chances of fulfilling the aims of rectification are enhanced the greater the availability of tangible rewards both in society at large and for participants in the process unless, of course, a fundamental attack on the desire for such rewards is an overriding objective. Moreover, "coercive persuasion" is much more effective than Stalinist terror not only for attitudinal compliance but also for positive and negative behavioral compliance as it recognizes the inherent limitations of coercion. But the mix of coercion and persuasion will vary considerably with the objectives sought. The most basic consideration is the degree of change sought in a given movement, but other factors such as conflicting goals and diverse target groups must also be taken into account. This complexity suggests, to say the least, considerable difficulty in obtaining optimal effectiveness from "coercive persuasion."

Problems of Implementation

Effectiveness also depends on the performance of small groups and higher level authorities responsible for implementing the rectification process. The small group plays a crucial role at every stage of attitudinal change. During "unfreezing" it creates psychological pressure for rejecting prior beliefs by treating as alien those holding proscribed views. Once "changing" begins the small group becomes a key source of information from which new beliefs are formed. In seeking to identify with the group the subject of the process adopts its values and behavior. A final stage, "refreezing" or making new attitudes last, also relies on the small group. Given the importance of acceptance by the group, constant reinforcement of desired attitudes in group interaction deepens the individual's commitment to those attitudes.[43]

As both Chinese and Western commentators have observed, however, small groups will not necessarily function in the manner described above. Groups can generate conformity which either supports or resists views promoted by the authorities. If the dominant group attitude opposes the official line, social pressures will operate to reinforce resistance. While small groups are unlikely to offer overt opposition, strong deviant opinions can generate an undercurrent of opposition limiting the effectiveness of the group in achieving official goals.[44]

More significant are problems created by other weak points of the small group. For small groups to work well both a high degree of control over group activities and solidarity among its members are required. The control necessary to manage "coercive persuasion" properly is not easily attained; the pressures of a unit's regular tasks can divert time and energy from small group activities. The absence of solidarity can be detrimental in several senses. If deep frictions exist within a group, whatever their cause, the ability of the authorities to mobilize the group will be seriously undermined since the need to belong to the larger unit will not exist. Indeed, one faction may resist the official line simply on the grounds that another faction embraces it. In cases where such frictions do not exist but the general sense of group identity is weak, social pressures for compliance will be diluted by the member's limited involvement with the group. Moreover, experiments have shown that regardless of the number of people within a group who articulate views challenging those of an individual, if a single other individual affirms his view the tendency to yield to the pressure exerted by the larger group is almost totally wiped out. Thus if a person under attack can gain the support of others, his resistance to the rectification process will increase markedly.[45]

Perhaps the most important frailty affecting small groups concerns the quality of members and leaders. Even if considerable solidarity and basic support for the Party exists, the effectiveness of the small group will be considerably impaired unless there is a high degree of understanding of and commitment to specific values and policies. It is likely, however, that many cadres, particularly those at the basic levels with a low cultural and political level, will not readily grasp official arguments. There may also be a tendency to adhere to traditional and particularistic attitudes rather than those officially promoted. For example, the traditional avoidance of conflict and considerations of "face" will inhibit small groups from engaging in effective self-criticism. Group members will often focus on inconsequential matters rather than exposing important problems. And while these shortcomings are serious enough in small group members, they are doubly damaging when found in group leaders. As group leaders must convey the objectives of the Party to the group and orchestrate group activities, any failure of understanding, skill or commitment on their part can prove disastrous. Thus the continuing difficulty of cultivating small group leaders who are both well grounded in their group and committed to Party goals is a major hindrance to effective rectification.[46]

While the key arena for implementing rectification is the small group, policies guiding the process are set by the highest Party authorities. For the process to be successful effective links must be established between policy making and implementing bodies. Two main methods have been used to achieve this end. One uses the regular chain of command. Party committees at each administrative level are charged with guiding rectification at their respective levels; higher committees oversee subordinate committees which in turn direct rectification work in the organs under their control. While special *ad hoc* rectification machinery is frequently set up to guide campaigns, it is staffed by personnel drawn from the established local leadership. At the basic levels leadership rests with the Party branches. The second method relies on work teams *(gongzuodui)* organized at higher levels and sent to participate in the rectification of subordinate organs. While the precise authority of these work teams relative to local leaders varies, they often have a clearly superior role.

Each method has its strengths and weaknesses. Reliance on established leaders to rectify their own units places authority in the hands of people with an intimate knowledge of concrete problems. They are able to tailor the "coercive persuasion" process to the needs of individuals and groups. However, if those leaders have serious shortcomings they will be able to deflect the movement away from themselves. They may also be unwilling to deal firmly with the errors of those under them for fear of arousing resentment which will complicate regular work. Work teams, on the other hand, are equipped to handle thoroughly the problems of leading as well as ordinary cadres. In so doing, however, work teams run considerable risks of acting without adequate knowledge of the local situation, thus undermining morale. If work teams deal harshly with mistakes, local cadres may be unwilling to resume official duties after the teams withdraw. And if local leaders are rudely brushed aside by work teams, they may find it difficult later to reassert their authority.[47]

We can hypothesize, then, that reliance on established local leaders is best suited for handling relatively manageable shortcomings, while work teams, besides being essential in areas of weak local leadership, are appropriate for more intractable problems. Subsequent chapters will examine whether this rule was in fact followed by the CCP in the period up to the Cultural Revolution.

Distortions and excesses inevitably appear during the rectification process. The delicate relationship between rectification and regular work is a recurrent problem. Ideally, rectification links general concepts and principles to concrete problems of work and individual behavior. But sometimes, especially in mild campaigns, participants will avoid relating rectification to their work. Instead, they will engage in abstract discussions while escaping serious self-criticism. Moreover, many cadres will avoid participating in campaign activities altogether on the pretext that they are too busy with their normal duties. Thus the compartmentalization of rectification and work, together with the assumption that work takes precedence, prevents improved work performance. During intense movements, however, a contrary tendency often appears. Priority is given to uncovering defects to the extent that the functioning of the organization is severely disrupted. Occasionally the entire work of a unit grinds to a halt. While interruptions to work are often justified as necessary to achieve a campaign's overall goals, administrative and economic costs frequently exceed expectations. Improvements due to eliminating deviant behavior are therefore offset to some degree by these costs.[48]

The effectiveness of rectification is enhanced by the recruitment of energetic new cadres into Party and state organizations, but recruitment is subject to its own deviations. In contrast to periods between political movements when restrictive practices normally predominate, during campaigns standards are often lowered as recruitment generally becomes a major task. Responsible officials under pressure to show results frequently slight official selection criteria and procedures in the effort to meet recruitment quotas. As a result, vacant posts may be filled by people lacking requisite ideological understanding or political commitment. If this tendency gets out of hand the achievements of rectification are to some extent undone. Instead of replacing tired and corrupt cadres with vigorous new blood, one form of inadequate leadership may give way to another.[49]

Rectification is also vulnerable to distortion by the individuals who manage the process. Responsible officials at all levels are supposed to pursue goals set by the central leadership, but the considerable powers of mobilization, investigation and punishment can also be used to advance personal interests. Such officials not only suppress criticism voiced against them during movements, they also settle accounts with subordinates who have given offense in the past. The fear of retaliation thus generated undermines rectification measures. Higher authorities, aware of this tendency, have taken steps to correct it but the danger remains and, we can imagine, becomes especially serious when campaign guidelines are unclear or divisions appear in high Party circles. The more precise the criteria defining deviant behavior the easier it is for higher level bodies to identify distortions of those criteria. Where the definition of error is ambiguous abuses are harder to detect. Conflict at the top is the most likely source of such ambiguity.[50]

Another common problem is the tendency of major movements to get out of hand. Such errors as excessive struggle and overly harsh disciplinary punishment are often inevitable once a mass movement is underway. With central authorities insisting on the necessity of rooting out dangerous evils—and even setting quotas for the guilty[q]—it is hardly surprising that excesses occur. Such excesses can be severely detrimental to the rectification process. They not only have caused considerable numbers of suicides but also a more pervasive nervous strain due, as one commentary put it, to "fear of the two characters *zhengfeng*."[51] While such anxiety may contribute to rectification goals in some circumstances, more generally the counterproductive aspects of coercion predominate.

Finally, a less dramatic but perhaps more serious distortion of rectification occurs when its processes become routine. Routinization involves more than superficial participation in rectification activities; it is the progressive development of such tendencies over time. Recollections of former mainland residents, together with the findings of clinical psychology, suggest that rectification and similar thought reform processes had their deepest impact in the early 1950s following the Communist takeover. Not only did important political circumstances—

[q] Explicit purge quotas were used in 1955 during the *sufan* campaign; see above, Introduction to the First Edition, n. 3. The implicit use of quotas is discussed in Chapter 4. Of course, quotas can also have the effect of limiting the extent of a purge.

especially initial enthusiasm for CCP successes in unifying the country, bringing internal peace and economic reconstruction—favor such efforts, but the fact that most people were experiencing these techniques for the first time considerably enhanced their vitality. Not knowing quite what to expect and often overawed by manifestations of CCP power, people had little opportunity to develop psychological defenses against political movements. Therefore, the "unfreezing" potential of "coercive persuasion" was at its maximum.

Repeated use of these techniques, however, tended to produce diminishing returns. Ritualized public displays replaced inner conviction as emotional involvement in the process ebbed. A number of factors are involved. First, an important aspect of compliance is social adjustment, both in the sense of adjustment to small group pressures and to demands by the authorities. In order to secure approval of the group and to avoid official sanctions, people comply behaviorally including public expression of orthodox attitudes. The first experience with rectification is a learning process in which many participants come to understand the roles they are to play and the responses they should make during the process. With such understanding new campaigns could be faced with greater confidence and unorthodox attitudes could be retained with minimum tension. Moreover, to the degree anxiety still existed, it centered on playing one's role adequately rather than on the attitudes in question.

Another factor is that repeated exposure to rectification, i.e., to the coercive aspects of the process, tends to generate hostility. Apart from excesses in any specific campaign a cumulative coercion from successive movements produces resentment. Such resentment may be expressed in outbursts against the Party when pressures are eased, as in the Hundred Flowers period (see Chapter 6), or they may create a protective inner passivity against officially approved ideas. Meanwhile, the passage of time between campaigns provides an opportunity to accumulate evidence—i.e., disconfirming experiences—which challenges official dogmas at a cognitive level. In this regard we can speculate about the effect of constantly shifting objectives and deviations from movement to movement. While such shifts may be rational by some criteria, it is likely—particularly where the shifts are rapid and approved behavior is transformed into deviant behavior—that many people will perceive only inconsistency and develop reservations about official beliefs.

In some cases where people are highly motivated, however, clinical psychology demonstrates it is possible for control over expression of unorthodox attitudes to extend to their expression as thoughts. Here the social adjustment function of beliefs completely eclipses the function of appraising objective reality. In such cases, however, there is an atrophy of the ability to think creatively and people are reduced to ritual responses to cues from authority. When such cues are not forthcoming they can only flounder without purpose. This type of ritualized behavior and thought undermines an important aim of rectification since the ideal cadre not only accepts orthodox beliefs but carries out his duties actively and imaginatively, deriving courses of action from general principles without benefit of detailed instructions.[52]

Repeated use therefore robs rectification of its effectiveness in obtaining attitudinal change and instead produces routinized responses based on calculation, resentment and skepticism. An "internal migration" results whereby actual views remain private. Even where attitudinal compliance is achieved it is often ritualized and devoid of creativity. Ironically, however, attempts to break down routinized rectification patterns may also have detrimental consequences. For cadres well versed in rectification procedures at least play their roles properly, thus providing behavioral compliance. On the other hand, drastic alterations in existing practices, as in the Cultural Revolution, confuse participants and produce less predictable behavior with no guarantee of greater attitudinal change.

Conclusion

Rectification techniques encompass a wide variety of measures which can be combined in a multiplicity of ways. When functioning optimally these techniques can be a powerful force influencing behavior and attitudes. Their successful utilization, however, is contingent on many factors and requires extremely skillful management of rectification movements. In addition to the many possible combinations of techniques, differences among various target groups and potentially conflicting goals greatly complicate the task of leading rectification. Naturally, the process is vulnerable to shortcomings of cadres responsible for campaign leadership. The effectiveness of rectification is also inextricably linked to broader social and political conditions. If the political system is adequately meeting the needs of society it will be much easier to reform and revitalize the elite than when failures produce widespread social malaise. Furthermore, there is an apparent link between effective rectification and leadership unity. With such unity it is possible to assign clear objectives and ensure organizational discipline, factors critically necessary for achieving behavioral compliance and attitudinal change.

Finally, successful rectification requires a careful blend of coercion and persuasion. Coercion is a source of vulnerability as well as potential strength. On the positive side, coercive methods are essential both to provide the environmental control which facilitates persuasive efforts, and to create conditions for far-reaching change. But while this was clearly recognized by Mao's injunction to "give the patient a fright," the thrust of rectification doctrine warns against excessive harshness. Similarly, our behavioral analysis of "coercive persuasion" shows coercion will be counterproductive if used to excess, especially when genuine attitudinal change, high morale and creative leadership are major goals. The traditional persuasive approach, then, is firmly rooted in the actual constraints of the disciplinary process.

3
The Origins of Rectification

The development of rectification theory and practice in the early 1940s was both an extension of and reaction to the earlier history of the CCP.[a] Official histories and some scholarly analysis identify rectification with Mao while asserting that other leaders advocated sharply contrasting approaches. Thus CCP leaders before 1935 purportedly pushed coercive disciplinary methods—dubbed "ruthless struggles and merciless blows" *(canku douzheng he wuqing daji)*—while Mao

---

[a] Two broader influences on rectification should also be mentioned—the Chinese cultural tradition and Soviet theory and practice. Many specific features of rectification have parallels in the Confucian tradition. Confucian doctrine stressed self-examination, attitudinal change, and educating rather than merely punishing wrongdoers. Moreover, Confucian practice, while resorting to purges to rid the elite of unorthodox viewpoints, was also marked by a reluctance to kill literati who strayed from the approved path. Indeed, Liu Shaoqi claimed "The national character of the Chinese people prefers leniency; they do not like harsh treatment" ("Self-Cultivation in Organization and Discipline" (July 1939), *CLG,* Spring 1972, p. 53). Finally, traditional culture emphasized interpersonal relations, group pressures, and preference for informal over legal mechanisms of conflict management. Still, it is difficult to find precedents for the intensive group indoctrination of rectification campaigns. See David S. Nivison, "Communist Ethics and Chinese Tradition," *Journal of Asian Studies,* November 1956; and Robert Jay Lifton, *Thought Reform and the Psychology of Totalism: A Study of "Brainwashing" in China* (New York: W.W. Norton & Company, 1961), pp. 389–98.

Soviet theory and practice had a major impact on CCP disciplinary methods from the founding of the Party and continuing into the period of Mao's dominance notwithstanding the rejection of Stalinist excesses. Apart from fundamental concepts such as democratic centralism, the CCP also took such basic methods as the systematic study of documents and criticism and self-criticism from Soviet experience. Moreover, before Stalin's terror those aspects of the Leninist tradition which encouraged far-ranging debate within the leadership and included a disinclination to act against dissenters undoubtedly had a significant influence on the CCP in its formative years. See Robert V. Daniels, *Conscience of the Revolution* (Cambridge: Harvard University Press, 1960).

attempted to foster systematic education. Mao's undoubted contributions to rectification notwithstanding, the following analysis argues that this view both overstates actual differences and overlooks the developing nature of Mao's position.

As we have seen, it has also been argued that a clear divergence emerged between Mao and Liu Shaoqi over the preferred approach to elite discipline: Mao assertedly favored thoroughgoing ideological struggle and the involvement of non-Party forces in the process, while Liu sought to curb struggle and limit mass participation. In Chapter 1 we rejected this view on the basis of the writings of the two men; here we deepen the analysis by examining the two rectification movements carried out before nationwide victory in 1949. This reveals not only that the "Liuist" campaign of 1947–48 involved deeper struggle and more meaningful mass participation than the initial "Maoist" effort of 1942–44, but that in fact an essential agreement existed between the two men in both instances. The substantial differences between the two movements must be attributed to leadership imperatives under contrasting conditions rather than to the predilections of individuals.

Of the factors affecting Party disciplinary methods in the pre-1949 period two stand out: the relative degree of leadership unity and the degree of threat from external sources. An overview of Chinese Communist politics during the entire period preceding the founding of the PRC leads to the following hypotheses: First, when a revolutionary organization during its struggle for power suffers from leadership cleavages, it tends to adopt coercive techniques of internal control; when the organization is unified it tends to adopt persuasive control techniques. Second, in situations where such an organization has a secure environment it may develop systematic educational methods, but where its external environment is threatening such methods are not possible and coercive means are often introduced.[b] The following discussion elaborates these hypotheses as they apply not only to the basic contrast between the "ruthless struggle" and rectification periods but to unfolding events surrounding the two pre-liberation rectification campaigns.

---

[b] These hypotheses do not assume any necessary relationship between the degree of leadership unity and a threatening or secure external environment. If both factors favor either persuasive or coercive control methods, then the likelihood of such methods is considerably enhanced. If the two factors operate in contrary directions, then a more complex pattern will result as in the 1947–48 case discussed below. Furthermore, the hypotheses exclude revolutionary regimes in power not simply because they are inapplicable to at least one major case—that of Stalin—but because the very fact of state power provides a qualitatively higher degree of security than that which could be attained during revolutionary struggle. How this higher degree of security both affected the impact of changes in the external environment on control techniques and influenced the relationship between Party unity and control techniques after 1949 is a problem examined in subsequent chapters.

The Legacy of Factional Politics

From the founding of the CCP in 1921 until Mao Zedong gained preeminence within the Central Committee in 1935, factional disputes concerning the course of the Chinese revolution deeply divided the Party. Retrospectively, Mao reserved his sharpest criticism for the leaders of the so-called "third 'left' line" from 1931 to 1934, men who largely belonged to the returned student faction. This faction, which had close Soviet ties and gained ascendancy in the Central Committee due to the direct intervention of Comintern agents, brought about Mao's temporary eclipse but was finally overcome by Mao without benefit of Comintern support following the fall of the Jiangxi Soviet. In interpreting the differences between himself and the proponents of the "third 'left' line" 10 years later, Mao depicted an unambiguous struggle between the allegedly adventuristic military posture and harsh political and economic policies of his opponents, on the one hand, and his own cautious military strategy and moderate social reforms, on the other, when in fact the situation had been far less clear-cut.[1] What is of special interest to this study is that Mao went beyond criticisms of revolutionary strategies and attacked the methods of handling disputes within the Party which had prevailed at that time:

> Whenever an erroneous political line became dominant, an erroneous organizational line inevitably emerged.... Accordingly, the various ... lines of the [1927–34] period opposed Comrade Mao [Zedong's] organizational line as well as his political line.... In particular, in order to enforce their will, the exponents of the [1931–34] line invariably and indiscriminately branded all Party comrades who found the wrong line impracticable and who therefore expressed doubt, disagreement or dissatisfaction, or did not actively support the wrong line or firmly carry it out; they stigmatized these comrades with such labels as "[r]ight opportunism," "the rich peasant line," "the line of conciliation" and "double-dealing"; waged "ruthless struggles" against them and dealt them "merciless blows," and even conducted these "inner Party struggles" as if they were dealing with criminals and enemies. This wrong kind of inner Party struggle became the regular method by which the[se] comrades ... raised their own prestige, enforced their own demands and intimidated the Party cadres.[2]

This attack not only reflected the past position of Mao whose supporters had been subjected to "merciless blows," it also supported Mao's efforts in the 1940s to create a new set of principles for handling tensions under his consolidated leadership. But the question remains: were there in fact two organizational approaches in the pre-1935 period emphasizing "ruthless struggle" on the one hand and systematic education on the other?

While the pre-1935 leaders did not develop systematic educational methods for handling cadre deviations despite repeated calls for study, and often treated their opponents harshly, it is also clear that they observed some restraints in handing out Party discipline. Although Chen Duxiu and other leaders were expelled from the Party, many of those who lost out in factional conflicts during the late 1920s and early 1930s retained Party membership and some—e.g., Qu Qiubai—regained important positions even before Mao assumed leadership. Moreover, Mao himself was reelected to prestigious posts when his actual power was at its nadir—a situation not unlike Mao's later practice of reserving Central Committee places for former opponents who had lost all real influence—and there is evidence of the returned student leaders seeking cooperation with Mao despite their differences.[3] Thus while Party purges in these years were extensive,[4] even under the returned students CCP practice reflected recognition of the need to limit inner Party conflict.

For Mao's part, the evidence suggests he was not fully committed to an educational approach. Although Mao's 1929 Gutian resolution, which was later resurrected as a rectification document, did call for systematic political education, its basic thrust was to bolster Mao's position *vis-à-vis* the Central Committee then under Li Lisan by placing army political officers under the authority of Mao's Front Committee.[5] The clearest example of Mao's willingness to ignore persuasion and opt for coercive methods was the Futian incident in late 1930. The incident began with Mao's forces arresting some 4,400 members of a Red Army corps and most of Li's local followers, assertedly because of connections with an "anti-Bolshevik league" set up by the GMD several years earlier. In response, a political commissar of the affected army corps led an attack on Maoist forces at Futian, freed most of the local leaders jailed there, and established a rival Soviet government nearby. Mao counterattacked and suppressed the rebellion after several months, reportedly making use of widespread executions and mass trials.

What is of particular relevance to us is that Mao's Central Committee opponents used the Futian incident to attack him in terms that were even harsher than those Mao later used against them. Thus Mao was accused of unprincipled factional struggles which sent many Communists to their deaths, excessive use of force, and indiscriminate use of torture and capital punishment—a "reign of terror"—while neglecting mobilization and education. Mao was not, of course, the only leader conducting harsh purges at this time. But those he carried out together with the struggles against alleged "anti-Bolsheviks" in other Soviet areas produced a reaction within the Party. By 1934, some curbing of political security bureaus and shaking up of security personnel had occurred, although the stark policy of "no mercy for class enemies" continued. However limited, opposition to merciless struggle developed before Mao gained predominant power and, ironically in view of later Maoist history, Mao's own acts were one catalyst of this opposition.[6]

In a more fundamental sense, the question is whether any leader could have instituted a systematic rectification program in the pre-1935 period. On balance, the answer appears negative. The youth of the CCP was clearly a factor; it takes time to build up an organization and develop organizational techniques. More significant was the precarious environment within which the CCP functioned. During the period of the GMD-CCP alliance up to 1927 the Party was able to function openly but was always exposed to Nationalist pressure and ultimately to the threat of GMD military action. From the 1927 split to 1935 the CCP was able to develop military forces and maintain scattered rural base areas, but Communist forces faced repeated GMD harassment which finally succeeded in destroying most of these bases. In this hostile environment mere survival had highest priority; while, ideally, educational measures could have strengthened the Party, under the circumstances more pressing tasks took precedence. Moreover, the tension created by the threat's immediacy reinforced tendencies to rely on harsh disciplinary measures for elite control.

Another factor inhibiting the development of a rectification approach at this time was the deep factional cleavages within the Party. These cleavages, which were intensified by repeated revolutionary failures, the imposition of vague yet demanding Comintern directives, and a diverse Party membership of labor organizers, young Soviet trained intellectuals and rural guerrilla leaders, were not conducive to mild methods of settling differences; bitter conflict made recourse to coercion all but inevitable. Moreover, even if in this situation a rectification program had been proposed by one group, it could not have been effective. With Party leadership fragmented, any effort to correct errors by rectification measures would have floundered in disagreement over the nature of those errors and the failure of dissident factions to carry out the campaign.

When Mao obtained preeminence within the CCP leadership in January 1935, the Party was still in the midst of the Long March and the time was not yet ripe for the introduction of systematic rectification. However, factors inherent in Mao's new situation can, in retrospect, be seen as inclining him to more persuasive, less harsh methods than had been the norm up to that time. First, the coalition which supported Mao not only objected to the disastrous military policies of the previous leadership, but many of its members had suffered from ruthless struggle. Although Mao was not without fault himself, it was nevertheless widely recognized that he had suffered badly at the hands of the returned students. As Chen Yi put it over 30 years later, "Chairman Mao's prestige ... is due to his having been humiliated the most and having been wronged. . . ."[7] Yet if Mao were to be credible as a leader who would break with such practices—particularly in view of his own blemishes—it was necessary that he adopt a conciliatory approach. Initially he patched up differences with former opponents and did not allow them to apologize to him[8]; eventually it meant restraint was used when these apologies were finally demanded. Closely related to the benefits to Mao of adopting a moderate posture were the limitations on his power; although preeminent within the new leadership his authority was far from absolute as even members of the returned student group retained important posts.[c] Mao could not have taken drastic action against his old opponents even if he desired to do so. According to Chen Yi, "Chairman Mao [in 1935] . . . described the loss incurred to the revolution [by the previous leadership] not as a mistake in political line, but only as a mistake in military line. If he pointed out at the time that the mistake was a political one, some people would definitely have found it unacceptable. . . . He pointed it out only in Yan'an 10 years later."[9] But while the need to build unity around Mao's fledgling leadership made conciliation the order of the day, it was not the same thing as a systematic rectification approach. Indeed, the necessity of conciliation delayed the reform efforts and concomitant demotions which marked the initial rectification movement.

The First Rectification Campaign, 1942–44

The first rectification campaign *(zhengfeng yundong)* was the product of the entire period following the arrival of Mao Zedong in Yan'an. Some of Mao's most significant writings in this period articulated the theme of the need to unify Marxist-Leninist theory and Chinese realities which came to play a major role in the 1942–44 campaign. Moreover, the development of Party schools in Yan'an provided a potent means for indoctrination in Mao's concepts. As early as the Central Committee plenum of September-November 1938 the CCP adopted a program of increased education and training for Party members. Subsequently a study movement involving 4,000 cadres in the Yan'an region was carried out in 1939–40 and cadre education was extended to other base areas. Party directives also called for screening cadres in conjunction with education, and a limited degree of purging took place.[10]

The period leading up to the rectification movement saw the gradual growth of Mao's power, a process which that campaign brought to its conclusion. Despite the official dating of Mao's accession to leadership in January 1935, he subsequently had to meet several challenges, most significantly from Wang Ming, a leader of the returned student faction who had left China in 1931. Wang's arrival in Yan'an in late 1937 apparently marked a setback for Mao on the critical issue of the nature of the new united front with the GMD. Although the united front debate, which had been under way well before Wang's return, was hardly as clear-cut as official histories claim, it does appear that Mao advocated subordinating some CCP goals but strictly maintaining the Party's independence, while Wang, reflecting Soviet interest in a bulwark of anti-Japanese power based on Chiang Kai-shek's armies, argued for closer cooperation with the Nationalists. It took nearly a year for Mao's line finally to emerge

[c]This may well still overstate Mao's position in 1935–36 when a returned student, Zhang Wentian, the newly appointed general secretary, was perhaps Mao's equal.

victorious at the September–November 1938 Central Committee plenum, a victory which marked an important milestone in Mao's consolidation of power.[11] It is significant that it was this plenum which initiated plans for inner Party education, for Mao's substantial success in achieving a consensus on his power and policies provided the basic unity of outlook and stability of leadership upon which the first rectification movement could be launched. Moreover, Mao's strategies of capitalizing on growing nationalist sentiment and extending CCP influence to large areas of North China behind Japanese lines resulted in a dramatic increase in both the territory under Communist control and in Party membership. According to CCP estimates, at the end of 1940 the areas of substantial Communist control encompassed 100 million people while the Party had grown by 20 times since 1937 to 800,000 members.[12]

The vast influx of new Party members caused problems as well as opportunities. Party leaders were unable to screen adequately the new members, and educational efforts since 1939 were judged unsuccessful. Moreover, the heterogeneous composition of that membership created obstacles to the achievement of Party programs. The bulk of CCP recruits consisted of illiterate peasants lacking knowledge of Marxism-Leninism and imbued with traditional values; they were bound by particularistic social relationships in conflict with Party goals. The other major stream of new membership consisted of students and intellectuals who had fled from the Japanese occupied urban areas of North China. Strongly motivated by nationalism, these elements possessed many skills in short supply in Yan'an but their ideals and ideology were as likely to be reformist as Marxist and, if Marxist, were frequently prone to a radical dogmatism abhorred by Mao. In addition, the CCP's united front and patriotic appeals tended to blur its revolutionary program and hinder the growth of Marxist-Leninist concepts among both peasants and intellectuals.[13] Despite these problems, the official retrospective judgment was that the CCP was already sound ideologically, politically and organizationally before the 1942 movement,[14] and, indeed, a base existed upon which further consolidation could proceed: the infrastructure of Party schools which had been built up provided a foundation for a more systematic and larger scale educational effort to overcome the Party's declared inadequacies.

More generally, the outbreak of the Sino-Japanese War and subsequent CCP gains dramatically lessened the threat to Party survival thus providing an environment in which rectification could be contemplated. The element of threat had not been entirely eliminated, of course, and security measures against saboteurs, enemy infiltration and "Trotskyism" in the late 1930s encompassed a continuing role for coercion.[15] Furthermore, despite the successes of Mao's united front policies, the continued presence of returned student leaders in important posts in the Party propaganda apparatus indicated that the final consolidation of the Maoist leadership was still to be accomplished.[16] Nevertheless, the more favorable environment overall was conducive to a persuasive approach to elite control.

In 1941–42, however, events were becoming more threatening to the CCP.

The Party's rapid expansion under Mao's united front policy precipitated sharp clashes with the Japanese and GMD. In 1941, following a major Communist military offensive, the brunt of Japanese attacks shifted to the Communists and resulted in a dramatic contraction of their base areas. Moreover, the GMD blockade of the Yan'an region, initiated in 1939, was tightened in 1941 and the Nationalists also cut off the subsidy provided to the CCP under the terms of the united front. These pressures created an immediate need for improved Party morale and discipline which the rectification campaign sought to provide. In this sense, the movement was at least in part a response to the worsening situation. However, it is important to note that the Yan'an area, where the campaign was implemented most thoroughly, faced a political and economic rather than a military threat. Thus the problems to be dealt with in Yan'an were suited to rectification methods, and the environment, despite increased dangers, was still sufficiently stable to enable the implementation of these methods.[17]

Finally, before turning to the first rectification campaign itself, it is important to emphasize the degree to which it was Mao's campaign. Not only were his theories and writings the main objects of study, but his personal initiative can be seen at every stage. Most significant for subsequent analysis is the lesser role played by Liu Shaoqi. Although Liu's writings were the most important of those studied apart from Mao's, and he did have a significant role in the later stages of the campaign, he was not in Yan'an in 1941 and most of the latter half of 1942 when key decisions concerning the movement were taken.[18] Thus in terms of day to day management it is clear that, in contrast to the situation in 1947–48, Mao rather than the Party's "organization man" was in charge.

The Targets of Rectification

The basic aim of the *zhengfeng* campaign was to build a unified Party out of its heterodox elements. Systematic and intensive education in basic concepts of Marxism-Leninism and in Mao's current policies and strategies was crucial to this goal in three respects: (1) to eradicate "non-proletarian" ideas; (2) to create primary loyalty to the Party over all conflicting personal, local and factional bonds; and (3) to provide the diverse elements of the Party with common goals and a common body of knowledge to use in solving concrete problems. To achieve these aims "three bad work styles" were singled out for extensive criticism—"subjectivism" *(zhuguanzhuyi)* in the study and analysis of problems, "sectarianism" *(zongpaizhuyi)* in political life and organizational matters, and "stereotyped Party writing" or "formalism" *(dangbagu)* in methods of expression.

As these three work styles have been dealt with at length elsewhere, we shall only examine briefly a few important aspects of the problems involved. Sectarianism, in addition to other problems, referred to poor relations between cadres and the peasant masses. This was partially due to the tendency of leading officials to stand apart from the populace and rely on bureaucratic methods of leadership. These officials had little first hand knowledge of social reality and consequently alienated people who were harmed by their uninformed decisions. In addition, estrangement marked the relations of many basic level cadres with the masses. This was due to harsh and arbitrary leadership methods employed by cadres, methods to a large extent made unavoidable because of heavy demands placed on the people by the difficulties of 1941–42. Nevertheless, the population came to resent local leaders who constantly increased their burdens without adequately explaining the reasons. All of this created the danger of a Party isolated from the masses and in turn led to a central theme of the movement: the need to develop mass line methods of close contact between leaders and led so the Party could both determine the views of the people and effectively promote its policies among them.

In attacking subjectivism, particular stress was attached to criticism of "doctrinairism" *(jiaotiaozhuyi),*[d] the pursuit of Marxist learning in abstract with no effort to relate it to the needs of the Chinese revolution. The campaign placed great emphasis on the need to adapt Marxism to actual conditions in China, the Sinifying of Marxism, which in turn led to harsh criticism of those who sought to base all action on Soviet experience. This, however, did not mean a denial of the significance of Soviet methods, many of which were repeatedly emphasized, but rather development of the habit of viewing political problems in their specific Chinese context. The leading "doctrinaires" attacked during the campaign were Mao's old antagonists, the returned students, people whose views had been formed to a significant extent in Comintern schools rather than by revolutionary practice in China. Similarly, in criticizing formalism in propaganda, a sphere where the returned students were still strong, pointed reference was made to "foreign formalism"—the practice of writing about Soviet experiences instead of illustrating points with Chinese examples readily understandable to native audiences. Thus the assault on subjectivism and formalism not only promoted a more pragmatic approach to problems on the part of Party cadres, it also asserted a critical attitude towards Soviet precedents and further eroded the influence of Mao's former Comintern backed opponents.[19]

Development of the Movement

The *zhengfeng* campaign actually began in 1941 with a series of directives, speeches and conferences. Most important of these was an enlarged Politburo meeting in September which discussed the Chinese revolution and particularly

---

[d]The other form of subjectivism to come under attack was "empiricism" *(jingyanzhuyi),* the tendency to become engrossed in concrete facts without applying the theoretical perspectives of Marxism-Leninism. This was most prevalent among poorly educated local cadres.

criticized Party policies before 1935. Thus from the very outset an important objective of the movement was to undermine the remaining influence of the returned student group despite its continued presence in the propaganda apparatus charged with the campaign's implementation. The Politburo also directed the "development of an all Party ideological revolution" and, subsequently, over 100 high level cadres in Yan'an began rectification study. Moreover, in December 1941 a drive against excessive bureaucracy was launched which became one of several key campaigns coordinated with rectification.

Guidelines for the movement were laid down by Mao in two speeches in February 1942. Discussions and investigations followed in committees, organs and schools directly subordinate to the Central Committee and in military units in the Yan'an area. In early April a formal rectification for the entire Party in Yan'an was announced and a General Study Committee under Mao was established to provide overall direction. This meant broadening the movement beyond the ranks of high level cadres and nearly 10,000 cadres participated in rectification study in Yan'an at that time. However, at meetings held in June to review the campaign, CCP leaders apparently concluded that a prolonged movement was necessary if rectification goals were to be achieved. In that month the Central Committee also ordered the extension of rectification to all Party members outside the Yan'an region and it was subsequently carried out in the various anti-Japanese base areas behind enemy lines.[20] The more hostile conditions in these areas, however, made impossible the thorough implementation of Yan'an—a fact later pointed out by the most important leader of areas behind Japanese lines, Liu Shaoqi:

> Some [rectification measures] can be used but much cannot be used. If you use Yan'an's method and hold a discussion meeting in which you say all you want to say, of course sometimes you talk one day, two days . . . you're not finished in a month! But before the talking is finished the enemy will break in. . . . So if you want to convene a discussion meeting it is just as well . . . not to talk so much, to keep it under your belt. . . . When you come back here [to Yan'an] you can relax a bit, it doesn't matter if the meeting breaks up in confusion.[21]

As rectification was extended to the anti-Japanese bases, the campaign in Yan'an itself underwent an important development with the holding of a senior cadres' conference from October 1942 to January 1943 under the auspices of the Party's Northwest Bureau. One of the crucial tasks of this conference was to render a verdict on Party history—in this case of the Shaanxi-Gansu-Ningxia (Shaan-Gan-Ning) Border Region. Significantly, nearly all top Party leaders made important speeches with the notable exception of members of the returned student faction. After Mao, the dominant figure at the conference was Gao Gang, Party secretary of the Northwest Bureau and a key leader of Communist guerrillas in Shaanxi during the early 1930s. At that time Gao and Liu Zhidan, the top local leader, had had serious differences with representatives sent to Shaanxi by the Party Center which remarkably paralleled contemporaneous disputes between Mao and Central Committee leaders over military and political strategies in Jiangxi. While undoubtedly oversimplifying differences as Mao did *vis-à-vis* developments in Jiangxi, the conference depicted the central representatives as pushing a strategy of positional warfare when Communist forces were weaker than their opponents, and a narrow political approach which alienated potential allies in contrast to the flexible guerrilla tactics and mild social policies assertedly advocated by Liu Zhidan and Gao Gang. Whatever the precise differences in fact, the bitterness of the conflict had resulted in the arrest of the local leaders by the central representatives in 1935, a move which had been voided by Mao upon his arrival in Shaanxi but only censured officially at the conference. In addition to these errors, the central representatives who had retained important local positions after 1935 were now charged with "right opportunism"—again the deviation of Wang Ming—after the new united front with the GMD was formed. Thus the judgment of the conference not only solidified Gao's position within the border region, but by virtue of close parallels to Mao's struggles with the returned students it also further consolidated Mao's position within the Party as a whole.[22]

The senior cadres' conference also engaged in extended debate on the tasks currently facing the Party and decided to intensify the mass line approach to transform society at the village level. Such measures had begun with the earliest stages of rectification in 1941–42 when the campaign for "picked troops and simplification" *(jingbing jianzheng)* and a "to the villages" movement *(xiaxiang)* had eased burdens by reducing the size of the bureaucracy and brought many intellectual cadres into direct contact with village problems and local cadres for the first time. In 1942, moreover, a campaign to reduce rent and interest utilizing cadres recently sent to the grass roots both enhanced the strength of Peasant Associations and eroded landlord power in the villages. The senior cadres' conference not only affirmed these developments, it also laid the basis for the vigorous development of cooperative and production movements in 1943 which involved both cadres and masses in the vital task of developing a stagnant agrarian economy. These measures, in addition to enlisting active popular participation in vital undertakings, reflected Mao's key rectification principle that Party work should be solidly anchored in Chinese social reality.[23]

In the spring of 1943 attention shifted from education to the work of investigating cadres' history *(shencha ganbu lishi gongzuo)*, a task concerning problems of counterrevolutionary activity. Party organizations had, as indicated previously, screened members for possible enemy agents since the late 1930s but had not been directed to conduct a widespread purge. The new emphasis on anti-subversion work had been presaged by Mao's call for increased vigilance "against spies" at a July 1942 meeting of the General Study Committee, and a "broad mass movement to fight spies" unfolded in 1943. As a result of these efforts by August 1943 some 4,000 "GMD agents" and other hostile elements had been uncovered in the Shaan-Gan-Ning Border Region while many times more people with undesirable past connections or who had merely committed errors in work confessed their shortcomings. In this process excesses occurred, however, as responsible officials confused general problems requiring rectification with counterrevolution where cadre investigation was necessary. These excesses included torture to extract confessions which brought harm to "good comrades." One reaction to this was to limit sharply the previously leading role of the security forces in cadre investigation. In any case, the use of coercive measures during the rectification movement reflected the continuing importance of hostile aspects of the CCP's environment.[24] Moreover, it appears coercion was more prevalent at the front and in border regions behind Japanese lines than in the secure Yan'an area.[e]

The CCP also turned its attention to the recruitment of mass activists for leadership roles as the weeding out of hostile elements unfolded. In June 1943 Mao implied at least some purging when he spoke of the need to replace failing leaders:

> In the process of a great struggle, the composition of the leading group in most cases should not and cannot remain entirely unchanged throughout the initial, middle and final stages; the activists who come forward in the course of the struggle must constantly be promoted to replace those original members of the leading group who are inferior by comparison or who have degenerated.[25]

While figures on actual recruitment and losses in Party membership are not available, overall membership figures indicate that after a decline in 1941–42, probably due mainly to the contraction of Communist held areas, a substantial buildup of Party strength took place in the final years of the rectification campaign to reach 1.2 million members by the time of the Seventh CCP Congress in April 1945, an increase of 50 percent since the end of 1940.[26] Much of this expansion was undoubtedly unrelated to rectification and its concomitant purges, but it does suggest that no deep purge of the Party occurred in this period.

The movement in its final major phase in 1944 once again returned to the question of Party history. In addition to the September 1941 enlarged Politburo meeting and the senior cadres' conference of late 1942-early 1943, the Politburo held several discussions on Party history in 1942–43 prior to launching similar discussions among senior cadres throughout the Party in the winter of 1943 and the spring of 1944. It was at this time, moreover, that many—although not all—of the returned student leaders were eased out of their posts in the propa-

[e] According to an August 1943 directive, *Zhonggong zhongyang guanyu shencha ganbu de jueding* [CCP Central Committee Decision concerning Investigating Cadres], investigations in Yan'an had not resulted in any killings but the peculiar circumstances at the front and border regions necessitated the suppression of certain individuals. I am indebted to Hong Yung Lee for calling this document to my attention.

ganda apparatus. A key role in the discussions was played by Liu Shaoqi who vigorously endorsed the Maoist version of the Party's past. This apparently cemented the alliance between Mao and Liu which had been developing since they joined forces in the united front discussions of 1937–38. The benefits of the arrangement for Liu were underlined as many of his subordinates in the base areas behind Japanese lines began to assume key Central Committee posts in organization and propaganda work, including those vacated by the returned student group. All of this served as preparation for the Seventh Congress which assertedly attained "an ideological and political unity without precedent in the history of the . . . Party" and issued the detailed resolution on historical questions declaring Mao the embodiment of correct policies for the revolution as a whole and Liu the model of correct tactics in "white areas" *(baiqu)* under enemy control. Thus attacks on the returned student group served to unify disparate elements of the Party from Gao Gang to Liu Shaoqi around Mao's leadership both by reviving past grievances and providing immediate benefits.[27]

As before, the rewriting of Party history served to strengthen Mao's position but now it was accompanied by a burgeoning cult of Mao. Apart from raising his personal status to heights without precedent in CCP history, the exaltation of Mao, together with the rectification theme of making Marxism-Leninism relevant to Chinese conditions and extensive criticism of earlier CCP leaders who had been heavily influenced by Comintern directives, represented a dramatic assertion of Chinese independence of the Soviet Union. The whole question of Party history clearly involved more than settling old scores within the CCP; it necessarily raised questions concerning Soviet responsibility for major setbacks to the Chinese revolution. While public assessments of the Soviet role were withheld, CCP leaders made it abundantly clear that there were many imperfections in Soviet practice and China could not simply copy the Russian example.[28] Despite Mao's continuing deference to Soviet authority on theoretical matters, by the conclusion of the rectification campaign he and his colleagues had clearly declared their right to determine concrete policies based on their own reading of Chinese conditions.

Rectification and the Literary Intelligentsia

As would be the case in several post-1949 rectification campaigns, the creative intelligentsia of writers and artists played a special role in the initial movement. These radical intellectuals—especially the significant numbers who flocked to Yan'an after the outbreak of the Sino-Japanese War but also Party members and sympathizers who went to GMD areas—posed a sensitive problem both because they were deeply affected by the heterodox ideologies of the cities and because their work had a considerable impact on public opinion within and without the liberated areas. Moreover, the handling of literary intellectuals during the 1942–44 movement is of particular interest due to some striking similarities to the Hundred Flowers Campaign fifteen years later.

Following Mao's February 1942 speeches which set the tone of the movement, many writers apparently took heart from the criticisms Mao made of narrow minded tendencies within the Party and hoped the leadership would listen to their own criticisms of CCP shortcomings. In March they issued a barrage of critical essays which were published in *Jiefang ribao* [Liberation Daily], the official Party daily. These essays attacked, often savagely, bureaucratic aspects of Yan'an life and painted the Party as an emerging new elite. In this the writers now used against the CCP the same polemic talents they had previously employed against the GMD. Moreover, they asserted their right of independent creativity unhindered by Party policies and directives. The official reaction was not long in coming. In early April the writers were no longer allowed to publish their views. At the start of May the CCP convened the Yan'an Forum on Literature and Art where Mao laid down authoritative policies on the creative arts. Mao rejected claims of creative independence and insisted on the strict subordination of art to politics; writers were to fashion optimistic and heroic accounts of life in the liberated areas and reserve criticism for the Party's opponents.[29]

In the two months following Mao's talks organized attacks unfolded against the dissidents. The only figure singled out for public denunciation was Wang Shiwei, the most caustic of the critics who was also vulnerable because of past Trotskyite ties, but many other writers confessed their errors as the pressure mounted. Once criticism and confessions sessions concluded, leading critics generally lost their positions in the literary bureaucracy and were sent to factories or the countryside for reform through labor. And Mao later acknowledged that the most serious offender, Wang Shiwei, was executed by security forces.[30] Thus coercive measures quickly supplanted the persuasive emphasis of rectification with regard to this small but significant group. Yet it should be stressed that this development came only in response to what was seen as a severe provocation by people of questionable bourgeois origins. It apparently did not alter the reform thrust of the movement as applied to the vast majority of Party members and cadres.

While the outpouring of intellectuals' criticisms followed by a severe official reaction has obvious parallels to the situation fifteen years later, the similarities should not be overstated. In contrast to the Hundred Flowers period when repeated efforts were made to solicit the views of the intelligentsia, Mao's February 1942 speeches contained no explicit or implicit invitations for criticisms of the Party by writers and artists. Indeed, it took considerable naïveté to interpret Mao's remarks which were replete with barbs directed at bookish intellectuals as reflecting a willingness to expose the Party to the attacks from that quarter. Moreover, since some of the critical writers had ties to the returned student faction it was doubly dubious that their views would be welcomed by the Maoist leadership. Perhaps the simplest explanation of their miscalculation is that they were not long removed from the free-wheeling, contentious atmosphere of Shanghai literary circles and had not been sufficiently socialized in the disciplined life expected of Party workers. The intensive education of the unfolding rectification campaign provided the first taste of that socialization.

Summary and Evaluation

Several results of the initial rectification campaign are clear. Mao, whose leadership had gained strength steadily in the years preceding the movement, now attained unprecedented power with the systematic undermining of the returned student group. Moreover, the Maoist leadership which solidified in this period, in no small part due to the successes of Mao's policies, provided a more unified high command than the CCP had known at any time since its founding. It was this unity as much as Mao's Sinocentric revolutionary tactics which formed the basis for the CCP's unmistakable assertion of independence from Moscow during the rectification movement. In terms of the Party as a whole, a more thorough and extensive educational program was carried out than was previously possible, although it was necessarily limited in the more exposed anti-Japanese base areas. It was during the campaign that the small group methods central to rectification were developed on a large scale for the first time.

Although the emphasis was on education and official claims were made that disciplinary measures were seldom taken during the movement, it is clear that some very harsh punishments were meted out, especially to literary intellectuals and as a result of anti-subversion work carried on in conjunction with rectification. Moreover, while there are no reliable figures on the total number of purges, dismissals from Party and government posts did occur to some degree.[31] Still, any large scale expulsion of Party members at this time is doubtful. At the highest levels the stress was also on reform. While several of the returned student leaders—most notably Wang Ming—were reduced to politically insignificant posts, no expulsions of leading personalities are known, and even figures like Wang retained seats on the Central Committee elected in 1945 as living examples of Mao's tolerance. It should be recalled, however, that even in the days of ruthless struggle similar gestures were made.

What is more difficult to evaluate is the extent of the CCP's success in actually achieving ideological reform within its ranks. An official Party history published in 1958 hailed the rectification campaign as a monumental success which "wiped out the influences of doctrinairism . . ., helped many new Party members of petty bourgeois origin to discard their original stand, greatly raised the Party's ideological level and achieved an unprecedented unity of the whole Party. . . ."[32] During the Cultural Revolution, on the other hand, Zhou Enlai minimized the achievements of the movement and indicated that it was largely confined to high level cadres.[33] In this regard, a comment in the Party press during the rectification movement of 1947–48, a campaign under the direct leadership of Liu Shaoqi, is of special interest. This comment favorably compared the then current rectification to the original one in terms of mobilizing the masses for criticism of Party cadres rather than relying on reform "from the top down."[34] While the motive behind such an observation remains a moot point, it once again brings sharply into question the view that in matters of Party reform Mao consistently advocated thoroughgoing struggle and the direct involvement of the masses while Liu argued for restraints on struggle and sharp boundaries separating internal Party matters from areas of popular concern.

As will be seen below, the 1947–48 movement did involve intense struggles and mass participation which went beyond anything attempted in 1942–44. Still, the view implied in the 1947 commentary and Zhou's 1967 statement that the initial rectification campaign was largely an elitist affair is misleading. Not only did many of the measures undertaken in conjunction with rectification—e.g., the *xiaxiang* movement—affect the basic levels, but the entire emphasis of the movement on the need to understand Chinese social realities militated for a grass roots approach to leadership. Moreover, by 1943, rectification study itself had extended outside higher Party circles to lower levels and to fields beyond such as secondary schools in the Yan'an area. Nevertheless, it is undeniable that the movement did start at the top and was conducted most thoroughly at that level.

In another regard it was stipulated at the outset that non-Party people in organs undergoing rectification could voluntarily participate; in practice all non-Communists in such units took part. Yet while this indicates a blurring of the line between Party members and non-Party cadres, it should be stressed that the participation of non-Party people took place within a highly structured format and did not involve attacks on Party officials by outsiders as such. Another important aspect of the campaign was the great stress put on professional and technical improvement as well as ideological reform. Thus educational measures to raise levels of literacy and fundamental knowledge plus various in-service training programs to improve job related skills formed an important part of the overall rectification program. In this emphasis was not on thought struggle but on prosaic tasks nevertheless crucial to revolutionary success.[35]

Finally, in terms of general style it is fair to conclude that rectification itself as distinct from various coordinate programs was a "closed door" *(guanmen)* affair. William Hinton's description of the rectification experiences of a low level cadre is instructive:

> Cai Jin [the cadre] was delegated to take part in the *[zhengfeng]* movement. For a whole year . . . he sat in school, read, transcribed his thoughts, and talked. During that period he minutely examined every facet of his past, his outlook at various stages of maturity, the decisions he had made, both in his personal life and in the course of his work, and the class stand he had taken. All this was discussed and analyzed with the help of classmates whose background was similar to his own. . . . Slowly and painfully he built for himself a new class outlook, a code of loyalty.[36]

While there is little reason to doubt that the cadre discussed did undergo an emotionally taxing experience, it was clearly not an experience "in the midst of the masses." Instead, it took place in a school specially set aside where the participants were all cadres of similar social origins. In many respects, then, the first rectification campaign did have the nature of a movement designed to indoctrinate and train an elite which was clearly distinct from the masses in the eyes of top CCP leaders, despite their repeated urgings that the members of that elite get close to the masses and unite with them. As Mao had put it in 1937, it was wrong "to be indifferent to [the masses] and show no concern for their well-being [as this would mean] forgetting that one is a Communist and behaving as if one were an ordinary non-Communist."[37] For all its emphasis on the mass line, the Maoist rectification of 1942–44 stopped far short of exposing the Party to mass struggle.

Rectification and Land Reform, 1947–48

The rectification campaign *(zhengdang yundong)*[f] of 1947–48, in contrast to its predecessor, focused mainly on rural basic level Party organizations. With the exception of a "democratic movement" in the army, the campaign largely concerned problems arising from the implementation of land reform in liberated areas. Whereas the initial campaign had been most thoroughly implemented in the secure Yan'an area, now the major emphasis was on Northeast and particularly North China where the decisive battles of the civil war were being fought and Communist base areas were expanding.[38]

Another major difference between the two movements is, as previously noted, that Liu Shaoqi rather than Mao was in operational control of the movement. This was due not only to Liu's responsibilities as head of the Central Committee's land reform department, but also to the fact that the central leadership was organized into two groups as an emergency measure following the fall of Yan'an to GMD forces in March 1947. One group, headed by Mao, remained in the Shaan-Gan-Ning Border Region while the other under Liu went to the Shanxi-Suiyuan Liberated Area and then on to Pingshan county in the Shanxi-Chahar-Hebei Border Region; the two groups were reunited in May 1948 with Mao's arrival in Pingshan. During the period of separation Liu chaired two major conferences determining land policy and oversaw land reform in the crucial North China area. Mao, especially from late December 1947, also frequently commented on the agrarian and rectification questions but, as Mao himself later implied, Liu was directly concerned with guiding rectification in particular.[39]

---

[f]Although officially translated as "Party consolidation," and having a somewhat harsher tone in Chinese than *zhengfeng, zhengdang* is regarded as interchangeable with *zhengfeng*. See Zhao Han, *Tantan,* pp. 16–17.

By April 1948 at the latest, however, the Party leadership determined that there had been serious mistakes of a leftist nature during the land reform and rectification drives. While initially blame was placed predominantly on the basic level cadres themselves, some fault was attached to Liu and others for their direction of the campaigns. Liu's culpability was again raised during the Cultural Revolution when his stewardship in 1947–48 was characterized as " 'left' in form, right in essence" and—with some justification—explicitly compared to similar deviations during his leadership of the Socialist Education Movement in 1964 (see Chapter 11).[40] But the question to be examined here is whether differences over the actual direction of policy existed between Mao and Liu during 1947–48, or did Mao also support policies which produced the results subsequently labelled "leftist deviations"?

Finally, in an important sense a richer understanding is possible of the 1947–48 campaign than of the 1942–44 movement because of the existence of a lengthy, first hand account of its progress within a basic level unit in William Hinton's *Fanshen.* Hinton's account of land reform and rectification in Long Bow, Shanxi, tells only of developments in one village out of tens of thousands—a village which had many but clearly not all of the problems faced elsewhere by the twin movements. But whatever their uniqueness, the unfolding developments in Long Bow both provide a useful check against official histories and illuminate the impact of rectification on the ordinary rural cadre upon whom so much of the revolution's success depended.

Land Reform, 1946–47

The growing tensions between the GMD and CCP which culminated in full scale civil war in 1946 brought about important changes in many CCP policies, not the least of which concerned land reform. The united front approach of relying on rent reduction in order to avoid alienating rich peasants and enlightened gentry, i.e., landlords willing to cooperate with the Party, gave way to land confiscation and redistribution. This occurred in the context of growing class polarization in the countryside which required new policies. On the one hand, landlords and rich peasants tended either to side with the GMD or withhold their support from the CCP in hopes of a Nationalist victory. At the same time, the less well-off peasants who were the Communists' natural allies were called upon for increasing sacrifices to the Party's cause in terms of military manpower, supplies and labor; clearly concrete gains for these people were necessary to sustain their revolutionary enthusiasm. The Party leadership, however, did not quickly or fully grasp the implications of the new situation; as late as February 1947 Mao spoke of a united front as broad as that of the anti-Japanese period and which included the enlightened gentry.[41] Indeed, as Tanaka Kyoko has shown, the radicalization of CCP Policy in 1946–47 actually followed the appearance of radicalism at the grass roots in North and Northeast China. It was in these areas where memories of especially harsh exploitation by collaborators with the Japanese were fresh, and the danger of losing social and economic gains to GMD backed local elites was immediate, and not in the more stable Shaan-Gan-Ning Border Region, that the impetus for a more thoroughgoing land revolution originated.[42]

The first major change in land policy came shortly before the outbreak of full scale war but at a time of increasing GMD gains in clashes with CCP forces. The May Fourth (1946) directive, which followed a period of increasing land confiscation at the basic levels, shifted the emphasis from rent reduction to land redistribution for the first time since 1937. Despite being hailed as an effort to "eliminate the feudal land owning system," the directive was in fact a vague and cautious document which did not call for confiscation of landlord land (apart from that of collaborators) but instead suggested ways in which such land could be purchased and distributed to the peasants. In the year following the May Fourth directive, land policy gradually placed more emphasis on confiscation in response to seizures by the peasants. Still, throughout this period Mao and his associates remained ambivalent in their attitudes towards land reform; while calling for its vigorous implementation they also warned against excesses, particularly against encroaching on the interests of middle peasants. Meanwhile actual developments also presented contradictory aspects. In some areas land reform was at best superficial with little popular involvement and local power still largely in the hands of landlords. In other areas, however, radical land reform measures exceeded Party policies, resulted in the killing of innocent people, and seriously alienated broad segments of the rural population. While later official criticisms emphasized the excesses of 1946–47, by mid-1947 Party leaders had apparently concluded that the main danger facing the movement was insufficient mobilization of the masses.[43]

The beginning of intensive efforts to mobilize the masses fully for land reform was apparently a regional campaign in the Shanxi-Suiyuan Liberated Area in the spring and summer of 1947. Based on the experiences of this campaign in which Liu Shaoqi and Kang Sheng played leading roles, a conference was called by the Shanxi-Suiyuan Party Sub-bureau in June. This conference was to be criticized by Mao in April 1948 for adopting ultra-left policies,[44] but his overall assessment was that, by overcoming rightist deviations, it had been a success without which land reform and Party rectification would have failed. Moreover, Mao's enthusiastic comments in July 1947 on a letter from Liu to Shanxi-Suiyuan cadres indicate contemporaneous support for the radical line.[45]

The final step in formulating a radical land program was a National Land Conference convened by Liu in Pingshan in September 1947 which adopted an Outline Land Law of China. This law, which was considerably more detailed and radical than the May Fourth directive, reportedly corrected "a certain lack of thoroughness" in that directive. The Outline Land Law not only abolished the land ownership rights of all landlords and decreed equal distribution to all members of the rural population apart from traitors; it also stipulated requisition and distribution of "surplus property" of rich peasants while failing to mention the need to protect the interests of middle peasants. Authority for carrying out these provisions was vested in the peasants themselves, i.e., in Peasant Associations *(nonghui),* including middle peasants, and Poor Peasant Leagues *(pinnongtuan)* restricted to the poorest elements in the villages. Although this program was shaped by Liu's land conference, the fact that it was issued in October by the Central Committee strongly suggests Mao's assent.[46]

The timing of the final step in the radicalization of CCP land policy was closely linked to a fundamental turning point in the course of the civil war. In the July–September 1947 period the PLA went on a nationwide offensive and carried the battle into areas held by the GMD. Thus a new and deeper security was gained for the liberated areas and land reform and Party rectification could proceed in a more thoroughgoing fashion without worries about enemy disruption. It was not mere coincidence that on the same day that the Central Committee approved the Outline Land Law the PLA issued a manifesto, written by Mao, proclaiming confidence in the coming victory. In this favorable situation large cadres' conferences dealing with land reform and the associated task of Party rectification were held in practically all liberated areas in the months following the adoption of the law; their emphasis was on criticizing rightist ideas and satisfying the demands of poor peasants and hired laborers. By early 1948 the Party was organizing work teams to go to selected keypoint areas *(zhongdian)* and systematically implement the new program.[47]

The Need for Party Rectification

The task of land reform ultimately depended on Party cadres at the village level and it had been apparent for some time that these local leaders had serious shortcomings. Higher authorities saw two interrelated problems—widespread cadre misbehavior and the "impure" *(bu chun)* class status of many cadres. Cadre behavior was judged faulty in a number of respects. One major concern was the previously mentioned tendency of failing to carry out land reform thoroughly. Local cadres, often fearful of continuing landlord influence and the possibility of a GMD revival, in many areas compromised with the landlords and failed to mobilize the peasants to struggle against them. Another important category was petty corruption and the arrogation of special privileges by village leaders. Hinton graphically portrayed a wide variety of cadre malfeasances including taking choice articles from confiscated landlord property, refusing to contribute labor service, avoiding military service, stealing from the public warehouse, and forcing their attentions on village women. By these and other acts cadres began to behave as a new elite and caused considerable resentment among the people. A final category concerns harsh and arbitrary leadership practices. These were clearly present in leftist excesses during land reform when local cadres often played a key role in mass struggles resulting in excessive beatings, killings and suicides of landlords and others considered enemies of the Party. Many cadres also engaged in high handed if less extreme behavior towards ordinary peasants which was subsumed under the label "commandism" *(minglingzhuyi)*. It is important to note that commandism could be associated with either leftist or rightist deviations. Both those cadres zealously carrying out radical land reform and those merely administering routine tasks while land reform lagged frequently used force rather than persuasion to obtain popular compliance. Thus even where no attempt to gain personal advantage was involved, local leaders often exacerbated relations with the masses.[48]

These faults led to efforts to reform basic level cadres through a "wash your face" *(xilian)* campaign in spring 1947. The method adopted for this campaign was very similar to that employed during Party rectification a year later. It involved bringing the masses into the process by requiring all cadres to face criticism by a council of delegates elected by the peasants. Once criticism began, however, it began to get out of hand, at least in part because individuals dissatisfied with the new order used the opportunity to attack the cadres. The reaction of the Party in Long Bow was typical:

> Instead of allowing this storm of criticism to rage and using it to educate the peasants to distinguish honest from dishonest opinions so that the cadres could reform and all the people profit from a living political lesson, the district leaders lost their nerve and retreated. They intervened on behalf of the cadres and in effect suppressed criticism, both honest and dishonest.[49]

Yet it appears that CCP leaders had little choice but to call off the campaign before it was fully under way. For at a time when the GMD was still on the offensive and the CCP's hold on many areas was under severe threat, it would have been a grave risk to undermine what experienced leadership there was in the countryside. By September 1947, however, the new situation created by the CCP's general offensive greatly enhanced the security of local Party organizations and reopened the possibility of systematically dealing with errant cadres.

The related problem—that of "impure" class origins—was an inevitable consequence of rapid Party expansion after the Sino-Japanese war under conditions of civil war. By autumn 1947 the CCP had 2.7 million members, more than double the mid-1945 figure, and the fluid battle situation had made controls over recruitment and indoctrination of new members extremely difficult. In these circumstances, many landlords, rich peasants and "riffraff"*(liumangfenzi)* reportedly "snuck into the Party" and gained control of some Party, government and mass organizations in the villages. By the September 1947 land conference these impurities together with an alleged rightist tendency to overlook them were considered serious barriers to the successful implementation of land reform, and both the conference and subsequent regional meetings placed heavy emphasis on the need to rectify the situation.[50] Thus it is hardly surprising that in Hinton's area a "quick and superficial check on the background of the comrades in the village branches [following a regional meeting] convinced the County Committee that at least 40 percent of the local Communists were of landlord or rich peasant origin." [51] Similar evaluations were apparently made in many other areas.

When the National Land Conference decided to launch Party rectification in conjunction with intensified land reform, the decision was based on several misperceptions. First, to judge by Hinton's evidence, estimates of the degree of infiltration of the Party by class enemies were grossly exaggerated.[52] Moreover, the tendency to link cadre class status and misbehavior overlooked the fact that a great deal of that behavior was committed by officials of poor peasant origins. In any case, both left and right deviations during land reform came largely from cadre inexperience, popular pressures for radical action or, conversely, restraints created by unstable circumstances, and the ambiguity of CCP agrarian policies in this period. Finally, by identifying the main danger as a rightist tendency despite the fact that much cadre misbehavior could just as easily be associated with leftist deviations—and bolstering this with class analysis—Party leaders inevitably created a situation where radical excesses could flourish.

The Excesses of Land Reform and Rectification

By all subsequent accounts the measures taken as a result of the National Land Conference overcame existing rightist tendencies thus achieving a thoroughgoing implementation of land reform and the cleansing of Party branches of class enemies and degenerates. But inevitable excesses accompanied this achievement. They took a variety of forms. The indiscriminate beating and killing of landlords and rich peasants which had appeared earlier continued to mark both land reform and the suppression of counterrevolutionaries after the September conference. This resulted in substantial popular alienation, and in some areas "bad elements" *(huaifenzi)* reportedly exploited the situation to take revenge by murdering working people. But excessive violence was far from universal, and in Long Bow the beatings and killings which accompanied land reform following the village's liberation were not repeated under the new law.

Another set of problems arose from the official insistence that land reform had not been thorough; in simplest terms this meant that not enough property had been taken from the rich and given to the poor. One result was sweeping confiscation of the rich's property including daily necessities, the diversion of energy into often futile efforts to uncover landlords' imagined hidden wealth, and seizure of industrial and commercial holdings—particularly those owned by landlords and rich peasants—despite explicit protection granted such enterprises by the Outline Land Law. It was not only the upper strata who were disadvantaged by the renewed emphasis on redistribution, however. Given the land law's call for equal distribution per capita, it was inevitable that some better-off middle peasants were forced to give up property. Additional dimensions of the problem are illuminated by Hinton's account of developments in Long Bow, a village where redistribution had originally been thorough, but due to the prevailing assumptions the work team in charge had declared land reform stillborn. Following Central Committee regulations, a new classification of all families was undertaken. Although the tendency, criticized elsewhere, of broadening the categories of landlord and rich peasant to include unjustly middle peasants and other working people did not occur, the intrinsic importance of classification (i.e., how a family was classified determined whether it would benefit or suffer from the new redistribution) generated considerable anxiety and conflict within the village. Moreover, the assumption that land reform had not been thoroughly implemented led to an overestimate of the number of poor peasants and therefore increased the threat to the limited resources of those placed in higher categories. Furthermore, the relative lack of surplus property in the community, given the actual thoroughness of the earlier distribution, meant bitter disappointment for the poor whose hopes had been raised. Finally, in these circumstances attention turned to imagined cadre graft as a solution to the puzzle of where the presumed excess wealth due to the poor had gone. As actual graft had been small scale this did not uncover significant property but it did demoralize local cadres.[53]

The above problems to a significant extent reflected two intertwined tendencies later denounced as the "poor peasant-farm laborer line" *(pin-gunong luxian)* and "tailism" *(weibazhuyi)*. The notion expressed in the official media that poor peasants and farm laborers should rule and the government should be responsive to them first of all rural elements inevitably caused disregard of middle peasant interests. Middle peasants were often excluded from peasants' representative bodies in addition to being subject to confiscations and erroneous classification. Moreover, the slogan, "Do everything as the masses want it done," which came out of Liu Shaoqi's June 1947 conference, purportedly resulted in the uncritical acceptance by many cadres of the views and demands of poor peasants rather than the exercise of the Party's educational and leadership roles. Actually, leadership, especially that provided by work teams dispatched to carry out land reform, was crucial in mobilizing poor peasants, but once mobilization was under way responsible cadres would often bend to the will of the newly organized poor. Thus the work team cadres sent to Long Bow, with the county Party secretary's injunction that "He who cannot find poor peasants in the villages doesn't deserve to eat!" ringing in their ears, devoted their entire first week in the community to visiting poor peasants, soliciting their opinions, and selecting activists who would play a key role in subsequent classifications—i.e., to "striking roots and linking up" *(zhagen chonglian)*, the method which would also be used and criticized during the Socialist Education Movement in 1963–64. In this instance the work team cadres in no sense abdicated leadership and sought with considerable success to moderate excessive demands as the movement developed. Nevertheless, in Hinton's words, they "were pushed now one way, now another [by the views of different groups and] more often than was wise they allowed their weight to fall on the side of extremism among the poor."[54]

In many respects the excesses which appeared during Party rectification mirrored those of land reform. Rectification in some places involved intense struggle resulting in unwarranted beatings and overly harsh disciplinary punishment including sweeping dismissals of erring cadres. In implementing the "three checkups" into cadre class origins, ideology and work style, work teams often either overestimated the number of rich peasants or landlords in Party branches or evaluated cadres on the basis of class background alone, thus ignoring their contributions to the revolution. Moreover, spurred on by attacks on the rightist tendency of ignoring the problem of impure elements and by the influence of the poor peasant-farm laborer line, some work teams concluded, on the basis of uncovering cadre misbehavior or individual Party members with landlord and rich peasant ties, that entire branches were under the influence of class enemies. As a result, instead of retaining Party branches as leading organs and working to reform their members, work team cadres either dissolved branches or set aside their powers and relied on Poor Peasant Leagues and Peasant Associations to spearhead rectification work.[55]

The crux of the problems arising during rectification lay in the triangular relationship between work teams, local cadres and peasant masses. Armed with the authority to conduct basic level rectification, work teams undercut the authority of local cadres even if they did not go to the extreme of dissolving the Party branch. The Long Bow work team, for example, assumed local cadre guilt for an attack on one of its members and took the drastic steps of suspending all village cadres, dissolving all mass organizations, and effectively ending all the normal activities and responsibilities of the Party branch. And even after these measures were rescinded several weeks later on the instruction of higher levels, and the local cadres returned to their posts, the village continued to look to the work team for leadership. The method of conducting rectification also profoundly altered the relationship of cadres and masses. In contrast to the campaign in 1942, Party rectification was not carried out within the confines of specific organizations but instead the entire process was thrown open to active participation by ordinary peasants who had the right not only to criticize but to take part in the determination of disciplinary measures. This was possible only in the context of the changed military situation; only with the CCP's general offensive was there sufficient security to open up the hitherto secret life of the Party. In Long Bow this process took the form of a "gate," a forum where each member of the Party branch[56] had to face delegates elected by the villagers from their own number. Only when the delegates were satisfied that a cadre had sincerely owned up to all his malfeasances, that his case was not so serious as to require legal action and that he would return any graft, would they allow him to "pass the gate" *(guoguan)* and resume his official duties. Cadres who had previously exercised unchallenged local power now had their fate placed in the hands of the masses.[57]

The potential in this situation for destroying the morale of village cadres and critically weakening Party leadership at the basic levels was clear. In this regard the Long Bow case is particularly revealing since an extreme situation did not arise. As with land reform the work team mobilized the masses for rectification and carefully guided the process. In this the team leaders were very successful in tempering sentiments of revenge among the peasants; although some villagers advocated beating offending cadres the majority favored a moderate approach which recognized the contributions cadres had made in earlier struggles. Moreover, the examination at the gate revealed that the great majority of local Communists were poor peasants and graft involved minor amounts rather than gross misappropriations; thus the delegates took a lenient attitude, emphasizing education and reform rather than punishment and let all but four of the village's 22 Party members pass the gate. The relative mildness of the process—which avoided the cadre suicides that occurred in other villages in the same county—did not, however, prevent substantial estrangement on the part of local Communists. Anxiety gripped Party members during their confrontations with the peasant delegates at the gate. Many responded to the pressures of the situation by admitting things which were untrue, while those who refused to confess to false charges were not allowed to pass the gate. Thus even after passing the gate cadres reflected with bitterness on the sharp and often unfair attacks they had received after having taken the lead in the local revolution at great personal risk. Moreover, the new role of the masses in village affairs together with prohibitions on the use of force by cadres had resulted in a situation of "extreme democracy" where peasants refused to obey cadre orders or undertake public duties. Thus increasing burdens fell on cadres at the cost of time they would normally devote to their own land. Finally, the prestige of Party members remained low even after passing not only the initial gate, but also a final gate a few months later. Villagers continued to treat them with animosity, scorn and derision. In these circumstances it is not surprising that various local Communists concluded there was little to be gained from being a cadre. Presumably, the situation was much more serious in villages where Party rectification had not been as restrained as in Long Bow.[58]

Curbing the Excesses: The Roles of Mao and Liu

The problems caused by excesses in the implementation of land reform and rectification gradually became clear to CCP leaders and eventually led them to emphasize the importance of curbing leftist deviations. The official *ex post facto* view, one articulated by both Mao and Liu Shaoqi, was that starting with a Central committee meeting in December 1947 in northern Shaanxi and Mao's report, "The Present Situation and Our Tasks," the Party rapidly corrected these deviations.[59] Other evidence, however, suggests that the official version overstates the leadership's perception of the problem in December 1947 and that it was only in late March or April 1948 that the Party came down unambiguously against the excesses of the twin movements. The question of timing gains significance in view of subsequent suggestions that Liu was responsible for the leftist tendencies of the period. For if Mao had indeed come out clearly in December 1947 against the policies which produced the leftist trend while Liu continued to push those policies, then there would be a substantial basis for assertions of a Mao-Liu split over land reform and rectification.

Considerable difficulties surround any effort to uncover the precise positions of Mao and Liu. In the case of Liu only one statement—albeit an important elaboration in February 1948 of rectification measures—is available.[60] Although 11 statements by Mao dealing with the land and rectification questions exist for the period December 1947-April 1948, all but three are available only as they appear in the *Selected Works* after 1949.[61] Thus it is possible that alterations were made in Mao's actual statements in early 1948 which changed their emphasis; in any case, the thrust of the following analysis is sustained by the versions in the *Selected Works.*

Mao's December 1947 report did indeed warn against repeating the ultra-left mistakes of 1931–34 in land reform. But this in itself does not indicate decisive action against leftist errors. Directives and statements by Party leaders generally hedge against tendencies that might be anticipated from over zealous implementation of approved policies. What is critical is the overall emphasis—the main orientation which provides clues for the priorities of lower level officials. The overall emphasis of Mao's report was support for the Outline Land Law—a document which encouraged radicalism.[62] Mao's position, although calling for attention to middle peasant interests, did in fact provide a basis for the poor peasant-farm laborer line:

> To carry out the land reform resolutely and thoroughly, it is necessary to organize in the villages . . . not only Peasant Associations on the broadest mass basis, including farm laborers, poor peasants and middle peasants in their elected committees, *but first of all Poor Peasant Leagues composed of poor peasants and farm laborers and their elected committees; and these Poor Peasant Leagues should be the backbone of leadership in all rural struggles.* Our policy is to rely on the poor peasants and unite solidly with the middle peasants to abolish the feudal and semifeudal system of exploitation by the landlord class and by the old type rich peasants. . . . Here two fundamental principles must be observed. First, *the demands of the poor peasants and farm laborers must be satisfied, this is the most fundamental task in the land reform.* Second, there must be firm unity with the middle peasants, and their interests must not be damaged.[63]

Significantly, Mao's emphasis on the first principle was reflected in the basic level implementation of land reform at the expense of the second principle, something which subsequently came under attack.[64] Similarly, Mao's remarks on the state of Party organs—which included *no* warnings against possible excesses—could only encourage radicalism in rectification work:

> ... [I]n the Party's local organizations, especially the organizations at the primary level in the countryside, the problem of impurities in the class composition of our ranks and in our style of work is still unsolved. ... Many landlords, rich peasants and riffraff have seized the opportunity to sneak into our Party. In the rural areas they control a number of Party, government and people's organizations, tyrannically abuse their power, ride roughshod over the people, distort the Party's policies and thus alienate these organizations from the masses and prevent the land reform from being thorough. This grave situation sets us the task of educating and reorganizing the ranks of our Party. We cannot make headway in the countryside unless we perform this task.[65]

From January to mid-March 1948 Mao made seven statements on or relating to land reform or rectification but only one of these—a brief commentary—is available in the original. These statements tended carefully to lay down guiding principles for the movements rather than call for a mass upsurge. Moreover, they devoted more attention to leftist errors than rightist ones—although it is interesting that the commentary available only in the original listed commandism (the abuse of cadre authority) ahead of tailism (a shortcoming resulting in mass excesses).[66] In any case, Mao's directives in this period did not alter the basic evaluation of the situation laid down by the Outline Land Law. For example, in early February Mao declared that in areas liberated since the Japanese surrender up to the launching of the CCP's general counteroffensive (i.e., from September 1945 to August 1947) the land problem had not been thoroughly solved, poor peasants were demanding land, and preparations for a new land distribution should be made. Moreover, in January, Mao had proclaimed the right of the masses not only to criticize cadres but even to dismiss them from their posts.[67] Thus despite the distinctly moderate tone of Mao's writings from this period, conceivably aided by the editors of the *Selected Works*, his overall assessment remained compatible with extremism.

In February 1948 Liu Shaoqi made his major statement on land reform and rectification—a summary of the experience of Pingshan county where his Working Committee of the Central Committee was located. This experience was hailed by Mao at the time as a model for work in old and semi-old liberated areas (i.e., those under CCP control before September 1945 and August 1947 respectively) and for rectification generally, it formed the basis of a key Central Committee directive of February 22, 1948, on the two movements, and it was subsequently—at least prior to the Cultural Revolution—cited as a major turning point in curbing leftist excesses.[68] As with Mao's initiatives, these claims seem overstated. Although Liu did criticize work teams for the leftist mistake of forcing the peasants to struggle against landlords who had already been struggled against, the Central Committee directive based on the Pingshan experience led directly to land reform excesses. This directive set up a threefold classification system according to how thoroughly land reform had been carried out, and stipulated that the entire process should be started from scratch in the most backward villages—those, classified as the third type, where feudal relations of production were still dominant. Given the view that land reform had not generally been thorough in semi-old liberated areas, the tendency to underestimate the degree of land reform during the classification process was inevitable. As long as the basic assessment of the thoroughness of land reform was pessimistic, the various warnings by Mao and Liu against leftist excesses were bound to be less than totally effective.[69]

The bulk of Liu's summary dealt with Party rectification. In analyzing the source of problems in rural Party branches Liu cited the infiltration of landlords and riffraff—an analysis conducive to leftist excesses. Moreover, the February directive, in addition to the progress of land reform, also called for a tripartite classification of Party branches according to the class origins and behavior of their members. As with land reform itself, classifications tended to paint a more gloomy picture than in fact existed. The directive also stated that in areas where feudal forces had in general been eliminated peasant dissatisfaction focused on cadres who "usurp the fruits of land reform," thus contributing to the belief that widespread cadre graft had occurred.[70] Most significant, Liu's criticism of defects appearing during rectification included rightist as well as leftist tendencies:

> First, the masses rose to struggle against the bad Party members and cadres. In many districts Party members and cadres were arrested and beaten, causing panic among other members and cadres. Second, the landlords and rich peasants who had been struggled against intrigued to take revenge and incite the masses to struggle against Party members and cadres in a confused manner. Third, the work teams insisted, rather mechanistically, on hitting the landlords first and solving the cadre question afterwards. They arbitrarily separated land reform from the democratic movement of Party rectification; they restrained the masses from carrying out struggles against Party members and cadres, or removed large groups of Party members and cadres whom the masses opposed to other places like "stones." Consequently, the work teams created a situation whereby they were isolated from the masses.[71]

While the correction of the first two tendencies would require dampening mass struggle, countering the third demanded opening up Party rectification to mass participation. The Pingshan experience, Liu continued, provided such an "open door" *(kaimen)* method by inviting ordinary poor and middle peasants to attend branch meetings which lasted for up to 24 hours. These meetings reportedly received an enthusiastic response particularly as the branches were enjoined to mete out prompt punishment in accord with popular opinion. This device, while undoubtedly enlivening rectification in areas where it had been "behind closed doors," was also designed to provide a modicum of control over the process and thus prevent the beating of cadres and other excesses. As Liu put it, once drawn into the bosom of the Party branch "the peasants who come with grievances to vent through vilification and revenge find their attitude is unconsciously changed to one of 'treating the illness to save the patient'. . . ." Nevertheless, the Pingshan method of rectification clearly promoted vigorous mass criticism of cadres and, shades of tailism, advocated quickly turning popular views into accomplished fact.[72] Thus in pushing this method Liu violated his own (and Mao's) strictures of a few years earlier concerning the need to limit mass participation in Party discipline. In the case of Long Bow, excesses and problems were the responsibility of a work team thoroughly versed in Liu's policies as of February 1948[73]; the Long Bow "gate" can be viewed as a local version of the Pingshan experience. And while it made successful efforts to keep the entire process under control, the work team's basic thrust was in accord with the radical assumptions of the Outline Land Law.

The decisive turning point against leftist excesses came in late March and April. The earliest indication was Mao's "Circular on the Situation" of March 20, 1948, in which for the first time he explicitly identified leftist deviations as the main ones.[74] Mao reiterated this view in two early April speeches in the Shanxi-Suiyuan Liberated Area when he was in transit from North Shaanxi to reunite with Liu in Pingshan. Moreover, policy at the basic levels now emphasized moderation. The Long Bow work team, together with others in the area, was called to a county conference in late April where the county leadership sharply rebuked the teams for "left extremism." A new assessment of the situation and new policies were introduced at the conference. The view was now taken that the thoroughness of land reform had been underestimated and most peasants had enough land even in the worst organized villages; the county ordered all keypoint villages to be reclassified as the first type, advanced villages where land reform was successful. Work teams had assertedly erred by seeking support solely from poor peasants, neglecting middle peasants and treating Party members as class enemies. The policies adopted reflected a shift of emphasis to Mao's second principle—the need for firm unity with middle peasants; the measures included a broadening of the criteria for classifying middle peasants and the decision to return confiscated property to "wrongly struggled middle peasants." Moreover, it was determined that apologies would be given to cadres who had been arrested, those who had not yet passed the gate would receive another chance, and efforts would be made to restore local Communists to positions of leadership.[g] A subsequent county cadres' conference in June reaffirmed

---

[g] In still another parallel, developments in the Socialist Education Movement in 1965 took a course very similar to that which evolved in spring 1948. Moreover, a Cultural Revolution source claims that Peng Zhen, who later guided the moderation of socialist education in 1965, had also directed the new cadre policy after April 1948. *Qianjunbang* [The Massive Cudgel] (Tianjin), April 1967, in *JPRS*, No. 41, 858.

and extended the new analysis and policies; in particular it declared that the class composition of Party branches in keypoint villages was pure, and it set production—the strong point of the middle peasants—as the main task for the future.[75]

Of particular importance is that only in April did cadres actually implementing land reform and rectification perceive a basic change in policy. Up until that point efforts made by Mao and Liu to curb leftist tendencies had not been totally effective. While measures taken before April such as the propagation of Liu's Pingshan experience apparently had some effect in containing (if not eliminating) excesses, it took a clear-cut analysis of the left as the main danger finally to turn the tide.

In sum, allegations that shortcomings in land reform and Party rectification in 1947–48 were uniquely Liu's responsibility will not bear scrutiny. Mao's indirect April 1948 rebuke to Liu for the leftist errors of the June 1947 land conference has all the earmarks of an *ex post facto* judgment; Liu's operational responsibility for intensified land reform made him vulnerable to criticism but there is no evidence that Mao had any misgivings at the time. When Cultural Revolution accusations widened Liu's culpability to include the full range of 1947–48 excesses they not only glossed over the ambiguities of Mao's position but also the inherent tendency of mass movements to extremism. Overall, the weight of available information indicates that Mao and Liu were in essential agreement: in the second half of 1947 both emphasized the need for thoroughgoing land reform and rectification to overcome very serious problems, while in the first quarter of 1948 they sought to correct the excesses which had become apparent without altering their basic evaluation of the situation. To the extent that leftist deviations reflected leadership errors rather than the passions of social revolution, Mao as well as Liu must share the blame.

The Legacy of Rectification

The impact of the 1947–48 rectification movement in terms of numbers of cadres purged, i.e., those who remained expelled from leadership posts even after the introduction of measures to ameliorate the treatment of cadres, cannot be stated with confidence in the absence of official figures. However, the fact that the annual increase in Party membership in 1947–48, a period of great expansion of areas under CCP control, was roughly one-fifth of the previous year's despite efforts to recruit activists into the Party as part of the rectification process suggests the possibility of a substantial weeding out of undesirables.[76] In any case, an equally significant legacy of the campaign was its detrimental effect on the morale of cadres who continued to serve as the backbone of leadership at the basic levels. As we have seen, the resentment felt by village cadres at the treatment they received during Party rectification was substantial. Although Hinton's account of Long Bow indicates some improvement in basic level morale in subsequent months due to the more moderate cadre policy, local Communists were generally unwilling to exert vigorous leadership as confusion and despair were still widespread within their ranks. In this situation not only did "extreme democracy" thrive, but there was also a general lethargy and lack of interest in political affairs among the villagers.[77]

Work team cadres in Long Bow and nearby villages also suffered from the general malaise following the adoption of the new line. In part, this was because they faced some of the same problems as the village Communists described above. These cadres had themselves undergone intensive examination by county authorities and, in their own villages where their status was still that of ordinary Communists, had been required to go before local gates. Moreover, the farming assistance which their families formerly received during their absence from mutual aid teams was no longer forthcoming due to the hostility and suspicion felt towards cadres as a group. Another important factor in low work team morale was the harsh criticism of their performance in land reform and rectification presented at the April conference. Furthermore, at both the April and June meetings, there was a feeling of uncertainty as to how the new policies could be realized. Thus land reform cadres did not see how they could return property to "wrongly struggled middle peasants" and at the same time continue to redistribute land to poor peasants given the shortage of surplus property in the villages—even with the new assessment drastically reducing the estimate of poor peasants who still had not received land.[78]

Probably the greatest source of discontent among work team cadres, however, was the feeling that even if they had committed serious errors it was unfair to focus the blame on them. The attacks by the county leaders engendered anger and bitterness not only because those same leaders had approved specific acts now criticized but because a county conference in February which trained the work teams had set the tone for the excesses which followed. But while resentment focused most sharply on county officials, a more generalized disenchantment with higher level leadership arose since even the Central Committee's own newspaper had promoted the "poor peasant line."[79] This disenchantment stemmed not only from feelings that they were being made scapegoats for mistakes committed above, but from the difficulty of work team cadres in comprehending why such a rapid and sharp shift of line had been necessary. This difficulty was sufficiently widespread—among village cadres as well as work team members—to bring about a defense of the leadership by an administrative district secretary at the June conference:

> The land reform policy laid down by Mao Zedong has not only been consistent, it has been correct. Is there anything wrong with the formulation, "Depend on the poor peasants, unite with the middle peasants, join with the anti-feudal forces to destroy the feudal land system and institute the system of land to the tiller"? No. That has always been the policy, is still the policy, and

will be the policy wherever the feudal system has not yet been uprooted.

Our problem is that we have applied this policy to a county and to villages where the feudal system no longer exists. . . .

Who then is to blame for the wrong estimate and for the policies which flowed from this estimate? The county and regional leaders are responsible. But the cadres in the field must also be self-critical. Is it not on their reports of conditions that the leaders in the county seat make their estimates? And have not the local cadres sometimes interpreted policy carelessly? Have they not been prone to seize on a single aspect that suited their prejudices and thus neglect the whole? "Depend on the poor peasants" is part of our agrarian policy, but it certainly is not the whole of it. Yet the cadres in the villages have emphasized it out of all proportion.[80]

The willingness of higher cadres to assume some blame—a tendency which became less guarded as the June conference unfolded—helped dispel some of the bitterness of the work team cadres but the effort to uphold the Center's correctness left many unconvinced and at least some still hostile.[81] Such skepticism seems indeed to have been justified since the highest leaders were responsible for the estimate of the situation from which, in the words of the administrative district secretary quoted above, erroneous policies flowed.

Conclusion

The development of rectification doctrine and techniques in the revolutionary period was closely linked to the consolidation of Mao Zedong's leadership. This was true not only in the obvious sense that the initial rectification campaign marked the ultimate defeat of the returned student faction, but also in that it contributed to a viable, largely non-coercive approach to handling differences within the leadership. As already argued in Chapter 1, by establishing norms of inner Party behavior which, in effect, promised at most criticism of minority views, Mao facilitated both vigorous, beneficial debate within Party councils and a high degree of loyalty from diverse CCP leaders. Given the difficult and complex tasks facing the Party, only such a self-assured and unified leading core could achieve the revolutionary successes which were the ultimate source of Mao's power. These successes were also due to the impact of rectification on the Party rank and file. By widely disseminating methods and attitudes essential for peasant mobilization, rectification measures helped forge the effective cadre force essential for victory.

The relationship of rectification to Mao's power as well as his considerable substantive contribution to the process should not, however, lead to an uncritical acceptance of the view that he consistently pushed his concept of inner Party discipline in opposition to the conflicting approaches of other leaders. While rectification does have a decidedly more educative aura about it than the methods employed by the returned student leadership, Mao himself contributed to the excesses of ruthless struggle in the early 1930s. The conciliatory approach adopted by Mao in 1935 reflected a shrewd sense of the grievances shared by many in high Party councils and an appreciation of the severe limits on his newly attained powers; it had not yet evolved into a systematic program of inner Party education. When that program did emerge in the early 1940s there was no sign of opposition to educational methods *per se,* although clearly the returned students resented being made targets of the initial campaign. Moreover, there had been efforts to curb excessively harsh methods of handling inner Party disputes in the days of ruthless struggle and the practice of retaining erring comrades in official posts predated Mao's leadership. While Mao certainly deserves credit for institutionalizing the "save the patient" approach, it appears that both cultural factors and the Leninist tradition militated for the amelioration of struggle within the Party even under conditions far less favorable to moderation than those which existed in Mao's Yan'an.[82]

While the differences between Mao and the returned students have been overdrawn, arguments that Mao consistently favored intense ideological struggle and the opening of the rectification process to mass participation, while Liu Shaoqi sought to circumscribe both are not borne out by the development of the two pre-1949 rectification campaigns. It was the Liuist rectification of 1947–48 which adopted open door methods while the 1942–44 Maoist movement was, by comparison, a closed door affair. But it would be equally misleading to accept the Cultural Revolution version of Liu's 1947–48 activities as undermining basic level Party morale while Mao remained solicitous of ordinary cadres. The evidence indicates a basic unity of views between Mao and Liu on both rectification efforts of the 1940s. While in each case one leader had predominant operational authority over the campaign, the other also played a key role and expressed approval of the general trend of events on more than one occasion. Where there were ostensible differences—as in Mao's implied criticism of Liu in April 1948 and perhaps in Liu's 1944 statement that *zhengfeng* methods were not entirely suited to anti-Japanese base areas—they are better explained as reflecting different perspectives of time or location than fundamentally conflicting approaches.

More generally, the 1942–44 and 1947–48 campaigns were keyed to different tasks and this, not the roles of individual leaders, explains the differences between them. The original campaign dealt with important policy disputes in the CCP's past and sanctified the rise of a Sinocentric leadership; by necessity the center of gravity was at the higher levels where mass participation could not be meaningful. The 1947–48 movement, on the other hand, was linked to a vast social revolution in the villages of North and Northeast China which made mass participation not only feasible but desirable for sustaining popular support. Moreover, the problems addressed in 1942–44 concerned, as Mao said,[83] basic orientation—general principles of leadership with particular attention to the relationship of theory and practice—matters suited to discussion in fairly cloistered settings. In 1947–48, however, concrete policy implementation was at issue and such questions as how local cadres had behaved towards the masses could be illuminated by an open airing of views.

Finally, our hypotheses concerning the relationship of persuasive and coercive techniques of internal control to both the degree of leadership unity and external threat can be examined in greater detail. Of course, the CCP faced armed enemies throughout the period from 1927 to 1949, but in terms of actual threat to its continued existence it is clear the danger was far greater in the late 1920s and early 1930s—the period of ruthless struggle—than at any point in the 1940s. Moreover, although short term increases in external threats such as the intensified Japanese and GMD pressure of 1941–42 and the renewed outbreak of civil war in 1946 created problems dealt with by rectification, relative security was a precondition for Party reform.[84] This was illustrated both by the greater applicability of the 1942–44 movement to Yan'an, where the enemy could not disrupt the process, and by the development of rectification in 1947–48 as the tide of battle shifted and the CCP went on the offensive. Still, both campaigns involved significant purging and coercive punishment due in no small part to hostile aspects of the environment, particularly as manifested in the infiltration of the Party by subversive elements. The apparently greater use of coercive means during the 1947–48 movement, however regretted later, was due to objective and conceptual considerations concerning hostile external forces even though the CCP was far closer to final victory during the latter campaign. Objectively, the severe struggles in North and Northeast China during the anti-Japanese and civil wars created a much higher level of social tension than had been present in the stable Yan'an area. Conceptually, the CCP view of the later 1940s as a period of sharpening class contradictions led to considerably more stringent policies than had been the case during the united front period. Thus while in the largest sense the Party's environment was more favorable in 1947–48 than in 1942–44, class contradictions—which are inevitably reflected within the Party according to rectification doctrine—were more intense in the later period justifying a relatively harsher approach to inner Party discipline.

Apart from a precarious external environment, the period of ruthless struggle was marked by bitter factional divisions within the Party leadership. By the time Mao launched the initial rectification campaign, in contrast, a substantial consensus had formed approving both his preeminence and programs. The weakness of the returned student group by the early 1940s, moreover, meant relatively lenient methods would suffice for the final undermining of their influence. Coercive measures were largely restricted to those uncovered during anti-subversion work and dissident intellectuals. The basic thrust of the movement for Party members generally was educative since, in the absence of substantial opposition, the task was largely one of propagating Mao's approach to a receptive audience. Although by 1947–48 Mao's leadership had solidified even further, rectification nevertheless took on a more punitive tone. But while leadership unity did not preclude coercive measures where class infiltration was perceived, such coercion was aimed at the basic levels and the unified upper echelons of the Party were basically immune. The larger lesson of the pre-1949 period confirms both official doctrine and our analysis of "coercive persuasion": the rectification approach emphasizing education, although an important element in the development of Party unity, is only viable where that unity is already substantial.

PART II

Rectification According to the Norms, 1950–1957

4
Rectification and the Consolidation of Power, 1950–1953

Nationwide victory did not mark the fulfillment of the Chinese revolution. It was but one step in a more protracted process of social transformation which would require further stages and struggles before a Communist society could be realized. That one step, however, meant the tasks, opportunities and problems facing the Party were profoundly different from those of the revolutionary period when rectification was first developed.

Rectification now became an integral part of the overall consolidation of national power which was the central feature of the early years of the PRC.[1] Military success and the crumbling of organized resistance shifted leadership energies from seizing power to administering and using it. The most pressing task was social and economic recovery from the dislocations of civil war. Once that was achieved China's new modernizing elite would embark on the initial phases of ambitious programs for construction and development. As a Marxist modernizing elite, moreover, CCP leaders consciously sought to restructure society, altering the distribution of power, wealth and status among various social groups in a far more comprehensive fashion than had been possible earlier in the revolutionary base areas. In undertaking the twin tasks of development and social transformation, Party leaders found their circumstances altered in other significant respects: the rural based revolutionaries of the recent past now operated in China's urban centers and controlled vast territories almost totally lacking the organized masses and indigenous Party members crucial for previous successes. In all these respects victory created a new situation requiring considerable adaptability from the CCP.

Adapting to the new situation naturally placed a heavy strain on the Party's organizational resources. Problems of elite performance inevitably arose both from inadequate personnel for coping with new conditions and from the tension created between long standing work methods and unfamiliar tasks. Throughout the consolidation period, the rectification approach developed before 1949 was utilized to correct shortcomings and expel those unable to meet the demands of the post-liberation era.

The first major effort was the rectification campaign *(zhengfeng yundong)* of 1950,[2] a movement focusing on defects in local organs from the large administrative regions to the lowest levels in rural and urban areas. This movement, which lasted from May 1950 to the end of the year, took place while overall CCP policy heavily emphasized the goals of restoring production and alleviating popular fears of the new regime. Although efforts to extend Party control of society and implement social reforms were also under way, socialist transformation was largely a matter for the future. In terms of the ongoing rhythm of Chinese political life, the PRC was clearly in a consolidation phase, although preparations for a great mass movement—land reform—were a major feature of the period. Moreover, administration in 1949–50 was heavily decentralized with six large administrative regions performing functions beyond the capabilities of a fledgling central authority.

Despite claims of great results for the 1950 campaign, a new rectification movement *(zhengdang yundong)* was soon launched in early 1951. This new undertaking, which emphasized the work of Party recruitment as well as rectification, continued for three years until early 1954. In actual fact it lacked many of the attributes normally associated with nationwide campaigns, being extremely diffuse and conducted in different localities at widely disparate points in time. It often took on definite shape during two coordinate rectification movements, the more compact Three Anti Campaign of 1951–52 and New Three Anti Campaign of 1953. Moreover, by spanning such a substantial period, the course of the 1951–54 movement reflected a change in emphasis in overall Party policy from economic recovery—with its explicit encouragement of private economic forces in both urban and rural areas—to increasing Party control of society and the economy as the basis for socialist transformation and planned development was laid. The movement also encompassed both a predominantly mobilization phase marked by several major campaigns (see below) in 1951–52 and a consolidation phase in 1953, as well as unfolding during a steady process of administrative centralization.[a] Throughout this period the rectification campaign focused on reforming and strengthening basic level Party branches to provide a firm organizational basis for the CCP's ambitious programs.

---

[a] While great power was initially vested in the six large administrative regions which combined Party, governmental and military authority, centralizing tendencies soon appeared as leading personnel were transferred from the regions to Beijing. Administratively, the status of the large regions was downgraded in the winter of 1952–53 as the regional Military and Administrative Committees were redesignated Administrative Committees and the central government was granted increased authority over the regional bodies. The process of centralization culminated in 1954–55 as the regional Party, government and military structures were disbanded.

The Three Anti Campaign *(sanfan yundong)* from late 1951 to mid-1952 against "corruption, waste and bureaucratism" *(tanwu, langfei, guanliaozhuyi)* was an integral part of intense mobilization efforts as well as the key vehicle for Party rectification in China's cities.[b] These mobilization efforts, which were probably influenced by the threatening atmosphere created by the Korean War,[c] sought to solidify CCP control by eliminating the independent power and prestige of old elites, raising the status of groups formerly subordinate to such elites, and recruiting activists from these groups for newly created or vacant official positions. In the countryside, the main methods were an intensification of land reform in newly liberated areas together with the development of mutual aid and cooperativization in areas where land reform was complete. In urban areas, following the suppression of counterrevolution *(zhenfan)* and democratic reform *(minzhu gaige)* movements which attacked secret societies, independent labor bosses and other potential alternatives to Communist authority,[3] the Three Anti Campaign, together with its sister Five Anti *(wufan)* drive directed against businessmen and the ideological remolding of the intelligentsia, comprised the most significant political mobilization of the early post-liberation period. The primary importance of the Three Anti Campaign is that it dealt with problems created by the arrival of Party authority and personnel in an urban environment following nationwide victory. The injunction to oppose corruption, waste and bureaucratism was shorthand for CCP efforts to grapple with the complex influence of urban life on the governing elite.

Finally, in the first half of 1953 the New Three Anti Campaign *(xinsanfan)*,[4] more formally known as the "struggle to oppose bureaucratism, commandism and violations of law and discipline" *(fandui guanliaozhuyi, minglingzhuyi he weifa luanji de douzheng)*, reflected the consolidation phase which followed the mobilizations of 1951–52. In rural areas, the mutual aid-cooperativization and land reform movements continued in old and new liberated areas respectively. But land reform was in its concluding stages and the rate of mutual aid and cooperativization slowed considerably following excesses in 1952.[5] Meanwhile, the high powered urban campaigns of 1952 had abated by the middle of that year. More broadly, 1953 saw the start of the First Five Year Plan (FFYP) for economic growth and a concomitant emphasis on regularizing and rationalizing institutions and procedures, aims that were hardly congruent with the dislocations accompanying mass movements in 1952. In this context, the new rectifica-

[b] The *sanfan* campaign was also carried out extensively at the county level and there was even an effort to extend it to villages. However, when the movement was developed experimentally in rural district *(qu)* organs, many problems arose which disrupted agricultural production and resulted in abandonment of the experiment. NCNA, Beijing, February 9, 1953, in *SCMP*, No. 514.

[c] Most of the mass movements of the period were not launched until after Chinese entry into the Korean War while land reform took on a decidedly more severe cast shortly after China intervened.

tion campaign focused on problems resulting from the earlier upsurge, particularly those in rural areas at lower and intermediate levels which had to a large extent been ignored by higher level officials preoccupied with *sanfan* and *wufan* tasks in 1952.

While these rectification efforts differed in target groups, deviations to be rectified and intensity, they all had the goal of strengthening the new regime and facilitating further social revolution and economic development. In pursuing this goal, moreover, they adhered to the organizational norms laid down in the early 1940s.

Debate and Consensus within the Leadership

The number and complexity of tasks facing the CCP in the 1950–53 period inevitably led to different opinions within the leadership. The overall picture, however, is of a highly unified leadership sharing a common view of the problems facing China and the measures required to deal with them. The reasons for this unity are twofold. First, a substantial consensus existed on the desirability of following the Soviet model. Although Mao overstated matters when he subsequently said, "Since we had no experience . . . we could only copy the Soviet Union and our own creativity was small,"[6] with the aid of Russian advisers China did undertake extensive institutional borrowing from her Soviet "big brother," particularly in economic strategy and organization, governmental organization, education and military affairs. Nevertheless, CCP leaders made significant alterations in the Soviet model not only in specific areas such as policy toward counterrevolutionaries,[7] but most basically by adopting a gradualist approach to socialist transformation. Clearly Mao and his colleagues were prepared to learn from the negative as well as positive aspects of the Soviet path. This created an area of debate: precisely what are the positive and negative features of Soviet experience? How should China adapt her policies accordingly? How fast should the Soviet path be implemented?

That these questions did not cause deep strains within the leadership was due in significant measure to the second factor—the undisputed leadership of Mao. With the success of his revolutionary strategy a fresh memory Mao's prestige was enormous. During the consolidation years Mao's colleagues placed considerable stress on his personal contributions.[8] For his part Mao played a dual role: he defined the nature of the period and served as the final arbiter of policy disputes. In this context of stable power relations little advantage would accrue to any leader who exaggerated policy differences in an effort to outmaneuver potential rivals.

The stability of the leadership was further enhanced by the fact that Mao's position in these years was orthodox and mainstream. To the extent he displayed idiosyncrasies which set him apart from his associates, these seem limited to an unusual sensitivity to dangerous tendencies in the arts.[9] In most matters Mao shared with his colleagues a deep commitment to economic and technical advance, a keen awareness of objective limits to Party policies, a determination to steer a course between leftist excesses and rightist timidity, and a confident optimism that progress would be achieved by following the Soviet path.[10] Thus when debate did occur, Mao's moderate centrist position served to ameliorate conflict and build a consensus rather than polarize differences within the leadership. This in turn allowed the Chairman to play his role as final arbiter of policy disputes within the boundaries of Party organizational norms. By pursuing consensus politics Mao could secure the majorities required by the principle of collective leadership.

As to the concrete policy disputes of the consolidation years, it is easier to identify areas of debate than the nature and degree of conflict among individual leaders. While it may be that some officials (notably economic planners) were relatively consistent in their positions on such matters as whether to increase the tempo of socialization, it appears that figures of the level of Mao and Liu Shaoqi tended to shift ground as their perceptions of conditions changed.[11] Thus it is particularly difficult to evaluate Cultural Revolution charges of Mao-Liu conflict since, apart from questions of reliability of sources, rarely is "evidence" presented of different views held by Mao and Liu *at the same point in time.* In any case, fewer accusations were raised against Liu (and Mao's alleged opponents generally) for their activities during the consolidation years than for any other period after 1949.[12] Moreover, some of the most prominent charges—e.g., those concerning Liu's conciliatory policy toward capitalists in Tianjin in 1949[13]—are clearly gross distortions since Liu's activities were fully compatible with Mao's own position.

Mao's own words indicate that the initial consolidation measures were relatively non-controversial, but "on the question of forming [Agricultural Producers'] Cooperatives (APCs) there [were conflicting] attitudes."[14] This issue, the question of how to modify the Soviet practice of collectivized agriculture to suit Chinese conditions, involved such matters as the rate of industrialization, the relation of technical reform (mechanization) to institutional reform (full collectivization), the supply and control of grain, and especially the rate of cooperativization. It is clear that the debate on these issues was extensive, although Cultural Revolution accusations against specific leaders in this regard are problematical.[15]

The agricultural cooperativization issue, however, was only part of a broader debate on when and how to shift the emphasis from reassuring key groups in society to social transformation. Such reassurance was initially crucial to the task of reviving economic activity after years of war. In the urban sector, the new government encouraged the entrepreneurial class to resume production by sanctioning the profit motive, bolstering managerial authority and curbing workers' demands. Similar policies were pursued in rural China, not least in the newly liberated areas where Communist control was gradually extended outward from the cities in contrast to North China where Communist power had formed in the countryside surrounding the cities. In rural areas, small scale private production, including that of rich peasants, was reaffirmed.[d] By these various measures—and by a very narrow definition of enemies limited to landlords, "bureaucratic capitalists" and "reactionaries" linked to the GMD and imperialism—the CCP created an extremely broad united front.

From the first, however, the policy of reassurance was in tension with the imperative of establishing firm organizational control. Most official policies whittled away at the autonomy of groups whose cooperation was sought for reconstruction. Thus private capitalists, despite official encouragement, were subject to a policy of "use and restrict" which enforced various external controls (*via* taxes, government contracts, price manipulation, control of raw materials, etc.) and created uncertainty about how long the relatively favorable situation would last. In establishing administrative control veteran Communists increasingly penetrated the state bureaucracy and new elements presumably loyal to the emerging system—most notably intellectual youth—were recruited extensively in conjunction with rectification and other political movements. Personnel expanded enormously[16] and the position of holdover officials from the GMD regime who initially had been encouraged to stay at their posts became increasingly precarious.

Closely tied to the extension of Party control was "socialist transformation" along Soviet lines, but with substantial modification in timing. From the outset, socialist transformation centering on ownership of the means of production was conceived of as a step-by-step process which would take a fairly long period to complete.[e] The thrust of public pronouncements—aptly captured by the slogan

---

[d] Cultural Revolution sources have extensively attacked Liu Shaoqi for advocating policies upholding the "rich peasant economy." While Liu did indeed speak in support of such policies in mid-1950, Mao pushed this course at the same time. Liu Shao-ch'i, "Report on the Question of Agrarian Reform," in *The Agrarian Reform Law of the People's Republic of China and Other Relevant Documents* (Beijing: Foreign Languages Press, 1959), pp. 66–67; and *SW*, V, 29. Moreover, the views of Mao and Liu on this matter *after* 1950 are unclear. Although Mao criticized slogans encouraging private peasant production in mid-1953 (*SW*, V, 94), his available statements for 1951–52 give no indication of his attitude on the rich peasant question.

[e] All Party leaders who spoke on the subject, including both Mao and Liu Shaoqi, depicted a relatively long period before socialism would be realized. There are conflicting indications of just how long a period was envisioned. Liu was accused during the Cultural Revolution of having advocated twenty years (*Xin Nongda* [New University of Agriculture], May 10, 1967, in *SCMP-S*, No. 186). In a 1950 speech, however, Liu seemed to suggest a period of six to nine years (*Collected Works of Liu Shao-ch'i, 1945–1957* [Hong Kong: Union Research Institute, 1969], p. 238), while Mao still saw a 15-year transition to socialism in 1953 even while criticizing others for wanting a slower pace (*SW*, V, 93–94).

"Temporarily maintain the existing situation, introduce reforms gradually as necessary and feasible"[17]—was to downplay the immediacy of change. But while emphasis on the long term viability of capitalism and guarantees for private peasant production reassured key groups, it also raised fears within Party circles that capitalist features of the new order would be unduly strengthened and socialist reforms unconscionably delayed. Thus although the overall approach remained gradualist throughout the consolidation period, as time passed efforts were made to push forward the socialization process which in turn antagonized various groups, disrupted production, and generated pressures for relaxation. This dialectic was particularly pronounced in the rural sector where the movement to build mutual aid teams and lower level cooperatives went through a cycle of organizational expansion, retrenchment, and renewed expansion from late 1951 to the end of 1953.

The debate which inevitably revolved around the dialectic of reassurance and advance concerned both overall emphasis and specific policies. In both regards, albeit rather tangentially, leadership differences were ostensibly linked to rectification efforts. This was particularly the case concerning standards for Party membership which were laid down in early 1951 as guidelines for the 1951–54 rectification campaign. During the Cultural Revolution Liu Shaoqi was accused of advocating the slogan "Consolidate the new democratic order" and incorporating it into the standards for membership.[18] Although there is no evidence of conflict over this slogan *in 1951* and the charges against Liu are clearly distorted,[f] by 1953–54 Mao and other leaders were criticizing emphasis on new democratic programs as inhibiting socialist transformation.

---

[f]Not only was Mao's June 1953 critique of new democratic programs mirrored by Liu in a 1954 report, but the relevant section of the membership standards looked beyond the new democratic period: "All members must struggle for the ultimate goal of the realization of the Communist system, first for the consolidation of the new democratic system, then proceeding to the nationalization of industry and collectivization of agriculture, and finally attaining Communism." See *SW,* V, 93–94; *Collected Works of Liu 1945–57,* p. 285; and *RMRB,* July 1, 1952, in *CB,* No. 251.

In any case, a Red Guard source claims Mao was angered by the standards Liu had drafted and demanded to know what they meant and why they hadn't been brought to his attention. The source suggests other contentious issues involved in this affair were the placing of the study of Mao's Thought last among the standards, and the alleged inclusion (not borne out by the 1952 published version) of the notion that the CCP was led by the working class in the cities and a semi-proletariat, presumably peasants, in the countryside. The downgrading of the proletariat implied by the last charge is also seen in the accusation that during the 1950 rectification campaign Liu opposed Mao's call for stepped up recruitment of workers into the Party, arguing that the credentials of the urban working class were suspect. *Ziliao zhuanji* [Collected Materials], November 1968, in *SCMP-S,* No. 246. If true, note that these instances indicate a more complex situation than the stereotype of Liu placing his faith in the industrial proletariat in contrast to a peasant oriented Mao. Moreover, the extremely slight attention given to any of the above issues in Cultural Revolution polemics suggests that any differences were not of great significance.

Similarly, the specific policies for restoring rural production by protecting rich peasant interests—the so-called "four major freedoms" to buy and sell land, hire labor, lend money and lease land—apparently soon became a source of tension within the leadership despite Mao's open advocacy of the "rich peasant economy" in 1950. Liu, in addition to being subsequently belabored by Red Guards for *his* support of rich peasant interests, was further charged with decreeing in 1951 that members of rich peasant origin could remain in the Party and that Party members generally could hire labor.[19] Whatever debate there may have been within the leadership at that time on these issues, it is clear that the basic problem was one of *evolving* Party policy as conditions and tasks changed. This can be seen in the speeches of a single leader, Gao Gang, Party chief of the Northeast, who in 1950 took a tolerant view of Party members seeking individual riches but in 1952 sharply condemned Communists who hired labor and lent at usurious rates.[20]

The fact that debate in the 1950–53 period centered on shifting emphases, rates of development and timing rather than on fundamental approaches meant the full leadership could rally around decisions committed to gradual development along the Soviet path. It also facilitated elite discipline according to established principles. With no drastic alternatives being offered, there is little indication of purging or other sanctions being invoked for policy related matters during the early 1950s. A partial exception concerned Bo Yibo, one of the CCP's leading economic specialists. In August 1953 Mao launched a strong attack on Bo within the Party, criticizing in particular his new tax system which included certain concessions to the private sector. Arguing that this system "would have led inevitably to capitalism," Mao characterized Bo's errors as "mistakes of principle" which showed that "To some extent he has been corrupted both politically and ideologically." However, the Chairman implied the matter was not simply one of policy sponsorship by claiming Bo had failed to make adequate reports to the Central Committee.[21]

The seriousness of these strictures notwithstanding, the approach adopted was educational with Bo's case used to stimulate criticism of similar laxness towards the bourgeoisie in several spheres of work. Furthermore, no formal disciplinary action was taken against Bo. In September, however, Bo was relieved *(mianzhi)* as Minister of Finance, although he continued to serve in other important economic posts and gained major new responsibilities in this area when the central government was reorganized a year later.[22] While, as rectification principles advise, Bo had not been formally punished and his talents continued to be used, his loss of a key post suggests the dangers of policy advocacy even in a period of high leadership cohesion. But in the last analysis, the exceptional nature of Bo's case together with the mildness of the measures taken indicate the viability of rectification norms during the consolidation years.

Finally, it appears that the leadership unity of the early 1950s was especially strong with regard to rectification, discipline and recruitment. In contrast to subsequent periods, there is little to indicate substantial divisions on these questions. The charges concerning such matters made during the Cultural Revolution[g] were extremely few in number and frequency, and generally unpersuasive. Corresponding to the broad consensus on overall policy, agreement was easily obtained on an organizational approach upholding traditional principles.

Major Problems and Deviations during the Consolidation Years

A variety of problems and deviations were dealt with by the rectification movements of the early 1950s. Harsh leadership methods—commandism—were a major focus of the 1950 and 1953 campaigns, while the closely related problem of bureaucratism was criticized throughout the period. The adjustment of tensions among different groups within the elite was another key problem during the 1950 movement and remained a matter of concern during the consolidation years although policy towards one major group—personnel retained from the GMD administration—changed markedly with the passing of time. Even among cadres of politically respectable backgrounds serious shortcomings arose; low levels of ideological awareness were a worrisome deficiency which, together with organizational weaknesses, presented considerable obstacles to effective rule. Moreover, shifting policies toward private peasant production contributed to attitudes and behavior by rural cadres judged dangerous by the Party leadership. Rural cadres were also vulnerable to various blandishments and particularistic ties linking them to the old village elite. Meanwhile, similar phenomena appeared in the cities concerning the relationship of Party and state officials to the bourgeoisie. Each of these problems had to be overcome before the authority of the new regime could be fully consolidated.

Commandism and Bureaucratism

Harsh leadership practices were the central problem attacked during the initial campaign. The attention given commandism at this time indicated fear of a serious strain in the Party's relations with the masses while popular attitudes were still in their formative stage. The development of the problem was attributed partly to the conceit and pride of old Party cadres who, in the flush of their success, looked down on the people, and also to the remnant influence of the "GMD style" of governing on newly recruited cadres and personnel held over from the old regime. Manifestations of harsh leadership included cursing, beat-

[g] In addition to the cases discussed above, the only further instance of a rectification issue from the early 1950s found in Cultural Revolution sources was the accusation that Liu Shaoqi "switched the Three and Five Anti Campaigns to the right." "Long Live the Invincible Thought of Mao Zedong!" (Red Guard pamphlet), in *CB,* No. 884. While the campaigns did moderate, or "switch to the right," in their later stages, there is no evidence that this was a matter of dispute within the leadership.

ing, tying up, illegal arrests, and various forms of torture, sometimes resulting in the death of innocent people.[h] While it is not easy to gauge the extent of such deviations, a report that over 50 percent of district *(qu)* cadres in a Henan special district were guilty of striking people suggests the problem was considerable.[23]

The New Three Anti Campaign also focused on commandism which apparently was again fairly widespread in the Chinese countryside in 1952–53. One report estimated 15 to 21 percent of rural Party members in Shanxi were guilty of such behavior.[24] The situation was similar to that immediately after nationwide victory when the CCP's rural administrative machinery had been overburdened with the manifold tasks of rule. Now tasks once more increased as the Party introduced an increasing number of programs to the countryside ranging from literacy movements to anti-drought movements to agricultural cooperatives; these, in turn, led directly to crude leadership methods. For example, during a campaign for drilling wells to prevent drought in parts of Shandong some district and administrative village *(xiang)* cadres, without proper investigation, allotted drilling tasks by households, proceeded to mark the land of the people, and forced them to drill wells in accordance with these markings. In some villages militia men were posted to enforce the drilling. There were even cases where market towns were suddenly blockaded and people attending market forcibly conscripted for drilling work.[25]

Officially defined as "the practice of attempting to carry out Party or government work merely by issuing orders or by making use of administrative machinery without taking the trouble to mobilize, . . . educate and convince the masses,"[26] commandism thus reflected tension between the revolutionary traditions of the mass line and escalating governmental demands. Implicit in the definition are several assumptions clearly articulated during the course of the 1950 campaign in particular. One was that the people were relatively backward ideologically and did not automatically accept measures truly representative of their interests. It was also assumed, however, that Party policy was consistent with the views of the people, although on a higher ideological level. The "scattered and fragmentary" opinions of the masses were "concentrated" by Party policy and assumed a different form. Through careful education and propaganda work the people can be convinced that official policy is consistent with their "real" interests. Thus complaints by cadres that "the masses are too backward and we must resort to commandism" were viewed as confessions of deficient propaganda work.[27] It was claimed that if well tested mobilization techniques

[h] Most of these phenomena together with interference in the freedom of marriage, persecution of those making criticisms, false accusations against good people, sheltering counterrevolutionaries, rape, forcing people to commit suicide, and killing people were attacked as violations of law and discipline during the 1953 campaign. These violations assertedly could take place on a significant scale because of the bureaucratic tendencies of higher level officials who failed to keep in close touch with basic level conditions. NCNA, Beijing, February 9, 1953, in *SCMP*, No. 514.

were utilized, then popular consent would result in successful policy implementation.

Rough leadership methods can be better understood by examining conflicting pressures placed on cadres charged with implementing Party policy by the PRC administrative system. Most important was the contradiction between "policy" *(zhengce)* and "tasks" *(renwu)*. Officially no contradiction exists. As Chen Yi put it, "Policy sets the tasks of concrete struggle or construction, while tasks are the concrete embodiment of policy."[28] In practice, however, there was considerable tension between *renwu*, frequently a quantitative target set by the state, and *zhengce*, which prescribed the proper methods for fulfilling tasks and thereby limited the legitimate means available for meeting targets. Since tasks can often be measured in quantitative terms, higher level cadres found it less complicated to evaluate the performance of subordinate units in task fulfillment than to give comparable attention to whether the limitations of policy were being observed. For lower levels to meet their quantitative goals, violations of policy were often the easy or only way out.[i] Some cadres felt that "to complete tasks is easy, to carry out policy is difficult, and to change one's work style is even more difficult." Thus a major source of the problem was demands from higher levels of the administration for exceeding quotas and eagerness of the lower levels to meet such demands while neither paid attention to actual conditions or the requirements of policy.[29]

An area where the contradiction of *renwu* and *zhengce* was particularly severe was agricultural taxation. Here *renwu* is the tax quota assigned a specific area in terms of a set amount of grain; *zhengce* is the detailed stipulations of the tax law concerning what and who could be taxed and the differential rates to be used in various circumstances. When taxes were actually collected, however, tax cadres came under heavy pressure to meet their tax quotas. Often they would introduce flat tax rates ignoring tax law distinctions, or rates in excess of the stipulated limit. For example, in one administrative village the responsible cadres ignored the law and placed an undifferentiated tax of over 14 percent on all production, and when this failed to meet the quota they merely increased everyone's tax by a

[i] However, during the 1950 campaign the media also attacked excessive caution and overemphasis of *zhengce* which resulted from rectification efforts. One target was tax cadres who reportedly felt, "This year the summer tax work does not lie in the amount of *renwu* one achieves, one only has to conform to *zhengce;* if one's *renwu* is not completed he will receive higher level criticism and be sent to the supervision authorities, but one cannot overtax the people since they will appeal to the people's court." Thus a tendency to underestimate production output and tax quotas arose. Similarly, in public security work, an area which received strong criticism for harsh methods, warnings were issued against misinterpreting policy to cause excessive leniency in handling criminals and counterrevolutionaries. In the official view, the response to attacks on commandism could be overdone and adversely affect the delicate balance of *zhengce* and *renwu. RMRB,* August 7, September 6, December 28, 1950.

flat 25 percent. The resentment engendered by such practices is indicated by the killing of over 3,000 tax cadres as they attempted to collect the grain tax in the PRC's first year.[30]

Cadres offered a variety of excuses for breaching policy. One was that lower level commandism was a direct outgrowth of bureaucratism at higher levels, an excuse only partially acknowledged in 1950. According to official statements, where cadres encountered bureaucratic behavior at higher levels, they had a duty to bring the actual situation to the attention of their superiors rather than to use it as a pretext for their own shortcomings. Furthermore, some lower level cadres were said to have carried harsh leadership practices to irresponsible lengths which in no way could be attributed to higher level errors.[31]

Cadres articulated many additional excuses for their behavior: tasks were too pressing and complicated, not enough time was allowed for their realization, and the people's consciousness was inadequate. Force was necessary when demanding sacrifices from the masses, for "only in giving things to the masses is there no need for force." Without rough methods people would cause trouble and tasks could not be met, thus small mistakes were necessary to avoid big ones. Special conditions were also cited, e.g., in newly liberated areas the particular backwardness of the masses made a coercive approach necessary. Some worker and peasant cadres claimed their unsophisticated nature prevented them from understanding the fine points of Party policy. In addition, some cadres saw their harsh methods as activism, a demonstration of loyalty to the Party. All of these attitudes were officially denounced as unacceptable rationalizations for crude basic level leadership.[32]

While a link between commandism and bureaucratism had been noted during the 1950 movement, it was only during the New Three Anti Campaign that major blame for such behavior was placed squarely at the door of higher level cadres guilty of bureaucratic practices. In 1953 An Ziwen, deputy head of the Party's organization department, discussed the responsibility of higher level cadres in great detail:

> Many workers in leadership organs do not understand the true conditions of lower levels or the sufferings of the masses. They frequently conduct work not on the basis of objective factual conditions, but rather on the basis of their own wishful thinking. Accordingly they often demand the carrying out of tasks too numerous and too heavy, and the urgency with which these demands are made leave those at lower levels under a state of great tension . . . so that a good job cannot be done. They are interested only in employing the services of cadres, but not in the education of cadres. In the allotment of tasks *(renwu),* they often emphasize the need for fulfillment, but fail to reveal clearly and concretely the policies *(zhengce),* the demarcation between what should and what should not be done. . . . After allotting tasks, they further fail to carry out inspections, and are satisfied with superficial achievements stated in reports submitted by the lower ranks without paying attention to actual results. Sometimes they only

> see the good side of a task but not the bad side. At other times they seek only quantitative results without bothering about quality. They are often oblivious of the various serious phenomena which endanger the interests of the people, and do not take active steps to support the good, punish the bad. . . . All these cannot but help to foster among the [lower] cadres the growth of commandism . . . so that the interests of the people suffer serious damage.[33]

Such practices by complacent high level officials who sat in their offices issuing directives without first hand knowledge of grass roots conditions led to excesses in the implementation of many programs. A major example was the mutual aid and cooperativization movement where leading cadres assertedly were seriously imbued with subjectivism and wished to achieve cooperativization with great speed. Believing that merely issuing orders would get things done, they overlooked the backwardness of small producers, excessively interfered with the peasants, and simply handed down numerous tasks calling for increased numbers of households in APCs, causing forced enrollment and peasant dissatisfaction.[34] The catalog of bureaucratic sins also included the syndrome of demanding results, receiving questionable reports which precluded sound planning, yet proceeding to implement policy on the basis of such reports. There was a saying among district and village cadres that results were "pressed for by the special district, demanded by the county, collected by the district and concocted by the village."[j]

Apart from contributing to harsh leadership methods and poor work performance, the tendency to rely on official communications also abetted serious illegal behavior. During the Three Anti Campaign the occurrence of corruption on a big scale was largely attributed to the bureaucratic behavior of responsible officials. Immersed in routine, failing to investigate at the basic levels, leading cadres often overlooked corruption. A prominent example concerned two Party secretaries of Tianjin special district, Hebei, who led a decadent life and engaged extensively in illegal business with state funds. The case went undiscovered for a period because leading provincial Party secretaries evaluated the situation on the basis of written and oral reports rather than undertaking penetrating investigation.[35]

Another bureaucratic shortcoming was inadequate coordination of the many programs initiated in the countryside, a tendency toward "dispersionism"

---

[j] NCNA, Beijing, June 25, 1953, in *SCMP,* No. 602. Such problems were not simply the result of shortcomings in the work of higher officials; they also reflected serious personnel shortages in the early post-liberation years. First, the weakness of basic level Party organizations both in numbers and performance (see below) hindered the gathering of comprehensive and accurate information on actual conditions in the villages. Moreover, the small staffs and weak leadership widely found at the *qu* level caused a crucial bottleneck which hampered higher levels in checking up on information provided by basic level units, and in assuring that directives sent down the chain of command were heeded. See NCNA, Beijing, February 9, 1953, in *SCMP,* No. 514.

(fensanzhuyi) as each department emphasized its own tasks and went its own way in the absence of unified Party leadership. As emphasized by attacks on the "five too many" *(wuduo)* in summer 1953, this was in large measure due to the surfeit of tasks, meetings, concurrent posts, documents and organizations which simply overburdened cadres and made it impossible for them to bring a sense of priorities to the basic levels. For example, in one administrative village pressure from various higher level departments resulted in 10 big tasks, 22 small ones, and five movements being carried out simultaneously. Cadres in this *xiang* had to attend anywhere from 10 to 30 meetings a month and became befuddled and confused in their work. Thus a "pure business viewpoint" *(danchun renwu guandian)* arose in which specific tasks were performed without any effort to integrate them around the overall goal of socialist transformation.[36]

Paradoxically, then, bureaucratic practices led not only to confusion and harsh methods as basic level cadres sought to implement directives from above, but also to the loss of control over subordinate officials at various levels who were able to go their own way in the absence of systematic checkups by higher authorities. In a situation where a complex, rapidly expanding bureaucratic structure was taking shape, individual units sought to take advantage of the difficulty of supervision to maximize their own resources. During the Three Anti Campaign criticism was directed at this tendency at a relatively high level in the case of leading provincial authorities in Jiangxi, Governor Shao Shiping and Vice Governors Fan Shiren and Fang Zhichun. At issue was concealment of grain output by sub-provincial levels. The provincial leaders took no action, despite pressure from Central-South regional authorities. In fact, these leaders were not merely being bureaucratic, they had actually encouraged such concealment. In a joint self-criticism, Shao, Fan and Fang admitted that they had engaged in such activities because they feared that the 1951 cut in national expenditures would cause a cut in provincial allowances and make concealed resources necessary for various projects in Jiangxi. Thus they confessed to "departmentalism" *(benweizhuyi),* "the vestige of the old outlook of scattered management . . . which one-sidedly stresses local partial difficulties and fails to realize the circumstances of a unified national political regime."[37]

The more extreme instances of bureaucratic and local units going their own way were attacked as "independent kingdoms" *(duli wangguo).* This was a central issue in the Huang Yifeng case, a case which came under heavy criticism during the New Three Anti Campaign.[38] In addition, the Huang affair involved other problems which reflected both the transition from revolution to rule and endemic difficulties of the PRC administrative system. Huang, who was director of the communications department of East China and president of the regional institute of communications, had been a Party member since 1941 and served in both the New Fourth Army and with PLA forces in Manchuria. After liberation, Huang is said to have treated his units as independent kingdoms by deceiving higher levels, equating Party discipline with obeying his word, and arbitrary personnel policies. He was alleged to have placed many of his students, personal friends, relatives, schoolmates and old colleagues in important posts. He considered them "my own people" and gave them unwarranted promotions. Furthermore, he transferred to other units or removed from active duty able cadres who dared question or criticize him. Huang was also accused of "meritorious thought" *(gongcheng sixiang);* he allegedly used the celebration of the CCP anniversary to brag about his own "glorious history." He reportedly became disgruntled when he was passed over for the position of head of the Shanghai railway bureau, arguing that his rank and revolutionary achievements had been disregarded.

Huang's case was triggered by a relatively mild anonymous letter to *Renmin ribao* in December 1951 from a group of students in the communications institute which complained in impersonal terms about "chaotic conditions" at the institute. Huang, however, was resentful over this affront, uncovered the student who actually wrote the letter, and made life so unbearable for him that he left school. This act of "suppression of criticism" *(yazhi piping)* was reported to the Party's East China Bureau which organized an inspection team to handle the case. Huang, rather than showing repentance, resisted the investigation by requiring all students to tell the same story and attempting to use his revolutionary record to intimidate the investigators. He allegedly "put on the badge of the North China liberation" and said, "let me scare those bastards." For this attitude Huang was expelled from the Party.

Besides violating CCP concepts of democracy, suppression of criticism was also an important factor in maintaining independent kingdoms. In reviewing the Huang Yifeng case, official statements held that it was typical of many leading cadres from village chiefs on up to treat their units as personal fiefdoms. Leaders implemented only policies they liked, were unwilling to cooperate and coordinate activities with other units and, as in the Jiangxi case during the *sanfan* campaign, used resources and personnel to further the narrow interests of departments or areas at the expense of broader national goals. The ability of leading cadres to engage in such practices was in large measure due to their control of communications channels within the bureaucracy. Their freedom was therefore jeopardized when critical information reached higher levels through such devices as letters to newspapers. Thus it is hardly surprising that leading cadres sought to prevent criticism which might result in higher level scrutiny of their units. Some are said to have taken the view that "I am the Party" and "my word is discipline," and anyone who challenged them within their own bailiwicks was denounced for "committing the error of anarchy and lack of discipline." As long as criticism was successfully suppressed, the capacity of leaders and their units to depart from strict adherence to Party programs would remain great.[39] At a time when steps toward administrative centralization and economic planning were well under way, such independent tendencies were a particularly serious matter.

Another persistent problem given prominence by the Huang Yifeng case was "meritorious thought." The belief that one was entitled to special privileges because of past contributions extended well beyond Huang's exaggerated view of himself. The lenient handling of the case in its earlier stages was apparently due to the misplaced trust of higher authorities in a cadre with a long record of revolutionary service. Moreover, the tenacity of these attitudes was reflected in the sympathy some cadres had for Huang even after he had been subjected to extensive criticism. The appearance of sentiments such as "it is going too far that an important cadre is purged as a result of a student's criticism . . ." indicate how deeply ingrained notions of status and special privilege were.[40] The tendency of veteran revolutionaries in particular to believe such status and privilege were theirs as a matter of right was a major cause of tensions among different segments of the elite in the early post-liberation period.

Inner Elite Tensions

As the CCP rapidly achieved nationwide victory in 1949 its personnel resources were grossly inadequate to the tasks of governing. It was therefore necessary to throw together hastily a heterogeneous elite to perform these tasks. Tensions quickly arose within this elite; ameliorating conflicts among various types of officials thus became a major aim of the 1950 campaign and remained a concern of subsequent rectification efforts. There were three broad groupings of personnel within the new governing elite: old cadres *(laoganbu),* new cadres *(xinganbu)* and retained personnel *(liuyong renyuan).* Old cadres were those who fought for the CCP during the critical days of the "third civil war" of 1946–49 or earlier; thus they stood with the Party when victory was by no means guaranteed. There were at least two to three million of them serving in the period immediately after the takeover of power.[41] New cadres were recruited to the Party's cause toward the end of the third civil war when victory was in sight or after the establishment of the PRC. This group included many students and intellectuals with talents needed for administration and economic recovery. By mid-1950 there were approximately two million new Party members among them[42] and many more new cadres who had not been admitted to the Party. Retained personnel were officials of the GMD regime with skills vital to the functioning of complex urban societies in particular who were kept in their posts after 1949. Their numbers are difficult to estimate, but they were a substantial force: for instance, in 1950 a majority of cadres in public security work were retained personnel. Although normally new cadres and retained personnel were treated as distinct categories, the two groups were sometimes combined into the single category of new cadres. Thus there were reports that in some newly liberated areas "new cadres" made up over 90 percent of the total cadre force.[43]

The conceit or "meritorious thought" of old cadres contributed to mutual dissatisfaction between them and other personnel. Many old cadres considered themselves well tested by years of revolutionary struggle and felt far superior to new cadres and retained personnel whom they regarded as politically untrustworthy. Moreover, these old revolutionaries believed they had earned a share of the fruits of victory. They stressed the importance of seniority and rank in assignments and promotions, and despite official claims that old cadres had generally been promoted they complained of insufficient attention to their status and problems.[k]

The key factor in the smoldering dissatisfaction of old cadres was the important positions recently obtained by their juniors, the new cadres. Faced with expanding administrative demands, CCP leaders had to staff choice posts with young intellectuals possessing the requisite literacy and skills old revolutionaries often lacked. Thus ability to perform pressing tasks often took precedence over proven loyalty. The adjustment was often painful for old cadres. A case widely publicized in the Party's theoretical journal, *Xuexi* [Study], concerned a cadre who was happy when transferred to an urban area after ten years in the mountains but soon became disillusioned upon finding that a majority of his new colleagues were fresh out of school. Distressed to find himself on an equal footing with such untested youngsters, he plaintively asserted that "the fruits of victory which we paid for in blood and flesh are now being enjoyed by those who contributed nothing and deserve less."[44] In addition, old revolutionaries were vexed by the fact that retained personnel continued to receive salaries while they received only daily necessities under the revolutionary supply system. The depth of these frustrations was reflected in a saying attributed to old cadres: "Old revolutionaries are treated worse than new revolutionaries; new revolutionaries are treated worse than non-revolutionaries; and non-revolutionaries are treated worse than counterrevolutionaries."[l]

New cadres, for their part, resented the domineering attitude of old cadres who they felt often received preferential treatment. Some new cadres, viewing the allocation of praise and blame between old revolutionaries and themselves, claimed "achievements belong to you while commandism is attributed to us." In response to this mutual ill will, the Party press strongly rebuked old revolutionaries for acting as heroes and seeking enjoyment after liberation. They were told the proper concern of a good Party member was not his own position but the good of the people, and that ability and work accomplishments had to take

[k] *CJRB*, September 5, 1950; *RMRB*, October 10, 1950, in *CB*, No. 180; and *Xuexi* [Study], January 1, 1951, in *CB*, No. 180. Within the ranks of old cadres, moreover, similar tensions existed. Some old cadres from the revolutionary base areas looked down on veteran underground workers behind enemy lines as "retained Party members" whom they had "liberated." *XHYB*, November 1950, p. 27.

[l] Ezra F. Vogel, "From Revolutionary to Semi-Bureaucrat: The 'Regularisation' of Cadres," *CQ*, No. 29 (1967), p. 39. Another practice which must have been galling to old cadres was the promotion to ordinary cadre status of some younger retained personnel who utilized their intellectual advantages to master Marxism-Leninism and Mao's Thought. See *ibid.*, p. 56.

priority over seniority in assignments. On the other hand, the documents studied during the 1950 campaign enjoined new cadres to respect the past accomplishments of old revolutionaries and to develop amicable relations with them. The two groups were handled differently during the campaign: old cadres underwent rectification of thought and work style; new cadres, who previously had no systematic training, received a more intensive education in basic Party principles. Beyond this the CCP denounced the sectarian attitudes of Party members, both new and old, which discriminated against retained officials and other non-Party personnel.[45]

While the subsequent rectification efforts in the early 1950s continued to reflect concern over relations between old and new cadres, the solicitude of the 1950 movement towards retained personnel was a more transitory phenomenon. Clearly those who had served the GMD were a suspect group and Party leaders were eager to reduce their dependence on such people. As new cadres trained under the new regime became available it was possible to replace retained personnel. Indeed, as we shall see, a main function of the Three Anti Campaign was to remove former GMD officials who were regarded as unsuited to the tasks of socialist transformation.[46]

Weaknesses within the Party: Organizational Inadequacy and Low Political Awareness

While CCP leaders wanted to shift the burden of governmental leadership to Party cadres and organizations, shortcomings within this most trusted segment of the elite created major obstacles to their goals. The 1951–54 rectification movement dealt most directly with these problems; the overriding concern of the campaign was the weakness of CCP basic level organization. This included the sheer shortage of Party branches and members for the tasks facing the new regime as well as political shortcomings of existing organizations. Thus recruitment of new Party members and strengthening of branches in industry was seen as vital if the Party was to provide firm guidance for large scale economic construction. In the countryside, large areas, particularly in the newly liberated regions, were without basic level Party units to provide leadership. For example, in the Southwest in 1952, 93 percent of all administrative villages lacked Party branches.[47] Therefore, key undertakings such as land reform had to be delayed or were implemented improperly.

Besides the shortage of Party branches, major problems concerned the activities and role of those branches which did exist. In many cases the regular "organizational life" *(zuzhi shenghuo)* of Party branches atrophied. In some units many cadres avoided participating in branch meetings and study sessions for as much as five months. In others such activities were not held at all for long periods. The lack of vitality in many Party branches was reflected in other aspects of political life, as in one village where attendance at Peasant Association meetings declined and the militia disarmed itself. Where organizational life did continue on a regular basis, it was often formalistic. In some cases documents were blindly memorized, while in others regular work was substituted for political study.[48]

This atrophy of Party branches was further reflected in their frequent failure to play a leading role in administrative and production units. For example, in some factories and mines leading cadres felt that the overall work guidance was the responsibility of superior economic organs and paid little attention to the opinions of Party branches. Similarly, the role of rural Party branches was often undercut by administrative personnel of APCs in those areas where cooperativization had developed. Thus an investigation in Jilin found that in 11 of 12 APCs the leadership core was not formed by the Party branch. Instead, leadership was frequently provided by the cooperative director who, in some cases, assumed the power to call or prevent Party branch meetings.[49]

The weakness of basic level organization was also due to a very low level of political and theoretical knowledge on the part of many Party members, a state revealed by examinations carried out as part of the 1951–54 movement. In a test given to special district and county cadres in Quzhou special district, Zhejiang, many cadres were unable to answer such questions as "why should we launch the suppression of counterrevolutionaries?" Such ignorance of official policies was, of course, in no small part due to widespread illiteracy and semi-literacy, especially among rural cadres. In particular, many cadres and Party members of peasant origin were unable to understand the concept of working class leadership. Thus when 114 Party members in four branches under the Tangshan Municipal Committee were asked what class the Party represented, some replied it was a peasant party, still others that it was the party of the poor. After two or three days study, there were still only 70 to 80 percent who could give the "correct" answer that the Communist Party was a working class party. Moreover, peasant cadres argued that urban workers had not made a significant contribution to the revolution and only declared their loyalty to the CCP after liberation by the rural based Party.[50]

Party members also held many simple notions of Communism. Some members could only speak of Communism in crude materialistic terms of eating bread and riding about in cars. These people had no notion of class struggle and production struggle being necessary for the realization of a Communist society. Others considered Communism in terms of common property, eating out of the same bowl and wearing the same clothes.[51] The egalitarian tone of their views clearly reflected the radical aspect of social revolution which also contributed to "agrarian socialist thought" (see below). Such attitudes indicated the inability of many cadres and Party members to grasp the complex nature of the Party's short term and long term goals, and the fact that the attainment of those goals would be a prolonged and intricate process. Lacking sufficient political consciousness, many Party cadres could not adequately perform the leadership roles required of them at a time of shifting policy lines.

Ideological Deviance and Official Policy: Agrarian Socialist and Rich Peasant Thought

The low level of ideological and political awareness among Party officials was not simply due to illiteracy and the lack of systematic indoctrination. This problem was further caused by ambiguities in Party policies concerning the relative emphasis between stability and transformation, between production and social revolution. While such matters were debated in high Party councils, low ranking cadres were frequently confused by conflicts among the CCP's various long and short term goals.

This was clearly the case with "agrarian socialist thought" *(nongcun shehuizhuyi sixiang),* a tendency attacked in both the 1950 and 1951–54 campaigns which reflected an important contradiction in CCP rural programs. While land reform undercut rich peasants politically to advance social revolution in the countryside, their economic position—i.e., the "rich peasant economy"—was initially protected in order to restore production. Rural cadres found these imperatives difficult to reconcile and some tried to apply the land reform policy of "depend on farm laborers and poor peasants, unite with middle peasants" to production problems. This meant, in effect, resisting official policies of freedom for money lending, buying and selling land, hiring labor and leasing land which were aimed at reviving the rural economy. Thus an overly zealous adherence to class distinctions stressed during the civil war and retained in the post-liberation land reform program hindered current economic policy.[52]

The official preoccupation with restoring production in the immediate post-1949 period, however, led many basic level cadres to overlook the longer range goals of the CCP. During the 1951–54 movement particular concern was voiced over those who held that with nationwide victory or with the completion of land reform the aims of the revolution had been realized and there was no need for further struggle. Some Party members were reported to have felt that since no more revolutionary work remained, the time had come for the Party to reward them for past achievements. Others felt there was no need for continued sacrifice and they should take the land, cows and houses gained during land reform and retire from politics. Such sentiments as "with land reform over an old cadre should quit," and "I will no longer serve as a cadre but will engage entirely in production" apparently were widespread even in old liberated areas. For example, a survey of 87 branches in Shanxi showed only half of over 1,000 members were politically active while in a district in newly liberated Zhejiang eight of 10 *xiang* cadres wanted to devote their time to production rather than politics.[m]

---

[m] *XHYB,* July 1951, p. 536; *CJRB,* March 1, 1952, in *SCMP,* No. 299; and *Shanxi ribao* [Shanxi Daily], January 8, 1953. This, of course, was due to more than the official emphasis on production. It also resulted from the great burdens of local leadership. As some basic level cadres complained: "If we don't do a good job, we get criticized by the higher level. If our attitude isn't good the masses complain. If we neglect our farms, the wives grumble. So, the best thing is not to be a cadre." *Zhejiang ribao* [Zhejiang Daily], January 27, 1952.

CCP policies contributed not only to the withdrawal from political involvement, but also to "rich peasant thought" *(funong sixiang)*—another target of the 1951–54 rectification movement. Rich peasant thinking included but went beyond emphasizing production at the expense of political matters. Cadres not only promoted activities such as the "four major freedoms" which were officially viewed as exploitative but permissible as transitional measures, they also engaged in such activities themselves. Of all measures to restore production in the consolidation years, these were the most risky politically and required constant attention to prevent their getting out of hand. In some areas, however, cadres were said to have pushed the four freedoms enthusiastically without appropriate restraints. Thus reports spoke of rural cadres propagating "the glory of money lending." Such action naturally led to inadequate attention to the needs of poor peasants and hired hands. In granting official loans the sole criteria sometimes was ability to repay, with the result that most loans went to middle peasants. Efforts to encourage patriotic production drives rather than individual enrichment were also hindered, as was the development of collective forms of production—the mutual aid teams and APCs.

Even more disturbing were indications that Party members themselves were actively pursuing individual enrichment *via* the four freedoms, including such extreme forms as usury and speculation. Basic level Party members rationalized these activities with such statements as "hiring a long term laborer is not exploitation but taking the lead in developing production." As with the more general problem of withdrawal from political activities, this behavior was found in old as well as newly liberated areas. Thus an analysis of 185 rural Party branches with over 5,000 members in Shanxi concluded that in 21 percent of the branches members either engaged widely in various forms of exploitation or had deteriorated in that direction. And an investigation of a Shandong village revealed that a third of its Party members had been hiring labor for years. With such blatant pursuit of private gain widespread, it is not surprising that many cadres either refused to participate or only formally participated in mutual aid teams. It was found that only 30 percent of Party members in 3,847 rural Shandong branches joined mutual aid teams, and even in comparatively advanced areas the figure was only 40 to 50 percent. This evidence demonstrates that in a context where capitalist activity was encouraged, exploitative activity tolerated and cadres themselves were upwardly mobile property owners, rich peasants, in Thomas Bernstein's words, had become a reference group. They served as a model not only for the mass of ordinary peasants, but also for a significant segment of basic level Party leaders.[53]

With ambivalence existing at the highest levels concerning the emphasis on economic recovery and social transformation, it is not surprising that semiliterate basic level cadres were unsure of the direction of rural policy and many seized upon official encouragement of individual enrichment to justify their personal inclinations.

The Cadre in Rural Society

The strength of rich peasant ideas among rural cadres and Party members indicates how deeply they were influenced by their immediate environment. Another aspect of this problem was the complex web of particularistic ties which entangled the new elite and impeded social revolution in the Chinese countryside. Cadres reportedly were guilty of the "five sames" *(wutong jiyi),* that is, trusting their own relatives, brothers, co-workers, schoolmates and fellow townsmen without bothering to check into their political background.[54] A striking example of the importance of family relations occurred in a village where meetings of the Party branch were held in the home of the propaganda committeeman. The mother of the committeeman, who was not a Party member, participated in the branch meetings and her disapproval could change branch decisions. The village masses were said to believe that she was the real head of the village and called her "the queen mother."[55] In situations such as these it was obvious that Party branches could not be an effective force for political and social change.

A major concern of rectification in the early 1950s was to root out of the Party "alien elements" *(yijifenzi)*—landlords, counterrevolutionaries, secret agents, people with links to the GMD, former members of religious sects, and corrupt officials—who utilized the power of their positions to sabotage official policies, pursue personal enrichment and engage in despotic conduct toward the peasants.[56] But an even more significant obstacle to revolutionary change was the subtle involvement of Party members and cadres with such alien forces outside the Party, particularly the landlord class.[57] This involvement was demonstrated by the Little Pine Hill Murder incident which was exposed in Central Guangdong in 1952.

The Little Pine Hill Murder case concerned the murder of a landlord by his wife's lover, also a landlord, in this rural area. The murderer then plotted with other landlords to frame a peasant leader who had been causing trouble. The frame-up succeeded and the peasant leader was executed. When the case subsequently came to light, it was revealed that the guilty landlord entertained and gave gifts to county court personnel sent to investigate the case. When these cadres nevertheless proceeded to arrest the wife of the slain man, the guilty landlord bribed them, obtained her release, and arranged the frame-up of the peasant. The investigation of the case disclosed that a high percentage of the officials involved had served under the GMD regime including five of the preliminary investigators, the chief of the investigation section of the country public security bureau, and a judge of the Central Guangdong People's Court. The investigation further revealed that over 20 former GMD officials and landlords held important posts in the county government, public security bureau and court.

This case illuminated several key factors in the continuing landlord influence. One was the use of material blandishments ranging from the subtle use of entertainment to outright bribery. Another factor was the large number of retained personnel in official positions due to the lack of trained Communist cadres. Such personnel were used to dealing with the old rural elite and predisposed to their interests. By relying on such people Party officials were also drawn into favoring those interests. But perhaps the most important factor was the influence of "feudal" ties, particularly clan ties, on the behavior of leading Communist officials. Overall responsibility for the Little Pine Hill Murder incident was laid at the door of county magistrate Zheng Dingnuo. A revolutionary guerrilla for over 10 years, Zheng was said to have been responsible for the large scale recruitment of former GMD personnel and landlords into government organs. The role of clan ties was crucial, for Zheng had never severed his ties to the landlords of his clan and after liberation gave many of them government posts. When he assumed office these landlords are reported to have said, "now the Zheng clan has a magistrate in Uncle Dingnuo," and the people referred to the county government as "the family shrine of the Zheng clan."[58]

The persistent strength of clan and family, and of other traditional ties such as nationality, native place and school ties, clearly had a deep influence on rural politics. Not only were many cases of shielding landlords traced to attempts to protect relatives, but the overall impact of such influences also retarded the restructuring of society. In areas where cadres had extensive clan ties, they were apparently unwilling to implement enthusiastically such programs as land reform. Even where social transformation ostensibly proceeded actively, the influence of clan relations still existed as in an "advanced" Henan *xiang* where active struggle was carried out against the landlords of one clan, while those of other clans were protected.[59] While land reform and other rural policies directly undermined the political and economic power of the traditional upper strata, Party rectification combatted the above forms of residual old elite influence on the new rulers of rural China.

Urban Life and the Erosion of Revolutionary Values

In the cities the Three Anti Campaign dealt with similar problems which went well beyond the "three evils" of corruption, waste and bureaucracy. Although claiming that corruption was much less of a problem than under the GMD, *Renmin ribao* declared its extent so great as to represent an "attack by the bourgeois camp."[60] As official statements elaborated the nature of this attack it became clear that concern was as much with the entire pattern of interrelations of Party and state officials with the bourgeois class as with actual acts of corruption. Much as Party rectification in rural areas attacked involvement of cadres with remnants of the old social structure, the *sanfan* movement reflected an effort to rectify such relationships in urban China.

The consequences of the CCP entering the cities were frequently discussed during the campaign. A *Renmin ribao* editorial early in the movement depicted the effect of urban life on many tested revolutionary cadres:

> . . . [A]fter their arrival in the cities the longstanding revolutionary cadres were exposed to the evil influences of imperialism and feudal bureaucracy handed down by the GMD reactionary clique, and they quickly degenerated, accepted bribes to prevent justice, profited from fraudulent practices, and became harmful insects in the activities of the people's revolution.[61]

As in the countryside, many cadres felt that with victory attained the time had come to enjoy its fruits. The bourgeoisie was accused of taking advantage of this situation by adopting two tactics—the methods of "pulling over" and "sending in." The former method involved corrupting cadres already serving in official organs. The latter concerned introducing prospective employees to state enterprises and government organs. An example of "sending in" was the Dalian General Goods Company where 1,200 of 1,300 employees were alleged to have been appointed through introductions from private merchants. The inference was that they remained beholden to these merchants.[62] Regarding "pulling over," a suggestive descriptive was given of various blandishments used by the bourgeoisie:

> The bourgeoisie wins over cadres by first propagating the bourgeois life style, then introducing them to dinner parties, gifts, commissions, etc., then engaging them in corrupt activities, partnerships, contracted marriages . . . .[63]

Of particular concern to CCP leaders was the adoption of bourgeois values, attitudes and life style by Party and government officials. Apparently many cadres viewed corruption and waste as natural and acceptable. They reportedly said: "corruption and degeneration are minor things and have no bearing on the cause of revolution"; "it does not matter if one squeezes [graft] as long as it is not discovered"; "waste is unavoidable"; "having left the rural areas for the city one has to live a little better to suit the environment"; and so forth. Moreover, the "grand manner" and "style" of the bourgeoisie were admired, officials who wasted money were regarded as "generous men," and cadres who fattened themselves at the expense of the public were considered "capable" and "competent." In contrast, those who were frugal and adhered strictly to discipline were called "niggardly" and "country bumpkins."[64] In addition, the united front policy calling for the continued existence of the national bourgeoisie was said to have been misinterpreted to allow unlawful acts by capitalists. Officials sympathized with capitalists and were impressed with their abilities, saying "capitalists are such capable businessmen we must rely on them." These attitudes resulted in such tendencies as compromising with speculation by private merchants and granting them favorable tax breaks.[65]

Such sentiments were in large measure attributed to inadequate political education. Faced with problems of economic restoration and construction, urban cadres were said to have felt "one can work without political study but one can't earn bread without technical ability." But as with similar problems in the countryside, certainly much of the susceptibility of urban cadres to bourgeois values can be attributed to the nature of CCP policies in the 1949–51 period. In addition to the emphasis on a broad united front, the substantial role given to private industry and commerce in reviving the economy, marked as it was by extensive efforts to encourage and reassure capitalists, inevitably led to close and even cordial relations between government officials and the bourgeoisie. Official policy of course was two-edged with restrictions placed on capitalist development, but as long as economic recovery was a high priority goal, orthodox Marxist suspicion of the bourgeoisie was played down. Particularly vulnerable under these circumstances were the large numbers of new cadres and retained personnel who had to be relied on in the early post-liberation period. Not only were these types lacking in political education, but retained personnel often had well developed ties with businessmen dating from the pre-liberation period. Thus it is not surprising that the official media reported they were the most affected by the "three evils."[66]

The vulnerability of new cadres and especially retained personnel to corruption was indicated by several reports claiming that over 98 percent of all corruption in given areas was committed by these groups.[n] Party leaders, however, were also deeply concerned with corruption committed by significant numbers of old cadres. A typical case concerned five cadres in Wuhan's urban-rural liaison division. These cadres, including the Party branch secretary and Youth League secretary, were all old cadres who had joined the Party in the 1940–46 period. Despite their revolutionary background, these officials became corrupt while exercising power. They embezzled funds, recruited relatives and fellow townsmen of dubious political backgrounds, extorted sexual favors from female workers, and suppressed democracy within the unit.[67]

The great bulk of corruption was found in economic organs such as state factories and mines, state trading companies, government financial offices, communications departments, etc. The forms of corruption in financial and economic units were many: stealing state property; forging accounts and misappropriating funds; accepting bribes; selling economic information to capitalists; colluding with businessmen in the use of inferior materials, overcharging and evading taxes; smuggling; engaging in black market activities; and acting as agents of capitalists when handling labor disputes.[68] Apart from economic departments,

[n] *RMRB,* November 23, December 9, 1951. This claim, as well as the general assertion that these groups were the most affected by the "three evils," conceivably was an attempt to justify the purge of retained personnel (see below) rather than an objective statement. But given the pre-1949 ties of retained personnel to the bourgeoisie and past instances of Party cadre hostility toward urban businessmen (see Kenneth Lieberthal, "Mao Versus Liu? Policy towards Industry and Commerce: 1946–49," *CQ,* No. 47 (1971), pp. 496–99, 511–12), it appears likely that there was an objective basis for such assertions.

perhaps the most significant arena for corruption was legal institutions. Judicial officials were reported to have taken bribes from lawbreaking capitalists and counterrevolutionaries or conversely extorted money from them.[69]

Closely linked to corruption were various "degenerate" *(tuihua)* acts committed by urban cadres. Much of this was alleged to have grown out of close personal contact with capitalists and other questionable elements. Officials joined such people in eating and drinking parties and on visits to brothels. A frequent charge concerned the involvement of cadres with women from the bourgeois and landlord classes which was especially galling when officials deserted their cadre wives of worker and peasant origin. In one case a high police official was alleged to have allowed a female GMD spy with whom he was sexually involved to travel back and forth to Taiwan. The net result of such involvements was to shield capitalists and landlords from punishment and often to collude with them in illegal acts.[70] As with corruption, the CCP's concern was as much with the implications of a political alliance between members of the official elite and suspect social groups as with the degenerate acts themselves. Revolutionary programs could only be sustained in China's cities if such links were thoroughly broken.

The Implementation of Rectification

In combating the deviations of the early 1950s, rectification movements varied in the sections of the elite singled out as targets, the instrumentalities used to conduct the process, and the relative emphasis on persuasive and coercive methods. In terms of geographic, functional, urban/rural, Party/non-Party and administrative level focus, some clear differences appeared despite the nationwide nature of each campaign.

As befit the relatively decentralized conditions of the period, the implementation of rectification often varied by area. In the 1950 campaign a fundamental distinction was made between the newly liberated areas of East China, the Central-South, the Northwest and the Southwest where rectification was to be concluded before winter so that land reform could begin, and Northeast and North China were it could continue until spring planting in 1951. Furthermore, the campaign had different emphases in different areas—e.g., the Central-South's rectification plans were closely integrated with preparations for land reform while those in the Northeast, China's most advanced industrial area, stressed economic work. Regional variations naturally were also pronounced in the 1951–54 Party rectification given its prolonged duration. This movement began in the old liberated areas of Northeast and North China were the CCP organizational structure was most developed and it spread gradually to the newly liberated regions. Similarly, the Three Anti Campaign was initially carried out in an old liberated area, the Northeast, where both the relatively strong CCP organization and the concentration of industry provided optimal conditions for a trial run of a campaign centering on China's economic institutions.[71]

The Three Anti Campaign was the only rectification effort of the period with a clear functional focus: in addition to financial and economic units, police and legal organs as well as cultural and educational units received particular attention due to their vulnerability to corruption. Moreover, given the stress on breaking the ties between the elite and the bourgeoisie and the claim that the overwhelming majority of Three Anti corruption cases occurred in collusion with private businessmen, the movement virtually merged with the Five Anti Campaign opposing bribery, tax evasion, theft of state property, cheating on government contracts, and stealing state economic secrets for private speculation which centered on private enterprises. In contrast to this urban emphasis, the New Three Anti Campaign focused on the problems of rural areas which had been neglected during the Three and Five Anti period while the 1950 and 1951–54 movements dealt equally with rural and urban institutions.[72]

Apart from the concentration of the 1951–54 Party rectification on basic level branches, the other movements of the consolidation years encompassed all administrative levels up to central Party and government bodies. In the 1950 movement, however, there was only minimal involvement of central ministries as the explicit focus was on the large administrative regions and their subordinate levels, particularly the basic levels where the main deviation under attack—commandism—was primarily a problem. Similarly, when commandism was again criticized in 1953 the rural district and village levels were singled out along with bureaucratism at the county level.[73] As we shall see, it was only in the Three Anti Campaign that rectification in central units apparently resulted in significant disciplinary measures. Moreover, the *sanfan* drive was the only one to affect (marginally) those making up the powerful elite of Central Committee members, Government Administrative Council (GAC) members, ministers and vice ministers, members of large region administrative committees, provincial Party secretaries, governors and vice governors, and Party secretaries, mayors and deputy mayors of major cities.

In all rectification movements of the early 1950s non-Party personnel were drawn into the process. This was not only due to the importance of correcting deviations among the vast numbers of non-Party cadres, but also—as in the 1951–54 campaign—in order to recruit non-Party activists into the new expanding elite. But in only one case—the Three Anti Campaign—was a particular segment of the elite, retained personnel, apparently singled out as a special target for disciplinary sanctions.

Coercive and Persuasive Methods

The rectification efforts of the early post-liberation period differed considerably in the degree of coercion and persuasion invoked. The 1950 and 1953 campaigns were by all evidence persuasive in emphasis as one would expect in consolidation phases where relatively manageable shortcomings were at issue. The 1951–54 movement, on the other hand, had the highest Party purge rate—effectively 10 percent—of any post-1949 campaign for which figures are available.[o] And the Three Anti Campaign made substantial use of the most severe sanctions at the disposal of the CCP.

Despite the silence of official reports on the extent and types of disciplinary measures taken, by most available indications the 1950 movement was a mild one. Apart from evidence that the most visible national, regional, provincial and municipal level leaders were virtually untouched,[74] the emphasis of the campaign was explicitly to educate the majority rather than punish a minority. Moreover, reports on the movement in the villages of old liberated areas imply very few expulsions of Party members.[75] Finally, an examination of Party membership figures does not indicate a significant purge. From the June 1950 Central Committee plenum when Mao called for a virtual halt to rural Party recruitment to the end of the year CCP membership increased by about 1.3 million. While it remains possible that the overall increase hides a substantial number of expulsions, this seems unlikely given the stringent restrictions on recruitment in the villages while rectification was in progress.[76]

The mildness of the campaign can also be deduced from its practical orientation reflecting a high priority attached to the efficient performance of governmental functions. Great emphasis was placed on integrating rectification and regular work; documents under study included detailed policy decisions on current tasks as well as theoretical tracts on self-criticism.[77] Press reports insisted the proper way to implement the campaign was to investigate the ordinary affairs of the unit concerned, and strong criticism was leveled at tendencies to carry out rectification in an abstract fashion without dealing with actual problems encountered in performing duties. This emphasis on the regular tasks of administrative units indicates not only minimum disruption of work routine, it also implies strict curbs on coercive measures which would result in such disruption.[p]

---

[o] As later chapters indicate, the purge rate in rectification efforts from 1959 to 1965 may have been higher than in the early 1950s, but no comprehensive statistics exist to document the point.

[p] A few reports appeared which did not fit the above picture of a mild campaign. These accounts indicated considerable uneasiness and fear on the part of participants. Some anxiety was no doubt reasonable, but reports that when a meeting was called cadres desperately sought to learn whether it was a rectification meeting, and felt relieved if it was not, suggest tension out of all proportion to the methods employed. It is noteworthy, moreover, that none of the media descriptions of such fears linked them to excesses in the actual conduct of rectification. While an explanation must remain speculative, some evidence indicates that significant numbers of old cadres may have been made uneasy by memories of the 1947–48 campaign, while new cadres who faced rectification for the first time grappled with fear of the unknown. On balance, it does not seem that deep anxieties were especially widespread during the 1950 movement. See *CJRB,* July 10, 31, August 9, 1950.

The apparent persuasive orientation of the 1950 campaign was appropriate to the problems confronted—problems which were seen as non-antagonistic contradictions stemming from difficulties cadres had in adjusting to new responsibilities and policies, uneasy relations of diverse types within the new administrative structure, and the general inability of Party authorities to provide adequate ideological training in the final days of the civil war. These were all matters of achieving a proper understanding of a new and complex situation, and thus suited to an educational approach.

Many of the same factors applied in 1953 during the New Three Anti Campaign, again resulting in lenient rectification methods. The central problems under attack—bureaucratism and commandism—were again non-antagonistic, and the system had entered a new consolidation phase. Despite the fact that some violations of law and discipline clearly called for coercive measures, disciplinary action was supposed to supersede education only where serious errors led to great damage and the guilty refused to reform. In addition, a persuasive approach was facilitated by injunctions that the campaign should not disrupt regular work and its emphasis on improving administrative efficiency as tasks multiplied in rural China.[78]

In the absence of comprehensive statistics no precise picture can be drawn of the disciplinary sanctions employed in the *xinsanfan* campaign. While it does appear that in basic level Party organizations the high weeding out rate of the coordinate 1951–54 movement continued (see below), other evidence suggests an infrequent use of harsh sanctions. Not only were there no identifiable dismissals of officials of Central Committee rank, ministers and vice ministers, top regional leaders, or provincial and municipal Party and government leaders,[79] but no mention was made of disciplining lower ranking central officials in reports on anti-bureaucratic struggles carried out in a number of ministries. There were some reports, however, of dismissals and lesser disciplinary measures in cases involving lower ranking regional, provincial and municipal cadres, as well as of purges of special district, county and village leaders.[80] While the frequency of disciplinary sanctions cannot be measured, reports of formal measures were far less frequent than in 1951–52 and there is no indication that the New Three Anti Campaign saw the severe legal punishments, intense struggle sessions or cadre suicides which had been a feature of the *sanfan* drive.

In many ways the Three Anti Campaign was the most severe rectification movement of the 1950–53 period. This was not simply a reflection of the sanctions employed. In a sense, the implementation of the campaign was a classic attempt to manipulate coercive techniques by shifting from "assault" to "leniency," although the success of this effort is open to question. This can be seen by examining the unfolding of the various stages of the movement.

After an initial stage of "democratic inspection" involving the discussion of general problems within individual units and the exposure of small scale corruption cases, the movement underwent a significant intensification as it entered its second, critical stage—that of "tiger hunting" *(dahu)*. The pressures brought to bear in this stage resemble the "unfreezing" phase of attitudinal change. The aim was not only to expose major corrupt elements, "big tigers," but also to demoralize those "tigers" thoroughly and arouse mass hatred of the bourgeois class. Thus emphasis was placed on links between acts of corruption and more general bourgeois exploitation of the working class past and present. No precise definition of "tigers" was given, but it was estimated that Guangzhou's 500 to 600 "big tigers" took on the average ¥200 million in graft, while the average graft of its 4,000 to 5,0000 "medium and small tigers" was placed at ¥30 million. "Tigers" were considered the most resourceful and hardest to expose of those guilty of corruption. Because their defiant attitude was supposed to have a detrimental effect on others, breaking their resistance was crucial to the success of the movement.

The assault on "tigers" was led by "tiger hunting teams" *(dahudui)* of activists selected from ordinary unit personnel. These teams gathered information on corruption and led struggles against selected targets. The severity of the "tiger hunting" stage was evident in several ways. Struggle meetings within units were frequent and intense; psychological pressure and verbal abuse were sometimes accompanied by physical blows. As a result, suicides by those suffering humiliation were frequent. Moreover, during this stage many institutions stopped work entirely, others worked half day shifts, and still others kept only skeleton staffs at work so that as many as possible could participate in the movement. The result was considerable disruption of production and administrative routine. Severity was also manifested in mass trials and harsh criminal punishments. for example, a mass trial of seven major corrupt elements was held in Beijing on February 1, 1952. The accused included the former head of the administrative office of the Ministry of Public Security and a former deputy director of the rear supply office of the People's Revolutionary Military Council. All seven received heavy sentences and two were executed on the spot.[81]

Following this fierce "assault," a shift to "leniency" came with the third stage of disposing of cases. This involved systematically meting out penalties to corrupt elements exposed earlier in close coordination with efforts to recover funds which had been lost as graft. General principles and a detailed set of guidelines for the handling of *sanfan* cases were approved by the GAC on March 8, 1952.[82] These general principles highlighted the reform element. Cases were to be handled with "an attitude of serious treatment and magnanimity," and with "a policy coordinating reform with punishment." More specifically, severe punishment was prescribed for those who refused to admit guilt, and leniency for those who made frank confessions and performed "meritorious service" by exposing others or returning stolen funds.

Detailed regulations divided corrupt elements into four categories on the basis of the amount of graft: (1) less than ¥1 million; (2) ¥1 to 10 million; (3) ¥10 to 100 million; and (4) over ¥100 million. The higher the amount of graft the harsher punishment tended to be,[q] although confessions and "meritorious service" could ameliorate even the most serious cases. in addition, a similar scheme of seven categories of waste was defined together with suggested penalties. These penalties, however, were considerably milder than those for corruption and throughout the campaign cases of waste and bureaucratism were generally treated with considerable leniency.

This distinction supports the hypothesis advanced in Chapter 2 that while coercion is appropriate for serious anti-social acts, persuasion is better suited to remedying relatively minor shortcomings of cadres who basically accept the official value system. Notwithstanding the tolerant attitudes attributed to cadres and the social acceptability of personal favoritism, large scale corruption was dubious behavior according to non-Communist as well as official values. Therefore, propaganda directed at broad groups, most notably workers, not only was undoubtedly effective in spreading antagonism toward corrupt activities and in undermining the social status of businessmen by linking them to corruption, it probably was also a significant factor in obtaining popular acquiescence to coercive measures against the relatively narrow group alleged to be guilty of such acts. For less serious problems such as bureaucratic shortcomings, however, it is unlikely that popular distaste of a similar intensity could be tapped, quite apart from the problems of cadre morale that would have been created by a harsh approach to such deviations.

Although the GAC regulations sanctioned a broad range of penalties including capital punishment, steps were taken to uphold the traditional emphasis on education and reform embodied in the decision. When the principle of leniency for confession was not strictly implemented at first and corrupt elements generally received severe punishment regardless, meetings were called to stress the educational function.[83] The importance attached to changed attitudes and "meritorious service" also helped recover graft since there would be no better evidence of reform than surrendering one's tainted gains or exposing others who had stolen from the state. More broadly, the shift in emphasis from "assault" to "leniency," from a heavily coercive approach to a more persuasive one, should have enhanced the overall effectiveness of the campaign in achieving attitudinal change. But evidence drawn from refugee accounts in particular casts doubt on the success of the movement in this respect. This evidence indicates that the

[q] According to a non-Party participant in the drafting of these regulations who later defected from the PRC, there was debate concerning the amount of graft for which the death sentence could be imposed. Figures of ¥15 and ¥30 million were proposed, but Peng Zhen is reported to have objected that these limits were too low and would result in widespread killing of middle echelon cadres. Ultimately, no specific limit for the death penalty was set as Party leaders became aware that numerous cases of large graft existed and to have set a figure could have resulted in excessive executions. Chow Ching-wen, *Ten Years of Storm: The True Story of the Communist Regime in China* (New York: Holt, Rinehart and Winston, 1960), pp. 124–25.

assault frequently went too far and crossed the threshold beyond which coercion becomes counterproductive, resulting in alienation, paralyzing fear and unresponsiveness to "rational" argument among many of those who did not take the extreme course of suicide.[84] Nevertheless, the relaxation of tension did limit demoralization and thus help restore production and administrative activity, however limited its contribution to creating new values within the target groups may have been.

The final stage of the movement, together with the conclusion of the Five Anti Campaign, combined tangible blandishments with leniency in an effort to offset economic disruption. Loans and government orders were given to private enterprises where *wufan* disruptions had caused a serious business slump, tax assessments were lowered, and fines drastically reduced. Moreover, in state enterprises where emphasis on Three Anti work and neglect of production resulted in unfilled vacancies left by purged personnel, increased accidents, and decreased quantity and quality of production, attention was now given to production leadership. Responsible officials were instructed to take technical and work ability into consideration as mitigating factors when handling cases of corruption.[85] These measures further dissipated tensions created by the coercive approach earlier in the Three and Five Anti Campaigns.

Tangible appeals were also emphasized in the recruitment and promotion of cadres, another prominent feature of the final, "constructive" stage of the *sanfan* movement. Calls for the "bold promotion" of cadres cited the need to replace large numbers of corrupt elements dismissed from government organs and state enterprises. The number of activists emerging during the *sanfan* movement is said to have exceeded by far those ousted for corruption; the best were trained and given responsible positions. According to one report, 88,400 cadres were promoted in the latter part of the Three Anti Campaign, including 5,649 to leadership posts at the county level. A later report stated that, in the months following the *sanfan* movement, over 375,500 cadres were promoted including 24,500 at the county level and above. Moreover, efforts were made to recruit *sanfan* activists into the Party in coordination with the 1951–54 rectification movement.[86]

While the *sanfan* movement clearly was a severe one, the precise contours of the purge accompanying it are not easily definable. The evidence does suggest, however, that in terms of purge rate the movement was less severe than the coordinate Party rectification. On a nationwide basis, the only statistic found simply reported that during the Three Anti Campaign 4.5 percent of all "government employees" *(guojia gongwu renyuan)* were found guilty of varying degrees of corruption, waste and bureaucratism, and received (unspecified) disciplinary action accordingly.[87] Since a total of 3,836,000 officials at the county level and above reportedly participated in the movement, the number of cadres at these levels who received some form of disciplinary punishment can be estimated at about 173,000. Of these, 105,000 (2.7 percent of the total participating) were found guilty of extracting ¥10 million or more by corrupt practices and thus were potentially subject to criminal punishment under the GAC regulations.[88]

While no figures were given on the numbers actually expelled from the bureaucracy, it seems reasonable to conclude that most (although not all) of the officials found guilty of ¥10 million or more graft were ousted while only a minority of those guilty of lesser graft were removed. Thus the purge rate for all state officials would be of the order of 3 percent, decidedly less than the 10 percent weeded out during Party rectification. Of course, the fact that cadres in basic level economic enterprises may not have been included in the "government employee" category could understate the disciplinary impact,[r] but there is little to indicate that *sanfan* purges of basic level urban cadres reached the 10 percent figure. Where statistics were found on basic level economic enterprises, although it was often reported that 30 to 40 percent of the personnel were guilty of some form of corruption, the great majority of these acts were considered minor and handled without disciplinary action. When listing the various means used to dispose of cases, the most frequently recorded measures were voluntary confession *(zidong tanbai)* or exemption from disciplinary action.[89]

When disciplinary sanctions were meted out, they took the form of legal sanctions in a significant number of cases. While it is difficult to estimate the frequency of legal as opposed to administrative measures, one report for industrial departments and factories in East China held that legal sanctions were applied in 30 percent of the cases, the remainder being handled administratively.[90] As to the severity of criminal sanctions, again little can be said with precision. There were voluminous references to prison sentences of varying lengths and reform through labor apparently was used on a wide scale.[91] Although the death penalty was reported infrequently, there were enough references to capital punishment to indicate it played an important role.[92] Thus although formal disciplinary measures seemingly were invoked on a relatively modest scale, once used they tended in a significant proportion of cases to be criminal sanctions, including the most severe, as would be expected in a movement with pronounced coercive overtones.

As indicated earlier, there are many indications that the campaign was primarily directed at retained personnel. Apart from official assertions that such people (along with newly recruited cadres) were most susceptible to the "three evils," refugee accounts view the removal of holdovers from the GMD and their replacement by cadres loyal to the new regime as *the* aim of the movement. Such accounts suggest that while corruption was a genuine target of the movement, *sanfan* attacks were frequently leveled at people with ties to the old regime

[r] "State cadres" *(guojia ganbu)*, which may or may not be equivalent to "government employees," apparently have included administrative cadres in state enterprises. Whether this was the case at the time of the *sanfan* campaign is uncertain. Moreover, it is also unclear whether cadres in joint state-private and private enterprises were so classified.

whose sins were more a lack of wholehearted commitment to the Party's cause than any actual graft. Indeed, official propaganda directed at bourgeois *values* lends credibility to this view. Moreover, reducing dependence on retained personnel was a CCP goal since the founding of the PRC. By the time of the Three Anti Campaign enough new personnel had been recruited and trained to make significant dismissals of GMD holdovers feasible. Nevertheless, it is clear that the *sanfan* drive did not mean a clean sweep of all retained personnel. Not only were many kept on only to fall in later movements such as the 1955–57 purge of counterrevolutionaries, but the overall disciplinary rate indicates the great majority were kept in government service. For while it is likely that the 4.5 percent figure hides a higher disciplinary rate for retained personnel, their numbers in official positions were clearly large enough that any unusual purge of the group (say, over 15 percent) would have driven the overall rate above 5 percent. In any case, the sharp struggles of the *sanfan* movement undoubtedly did at least as much as actual purging to weaken the position of holdover officials.[93]

As would be expected, given both the focus on retained personnel and the apparent absence of leadership conflict over the course of the movement, the highest national policy makers were unaffected by *sanfan* discipline. Looking at the top political elite more broadly yields a similar finding; no Central Committee members, ministers or vice ministers were purged at this time.[94] Nevertheless, significant purging did take place in central ministries at less exalted ranks; numerous cases of dismissals from bureau *(qu)*, office *(shi)* and division *(chu)* posts were reported. The same pattern appeared at the large region level with the top Party and administrative figures unscathed but purges of department *(bu)*, office and division leaders reported in most areas. Another significant category of officials dismissed during the movement was leading personnel in nationally and regionally important state enterprises.[95]

At the provincial level, some of the very highest officials were affected by the movement. As already noted, the governor and vice governors of Jiangxi undertook self-criticism, as did Party secretaries in Hebei. There is direct evidence, however, of only one official of this rank actually receiving disciplinary punishment: Jilin Governor Zhou Chiheng was charged with "violation of law" and dismissed in April 1952.[96] On the other hand, there is ample evidence of dismissals and expulsions at the departmental *(bu* or *ting)*, bureau and division levels of provincial Party and government bureaucracies. Similarly, at the municipal level, at least one Party secretary and six mayors and deputy mayors of cities of various sizes were removed from office, as well as many lower ranking officials in Party and government organs.[97]

Moreover, the Three Anti Campaign also had a disciplinary impact at rural intermediate levels. Cases of dismissals of county Party secretaries and magistrates, in addition to lower ranking figures, were reported from all areas of China. In a number of cases, corruption was so widespread that entire county Party committees were disbanded.[98] And in at least one case a corrupt special district Party secretary was sentenced to death during the *sanfan* drive.[99] Of course, the most voluminous reports of disciplinary measures (although regrettably scanty in comprehensive statistics) deal with basic level economic organs.

In sum, the coercive nature of the Three Anti Campaign led to far harsher and more widespread disciplinary sanctions than was the case in the 1950 and 1953 movements. This was not simply due to the use of extreme criminal punishments and severe struggle; it was also reflected in the level of people affected. Unlike the other movements, cases of sanctions in central organs were reported, including the most severe against Party members of considerable rank. Similarly, there were far more reports of discipline at the regional, provincial and municipal levels, including leading political figures such as governors and mayors who had been untouched in 1950 and 1953. Nevertheless, there was a similarity to the other campaigns: the lower the administrative level concerned the more likely the most responsible political figures were involved. Moreover, where responsible leaders at the higher levels were involved, they were brought to judgment not for policy advocacy but for some of the most flagrant breaches of law and discipline. Finally, despite the rooting out of corrupt individuals of both high and low station within the Party, the main thrust of the attack on corruption was directed at retained personnel with past ties to the GMD. The Three Anti Campaign ranged far and wide in Party and state bureaucracies as well as economic enterprises, but it tended to shy away from politically significant figures in the upper echelons while reserving the greatest harshness for the most vulnerable segment of the elite outside the Party.

In terms of severity, the 1951–54 Party rectification stood somewhere between the 1950 and 1953 movements, on the one hand, and the Three Anti Campaign on the other. While it is tempting to attribute this to the fact that the 1951–54 movement spanned both mobilization and consolidation phases, the evidence available cannot sustain such an interpretation and indeed argues against it: the relatively high rate of weeding out Party members during rectification apparently was unchanged for the duration of the movement.

In the absence of any real detail on the disciplinary techniques used against those weeded out of the Party, it is largely the purge rate itself which leads to the conclusions that the campaign was a relatively harsh one. In contrast to the 1950 and 1953 emphasis on avoiding indiscriminate punishment of cadres, the guidelines laid down in early 1951 made purging *(qingchu)* "bad elements" and taking "suitable measures" to oust Party members unwilling or unable to respond to education key measures for implementing Party rectification.[100] The scope of purging only became apparent during a February 1953 report by An Ziwen on the first two years of the movement. An announced in formula-like manner that 90 percent of Party members examined were found qualified for membership and 10 percent unqualified. Of the 10 percent, 3 to 5 percent were "bad elements" expelled from the Party; while 5 to 7 percent were (1) people who, after explanations were made to them, realized they lacked the qualifications of Party members and resigned voluntarily, and (2) "passive and backward elements" who resigned on advice of Party authorities.[101] While only the 3 to 5 percent were technically purged, the resignations under pressure bring the *de facto* purge rate to 10 percent.

An's assessment was made when the movement was far from complete. The formula, however, was repeated in April and again in July of 1953 when the movement was basically completed in the cities and in nearly twice as many rural branches as in February.[102] The absence of any revised estimate as the movement was implemented under changing conditions suggests that the 10 percent figure was as much an informal guideline as to how many *should be* removed from Party rolls as a statistical report on how many actually *had been* removed. The early 1953 report ostensibly summed up rectification results during a harsh period marked by the initial stages of PRC involvement in the Korean War and intensifying social policies in 1951–52. Yet the same degree of weeding out was indicated by the later statements which came as the war concluded and internal policy underwent a significant relaxation during the consolidation phase of 1953. Moreover, scattered local reports on the progress of rectification covering various periods from mid-1951 to the end of 1953 all indicated purging on the order of the 10 percent formula.[103] Thus it appears that during the mobilization phase of 1951–52 an informal purge quota was laid down which was sustained even after major changes in the political climate.[104]

Apart from the purge rate, evidence of coercive tendencies was provided by scattered reports of excessive harshness in overestimating "historical debts" *(lishishang de jiuzhang),* i.e., anti-Party activities before liberation, in treating problems requiring education as violations of law or discipline, and in reviving previously corrected mistakes as the basis for new disciplinary action. Such tendencies reportedly caused fear of rectification resulting in cadres running away or even committing suicide.[105]

Presumably, the threatening environment created by the Korean War may have been a factor in such phenomena and the high purge rate. Other more basic factors can also account for the extent of the purge, however. The rapid expansion of the CCP during the civil war and early post-liberation period, together with inadequacies in educational programs, meant many unqualified people had entered the Party. The worst of these clearly had to be expelled if ambitious programs of social transformation were to be realized. But despite the extensive weeding out of questionable Party members, the 1951–54 movement involved neither the calculated tension of the Three Anti Campaign nor the spontaneous excesses of the 1947–48 rectification. While conducting a needed purge, the leadership was determined that it not get out of hand and threaten the Party's existing organizational base. Not only was the lenient principle of "magnanimous treatment for past deeds, but rigorous treatment for new deeds" prescribed, but scattered reports suggest far fewer members were dismissed than were judged guilty of various offenses.[106] Most importantly, at the outset of the movement Mao warned that in persuading people to leave the Party, ". . . [We must] make sure that they withdraw of their own free will and that their feelings are not hurt. Don't repeat the practice of 'removing stones' as in 1948."[107] As we shall see, this limited the role of the masses in rectification as well as apparently avoiding the widespread use of extreme sanctions.

As had been the case during the Three Anti Campaign, the 1951–54 rectification campaign also made use of tangible appeals in the form of recruitment. The growth of the Party was substantial in these years with a net increase of about 800,000 from the end of 1950, when the Party had 5.8 million members, to the end of 1953 when the figure reached 6.6 million.[108] Since the 10 percent purge rate meant the weeding out of somewhere on the order of 580,000 members, roughly 1.38 million new members, or about 20 percent of the total membership as of the end of 1953, were added during the course of Party rectification.[s]

In addition to the high purge rate, other features of the period also enhanced the importance of Party recruitment and the related recruitment of cadres: the basic shortage of personnel at the time of takeover, the need to fill new posts created both by economic construction and by socialization measures in industry and agriculture, and the desirability of diminishing dependence on personnel retained from the GMD administration. Recruitment focused on activists who distinguished themselves during the movement and its coordinate campaigns, particularly the Three Anti Campaign. Moreover, it was a period of considerable upward mobility for those already in the Party, particularly as new positions were opened up by socialist transformation. Thus the tangible benefits available to those who participated actively in rectification and other political campaigns were considerable and played an important role alongside coercive and persuasive sanctions.

Conducting Rectification: Work Teams, Regular Party Bodies, and Restrictions on the Mass Line

Both of the approaches outlined in Chapter 2, reliance on the regular chain of command and the use of work teams, were employed in the conduct of rectifica-

---

[s] The expansion of Party membership, however, was not sufficient to provide vital Party organs at all levels of society. Even in the Northeast where CCP power had been firmly established for a considerable period, severe weaknesses in Party membership were reported in mid-1954. Despite an overall 35 percent increase in Party membership in the Northeast since June 1952, Party organization was notably weak in the countryside with 10 to 15 percent of rural villages without Party branches. It was said to be worse in suburban areas where, for example, 30 percent of a sample of APCs near Shenyang had no Party members. Party organizational weakness was still more pronounced in newly liberated areas. For example, in a Yunnan special district 80 percent of administrative villages lacked Party branches after the conclusion of the Party recruitment. DBRB, July 1, 1954, in SCMP-S, No. 887; and XHRB (Chongqing), July 1, 1954, in SCMP-S, No. 887.

In addition, many of the new recruits were of dubious quality due to the practice of forcing people to join in order to meet membership quotas, lowering membership standards and substituting reliance on surface manifestations of activism for thorough investigations of candidates. *CJRB*, June 24, 1952, in *CB*, No. 200.

tion during the early 1950s. The 1950 movement and the Three Anti and New Three Anti Campaigns were basically administered by the established Party authorities at each level, while in the 1951–54 movement both methods were used. Regardless of the approach adopted, throughout the consolidation years efforts were undertaken to prevent the excesses which had accompanied mass participation in the 1947–48 rectification campaign.

The 1950 campaign was systematically implemented through the regular chain of command, an approach suited to the relatively manageable problems of commandism, bureaucratism and inner elite tensions according to the hypothesis advanced in Chapter 2. The movement proceeded in orderly, level by level fashion from the top down on the theory that only personal involvement of leading personnel could provide proper leadership for the movement. Rectification measures were undertaken first by cadres at the large region level, and then at progressively lower levels, reaching down to village cadres in the countryside and factory and enterprise officials in the cities. A concrete example can be seen in the rectification plans of the CCP's North China Bureau. The North China plan called on the various provinces to select important cadres at the county and special district levels for rectification training before the fall harvest. After the harvest, county and special district committees could become training centers for district cadres. Finally, rectification of Party branches and training of village cadres would begin in the winter.[109] This procedure, by selecting leading cadres for training at higher levels and then returning them to their original units to lead rectification, facilitated control of the process by the established authorities at each level, and thus contributed to the non-disruptive, pragmatic orientation of the movement.

The 1950 movement's non-disruptive nature was reinforced by limits placed on mass participation. Although non-Party cadres were drawn into the rectification process as subjects and participants in criticism of work performance within individual units, they were denied a role in the determination of disciplinary sanctions. The guidelines for the campaign stipulated that discipline and purging were not the function of rectification meetings and training classes, but were to be handled by "specially responsible organs," presumably state supervisory and legal organs and Party control committees.[110] While there is no direct evidence of the activity of these "specially responsible organs," the very fact of separating the disciplinary function from the mass movement—in striking contrast to the village gates of 1947–48—suggests a conscious effort to prevent popular disruption of the disciplinary process.

Given similar circumstances in 1953, it is not surprising that the New Three Anti Campaign was also implemented through the regular chain of command without any significant mass initiative. Despite the use of high level inspection teams to monitor rectification in county, factory and village organs, and of work teams to teach local cadres administrative skills, these bodies did not clash with established local leaders.[111] More surprising, given the disruptive nature of the movement, was the implementation of the *sanfan* campaign by existing Party authorities. Although central and local Austerity Inspection Committees were set up to provide overall guidance, these were *ad hoc* bodies made up of key Party officials at each level. While these committees dispatched work teams to conduct checkups of keypoint basic level units, the inspection teams seemingly did not displace existing unit leaders as had occurred in 1947–48. Generally the functions of *sanfan* work teams appeared limited to conveying policies from above and gathering information on the campaign's progress. Cadres sent from higher levels did not usurp the functions of unit leaders but merely clarified Party policy for them so *they* could guide the movement. Moreover, while the ordinary unit personnel were mobilized to bring heavy pressure to bear against those singled out for attack, this was a highly orchestrated form of mass participation. As indicated above, the key role was played by specially selected "tiger hunting teams" which were usually organized by the unit leadership. These teams led the investigations which determined who would be objects of struggle, and provided cues for the "aroused" masses during struggle sessions.[112]

Reliance on the established leadership of units was also found in one major approach laid down in early 1951 for the conduct of the 1951–54 Party rectification. This approach, particularly used in rural areas of low population density and few Party members, involved selecting cadres and sending them to higher levels for rectification training. Afterwards they would return to their villages or units to lead the movement. A related method was to coordinate such training by concentrating cadres and activists from nearby villages in a *xiang* selected for rectification experimentation. The advantages claimed for these methods were that they only took a short time and created strong local leadership for rectification work. The disadvantages noted were the removal of those selected for training from production and the inability of Party members who remained in their units and villages to participate in rectification training. Under both variants, as well as through rectification offices *(zhengdang bangongshi)* established by Party committees at various levels to guide the movement, control remained with local Party authorities.[113]

But a second basic approach, used in rural areas of high population density and heavy concentration of Party members, was to dispatch work teams of higher level cadres especially trained for rectification work to the basic levels. This approach purportedly allowed relatively skilled rectification cadres to coordinate the campaign with production, draw the entire Party membership of the basic level unit into rectification, and encourage the participation of the whole population. The use of work teams, however, raised the danger of distortions such as those which had occurred during the 1947–48 rectification campaign. Despite warnings by Mao and other leaders to avoid the errors of 1947–48, cases of work teams monopolizing branch functions and brushing aside local leaders were again reported. In some cases, when work teams prepared to leave basic level organizations, instead of allowing the branch to elect a new leadership the team simply appointed one, thus further dampening the enthusiasm of branch members. Moreover, in some instances work teams used non-Party cadres and local activists to attack Party members, a situation similar to 1947–48 when poor peasant masses were mobilized against local Communist leaders. In the 1951–54 movement, however, this phenomenon was due to the initiative of individual work teams and in violation of guidelines attempting to keep mass participation within strict limits. Overall, CCP leaders seem to have been successful in keeping such problems under reasonable control.[114]

The use of work teams and reliance on existing unit leaders during the 1951–54 movement did not reflect the rule advanced in Chapter 2 that work teams are most suited for relatively intractable problems and local leaders for more manageable ones. Moreover, the official guidelines also fly in the face of the common sense notion that work teams are most needed where basic level leadership is weak. A weak Party branch with few members would be most vulnerable to pressures from the old society, but the guidelines called for conducting rectification through the leadership of such branches. Data unfortunately are insufficient to determine to what degree this practice dissipated the impact of the campaign. Moreover, there are no data to indicate whether rectification by work teams resulted in a higher purge rate than that conducted by established local leaders. But it is clear that, apparently for reasons of administrative feasibility (work teams presumably could get around easier in areas of high population density), methods were adopted which theoretically were not optimal purveyors of rectification.

Conclusion

In any period, the deviations selected for rectification will be drawn from among endemic defects of the Chinese political-administrative system, tensions derived from the dialectic of consolidation and mobilization phases, and problems reflecting the overall goals and concrete policies of the period. Throughout 1950–53, endemic problems of excessive bureaucracy appeared. Manifold shortcomings were subsumed under the label of bureaucratism. Excesses similar to those of traditional bureaucracy—too many documents, numbing routine, isolation from the people—reappeared despite repeated efforts to combat them. These defects were particularly abhorrent in a bureaucracy guided by a populist ideology and committed to rapid modernization and expanding governmental programs. Yet the ambitious nature of Party programs intensified the problem. In both consolidation and mobilization phases the heavy pressure of work kept officials in their offices coping with the staggering flow of paperwork. This pressure further complicated the perennial bureaucratic problem of obtaining accurate information. Lower level units, pressed for results, often fabricated them. Higher level officials, overwhelmed with work, could often do no more than read and approve reports sent up from below.

Another bureaucratic distortion which appeared at various times in this period was departmentalism or independent kingdoms, the tendency of units or localities to manipulate information, personnel and resources in order to further their bureaucratic independence and goals even at the cost of distorting overall policy. Under such tendencies, appointments were made on the basis of personal loyalty, assets were hidden, and funds wasted on prestigious local projects rather than spent on programs of national significance. Those who attempted to reveal such deviations to higher authorities were harassed. Having established a more elaborate and ambitious hierarchical administrative system than ever before in Chinese history, CCP leaders now faced problems inherent in complex modernizing bureaucracies as well as in traditional ones.

Tensions generated by the dialectic of consolidation and mobilization phases are also endemic to the Chinese system. The seriousness of some problems apparently varies according to phase. Thus information distortion seems greater in mobilization phases when the demands of the administrative system are most intense. At the least, consolidation stages designed to correct excesses of previous mobilization efforts devote more attention to the problem. In the early post-liberation period, however, the dialectical aspect of problems singled out for rectification appeared less pronounced than at some other times. For example, commandism, a deviation presumably most serious during high pressure mass campaigns, was a primary target of criticism in both the 1950 and 1953 consolidation phases, but only in the latter were the problems derived from an earlier mobilization. While the rural campaigns of 1952 gave rise to harsh leadership practices attacked during the New Three Anti Campaign, the 1950 rectification movement dealt with such practices originating within the consolidation phase itself. More broadly, the relative weakness of the correlation between rectification goals and the ongoing rhythm of consolidation and mobilization may be attributed largely to the following factors: the segmented quality of political life in a system still not fully centralized, so that there was geographical variation in policy implementation and deviations under attack; the shifting foci of Party programs independent of alternating phases; and the close link between the shortcomings criticized and the peculiar conditions of the 1950–53 period.

Most important was the link between shortcomings and early post-liberation conditions. In several campaigns, Party leaders described the conditions which were generating the problems they were facing in similar terms: the heavy tasks of the civil war and reconstruction period which prevented systematic Party education, the rapid and to a certain extent uncontrolled expansion of CCP membership and the state bureaucracy in the same period, and the involvement of revolutionary cadres with old elite elements were repeatedly cited as causes of deviant behavior. Of course, similar problems appeared in later periods. For example, neither low political awareness of cadres nor inadequate numbers of Party branches were unique to the takeover years. Nevertheless, these problems were more serious because of the sudden extension of Party control to the entire nation. As a result, a new and widely heterogeneous elite was hurriedly thrown together including not only callow students with minimal if any revolutionary experience, but even holdovers from the enemy regime. In China after liberation the tasks that needed to be undertaken were well ahead of organizational capabilities, thus forcing dependence on politically suspect elements as a stopgap measure.

Similarly, tensions generated within the elite by its heterogeneous nature were very much the product of the times. Conflict between Party members and non-Party cadres and old and new cadres reappeared later, but the deep suspicion between revolutionary veterans and retained personnel was a transitional phenomenon largely if not completely resolved by weeding out old regime officials during the initial post-1949 period. Moreover, the tension between young, administratively competent new cadres and politically tested old cadres can be distinguished from later conflicts of "red and expert." The tension between those representing political loyalty and technical proficiency was real enough, but it did not reflect leadership ambivalence over expertise *per se* as was the case later in the post-Hundred Flowers period. During the 1950 rectification campaign, official statements valued the administrative abilities of new cadres as well as the political achievements of old cadres. In fact, the emphasis was on the need to promote administratively competent newcomers at the expense of old revolutionaries as befitted the needs of the situation.

In the case of "agrarian socialist thought" and "rich peasant thought," the shortcomings criticized were direct products of specific shifting Party policies reflecting the larger objectives of the takeover period. The immediate imperative of economic recovery necessitated a relatively free rein for rural capitalism. As a result, rectification efforts in 1950–51 focused on curbing crude egalitarian notions of Communism. However, these efforts, in a dialectic of their own, contributed to basic level cadre attitudes and behavior incompatible with socialist transformation. As socialist transformation gradually supplanted economic recovery as the overall goal of the period, criticism then focused on self-seeking cadre behavior.

Of all the shortcomings attacked in 1950–53, those concerning involvement of the new rulers with remnants of China's old elite—the landlord class in the countryside and the bourgeoisie in the cities—were most peculiar to the period. In the broadest sense, the aim of rectification was to destroy the prestige of these groups so that they could no longer exert influence against CCP objectives. This aim was largely accomplished. The impact of the old rural elite on Party cadres was sharply curtailed at least until the severe economic crisis of 1960–62 which generated a certain resurgence in landlord influence. And while corruption reappeared within a few years[115] and became a target of later movements, large scale urban corruption based on the interconnection of officials and private businessmen was finished.

The success in cutting ties with the old elite was due to the coordination of rectification with other movements which fundamentally undermined the position of that elite. In the countryside, land reform overturned the traditional social structure by eliminating some of the most powerful landowners, raising poor peasants to positions of village leadership, and destroying the economic basis of the landlord class through land redistribution. Similarly, in the cities the prestige of the bourgeoisie was gravely damaged by the Five Anti Campaign,[116] while the economic basis of that class was being weakened by the initial phasing out of the private sector as the socialist transformation of industry and commerce got under way.[t] Clearly, the effectiveness of rectification was greatly enhanced by structural changes in Chinese society during the consolidation years.

During 1950–53 the pattern of deviations, Party aims and policies on the one hand, and the severity, methods and foci of the rectification process on the other, with some modifications confirms the propositions advanced in Chapter 2. The degree of persuasion or coercion applied in dealing with different types of deviations largely followed the theoretical prescription. For relatively minor violations of official norms which were widespread among basically loyal cadres, as in the case of commandism and bureaucratism in 1950 and 1953, mild methods emphasizing education were adopted. To put it another way, CCP leaders tacitly recognized that such shortcomings were inherent in the situation and system and could best be ameliorated by a persuasive approach which did not create alienation. But deviations seriously violating the law (and involving links with potentially hostile elements) such as *sanfan* corruption were dealt with by a harsh, coercive approach. Similarly, in 1950–53 the relative severity of the campaigns generally varied as expected with the political phase. During the consolidation phases of 1950 and 1953 mild methods predominated, while the *sanfan* mobilization was marked by the harsh approach necessary for far-reaching social change.

There were, however, important exceptions to the above relationships during the 1951–54 Party rectification. During this movement the high 10 percent purge rate (i.e., expulsions plus withdrawals) remained basically stable regardless of political phase. Moreover, the purge rate was a response to shortcomings such as the low level of political awareness and "rich peasant thought" which were essentially problems of ideological understanding, and thus theoretically suited to persuasive techniques. As suggested earlier, the apparent lack of variation in the purge rate was probably due to an informal quota being set during the 1951–52 mobilization phrase, a phase which was also marked by an external

[t]The Five Anti Campaign contributed directly to this process since Five Anti fines paid by private enterprises were converted into shares in newly constituted joint state-private enterprises, the first stage of socialized industry. In addition, the Three and Five Anti Campaigns furthered state control of the economy by increasing the role of trade unions as a check on private management and obtaining information on the inner workings of private business.

threat (see below). The use of this somewhat more coercive approach, however, is probably better explained in terms of the actual seriousness of the problem. While not serious in the sense of flagrant violations of law, low political awareness and related problems were serious obstacles to achieving Party objectives. For socialist transformation could be successfully implemented only if basic level Party members were committed to that program. In turn, a substantial weeding out of those most imbued with "rich peasant" attitudes as well as education for those less tainted was required.

The matter becomes clearer if we consider the campaigns of the 1950–53 period in terms of the persuasive-coercive continuum developed in Chapter 2.[117] While Party and administrative discipline, including purging, indicates a move away from a persuasive approach, a greater coercive component is achieved by criminal sanctions and intense, psychologically unnerving struggle and mass trials. In the 1951–54 movement there is little evidence of the high purge rate being accompanied by either extensive struggle or criminal sanctions,[118] in sharp contrast to the Three Anti campaign where the more coercive measures were widely used. With this refinement the original proposition gains reaffirmation: the more blatant violations of official norms tended to be dealt with by more coercive means. Equally significant is that less flagrant breaches of official norms receiving relatively persuasive (or less coercive) handling were distributed widely throughout the elite. In contrast, more serious violations dealt with by criminal sanctions and struggle were to a significant degree concentrated with a suspect segment of the elite, personnel retained from the GMD regime.

The rectification movements of the 1950–53 period were largely implemented through the regular chain of command. Work teams and inspection teams were used largely to gather information, transmit policies from above, and teach needed skills to lower level cadres. Only in the 1951–54 movement was there evidence of pushing local leaders aside as happened in 1947–48, and that apparently occurred on a limited scale. During the *sanfan* drive, the masses were mobilized not against existing leaders but largely against targets selected by those leaders. Moreover, although in most campaigns efforts were made to coordinate regular work with rectification so that ongoing administration was not disrupted, in the Three Anti Campaign extensive disruption occurred despite the control of established leaders.

Superficially, these last developments appear at variance with the general propositions advanced in Chapter 2. Work teams in theory were better suited for handling the serious deviations and harsh sanctions of the *sanfan* campaign than regular unit leaders. However, since the deviations and sanctions generally centered on a suspect group which did not have close links to Party leaders at each level, these leaders could act decisively against that group without risking their own position. For the same reason the tendency of established leaders to try to prevent disruption was less pronounced than it might otherwise have been. Unit leaders were able to look forward to the infusion of vigorous young activists into the organization in place of retained personnel, thus offsetting the administrative costs of the campaign. The extension of Party control and increased availability of state investment funds from *sanfan* and *wufan* fines were additional benefits making CCP leaders at all levels reliable administrators of a disruptive movement.

Chapter 3, moreover, advanced the following hypotheses: (1) when a revolutionary organization suffers from leadership cleavages it tends to adopt coercive techniques of internal control, when the organization is unified it tends to adopt persuasive control techniques; and (2) in situations where such an organization has a secure environment it may adopt systematic educational methods, but where its external environment is threatening such methods are not possible and coercive means are often introduced. How do these hypotheses stand up for the 1950–53 period, a period of rule rather than revolution?

It can be argued that the achievement of power created new conditions which potentially could alter these relationships. A hostile environment during revolutionary struggle posed a much more palpable threat to the Party than a hostile international situation after 1949, even when it involved war *beyond China's borders* in Korea. During the ebb and flow of civil war the enemy frequently penetrated Communist areas or was close enough to doing so to make extensive educational efforts impossible. But after the establishment of the PRC, the threat of the enemy "breaking in," while real, was still contingent on a whole series of international developments which might not materialize even if the fighting in Korea went against Chinese forces. In the case at hand, in 1950–53 CCP authorities had adequate control over the country to carry out whatever type of campaign they felt necessary. Thus following the entry of Chinese forces into the Korean War the CCP undertook extensive rectification efforts—much as it had in the secure Yan'an area in 1942–44. However, the linkage between external threat and severity tended to be borne out by the relative harshness of the movements conducted during the fiercest fighting—the intense struggles of the *sanfan* campaign and the high purge rate apparently set for Party rectification in this period. And although there were clearly other, perhaps more important factors, in 1953 with the war stalemated and a negotiated settlement near, the New Three Anti Campaign was markedly milder than its immediate predecessors.

Similarly, the relationship between leadership unity and control techniques might be different once power is achieved. In the Soviet case, certainly, Stalin's greatest use of coercion occurred *after* he had consolidated his leadership. It could be argued that once the revolution is successful, there is less incentive for a persuasive approach toward colleagues who always remain *potential* threats to a given leader or faction even when there is substantial agreement on policy and the allocation of power. Under conditions of civil war leadership purges might disrupt the cohesion necessary for confronting the enemy; with victory international enemies will most likely remain at bay even during extended factional conflict.[u] In China during the early 1950s, however, the unity of the later revolutionary period was, if anything, strengthened. Not only were general policy debates kept well within manageable parameters, but only very marginal differences appeared over the various rectification efforts of the period. Yet highly coercive techniques were used during one movement, the Three Anti Campaign. In broad perspective, nevertheless, even the *sanfan* experience affirms the hypothesis. For here, as in all movements of the period, the highest policy makers were unscathed. Moreover, the campaign followed the general early 1950s pattern of markedly less purging and discipline directed at politically sensitive cadres than at lesser high level officials, and particularly at intermediate and basic level cadres. Thus a relatively persuasive approach was adopted toward key decision makers and administrators, even though individuals of high rank received severe sanctions.

In addition, the approach toward ordinary cadres generally was still comparatively persuasive throughout the period. Although basic level cadres were assigned a perhaps unfair degree of blame for commandism in 1950, they were dealt with largely by education. And in 1953 not only was the emphasis again on persuasion, but considerable responsibility for deviations was attributed to higher authorities. Even the high purge rate of Party rectification, as we have seen, fell considerably short of a severely coercive approach. Only during the Three Anti Campaign, in marked contrast to the handling of Party members during the 1951–54 rectification, were strongly coercive measures applied—but disproportionately to a group of non-Party officials who had served the GMD. This channeling of coercion toward elements considered potentially hostile to the new order provides an important modification of our hypothesis. Overall, however, the relationship between leadership unity and persuasive techniques generally held during the initial post-liberation period.

In nearly all respects, Party norms developed in the early 1940s functioned throughout the 1950–53 period. Not only were rectification methods, apart from those focusing on retained personnel, relatively persuasive, but mass participation was kept under tight rein. Moreover, discipline was reserved for questions of work style and organizational purity. Debate within the framework of consensus on the Soviet path, with Mao adopting a centrist position, basically respected both minority rights and collective leadership. Despite informal steps against Bo Yibo, policy advocacy was not a rectification target. The Party unity strengthened by these circumstances not only facilitated the traditional "save the patient" approach, it also contributed to the effectiveness of rectification.

One measure of this effectiveness is the number of key problems decisively dealt with—ties to the old elite, large scale urban corruption, reliance on functionaries of suspect loyalties. Another is that overall CCP programs—restoring the economy, extending political control to the grass roots, launching socialist

[u] The most obvious example is Soviet inaction during the Cultural Revolution.

transformation and planned economic construction—were successfully implemented. While rectification was only one factor in these achievements, its impact should not be underestimated.

In particular, the rectification of rural basic level Party units and recruitment of new members was vital in providing an organizational base upon which socialization of the countryside could proceed. It could further be argued that the link between rectification efforts and concrete tasks of social transformation and economic betterment was crucial to their overall effectiveness. During the takeover period cadres were engaged in a dynamic social experiment and rectification was aimed at furthering that experiment. Since the new elite benefited from this program the impact of rectification was significantly enhanced. In sum, the ability of the CCP to offer ample tangible rewards—not only official posts for activists and promotions for tested cadres but broad social gains for the groups from which the elite was drawn—made the message of rectification eminently persuasive.

5
The Purge of Gao Gang and Rao Shushi

The purge of Gao Gang and Rao Shushi was the first major leadership struggle within the CCP after 1949, and to this day remains one of the most obscure. The principals held some of the most powerful posts in the PRC in the early 1950s: Gao was a Politburo member, one of the six vice chairmen of the Central People's Government Council, a vice chairman of the People's Revolutionary Military Council, chairman of the State Planning Commission, and the top Party, government and military official of the Northeast region; Rao was director of the Central Committee's organization department, a SPC member, and Party secretary, government chairman and political commissar of the East China region. When they disappeared in early 1954, no explanation was given. Subsequent official accusations against Gao and Rao in 1955 and Red Guard revelations during the Cultural Revolution were both extremely skimpy, leaving many crucial aspects of the affair in the realm of the unknown.

Various speculative interpretations have been advanced concerning the Gao-Rao affair. Some have emphasized possible policy differences,[1] others regionalism,[2] and still others ties between Gao Gang and the Soviet Union.[3] This analysis, while not excluding possible tangential roles for these factors, finds none of them persuasive as an explanation of the purge. Instead, as does the official version, it focuses on violations of established Party organizational norms by Gao and Rao in a bid to extend their own power. Theirs was a classic case of "factional activities" *(paibie huodong)*—of building support by dubious means outside regular Party bodies. Since Party norms had functioned smoothly in the consolidation of power period, why the challenge to these norms? As argued in Chapter 1, the successful functioning of the norms is dependent on political circumstances. The most relevant here are a broad policy consensus and stable power relationships within the leadership. The previous chapter has demonstrated that a broad policy consensus did exist through 1953 when the affair came to a head. However, Cultural Revolution sources suggest, at this time Mao's health was in question. The resultant uncertainty over the allocation of political power, we argue, created the conditions for the "conspiratorial" maneuvers of Gao and Rao.

The Gao-Rao affair went through three stages. First, the case became a major problem behind the scenes in the latter half of 1953 while Gao and Rao remained active political figures. The second stage began with the February 1954 Fourth Plenum of the Seventh Central Committee which focused on the problem of Party unity and clearly indicated that very high ranking but unnamed cadres had breached this unity. This plenary session marked the political defeat of Gao and Rao who subsequently dropped from public view. Over the next six months, meetings convened by Party committees of various levels to discuss the results of the Fourth Plenum, editorials and articles provided some elaboration of the issues involved. The third stage began with a CCP National Conference in March 1955 which openly denounced Gao and Rao, detailed their "crimes," and expelled them from the Party. In the following months, new articles and meetings further discussed the case.

The critical first stage took place in the context of the latter consolidation years, a period (as discussed in Chapter 4) marked by a decided shift in emphasis to planned economic construction and social transformation, increasing administrative centralization, and a general relaxation of the political climate. Once Gao and Rao had been defeated, in the second and third stages CCP authorities organized extensive study of matters related to the case, but these efforts fell short of a true rectification campaign.[4] Nevertheless, official propaganda repeatedly drew parallels between the behavior of Gao and Rao and that of lesser cadres with no connection to the case. This occurred in an overall context reflecting broad continuities with the initial stage although a speedup in the rate of agricultural cooperativization in 1954 brought about partial mobilization within a larger consolidation phase before a slowdown was decreed in early 1955.[5] Thus despite the fact that the affair involved political maneuvering at the highest levels unique in the period since the solidification of Mao's leadership, given the continuities with the earlier period it was utilized to attack deviations similar to those criticized in the movements of 1950–53.

Political Profiles of Gao and Rao[6]

Gao Gang

Gao, born about 1902, was one of the earliest CCP members in his native Shaanxi. He attended a military and political academy established by warlord Feng Yuxiang in cooperation with the CCP, but in mid-1927 Feng broke with the Communists and suppressed their movement throughout the province. In response, Liu Zhidan, a friend of Gao's since middle school, led an unsuccessful insurrection in spring 1928 and was soon joined by Gao in remote Northwest Shaanxi. Together they built the Shaanxi guerrilla movement.

As noted in Chapter 3, throughout the early 1930s the local Shaanxi Communists led by Liu and Gao had serious differences with representatives sent to Shaanxi by the Party Center which paralleled disputes between Mao Zedong and Central Committee leaders over the correct political and military strategies to be followed in the Jiangxi Soviet. Thus Gao and Mao had independently developed similar policy positions. Their ties became more tangible with the arrival of the Long Marchers in Shaanxi and Mao's release of the local leaders who had been arrested by representatives of the old Party Center. Gao, who became the most important figure from the old North Shaanxi base area following the 1936 death of Liu Zhidan, soon assumed a key role among officials active in the Yan'an area under Mao. Throughout the Sino-Japanese War he held a number of key posts in the Shaan-Gan-Ning Border Region, second in importance only to Lin Boqu, the border region's chief executive officer. As we have seen, during this period Gao took a leading role in the 1942–44 rectification campaign and evidently further won Mao's confidence.[a]

Gao remained in Yan'an until the fall of 1945 when he was sent to the Northeast along with other prominent leaders. By 1947 he was deputy commander and deputy political commissar of the Northeast Military Region under Lin Biao. With the departure in 1948–49 of nearly all other top leaders, Gao assumed the predominant role in the area. This was followed by his increasing national stature in the post-1949 period. With the attainment of Politburo status by 1952, Gao became only the second figure whose early career had been in North China to break into an inner circle dominated by men intimately associated with the pre-1935 South China revolution.[7]

Rao Shushi

Rao, born about 1901 in Jiangxi, reportedly studied at Shanghai University in the early 1920s. About the same time he was active as a labor organizer in Wuhan, joining the Party in 1925. In 1929 he was active in the Manchurian underground—i.e., "white area" work—under Liu Shaoqi. Rao apparently spent much of the next decade abroad, but by 1939 he was back in China and soon became deputy political commissar of the New Fourth Army and deputy secretary of the

---

[a] See Mao's praise of Gao in 1942 for his knowledge of local conditions in the Yan'an area; Compton, *Mao's China*, p. 25. In addition, Taiwan sources claim Gao was Mao's personal choice at the end of the Sino-Japanese War for the post of secretary of the Northeast Party Bureau, but Mao accepted Liu Shaoqi's candidate, Peng Zhen, on the understanding that both Gao and Lin Biao would receive key regional posts. See Carroll Robbins Wetzel Jr., "From the Jaws of Defeat: Lin Piao and the 4th Field Army in Manchuria," Ph.D. dissertation, The George Washington University, 1972, pp. 51–52.

Central China Sub-bureau, again serving under Liu Shaoqi for about a year.

After the Sino-Japanese War, Rao was sent to Beijing to serve as a senior political adviser to the CCP mission established under the January 1946 cease fire agreement with the GMD. When the civil war intensified in mid-1946, Rao returned to East China as political commissar thus resuming his association with Chen Yi, former commander of the New Fourth Army and still military leader in the area. After liberation, Chen served as second secretary of the CCP East China Bureau under Rao.

When Rao Shushi took up his duties at the Party Center in 1952 and allegedly began his conspiracy with Gao Gang, the two had clearly divergent career patterns. While the incomplete nature of biographical information mandates caution, it appears that no substantial ties had developed between Gao and Rao during the revolutionary period. Judging Rao's career as a whole, his most important career ties apparently were with Chen Yi, and to a lesser extent Liu Shaoqi—although such links do not necessarily mean that a cordial relationship always existed.[b]

The Genesis of the Crisis: Developments in 1953

Despite charges of earlier deviations by Gao and Rao, several major CCP pronouncements later declared the "anti-Party alliance of Gao Gang and Rao Shushi" *(Gao Gang, Rao Shushi fandang lianmeng)* had initially appeared in 1953. Specifically, they assertedly engaged in activities threatening Party unity at the National Conference on Financial and Economic Work in the summer of 1953, and again at the National Conference on Organization Work in September and October of the same year.

Cultural Revolution sources provide further information concerning the 1953 financial and economic conference which appears to be the first major instance of political maneuvering by Gao, Rao and others linked to them. Gao himself was absent from at least part of this conference having been dispatched to Moscow to attend a special meeting concerning Hungary's resistance to new Soviet economic policies. The information available on the conference itself focuses on the activities of two East China officials with career links to Rao Shushi, re-

[b] A Cultural Revolution document, "Evidence of the Crimes of the Renegade, Traitor and Scab Liu Shaoqi—Major Evidence of His Traitorous Activities in 1925, 1927 and 1929" (October 18, 1968), in *Issues & Studies,* March 1971, p. 96, asserts that Liu revealed the identity of members of the Manchurian Provincial Committee including Rao when arrested by forces of the warlord Zhang Xueliang. If true, this could have been a source of tension between the two men. On the other hand, another Cultural Revolution source asserts that both Rao's wife and Xiang Ming, the only officially identified member of the Gao-Rao "alliance" from Rao's East China region, had served as Liu's personal secretary; "Down with Liu Shaoqi—Life of Counterrevolutionary Liu Shaoqi" (Red Guard pamphlet), May 1967, in *CB,* No. 834.

gional Third Secretary Tan Zhenlin and Shanghai Fourth Secretary Chen Pei-xian. Tan, allegedly known as the "big gun," and Chen, the "little cannon," reportedly circumvented established Party norms by conducting activities outside the conference sessions. Both Tan and Chen reportedly held "secret talks" with Gao and Rao; e.g., when Gao returned from Moscow he sought out Tan privately rather than first report to the Party Center. Tan, moreover, visited conference participants at night in their guest houses, lobbying for support and spreading rumors. He assertedly built up Gao as "young and capable" and Rao as an "outstanding Marxist of China" while attacking other Party leaders by claiming "there are sinister ministers around the Center." Chen also allegedly spoke unfavorably about leading central comrades. The activities of these officials were not all covert, however. Chen openly raised policy grievances at the conference by attacking state banks for "gobbling down all private banks in Shanghai" and arguing that "the worker-peasant alliance is breaking up." It may also have been at this conference that Tan and Chen allegedly authored an open letter to Mao asking that he "take a rest" (to be discussed subsequently), a move which could not be regarded as conspiratorial. As for Gao and Rao themselves, apart from their alleged consultations with Tan and Chen, the only charge made was Mao's vague 1955 statement that they "worked hand in glove" during the conference.[8]

The financial and economic conference thus apparently involved both policy criticisms, legitimate under existing rules, and unacceptable factional activities. This was further indicated by Mao in 1956 when he distinguished "some comrades who said the wrong thing and were subject to criticism [at the conference]"—a description which would fit Bo Yibo and his tax policies[9]—from the "destructive" activities of Gao and Rao.[10] Even the alleged activities of Tan and Chen, as we have seen, involved open as well as behind the scenes aspects, a fact which perhaps explains the relative leniency of the treatment of these officials following the Fourth Plenum in 1954. In any case, Mao claimed the top Party leaders "realized [Gao and Rao] were not behaving normally" after their "goings-on" prior to and at the conference, and rebuked them for these activities. This seemingly led to an end to open maneuvers and, according to Mao, "from then on they switched over completely to undercover activities." Information concerning developments at the fall organization conference is even more elusive, the only accusation being that this occasion was used to circulate a list of prospective Politburo members "illicitly" drawn up by An Ziwen[c] in an apparent effort to gain support for the "alliance."[11]

---

[c] An may simply have been acting as Rao's deputy in the organization department. It is also unclear how "illicit" this activity was since the list was apparently circulated openly. Such a list is perhaps explainable given proposals for a reallocation of offices in view of Mao's health (see below). It may also have been logical given the new tasks and positions created by the launching of the FFYP and the process of centralization. In any case, An was let off with a disciplinary warning *(jinggao)*. *SW*, V, 161.

The only public manifestation of the problem in 1953 was a November 26 *Renmin ribao* editorial entitled "Seriously Carry Out the Collective Leadership System." The editorial raised a number of themes in general terms which were later developed at the Fourth Plenum without suggesting the high levels involved. According to its analysis, deviations from collective leadership could be found at any level of the Party apparatus:

> ... [S]ome comrades are in the habit of making decisions on problems themselves and are unaccustomed to appreciate the value of collective leadership, ... [they] are not adept in leaving important problems to the discussion and decision of the Party committee. Sometimes, the principle of collective leadership is even violated....
>
> ... In some places, individualists have taken advantage of the failure of the Party committee to practice criticism and self-criticism ... to sabotage the unified leadership of the Party committee and even attempt to substitute individual leadership for the collective leadership of the Party committee.

The editorial dealt mainly with various perversions of the Party committee system: unilateral decisions by Party secretaries instead of committee discussions; formalistic discussions which effectively left decision making to concerned departments; action by departmental leaders on important policy problems without committee discussion; the refusal of departments to carry out committee decisions or to allow committee members to look into departmental work; and, conversely, attempts to settle everything in committee including minor routine matters. These were all recurrent concerns, but in the context of late 1953 the emphasis on collective leadership had deeper implications for Party unity.

The issue evidently came to a head at a December 24 enlarged meeting of the Politburo. According to Mao, it was only in the fall and winter of 1953 that the conspiracy was detected, with Gao apparently exposed at the meeting itself. At this gathering, Mao claimed, "I said there were two headquarters in Beijing. The first headed by me stirred up an open wind and lit an open fire. The second headed by others stirred up a sinister wind and lit a sinister fire; it was operating underground." With the "alliance" exposed, the Politburo unanimously endorsed Mao's proposal for "strengthening Party unity," and formulated a draft resolution on the subject for discussion by the Fourth Plenum.[12]

Throughout the latter part of 1953 both Gao and Rao made significant public appearances in a variety of official roles. Following the December Politburo meeting, however, Gao made fewer appearances, the last one at a rally on January 20, 1954; while Rao appeared only once on New Year's Day. Meanwhile, other key leaders—most notably Liu Shaoqi and Zhou Enlai—were active both before and after the December Politburo meeting. Most significant, however, were the activities of Mao himself. Throughout the latter half of 1953 Mao performed a variety of public roles until December 15 when he received the new Soviet ambassador. For the next three months, until March 23, 1954, Mao made no public appearances and was even absent from the crucial Fourth Plenum.[13] This mysterious absence was a key to the entire Gao-Rao affair.

The Fourth Plenum and Its Aftermath

The dominant figure at the Fourth Plenum from February 6 to 10, 1954,[14] was Liu Shaoqi. According to the plenum communique, "Comrade Mao Zedong was away on a holiday" and the report of the Politburo dealing with the critical question of Party unity "was entrusted to [Liu] by . . . Comrade Mao." Apart from Liu, "important speeches" were made by Zhu De, Zhou Enlai and 42 others.

While no names were mentioned, the communique clearly indicated that the threat to Party unity concerned the highest levels:

> The "Resolution on Strengthening Party Unity" . . . points out that the unity of responsible comrades of the Central Committee and the provincial (municipal) and higher level committees, and of the high ranking responsible comrades in the armed forces, is the key to the unity of the entire Party.

The seriousness attached to the problem was suggested by symbolic statements alleging efforts by imperialists and counterrevolutionaries to cultivate agents and stimulate factional activities inside the Party "because the enemy knows . . . a fortress can most easily be taken from within." Moreover, although the traditional policy of "treating the illness in order to save the patient" was advocated, the plenum stipulated strict disciplinary action including expulsion from the Party against those who deliberately carried out "factional splitting activities," undermined Party unity and collective leadership, and refused to repent.

Such measures were required since "a most dangerous kind of conceit" assertedly grew among some high ranking cadres:

> [Some cadres] exaggerate the role of the individual and emphasize individual prestige. They think there is no one equal to them in the world. They listen only to others' flattery and praise but cannot accept others' criticism and supervision; they suppress and revenge themselves against those who criticize them. They even regard the region or department under their leadership as their individual inheritance or independent kingdom.

This behavior, which was attributed to Gao and Rao a year later, was common among middle and low ranking officials enmeshed in the Chinese bureaucratic environment; thus criticism of such phenomena had broad applicability within the elite. Only Gao and Rao were highly enough placed, however, that their activities could threaten the established leadership.

While nothing explicit was openly said about Gao Gang or Rao Shushi, the

Fourth Plenum clearly sealed their political defeat. The dominant role of Liu Shaoqi (apparently, as we shall see, Gao's main target), the affirmation of the "Resolution on Strengthening Party Unity" which attacked behavior later laid at the door of Gao and Rao, and their absence from public life following the plenum all indicate that their fate had been settled by February 1954. Moreover, a year later it was claimed that the entire period from the Fourth Plenum to the March 1955 national conference had been devoted to exposing their conspiracy. Cultural Revolution sources, furthermore, suggest that Gao's defeat did not meet with significant dissent within the Party. Only a single report was found indicating opposition to the resolution adopted at the plenum; East China Fourth Secretary Zhang Dingcheng was said to have openly voiced his disapproval and then returned to his home town.[15] Thus the year's delay in making the case public seemingly did not reflect resistance to the purge. In all likelihood it was due to the desire to deal with such a sensitive matter within the elite first and to conduct investigations into the extent of the conspiracy. It may also have reflected the CCP rectification practice of offering erring officials the opportunity to repent.

Press Criticism after the Plenum

In the months following the Fourth Plenum, press editorials and articles elaborated the themes of the meeting and hailed its results, claiming that many cadres were educated in the acute nature of class struggle although liberalism, e.g., regarding improper speeches and actions as "nothing serious," still required attention.[16] This press commentary apparently had two purposes: (1) to inform the public indirectly that a serious problem had developed high in the Party hierarchy and measures had been taken to deal with it; and (2) to combat tendencies permeating the entire Party and state structure which bore similarities to the deviations of Gao and Rao. The discussion of these tendencies, while a tangential aspect of the case, nevertheless involved matters of concern to CCP leaders in the period following the political defeat of the Gao-Rao group.

Press reports discussed questions concerning the correct functioning of the Party committee system which had been raised by *Renmin ribao* the previous November. One deviation was the tendency of Party secretaries, particularly in lower level organs, to monopolize decisions rightfully belonging to full committees on the pretext that collective leadership was too much trouble and too time consuming. Frequently, even though Party committee meetings were held, no real collective decision making took place due to the domineering role of the secretary. Secretaries reportedly formed definite opinions on matters prior to meetings and began committee sessions with long speeches advocating those opinions, thus in effect lecturing the committee members instead of encouraging a genuine exchange of views. Secretaries even deprived committee members of opportunities to express themselves or seized upon isolated defects in their speeches to discredit their views.[17]

Also threatening the committee system was the dispersion of authority to specialized business departments. Many departmental leaders regarded Party committees as unfamiliar with specialized work and often bypassed them in carrying out tasks. Instructions from business departments of superior levels went directly to subordinate departments rather than being submitted to Party committees of subordinate levels for discussion. In addition, departmental leaders returning from higher level business meetings would not report to Party committees or, if they did, often presented a mass of technical data to show off their expertise and make it difficult for committee members to express opinions. In cases where no reference material or agenda was prepared, committee members found it even more difficult to comment. If committee members did express views, departmental leaders allegedly took the attitude, "you know nothing but I know [much], approve it and don't worry," and refused to revise their instructions according to the committee's views. The failure of administrative cadres to respect the authority of non-expert Party committees reflected a larger tendency to regard economic work as vital without giving any attention to politics.[18] It further reflected inherent tension between parallel specialist and political bureaucracies. Although Party committees were by no means devoid of expertise, they were largely oriented to overall political questions during a period of growing influence for vertically organized specialist departments. Thus the attention given to the Party committee system indicated efforts to strengthen both territorial *vis-à-vis* vertical control and "redness" *vis-à-vis* expertise, but without a fundamental change in either relationship at a time when administrative centralization and economic construction were dominating themes.

Another major target of media criticism was seriously conceited leading cadres who let promotions and departmental achievements go to their heads. They exaggerated the role of the individual in accomplishments and created an atmosphere of worship and sycophancy in their units. "Dizzy with success" and citing the peculiarities of their areas, they frequently refused to execute policies established by the Party Center and took the attitude that "if there is trouble I will fight back." Most seriously, individual conceit resulted in the pursuit of power and positions and caused factional activities which assertedly "helped the enemy to split the Party."[19]

Conceit was not the only stimulant to factionalism. As in the 1950–53 period, another powerful force was the frustration and resentment of cadres who failed to gain promotions and recognition of their services to the revolution. They often expressed unhappiness when others received advancement and rewards. Clique activities reportedly grew because such cadres felt the Party was not "warm" to them and sought "warmth" from people who "showed concern" for them. Another important factor was parochial perspectives, particularly where large numbers of native cadres and outsiders worked in the same area. Here differences in living habits and work style created mutual distrust and suspicion. A further division which generated conflict was between cadres newly transferred to a unit or area and old cadres already stationed there. Old cadres reportedly resented the superior positions they felt newly transferred cadres too often received, while recent arrivals were unhappy with the conditions they discovered, complained and "put on airs."[20] One factor which apparently was not a major cause of factional activities, however, was policy differences. A statement foreshadowing allegations against Gao and Rao claimed, "In our work, disagreements over principle or policy are seldom developed into controversies and what is frequently witnessed is a 'disturbance of relations,' [i.e.,] lack of unity and lack of mutual respect. Actually it is due to conceit."[21]

To exploit tensions among cadres and build factional alliances, ambitious officials reportedly used a variety of methods. One was to ignore CCP cadre policy emphasizing [business] ability *(cai)* and [political] virtue *(de),* and instead to select and promote cadres on the basis of individual relationships and personal loyalty. At the same time such officials disciplined and denied promotions to cadres who criticized defects and "persisted in the truth," much as Huang Yifeng allegedly had done several years earlier.[22] In addition, an analysis similar to later accusations against Gao and Rao pointed to a potent mixture of cajolery and intrigue used by leaders intent on building a personal following:

> If they want to win over a person, they would liberally promise him promotions and flatter him, speaking highly of him in the presence of others in order to make him feel grateful and fall into the trap.
>
> Another method ... is to sow discord ... to bring about inner Party strife. For instance, they would utilize certain defects and mistakes in Party work or defects and mistakes of individual comrades to spread falsehoods and sow discord ... exaggerating unimportant questions and exaggerating individual, temporary and already rectified defects and mistakes as systematic and consistent defects and mistakes. They are also adept at creating contradictions within the Party and setting one against the other by speaking against B in the presence of A and speaking against D in the presence of C, by saying one thing at one place and another thing at another place. . . .[23]

Factional activities inevitably included establishing independent kingdoms. The units and areas allegedly turned into such kingdoms were not indicated, but reports spoke of cadres independently assuming control of a "county area or more," or of "important departments." As during the New Three Anti Campaign, attacks on independent kingdoms pointed to the use of accomplishments to build individual prestige at the expense of Party prestige, the manipulation of cadre policy and the refusal to implement unwanted central policies. Another familiar feature was manipulating information reaching higher levels and generally blocking off any avenues of control from above or below; rulers of these satrapies included only favorable information in reports to superior organs. Moreover, they rejected both mass supervision and criticism within the unit. Among the methods used to reject criticism were ridicule, exploiting defects in the content or wording of criticism, and claiming one's private life was not a legitimate target of criticism. Finally, as in the Huang Yifeng case, bosses of independent kingdoms resisted the supervisory and inspection machinery of the Party. As noted, departmental leaders often refused to cooperate with Party committees of the same level. In addition, they resisted the authority of checkup teams sent from higher levels. Thus cadres who treated their units as personal fiefdoms reportedly regarded it an insult when inspectors from superior organs discovered defects in the work of their units, and they would seek ways to "deal blows" to those inspectors.[24] In sum, although some problems subject to press criticism seem closely patterned on the Gao-Rao affair and others, although more general phenomena, had not been dealt with by the rectification efforts of 1950–53, many were ingrained features of the Chinese bureaucratic system and had been targets of earlier post-liberation movements.

Regional and Local Party Conferences

In the half year following the Fourth Plenum, regional Party bureaus and sub-bureaus plus provincial and municipal Party committees throughout China convened enlarged conferences to transmit the resolution of the plenum and discuss the question of Party unity. These conferences also involved criticism and self-criticism and checking up on leading cadres. The meetings generally took one to three weeks and usually were attended by 200 to 300 officials including cadres of the county, special district and urban district levels. Starting in June there were some reports of Party committees at the rural district, county and special district levels convening conferences to discuss the decision of the plenum. Many reports also indicated that study and self-examinations based on the Fourth Plenum were being carried out among Party and non-Party cadres alike in various Party, government, economic and military organizations.[25] The regional, provincial and municipal meetings were the crucial ones, however.

In most areas reports on the enlarged conferences were bland and focused on regional and local problems. The conference usually declared confidently that Party organs of the region or province were basically united, normally observed the principle of collective leadership, and were consistently firm in carrying out the Party line. The shortcomings which were admitted were of a comparatively minor type and suggestions for strengthening Party unity and collective leadership were accordingly mild. The overall thrust seemed to be that although the general question of Party unity was a serious one, in the regions, provinces and cities where the conferences were held the problem was well under control and no drastic remedies were required.[26]

In East China and the Northeast there were notable departures from the tone and substance described above. In contrast to other areas, East China conferences identified specific figures who underwent self-criticism. In Shanghai three leaders reportedly made "strict self-criticisms": Chen Peixian, First Deputy Secretary Pan Hannian,[d] and Second Deputy Secretary Gu Mu. In somewhat blander references, Tan Zhenlin and East China propaganda chief Shu Tong were said to have "carried out criticism and self-criticism of the work of the East China Bureau and their own work"; while Fujian Deputy Secretary Zeng Jingbing made a self-criticism of his work over the previous few years.[27] Further information on the East China conference is provided by Cultural Revolution sources. According to these sources, Tan Zhenlin and Chen Peixian were afraid of being uncovered following the Fourth Plenum and conspired to present "false self- examinations" to the regional conference. In these self-examinations Tan and Chen reportedly distorted their activities on behalf of Gao and Rao at the 1953 financial and economic conference by admitting only "bad temper" and "arrogance." Chen then called a municipal conference in Shanghai where the central issue was again avoided. Tan, however, assertedly worried that Chen had been too blatant, convened the East China Bureau and hypocritically attacked the Shanghai Municipal Committee and Chen for failing to "make a profound criticism" of Rao's influence on the work of the committee. Chen, after feigning disagreement, soon pretended to repent and thus escaped punishment. Whatever the accuracy of this account, together with contemporary reports it indicates that meetings held in East China were much more serious affairs than those in most other regions.[28]

Most striking of the contemporary reports was the generally harsher tones of those dealing with conferences in Gao Gang's Northeast. The clearest example was the March 26 to April 24 conference of high ranking Party cadres held by the Northeast Bureau. The meeting's seriousness was indicated by its being "held under the close concern and guidance of the CCP Central Committee" and involving more than twenty days of "fervent discussion." According to the conference report, the conceit of high ranking cadres had resulted in failure to resolutely implement central instructions and in "intolerable speeches and deeds" undermining Party unity.[29] Thus the regional responses to the Fourth Plenum clearly indicated that the major ramifications of the effort to strengthen Party unity were felt in the home areas of Gao Gang and Rao Shushi.

Defining the Scope of the Purge

A major aspect of the period between the Fourth Plenum and the 1955 National Party Conference was determining who had been linked to the activities of Gao and Rao and defining the scope of the purge. While Gao and Rao themselves had

---

[d] Pan was purged in 1955 during the *sufan* movement for alleged ties to GMD espionage organs. Despite some indirect suggestions of involvement with Rao, there were no direct charges of Pan's participation in Gao-Rao activities at the time of his purge or subsequently. However, Pan's purge was linked to that of Shanghai public security chief Yang Fan who was explicitly tied to the "alliance." See n. 43, this chapter.

clearly been removed from power by February 1954, Party leaders seemingly spent the period following the plenum examining the involvement of individual officials with Gao and Rao before taking definitive action. Thus some who apparently played a role in the affair, e.g., Chen Peixian, were judged involved to a degree requiring no more than self-criticism; others were found more deeply tainted and quietly demoted or purged;[30] and still others were found part of a core group around Gao and Rao and publicly denounced with them in 1955. At the March 1955 conference Mao affirmed that different individuals had "[fallen] under the influence of Gao and Rao ... in varying degrees. Some were influenced in a general way.... A few comrades were deeply influenced ... [and] carried on clandestine activities...." The previous year apparently had been used to determine who fell into these broad categories, and what action was appropriate in each case.[31]

The still tentative attitude of CCP leaders toward the case in the period between the Fourth Plenum and the 1955 Party conference was even seen in the cases of two officials subsequently identified as being in the core of the Gao-Rao "anti-Party alliance." One, Zhang Mingyuan, a leading Northeast official, was reported greeting a North Korean delegation in March 1954 *after* the plenum.[32] The second, Shandong Sub-bureau Second Secretary Xiang Ming, delivered a report on the Fourth Plenum with no apparent self-criticism in the same period.[33] Cultural Revolution accusations shed further light on the sorting out process after the Fourth Plenum as it applied in the case of Xiang Ming. Xiang, according to these allegations, had attempted to build an independent kingdom in Shandong using Rao's influence. He not only pursued erroneous policies, e.g., developing the "rich peasant economy," but supplied Gao and Rao with "anti-Party 'stones,' " i.e., information with which to attack certain central policies and leaders. Thus he "virtually" joined the Gao-Rao alliance, the qualifying adverb suggesting his involvement was something less than total participation in their machinations. In any case, before the Fourth Plenum Tan Zhenlin, in the name of the East China Bureau, assertedly supported Xiang against his critics within the Sub-bureau causing him to be even more intolerant of opposition. The plenum, however, brought the "Shandong problem" to light and a central checkup team was dispatched to the province. Despite alleged cover up efforts by Tan, the checkup resulted in linking Xiang to Gao and Rao.[34]

Apart from attempting to determine the precise involvement of specific officials in the Gao-Rao affair, the circumspect approach of the period leading up to the 1955 Party conference reflected rectification principles. Even those deeply involved in the affair were encouraged to reform themselves. As Mao put it at the conference, "All comrades who have committed mistakes [but] have awakened and are willing to make progress not only must be observed but also must be helped."[35] Such an approach furthermore eased anxieties and reduced potential opposition by those who may have been peripherally or even significantly involved with Gao and Rao.

The Case against Gao Gang and Rao Shushi

More than a year after the decisive Fourth Plenum, the CCP finally denounced Gao Gang and Rao Shushi by name at the March 21–31, 1955, National Party Conference. This conference was chaired by Mao who gave the opening and concluding speeches, and featured two major reports, one (apparently unrelated to the case) by Chen Yun on the FFYP and the other by Deng Xiaoping on the "Gao Gang-Rao Shushi anti-Party alliance." "Fervent discussion" followed the two reports including speeches by all Politburo members. This discussion also included self-criticisms by "many people" who had been influenced by Gao and Rao to greater or lesser degree. In Mao's words, the conference was "another rectification meeting, following the rectification of the Yan'an days."[36]

Also on the agenda was "the establishment of central and local control committees of the Party," a measure explicitly designed to prevent future Gao-Rao cases. On the last day of the conference, it passed three resolutions—on the draft of the FFYP, on the "Gao-Rao anti-Party alliance," and on the establishment of Party control committees. The resolution on the "alliance" further emphasized CCP rectification doctrine as it reported the final disposition of the case. In a classic statement, it declared that "Gao Gang not only did not admit his guilt . . ., [he] even committed suicide as an expression of his ultimate betrayal of the Party"; while Rao Shushi was assertedly unrepentant and "persisted in an attitude of attacking the Party." Both were formally expelled from the CCP.[37] In summarizing the results of the conference, the resolution claimed that a greater unity and solidarity existed than ever before. Immediately thereafter, meeting in its Fifth Plenum on April 4, the Central committee elected Lin Biao and Deng Xiaoping to the Politburo.[38]

The official case against Gao and Rao was stated in the National Party Conference's resolution on the affair; a press campaign in subsequent months elaborated somewhat but made no substantial new revelations. In later years the official media rarely commented on the case. During the Cultural Revolution, however, scattered official and unofficial reports provided valuable information and insights, and in 1977 publication of Volume V of Mao's *Selected Works* gave additional data. Combining the official 1955 view with these later reports, and also using personnel data where relevant, makes possible an evaluation of the case against Gao and Rao and an interpretation of the entire affair.

The Central Charge: Factional Activities to Seize Power

The main charge against Gao Gang and Rao Shushi was that they engaged in secret factional activities with the aim of "seizing the leadership power of the

Party and state." These "conspiratorial activities" *(yinmou huodong)* were assertedly "first and foremost [directed] against the central Politburo, in an attempt to overthrow the long tested nucleus of leadership of the Central Committee headed by Comrade Mao Zedong." The resolution of the March 1955 meeting defined the essence of the conspiracy:

> The characteristic of the Gao Gang-Rao Shushi anti-Party alliance was the fact that they never openly put forward any program against the Central Committee of the Party in any Party organization or at any Party meeting among the public. Their only program was to seize the supreme power of the Party and state by conspiratorial means. They did their utmost to cover up their true character before the Party organizations and Party meetings. . . . Theirs was an unprincipled, conspiratorial group which arose within the Party under the particular circumstances of the present class struggle. . . .[39]

Mao underlined this theme at the conference by introducing a slogan which would become especially significant in the 1970s: "[W]e must all *be open and above board* politically, always ready to express our political views openly . . . on each and every important political issue. We must never follow the example of Gao Gang and Rao Shushi and resort to scheming."[40]

Gao Gang's efforts to split the Party were traced to 1949. From that year on he allegedly spread rumors slandering the Central Committee, stirred up dissatisfaction with leading Party figures, turned the Northeast into an independent kingdom and formed his own anti-Party faction. After his transfer to the Center in 1953, Gao's anti-Party activities reportedly became "even more outrageous." At this point Rao Shushi, who allegedly had resorted to deception on many occasions from 1943 to 1953 to gain power for himself, reportedly came to believe Gao was about to succeed in seizing power and joined forces, using his powers as Party organization head to carry out further splitting activities.[41]

Gao and Rao apparently used several methods to create a factional following. Two were the closely related measures of promoting their individual prestige and creating an organizational power base. They assertedly usurped the work achievements of the Northeast and East China as their own personal merits and stimulated the type of individual worship which had been denounced at the Fourth Plenum. They created the myth that they were "always correct," "men of great ability," and "well trained in theory." The public media were used extensively to increase Gao's personal prestige: e.g., the Northeast People's Publishing House put out volumes of his reports and exhortations on various topics allegedly to picture him as the only person capable of handling key problems of national construction and thus rationalize his accession to greater power.[42] It must be noted, however, that Gao necessarily played an extremely active public role in the early 1950s since the Northeast, as the region of greatest economic development, was often used to give important policies a trial run. In any case, the public exposure Gao gained in national as well as regional media as a result clearly had the acquiescence of central authorities, however he may have tried to use it for factional purposes.

The effort to create an organizational power base focused on Gao Gang's Northeast. This was illustrated by the core group of followers who were denounced with Gao and Rao in 1955.[43] Table 1 lists these officials together with the posts they held in the post-1949 period.[e] It shows six of the seven members of this group had close ties to Gao within Northeast Party and government organizations, collectively dominating leading Party executive posts and positions controlling personnel and discipline. Together with other Northeast officials removed in the wake of the affair, they provided a substantial organizational base although, as we argue below, considerably less than complete control of the area. One official, Ma Hong, apparently accompanied Gao to Beijing and worked under him in the SPC, but the lack of dismissals of other SPC personnel suggests no solid base was established there. As we have seen, Xiang Ming, the one core group member who did not work in the Northeast, assertedly developed ties to Rao during his service in East China. But despite the self-examinations of other local leaders, the East China region as a whole does not appear to have been a well developed organizational base for Gao and Rao since very few regional officials had their careers disrupted as a result of the case.[44]

Independent Kingdoms

As the above suggests, in building an organizational base Gao and Rao inevitably engaged in practices falling under the category of creating independent kingdoms. Fittingly, the term was applied only to the Northeast, although the charge that Rao Shushi "destroyed collective leadership and sought to establish personal prestige in East China" was undoubtedly aimed at similar phenomena. Both Gao and Rao were accused of claiming a "special nature" for their areas in order to justify arbitrary deviations from the Party line. In the Northeast, Gao assertedly refused to implement central directives or allow central organs to investigate local work performance, setting "various leftist or rightist policies against the correct policies of the Center [on the pretext that] the Northeast has always been more advanced."[45] Such charges, of course, ignore the fact that regional decentralization in the early 1950s was designed to give regional leaders flexibility to adjust to special local conditions. Moreover, while it may be tempting to see the centralization measures of 1954–55 as the Center's reaction to its presumed inability to control Gao and perhaps other regional leaders, the official rationale that planned economic construction required greater central coordination (thus making the regions dysfunctional) is sufficient explanation particularly since

[e]These officials, however, were distinguished from Gao and Rao in that they were still referred to as "comrades" and the disciplinary measures taken against them were unspecified —presumably less than expulsion. But there is no record of their appearing after 1955.

Table 1

Members of the "Gao-Rao Anti-Party Alliance"

Official	Post-1949 Positions
Xiang Ming	2nd secretary, Shandong Sub-bureau, 1950–54; vice governor, Shandong, 1951–55.
Zhang Xiushan	deputy secretary, NE Bureau, 1952–54; director, NE organization dept., 1950–53; chairman, NE supervision com., 1950–54; secretary, NE discipline inspection com., early 1950s; deputy political commissar, NE Military Region, early 1950s.
Zhang Mingyuan	3rd deputy secretary and secretary-general, NE Bureau, 1952–54; vice chairman, NE govt., 1953–54; secretary-general, NE govt., 1952–54; vice chairman, NE supervision com., 1950–52.
Zhao Dezun	secretary, Heilongjiang, 1950–54; governor, Heilongjiang, 1952–53; deputy director, NE organization dept., 1951; director, NE rural work dept., 1954.
Ma Hong	deputy secretary-general, NE Bureau, 1952; member and secretary-general, SPC, 1952–53.
Guo Feng	secretary, Liaoxi, 1950–54; deputy director, NE organization dept., 1952–53; director, NE organization dept., 1953; director, NE personnel dept., 1952; deputy secretary, NE discipline inspection com., early 1950s.
Chen Bocun	2nd secretary, Lüda, 1952–53; deputy director, NE organization dept., 1950–51; director, NE personnel dept., 1952; deputy secretary, NE discipline inspection com., early 1950s; member, NE procurator's office, 1951.

centralizing steps were taken systematically throughout the 1950–55 period.[f]

As indicated in the media campaign following the Fourth Plenum, an important factor allowing the existence of independent kingdoms was the impotence of the CCP's control machinery—the discipline inspection committees. The key shortcoming of the discipline inspection committees was their complete subordination to Party committees or bureaus of the same level. Thus in the Northeast the regional discipline inspection committee was staffed by Zhang Xiushan, Chen Bocun and Guo Feng, all officials of the Northeast Party Bureau and members of the Gao-Rao "alliance." As a result it was unable to provide a check

[f]See NCNA, Beijing, September 24, 1954. However, the *Selected Works* version of Mao's April 1956 speech, "On the Ten Great Relationships," implies a link to the Gao-Rao affair: "[The large regions] had shortcomings which were later exploited to a certain extent by . . . [Gao Gang and Rao Shushi]. It was subsequently decided to abolish [them] and put the various provinces directly under the central authorities." *SW*, V, 293–94. But even if the Gao-Rao case served as a catalyst for the dismantling of the large regions, the trend toward centralization was clearly well established before the surfacing of the affair.

on the activities of Gao Gang. Another example occurred in Shandong where Xiang Ming allegedly used his power in the Party sub-bureau not only to "outrageously restrict" the work of the provincial discipline inspection committee, but also to "drive out of Shandong" staff members of the central discipline inspection body who had been sent to carry out investigations.[46] Events such as these undoubtedly explain the National Party Conference's decision to revamp the Party control system and replace the discipline inspection committees with more powerful control committees.[47]

The question remains, however, to what extent the Northeast under Gao Gang was an independent kingdom in the sense of a sealed off area more loyal to local leaders than the Party Center. Despite charges that Gao refused to implement central directives, the overall picture projected by the Northeast in the early 1950s—as illustrated by the Three Anti Campaign in 1951—is that of a trailblazer, the area where policies were tested and refined before adoption on a nationwide basis. In those years the national media treated the Northeast as a model area to be emulated by the rest of the nation. Moreover, the Northeast's response to central policy directives insofar as can be judged by public statements was consistently prompt and vigorous endorsement. Thus while Gao, and many other local leaders, may have bent or ignored central directives as they saw fit, there is little to indicate he developed a distinctive set of policies in the Northeast at variance with the Center's programs.[48]

Another perspective, that of personnel developments surrounding the case, provides further insights into this question. First, the strength and penetration of the "alliance" in the Northeast was extensive. Gao and his core followers had a stranglehold on the leading positions of the regional Party bureau; of eleven bureau leaders only First Deputy Secretary Lin Feng and three propaganda officials[49] were not dismissed. Moreover, in contrast to all other regions, there is evidence of considerable repercussions of the Gao-Rao affair on leading provincial and municipal personnel. In four of the six Northeast provinces and in each of the region's six major cities, careers of high Party and government officials were affected.[50] In some cases, e.g., Governor Chen Lei of Heilongjiang who became a provincial department head, demotions occurred; in other cases, e.g., Secretary Han Tianshi of Anshan, quiet removals from office apparently took place. Finally, the ramifications of the case on the Northeast military command bear comment. Not only had Gao served as commander and political commissar and Zhang Xiushan as deputy political commissar, but Deputy Commander He Jinnian, Chief of Staff Duan Suquan and Air Defense Commander Zhou Shichang apparently suffered severe career setbacks after 1954–55.[51]

Although the above suggests the strength of Gao's organizational base in the Northeast, a broader view indicates its limitations. If the entire leadership serving under Gao in key Party, government and military positions in the post-1949 Northeast is examined, the great majority of key officials continued their careers uninterrupted following the Gao-Rao affair. Of 40 Northeast leaders for whom pre-1949 career data are available, only three suffered from Gao's purge.[52] Further analysis, moreover, reveals that the surviving 37 officials had diverse pre-1949 revolutionary experiences including participation in the Jiangxi Soviet, Long March and other major events in South China, as well as service in the New Fourth Army. Thus these leaders had developed career ties quite independent of Gao Gang and were by no means totally beholden to him.[53]

A career illustrating experiences and contacts separate from Gao prior to Communist entry into the Northeast in 1945–46 is that of Lin Feng, Gao's immediate deputy in the Northeast Bureau. Lin joined the CCP in 1927 and held a number of posts during the 1930s in North China which undoubtedly involved underground work—i.e., work in the "white areas"—and brought him into contact with Liu Shaoqi, whom he served as a personal secretary. In the early years of the Sino-Japanese War Lin served as a political officer with He Long's forces in Northwest Shanxi; for the remainder of the war he was active in the Shanxi-Suiyan area. The importance of Lin's position by the war's end was indicated by his election to the Seventh Central Committee in 1945, apparently before any career ties to Gao Gang developed. Shortly thereafter he was dispatched to the Northeast where he served as a member of the regional Party bureau's standing committee, first under Peng Zhen and then under Gao Gang. In the early 1950s Lin was clearly the number two man in the Northeast, although far overshadowed by Gao. After Gao's purge, Lin was transferred to Beijing where he was named head of the State Council's Second Staff Office dealing with cultural and educational affairs and became one of the regime's most influential officials.[54]

Thus despite his immense powers in the Northeast, Gao Gang did not rule over a clique of personal followers. Indeed, most of his pre-1935 associates in North Shaanxi had remained in the Northwest following the Japanese surrender. As the case of Lin Feng demonstrates, an important part of the Northeast leadership had independent political connections to support their careers. This factor undoubtedly impeded any efforts to draw such leaders into the "alliance" and thus create a truly airtight independent kingdom. Indeed, what is particularly striking is the contrast between such officials and the people who fell with Gao, none of whom (excepting Rao and Xiang Ming) are known to have had significant careers independent of Gao's influence.

Personnel data can be used in other ways to test the extent of Gao's independent kingdom. Presumably, if the Northeast had become a "camouflaged power center beyond the effective control of Beijing,"[55] there would be evidence of adverse effects on career advancement of the total group of officials serving under Gao. Yet this is not borne out by the available data. An examination of ministers and vice ministers serving in 1965–66 prior to the Cultural Revolution reveals that the Northeast more than held its own in comparison with other pre-1954 large administrative regions in staffing high level central positions.[56] Especially interesting is the fact that officials with pre-1954 Northeast experience made up the largest group of 1965 vice chairmen of the SPC, an indication

Table 2

Background of Leading Provincial and Municipal Officials in the Northeast, 1955

Served in NE under Gao	72	92%
Served in same province or city	(53)	(68%)
Served elsewhere in NE	(19)	(24%)
Sent in from other areas	4	5%
Previous work locale unknown	2	3%
Total	78	100%

that functional considerations—i.e., the need for cadres with economic expertise which the advanced Northeast could provide—far outweighed any possible stigma attached to people who had worked with Gao.

Another likely response by the central leadership to a perceived loss of control over the Northeast would have been to break the continuity of leadership in the region; again, the data do not bear this out. The personnel shake-up resulting from the purge provided ample opportunity for the Center to send in outside personnel to assume leading roles. Yet, as Table 2 indicates, this happened in only a small fraction of cases. The great bulk of vacant positions was filled by officials who had worked elsewhere in the Northeast under Gao or who were promoted from within the same organizations. Furthermore, on a comparative basis, the proportion of Northeast provincial Party secretaries in the post-1956 decade who served in that area prior to 1954 was of the same order as that for other regions.[57] Finally, although the data on the post-1954 Northeast military command are far more sketchy, four of the seven leaders who could be identified had served under Gao and two others had served in Korea, and thus probably had dealings with Gao's command during the war.[58]

In sum, the key posts held by Gao Gang and his followers in the Northeast, particularly in the regional Party apparatus, placed them in an excellent position to magnify their personal prestige, affect the implementation of policy in ways which conceivably could annoy the Party Center, and generally influence the political life of the region. Nevertheless, Gao's power and authority within the Northeast undoubtedly derived from his position within the national leadership of the CCP. There is little to indicate that the overall Northeast leadership, which included many key figures who survived Gao's purge, was bound by cohesive ties either to Gao Gang as an individual or to the Northeast as a regional power center. The career patterns of major regional leaders were too diverse to easily lead to a narrow clique. The proportionate role which Northeast cadres continued to play in the political life of the nation and the high degree of regional continuity in Party, state and military leaders further indicates their basic loyalty as a group to national goals and authority. Thus without denying Gao's great organizational strength at the regional level, the existence of an independent kingdom impervious to central direction is most doubtful.

A Soviet Connection?

One additional variant of the argument that Gao Gang had indeed set up an independent power center in the Northeast requires analysis—the view that Gao's independence was supported by the Soviet Union under Stalin. This speculative interpretation has been advanced by foreign observers on the basis of Stalin's known penchant for extending his control to foreign Communist parties, Russia's historical interest in Manchuria, and such concrete facts as Gao's July 1949 mission to Moscow concluding a trade agreement between the Soviet Union and the Northeast government before formal governmental relations existed between Moscow and Beijing. Most important, an undeniably significant role was played by Soviet economic aid and advisers in the Northeast during the early 1950s and Gao necessarily developed close contacts with Russian representatives.

The possibility of a Soviet connection gains some support from both Chinese and Russian sources. On the Chinese side, most significant is Mao's November 1956 statement made during a discussion of Sino-Soviet relations:

> Here I'll speak on the question of "having illicit relations with foreign countries." Are there such people in our country who provide foreigners with information behind the back of the Central Committee? I think there are. Gao Gang is a case in point.[59]

Moreover, Mao later observed that Stalin liked Gao very much and gave him an automobile while Gao sent Stalin congratulatory telegrams on each anniversary of the Japanese surrender.[60] Recent Russian sources in the context of Sino-Soviet polemics have been somewhat more explicit in linking Gao's downfall to his relations with Moscow, claiming, e.g., that Gao's "offense" was his "friendship with the Soviet Union."[61] Other Soviet sources, however, suggest Gao's enthusiasm for the USSR was less than wholehearted.[g]

---

[g]*Kommunist,* No. 7, May 1964, trans. in *CQ,* No. 19 (1964), p. 191, reported that a Northeast faction headed by Peng Zhen and Lin Feng was hostile to the Soviet Union in the period following Japan's surrender apparently because of the Soviet policy of stripping Manchurian industry. In 1949 the Northeast Bureau under Gao conducted criticism of anti-Sovietism (something fully compatible with Mao's "lean to one side" policy) but, according to the Soviet account, it was of a perfunctory nature.

In addition, there is other information which calls into question Gao Gang's purported links to the Soviet Union. Alex B. Ikonnikov, a White Russian raised in China who worked as a translator in the Northeast in these years and dealt with Gao Gang on several occasions, views Gao as a strong Chinese nationalist with pronounced anti-Russian sentiments. It is also of interest that several statements—e.g., NCNA, Shenyang, July 1, 1955, in *SCMP,* No. 1087—linked the need to eliminate Gao's influence in the Northeast with the necessity of following the advice of Soviet experts, something one would hardly expect if Gao's relations with such experts had been a device for maintaining his alleged independence of Beijing.

What, then, are we to make of Mao's 1956 remarks about "illicit relations"? The answer may be provided by Khrushchev's memoirs. Khrushchev, who apparently did not have a particularly close knowledge of the matter, reported that Gao had revealed the true feelings of Chinese leaders towards the Soviet Union to the Soviet ambassador, assertedly claiming that Liu Shaoqi and Zhou Enlai (the main targets of the conspiracy)—but not Mao—were vocal opponents of Moscow. Mao became aware of this since Stalin, in an effort to win his confidence, turned the ambassador's report over to the Chairman.[62] Thus we have a possible instance of "providing foreigners with information behind the back of the Central Committee." But the questions remain whether Gao's actions, if true, implied close ties with Stalin, whether they were unique, and whether they represented a clear violation of existing Party norms.

The incident as described seems fairly innocent. Gao, who had been designated an official representative of the Central Committee for communication with the Soviets, could be seen as engaging in an indiscretion by speaking ill of Liu and Zhou, but it hardly represented a close working partnership. Moreover, in the context of the early 1950s, far-ranging discussions with the Russians were a matter of course since the central leadership was strongly committed to the Soviet model. Mao himself repeatedly engaged in such discussions and, according to Khrushchev, was less than generous in *his* comments on other Politburo members. There is, moreover, no firm evidence of clear-cut guidelines on what was or was not a violation of organizational norms regarding dealings with the Soviet "big brother." It is instructive that in contrast to Mao's 1956 statement which came in a highly critical evaluation of the Russians at a time when strains had already appeared in Sino-Soviet relations, Mao's remarks at the March 1955 conference concerning the Soviet Union were favorable and contained no hint of criticism. What became "illicit" subsequently was seemingly less offensive at the time of the Gao-Rao affair.[63]

On balance, the evidence is insufficient to support the theory that close Gao-Soviet links led to his purge. The absence of more detailed information linking Gao and Stalin is particularly striking. There would have been, of course, many reasons in the 1950s for both Beijing and Moscow to maintain silence if such ties had existed. But it is noteworthy that so little was said about Gao Gang in the Sino-Soviet polemics of the 1960s and in Red Guard publications which paid scant attention to potentially embarrassing aspects of their revelations. Especially interesting is the failure of Mao in his candid criticisms of Stalin to denounce Gao explicitly for involvement with the Soviet leader. Lack of information can hardly prove the non-existence of a political relationship, but in view of the uninhibited nature of Cultural Revolution sources its absence in this case is significant.

Ultimately, the most convincing argument against the Soviet connection theory is that such ties were not only not needed for Gao to make a bid for supreme power, but would actually have been detrimental to any such effort. Gao was in a position to try for national leadership because of his position in the highest Party body, the Politburo, and the acceptance he had gained from Mao and other leaders over the years in a purely *Chinese* context. Moreover, given the blunders of Comintern leadership during the Chinese revolution and the CCP's assertion of political independence from Moscow during the first rectification campaign (in which Gao played a key role), any leader attempting to gain support for a power bid would have been seriously disadvantaged by excessive involvement with the Soviet Union. The route to power within the CCP was through Beijing and not Moscow.

Building a National Faction: Methods, Tactics and Timing

The organizational base in the Northeast, even without the albatross of Soviet backing, clearly was insufficient for a bid at national power. As suggested above, to have a chance at success Gao and Rao had to win over more powerful figures at the central and regional levels. What appeals did they use in this effort? Not surprisingly, official descriptions of their alleged conspiratorial methods were vague and elusive. Gao and Rao were said to have been aware that their project was a gamble and assertedly changed methods at different times and under different circumstances so as to adapt to the "political climate." They posed as staunch revolutionaries and performed useful work in order to win the trust of the Party while creating dissatisfaction with individual leading cadres by "spreading rumors" and "sowing discord."[64]

A full reading of the evidence suggests Gao and Rao essentially relied on two tactics: (1) attempting to play off officials with certain career backgrounds against those with different revolutionary careers; and (2) dangling the prospect of leading positions under a Gao-Rao regime before ambitious officials. But before examining these tactics, it is necessary to comment on the apparent failure of policy issues to be a major factor in the effort to build the Gao-Rao faction.

The Minor Role of Policy Issues

As we have seen, the "Resolution on the Gao Gang-Rao Shushi Anti-Party Alliance" asserted that Gao and Rao had engaged in unprincipled activities. The implications of this charge are twofold: (1) Gao and Rao violated traditional Party procedures concerning the airing of dissident views; and (2) policy concerns were not central to the formation of their clique. In contrast to principled differences over Party policies which were legitimate subjects for debate within authorized Party bodies, the unprincipled disputes fostered by Gao and Rao reportedly centered on personalities and individual gain. Rather than oppose Central Committee policies in duly constituted forums they "lied consistently within the Party organization" and formally supported the Center; but outside

Party meetings Gao and Rao covertly spread their grievances in hope of winning over others in opposition to individual leading cadres.[65]

Whenever policy issues were raised in official charges they concerned the period *before* the conspiracy surfaced. Thus Rao was accused of rightist deviations during his tenure in East China by assertedly delaying social reforms in the cities, failing to mobilize the masses in rural work or smash the feudal order, and instead "surrendering to the capitalists, landlords and rich peasants." Rao was also held guilty of one-sidedly stressing magnanimity to protect counterrevolutionaries.[66] Whatever the truth of these allegations, they do not refer to issues which were policy questions in 1953 when the factional activities of Gao and Rao were most intense. The reference to the failure to smash the feudal order clearly concerns implementation of land reform, but by 1953 the main policy decisions in the countryside concerned the rate and nature of cooperativization. The question of "magnanimity" concerning counterrevolutionaries was an important issue in the winter of 1950–51, not 1953. Moreover, while Gao had allegedly implemented "various leftist or rightist policies" in the Northeast, as indicated above, that region was regarded a model for the rest of the country in the early 1950s. Thus these accusations do not contradict the view that the Gao-Rao faction was neither the product of fundamental policy differences, nor did it find its essential expression in such differences.

Nevertheless, it is difficult to conceive of factional politics where policy issues do not come into play at least as tools of conflict. Moreover, there may have been reasons for CCP leaders to suppress evidence of policy differences—e.g., to maintain the image of unanimity behind the general line or to keep open policy issues on which Gao and Rao may have taken stands without prejudicing the argument by associating a particular view with the discredited conspirators. Thus it is necessary to examine further the possible involvement of policy issues. Of the issues raised by Western scholars, the most systematic case has been made regarding alleged differences over the form of industrial management.[67]

In the early 1950s the CCP introduced the Soviet Union's "one man management" *(yizhangzhi)* system of factory organization. This system was never fully implemented throughout China. It focused on the economically advanced Northeast, especially key industrial projects aided by Soviet loans, equipment and technical experts. Under one man management the sole authority for business operations was vested in a technically competent factory manager, and under his authority individual heads of shops and production teams had unchallenged control of their units. This reduced the role of the factory Party committee and thus ran counter to the traditional CCP emphasis on collective leadership by Party committees which was emphasized following the Fourth Plenum. In terms of the distribution of power within the political system, it strengthened vertically organized economic ministries at the expense of territorially based Party committees. As the end of the FFYP approached in 1956, however, CCP leaders became increasingly aware that the Soviet model was not fully applicable to China. One man management was a case in point since China lacked the solid core of capable managerial personnel on which the system depended, and at the Eighth Party Congress it was officially scrapped in favor of "factory manager responsibility under the leadership of the Party committee" *(dangwei lingdaoxia de changzhang fuzezhi)*, a new arrangement which conferred greater powers on Party committees *vis-à-vis* factory managers.

Since the one man management experiment focused on the Northeast, since Gao had endorsed it,[68] and since the implications of the system ran counter to the themes of the Fourth Plenum, it has been argued that this issue was a key factor in the purge of Gao and Rao. Yet the purge was not decisive on this question; one of the major statements articulating the advantages of one man management appeared three months *after* the Fourth Plenum.[69] Moreover, while a few statements charging Gao with downgrading Party organizations in industrial enterprises appeared following the rejection of one man management in 1956, Gao was on record in 1952 in support of Party leadership within such enterprises.[70] On balance, it is unlikely that industrial management policy was a major issue around which Gao rallied support for his cause, particularly as others who had advocated similar views in this sphere survived Gao's fall.[71] In any case, although one man management enhanced the authority of central economic organs, this was not necessarily to Gao's advantage in view of his limited power base in these organs: apart from Gao, Rao and Ma Hong on the SPC, the entire central economic apparatus of the PRC apparently was unaffected by the purge. In contrast, given Gao's dominance of the Northeast Party Bureau, a managerial system stressing Party committee authority would have been more conducive to maximizing his control of China's key industries than a system emphasizing vertical ministerial control.

The preceding discussion suggests a paradox: in the period spanning the purge of Gao and Rao there were many policy differences yet policy issues were tangential to the purge. The key to this paradox was the broad policy consensus on the Soviet model during the first half dozen years of the PRC. As indicated in Chapter 4, adjustments were made to take account of Chinese conditions. Nevertheless, the Soviet model was widely accepted as a proven path to both great power status and a socialist society. Agreement on the overall course of development did not eliminate issues of contention; in addition to industrial organization, the rate of economic growth, the role of private capital in economic reconstruction, the rate of cooperativization, and a host of other questions provided ample opportunity for spirited debate within the framework of consensus. But precisely because of the confidence in a well charted path to obtainable goals, freewheeling debate over pace and methods raised little danger of polarization within the leadership. As minister of Finance Li Xiannian put it in November 1955 concerning agricultural cooperativization, "We did not have any doubts about the general line ... [but only deviated] in our view of the speed of development."[72] In this context even "erroneous" views during policy debates could not shake the firm foundation of shared principles. Only in less certain times, with the policy consensus eroded and fundamental choices to be made, would the permissible limits of debate shrink and policy conflict lead to a major leadership purge (see Chapter 9).

In these circumstances, it is not surprising that any policy aspects of the Gao-Rao conspiracy were secondary at best. In a situation where a free exchange of opinions within the top elite was the norm, Gao and Rao undoubtedly found themselves in varying degrees of agreement and disagreement on a wide range of issues with many CCP leaders. But given the overall consensus, it was unlikely that any program could be formulated which both appeared distinctive from what other leaders advocated and necessary to meet urgent problems. Indeed, to the extent Gao and Rao advanced policy related views, it appears they were less concerned with fashioning a coherent program than with attacking the performance of other leaders. According to Mao in 1959:

> The Gao-Rao anti-Party clique were too extreme, they went beyond the limit. They opposed [Liu] and Zhou, and [Liu] was the key point. . . . They negated everything, attacked one point which was not as good as the remainder and exaggerated the one point to cover everything. . . .[73]

Since the time was not ripe for mobilizing support along programmatic lines, Gao and Rao apparently were reduced to carping criticism of others' efforts to carry out Party policies. This situation further meant they had to resort to even less principled appeals to advance their cause.

"Revolutionary Bases" against "White Areas": The Effort to Manipulate Career Tensions

Gao Gang attempted to win support by appealing to presumed grievances of leaders with certain types of revolutionary experience against those with contrasting pre-1949 careers. The resolution on the "alliance" outlines this effort to "distort history":

> [Gao] even tried to instigate Party members in the army to support his conspiracy against the Central Committee of the Party. For this purpose he raised the utterly absurd "theory" that our Party consisted of two parties—one, the so-called "party of the revolutionary bases and the army" *(genqu de he jundui de dang),* the other, the so-called "party of the white areas" *(baiqu de dang)*—that the Party was created by the army. He claimed himself as the representative of the so-called "party of the revolutionary bases and the army" and [that he] should hold the major authority, that the Party Central Committee and the government should therefore be reorganized in accordance with his plan and that he himself should for the time being be general secretary or vice chairman of the Central Committee and premier of the State Council.[74]

This account claims Gao attempted to enlist leaders whose revolutionary careers largely involved work in guerrilla base areas—e.g., the Jiangxi Soviet before 1935 and the Yan'an area during the Sino-Japanese War—and Red Army service against those who had done extensive work in areas of enemy control, the so-called "white areas." "White areas" refers both to places, particularly cities, under the GMD regime following the 1927 CCP-GMD split, and to Japanese controlled regions during the Sino-Japanese War. The leading Party figure most closely identified with "white area" work was Liu Shaoqi. Of the remaining two dozen or so top leaders of the PRC, Peng Zhen, a Politburo member, and Bo Yibo had the closest career ties to "white areas." Moreover, although service in the wartime Communist delegation to the Nationalist government was not generally termed "white area" work, it certainly was a distinct career pattern within GMD territory contrasting to that of army and base area cadres. At the Politburo level, Zhou Enlai and Dong Biwu represented this career line. Taking the Politburo as a whole, at least two-thirds of the dozen members had some "white area" experience, although in terms of total careers "revolutionary base area and army" service was more significant for most.[h] In this situation Gao and Rao were apparently attempting to fan resentment on the part of "base area and army" cadres over the fact that while they assertedly had won the revolution, "white area" figures Liu Shaoqi and Zhou Enlai held the second and third ranking positions in the Party after Mao. That Liu and Zhou were the key targets of the conspiracy is indicated both by Mao's words quoted above and by the posts Gao allegedly sought: the premiership was held by Zhou; and while neither the Party general secretary[i] nor vice chairman positions existed, the creation of either post for Gao would presumably have meant his replacing Liu as the second ranking Party figure.

---

[h] This analysis is at variance with that of Roderick MacFarquhar, "On Photographs," *CQ*, No. 46 (1971), p. 294. Based on an examination of biographies of each Politburo member, we make the following categorization: (1) pure "base area and army"—Mao, Gao, Zhu De, Peng Dehuai; (2) overwhelmingly "base area and army" but some "white area" work—Chen Yun, Zhang Wentian; (3) important "white area" experience but predominantly "base area and army" careers—Lin Boqu, Kang Sheng (?); (4) critical "white area" service but important "base area and army" work as well—Liu, Zhou, Dong, Peng Zhen. Kang Sheng is especially difficult to categorize because of large gaps in the data on his career.

[i] The general secretaryship *(zongshuji)* had been a powerful post in the early 1930s before being discontinued. In that period the less significant post of secretary-general *(mishuzhang)* also existed. NCNA, Beijing, May 3, 1954, identified Deng Xiaoping as *mishuzhang* and in 1956 he was elected *zongshuji*. Thus it is possible that Gao's desire to be general secretary was partially designed to curtail the rise of Deng, a hypothesis reinforced by the fact that Deng gave the 1955 report on the "alliance," was immediately elected to the Politburo, and rose to the general secretaryship over a good number of officials with more impressive career credentials. Deng, however, had a predominantly "base area and army" career although he served briefly in Shanghai in the late 1920s.

While Liu and Zhou were clearly the major targets of the conspiracy, who were the allies Gao and Rao sought? Within the Politburo the figure with the closest career ties to Gao Gang was Lin Boqu, Gao's old associate in the Shaan-Gan-Ning Border Region. Yet Gao apparently was unable to win over Lin or any other high ranking officials who had served in the Shaan-Gan-Ning area apart from Zhang Xiushan and He Jinnian. A partial explanation for this failure is that generally the career connections of these officials to Gao were of limited duration; many leading Shaan-Gan-Ning officials including Lin had previously participated in the southern phase of the revolution while very few later served under Gao in the post-liberation Northeast. Similarly, Politburo figures who had worked with Gao in the Northeast in the late 1940s had separate careers before and after that period.[75] Among the outstanding PLA figures Gao probably tried to win over were Zhu De, Peng Dehuai and Lin Biao.[76] Both Lin Biao and Peng Dehuai had previous dealings with Gao—Lin as leader of the armies entering the Northeast in 1945–46 and Peng as commander of Chinese forces in Korea while Gao ruled the adjacent Northeast—while Zhu De was linked to the case by unofficial Cultural Revolution sources. Yet here again Gao's blandishments seemingly failed: both Peng and Lin rose in prominence during the period of the purge. Peng became Defense Minister in September 1954 while Lin was elevated to the Politburo following the 1955 national conference. A possible interpretation is that their increased stature was partially a reward for rejecting Gao's appeals.[j]

It is also possible, however, that some military leaders had been involved with Gao and Rao despite their continued prominence following the purge. Red Guard allegations concerning Zhu De are too few and too vague to be convincing proof of active participation in Gao-Rao activities,[77] but more weighty evidence exists concerning Peng Dehuai. The secret 1959 resolution on Peng's dismissal claimed Peng, together with Huang Kecheng and Zhang Wentian (also a Politburo member in 1953), had participated in the "alliance":

> During the struggle against [Gao and Rao] the Central Committee ... was already in possession of certain facts about Peng's and Huang's participation, ... seriously criticized them, hoping they would ... repent, and did not go deeply

[j] Some analysts, however, have speculated that Lin's rise may have reflected displeasure with Peng. Indeed, Lin was listed above Peng in the list of vice premiers selected at the First National People's Congress in September 1954 despite his lower Party rank, lack of ministerial portfolio and apparent inactivity. Nevertheless, Peng was third on the list of vice premiers and the general conclusion that his status in the 1954–55 period was enhanced, or at the very least did not decline, remains valid. For further evidence of Peng's increased stature in this period, see MacFarquhar, "Photographs," pp. 295–96.

> into the matter. Ostensibly [they] made a self-criticism; actually . . . they concealed certain important facts concerning their participation. . . .[78]

Cultural Revolution sources further claim that Peng developed close ties to Gao during the Korean War and wanted Gao for his chief of staff, a relationship which if true presumably could have predisposed Peng to listen to Gao's ideas on national leadership. In any case, when Peng sought to reopen his case in January 1962 Mao and Zhou reportedly interrupted a discussion of Peng's part in the Gao-Rao affair by Liu to assert that Peng had been a "principal member" and even "the leader" of the clique. However, since these statements came after Peng was in political disgrace for other reasons, they are particularly difficult to evaluate.[79]

Even accepting some involvement on Peng's part, a number of alternatives are possible. Peng might have listened to Gao briefly and then reported his activities to Mao and Liu, thus playing an active role in Gao's downfall. Alternatively, he might have played a tangential role in Gao's group but sided with Liu and Zhou when the issue came to a head. A third possibility is that other leaders were simply unaware at the time of how deeply committed Peng had been to Gao.[80] Or Peng could indeed have been recognized as a "principal member" but allowed to repent by the dominant group in order to minimize dissent and opposition. It should be noted that a self-criticism by Peng is compatible with all of these possibilities, including the first. But under the last and, to a lesser extent, second alternatives, it is difficult to explain Peng's new post as Minister of Defense and his rise in prominence particularly since the Gao-Rao conspiracy seemingly was so feeble (see below). In any case, whatever their degree of involvement, Peng and all other Politburo members supported Liu and Zhou at the critical Fourth Plenum.

Implicit in the appeal to "base area and army" cadres was a redistribution of power and positions at the expense of leading "white area" figures. This may have included a reshuffle of the Politburo, as suggested by the circulation of An Ziwen's list at the 1953 organization conference. The promise of important posts in a future Gao-Rao government was more graphically illustrated by an unofficial Cultural Revolution source purporting to tell of Gao's approach to Tao Zhu, then the leading Party official in South China and a former associate of Gao's in the Northeast before 1949. According to this report, Gao and Zhang Xiushan went to Canton in 1953 to hold secret talks with Tao. They told Tao that there was wide support for Gao to be Party vice chairman and asked his opinion. Tao reportedly replied, "You are most experienced in practical work," and Gao responded by dangling a vice premiership before Tao's eyes. When the case broke against Gao, Tao hurriedly made a "false confession," claiming he thought Gao had been indulging in idle gossip and was merely "sounding him out," and proclaimed his support of Liu Shaoqi.[81] Indeed, it seems Gao and Rao were proceeding in a circumspect manner. Following the purge official sources expressed concern over the lax attitude of officials who had been aware of Gao's activities but did not consider them a serious matter.[82] Together with the account of the approach to Tao, this suggests the lure of office was used only tentatively and the conspiracy never reached the stage of elaborate bargains on the shape of a future regime.

Why did the attempt to rally support around the banner of the "base areas and army" fail? Several reasons can be offered. First, grievances of "base area and army" leaders probably were minimal. The leaders of the southern guerrilla bases who followed Mao on the Long March dominated the Central Committee,[83] while PLA military and political officers moved into leading Party, government and army positions at all levels after liberation. As stated above, "base area and army" experience predominated in the Politburo despite significant "white area" representation. Thus especially at the Central Committee level and above, "base area" officials could hardly feel themselves the victims of systematic discrimination.

Second, the personal histories of Liu Shaoqi and Zhou Enlai, as of many other key leaders, were too complex to be easily identified with a particular career type. Liu, for example, in addition to his extensive experience in "white areas," worked in the Jiangxi Soviet, took part in the hallowed Long March, spent much of the Sino-Japanese War in Yan'an, and played a leading role in many distinctive "base area" policies. Moreover, his activities with the New Fourth Army in 1941–42 gave Liu close contacts with one of the main career lines within the army. From the early 1940s on he became Mao's trusted collaborator at the Party Center and as a result greatly extended his contacts and power within the top leadership. Similarly, Zhou had a diverse career including early contacts with key army figures such as Lin Biao, a central role in the Jiangxi Soviet, and participation in the Long March with Mao. Thus any effort to isolate Liu and Zhou as "white area" representatives faced considerable obstacles.

Furthermore, any attempt to polarize the Party along "base area"-"white area" lines clashed with existing leadership arrangements, the unified nature of that leadership, and with well established Party norms. Much as the broad policy consensus had inhibited Gao and Rao from developing a distinctive program, past successes based on the cooperation of different groups within the Party, together with a liberal sharing of power along well defined lines, drastically limited the effectiveness of efforts to fan factional resentment. In the early 1950s the pecking order of the top leadership was clear—after Mao stood Liu, Zhou and Zhu De.[84] Mao, moreover, had clearly made the unity of diverse groups a key principle of his approach to leadership; whatever past confidence he had in Gao would have been shattered by knowledge of divisive activities conducted outside formal Party channels. Even in a situation of Mao's possible incapacitation, other leaders undoubtedly had a strong commitment to norms of leadership which allowed their vigorous participation in Party councils with relatively little fear of punishment for "erroneous" views. It is not difficult to imagine reluctance to cast their lot with someone threatening those norms.

Under different conditions of an eroded policy consensus or increased factional tensions Gao's efforts might have had greater chance of success. In a hypothetical showdown between "base area" and "white area" factions (and the Gao-Rao case did not represent such a simple polarization as Rao himself had "white area" experience), the "base area" side undoubtedly would have emerged victorious. For despite the strong position of "white area" types in the central Party apparatus and their substantial representation within the Politburo, any vote in the Politburo and particularly Central Committee would in all likelihood have gone against the "white area" group. Moreover, if Party legality was overthrown completely the "base area" group would certainly have prevailed due to its control of the instruments of coercion—the army and (less clearly) the public security apparatus.[85] But while new leadership arrangements were a definite possibility in 1953–54 due to organizational changes accompanying centralization and the FFYP as well as to uncertainty over Mao's health, divisive votes on factional lines, much less extra-legal means, would have clashed fundamentally with the existing style of leadership. Party leaders as a whole were predisposed to continuing the sharing of power among various groups,[k] ratifying existing succession arrangements which could only benefit Liu Shaoqi,[l] and rejecting any bid to upset the applecart.

Finally, even if substantial resentment against "white area" officials had existed and conditions were more favorable to polarization, Gao Gang lacked the contacts to represent the "base areas and army." Gao's pre-1935 experiences were isolated from the main stream of CCP development in the south and thus he could not at an early stage develop ties with the men who became the most important leaders of the PRC. Moreover, the most influential officials who had served in the old North Shaanxi base area developed independent careers in the Northwest after 1945; thereafter they had neither close contact with nor career dependence on Gao Gang. The relatively undistinguished careers of those Gao did draw into the "alliance" underlines the limits of his connections. Apart from all other factors, Gao Gang failed because he was the wrong person to build a faction purporting to represent either the revolutionary base areas or the army.

---

[k] Evidence of this is suggested by developments at the March 1955 conference. Both new members of the Politburo, Deng Xiaoping and Lin Biao, were essentially "base area and army" men, while the head of the new Party control apparatus, Dong Biwu, had been deeply involved in "white area" work.

[l] The dating of Liu's emergence as Mao's successor is unclear but one report places it at the Seventh Congress in 1945; see *Hongqi* [Red Flag] (Beijing Red Guard newspaper), April 4, 1967, in *SCMP-S*, No. 180. Even if this report is erroneous and his 1959 appointment as State Chairman (which was apparently agreed upon in late 1957) is a more accurate date, in 1953–54 Liu was the second ranking member of the Politburo and thus the logical candidate for preeminence in any succession situation.

Mao's Illness and a Premature Succession Struggle

Throughout the official version of the Gao-Rao case runs a contradiction—although accused of seeking to "overthrow the long tested nucleus of the ... Central Committee headed by Comrade Mao Zedong," the details of the charges against Gao and Rao suggest that their primary targets were the leaders directly *below* Mao, Liu Shaoqi and Zhou Enlai. The absence of Mao from public view between December 1953 and March 1954 deepens the mystery. While Mao clearly played a crucial part in the events of this period through his attack on Gao and Rao at the December Politburo meeting, what was his overall role and can it illuminate the timing and motivation of the Gao-Rao conspiracy?

Cultural Revolution revelations provide the key to the mystery—Mao's health. Mao's absence apparently was the culmination of a period of serious illness. Tan Zhenlin and Chen Peixian, whose alleged activities at the 1953 financial and economic conference were previously discussed, reportedly initiated about that time a joint letter requesting Mao "take a rest" and give up at least some of his posts. Chen was accused, furthermore, of teaming up with Gao and Rao to seek Mao's abdication, saying "Gao is young and capable [while] some people are old and do not look fit." Chen defended his actions by claiming the purpose of the letter, in traditional Chinese fashion, had been to protect Mao's health by reducing his burdens.[86] While the precise role of Gao and Rao in this joint letter, if any, is obscure,[m] this incident and other Cultural Revolution revelations concerning the same period indicate that Mao's health and its consequences for Party and state leadership were important issues in 1953–54.[n]

With Mao presumably ill and facing the prospect of semi-retirement, or even death, the timing and motivation of the Gao-Rao affair begins to make sense. The conspiracy can be seen as jockeying for position and seeking support in

---

[m] No sources were found alleging that Gao and Rao were personally involved in drafting the letter, only that the "Gao-Rao group" wrote it and its intent was to let Gao and Rao usurp Party and state power. Moreover, as Philip Bridgham, "Factionalism in the Central Committee," in John Wilson Lewis, ed., *Party Leadership and Revolutionary Power in China* (London: Cambridge University Press, 1970), p. 206, points out, the letter was an open effort using accepted channels of communication within the Party in sharp contrast to the alleged conspiratorial activities of Gao and Rao. Also, the fact that Tan and Chen were only required to undergo self-criticism suggests a tenuous link at best between the letter and Gao-Rao maneuvers.

[n] Scattered reports alleged that Zhu De (who assertedly desired to be Party Chairman himself) and Peng Dehuai advocated exercising leadership by rotation, a proposal which makes sense as an *ad hoc* measure given Mao's possible incapacity. As with the joint letter, the link of Gao and Rao to this proposal is obscure although it allegedly would have facilitated their usurpation of power. *Dongfanghong* [The East is Red] (Beijing), February 11, 1967, in *SCMP-S,* No. 172; "Chairman Mao's Successor—Deputy Supreme Commander Lin Biao" (Red Guard pamphlet), June 1969, in *CB,* No. 894; and Bridgham, "Factionalism," p. 206.

anticipation of the succession. In this situation attacks on Liu Shaoqi and Zhou Enlai and maneuvering over the posts of Party vice chairman, general secretary and premier are understandable. On the other hand, if Mao had been healthy, 1953 would have been an inauspicious time to challenge *his* leadership. After eighteen years of Mao's stewardship the CCP had achieved nationwide victory and successfully completed the tasks of economic recovery and consolidation of power. The period of socialist transformation and planned economic construction was just beginning on a basically optimistic note, and the inadequacies of the Soviet model for China would not become apparent for several more years. Moreover, 1953 marked the liquidation of China's most pressing international problem, the Korean War. Given the solidity of Mao's personal authority backed by a broad policy consensus, the activities of Gao and Rao are understandable only if uncertainty was injected into the situation—and the evidence indicates that Mao's health was the unpredictable factor. Unfortunately for Gao and Rao, the succession did not materialize and their struggle was, at best, premature.

Conclusion

The campaign to promote Party unity in 1954 and the open attacks on the "Gao Gang-Rao Shushi anti-Party alliance" in 1955 were major events in the political history of People's China. While such methods as the study of documents, criticism and self-criticism, and the examination of individual cadres were used, they never developed into a full fledged rectification campaign. In most areas the exposure of low ranking cadres to the case undoubtedly was restricted to reports and propaganda. Although the affair was of particular relevance to high ranking cadres, the campaign to promote Party unity and also criticism conducted in 1955 dealt with endemic problems of the political system affecting cadres at all levels, many of which had been targets of rectification in the consolidation of power period. Only in the Northeast, and to a lesser extent East China, did these activities show signs of any intensity. In the Northeast, the "close guidance" of the Central Committee had been invoked in 1954, and local conferences following the 1955 national meeting were also more intense than those elsewhere.[87] In other areas local authorities themselves conducted low key activities to combat problems widespread in the complex bureaucratic system being refined in the mid-1950s. The overall mildness was suited to a period of no major external threat[88] where policies still reflected a predominantly consolidation phase, but the key reason undoubtedly was the fundamental lack of relevance of the Gao-Rao affair for ordinary cadres.[o]

[o] Despite this mild approach affirming rectification principles, the purge of Gao and Rao apparently made some officials anxious and led to a decline in the vitality of inner Party debate. According to Mao in April 1956, "[The Fourth Plenum's] resolutions were very necessary.... But they have produced an overcautiousness about everything, and some [people] do not dare to speak of national affairs...." *MMT*, I, 31.

The Gao-Rao case is mainly significant as a conflict at the apex of power. apparently stimulated by Mao's illness in 1953, the conspiracy never came close to fruition. In retrospect, what is most striking is the weakness, even ineptness, of the Gao-Rao plot. Its organizational base was largely restricted to one pre-1954 large administrative region, albeit the most economically advanced. Even in the Northeast, however, Gao Gang's independent kingdom was far from airtight. Using the most liberal definition to include apparent demotions and people who dropped from public view, only slightly over two dozen leading regional Party, government and military officials seem to have been affected by Gao's purge. Moreover, a significant number of important Northeast leaders survived his purge to play major roles at the national level. In any case, Gao's regional base was clearly a limited device for conflict at the Politburo level.

Another weakness was the inability to produce a distinctive policy platform. This was inevitable given the broad policy consensus existing at the time. While support could conceivably had been obtained on individual issues, the situation was not ripe for polarization around specific policies. The tactics adopted by Gao and Rao in these circumstances had several shortcomings. First, to take on under the "white area" theory both the second and third ranking CCP leaders, as well as the powerful Peng Zhen, was to take on enormous strength; a more prudent approach might have sought to enlist Zhou against Liu. Second, in any contest of contacts within the highest CCP circles, Gao was clearly outgunned. Gao had not participated in the events of the pre-1935 southern phase of the revolution and even his closest early associates took separate paths after 1945. In contrast, neither Liu nor Zhou could be simply viewed as representatives of a narrow "white area" group; their careers were entwined with many of the major events and figures of the Chinese revolution.

Furthermore, the conspiracy seems never to have gotten off the ground. Cultural Revolution revelations picture Gao approaching other leaders and tentatively feeling out their attitudes towards his prospective leadership; few if any concrete deals are asserted.[89] The failure to expel from the Party even officially designated members of the "alliance" besides Gao and Rao themselves, the silent removal from office of others, and mere self-criticisms by still others suggests highly differential degrees of involvement in the plot. Thus for at least some of those involved, the conspiracy meant far less than carefully planned factional activities. The largely unformed nature of the plot, in turn, reflects the weakness of its tactics and resources. Once even tentative moves by Gao and Rao came to the attention of Mao, Liu and Zhou, the "alliance" was crushed within a relatively short period.

The ease with which the entire matter was handled supports the above analysis. For a case involving an attempt to seize Party leadership, the limited extent of the purge is striking. While study and criticism were directed at the highest levels, measures taken against leading figures were on the whole extremely mild.

Gao and Rao themselves were the only significant figures serving in Beijing to be purged, and there is no evidence of a personnel shake-up in central Party and government organs. At the regional, provincial and municipal levels outside of the Northeast, Xiang Ming in Shandong is the single significant figure explicitly disciplined in connection with the case, and only a few others were required to undertake self-criticisms. The relatively severe disciplinary impact in the Northeast probably was as much an effort to eradicate totally Gao's prestige in the area of his former dominance as an indication of widespread active participation in the conspiracy. Moreover, even taking Cultural Revolution accusations at face value, apart from the core group ousted in 1955, only 11 prominent national and local leaders were linked to the activities of Gao and Rao—and for many if not all of these the charges were extremely vague and, if true, indicate only the most tenuous ties to the conspiracy.[p]

Finally, there is little indicating disruption of CCP programs and policies during the period of the purge. In addition to the general blandness of the regional meetings on Party unity following the Fourth Plenum, propaganda on the case following the 1955 conference lasted no more than three months. Unlike the campaign launched following Peng Dehuai's 1959 dismissal, and in direct contrast to the rectification efforts of 1950–53 which focused on intermediate and lower levels, discipline apparently did not extend below significant political leaders at the national, provincial, regional and municipal levels. The case was not entirely dead in leadership circles as reports of examinations of individual cases in 1955, 1957 and 1962 indicate.[q] Nevertheless, again in striking contrast to events following Peng Dehuai's ouster, there was little effort to reopen the affair and no indication that the verdict on Gao and Rao was regarded as anything but just.[90] The lack of post-purge sympathy for leaders who had violated

---

[p] References were found implicating the following leaders in the Gao-Rao affair: Zhu De, Peng Dehuai, Zhang Wentian, He Long, Huang Kecheng, Tan Zhenlin, Luo Ruiqing, Tao Zhu, An Ziwen, Xi Zhongxun and Chen Peixian. In addition, Yang Shangkun and Kai Feng (who last appeared in 1952) reportedly were active about 1950 in promoting Gao Gang; *Pi Tao zhanbao* [Criticize Tao Combat Bulletin], April 10, 1967, in *SCMP*, No. 3962. But no accusations that Yang or Kai were active in the crucial 1953 maneuvers were uncovered.

[q] Tan Zhenlin and Chen Peixian reportedly conspired to conceal their activities at the 1953 financial and economic conference during self-examinations at a 1955 Central Committee meeting (presumably the October plenum), while Xi Zhongxun assertedly was "dragged out" and his role in the Gao-Rao affair detected at the September 1962 Central Committee plenum where Tan and Chen were apparently forced to address the subject again. Xi's downfall may have been more related to the Peng Dehuai affair than the Gao-Rao case, however. *WHB* (Shanghai), May 20, 1968, in *SCMP*, No. 4205. Tao Zhu reportedly was required to examine himself on the Gao-Rao question twice at a central work conference in 1957; his first statement was not approved and his second assertedly "barely passed." *Pi Tao zhanbao*, April 10, 1967, in *SCMP*, No. 3962; and "Important Speeches Made by Responsible Comrades of the Center on the Question of Tao Zhu" (Red Guard pamphlet), January 12, 1967, in *SCMP-S*, No. 232.

established Party norms is one further indication of the weakness of the conspiracy. Following the 1955 propaganda onslaught against them, Gao Gang and Rao Shushi were relegated to the dustbin of history and, with few exceptions, excised from the public memory as well.

6
The Hundred Flowers Experiment

One of the most dramatic developments since 1949 grew out of an overture to China's intellectuals under the slogan "Let a Hundred Flowers Bloom, a Hundred Schools of Thought Contend" *(baihua qifang, baijia zhengming)*. This overture, initially launched in spring 1956, was linked to a new rectification campaign *(zhengfeng yundong)* by Mao's personal initiative a year later only to result in unacceptable levels of criticism directed at the CCP. The most thorough scholarly analyses of the Hundred Flowers experiment view it as the cause of sharp, divisive debate within the top Party leadership. Mao's initiative is seen as systematically opposed in 1956 and in the first half of 1957 by a major group within the Politburo headed by Liu Shaoqi and Peng Zhen.[1] The following interpretation, while agreeing that significant opposition to the new rectification program did exist within the CCP, argues that whatever misgivings may have been expressed within the Politburo the debate was conducted according to established Party norms and did not result in a deep split among China's top leaders.

The innovations of the Hundred Flowers were themselves seen by many Party members as a violation of traditional procedures. For now non-Party intellectuals were encouraged to criticize the CCP in contrast to the rejection of extra-Party criticism following the excesses of 1947–48. Moreover, the source of criticism was suspect bourgeois intellectuals rather than the peasant masses of the earlier case. Nevertheless, the new experiment, as originally conceived, was still well within existing principles in important respects. Criticism was to be of a low key nature, like a "gentle breeze and mild rain" *(hefeng xiyu)*, and not to result in harsh disciplinary sanctions. While intellectuals might criticize both the Party and individual cadres, officials were assured that the actual conduct of rectification would follow the "closed door" precedent of the 1942 campaign. Thus while the new departure was clearly cause for concern, in its conception the innovative methods were not intended to alter the established persuasive approach.

The Hundred Flowers experiment was part of a classic shift to a consolidation phase following the mobilization efforts of the "socialist high tide" which saw rapid advances in agricultural cooperativization and the socialization of industry and commerce in the second half of 1955 and 1956. This shift, moreover, reflected a new overall assessment that, as Mao put it, a "fundamental change in the political situation" had taken place due to the basic victory of socialism over capitalism in 1955.[2] As a result, in contrast to the severe class struggle of socialist transformation, a decided attenuation of class conflict was forecast for the new period[a]—a situation where attitudinal change by persuasive methods was more possible than ever. With the basic political struggle largely won, priority was now given to economic development with the aim of, in Mao's words, "wiping out China's economic, scientific and cultural backwardness within a few decades and rapidly getting abreast of the most advanced nations in the world."[3] In seeking economic growth the leadership continued to operate within the framework of the Soviet model, but with a growing awareness of the inadequacy of that model for Chinese conditions and a willingness to tinker marginally with the imported strategy. To this was added concern over the quality of Soviet political leadership as reflected in Communist bloc events in 1956—Khrushchev's denunciation of Stalin, the Polish October and the Hungarian revolution—events which had a direct impact on CCP policies towards rectification.

Throughout this period Mao's authority and leadership unity remained strong. On top of Mao's victorious revolutionary strategy and the achievements of the consolidation of power years, the success of the stepped up pace of cooperativization which Mao had strongly advocated in 1955 further bolstered the Chairman's prestige. None of the problems which emerged in 1956–57 were serious enough to change this situation. Although the personality cult surrounding the Chairman was toned down and the "Thought of Mao Zedong" was excised from the 1956 Party Constitution, this was virtually required by Soviet bloc politics following Khrushchev's attack on Stalin and Cultural Revolution evidence indicates Mao fully concurred with these measures. Moreover, vigorous debates, similar to that over cooperativization from 1952 to 1955, occurred

[a] Cultural Revolution sources have portrayed this view as a particular heresy of Liu Shaoqi, and some scholars have seen a significant difference of emphasis between Mao and Liu on this point. Close analysis, however, reveals a substantial consensus existed. Mao's statements of 1956 and early 1957 do not take up the theme of class struggle as a continuing long term process except for spring 1957 speeches as they appeared in edited form *after* the Hundred Flowers experiment got out of hand. Moreover, even the edited versions spoke of "large scale, turbulent class struggle" as having basically concluded. In later years, furthermore, Mao admitted that during this period he wrongly believed the bourgeoisie would be eliminated and had failed to speak about the class struggle on the ideological front. See *PDA*, pp. 281, 288–89; *Speech at the Chinese Communist Party's National Conference on Propaganda Work* (Beijing: Foreign Languages Press, 1966), pp. 2–3, 25–27; and "Talk at Core Group Meeting" (August 1962), in *JPRS*, No. 52029, p. 22.

within the framework of a broad consensus on the need for policy adjustments following the victory of socialist transformation. In this context Mao continued to fulfill the role of final arbiter, a role he played within the parameters of existing norms. Thus in mid-1956 the Chairman accepted the consensus of the Party's economic specialists on the need to "oppose reckless advance" *(fan maojin)* despite his own preference for a faster rate of growth and a "leap forward" in production.[b] Notwithstanding such disappointments, Mao's confidence in his own ultimate power and the loyalty of his Politburo colleagues was demonstrated by steps he initiated to prepare for an orderly succession. This process apparently began with the notion of "two lines" of leadership first advanced in 1956 under which Mao would retreat to the "second line" leaving day to day administrative decisions increasingly to Liu Shaoqi and others on the "first line."[4]

Pressures for Rectification: Adjusting the New Socialist System

The situation created by the victory of socialist transformation placed adjustment of the new system high on the list of CCP priorities. With class struggle on the wane, tensions in society were seen as predominantly manifestations of legitimate divergencies of interests (i.e., "contradictions among the people") resting on a basic unity in support of socialism. The task of government, then, was largely one of managing forces favorable to socialism—"uniting all forces which can be united"—and mediating the claims of different economic sectors and social groups. In addition, the need for adjustment was created by the very novelty of the new system. As Mao put it in his early 1957 speech "On the

[b] In early 1956 Mao sought to stimulate the same type of rapid development then being achieved in socialization on the production and construction fronts. This effort to leap forward soon ran into difficulties including unrealistic targets, faulty planning and poor quality products, and this in turn led to demands for greater realism from economic officials. Mao initially sought to accommodate many of the objections raised and in April produced an overall guideline for the economy in his "Ten Great Relationships," a speech, he later observed, that "made a start in proposing our own line for construction [which] was similar to that of the Soviet Union in principle, but had our own content." The specific measures taken in conjunction with the "Ten Great Relationships," however, did not arrest economic dislocations and the view that further efforts were needed to curb excesses gained predominance resulting in a mid-June policy reassessment. As Roderick MacFarquhar has observed, while the April measures sought to "restrain . . . adventurism within the framework of a continuing production drive," the June actions amounted to a "brake on the drive itself." Mao, whose views were apparently shared by Liu Shaoqi, was clearly unhappy with the turn of events yet seemingly acquiesced to the wishes of the planners in an area where, by his own subsequent admission, he lacked competence. See *MU*, p. 101, 122; *JPRS*, No. 50792, p. 50; and MacFarquhar, *The Origins of the Cultural Revolution, 1: Contradictions among the People 1956–1957* (New York: Columbia University Press, 1974), pp. 57–62, 87–90.

Correct Handling of Contradictions among the People," "time is needed for our socialist system to grow and consolidate itself, for the masses to get accustomed to [it], and for government workers to study and acquire experience."[5] Any adjustments would inevitably be linked to the rectification of Party and state cadres, particularly since the new order marked the full elaboration of the "totalitarian" system in China. By 1956 a vast centralized bureaucracy had been established to provide a more far-reaching administration of the nation than had been possible in the consolidation years following 1949. Moreover, the new institutions of socialism in urban and rural areas meant a significant enhancement of the Party's capacity to penetrate society. Thus tensions within society were much more extensively bound up with official policies and much more subject to Party management than had previously been the case. The CCP's leadership performance naturally became subject to scrutiny.

Adjusting the new socialist system involved the broadest range of problems. Here we deal briefly with a number of important questions which became involved in the unfolding rectification process: economic policy, agricultural cooperatives, crude leadership methods, counterrevolutionaries, national minorities, and the problems of a bloated, overly rigid bureaucracy. Virtually all these questions were under discussion throughout most of 1956 and the first half of 1957. They had been raised in Mao's spring 1956 overview of the situation, "The Ten Great Relationships," discussed again at the Eighth Party Congress in the fall, raised once more in Mao's early 1957 "Contradictions" speech, and manifested in various stages of the ensuing rectification movement. The discussion will then turn to the key question of the Party's relationship with the intellectuals which became so central to the launching of rectification.

Economic policy involved two interrelated but distinct questions: broad developmental strategy and current imbalances. The slight modifications of the Soviet model introduced by the "Ten Great Relationships"—marginal investment increases for light industry and agriculture—were reaffirmed in the outline of the Second Five Year Plan approved at the Eighth Congress. Short term policy grappled with problems created by overexpansion of the economy due to the early 1956 leap forward: careless control of expenditures, a national deficit of ¥1.83 billion, and inflationary pressures. In the months following the Eighth Congress, Party leaders increasingly turned to the fundamental problem of the Chinese economy—the lag of the agricultural growth rate. At the conceptual level the CCP moved even further from the Soviet model by quietly dropping the Congress proposals and emphasizing even more the importance of agriculture for industrial growth. Concrete measures included improved financial management and adequate credit for APCs, as well as increased material incentives for peasants through private plots and limited free markets. Considerable attention was also devoted to APC mismanagement. Criticism was directed at extravagance and waste, failure to provide overall production plans, failure to adjust directives to local conditions, excessively high production targets, and insufficient concern with the daily needs of APC members. Efforts to overcome mismanagement involved reducing the size of APCs and even resulted in the dissolution of some cooperatives in certain areas. These policies thus reflected an amalgam of adjustments in economic growth strategy which Mao pushed plus retrenchment measures advocated by economic specialists and grudgingly accepted by the Chairman.[6]

Substantial media comment was devoted to deviant cadre behavior which resulted from the effort to leap forward in production. "Impetuous sentiments" had assertedly been responsible for impractical plans as various departments competed with one another and "set too high targets . . . lest they be accused of right conservatism." In pursuit of such targets basic level cadres frequently resorted to crude leadership methods—commandism—a fault which, as in earlier campaigns, was linked to subjective and bureaucratic attitudes of higher level officials who demanded the rapid completion of excessive tasks. Of particular concern were not only such long standing practices as cursing, tying up, and applying political labels, but also using the new economic powers of the APCs to deprive unresponsive cooperative members of work or to reduce their wages. Apparently many APC cadres felt leadership tasks could easily be implemented without intensive education since "the land has been taken over by the cooperative, the peasants are in our tight grip and we can do what we want with them."[7]

Adjusting the new order also meant new policies concerning suspect groups who, in the changed circumstances created by the victory of socialism, lacked the capability of threatening the regime and/or possessed skills required for construction. Intellectuals were the most important of these groups, but pressure was also eased toward the bourgeoisie, landlords, rich peasants, and counterrevolutionaries. A significant move was relaxing the purge of counterrevolutionaries *(sufan)* campaign which had begun with considerable ferocity in mid-1955. Now a much more lenient approach was adopted toward counterrevolutionaries as Mao called for "fewer arrests and fewer executions," avoiding "irredeemable mistakes," and guaranteeing a "way out" for the guilty. By the time of his "Contradictions" speech Mao was even proposing a comprehensive review of *sufan* work by the National People's Congress (NPC) and Chinese People's Political Consultative Conference (CPPCC) Standing Committees and their lower level organs, bodies which contained large numbers of non-Party people. These ameliorative measures, while in no way indicating a disowning of past policies towards counterrevolutionaries, not only improved the position of this group but generally dispelled the social tension which the *sufan* drive had created. In dealing not only with suspect groups but with society as a whole, a new emphasis was placed on persuasive methods as we would expect in a situation perceived as fundamentally secure where the major tensions were nonantagonistic.[8]

Another source of tension, one which would become a major rectification issue in 1958 (see Chapter 8), was relations with national minorities, in large part due to attitudes of racial superiority on the part of Han Chinese. Particularly troublesome was the tendency of many Han officials in minority areas to brush aside local representatives and take everything into their own hands. The official assessment, which was to last to mid-1957, regarded "Han chauvinism" *(da-Hanzuzhuyi)* as the major danger and treated "local nationalism" *(difang minzuzhuyi)*, i.e., centrifugal tendencies among the nationalities, as relatively unimportant and, in any case, to a significant degree a reaction to the overbearing behavior of Han Chinese. The gradual social transformation of national minorities, as other matters, would be accomplished by lenient, persuasive means.[9]

Also requiring adjustment was the massive Party and state bureaucracy. Such endemic features of bureaucratism as being divorced from actual problems, red tape, buck passing, and overstaffed and overlapping organizations were sharply criticized in 1956. Under Mao's prodding, an effort to combat such tendencies was launched in winter 1956–57 through a retrenchment of personnel and simplification of organs drive. Closely related to structural obesity was overcentralization and administrative rigidity. In the "The Great Relationships" Mao stressed the need for greater local initiative while the major reports to the Eighth Congress criticized central departments for overly elaborate regulations binding lower level authorities and ignoring special conditions. Such rigidity could only lead to deception by lower levels and thus decrease actual control. This was graphically indicated by a report from Sichuan where a district Party secretary allegedly came to county level meetings with two reports in his pocket. As the meetings proceeded he would watch the trend in others' reports and the reactions of the county secretary and then decide which report to give. To avoid such problems, CCP leaders called for greater administrative flexibility with lower levels having defined functions and the right to deal with local questions. In addition, the revelations concerning Stalin focused attention on more serious problems inherent in bureaucratism. In its official response, *Remin ribao* warned that in China too alienation of the masses through arbitrary behavior was a danger requiring remedial action.[10]

Policy toward Intellectuals

The underlying rationale for a relaxation of policy toward other suspect groups was particularly relevant for China's intellectuals. First, with the victory of socialism intellectuals assertedly recognized they no longer had any viable alternative to supporting the regime. Thus predisposed, they would be more responsive to a milder, more persuasive approach than had typified the thought reform efforts of the past when their resistance was assumed to be higher. Secondly, their talents were urgently required for economic and cultural development. As Mao put it, "Now we are undertaking technical revolution and cultural revolution in order to do away with ignorance. It won't do not to have [intellectuals] and only rely on us old rustics."[11]

A policy of relaxation gained further impetus from the "thaw" in Soviet treatment of intellectuals which had begun in late 1955. As D.W. Fokkema has shown with regard to literature,[12] both intellectuals and Party officials responsible for the arts and sciences paid close attention to Soviet developments, often utilizing them for vastly divergent aims. Thus as a more accommodating posture was adopted toward the intelligentsia CCP officials cautiously incorporated liberalized Soviet doctrines into their own policy pronouncements while writers and artists exploited the more audacious opinions of their Russian counterparts in an effort to expand their own creative freedom. All this, however, was only possible because the Soviet "thaw" coincided with the victory of socialism in China. Moreover, it did not mean the eventual linkage of the Hundred Flowers and Party rectification drew its inspiration from Soviet experience. On the contrary, both Chinese and Soviet sources indicate the Russians were deeply suspicious of this development where Mao himself played the leading innovative role.[13]

CCP policy unfolded gradually. Following a series of democratic party forums convened in late 1955 to uncover problems facing intellectuals, Zhou Enlai laid down official policy in a January 1956 report. Zhou called for improved salaries and living conditions, the provision of better working conditions and resources, a reduction in excessive secrecy and the mechanical copying of Soviet experience, more effective and suitable employment of specialized skills, and more rapid promotions and easier admission into the Party. While Zhou also criticized the sectarian attitudes of Party cadres who looked down upon non-Party intellectuals, he stated the basic aim of the new policy was to strengthen Party leadership over the scientific and cultural sphere. Moreover, Zhou noted a continuing need for thought reform and criticized Party cadres for compromising with intellectuals as well as for sectarianism.[14]

The next major step came when Mao launched the Hundred Flowers slogan in spring 1956. Lu Dingyi, head of the Central Committee's propaganda department, elaborated the new policy in May. Lu argued the victory of socialist transformation and a fundamental change in the political outlook of intellectuals created conditions for the Hundred Flowers. He held that free discussion and independent thinking were necessary to avoid academic stagnation and declared the imposition of narrow, doctrinaire restrictions on intellectual life the "bitter enemy" of true Marxism-Leninism. In literature and art methods besides socialist realism were allowed. Lu went on to criticize cases of excessive criticism of intellectuals in the past, the tendency of some Party cadres to monopolize academic studies in philosophy and the social sciences, and sectarian attitudes of Party members generally. These liberalizing trends, however, were circumscribed by Lu's assertion of the continued need to criticize the backward and struggle against "idealist" *(weixinzhuyi)* thought. Moreover, Lu's injunction that intellectuals study documents from the 1942–44 rectification campaign was an ambiguous behest. The reference to an inner Party movement suggests the possibility of an active intellectual role in any new undertaking was already being canvassed, but the anti-intellectual overtones and carefully controlled nature of the first rectification campaign imply that any such role would be sharply circumscribed.[15]

Despite considerable caution on the part of intellectuals, the new atmosphere did result in significant debates in a number of academic fields—e.g., on heredity, the periodization of history, the role of Marxism-Leninism in philosophy, and socialist realism in literature. Moreover, in journalism changes included a more lively style, greater space devoted to free discussion, the encouragement of professionalism including Western style pursuit of the full story, and greater use of Western news sources, at least in restricted publications. Finally, from roughly the time of the Hundred Flowers initiative the harsher aspects of ideological education such as continuing attacks on the writer Hu Feng, a major target of the *sufan* campaign in 1955, gave way to relaxed study of Marxist theories.[16]

A second major policy initiative concerning intellectuals was "long term coexistence and mutual supervision" *(changqi gongcun, huxiang jiandu)* between the CCP and democratic parties. Mao raised the slogan in the "Ten Great Relationships," arguing that the views of these minor parties, "so long as they are reasonable," could be beneficial to socialism and should be accepted. Further statements provided a rationale for the continued existence of democratic parties which, according to Mao, would function as long as the Communist Party itself. Although the victory of socialist transformation theoretically meant the elimination of their economic basis, these parties assertedly survived because the persistence of bourgeois ideology preserved their social foundation among intellectuals and other bourgeois groups. Assuming the basic unity of the Chinese people, democratic parties represented legitimate interests of their strata, interests which had to be taken into account in the adjustment of tensions. A substantial note of ambiguity was introduced, however, by Mao's reminder that some members of democratic parties had equivocated in their support of Party policies and had formed a *de facto* opposition. But assuming patriotism would prevail and result in reasonable suggestions, and given the CCP's admitted shortcomings, supervision by these parties would be particularly valuable by providing a new angle for viewing problems. A July 1956 work conference convened by the CCP's united front department urged the minor parties to take the initiative in criticisms and discussions particularly of government work and also of Party united front work, and asserted the Party would never impose its political outlook on other parties. The new policy was further manifested in inspection tours to check up on state performance by democratic party members in their capacities as NPC deputies and CPPCC committee members and in organizational expansion of the parties. Acting with the backing of Party united front officials, democratic party leaders called for increases in both membership and full-time officials and by the end of 1956 their combined membership had probably tripled.[17]

While the new policies resulted in a relaxation of tension for intellectuals, many uncertainties remained. Despite declarations of a basic change in the attitudes of intellectuals, ideological reeducation was still called for and their asserted vacillating nature was not forgotten. Perhaps even more important was the ambiguity surrounding the question of leadership in specialized fields. Sectarianism, perhaps the most vigorously criticized cadre deviation in 1956, was a particularly acute problem in areas involving professional expertise which responsible Party cadres lacked. Such Party cadres were now told to admit their lack of knowledge and let non-Party experts assert initiative in dealing with work problems. To paraphrase Merle Goldman, the new policies of 1956 had the effect of shifting the blame for intellectual stagnation from the ideological shortcomings of professionals to the crude, bureaucratic attitudes of Party functionaries. Scientists and engineers, at least, were bold enough to seize on this to question the technical competence of cadres. Yet the principle of Party leadership was still asserted. Intellectuals could have more freedom within the framework of Party leadership, but the boundaries between such freedom and impermissible breaches of the leadership principle were never clearly defined.[18]

The Hundred Flowers policy, in fact, initiated a period of testing those boundaries, a process which took on increasing importance due to the nature of the new period. For with the victory of socialism and the priority assigned to construction, a new system was beginning to crystallize which presumably would last for a relatively long period and put a premium on the successful management of technical resources. From the point of view of the top leadership the key question was how to secure the enthusiastic participation of skilled experts outside the Party while preventing the creation of autonomous professional spheres. For intellectuals and Party officials charged with overseeing their work, questions of power, prerogatives and status would arise daily in efforts to implement the new line. What was involved was nothing less than an attempt to redefine Party leadership in circumstances where social revolution had given way to economic development as the main task.

Thus it is hardly surprising that there were contrasting responses to the Hundred Flowers policy. The general response of non-Party intellectuals, especially in the vulnerable literary and cultural spheres, was to tread with considerable caution; their statements tended to emphasize the limits of the new policy.[c] A striking example was a July 1956 article by the non-Party head of the Academy of Sciences, Guo Moruo, which argued that contending schools must be like instruments in an orchestra and play harmoniously under Party direction, carefully avoiding "confusion." The reaction of Party cadres responsible for im-

[c] This assessment is based on the open media of the period. A bolder response was suggested by Mao's remarks to provincial level leaders in January 1957: "There is queer talk among some professors . . . such as that the Communist Party should be done away with, the Communist Party cannot lead them, socialism is no good, [etc.]. Before they kept these ideas to themselves, but since the policy of letting a hundred schools of thought contend gave them an opportunity to speak up, these remarks have come tumbling out." *SW*, V, 353. It is impossible, however, to judge the extent of such views from this one statement of Mao's.

plementing the policy was more complex. On the one hand, official interpretations of the Hundred Flowers were generally more liberal than those of non-Party figures. Thus Guo Moruo's argument was refuted by a *Renmin ribao* "Commentator" who noted that "contention" meant there could be no guarantee of "no confusion." Moreover, the most vigorous "blooming and contending" in literary circles largely came from figures in the cultural bureaucracy who were either Party members or had close ties to leading Party officials. At least two explanations for their relative enthusiasm can be suggested. First, as creative writers themselves these figures may have genuinely welcomed a loosening of Party controls. Or second, they may have been implementing the policy as disciplined cadres in the knowledge that widespread skepticism in non-Party circles required special efforts to overcome lingering fears and doubts. In any case, the two motivations are not mutually exclusive.[19]

Many responsible cadres, on the other hand, were criticized in the official media in summer and fall 1956 for adopting an obstructionist attitude. One official responsible for literary and art work in the PLA reportedly went so far as to order the removal of the Hundred Flowers slogan from an army literary festival. Such resistance was apparently fueled by anxiety that "blooming and contending" would both undermine ideological orthodoxy and erode cadre authority *vis-à-vis* intellectuals. Increased prerogatives for intellectuals reportedly made cadres "afraid it would lead to the emergence of a privileged class with an undesirable sense of superiority." Here an ideologically motivated distrust of bourgeois intellectuals combined with an unwillingness to yield authority within spheres of bureaucratic responsibility to produce significant Party opposition to the Hundred Flowers.[20]

Party leadership as previously understood was further challenged by the long term coexistence and mutual supervision policy. As Benjamin Schwartz correctly noted at the time, "the very notion that there should be 'mutual supervision' between democratic parties and the Communist Party inevitably lowers [the CCP] somewhat from its dazzling heights."[21] Yet clearly there would be problems in defining a "mutually" critical relationship between parties representing vacillating groups only recently reconciled to socialism and the Party of the proletariat, and sharp differences of opinion soon arose. In August 1956 one article gave a very restrictive interpretation of the policy: "The Communist Party assumes the role of leadership and supervision toward the democratic parties while the latter supervise one another." In September, a second article asserted that the essence of the new policy was "first of all supervision of the Communist Party." While the former position was clearly a distortion of Mao's cautious formulation of the policy in the "Ten Great Relationships," it is by no means clear that *at this time* Mao's views went as far as the latter statement. In any case, by merely stating that democratic parties had a critical function with regard to the CCP, this policy raised much more directly than the Hundred Flowers the possibility of outside participation in Party rectification. The potential modification of Party leadership over its own internal discipline was bound to be a source of conflict.[22]

Moves toward Rectification, Mid-1956 to Early 1957

While the Hundred Flowers and mutual supervision policies had implications for rectification, a series of more direct steps began in mid-1956 with a Central Committee notice on the study of rectification documents. In the following months local authorities carried out study and in one instance launched a rectification campaign. When the Eighth Party Congress was convened in September, further impetus was given to rectification by calls to correct various erroneous work styles. The Congress was followed by intensified study of the rectification documents in conjunction with the documents of the Congress itself. Then, following the Polish October and Hungarian uprisings, at a November Central Committee plenum Mao indicated a rectification campaign would be carried out some time in 1957. In mid-January, however, a "recent" decision was announced to schedule nationwide rectification—but only for 1958.[23] This postponement suggests debate and uncertainty in the Politburo over the implications of East European developments for rectification and an apparent decision to give priority temporarily to other problems, especially economic construction. In addition, in early 1957 a series of developments occurred indicating resistance to possible directions which rectification and the Hundred Flowers might have taken. In this context Mao reacted with major speeches in February and March 1957 which significantly upgraded the priority of Party reform.

The June 1956 Notice and Subsequent Study

The June notice stipulated that within a year cadres of the county secretary level and above, personnel of higher and middle Party schools, personnel in research organs, in philosophy, the social and natural sciences, and graduating students from institutions of higher learning would undertake the study of five documents: three speeches by Mao which laid down the themes for the 1942 rectification, the 1945 resolution on historical questions which gave the official version of Mao's struggle with the returned student faction, and "On the Historical Experience of the Dictatorship of the Proletariat," the April 1956 *Renmin ribao* editorial on Stalin. By July the PLA's General Political Department (GPD) ordered the study of the same five documents by officers of regimental rank. The documents selected are significant from several points of view. First, the documents had either been authored by Mao or had his strong approval,[24] thus suggesting at the very least the Chairman's assent to the study program. Second, as indicated by the emphasis on 1940s documents, the projected rectification campaign was regarded in many ways as a latter day Yan'an rectification. At the most general level, both 1942–44 and 1956–57 marked new stages in CCP development requiring systematic education to equip the Party to deal with the problems and opportunities of a more favorable overall situation. Specifically, the June notice singled out subjectivism—the ranking evil of the 1942–44 movement—as the shortcoming to be overcome by study. In the current situation, as Liu Shaoqi was to observe at the Eighth Party Congress, there were many problems with which Party cadres were unfamiliar requiring both the attainment of new knowledge and the integration of Marxist-Leninist theory with new realities. Subjectivism, of course, encompassed both doctrinairism and empiricism, but doctrinairism was the greater danger. Thus study in the army stressed avoiding mechanical copying of foreign [i.e., Soviet] military methods and reaffirming the PLA's own traditions. As during the Yan'an rectification (and as suggested by the CCP's recent evaluation of Stalin), emphasis was placed on the critical evaluation of Soviet experience and its adaptation to Chinese conditions. At a time when CCP leaders were taking their first cautious steps in modifying the Soviet economic model, this was singularly appropriate.[25]

Finally, it is noteworthy that the study documents included the four recommended to intellectuals by Lu Dingyi in his exposition of the Hundred Flowers policy. The almost identical study course further hints the possible involvement of non-Party intellectuals in inner Party rectification. Yet, as already argued, harking back to the 1942–44 campaign where the participation of outsiders was strictly regulated within regular work units paradoxically suggests that any innovations contemplated on this score would be limited. It is most likely that with full scale rectification not yet scheduled, CCP leaders had not worked out the modalities of the future effort in any detail.

In the months following the June notice study began in various provinces and was linked to examinations of concrete work problems. In at least one province, Shanxi, the measures adopted went beyond study and a provincial rectification campaign was launched which in some areas went below the county to village and APC levels. The methods used included systematic criticism, self-examinations, and *ad hoc* rectification offices and investigation teams. Bureaucratism was declared the main target of the campaign which focused on subjectivism as well as bureaucracy at higher levels and commandism and sectarianism at lower levels. This would seem to suggest a degree of local autonomy in selecting the targets of rectification. Moreover, in Shanxi and elsewhere a variety of specific work problems were cited. These included not only matters derived from Mao's analysis in the "Ten Great Relationships"—e.g., overemphasis of the state and collective interests at the expense of individuals—but also the overambitious production goals which had been attacked by the economic planners as "reckless advance."[26]

The Eighth Party Congress

The Eighth Party Congress in September–October 1956 did not raise the priority of rectification among the tasks facing the CCP; the subject was not raised in the political resolution of the Congress. Nevertheless, additional impetus was given to rectification measures already underway by lengthy discussions of shortcomings in the Party's work. In his brief opening address Mao singled out the three major deviations and called for continuing efforts to combat them:

> [W]e still have serious shortcomings. Among many of our comrades there still are standpoints and styles of work which are contrary to Marxism-Leninism, namely, subjectivism in their way of thinking, bureaucracy in their way of work, and sectarianism in organizational questions. . . . Such serious shortcomings in our ranks must be vigorously corrected by strengthening ideological education in the Party.[27]

Given evidence of resistance to policies related to rectification—the Hundred Flowers and mutual supervision—the question arises whether conflicting attitudes were adopted by top Party leaders at the Congress. The answer is by no means obvious. As MacFarquhar's penetrating analysis has shown, different nuances appeared in the reports of Liu Shaoqi and Deng Xiaoping: Liu cited subjectivism as the main danger and downplayed the supervisory role of non-Party forces over the Party; Deng emphasized bureaucratism, noted the importance of supervision from extra-Party sources, and placed considerably more emphasis on the mass line. But what are the implications of these differences? As Liu and Deng were both reporting in the name of the Central Committee, the question arises whether different emphases reflected individual views or were part of a prearranged division of labor. The division of labor thesis is supported by Deng's own words. The newly appointed general secretary noted that he would not cover ground already dealt with by Liu but instead would elaborate on the mass line.[28] On balance, it seems likely that each report basically reflected an overall Politburo view although there inevitably would be room for individual opinions.[d]

But even assuming differences in the reports reflected the attitudes of Liu and Deng and that these were of some moment, the question remains concerning Mao's attitude. To the extent a judgment can be made, it appears Liu's version was closer to Mao's position *as it had been expressed up to that point.* It was, after all, Mao's opening address which listed subjectivism ahead of bureaucratism in the trilogy of evils to be overcome. Moreover, subjectivism had been the chief target of Mao's writings studied since June. On the question of supervision by non-Party forces, Mao's opening address mentioned neither the Hundred Flowers nor mutual supervision. In addition, the political resolution's statement that the Party "must be skilled in . . . listening to [the masses'] criticism and suggestions," a position reflecting Liu's report, was essentially a paraphrase of Mao's remarks in the "Ten Great Relationships" concerning the opinions of democratic parties.[29] While Deng's more positive remarks on the role of mutual

---

[d] This analysis is significantly influenced by the views of Alex B. Ikonnikov who translated drafts of the Congress documents in summer and fall 1956. According to Ikonnikov, the drafts emerged from Politburo discussions and did not bear the imprimatur of any individual. Moreover, to the extent individual views were expressed, they were not necessarily those of the speaker. E.g., Peng Zhen reportedly drafted the key section on the political life of the state in Liu's report; see MacFarquhar, *Origins 1,* p. 100. In addition, the practice of the time was to label individual views as "personal opinions" (see *ibid.,* p. 63), and this did not occur in the reports of Liu and Deng.

supervision possibly reflected a development in Mao's thinking on the matter, the absence of indications of the Chairman's vigorous support of Deng's position in the period leading up to the Congress suggests it was not yet an issue on which Mao had forcefully declared himself.

Other evidence suggests that Mao prevailed on issues relating to Party reform at the Eighth Congress. The treatment of deviations in the reports of both Liu and Deng were broadly phrased and did not cite manifestations of "reckless advance" as examples of subjectivism. Indeed, where rashness was noted it was placed after "right conservatism" *(youqing baoshou sixiang),* thus demonstrating a careful respect for Mao's sensibilities.[e] Moreover, despite suggestions in Cultural Revolution sources to the contrary, the best evidence indicates that any reservations Mao had about the political resolution of the Congress developed only *after* the Polish and Hungarian developments of October–November.[f] This further conforms to Mao's testimony that the East European events were crucial in the development of his views on the importance of rectification (see below).

---

[e] *Eighth National Congress of the Communist Party of China* (3 vols., Beijing: Foreign Languages Press, 1956), I, 100–103, 182–84. Although also warning against " 'left' adventurism" *('zuo'qing maoxian),* in late 1955-early 1956 Mao identified right conservatism as the main danger. See *PDA,* p. 118. His unhappiness with the economic retreat of mid-1956, moreover, suggests a continuing preference for this ordering of dangers regardless of the concessions required in practice.

[f] Liu's October 1966 confession claimed that Mao took exception to the political resolution's discussion of the main contradiction which emphasized China's economic backwardness rather than defects of the political system, but "there was no time to revise [it]." Other Cultural Revolution sources quote Liu's wife and Zhou Enlai as indicating Mao may not have seen the resolution and even Liu may only have read it in a hurry. See MacFarquhar, *Origins 1,* pp. 101, 119–21, 349–50. These accounts are simply not credible. First, there is the evidence of Alex B. Ikonnikov (see above, p. 178n), who reports that while extensive revisions of the documents did occur up to the last minute—e.g., concerning national minorities—the theoretical sections were unchanged from the initial draft in mid-1956. Moreover, it strains belief to think the Politburo would leave the key theoretical question of the first Party Congress in more than a decade to the last minute or that Mao and/or Liu would only inform themselves on the matter cursorily at the eleventh hour. In any case, the role of Mao's (then) close theoretical collaborator Chen Boda in the drafting of the resolution strongly suggests Mao's agreement. Perhaps the best explanation for Liu's peculiar remarks is that they were designed, as other "admissions" may have been (see MacFarquhar, *Origins 1,* p. 326), to indicate his innocence of any wrongdoing. Educated listeners would know that while Mao *later* objected to the resolution's formulation of the main contradiction, this was not the same thing as opposing it at the time. The remarks of Mme. Liu and Zhou could indeed have reflected last minute haste concerning Congress arrangements and the resolution as a whole, but the question remains whether it is credible that this would apply to the key theoretical formulation of the Congress.

As to the timing of Mao's rejection of this version of the main contradiction, his misgivings were first expressed (in available sources) in spring 1957, the same period Liu was indicating *his* doubts. *MMT,* p. 69; and Liu, "Speech at Meeting of Party Members and Cadres in Shanghai" (April 1957), in *SCMM-S,* No. 35.

Ultimately, this reconstruction rests on the conviction that Mao, regardless of his grudging acquiescence on economic policy in mid-1956, remained in control of the Party on key political matters which had always been his strength. In particular, Mao's moves to establish "two lines" of leadership at the time of the Congress indicates a confidence in his colleagues we would not expect if he were being directly challenged on political issues. In sum, prior to the Hungarian uprising it is unlikely that Mao had spelled out any innovations in a future rectification movement which still was not at the top of the Party's current list of priorities. Liu's political report appears to be a summary of the agreed upon position as it existed in fall 1956. While aspects of Deng's report were a harbinger of things to come, the issues raised were not yet the source of marked conflict at key policy levels.

Following the Congress, rectification efforts were further bolstered by extensive study of its documents in conjunction with the five June documents. This study movement was implemented widely among cadres and Party members throughout China, and also extended to the general population. As in the study campaign carried on before the Congress, this drive involved rectification of concrete work problems. Unlike the reports to the Congress, but similar to the pre-Congress study, examples of subjectivism included unrealistic production targets and blind implementation of overly ambitious programs—thus accommodating criticism to the view of those opposing excessively rapid development. Moreover, varying measures, including the launching of provincial rectification campaigns in Henan and Shandong, indicate the modalities of Party reform were still left to the localities in the absence of a central decision on the question.[30]

East Europe, the November Plenum, and the Scheduling of Rectification for 1958

The Polish October and particularly the abortive Hungarian revolution sent shock waves throughout the Communist world. China was not immune as Mao indicated in his "Contradictions" speech:

> Certain people in our country were delighted when the Hungarian events took place. They hoped that something similar would happen in China, that thousands of people would demonstrate in the streets against the People's Government. . . . There were other people in our country who took a wavering attitude towards the Hungarian events because they were ignorant about the actual world situation. They felt that there was too little freedom under our people's democracy and that there was more freedom under Western parliamentary democracy. They ask for the adoption of the two party system of the West, where one party is in office and the other out of office. . . .[31]

Mao's overall assessment, however, was that the basic reaction had been one of calm. Clearly the domestic situation was regarded as far more stable than conditions in the East European satellite states. Nevertheless, the East European developments emphasized the danger of letting problems fester. Mao subsequently claimed Hungary and Poland convinced him of the need to handle contradictions correctly.[32]

When the Central Committee met in the wake of Hungary from November 10 to 15, the proceedings were predominantly concerned with the international situation and the economy. On the latter question further retrenchment in line with opposition to "reckless advance" was decreed. But Mao, in his summary remarks, dealt extensively with political leadership and announced "a rectification movement next year" to be aimed at subjectivism, sectarianism and bureaucracy. In reviewing recent internal political developments, Mao spoke favorably of "great democracy" *(daminzhu)* which included not only mass movements under the CCP's control but also strikes and demonstrations against bureaucrats which he declared positive phenomena in cases of unresponsive officials. Such statements, however, were balanced by his assessment that the fundamental problem in East Europe had been the insufficient waging of class struggle against counterrevolutionaries.[33] Moreover, the Chairman's specific comments regarding rectification pointed to a restrained approach. Mao called for a period of time between officially announcing the campaign and starting its implementation so that individuals could make amends for their shortcomings:

> Rather than meting out "punishment without prior warning," make an announcement beforehand and then start the rectification movement at the specified time—this is a method of applying small democracy *(xiaominzhu)*. Some say, if this method is adopted, there probably won't be much left to rectify. . . . That is precisely the end we hope to achieve. . . . From now on, all problems . . . inside the Party are to be solved by means of rectification, by means of criticism and self-criticism, and not by force. We are in favor of the method of the "gentle breeze and mild rain," . . . the overall intention is to cure the sickness and save the patient. . . .[34]

Mao's unorthodox statements about strikes and demonstrations notwithstanding, in the Chairman's immediate post-Hungary assessment actual Party discipline was to follow longstanding CCP procedures.

In the following weeks, Mao and his colleagues apparently gave increasing attention to the warnings contained in the Polish and Hungarian events regarding the dangers of undermining Party control. This was underlined in the definitive CCP evaluation of the East European events, the late December *Renmin ribao* editorial, "More on the Historical Experience of the Dictatorship of the Proletariat," which Mao later said "exactly" reflected his views.[35] Although regarding the need to overcome bureaucratic and undemocratic tendencies a major lesson, the editorial depicted the Hungarian affair as primarily due to the machinations of imperialism and indicated that excessive reforms ran the risk of revisionism:

> We shall continue our efforts to correct and prevent errors [of doctrinairism] in our work. But opposition to doctrinairism has nothing in common with tolerance of revisionism.... In the present anti-doctrinaire tide, there are people both in our country and abroad who, on the pretext of opposing the mechanical copying of Soviet experience, try to deny the international significance of the fundamental experience of the Soviet Union and, on the plea of creatively developing Marxism-Leninism, try to deny the significance of the universal truth of Marxism-Leninism.[36]

While the main target of this analysis was international critics of Soviet action in Hungary, the existence of criticism of doctrinairism within China as part of rectification study since June meant it had direct domestic implications as well. Thus Mao's "exact" views on international developments cast an air of uncertainty over the future of CCP reform efforts.

Mao's views in two talks to a January meeting of provincial level secretaries provided additional ammunition to those concerned lest Party reform get out of hand. Mao noted that a "right opportunist wind" and an "anti-socialist tide" had appeared in the latter half of 1956 which had to be defeated, albeit by persuasive methods. It was in this context that Mao reaffirmed the Hundred Flowers policy. In his discussion the emphasis was not on helpful criticisms aiding Party reform but on the utility of the policy in strengthening the Party through struggle with "poisonous weeds" *(ducao)*. While taking a relatively relaxed attitude toward the presence of such "weeds" so long as they did not occupy a dominant position, Mao chided those who took a one-sided view of the policy and talked only about the blooming of "fragrant flowers" *(xianghua)* and not about getting rid of "poisonous weeds." He called for the forceful refutation of "harmful" statements, as well as the prohibition of "counterrevolutionary" utterances. Moreover, the Chairman complained that since the launching of the Hundred Flowers policy there had been a neglect of the ideological remolding of intellectuals, and he called for enforcing dictatorship and expelling Party members in cases of disturbances in schools. By these comments Mao put a decidedly restrictive gloss on the Hundred Flowers experiment.[37]

In these circumstances the decision to schedule full scale rectification in 1958, not 1957, was announced. That the movement would not begin for another year suggests the uncertainties of the current situation were such that an extended period of careful preparation was deemed essential. At any rate it does not appear that the form of the projected 1958 campaign had been decided in early 1957. Mao's remarks on the Hundred Flowers made no attempt to link this policy to rectification and he did not even mention mutual supervision. His comments, moreover, did not bode well for the democratic parties which he implicitly compared to "weeds" and imperialist agents.[38] Thus at the start of 1957, far from advocating radical departures in rectification procedures, Mao's position was conducive to a markedly cautious approach.

Issues under Debate, January–February 1957

About the time of Mao's talks, debate on a number of issues linked to rectification burst forth in the official media reflecting the more restrictive atmosphere since Hungary. The most striking development was an early January article in *Renmin ribao* by Chen Qitong, deputy head of the PLA propaganda department, and three colleagues which in effect advocated a limitation of "blooming and contending" in the literary realm. The authors feared an erosion of political criteria as satiric literature became more popular at the expense of works praising socialism. They warned that "If we do not take action . . . we will have the end of politics. . . ." This view, which contrasted with Mao's more relaxed attitude but at the same time drew sustenance from his comments about getting rid of "weeds," became the subject of considerable comment in the press, much of it favorable. The attitude was further reflected in controversy over a 1956 story, "The Young Newcomer in the Organization Department," which described bureaucratic phenomena in a Party office, a story now attacked as condemning the entire Communist system. In the educational sphere, the Ministry of Education expressed similar fears of relaxed ideological indoctrination and the neglect of collectivism and discipline. In general, attacks on "right revisionism"—undoubtedly stimulated by "More on the Historical Experience of the Dictatorship of the Proletariat"—began to rival criticism of doctrinairism and bureaucratism in the official media.[39]

The seriousness of deviations which had been censured by Party spokesmen since mid-1956 also became a topic of discussion. One writer in *Zhongguo qingnian* [Chinese Youth] offered the "personal opinion" that although bureaucratism was a problem, some people misconstrued it as a massive phenomenon and a product of the socialist system. These people, the article continued, felt all leading personnel were bureaucrats and regarded fighting upper levels a virtue. The writer also urged restraint in dismissing officials guilty of bureaucratism. In his view, the basic method to combat bureaucratism was for the Party to lead and the masses to respond. In addition, commandism received similar treatment in a January 1957 *Renmin ribao* editorial which argued this deviation had been unfairly charged to cadres in certain areas and APC overhaul sometimes resulted in excessive criticism. This, in turn, caused cadre unwillingness to continue in leadership roles. The editorial called for a moderate process of APC overhaul which would not jeopardize cadre morale and blamed much of the problem on higher level bureaucratism and subjectivism. This analysis was not too different from the 1956 view, but in the context of early 1957 the editorial represented another effort to restrict criticism of the system.[40]

Finally, in another "personal opinion," concern was expressed over whether strikes, parades and demonstrations as had occurred in 1956 were proper methods for forcing the leadership to correct mistakes. The writer concluded that such methods would result in chaos which could be exploited by counterrevolutionaries, and advocated taking grievances to Party leaders for solution rather than appealing directly to the masses. In this he was at variance with the view expressed by Mao in both November and January that strikes were not only legal, but that when reasonable they helped by pointing out shortcomings. However, the Chairman had also stated that disturbances were not to be encouraged and unjustified ones should be criticized. In any case, by emphasizing regular Party channels for redressing grievances the author tacitly opposed the more liberal interpretations which could be put on the Hundred Flowers and mutual supervision policies.[41]

However ambivalent Mao's position may have been from November to January, it seems clear that he both retained a strong commitment to Party reform and soon became displeased with the restrictive atmosphere which had developed. In the same period, moreover, several provincial organizations launched rectification movements. Inner Mongolia conducted a campaign against bureaucratism, sectarianism and subjectivism from December to March, and in mid-February Heilongjiang reported on the progress of its movement by noting that serious cadre shortcomings had come to light through the criticisms of intellectuals.[42] Thus rectification efforts were proceeding but in a national context unlikely to produce significant results. It was this atmosphere which undoubtedly led Mao to make his crucial speeches of late February and early March. At the same time the schedule for rectification was advanced by a full year.

Mao Intervenes: Rectification to the Fore, Spring 1957

Mao's two speeches were bold efforts to change the restrictive post-Hungary atmosphere. The first speech, "On the Correct Handling of Contradictions among the People," was given to a closed session of the Supreme State Conference attended by more than 1,800 leading Communists and non-Communists. Here Mao elaborated in detail the views and policies which had been developing over the past year concerning the nature of conflicts within China's new socialist society and the need for persuasive methods—including a revived Hundred Flowers policy—in dealing with them. Two weeks later, in his "Speech at the Chinese Communist Party's National Conference on Propaganda Work," the Chairman addressed over 380 leading Party cadres in cultural and educational work and more than 100 non-Party people active in these fields. In this speech Mao revealed that "the Central Committee has decided on another rectification within the Party to be started this year"[43] and attempted to convince his audience of the need for vigorous implementation of the new movement.

Mao's overall assessment of the situation in spring 1957[g] reasserted the fundamentally confident view of 1956 and its associated themes. Victory had been achieved in the socialist revolution, the country had realized unprecedented unity, and the face of old China was rapidly changing. It was in this situation that "large scale, turbulent class struggle" had on the whole concluded and the main problem facing the Party was to consolidate the system, gain experience in its operation, and help the masses become accustomed to it. Consolidation required adjusting imbalances and tensions in the economy and society—i.e., "contradictions among the people"—and the main danger was improper handling of contradictions, thus turning them into antagonistic ones. Proper handling meant persuasive methods. Persuasion was appropriate both because conflicting interests were, to a substantial extent, legitimate, and the groups holding those interests fundamentally supported the socialist system.[44]

Mao's optimistic analysis extended to his evaluation of China's intellectuals. This group was overwhelmingly patriotic: 80 to over 90 percent purportedly supported socialism. Moreover, Mao repeatedly emphasized the importance of intellectuals for economic and cultural growth. He noted that China needed as many intellectuals as she could get for construction, purportedly pointed out the greatest scientific advances were always made by intellectual rebels, and called for the development of "a scientific technical viewpoint." In addition, Mao lamented that the Party had "no great authors, great poets or great professors," and advocated the recruitment of some into the CCP. Overall he sought the recruit-

---

[g] Determining Mao's precise views in this period encounters considerable obstacles. First, his major addresses of February and March were only released under altered political circumstances: the "Contradictions" speech was published with "certain additions" by Mao in June 1957 when attacks were under way against alleged "rightists"; the propaganda conference speech was not made public until 1964 when it appeared in the context of a new rectification effort. However, some indications of the original version of "Contradictions" are available through the leak of lengthy extracts to a *New York Times* journalist by Polish sources and in accounts of refugees who heard recordings of Mao's words. In general, while the philosophical underpinnings of Mao's argument seem unchanged, the June version omitted specific revelations of Party shortcomings and added restrictive criteria to guide "blooming and contending." It apparently also added the ideas that the outcome of class struggle was not yet decided and that revisionism outranked doctrinairism as a danger. While the total effect of these changes was very substantial, even in altered form Mao's view was a remarkably strong call for reforms in the relationship between leaders and led.

In addition, Cultural Revolution collections of Mao's unpublished statements provide texts of three additional talks in the period from late February to mid-May. Taken in conjunction with the official texts and unofficial accounts of "Contradictions" and the propaganda speech, as well as spring 1957 media elaborations of Mao's themes, they provide a significant basis for determining Mao's position as articulated at the time. But even if all of Mao's remarks from the period were available, this would still not solve the problem completely. For Mao's efforts to get rectification going and encourage intellectuals to "bloom and contend," particularly when addressing non-Party audiences, may have led to statements giving a one-sided picture of his considered overall view. Cf. Loh, *Escape,* pp. 295–96.

ment of one third of all intellectuals into the Party, including 15 percent in 1957.[45]

This enthusiasm notwithstanding, Mao was well aware of the ideological shortcomings of intellectuals. Although 80 to over 90 percent supported socialism "in varying degrees," Mao declared only "over 10 percent, comprising the Communists and sympathizers, are relatively familiar with Marxism and take a firm stand. . . ." Nevertheless, Mao remained sanguine. While the remolding of intellectuals should continue this would be a relaxed long term process which could only be achieved by persuasion. Ideological shortcomings could not be simply blamed on intellectuals but reflected the Party's failure to be sufficiently convincing. Thus while ideological remolding would continue for at least another ten years, intellectuals were not targets of the new policies in the traditional sense.[h] The Hundred Flowers and participation of non-Party people in rectification would only have an incidental remolding effect on intellectuals. Primarily, these measures would "win them over" by alleviating their pent up grievances and bringing about a change in the attitudes of Party cadres toward them. Although Mao noted that others felt the time was not yet ripe for such measures due to the continuing need for ideological work with intellectuals, he dismissed such qualms by citing the nation's overall political stability and the widespread acceptance of socialism by the intelligentsia.[46]

It is clear, then, that for Mao the target of reform was Party cadres, not intellectuals. But what is less clear concerning Mao's spring 1957 outlook is how serious he considered cadre shortcomings and, to a lesser extent, how he ranked the various problems within the Party. Regarding the latter question, in his speech to the propaganda conference—i.e., the version made public in 1964—Mao listed the evils to be overcome as "subjectivism, bureaucratism and sectarianism," the same formula he used at the Eighth Party Congress. The rectification directive issued, apparently on Mao's initiative, at the end of April altered this order to read "bureaucratism, sectarianism and subjectivism."[i] Although Mao never explicitly stated which problems he considered most dangerous, the latter formulation seems to reflect his views more closely in this period. Although questions of ideological understanding—subjectivism—were mentioned, the Chairman's greatest concern was with human relations between rulers and ruled. Here Mao was primarily critical of bureaucratic distance from the people and failure to deal adequately with their needs. He particularly emphasized bureaucratism in discussing the causes of strikes and demonstrations in China and the Hungarian

[h] At one point in April 1957 Mao did say it was permissible to speak of the shortcomings of democratic parties and even to "knock over" *(dadao)* democratic personages; *SXWS,* II, 105. The basic emphasis of his remarks in this period, however, was more on "winning over" than "knocking over" the intellectuals.

[i] Variations in the order of rectification targets have led to speculation concerning differences within the top Party leadership. This analysis, in contrast, hypothesizes that a consensus existed in 1956 which placed subjectivism first to stress the need to become familiar with new conditions but that the Hungarian events led to a reevaluation emphasizing bureaucracy. (It is admittedly difficult to account for Mao's listing which placed bureaucratism last at the November 1956 plenum directly after the Hungarian events.)

uprising. In addition, as suggested above, Mao devoted considerable attention to high handed treatment of non-Party intellectuals by Party cadres—the sin of sectarianism.[47]

Least clear is how widespread and serious Mao saw these problems to be. The subsequently published official versions of his two major speeches were rather bland on this score. While "not a few shortcomings and mistakes" were admitted, achievements were declared the main thing.[48] In the original version of "Contradictions" and other talks in March and April, however, Mao indicated a somewhat graver attitude both through detailed examples of flagrant bureaucracy and by comments that bureaucratism was "serious among some of the cadres," high Party officials were guilty of "serious errors," "commandism is very serious" in APCs in many places, etc.[49] In addition, both Mao's linkage of the Chinese situation to the Hungarian events and his initiative in pushing rectification ahead by a year suggest considerable concern. Nevertheless, Mao's overall optimism concerning the situation in China makes it highly unlikely that he regarded Party cadres as basically unstable. The unprecedented unity of the nation was surely matched by unity of the cadres; the overwhelming support for socialism attributed to bourgeois intellectuals must have been at least equaled by Party members whatever their shortcomings. Moreover, the contradiction between leaders and led was non-antagonistic and cadre errors could therefore be dealt with by persuasive methods. The mild approach to rectification actually advocated by Mao (see below) further suggests a fundamentally sanguine attitude toward the Party. While a dramatic statement of shortcomings may have been necessary to launch a thorough rectification, Mao did not seem to be altering his longstanding confidence in the great bulk of Party cadres.

The innovations in Mao's spring 1957 position concerned the methods to be used during rectification. Now both the mutual supervision and Hundred Flowers policies were explicitly to involve criticism of the Party. As Mao put it to the propaganda conference:

> In building up the new China we Communists are not daunted by any difficulties whatsoever. But we cannot accomplish this on our own. We need a good

---

Despite this reevaluation Mao may simply have retained the old formula out of habit in March 1957 but altered it to reflect the changed priorities when the April directive was issued. As for the attitude of Liu Shaoqi, it is interesting that his usage, insofar as evidence is available, always followed the then current formulation. Thus in Shanghai on April 27, 1957—the very day the new directive was being drafted presumably at Mao's behest in Beijing—he used the old formula of "subjectivism, bureaucratism and sectarianism"; *SCMM-S*, No. 35. Once the directive was promulgated, however, Liu continued to use the new order of "bureaucratism, sectarianism and subjectivism" even after other Party leaders carelessly used varying formulations; *Collected Works of Liu 1945–57*, pp. 454, 463. Cf. MacFarquhar, *Origins 1*, p. 307. While any comment is necessarily speculative, it does appear that in this regard Liu lived up to his image of the disciplined cadre.

> number of non-Party people with great ideals who will fight dauntlessly together with us for the transformation and construction of our society in the direction of socialism and Communism. . . . [I]n order to be able to shoulder this task more competently and work better together with all non-Party people who are activated by high ideals and determined to institute reforms, we must conduct rectification movements both now and in the future, and constantly rid ourselves of whatever is wrong. Thoroughgoing materialists are fearless; we hope that all our fellow fighters will courageously shoulder their responsibilities and overcome all difficulties, fearing no setbacks or gibes, nor hesitating to criticize us Communists and give us their suggestions.[50]

The innovation here was not "optional" participation of non-Party people in Party rectification; this had been a common feature of every rectification campaign since 1942. In the past, however, such participation was largely confined to structured activities within work units. But now outside criticism of the Party would play a critical role and shape the course of rectification. This had only happened previously in 1947–48 and then the source of criticism was the disadvantaged rural poor. Now it was to come from the relatively advantaged urban intelligentsia.

To encourage a vigorous response to this invitation, Mao declared that those airing their opinions would not be punished and warned against stipulating Marxism-Leninism as the guiding ideology of the criticism process on the grounds that it would generate fear. The Chairman even went so far as to advocate that each province have two newspapers, one run by the Party and another run by people outside the Party to engage in mutual criticism. The evidence suggests, moreover, that the restrictive criteria for "blooming and contending" in the official text of "Contradictions" were added in June although Mao did indicate in March that he expected criticism to be "aimed at unity."[51] While not foreclosing responses to critics, Mao's thrust was clearly for a tolerant attitude toward criticism:

> In leading our country, two alternative methods can be adopted—to "open wide" or to "restrict." To "open wide" means to let all people express their opinions freely, so that they dare to speak, dare to criticize and dare to debate; it means not being afraid of wrong views and anything poisonous; it means to encourage argument and criticism among people holding different views, allowing freedom both for criticism and for countercriticism; it means not suppressing wrong views but convincing people by reasoning with them. To "restrict" means to forbid people to air differing opinions and express wrong ideas, and to "finish them off with a single blow" if they do so. That is the way to aggravate rather than to resolve contradictions. To "open wide," or to "restrict"—we must choose one or the other of these two policies. We choose the former, because it is the policy which will help to consolidate our country and develop our culture.[52]

This did not mean that Mao was oblivious to the possibility worrying many in the Party that some unpleasant side effects would appear. Mao advocated "blooming and contending" despite noting that it inevitably would cause "some confusion," although he subsequently denied having endorsed the harshly critical aspects of the "*big* blooming and contending" which developed in May. Similarly, he was undismayed at the prospect of "poisonous weeds" such as feudal plays and non-Marxist ideologies. In part, he argued as he had in January that Marxism would benefit from competition with erroneous viewpoints as a better understanding of such views would provide a vaccine against them. He further claimed, as he also had in January, that one should not be overly nervous about "poisonous weeds" as it often took time to determine which views were right or wrong and hasty action could stifle beneficial opinions.[53] But the fundamental reason for Mao's optimism and his insistence that "weeds" be given an opportunity to grow was the belief that under the new circumstances of socialist construction they were a temporary phenomenon representing only a minority viewpoint. In this vein, Mao discussed the appearance of feudal dramas:

> Recently, a number of ghosts and monsters have been presented on the stage. Seeing this, some comrades have become very worried. In my opinion, a little of this does not matter much; within a few decades such ghosts and monsters will disappear from the stage altogether and you won't be able to see them even if you want to.[54]

In the immediate context of "blooming and contending" the Chairman clearly envisioned that most opinions would truly be "fragrant flowers" designed to improve Party performance, while "poisonous weeds" could be tolerated because they would not have a significant influence.[j]

However optimistic Mao may have been concerning the likely content of criticisms of the Party, he laid down guidelines for the conduct of inner Party rectification which not only indicated an assumption that cadre ranks were basically sound, but also reassured Party members that the process would be kept under control despite the unprecedented methods adopted. The novel approach was partially offset by Mao's assertion that rectification should follow the precedent of the 1942–44 campaign, a campaign firmly guided by Party officials. The Chairman, who reaffirmed the existence of a distinction between the Party and those outside the Party, both advocated the Yan'an methods of study, criticism and self-criticism and emphasized the persuasive approach which assertedly set rectification apart from the "ruthless struggles and merciless blows" approach of the returned students. This implicit guarantee of a mild rectification was backed up by explicit assurances that the movement would be conducted as a "gentle breeze and mild rain," i.e., with the methods of "small democracy." Thus Mao,

[j] Mao was also optimistic concerning the appearance of small scale strikes and demonstrations. Although recognizing these as justified by serious bureaucratism, Mao regarded such phenomena as unusual and merely "supplementary measures" required in extreme cases while normal methods of criticism prevailed in most units. *SXWS,* II, 93–95.

as he had the previous November, promised Party cadres that they could avoid the intense struggle sessions and coercive sanctions associated with "big democracy" in the coming campaign. The Chairman apparently did not see any contradiction between this promise and encouraging bourgeois intellectuals to speak their minds.[55]

In sum, by spring 1957 Mao felt the new situation where contradictions were primarily "among the people" justified innovative methods of Party rectification. Criticism on a significant scale from non-Party sources was allowed for the first time since 1948—but now from a politically vacillating group albeit one which assertedly desired socialism. The optimistic assumption that a natural harmony of interests existed for all segments of "the people" led Mao to believe that intellectuals' opinions would be genuinely helpful. Any that were not would be overwhelmed by the weight of public opinion and no official punishment would be necessary. While "some confusion" could be expected this would be limited and no precise criteria concerning acceptable criticism were required. Party cadres, for their part, were basically good notwithstanding some serious cases of bureaucracy and could expect the traditional persuasive approach despite the innovative aspects of the movement. Mao's assessment, in short, attempted to reassure both the projected critics and targets of criticism in the new rectification campaign. In so doing he grossly underestimated both existing tensions in Chinese society and the conflict which would be generated by the striking departure from established political roles.

The Response within the Party to Mao's Initiative

Mao's Hundred Flowers and rectification policies met inner Party opposition well before the full extent of his miscalculation became apparent in May. In an April address to Shanghai cadres, the Chairman asserted 90 percent of Party comrades shared Chen Qitong's negative attitude toward the Hundred Flowers and added that "I have no mass base." Media reports on the conduct of the campaign, moreover, indicated cadre resistance was widespread. A mid-May report said "a very great portion of Party leadership cadres are antagonistic to [the Hundred Flowers] line." Such antagonism apparently led to restrictive practices in many localities. Thus an article which singled out the vigorous leadership of the Shanghai Party committee plaintively asked why Party committees elsewhere did not act similarly. To some extent, opposition reflected indifference due to the belief that other work was more important. But fears that the process would get out of hand were more basic. Some officials feared "blooming and contending" would force the Party into a passive position thus hampering effective leadership; others saw the creation of a chaotic situation. Opposition went beyond the failure to encourage "blooming and contending." Many cadres reportedly were overeager in defending the faith and indiscriminately attacked opinions as "poisonous weeds." Such behavior may have been furthered by Mao's failure to lay down precise criteria for criticism, but it clearly went against the thrust of his position.[56]

It is extremely difficult, however, to delineate precisely the opposition Mao may have faced in high Party circles. Subsequent analysis will examine two crucial areas of possible resistance—the propaganda apparatus functionally responsible for publicizing the new policies and much of the related organizational work, and Mao's Politburo colleagues. But first we shall discuss the specific measures taken in response to Mao's initiative of late February and early March.

The Implementation of Rectification: Timing and Methods

The revitalized Hundred Flowers drive only gained momentum gradually following Mao's speeches and did not become intense until May. The first important manifestation of the renewed policy occurred at a mid-March meeting of the CPPCC National Committee which overlapped the propaganda conference. The CPPCC meetings were carried out under the long term coexistence and mutual supervision policy in the spirit of "frank criticism and democracy." While considerable caution was shown by over 300 speakers, non-Party people did air conflicting views in plenary debates and group discussion on various important subjects including education, APCs, the economy, population growth, and national minorities and religious groups.[57]

Despite the CPPCC meetings, there was little evidence of wider efforts to revive the Hundred Flowers policy until late March when diverse views were published in the press, Party conferences were held on "contradictions among the people," and special non-Party forums were convened to air views on Party policies. Throughout April study and discussion of Mao's speeches were carried out extensively among cadres and intellectuals both at conferences and forums and through regular study mechanisms. In this manner accounts of the speeches reached cadres in factories and mines, school teachers, students in higher education, and rural cadres of the district level in addition to higher ranking personnel.[58]

One of the most significant initial steps following the CPPCC meetings were provincial and municipal propaganda conferences modeled on the national conference. These March-May meetings were under Party leadership and generally involved major reports by local first secretaries. In addition to leading Party officials and propaganda cadres, the conferences were attended by non-Party intellectuals including scientific workers, professors, engineers, literary workers and journalists. Beyond the study of contradictions, these meetings sought both to encourage intellectuals to "bloom and contend" by exposing irrational phenomena and to strengthen their ideological and political education. Provincial authorities also convened conferences in other functional areas such as rural work and industry to discuss contradictions peculiar to those fields.[59]

The most distinctive and innovative device was the forum of non-Party intellectuals. Li Weihan, head of the CCP's united front department responsible for relations with non-Party people, underlined this by declaring that "for the first time in the Party's history the united front department is being relied on to push forward rectification."[60] One type of forum consisted of opening the pages of the press to diverse viewpoints. More significant were meetings of non-Party groups; the opinions expressed were then selectively published in the official media. These gatherings involved a wide variety of groups and were held under diverse sponsorship. Sometimes local Party committees convened meetings as in Shanghai where First Secretary Ke Qingshi personally presided over ten forums in the latter part of April. Party and non-Party newspapers and various professional organizations all convened forums in urban centers from April to early June. Moreover, ministries and the State Council held meetings of their non-Party personnel to aid the rectification movement. Of all the forums held, the most important in terms of deepening the tide of criticism were those convened from May 8 to 16 and May 21 to June 1 by the united front department for leading democratic party figures. The extent of these efforts is indicated by a report that in Beijing alone 350,000 democratic party members had participated in forums by the end of April. As a result, virtually all elements of the urban intellectual elite had the opportunity to express themselves to the degree they judged prudent.[61]

From the above we can see that forums of intellectuals and other conferences were not only convened in response to Mao's initiative, but in many cases were organized by leading Party officials. Thus while these aspects of rectification were novel, to a substantial degree they remained in the hands of the established Party bureaucracy.[k]

While non-Party forums were proceeding, Party rectification was officially launched by an April 27 Central Committee directive apparently drawn up at Mao's insistence. This directive stipulated that the movement was to be guided by Mao's "Contradictions" and propaganda speeches, and called for renewed attention to the Hundred Flowers and mutual supervision policies. According to the directive, bureaucratism, sectarianism and subjectivism had grown for two reasons. First, "many comrades" did not understand the new conditions existing after the fundamental change in social relations. Moreover, as a result of the

---

[k] In the universities, however, a number of unsanctioned or reluctantly sanctioned devices spontaneously appeared among the students. These included *ad hoc* student groups for conducting criticism, unstructured debates among student factions, and unrestricted use of wall posters *(dazibao)*. It was in this context that not only the unprecedentedly wider use of big character posters but also "*big* blooming and contending" and "big debates" developed most extensively (see Chapter 7). These, Mao later claimed, did not arise from Party policies but had been the inventions of rightists who were not content with the gentler methods proposed for Party rectification. *SXWS,* II, 126–27, 133.

Party being in a ruling position, "many" fell into the habit of leadership by purely administrative measures while "some" were even contaminated by the "GMD style" of behaving as an oppressive ruling class.[62]

Concerning the conduct of rectification, the directive stipulated the "gentle breeze and mild rain" approach which Mao had advocated. Meetings would be limited to small scale discussion, individual "heart to heart talks" *(tanxin)* would be widely used, and no large scale criticism or struggle meetings would be held. Moreover, critics were asked to avoid excessive negativism and criticism could not be imposed on individuals who rejected it. Party members whose errors fell short of serious violations were to be exempted from organizational discipline. Non-Party people wishing to participate voluntarily in rectification would be made welcome and have the right to withdraw at any time. To overcome bureaucratism, the directive called for the systematization of participation in labor by leading Party, government and army personnel. It pointed out that labor, "however little," would help the "not a few comrades" who had drifted away from the masses. The campaign was placed under the personal leadership of local first secretaries and specially organized leading groups of key local Party officials. Thus the conduct of rectification was formally turned over to the Party's regular chain of command, an approach compatible with non-coercive Party reform. Finally, rectification would be coordinated with regular work so as to hinder neither and contribute to the solution of actual work problems, another familiar provision for mild campaigns.

Under plans made subsequently, the campaign was scheduled to last for six months in central government organs and go through three stages: (1) mobilization of cadres and study of documents; (2) examination of problems and criticism from below; and (3) summarization of experiences. By early May the movement was underway in central ministries of all functional systems. In each ministry the campaign was linked to solving important work problems. For example, rectification study in the Ministry of Public Security focused on cadres who had been active in suppressing counterrevolutionaries but could not adjust to the task of handling "contradictions among the people"; Ministry of Education cadres discussed problems of courses and teaching materials; and in the Ministry of Agriculture criticisms were made of unrealistic production plans. It was through focusing on concrete problems that contradictions were to be solved, an approach consistent with the repeated theme of not letting the movement conflict with regular work.[63]

Provincial level plans called for establishing rectification groups and offices at various administrative levels. First secretaries headed provincial rectification groups and, at least in Anhui, the standing committee of the provincial Party committee became the rectification group. In contrast to central organs, the movement in the provinces would last well into 1958 and have two basic stages: (1) rectification in Party and government organs of the county level and above, in large factories and mines, and in institutions of higher education lasting from three to eight months; and (2) rectification of cadres of sub-county levels down to basic level Party organizations for about five months after the conclusion of the first stage. As in central units, the movement was regulated so that rectification and ordinary work could be carried out at the same time.[64]

As rectification unfolded prominent Party officials began to participate in productive labor, a measure gradually extended to leading personnel in government, military, economic and cultural organs. This effort was aided by the *xiafang* program underway since the previous winter. In addition, rectification was coordinated with a production increase and austerity movement launched earlier to alleviate the stringent financial situation.[65] In all these respects Party rectification, following the April directive, took a markedly orthodox form despite the unorthodox backdrop of "blooming and contending."

Resistance in High Party Circles?

While the preceding account indicates a substantial bureaucratic response to Mao's initiative, it leaves unanswered the question of the locus, nature and intensity of opposition to the rectification *cum* Hundred Flowers policy. Although a full answer lies beyond the available evidence, as suggested earlier an examination of the Party propaganda apparatus and the Politburo may illuminate these matters.

The propaganda apparatus was responsible both for conveying Mao's message through the public media and, together with united front bodies, for organizing many of the conferences and forums of intellectuals where "blooming and contending" took place. Moreover, by virtue of their functional responsibility for culture and education, propaganda officials had complex and frequently tense relations with the higher intellectuals who were assigned a crucial role by the Hundred Flowers experiment. The available evidence indicates that the implementation of the new policies by these officials was sluggish at best. Certainly Mao felt his efforts were being thwarted. One report claims a frustrated Mao told friends in Shanghai "he would prefer not to be Chairman in order to get involved in 'A Hundred Flowers blooming and a hundred schools contending.' "[66]

Resistance was perhaps foreshadowed in an early March article commemorating the Yan'an rectification by propaganda chief Lu Dingyi. Although frequently citing Mao's contributions to the 1942–44 movement, Lu did not address himself to the role of non-Party critics in the "about to be launched" rectification which Mao had already raised at the Supreme State Conference.[l] It should be empha-

[l]*RMRB,* March 5, 1957, in *SCMP,* No. 1511. While an announcement of non-Party participation does not appear in the official version of the "Contradictions" speech, it appears to have been emphasized in the original. Loh, *Escape,* p. 292. It should be noted, however, that a danger exists in reading too much opposition into Lu's article. It was, after all, largely an historical and theoretical account of the first campaign, and in his remarks on the current situation Lu cited the need to implement firmly the Hundred Flowers and mutual supervision policies. For analysis stressing opposition, see MacFarquhar, *Origins 1,* pp. 190–91.

sized, in any case, that opposition was far from monolithic at the top of the propaganda apparatus. Deputy Director of Propaganda Zhou Yang and several of his subordinates in the literary and art field in particular were vigorous proponents of Mao's policies. But overall the initial media response following Mao's speeches was slow and contained sentiments out of tune with Mao's words. It took *Renmin ribao* a month and a half after Mao spoke to editorialize on the subject of contradictions. In mid-March the Party paper published criticism of Chen Qitong's views by Minister of Culture Shen Yanbing, but it was a cautious statement which even praised Chen's zeal in defending the Party line. Other articles in the official media clashed with Mao's position by imposing limitations on debate and focusing on cadre criticism of intellectuals. In short, by the end of March Mao's initiative was not adequately reflected in the Chinese press.[67]

Mao indicated his displeasure in early April with a stinging "Criticism of *Renmin ribao*":

> The Party press should promptly do propaganda on the Party's policies. It is a mistake that the conference on propaganda work has not been reported in the press. This conference was held jointly by Party and non-Party people, why then has it not been reported in the press? Why is it that no editorial has been issued on the Supreme State Conference? Why are the Party's policies being kept secret? There is a ghost here; where's this ghost? We used to say that the papers were run by pedants, now we should say they are being run by the dead. More often than not you play the role of the opposition in respect to the Central Committee's policies, and you do not approve of the Central Committee's policies.[68]

The apparent main target of this attack was *Renmin ribao* chief editor, Deng Tuo, who handled editorial policy.[69] In addition, Cultural Revolution sources have blamed Lu Dingyi and his propaganda department deputy, Hu Qiaomu, for blocking publication of Mao's speeches. Hu in particular was accused of using his supervisory powers over the Party press to prevent the propagation of Party policies.[70] If Lu Dingyi actually was at fault, moreover, then the affair affected the Politburo level since he was an alternate member of that body. But it is significant, as will be argued subsequently, that no more powerful members of the top Party council were linked to the blockage of Mao's speeches by Cultural Revolution sources.

Whoever was at fault, it is clear that Mao's unhappiness was also due to his belief that the spirit of "opening wide" had been negated. In early April the Chairman pointed approvingly to the non-Party Shanghai paper, *Wenhui bao* [Wenhui Daily], for its publication of critical opinions and made his suggestion that each province should have a non-Party as well as Party paper. On April 9 *Wenhui bao* published an interview with Zhou Yang attacking Chen Qitong. The next day *Renmin ribao* not only joined in with a sharp criticism of Chen and other opponents of the Hundred Flowers, but criticized itself for not having spoken out earlier. The Party paper concluded that the negative views of such opponents, abetted by its own silence, had sown ideological confusion in an attempt to force the Party to change its policy. The Party daily followed with a series of editorials and articles on the themes of Mao's speeches, as well as further attacks on the passive attitude of Party organizations and newspapers. Mao's insistence that "blooming and contending" be extensively developed was probably also behind a secret directive in early May that critics should be unanswered for a month.[71]

The response of *Renmin ribao* to Mao's criticism did not end questions concerning the performance of the propaganda apparatus. Throughout April and May two strains appeared in official Party pronouncements on the Hundred Flowers and rectification. The predominant strain reflected the thrust of Mao's position: it focused on bureaucratism as the main danger and encouraged "blooming and contending" by asserting the basic loyalty of non-Party people, attributing contradictions mainly to cadre shortcomings, attacking restrictive views, and declaring intellectuals' criticisms of the Party on the whole sincere and correct.[72] The second, lesser strain highlighted failures of subjective understanding and emphasized limits to "blooming and contending," the need to distinguish between "fragrant flowers" and "poisonous weeds," and the refutation of improper criticisms. It also reminded non-Party personnel that criticism of the Party was to be in the manner of a "gentle breeze and mild rain," upheld the guiding principles of Marxism-Leninism and Party leadership, and stressed the remolding of intellectuals on a long term basis.[73]

Any number of explanations can account for these two strains. To a certain extent they reflected ambiguities in Mao's own position. The Chairman, after all, had advocated "gentle breeze and mild rain" methods, did regard subjectivism as a major shortcoming, and had noted the need for continuing the ideological reform of intellectuals. Nevertheless, Mao had not emphasized such ideological remolding as a goal of the current campaign and emphasis on Marxism-Leninism ignored his warning that it would create fear among intellectuals. In general, although there was a degree of ambivalence in Mao's views, the picture presented by the media was a more cautious synthesis and on a few points occasionally came into clear conflict with the Chairman.[m] Another possible explanation is that the media accurately reflected central policy—a policy more balanced than Mao's personal position as a result of a compromise between

[m] The synthesis, however, was much more in tune with the official versions of Mao's speeches published subsequently. Thus the degree the propaganda apparatus departed from Mao's views depends on precisely how many changes were made in these speeches. For example, if Mao did in fact stipulate that countercriticism was allowed in his propaganda conference address (see above, p. 188), then the emphasis on refuting improper criticism was less a distortion of the Chairman's position than otherwise might be the case.

Mao and other Politburo leaders. In this case, while Mao might have been less than totally pleased at the outcome, he would not—according to CCP organizational principles—have much ground for dissatisfaction with the performance of the propaganda apparatus. A more radical alternative, one which this analysis rejects for the reasons given below, is that the media were used by different Politburo groups to fight out an issue on which the top leadership was sharply divided. Finally, the most likely possibility, differences of opinion within the Politburo, together with the absence of specific directives at various stages,[n] may have created a situation where propaganda officials were unsure of precisely what line to take but, at the same time, had scope to emphasize their own views which were considerably less sanguine than those of the Chairman.

The novel nature of Mao's rectification program made important differences of opinion within the top leadership likely. Moreover, there is evidence to suggest that this indeed was the case. The most explicit evidence appeared during the Anti-Rightist Campaign in the form of words allegedly uttered by various "rightists." One rightist was accused of saying: " 'The Party Center has split,' 'Chairman Mao is under the sectarian opposition of high level cadres. These high level cadres want to retaliate against him. . . .' 'Chairman Mao has had to compromise.' "[74] Another reportedly identified the main opponents: "The reason why 'blooming and contending' is not going well is because the Liu Shaoqi-Peng Zhen axis does not support [it]."[75] While the reliability of such information concerning closed Politburo debates may be questioned, these statements indicate that politically aware circles believed a division existed over rectification within the top leadership.

But what does a fuller reading of the evidence tell us? Peng Zhen, by the *public* record, would appear to have been a supporter of rectification. When Mao delivered his "Contradictions" speech Peng occupied a seat of honor well above his official status on the Chairman's immediate right—an event which by the normal rules of Pekinology would indicate Peng's approval and even strong backing of Mao's words.[76] Peng subsequently gained wide publicity for himself as a supporter of rectification through a report to a Beijing propaganda conference which strongly endorsed Mao's views and by being photographed engaging in manual labor. In his remarks to the Beijing conference Peng went to the heart of Hundred Flowers issue: "At present the main problem . . . is not enough blooming and contending."[77] These words and actions—in contrast to the silence of Deng Xiaoping—have led one analyst to view Peng as the main high level supporter of Mao within the Party

[n]MacFarquhar, *Origins 1*, p. 194, persuasively argues that the slow response of *Renmin ribao* to Mao's initiative must have reflected the lack of a final decision on rectification timing since it is virtually inconceivable that an official of Deng Tuo's rank would openly defy Central Committee policy. Note that the rectification directive was only drafted in late April; above, p. 192.

apparatus.[o] At the very least, it suggests that Peng—whatever reservations he may have expressed about rectification within the confidential councils of the Politburo—was putting on a public face of support as both organizational discipline and his own career interests would dictate.

Unlike Peng, in the case of Liu Shaoqi the public record—or more precisely the lack of one—does present a more credible case for opposition to Mao. Liu was absent from the picture released of the Supreme State Conference podium while Mao delivered his "Contradictions" speech. Moreover, Liu was virtually silent in public throughout the period from late February to mid-May. Nevertheless, it is clear that Liu was active behind the scenes particularly through an extensive provincial tour in March and April to explain the new policies and test local opinion. While it is impossible to determine precisely what views Liu expressed in his conversations with local leaders, partial Cultural Revolution texts of several speeches from this period give some indication of his position.[78]

One issue in spring 1957 was the nature of the major shortcoming within the Party. Mao, as we have seen, came to focus on bureaucratism—the high-handed attitude of cadres toward the masses. In a late April speech to Shanghai cadres which analyzed "contradictions among the people" in a manner faithful to Mao's views, Liu noted that "there are a considerable number of people within our Party who have . . . subjectivism, bureaucratism and sectarianism. . . ." Liu thus ranked subjectivism—problems of ideological understanding—first, but in so doing he was only adopting Mao's order of the previous month. In the course of his discussion Liu spent considerable time on ideological matters, but he also highlighted the danger of excessive bureaucracy:

> [T]here are . . . people who say the contradictions between the masses of people and leaders, or between the masses and bureaucrats, are principal contradictions, that these contradictions exist in large numbers and in concentrated form. . . . It may be generally right to say so. . . .
>
> It is very difficult to do away with bureaucratism entirely. I myself have a lot of bureaucratism. Bureaucratism under present conditions in China can hardly be avoided. Leading organs and leaders will be guilty of it in a greater or lesser degree. . . . I think no one can be free from bureaucratism. . . . Surely bureaucrats who are bad, very stubborn and opposed to the masses are in the

[o] Peter R. Moody, Jr., *The Politics of the Eighth Central Committee of the Communist Party of China* (Hamden: Shoe String Press, 1973), pp. 117–18. Moody's argument is also based on the fact that several other leaders who expressed pro-rectification attitudes had career links to Peng and on the rationale that Peng, who had been demoted at the Eighth Congress, was one of the "outs" in the Party apparatus and would have an interest in rectifying the Party machinery under Deng Xiaoping who had been promoted over him.

There is other evidence—assiduously compiled by MacFarquhar, *Origins 1*, pp. 181–82, 194–96, 203–207, 218–19, 228–31, 270–71, 284–85, 289–290—which suggests that Peng may have opposed Mao. The point is not what Peng's views actually were, which is unknowable, but whether his overall pattern of action reflected systematic, persistent resistance to Mao's line. On balance, the total evidence indicates this was not the case.

> minority. But in certain cases bureaucratism has assumed more serious dimensions, and has aroused the opposition of the people. Today cases of bureaucratism are not very few but quite many. . . .[p]

Ten days later in a talk at the Higher Party School in Beijing Liu addressed himself to rectification. In the course of his talk he stated that the most important political question was the relationship of the Party and masses and warned that if bureaucratism became an antagonistic contradiction the people would rise up and overthrow the socialist superstructure. Liu went on to complain that the mass line was in jeopardy:

> [S]ome of our comrades leave the mass line and people's democracy out of account and behave like overlords when dealing with such questions. The mass line is now increasingly neglected in our actual work. . . . From what people say it appears that some [cadres] are not willing to practise the "four togethers" [eating, living, working and studying together with the masses] and are only interested in sitting in their offices. Those also sit in their offices . . . divorce themselves from the masses and become bureaucrats. . . .
>
> Such instances of estrangement from the masses should be cited and drawn to the attention of all during the rectification campaign. . . .[79]

If Liu's Shanghai speech had been ambiguous regarding what he saw as the major problem facing the Party, when he spoke at the Higher Party School bureaucratism clearly received the greatest emphasis.

Perhaps the most critical issue facing the Politburo was the methods to be used during rectification. A number of analysts have argued that Liu sought to keep the movement as lenient and non-disputive as possible—i.e., to conduct it as a "gentle breeze and mild rain"—and that Mao was forced into a major compromise on this question in order to secure Politburo backing for the campaign. This, however, ignores both Mao's subsequent disclaimer of support for "*big* blooming and contending" and, more importantly, his consistent spring 1957 endorsement of the "gentle breeze and mild rain" approach. On close examination, moreover, there is little to choose between the expressed views of Mao and Liu on this issue. This can be seen in their comments on "small democracy" and "big democracy." As we have seen, these approaches had application both for dealing with cadres and the masses. "Small democracy" meant in

---

[p] *SCMM-S,* No. 35. Earlier in his speech Liu focused on the contradiction between proletarian and non-proletarian ideas but handled it in such a way as to indicate its relevance to bureaucratism: "According to the view of [some] comrades . . . the situation is probably like this: ideas among the masses, workers and students are non-proletarian ideas while ideas of our Party members, cadres and our leaders, factory directors, school principals, responsible government officials are proletarian ideas. . . . I think [this] is wrong." By this analysis the arrogant attitude of cadres who thought they alone possessed proletarian ideology was an important source of high-handed bureaucratic behavior.

essence the use of persuasive techniques: mild criticism emphasizing unity, patient education, and the avoidance of punitive sanctions. "Big democracy," in contrast, covered a number of more extreme phenomena. When used by the Party toward outsiders it took the form of mass movements and included repressive measures against enemies; within the Party it meant large scale struggle sessions and purges. In January 1957 Deng Xiaoping looked at "big democracy" from a somewhat different angle and linked it to undisciplined and unprincipled struggles where one group of leaders sought to overthrow another—the type of inner Party life which assertedly existed before Mao assumed command of the CCP. In still another sense, as Mao had argued since November 1956, "big democracy" was a method which could be used by the people to express discontent to the authorities outside normal channels when those channels were defective.[80]

In dealing with the people, both Mao and Liu consistently advocated "small democracy." This, after all, was the essence of Mao's "Contradictions" speech—the need to adjust methods of rule to a situation where "large scale, turbulent class struggle" was basically a thing of the past. Liu's April address to Shanghai cadres was a particularly forceful argument that Communist officials must adopt persuasive methods in dealing with the masses. Liu went on to make the observation that some not only opposed the Party's "gentle breeze and mild rain" policy as it applied to the people but also concerning inner Party discipline, and instead wanted to resort to purges for dealing with erring cadres. He rejected this approach in favor of "small democracy" within the Party—just as Mao had done in November 1956 and the rectification directive presumably drafted by Mao also did. These remarks and the directive deviated to a certain degree from the positions taken at the turn of the year by *both* Mao and Liu. In January Liu sanctioned "a little bit of big democracy" *(dian daminzhu)* for serious cases of bureaucracy, while Mao assumed a tolerant but hardly approving attitude toward strikes and demonstrations. At the Supreme State Conference Mao elaborated his view that such manifestations of "big democracy" were the inevitable outcome of the failure to allow any democracy in individual units and should be permitted as a supplementary method for combating bureaucratism.[81] Thus while the decision to adopt "gentle breeze and mild rain" methods while passing over "big democracy" in silence may indeed have meant a compromise for Mao, on the available evidence it could equally be seen as a compromise for Liu.

The preceding analysis is not to argue that Liu Shaoqi and/or Peng Zhen were in total agreement with Mao on rectification or even that they did not oppose him vigorously in Politburo debates. It is certainly difficult to believe that there would not have been important differences on such a novel policy. What it does argue is that the available evidence cannot conclusively demonstrate systematic resistance on the part of Liu and/or Peng—or even *whether* in fact they opposed Mao. In any case, Cultural Revolution evidence—or rather the lack of it—suggests that whatever differences existed they did not polarize the Politburo into sharply contending factions and that any debate was conducted according to accepted norms of decision making. An extensive examination of Cultural Revolution sources has uncovered *no* charges of opposition to "blooming and contending" or rectification against Liu or Peng or any other member of the Politburo except for Lu Dingyi.[q]

It could be argued, of course, that it would have been too embarrassing to level this particular charge given the failure of the Hundred Flowers. This ignores, however, any number of considerations. First, Mao's "Contradictions" speech, despite the many "un-Maoist" aspects of even the official version, was republished and widely hailed during the Cultural Revolution. Second, it would take no great dialectical skill to reinterpret opposition to Mao as " 'left' in form, right in essence." Third, particular officials—e.g., Lu Dingyi, Hu Qiaomu—were attacked for attempting to block Mao's directives, but this was not extended to higher ranking officials. If Lu and Hu had been explicitly encouraged by Liu and Peng, why not say so? Fourth, in his unpublished speeches Mao made several striking references to opposition to the Hundred Flowers, but at no point at the time or subsequently did he identify his Politburo colleagues as part of that opposition. And lastly, if Liu had indeed boycotted the Supreme State Conference as a deliberate sign of opposition, this is precisely the kind of personal affront which was grist for the Red Guard mill in numerous other instances. While the absence of evidence can never conclusively prove a point, sometimes silence speaks volumes.[r]

In sum, the lack of Cultural Revolution denunciations combined with existing evidence concerning the views and actions of Politburo members in spring 1957 suggests that any differences were contained by established procedures. There is important contextual evidence to support this conclusion. First, there was broad agreement on the nature of the new situation following the victory of socialist transformation and the need for relaxation in the CCP's methods of rule. This, in turn, was reflected in the optimistic assumptions upon which "blooming and contending" was based. While clearly it is likely that some Politburo members were more reserved in their optimism than Mao, particularly after Hungary, the generally confident mood undoubtedly served to mitigate the divisiveness of any differences.

---

[q] On the contrary, Liu and other Party leaders were attacked extensively in Cultural Revolution sources for pushing "opening wide" to encourage attacks on the Party. E.g., see NCNA, Beijing, May 24, 1967, in *SCMP*, No. 3949. Such accusations, of course, should be treated with extreme care as they involve both an effort to distort Mao's position at the time and to fix blame for excessive "blooming and contending" on Liu and others.

[r] The only concrete evidence we are left with is the statements attributed to rightists in summer 1957 asserting the opposition of Liu and Peng to Mao's policies (see above, p. 197). While no fully satisfying explanation of these statements can be offered, it should be noted that they were officially presented as slanders. It may have been that non-Party elements got wind of rumors concerning Liu and Peng—rumors which may or may not have had a basis in fact. In terms of our analysis, even if there were some basis for such rumors it would not necessarily indicate that opposition went beyond traditionally accepted bounds.

Moreover, Mao's views themselves were in a process of development throughout the entire period. The Chairman did *not* consistently push radical innovations in rectification for a full year, a situation which might have crystallized a well organized opposition, but instead he altered his views according to changing circumstances. When he delivered the "Ten Great Relationships" in April 1956 Mao devoted only one brief section to "the relationship between the Party and others" and gave a rather restrictive interpretation to the policy of mutual supervision. In subsequent months through the Eighth Party Congress, despite his concern with the issue Mao seemed to accept the consensus view that rectification was still a relatively low priority item on the Party's agenda. And while Mao's initial reaction to Hungary was to upgrade rectification, "More on the Historical Experience of the Dictatorship of the Proletariat" which "exactly" reflected the Chairman's views helped create the restrictive atmosphere of early 1957. Thus when Mao revived the Hundred Flowers and proposed striking innovations in Party rectification in February and March 1957 it probably resulted in extensive Politburo debate in the normal fashion, but a debate which was not engaged in by well articulated policy groups.

Most importantly, given the success of Mao's leadership over the previous two decades and the vitality of free debate within the Politburo as a leadership device, there was little incentive for Politburo members to violate Party norms in expressing disagreements. As Liu Shaoqi put it at the end of 1957, "Our Party has guarded its unity at all times, there's been no split, and the Party rules have been obeyed; no one has gone his own way, publicized his own ideas."[82] Finally, while such disagreements as existed may well have been substantial—and thus emboldened lower ranking officials to drag their feet—the restrained response of non-Party intellectuals until mid-May probably further served to limit the divisiveness of the issue at the highest level.

The Response of the Intellectuals

The complex response within the Party to Mao's initiative was paralleled by the reaction of the intellectual community. Many specialists made use of the relaxed atmosphere to push their views within their own spheres of expertise. For example, throughout the first half of 1957 water conservancy experts held a series of professional conferences, organized a professional association, and voiced their concerns and policy preferences in national newspapers and technical journals.[83] In a sense, this response was optimal in that it helped facilitate informed debate on technical subjects without challenging the authority of the Party. But it fell short of what Mao asked in spring 1957—that intellectuals criticize the shortcomings of the Party and its cadres.

Given the slowness of the media's response to Mao and the continuing articulation of different policy strains—together with past experience of ideological remolding—intellectuals initially adopted the same caution they had exhibited in 1956. Leading non-Party figures affirmed the basic correctness of Party policies while rebutting any harsh criticisms which had been aired at intellectuals' forums. Thus Zhang Bojun, a minor party leader and Minister of Communications who later became a major target of the Anti-Rightist Campaign, emphasized Party leadership at both the March CPPCC meetings and the May forums convened by the united front department. Different interpretations, moreover, resulted from the uncertainty surrounding the new policies. Some democratic party leaders stressed "boldly and widely blooming" with many views coming into play, but others emphasized the "picking of weeds," criticism of idealism, and the ultimate victory of "one truth."[84]

In view of such differences of opinion, it is hardly surprising that widespread doubts and anxieties existed in intellectual circles over the boundaries of permissible criticism and the entire process of "blooming and contending." Recalling past experiences where relaxation was followed by intensified pressure, many intellectuals doubted the Hundred Flowers policy would be a long term measure and feared reprisals for frank criticisms. Others complained that cadres were only giving lip service to the experiment. Some even saw the policy as a deliberate ruse designed to draw out the unwary so they could be easily identified and liquidated.[85] Despite such doubts, repeated official prodding and the fact that those who were bold enough to criticize the Party were not punished led to extensive criticism in May when the movement developed a momentum of its own and went beyond even the least ambiguous limits of CCP policy.

The outpouring of criticism which was eventually induced in spring 1957 touched upon a great many aspects of public policy and political life in China. The scope of opinions went well beyond immediate concerns of urban intellectuals, but the bulk of criticism dealt with problems and conflicts directly related to their roles and functions. Here we shall examine the content of Hundred Flowers criticism concerning these key problems and conflicts—relations of Party and non-Party personnel, the frustration of professional interests, the monopoly of power by Party officials, and institutional relations of Party and other structures—and only deal briefly with other topics raised during "blooming and contending." The crux of these issues was the degree of authority and influence exerted by non-political specialists at a time when China's leaders were hopefully anticipating rapid modernization. While similar questions underlay the professional activities of specialists in water conservancy and other fields, by facing the issues head on such criticisms inevitably raised the potentially explosive matter of the Party's competence to guide China in the new period.

In examining the content of "blooming and contending"[s] it is important to

---

[s] While their representativeness of intellectual opinion as a whole cannot be determined, the following views were widespread among a substantial proportion of Chinese intellectuals and provide a vivid picture of tensions within Chinese society. These views, with a few exceptions, are drawn from the media during the "blooming and contending" period itself rather than from accusations during the Anti-Rightist Campaign in order to minimize the possibility of distortion.

bear in mind that official criticism of "subjectivism, bureaucratism and sectarianism" since mid-1956 had opened the door for many of the opinions expressed. Indeed, as we shall see, it is striking how much of what was subsequently denounced as rightist can be traced to official CCP criticism of its own shortcomings.

Relations of Party and Non-Party Personnel

The key target of the Hundred Flowers policy from its inception in 1956 was overcoming sectarian attitudes of Party members toward non-Party people. Comments of intellectuals from all professions revealed manifold aspects of sectarianism and the depth of resentment it stirred. A basic manifestation was attitudes of Party members which ranged from aloof politeness to scornful condescension. Party cadres were accused of considering themselves made of "uncommon stuff" while looking down on non-Party people as knowing nothing of politics. These prejudices were not limited to those with proven revolutionary achievements; even newly recruited Party members would suddenly take on an air of superiority upon being granted membership. As a result, friendly interaction between Party and non-Party people became rare and many intellectuals felt that "high walls" and "deep moats" had been placed between them and Party cadres. While some admitted that intellectuals bore some blame for this situation due to their conceit, the dominant view was that the fault lay primarily with the arrogance and exclusiveness of Party members. This assessment corresponded with Mao's view that it was up to Party leaders to surmount the walls which separated people inside and outside the Party.[86]

Most intellectuals believed Party members made few sincere efforts to tear down the walls and fill in the moats. The most that could be expected was a show of solicitude when the Party decided it was necessary to utilize the talents of intellectuals or conciliate them—a show often devoid of practical consequences. Thus one critic summed up the attitude of the Party's united front department toward the suggestions of non-Party people as "we sincerely accept your criticism but have made up our mind not to make any changes." On other occasions, relations between Party and non-Party personnel were those between superior and inferior without even a veneer of consultation.[87]

Another aspect of the problem was discrimination which non-Party people in all professions suffered while performing their duties. For example, non-Party journalists frequently were denied access to information. In one instance, the Wuhan correspondent of *Dagong bao* had read halfway through a document at the municipal industry bureau when a bureau cadre suddenly asked whether the reporter was a Party member. The document was quickly snatched away when a negative answer was given. Non-Party cadres serving in government units also encountered heavy-handed practices. A former deputy director of the Tianjin meteorological bureau reported Party cadres regarded him with such suspicion that "Everyday, when I let off work to go home, they would make all sorts of clumsy attempts to search my briefcase to see what it contained." He added, with a degree of understatement, that he "thought this quite unpleasant." Non-Party intellectuals in every walk of life had similar "unpleasant" experiences which bolstered their sense of estrangement from the CCP.[88]

This estrangement was exacerbated by preferential treatment for Party members. Party (and Youth League) membership conferred many advantages. Intellectuals complained of special dormitories and dining halls which had been set aside for cadres and "aristocratic schools" established for the education of their children. Further criticism claimed university grades were unfairly weighted with political considerations to the advantage of Party and League personnel, and that these people had a virtual monopoly on opportunities for study abroad. Within the government bureaucracy, complaints were made that the rate of promotion for Party members was much more rapid than for non-Party cadres despite the better qualifications of the latter. Similarly, when administrative discipline was meted out, Party cadres allegedly received lighter penalties than their non-Party colleagues for comparable misdeeds. Favoritism in personnel matters extended beyond individual Party members to their wives and relatives. One democratic party member claimed the official policy of "employ only the virtuous and talented" had in fact been superseded by "employ only one's relatives and Party members.[89]

The combination of official privileges, common practices resulting in advantages for Party members, and status oriented behavior generally created an elite which seemed far removed from the mass line principles which CCP leaders had emphasized since 1956. One speaker at a democratic party forum summed up the situation by observing: "In leading the masses to carry through the revolution in the past, the Party stood among the masses; after liberation, it felt the position had changed and, instead of standing among the masses, it stood on the back of the masses and ruled the masses."[90] This view was not at great variance with the rectification directive's warning that the "GMD style" had appeared within its ranks. However, by speaking of the Party as a whole, this criticism, as many other expressions of dissatisfaction, implicitly went beyond an attack on deviant behavior and challenged the CCP as an institution.

The Frustration of Professional Interests

One of the most important causes of dissatisfaction among intellectuals was a widespread feeling that their professional interests were stymied by the system. A number of complaints focused on irrational practices which plagued intellectuals as they tried to perform their functions. Of particular concern was personnel mismanagement as in the case of law students who were assigned bookkeeping chores. Intellectuals also complained of inadequate resources for their work and unreasonable security restrictions on the accessibility of information. In addition, they viewed political education and requirements for attendance at meetings as excessive and detrimental to their professional performance.[91] The validity of this type of criticism, if moderately phrased, had been officially acknowledged as early as Zhou Enlai's January 1956 speech on intellectuals.

The basic problem, however, was the incompatibility of professional interests and the official view that all activities must ultimately serve the state. Thus journalists who saw their role as seeking out and publishing the truth declared themselves thwarted by political criteria even though concessions to professionalism had been officially encouraged in 1956. Moreover, individual creativity was stifled by restrictions, particularly in academic and literary fields. One writer, after listing all the political considerations he had to take into account when writing, said his former satisfaction from his work had faded and he often wrote solely to fulfill his duties. Here again, for roughly a year the Hundred Flowers policy had called for the relaxation of criteria governing artistic and scholarly creation.[92]

One of the major manifestations of the problem was the widespread existence of doctrinairism—the tendency to "suppress others by quoting from classical [Marxist-Leninist] writings," idealizing everything Russian, and negating everything Western. This was often exacerbated by cadres' lack of specialized knowledge. In the absence of technical expertise, responsible cadres frequently fell back on "dogmas as their sole blueprint," or they would be guided by blind faith in Soviet practices. Thus scientists protested attacks on Darwinism and the imposition of the ideas of the Soviet biologist Michurin. Sampling theory and other modern economic techniques were suppressed because of their "capitalist" origin while professional articles were largely reduced to quoting Marxist-Leninist tracts to the dismay of trained economists. An even more basic problem confronted scholars in certain Western oriented fields such as sociology and political science which were either eliminated as academic disciplines or reorganized beyond recognition to fit into a Marxist framework of analysis. These scholars used the "blooming and contending" period to ask that their subjects be reinstated in the university curriculum.[93]

While such criticism was often consistent with CCP strictures against applying foreign experience mechanically and excessive restrictions on academic debate, some intellectuals directly challenged the leading role of Marxist-Leninist ideology. Xu Zhangben, a professor at Qinghua University, argued that doctrinairism was a direct outgrowth of the dominant position of Marxism-Leninism and suggested that "Marxism-Leninism be abolished as our guiding ideology." Here Xu went beyond Mao who had warned of the effect of trumpeting Marxism-Leninism but never questioned the ideology's leading role in state affairs.[94]

The Monopoly of Power by Party Officials

In the final analysis, the crucial source of tension between Party cadres and non-Party intellectuals was the former's monopoly of power. In an opinion "offered to Chairman Mao and Premier Zhou" which later became a major object of attack during the Anti-Rightist Campaign, Chu Anping, editor-in-chief of the non-Party *Guangming ribao* [Guangming Daily], acidly summed up the situation:

> In my opinion, the key lies in the idea that "the world belongs to the Party." I think a party leading a nation is not the same thing as a party owning a nation. . . . Isn't it too much that within the scope of the nation, there must be a Party man as leader in every unit . . . or that nothing, big or small, can be done without a nod from a Party man? . . . For years, the talents or capabilities of many Party men have not matched their duties. They have bungled their jobs . . . and have not been able to command the respect of the masses with the result that the relations between the Party and the masses have been tense. But the fault has not lain with the Party members, but rather with the Party which has placed square pegs in round holes. I wonder if the Party acts this way because it entertains the idea that "every place is royal territory" and therefore has created the present monochromatic, one family empire appearance. I think this idea that "the world belongs to the Party" is at the bottom of all sectarianism and the root of all contradictions between the Party and non-Party people. . . .[95]

Non-Party personnel criticized the exclusive power of Party authorities from a number of perspectives. Intellectuals engaged in independent creative activity particularly objected to arbitrary interference in their work. Playwrights chafed when Party literary authorities required the insertion of new characters or scenes into plays or where "one sentence from a responsible comrade of the propaganda department" decided whether a play would be performed at all.[96] In these cases, what was objected to was the bureaucratic manifestation of doctrinairism—arbitrary assertions of authority backed by references to orthodox views. Curbing the exercise of such arbitrary authority had been another key Hundred Flowers objective since 1956.

Other non-Party people, however, desired more than simply to reduce Party control over their work. These individuals sought a positive role in the development of China and the exercise of real power. Many non-Party personnel in various fields complained they were denied the authority of their official posts, that they had "position without power"—a phenomenon which Liu Shaoqi criticized at the Eighth Party Congress. The case of Ma Yinchu, President of Beijing University, was typical. After Ma presented his opinions at meetings, the Party member vice president would offer "supplementary remarks" which revised Ma's views and demonstrated to everyone where real power lay. Even the power of non-Party ministers was tenuous at best. For example, Minister of Food Zhang Naiqi said that he had acquired power corresponding to his official position only through a long series of struggles. Huang Yanpei, a former vice premier as well as Minister of Light Industry, apparently was less successful in obtaining the substance of power. Huang had been denied a list of provincial industrial department directors on security grounds due to his non-Party background. These instances demonstrated that the policy of placing non-Communists in prominent positions produced only a minimal sharing of real power despite recent efforts to bolster the authority of non-Party officials.[97]

Institutional Relations: Proposals for Change

"Blooming and contending" was not limited to criticisms of the dominance of Party cadres. Many opinions concerned the institutional role of the Party *vis-à-vis* other organizations and how it might be changed. One of the most significant organizational relationships scrutinized by non-Party intellectuals was that between Party and government. One critic who later became a major target of attack saw Party encroachment on state authority as a basic factor in the deviations rectification was designed to combat:

> Tan Tiwu referred to the method by which the Communist Party led the state. There was now one set of structures in the government, and another set of structures in the Party. She referred to this as the double track system. She wondered if this were not the cause of all problems arising in work today—such as those relating to the "wall" and the "moat," and the three great "isms." She said ... it was originally claimed that the Party would undertake the control of ideology and policy only, but in practice this scope had already been exceeded, and the Party was directly issuing orders to the people, while the government departments did not have authority....[98]

Frequent complaints that "the Party has replaced the government" and "the Party's organization exercises control over virtually everything" indicated this was not an isolated opinion. The problem was seen as particularly severe at the county and lower levels where "one sees only the Party and not the government." Other critics focused on the CCP Central Committee's practice of issuing joint directives with the State Council. This undermined the authority of the governmental apparatus as lower level organs reportedly ignored ministerial or even State Council directives and obeyed only those bearing the concurrence of the Central Committee. To overcome these phenomena, non-Party intellectuals advocated a clear demarcation of functions between Party and government to allow government handling of administrative affairs without Party interference. In this they could draw implicit support from the Eighth Congress comments of Liu Shaoqi and Deng Xiaoping criticizing undue Party meddling in the administrative work of state organs.[99]

Criticisms not only demonstrated the limited authority of individual non-Party officials, they also revealed the lack of substantive power of official organs where non-Party personnel were strongly represented. Non-Party people charged that the Standing Committees of the NPC, officially the supreme organ of state power, and of the CPPCC, were poorly attended and only formally passed decisions previously made by the Party. Democratic party representatives in these bodies were particularly hampered by lack of prior knowledge of what was to be discussed or access to information necessary for forming effective opinions; thus proposals were made that they be given relevant information in advance. Concerning the democratic parties themselves, members complained not only about their exclusion from the policy making process but also about restrictions on recruitment even though membership had grown substantially under the policy of long term coexistence and mutual supervision.[100]

In this context, several cautious proposals were made. At the March CPPCC session, Zhang Bojun suggested an increase in the work of the CPPCC and, after calling attention to the two chamber parliamentary system of capitalist countries, advocated gradually turning it into "a democratic link in the parliamentary system required for the Chinese people's democracy." In May, at the forums of leading non-Party personalities, Zhang proposed a "political design department" which actually was only a request that the CCP cooperate fully with leading bodies of the NPC and CPPCC, democratic parties, and mass organizations in discussing major policies and problems. Although both suggestions were subjected to harsh criticism during the Anti-Rightist Campaign, it is clear that neither posed a basic threat to the Party. Both were phrased with great caution and explicitly recognized the leadership of the Communist Party. Here, as on other matters, non-Party figures could find sympathetic views in Liu Shaoqi's political report to the Eighth Party Congress which had called for "reinforce[d] supervision by the National People's Congress and its Standing Committee over the . . . Central People's Government," similar supervision by local people's congresses, and inspections by people's deputies to further this objective. Liu, moreover, later described the CPPCC as in a sense the "upper house" of the NPC, and he and Peng Zhen reportedly drew up plans for the creation of eight permanent committees of the NPC as a "supreme supervisory system" overseeing government work. On balance, it appears Zhang and others were attempting to gain maximum benefit from the official line of strengthening the role of the democratic parties by making specific, if vague, proposals to that end.[101]

Perhaps the most significant institutional target of intellectual critics—and certainly the subject of the boldest proposals for change—was the Party committee in educational and scientific institutions. Many felt this body had usurped the functions of academic administrators. Although some intellectuals, motivated by either caution or opportunism, upheld the capability and right of Party committees to lead educational and scientific work, the main thrust of opinions reported was to seek ways to circumscribe their role. Some demanded Party authorities refrain from interfering in everyday administration and non-Party people be given a greater share of decision making; others made the drastic proposal that the Party committee system in academic institutions be abolished. Thus the concrete form of Party leadership in the entire area of higher education and scholarship was under attack.[102]

Even here there is evidence suggesting non-Party critics were taking their cues from the most authoritative sources. In the most general sense, the view expressed by Lu Dingyi in May 1956 that Party members lacking specialized knowledge must "learn honestly and modestly from those who know" suggested a more discreet role for Party organizations in academic institutions. Cultural Revolution sources allege that key Party leaders went even further in their unpublicized remarks. Thus Zhou Yang allegedly said the Party had not led intellectuals well and true leadership in specialized fields must come from experts. Organizationally and financially, Zhou, Lu and others in the propaganda sphere reportedly advocated independent publishing houses and writers' associations. And, as we have seen, Mao himself suggested that each province have an independent non-Party newspaper. Moreover, the proposal that Party committees be abolished apparently gained impetus from the Chairman's critical remarks concerning the committee system in his never released April 30 address to the Supreme State Conference. During the Anti-Rightist Campaign Zhang Bojun and Minister of the Timber Industry Lo Longji were accused of distorting Mao's view that the system should be investigated into claiming that Mao had called for its abolition. In any case, the Chairman, in remarks to the Shanghai Party Bureau earlier in April, had advocated a reorganization of university Party committees including the reassignment of cadres to other duties. Whatever Mao's exact phraseology at the April 1957 Supreme State Conference, it seems clear his statements during this period stimulated radical proposals for the end of the Party committee system in academic institutions.[103]

Other Issues and Assessment

One of the most frequent targets of criticism in spring 1957 was the *sufan* movement. Intellectuals charged that this campaign had been overly harsh without producing sufficient results to justify its excesses. They argued the official 5 percent estimate of counterrevolutionaries made at the outset of the movement led to the creation of fictitious counterrevolutionaries. Moreover, the campaign was attacked as an instrument for seeking revenge. Unit leaders assertedly used the occasion to accuse falsely people they disliked or who had been critical of them in the past. Intellectuals further sought to reopen specific cases they felt had been wrongly decided. The writer Hu Feng in particular became a cause célèbre. Critics denied there was any proof Hu's literary faction was counterrevolutionary and demanded a new trial in open court.[104]

More fundamentally, Luo Longji sought to institutionalize the overturning of wrong decisions by advocating a special committee drawn from the NPC and

CPPCC to inspect deviations of the *sufan* drive as well as those of the Three and Five Anti Campaigns. Although this proposal subsequently came under heavy attack including critical remarks by Mao and Zhou Enlai, Luo had done no more than advance, in slightly expanded form, a suggestion made by Mao in his "Contradictions" speech. Luo not only denied later charges that he had advocated setting up "rehabilitation committees" *(pingfan weiyuanhui)* outside Party and state organs, but correctly pointed out that his proposal included Party members on the review body.[i] Here, even more clearly than in the case of abolishing Party committees in educational institutions, non-Party intellectuals cautiously advocated a radical suggestion—radical in terms of the prevailing norms of the political system—which had originated at the highest level, only to have that advocacy distorted during the Anti-Rightist Campaign. In any case, even though Luo's (and Mao's) proposal did not directly contravene Party authority, it did represent a far-reaching intrusion by non-Party elements into the critical area of public security work.

The *sufan* movement was only one instance of a recurring, politically charged atmosphere in official organizations and social intercourse generally which appalled many intellectuals. They felt fear and deception had become a commonplace feature of daily life particularly because of repeated political campaigns. As one account put it, "No one dares to let off steam even privately in the company of intimate friends, let alone speak his mind in public. Everyone has now learned the techniques of double-talk; what one says is one thing, what one thinks is another. . . ." Intellectuals also complained bitterly about indiscriminate labeling of those who expressed independent views as "ideologically backward," "capitalist element," etc., using a person's remarks out of context to attack him, the eagerness of activists to denounce people to prove fitness for Party membership, and the feeling of many people that they had to attack others to avoid being attacked themselves. A further indication of the widespread desire for a more normal atmosphere was criticism of the failure to enact criminal and civil codes. The "blooming and contending" period revealed a deep longing of non-Party intellectuals for a more predictable life than had been hitherto possible in People's China. In this they could find backing in Mao's reported winter 1956 comment that "The masses and cadres have had a hard time of it these past years with our movements, and we ought to give them a chance to catch their breath."[105]

Intellectuals also indicted a wide variety of bureaucratic phenomena including the tendency to "study and further study, consultation and further consultation, and

[i] Luo expanded Mao's proposal in that he included the Three and Five Anti campaigns in those to be reviewed while Mao mentioned only the *sufan* movement. Mao also indicated in April that *sufan* investigations should only check up on cases decided in 1955 and 1956. Luo was not specific about time but by raising the Three and Five Anti issue he was of course calling for the examination of events dating back to 1951. *SXWS,* II, 107; and MacFarquhar, *Origins 1,* pp. 271–73, 394.

procrastination and further procrastination" in handling differences between departments, rigid controls exercised by higher over lower levels, bloated administrative structures, and red tape and buck-passing.[106] In these criticisms non-Party intellectuals were not only well within the proper limits of "blooming and contending," they were of course echoing official attacks against bureaucratism since mid-1956.

Finally, a number of intellectuals criticized the basic policies of socialist transformation and construction and questioned claims of far-reaching achievements. Particular resentment was expressed over the official view that "achievements are the main thing, shortcomings and mistakes are secondary." This, they argued, was a ritualistic formula used by the Party to cover mistakes which created a danger of greater errors in the future. Among the charges against socialist transformation and construction were: economic construction in 1956 had been adventurously rapid; socialist transformation of industry and commerce had resulted in waste and inefficiency; planned buying and marketing was a mess and resulted in acute shortages of pork and other commodities; and living standards of the common people had not risen under Party rule.[107]

Although official pronouncements on these matters stressed the overall positive results of socialist transformation and economic development, here again considerable support for the critics' views could be gleaned from CCP sources. Opposition to the rapid growth of early 1956 had, of course, led to the emergence of a dominant "oppose reckless advance" position within high Party councils by the middle of the year. In addition, at the Eighth Party Congress speakers repeatedly articulated defects of the new socialist system, even alluding to such matters as food shortages. Yet on these issues a fundamentally different spirit often existed between official and intellectual criticisms. The former adopted the view, noted above, that shortcomings were unavoidable secondary aspects of the overall situation which hopefully could be overcome with the aid of specific, positive suggestions from non-Party sources. Many non-Party intellectuals, however, held a basically skeptical attitude toward key features of the new order.

What was it about the views aired by intellectuals in the spring which caused deep concern within the highest levels of the Party? On the whole, considerable caution was exhibited throughout "blooming and contending" and even sharp criticisms were not presented as explicit challenges to the existing order. Occasionally, extreme hostility was voiced toward the regime. For example, a lecturer at the Chinese People's University was quoted as defiantly warning the Party it would be overthrown and its members killed, and claiming this would not be unpatriotic since "the downfall of the Communist Party does not mean the downfall of China." [108] Such outbursts, however, were rare.[u] Undoubtedly more signif-

[u] This conclusion, based both on open media sources and the report of a Beijing resident at the time, concerns views expressed by adult intellectuals. As we shall see in Chapter 7, middle school and university students frequently were much more violent in both word and deed, and undoubtedly were a major factor shaping the crackdown of summer 1957.

icant were views which by implication questioned the system as a whole. Chu Anping, the editor of *Guangming ribao,* posed the problem by noting that the CCP was a highly organized and disciplined party and asking whether "defects of a nationwide nature have anything to do with the central leadership of the Party?" Others asserted the State Council itself was the root of bureaucratism.[109] That such views existed in significant degree after the victory of socialist transformation which, by Mao's logic, should at least have reconciled intellectuals to the necessity of working for socialism must have been unsettling.

But probably even more disturbing than the still relatively limited number of such critiques was the long catalog of complaints aired by non-Party intellectuals concerning their daily confrontations with Party authority. Even though many specific targets had been officially sanctioned, the depth of discontent could not have been anticipated. The strength of the attack on concrete Party leadership both resulted in a severe jolt to cadre morale[v] and raised questions about relying on bourgeois intellectuals for key contributions to national development. As this became apparent in May 1957 the days of the Hundred Flowers experiment were numbered.

Conclusion

By mid-1956 the stage was set for rectification according to traditional Party norms. Although a date for launching a new *zhengfeng* movement apparently had not been set, the circumstances were conducive to the persuasive, "save the patient" approach to elite discipline whenever the leadership was ready. Internationally, there was no major threat to China's security. Domestically, a new consolidation phase had begun. Many of the deviations then under criticism—extravagance and waste due to overly rapid growth, commandist leadership methods, and harsh policies toward suspect groups—were classic problems normally dealt with in periods of consolidation. In another sense, however, the successful completion of socialist transformation meant China was entering a fundamentally new period, a period where dealing with "contradictions among the people" rather than pursuing class struggle had become the main political task. This, in turn, required new policies, the most striking being the approach to intellectuals under the twin slogans of the Hundred Flowers and mutual supervision.

From mid-1956 to spring 1957 steps were taken toward rectification, steps which involved attempts to reconcile the traditional rectification approach with the innovative policies toward intellectuals. This undoubtedly involved signifi-

[v] According to Mao in October 1957, "When big character posters appeared [in May] in their thousands in factories, people in positions of leadership had a tough time. For ten days or so, some wanted to quit or resign, saying they couldn't take it any more, couldn't eat or sleep. That was the case with the secretaries of university Party committees in Beijing, they lost their appetites and couldn't go to sleep." *SW,* V, 505.

cant debate at the highest levels of the CCP. Yet whatever differences of opinion were expressed, they apparently did not involve persistent, sharp cleavages within the Politburo. While Mao himself was the main force behind the controversial effort to link rectification and the Hundred Flowers in spring 1957, his position over the entire period changed markedly according to events. His initial views on the role of intellectuals in Party rectification were cautious, and following the East European events of fall 1956 the implications of Mao's statements were decidedly restrictive. Only after the reaction to Hungary threatened to emasculate totally the Hundred Flowers did Mao emerge as the champion of intellectual criticism as an integral part of Party reform. But even in spring 1957 the Chairman continued to emphasize the need for "gentle breeze and mild rain" methods in dealing with Party cadres. Indeed, the one constant of Mao's view over the full period was that the persuasive approach developed in the 1940s must be the basis of the new rectification effort.

If debate on novel rectification methods within the Politburo was conducted according to established norms, clearly a significant degree of resistance appeared in the implementation of the new policy. To the extent such resistance can be located at high Party levels, it appears to have centered in sections of the propaganda apparatus, perhaps including propaganda chief Lu Dingyi himself. While bureaucratic footdragging in these circles may have reflected ambiguities in Mao's own position and awareness of differences within the Politburo, it also almost certainly was due to reservations based on the functional role of propaganda officials. Unlike Politburo members who operated from the commanding heights of the system and thus were to a certain extent insulated from concrete pressures and problems, propaganda officials dealt with intellectuals on a daily basis. They were faced with the difficult task of reconciling the promotion of enthusiasm for socialist construction with the need to maintain ideological orthodoxy and political leadership. It was their status and authority which was threatened by Mao's new policies.

In any case, the failure of the Hundred Flowers experiment cannot be attributed solely to bureaucratic resistance, resistance which was largely overcome by May. The failure was rather due to some fundamental misconceptions concerning the new situation in China. The Hundred Flowers was based on the assumption that non-Party intellectuals, despite their ideological backwardness, were basically in sympathy with CCP goals and could be counted on to make positive contributions to even so sensitive an affair as Party rectification. Since their differences with the Party were "contradictions within the people," there were no fundamental clashes of interest and few conflicts which could not be settled by persuasive methods. But bourgeois intellectuals as a group had been frequently subjected to severe pressure since the early days of the PRC, their interests as they conceived them had often been grievously violated, and their relations with Party cadres were marked by mutual mistrust. While there is evidence that many had high hopes that the new policies would mean a fundamental change in the

Party's attitude,[110] overall doubts and anxieties based on past experience were deeply entrenched. Thus considerable efforts were required to produce "blooming and contending." These efforts included statements and postures by key Party officials—as by Mao concerning the role of Party committees in education—which encouraged the articulation of unorthodox views by intellectuals. At root, intellectuals were being asked to perform an impossible task: to criticize boldly Party authorities whom they often feared and loathed, yet at the same time to do so in the spirit of a "gentle breeze and mild rain." That there should be deep seated caution on the one hand and bitter attacks on the other is hardly surprising. The problem was not merely that there were no clear criteria for "blooming and contending," but more basically that the entire process clashed with their total socialization under the Communist regime.

Party cadres too were placed in an unprecedented position. Criticism of such familiar evils as bureaucratism, sectarianism and subjectivism through the regular chain of command could have had some positive effect, however limited. But what was being asked in 1957 was that they redefine Party leadership in ways which were never precisely stipulated to take into account the views and talents of non-Party intellectuals. Moreover, they were themselves subject to the criticism of these individuals of suspect class origins and backward ideology, something which seemed most unjust. In the last analysis, the Party reform effort of spring 1957 was aborted because the assessment of contradictions following the victory of socialist transformation, however adequate as an overview of Chinese society, was not translated into a rectification strategy taking adequate account of the interests and expectations of the concerned groups. If the effort to ameliorate Party rule—to resolve the contradiction of leaders and led—had been conducted wholly by long tested methods, the result, whatever its deficiencies, would undoubtedly have been more palatable to both China's intellectuals and cadres.

7
The Anti-Rightist Campaign

The Hundred Flowers experiment came to an abrupt end with the launching of an "anti-rightist struggle" *(fan youpai douzheng)* in June 1957. The Anti-Rightist Campaign also saw the conduct of inner Party rectification return to traditional principles in all respects.[a] The end of the Hundred Flowers, moreover, removed a difficult issue from the agenda of the top leadership. Although some scholarly analysis argues divisions of the spring continued with Mao still focusing on internal Party deviations while Liu Shaoqi, Peng Zhen and others emphasized sharp rebuffs to intellectual critics, this interpretation sees Mao in the forefront of the anti-rightist onslaught. This did involve a major turnabout from his spring position, but the Chairman negotiated this shift without apology or apparent embarrassment. Mao not only took the key initiatives which began the readjustment, but CCP policies toward rightists and other aspects of rectification throughout summer 1957 all bore his imprint.[b]

---

[a] Strictly speaking, new methods continued to be used in rectification. According to Mao in October 1957, "A form has now been found for the rectification movement, namely, speaking out freely, airing views fully, holding great debates and writing big character posters." The Chairman went on to explain why these methods had not been used during the revolutionary period: "Because we were then in the heat of war and the class struggle was very acute, and if we had allowed a free-for-all within our own ranks, that would have been bad." *SW,* V, 498. Cf. Chapter 3, above, especially pp. 55, 79. Despite the degree of mass spontaneity implied, after spring 1957 these measures were under close Party guidance and thus in essence complied with the traditional approach.

[b] In addition to Mao's actions discussed below, this interpretation is also based on the lack of substantial contemporary evidence of Politburo conflict in summer 1957, and on relatively infrequent references to the Anti-Rightist Campaign in Cultural Revolution sources. What references were found generally made unconvincing assertions that Liu Shaoqi *et al.* opposed Mao through excessive leniency toward rightists. E.g., *RMRB,* December 19, 1968, in *SCMP,* No. 4330. Most significantly, while Mao continued to recall opposition to his views on the economy in 1956 and on the Hundred Flowers program (*SXWS,* II, 149–51), his unpublished speeches made no mention of major differences over rectification in summer 1957.

Whatever differences may have existed earlier, and whatever loss of prestige Mao may have suffered from his first major policy miscalculation of the post-1949 period, the Party rallied around him once he opted for a more orthodox course.

The anti-rightist phase[c] of the rectification campaign was distinguished by several features. First, the movement was essentially defensive in tone. Official arguments sought to refute rightist views and the overall aim was to restore Party control which had been weakened by the Hundred Flowers. Second, the primary focus of the campaign remained on urban units where "blooming and contending" had been conducted—and largely but not solely on non-Party intellectuals. But by August and September the movement began to extend to much broader groups leading to what became known as an "all people rectification" *(quanmin zhengfeng).* While the anti-rightist struggle in urban units attacked specific "slanders" on the socialist system, various programs of "socialist education" *(shehuizhuyi jiaoyu)* were carried out among different groups to supplement refutations with positive indoctrination in orthodox principles. In this context a significant rectification of rural cadres was carried out in conjunction with socialist education among peasants. Third, although the need to reform official work styles in urban organs too was still asserted in this period, it was only in the fall that the focus of the movement as a whole again shifted to cadre shortcomings, but now under tight Party control. Finally, the June–September period was one of continued moderate economic policies. Only as the Great Leap Forward strategy evolved in late 1957 did rectification shed its defensive, non-economic orientation and assume a forward looking posture as an integral part of a broad mass mobilization for economic development.

From "Blooming and Contending" to the Anti-Rightist Struggle

By mid-May repeated efforts to stimulate criticism resulted in "*big* blooming and contending." After four to five weeks of largely unchecked criticism, the Anti-Rightist Campaign was launched on June 8 by a *Renmin ribao* editorial, "What Is This For?" This action followed about three weeks of reassessing the situation at the highest levels. Undoubtedly the intensity and scope of intellectuals' criticisms were key factors in the new consensus which took shape. Also, it was clearly a direct response to growing student unrest (see below). Given the lead-

---

[c] Although anti-rightist struggles and purges continued well into 1958 in various units, the main anti-rightist period concluded in September 1957. In that month Teng Hsiao-p'ing (Deng Xiaoping), "Report on the Rectification Campaign," in *PDA*, p. 345, outlined the following stages: (1) full and frank discussions, i.e., "blooming and contending" [May 1957]; (2) counterattacking the rightists [June–September]; (3) emphasis on rectification and improvement [from October]; and (4) individual study of documents, criticism and self-review [to be completed by May 1958].

ing role of students in the recent Hungarian uprising and the major place of student demonstrations in Chinese history since the May Fourth Movement of 1919, leadership anxiety was to be expected.[1]

The first indication of a reassessment came from Mao himself in a May 15 article, "Things Are Changing," which was circulated among high ranking cadres on a restricted basis. Mao now asserted that during the recent criticism of doctrinairism no attention had been given to revisionism and warned that revisionists within the Party were more dangerous than doctrinaires as they negated everything, reflected bourgeois ideology, and opposed centralism and Party leadership. Mao's evaluation was still ambivalent, however, as he cited the need for a continued struggle against doctrinairism and warned that losses to the revolution brought about by the "left" were no better than those caused by the "right." Moreover, he still saw the necessity for securing the contributions of bourgeois intellectuals to economic development, declared most of the criticisms of old intellectuals correct, and called on Party cadres to trust them. But at the same time the Chairman lashed out at democratic party rightists who "In recent days . . . have shown themselves to be most rabid" through alleged efforts to seize the leadership of various cultural and educational fields and instigate the masses against the government. Mao further called for a struggle against the rightists but advocated the immediate tactic of "let[ting them] run amok for a while and . . . reach their climax."[2] Thus although other statements by the Chairman claiming the whole Hundred Flowers experiment had been a trap are unconvincing, this suggests a trap had been sprung in the sense that "blooming and contending" continued after it had been determined that some sort of counterattack was necessary.[d]

In his mid-May remarks Mao also signaled a major reversal in his attitude toward the press. Whereas in April he had been critical of the restrictive policies which inhibited "blooming and contending," he now denounced those who obliterated the differences between proletarian and bourgeois journalism and opposed Party control over newspapers—as he himself had at least partially done with his proposal that each province establish a non-Party paper. This amounted to an endorsement of restrictive practices to make sure that Marxism was not overrun by "bourgeois liberalism" in the media. It seemingly was the immediate cause, despite the early May directive that criticism should go unanswered for a month, of such mid and late May practices as withholding many "erroneous and reac-

[d] While a consensus on the need to strike back at the critics apparently formed quickly, there were differences over when this should be accomplished. In discussions with a Hungarian delegation two years later, Mao claimed that some local leaders had wanted to cut short "blooming and contending" but he adopted a wait and see attitude. János Rádvanyi, *Hungary and the Superpowers: The 1956 Revolution and Realpolitik* (Stanford: Hoover Institution Press, 1972), p. 28. On the other hand, Mao's May 1957 statement that "some people" felt the counterattack had begun too *soon* suggests that he may have been ahead of at least some other leaders concerning the timing of the crackdown. *SXWS*, II, 207.

tionary articles," official guidelines concerning what to print, and suppressing magazine issues which revealed too much about student discontent. In the last days of "blooming and contending," moreover, intellectuals directed criticism at *Renmin ribao* for allegedly seeking to restrain the development of the campaign. They cited detailed reporting of views supporting the Party against criticisms as attacking those who had responded to the call to speak out.[3]

The earliest public sign of a shift in policy came on May 20–21 as workers in Shanghai and Guangzhou reportedly denounced proposals by private capitalists that state representatives withdraw from state-private enterprises and interest payments to former owners be extended for a longer period. What is more important than the specific views rebutted is that for the first time Party officials had clearly organized sharp countercriticism to opinions expressed during the "blooming and contending" phase.[4] A number of events then occurred on May 25 further signaling a shift in policy. Most significant was a statement by Mao to a group of delegates to the Youth League Congress that "all words and actions that deviate from the cause of socialism are wrong." Significantly, this saying was quickly painted in large characters at Beijing University. Moreover, an important *Renmin ribao* article three weeks later revealed that Mao viewed the response of various newspapers to his warning as a key indicator of their political stand. May 25 also saw postponement of the annual NPC session from June 3 to June 20, perhaps indicating a desire for a breathing space in which a new line could be formulated. In remarks concerning the postponement Liu Shaoqi warned that people might go out onto the streets leaving the Party helpless if proper leadership were not exerted over the rectification campaign. Finally, on the same day, strong views were expressed at a democratic party forum in defense of the Party refuting various "incorrect" criticisms. One of the staunchest supporters of the pro-Party view at this forum was Lu Youwen, an assistant to the secretary-general of the State Council.[5]

A few days later, Zhang Zhiyi, deputy head of the united front department, left no doubt in a May 31 *Dagong bao* [Impartial Daily] article that there were limits to criticism and Party authority was not to be challenged, and he further argued that the danger of rightist behavior in China remained strong. On June 1 another straw in the wind appeared with the first recorded reference to individual rightists, "a very small minority of people who paid lip service to socialism, but actually admired capitalism . . . [and] the Euro-American type of government."[6] Then on June 6 Lu Youwen told a State Council forum that he had received an anonymous threatening letter as a result of his vigorous defense of the Party on May 25. This letter, whether real or manufactured, served as the pretext for the June 8 *Renmin ribao* editorial launching the Anti-Rightist Campaign:

> We regard this letter of intimidation an important event because it is indeed a warning to the broad masses of the people and is a signal given by certain people who exploit the rectification campaign for waging an acute class struggle. . . .

> [These rightists] try to take advantage of this opportunity to overthrow the Communist Party and the working class, overthrow the great cause of socialism, drag history backwards to the bourgeois dictatorship. . . .

A series of *Renmin ribao* editorials followed which further elaborated the new line. Moreover, forums held by various organizations abruptly shifted course as speakers began to attack selected rightists.

The transition from the Hundred Flowers to the anti-rightist struggle was marked by a lack of clear guidelines for determining which views should be attacked as several early editorials on the new policy warned against indiscriminate retaliation against well intentioned and correct criticisms.[7] Guidelines were eventually given on June 18 when the New China News Agency (NCNA) released the revised version of Mao's "Contradictions" speech including six criteria for correct criticism:

> [W]e believe that, broadly speaking, words and actions can be judged right if they:
>
> (1) Help to unite the people of our various nationalities, and do not divide them;
>
> (2) Are beneficial, not harmful, to socialist transformation and socialist construction;
>
> (3) Help to consolidate, not undermine or weaken, the people's democratic dictatorship;
>
> (4) Help to consolidate, not undermine or weaken, democratic centralism;
>
> (5) Tend to strengthen, not cast off or weaken, the leadership of the Communist Party;
>
> (6) Are beneficial, not harmful, to international socialist solidarity and the solidarity of the peace loving peoples of the world.
>
> Of these six criteria, the most important ones are the socialist path and the leadership of the Party.[8]

These guidelines left considerable room for interpretation, but they clearly indicated a bleak view of departures from the orthodox path. While they did not settle all problems, the formulation of criteria did create a basis upon which the anti-rightist struggle could proceed.

The Rationale and Implementation of the Anti-Rightist Campaign

Mao continued to play a crucial role in shaping the new policy as the Anti-Rightist Campaign developed in summer 1957. In addition to his May initiatives, the Chairman made several key statements in the following months. The most important came at the July conference of provincial and municipal secretaries in Qingdao where, according to Deng Xiaoping, Mao "made an overall estimate of the nature and conditions of the rectification movement and anti-rightist struggle and put forward a clear policy for the development of the movement."[9] This Qingdao statement subsequently became the basis for Deng's report to the Third Plenum of the Eighth Central Committee in September-October which laid down definitive policies on the future course of rectification.

The abrupt policy reversal reflected a massive shift in emphasis in Mao's position despite important continuities between his spring and summer views. Where the Chairman had previously raised important questions about the nature of Party leadership in a changing society, he now reaffirmed an orthodox definition of Party control. Where he earlier had assumed a basic consensus so firm that various "weeds" could be tolerated simply because they would be unable to attract a significant following, he subsequently argued that the left had been in danger of cracking under the onslaught of the bourgeois intellectuals. In addition, some of Mao's postures during the anti-rightist struggle can only be viewed as examples of either political duplicity or remarkable rationalization. Thus his remark that Luo Longji's proposal for a review of counterrevolutionary cases was supported in Taiwan and Hong Kong conveniently overlooked the similar proposal he had made in his "Contradictions" speech. Even more striking was his turnabout concerning the press, not only in terms of general principles but also in that Mao chose to launch his most bitter attack on *Wenhui bao* which had been one of the most faithful implementers of his "blooming and contending" policy, and whose criticisms he had praised as "beneficial" in April. Whatever his leadership colleagues or victimized intellectuals may have thought of such protestations, it appears that Mao was not above political expediency in an effort to escape responsibility for the Hundred Flowers miscalculation.[10]

The official rationale developed by Mao and other leaders for the Anti-Rightist Campaign pointed squarely to bourgeois intellectuals as the main target. Rightist activities were reported mainly in places where intellectuals were concentrated, i.e., in institutions where "blooming and contending" had developed. Moreover, leading members of democratic parties were singled out as the core of rightist groups although intellectuals within the CCP were also subject to vehement attack. Although contrived accusations that bourgeois rightists had programs, organizations and plans for the restoration of capitalism were put forward (see below), the basic shortcoming was clearly one of ideology. Party leaders concluded that although the bourgeoisie generally had not resisted socialist transformation in 1956, the revolution on the economic front was not sufficient to remold that class and its intellectuals. Moreover, specific political developments in 1956–57 assertedly caused many in this group to waver ideologically. The denunciation of Stalin and the Hungarian uprising in particular led to serious doubts among intellectuals concerning Communism. With the launching of the Hundred Flowers experiment and Party rectification, rightist intellectuals allegedly seized the opportunity to spread further bourgeois ideology. They converted "blooming and contending" from an artistic and scholarly affair into a political matter and even saw this development as leading to a Hungarian situation in

China. In view of this, although large scale class struggle was still considered in the main over, official pronouncements now reemphasized continuation of class struggle on the political and ideological fronts for a considerable period to come.[11]

The official analysis of bourgeois intellectuals divided them into three groups —the left, middle and right. Both the left and right were small in number, but rightists had substantial managerial, organizational and political capabilities. The great majority of intellectuals were classified as "middle of the roaders" who could be educated to accept socialism but were not under firm Party leadership and "provided a market for the activities of the rightists." Given this alignment, the official strategy was to isolate and split the right through sharp counterattacks, unite with and educate the middle elements, and thus swell the ranks of the left. Attacks on rightists and education of the middle of the roaders were mutually reinforcing; rightists would become more isolated as most intellectuals were reindoctrinated while refutation of their views was the most convincing education for middle elements. Party leaders argued that only when the rightists were discredited would the majority of bourgeois intellectuals gradually come over to the side of the proletariat. This was only the beginning of the CCP's task, however. The complete remolding of intellectuals was recognized as a difficult job involving a long term educational effort of ten or more years.[12]

The above suggests the bulk of intellectuals could be treated leniently using largely persuasive methods. But what of the relatively small number of rightists? Here a glaring inconsistency became apparent. On the one hand, the most sinister anti-Communist objectives were attributed to rightists. According to Mao at Qingdao and Deng at the Third Plenum, "the contradictions between the reactionary bourgeois rightists and the people are contradictions between ourselves and the enemy, are antagonistic, irreconcilable and life and death contradictions." At the same time, however, although advocating a month of turbulent anti-rightist struggle, Mao argued against punishing rightists under most circumstances and for magnanimous treatment of their problems, an approach associated with "contradictions among the people" and traditional rectification measures of reform, reasoning and "curing the illness to save the patient" were advocated for such cases despite Mao's harsher definition of the contradiction in abstract. Moderation assertedly was possible due to the state's basic stability which normally rendered organizational measures unnecessary. It was further justified on grounds of the need to avoid crude and simple methods and to distinguish between extreme rightists and other rightists as well as between rightists and people with temporary doubts. In fact, Mao pictured this approach as a prudent tactic toward intellectuals generally since "extreme policies produce bad results" while leniency could help win over substantial numbers of rightists. Nevertheless, these restraints implicitly recognized that many of the actual charges against rightists were not to be taken too seriously. In any case, official statements emphasized that the Party was offering "a way out" to rightists who confessed and repented, and claimed that many were indeed taking advantage of this offer as the movement unfolded.[13] But this persuasive aspect, as we shall see, only partially modified the coercion one would expect in a "life and death" struggle.[e]

The efforts to moderate the campaign were partly designed to avoid complete submersion of the original aims of rectification. Official statements held that the vast majority of opinions expressed by intellectuals during "blooming and contending"—including some sharply critical of the Party—were correct and efforts to encourage non-Party participation in the rectification movement should continue.[14] It was clear, however, that rectification could only proceed on the basis of successful completion of the anti-rightist struggle. According to Shanghai's Ke Qingshi:

> [T]he general policy of correctly handling contradictions among the people and the various [specific] policies, such as let a hundred flowers bloom, let a hundred schools contend and long term coexistence and mutual supervision, must and will continue to be implemented thoroughly, and definitely will not be abandoned halfway because of the anti-rightist struggle. *The anti-rightist struggle is precisely to create the appropriate conditions for this kind of political climate.* Since our people share no common language with the bourgeois rightists, *if we do not achieve victory in the anti-rightist struggle, this kind of climate cannot be created.* Accordingly, there is no basis for doubting that rectification, contending and blooming will be continued.[15]

Although the anti-rightist drive was given priority in summer 1957, continued attention to the goals of "blooming and contending" indicated that much of Mao's earlier analysis of the role of intellectuals and Party shortcomings remained in force. Clearly there was a strong desire to avoid totally alienating intellectuals whose technical skills were still valued by Party leaders. This attitude was fraught with ambivalence, however. A concrete manifestation was the treatment of the scientific and technical community. As Michel Oksenberg has demonstrated, in mid-June it did not seem the campaign would extend to China's scientific elite. In mid-July, however, the struggle began to have an impact in scientific and technical circles. In addition, signs appeared that the leadership was placing somewhat less importance on their skills although a significant role continued to be attributed to them.[16] Ambivalence was also found in Mao's July reassessment of bourgeois intellectuals. The Chairman declared they were un-

[e] MacFarquhar, *Origins 1*, pp. 280–85, 289–92, 305, argues the question of punishing rightists was a major source of leadership conflict with Mao advocating leniency while Liu Shaoqi, Peng Zhen and other Party leaders pushed harsh sanctions, but there is little persuasive evidence on this score. For example, Peng Zhen did compare bourgeois rightists to Chiang Kai-shek but went on to say there was no need to treat them as Chiang. Also, in summer 1957 Peng reportedly argued that the difference between the left and right was merely comparable to two sides of the same street and that the "save the patient" approach should be applied to rightists. *Ibid.*, pp. 289–90; and *WHB* (Shanghai), May 15, 1968, in *SCMP*, No. 4203.

willing to submit to the Party, thus necessitating a ten to fifteen year effort to build up an army of working class intellectuals. As to the utility of established intellectuals in the short run, Mao both denounced them as ignoramuses and, contradictorily, called for winning over individual "great intellectuals" who were "useful to us."[17] The strong criticism of the Hundred Flowers period had not only made intellectuals suspect politically, but led to second thoughts concerning their potential contribution to national development. In summer 1957, however, that contribution was still seen as substantial.

The continuing concern with deviations within the Party was strikingly illustrated by Zhou Enlai's work report to the June NPC. Although Zhou's report was couched in the hated "achievements are the main thing, shortcomings and mistakes are secondary" vein and refuted rightist opinions in detail, it was remarkable for the degree it admitted shortcomings which had been criticized during "blooming and contending." Zhou allowed that bureaucratism still existed to a serious degree, the legal system was not all it should have been, people suffered unnecessarily in political movements, the expansion of the economy had been excessive in 1956, rational features of the old educational system had been wrongly rejected while Soviet practices had not been sufficiently adjusted to Chinese conditions, and non-Party personnel often lacked the authority due their positions. Thus the Premier acknowledged some validity to opinions articulated in the spring and now denounced in the summer. He also emphasized the seriousness of these shortcomings by calling for further efforts to handle correctly "contradictions among the people" and overcome subjectivism, bureaucratism and sectarianism. That such words were backed with action was dramatically demonstrated shortly after the start of the Anti-Rightist Campaign by the dismissal of Guangxi First Secretary Chen Manyuan for bureaucratism which reportedly had contributed to famine deaths in his province.[18]

The need for ongoing Party rectification should not be confused with another development of summer 1957—the extension of the anti-rightist struggle to Party members. Mao, like Zhou, recognized this need and indicated that rectification should be launched twice every five years.[19] His overall summer estimate, however, reaffirmed that rectification within the Party should be conducted in a low key manner even though individual Party members had cast their lot with the rightists:

> Ideological struggle still has a further stage and must be carried out as a gentle breeze and mild rain. This is a rectification of the Party, a rectification of the Youth League. . . .
>
> . . . .
>
> Now the democratic parties are rectifying problems of line, rectifying the right opportunist line of the bourgeoisie. The Communist Party does not have problems of line but only problems of work style. . . . [But] within the Party there is a problem of line, i.e., the "revolting elements." These "revolting elements" are rightists within the Party and Youth League. . . .[20]

In this analysis Mao was clearly separating the rectification of work style from attacks on rightists within the Party. This was hardly an attack on the Party organization and its leaders; in mid-1957 Mao repeatedly emphasized the crucial importance of Party leadership. Since their problems were overwhelmingly questions of style, the Chairman advocated protecting Party and Youth League members during rectification. Anti-rightist measures would be limited to those Party members who had taken the same "anti-Party" positions as non-Party intellectuals.[21]

While critical opinions published during "blooming and contending" were attributed to non-Party people, charges made during the Anti-Rightist Campaign claimed many similar views had been advanced by Party members, including some whose Party history went back to the late 1930s.[f] Most of the Party members denounced during summer 1957 were themselves intellectuals holding posts in cultural, educational and publishing spheres. In the spring they apparently aired views reflecting their professional rather than Party interests. For example, the Party member vice president and deputy chief editor of the People's Publishing House assertedly advocated publishing houses run by professionals independent of Party leadership. Other Party members reportedly denounced the Party as a "privileged class," attacked various political movements for violating human rights, criticized official cadre policy as favoring unskilled veteran Party cadres at the expense of talented non-Party youths, found fault with the policy of unified purchase and sale of grain, and so forth. Given the nature of the above views, the insistence that rightists within the CCP be dealt with as severely as non-Party rightists can only be regarded as a defense of the Party *per se.*[22]

In essence, with the onset of the anti-rightist struggle the primary target of rectification shifted from the Party's leadership *style* to *attitudes* concerning Party leadership. While these attitudes often concerned specific CCP policies, the focus of rectification was not yet on *policy* as such. Rectification was not bolstering one policy line over another. In fact, the moderate policy line which most rightists implicitly supported remained in effect in many areas. But what was "rightist" about the attitudes in question? During the Cultural Revolution criticism of the Party was considered "leftist" or "ultra-leftist." In 1957, however, a number of factors made the rightist label appear appropriate to Party leaders. The source of criticism—bourgeois intellectuals—was by definition to the "right" of the Party. The content—attacks on many basic features of the

[f] While only a very small minority of Party members were said to be anti-Party and anti-socialist, rightist sentiments were more widespread. The minority were accused of organizing cliques, colluding with non-Party rightists, and inciting the masses. More general tendencies included seeking personal position, only agreeing with reformist aspects of Party policies, being passive in socialist construction, and paying attention only to professional matters. Most inner Party rightists assertedly joined the CCP about the time of liberation, but many were veteran Party members with ten to twenty years experience. See *ZZXX,* August 13, 1957, in *ECMM,* No. 103; and *RMRB,* July 28, September 11, 1957, in *SCMP,* Nos. 1590, 1616.

socialist system—also smacked of rightism. And the fact that Mao and his associates, despite tinkering with the concrete forms of Party leadership, still regarded the CCP as the mainstay of the Chinese revolution meant that any criticism weakening the Party would come from the "right." Only when the Party itself was seen as undermining the revolution could such attacks be conceived of as from the "left."

In an important sense, however, the behavior under attack was not rightist. The rightism of 1957[g] had little if anything to do with the right conservatism Mao had criticized in the first half of 1956. That variety of rightism clearly fit the normal definition of the term—excessive caution, unwillingness to mobilize fully the masses, and failure to achieve rapid advance. In contrast, the essence of the rightist position, according to Mao in mid-1957, was that mistakes outweighed achievements, the capitalist road was preferable to the socialist road, and the Communist Party was unfit for leadership. Despite the Chairman's later claim that the "anti-reckless advance" of 1956 stimulated the rightist onslaught of 1957, both intellectual critiques and official rejoinders only secondarily concerned economic matters.[23] Indeed, as suggested by actual developments in summer 1957, the basic political fruit of the struggle—restored Party control—was perfectly compatible with an economic moderation. Although the undermining of the intellectuals' position by the anti-rightist struggle may have been a contributing factor to the adoption of the Great Leap strategy, there was nothing inevitable in this development. With Party control reestablished concessions to intellectuals short of a leading role in rectification could again have been granted. Only a worsening economic situation and increasing awareness of the

---

[g] The official media of summer 1957 presented a picture of rightist views essentially compatible with what had been published during "blooming and contending." In terms of substantive issues, one of the few raised that had not been reported in the spring was direct attacks on the Soviet Union, particularly for alleged mistreatment of China. Moreover, proposals for institutional change now reported were far more basic than Zhang Bojun's "political design department." These included rotating democratic parties in power, establishing a genuine coalition government of all parties, allowing democratic parties to rule one province or municipality with their own laws and police, and replacing one party rule with popular elections choosing among competing parties. The Anti-Rightist Campaign also saw much more frequent reports of violently hostile views and opinions that problems were inherent in the system. Most basically, the *intent* of the critics was now at issue. Official statements insisted the aim of the rightists was to overthrow the Party and restore capitalism. See *PDA*, pp. 304, 307, 326; and *HF*, pp. 50, 57, 76, 221.

Finally, accounts of rightist behavior were distinguished from reports published during the spring by alleging direct attacks on individual Party leaders, particularly Mao himself. It was such accounts, using the words of rightists, which not only asserted the opposition of Liu Shaoqi and Peng Zhen to the Hundred Flowers, but also pictured Mao as favoring views under sharp attack by summer 1957. MacFarquhar, *Origins 1*, ch. 18, argues that publication of such "slanders" was a subtle attack on Mao organized by his opponents within the Party. While the matter remains obscure, it should be noted that Mao himself raised some of the same embarrassing issues in *his* attacks on rightists. See above, p. 221.

unsuitability of the Soviet model would lead to radical economic experimentation. By itself anti-rightism was reconcilable with right conservatism.

Implementation of the Campaign

The anti-rightist struggle adopted familiar methods: the study of documents, criticism and self-criticism, discussion and debate meetings, and wall posters. Organs which had used these measures to implement Party rectification in April-May now employed them to counterattack rightist views. Meanwhile, forums of non-Party groups continued but turned inward on rightists within those groups. Throughout June and the first half of July, the movement was largely directed against a few key rightists, generally leaders of democratic parties and prominent critics during "blooming and contending," and consisted of scathing attacks and efforts to extract abject confessions. In addition, meetings of workers were held in various cities to attack bourgeois rightists and demonstrate support for the Party.[24]

The NPC meetings from June 20 to July 15 were a major development in the Anti-Rightist Campaign. Zhou Enlai's government work report, the keynote address of the session, was a detailed if in some ways moderate defense of the Party's performance. A major item on the agenda was discussion of the revised version of Mao's "Contradictions" speech with its six criteria for acceptable criticism. Particularly important was criticism of rightists which came to dominate the proceedings in early July. Nearly all of the 408 deputies who spoke or submitted written statements attacked key rightists. Condemnations came from diverse sources including model peasants and workers faithfully articulating the new line, intellectuals anxious to disassociate themselves from the major targets, and veteran Party cadres relishing the opportunity to strike back at the spring critics. In the words of one analyst, "the spirit of a hysterical witch hunt" was created. Bowing to this pressure, towards the end of the session many of those attacked made self-criticisms, although these often were declared insufficient or insincere. Since the NPC meetings were widely publicized they served to communicate the aims of the anti-rightist struggle and intensify the campaign throughout the country.[25]

While attacks against leading rightists continued, the emphasis of the Anti-Rightist Campaign began to change in the post-NPC period. Massive counterattacks on a few key rightists gave way to more systematic and detailed criticism of rightist phenomena in various fields. In mid-July all government personnel were ordered to participate in the anti-rightist effort. Different organs focused on problems and rightists within their own ranks, an approach apparently initiated by Mao at Qingdao. By August the campaign was gradually extended beyond Party and government organs and higher intellectual circles to major factories and mines, primary and middle schools, and industrial and commercial circles, while at the same time it penetrated below the provinces and large cities and began to reach units in smaller cities, urban districts, special districts and counties.[26] As this unfolded in late summer, Party spokesmen claimed a decisive victory in the anti-rightist struggle in democratic parties and universities, among other intellectual spheres, and in organizations at and above the provincial and municipal levels. Now, as Mao had stipulated, intense struggle gave way to lower key political and ideological education to consolidate the gains of the movement. Programs for socialist education were developed both for organs and groups which had passed or were passing through the Anti-Rightist Campaign, and for workers and peasants who had not participated in the struggle. Meanwhile, however, harsher anti-rightist measures continued well into 1958 in units where rightists remained a major problem.[27]

The Anti-Rightist Campaign had a varying impact on different segments of the Chinese elite and larger population. Although the socialist education drive in the countryside developed considerable momentum of its own (see below), in summer 1957 the movement had an urban, non-Party focus centering on forums and organizations of intellectuals. Furthermore, the mid-1957 measures to push forward the anti-rightist struggle had some features of a mobilization phase, but in a highly limited and selective fashion. While broad sections of the population were drawn into related activities, the most intense pressures were restricted to various urban target groups. Moreover, no effort was made to link the anti-rightist drive to broader mobilization for economic development.

Coercive measures fell predominantly on urban non-Party groups. Certainly there can be little doubt that the more than 400,000 individuals labeled rightists in 1957–58 were largely intellectuals of various status.[h] Moreover, the most coercive informal sanction, struggle, was most frequently invoked against bourgeois intellectuals outside the Party. In contrast, inner Party rectification continued to use "gentle breeze and mild rain" methods although individual Party rightists were liable to expulsion. And while comprehensive figures do not exist, scattered data suggest the proportion of rightists was substantially higher in

---

[h] In 1961 Mao referred to rectifying over 400,000 rightists after "blooming and contending," while a Cultural Revolution source quotes Chen Yi as saying 400,000 had been seized in 1957. *SXWS,* I, 259; and MacFarquhar, *Origins 1,* p. 314. It is most likely the 400,000 figure refers to rightists uncovered during the full movement extending into 1958. In October 1957 Mao estimated that 50 to 60,000 rightists had been uncovered and that the figure might reach 150 to 200,000. In April 1958 he put the total at 300,000 and the following month said primary school teachers (i.e., "ordinary intellectuals") uncovered since December made up one third of this total. *SXWS,* II, 125, 180, 207, 215. This, together with the intense implementation of the movement in higher level educational institutions and other urban units, strongly suggests intellectuals made up the bulk of rightists. Within the intelligentsia, the evidence suggests the scientific and technical community was relatively protected and those dealing with social and philosophical questions were most vulnerable. See Mu Fu-sheng, *The Wilting of the Hundred Flowers: The Chinese Intelligentsia under Mao* (New York: Frederick A. Praeger, 1962), p. 240; and above, p. 223.

non-Party than Party circles. For example, over 5 percent of Shanghai industrialists and merchants, 8.5 percent of teachers at Fudan University, and 6.6 percent of the membership of the leading minor party, the China Democratic League (CDL), were declared rightists in comparison to only 1.9 and "about" 2 percent of Party members in Chongqing and Guizhou respectively. Finally, the few known instances of the use of the ultimate sanction—capital punishment—were limited to non-Party instigators of student riots.[28]

The precise degree of coercion actually used against urban intellectuals in general and rightists in particular remains murky, however. In 1958 Mao estimated that rightists made up only 1 to 2 percent of bourgeois intellectuals, while in mid-1957 he claimed that even in so volatile a place as Beijing University only 1 to 3 percent of students and 10 percent of professors were rightists. Thus the overwhelming majority of intellectuals were to be handled by education and criticism. Moreover, stipulations that punishment should generally be avoided and a "save the patient" approach adopted in rightist cases imply a mitigation of coercion here as well. Leniency was also reflected in Mao's directive that rightists generally should not be denied the right to vote and various individual rightists could continue to hold CPPCC membership and minor official posts. Furthermore, many of those who were denied their government and other posts were restored to official positions and had their rightist labels removed by the end of 1958 and 1959. Nevertheless, the severity of struggle sessions was demonstrated by reports of suicides. In addition, reform through labor apparently was meted out to rightists on a large scale and led to the establishment of new "labor reeducation" *(laodong jiaoyang)* camps to absorb rightists and others whose sins were considered less serious than those of individuals confined to labor reform camps. Thus notwithstanding measures to mitigate the struggle, the Anti-Rightist Campaign still ranked as one of the Party's more coercive rectification efforts. As Mao put it in 1958, "Towards the rightists we resort to a method rather coercive in essence, for no other purpose than to make them notorious."[29]

Despite the relatively coercive approach adopted during the anti-rightist struggle, the movement largely continued to be implemented through the normal chain of command rather than by work teams. With the onset of the anti-rightist stage Party rectification offices at various levels were simply rechristened anti-rightist offices *(fan youpai bangongshi)* and leadership of the campaign in government and Party units remained substantially unchanged.[30] The innovative devices of the spring, notably the forums of non-Party intellectuals, also continued but now under closer guidance by responsible CCP officials. Mao outlined the methods of Party organizational control in considerable detail in June:

> Get each of [the democratic] parties to organize forums with the left, middle and right elements all taking part. . . . We should tactfully encourage the left and middle elements to speak out . . . and refute the rightists. . . . When the opportune moment arrives, lose no time in organizing separate meetings of

> Party and League members to sort out the criticisms; accept those criticisms that are constructive and correct mistakes and shortcomings but refute those criticisms that are destructive. At the same time, organize some non-Party people to make speeches and state the correct views. Then, have a responsible Party cadre who enjoys prestige make a summing up speech that is both analytical and convincing to effect a complete change in the atmosphere. If all goes well, a month or so will see the whole process through and we can then switch to the inner Party rectification, which will proceed like "a gentle breeze and mild rain."[31]

Clearly a situation existed similar to that of the *sanfan* movement. The fact that sanctions centered on a suspect group lacking strong ties to Party cadres, cadres who had been angered by the developments of the spring, meant the established leadership could implement coercive measures without fear for its own position. Moreover, organizational interests were further protected by Mao's directive that production and other work should not be neglected at any time.[32] While the implementation of Party rectification through the regular chain of command in the spring served as a reassurance that those interests would not be excessively threatened, in the summer it guaranteed the enthusiastic prosecution of the anti-rightist effort.

In terms of effectiveness, the Anti-Rightist Campaign clearly obtained its immediate objectives of silencing the critics and restoring the authority of Party cadres. But the impact was counterproductive to the larger goals of the spring—goals which were not totally jettisoned with the launching of the anti-rightist struggle. While the Hundred Flowers experience raised high level doubts concerning the utility of China's intellectuals for economic development, the enthusiasm of those intellectuals was damaged in turn by the reversal of policy. Given that the worst fears entertained by non-Party specialists had proven true, many intellectuals undoubtedly were now more cautious in expressing opinions even on technical matters. Moreover, as indicated in Chapter 2, experimental psychology suggests that extreme stress results in significant damage to job performance, a phenomenon particularly marked where complex tasks requiring judgment and reflection are involved.[33] As far as Party cadres are concerned, although the end of "blooming and contending" may have restored a situation where traditional methods could have some effectiveness in combating deviations, the sin of sectarianism was presumably reinforced by the anti-rightist drive. More fundamentally, the general goal of developing a leadership style suited to the new socialist environment suffered a setback with the reassertion of orthodoxy.

Student Unrest and the Anti-Rightist Struggle in Education

"Blooming and contending" among China's university and middle school students was one of the most significant, if largely unreported developments of spring 1957. When reports finally appeared in the summer, it became clear that passions unleashed by free discussion led to student demonstrations and disruptions which spilled beyond the schools and universities. These passions were not simply aroused by the springtime debates. At the middle school level in particular they were fueled by reductions in new university students and declining employment prospects for graduates due to the economic slowdown of 1956–57.[34] Nevertheless, it was the opportunity offered by the Hundred Flowers experiment which opened the floodgates.

Beijing University (Beida) was in the fore of student "blooming and contending" as it so often had been during earlier Chinese student movements. As the Hundred Flowers unfolded at Beida it developed a number of distinctive forms. One was the virtually unrestricted use of wall posters. One of the earliest signs of unrest was the appearance of hundreds of *dazibao* critical of the Party on a so-called "democratic wall" at Beida on May 19. Another form was the open air meeting where thousands of students heard impassioned speeches and debated with speakers in an atmosphere compared to London's Hyde Park. In some instances, these meetings became accusation meetings aimed at Party cadres. According to the report of a Western student then at Beida, open air meetings were intensely emotional and marked by theatrical gestures, tears and shouts. Another development was the formation of *ad hoc* student organizations which took the lead in Hundred Flowers activities. The best known, the "Hundred Flowers Society," was denounced during the anti-rightist struggle for seeking to initiate a "movement for the thorough reform of the political system." Such charges notwithstanding, this society and other student groups apparently lacked clear-cut programs. The newspapers they published, however, were not only important for publicizing critical views within Beida, but also for spreading the student movement to other universities.[35]

By early June the student movement had reached universities in all areas of China and assumed similar forms to those adopted in Beijing. In addition to student publications and correspondence, in some cases the movement was spread by student delegations to nearby institutions. An important further development was the publication of reports on Beida in the *Guangming ribao* and *Wenhui bao* on May 26 and 27 respectively, reports which temporarily ended what one student leader called a "news blackout." But without extensive coverage in the official media, communication between different centers of student discontent could only be sporadic. As a result, the various universities were to a large extent isolated and no political program or organization could be formed on a nationwide basis.[36]

Generally student criticism concerned matters similar to those raised by older non-Party intellectuals, although more concentrated on problems of direct concern. A major demand was that Party committees be withdrawn from educational institutions or their powers be limited. Other issues included slavish imitation of Soviet educational practices, political favoritism in the allocation of job assignments to graduating students and selection of students for study abroad, and restrictions on the study of Western science and literature. In general, despite some views attacking the state system itself, the bulk of student criticism apparently was designed to elicit a more liberal educational policy and reforms within the universities.[37]

In comparison to criticisms offered by their elders, however, student views were considerably more vehement in tone. Student leaders not only dismissed the efforts of leading democratic party spokesmen as "insufficient," they indicated their ardor by continuing to post critical *dazibao* for days after the launching of the Anti-Rightist Campaign. Moreover, reports on student unrest frequently included statements of extreme hostility toward the regime: e.g., "exterminate the Communist bandits." These extreme views, however, should not be taken as indicative of student opinion any more than hostile opinions attributed to older bourgeois rightists were representative of non-Party criticism generally. Critical wall posters at Beida were usually surrounded by others defending the Party and most of the critics expressed support of Marxism. Perhaps typical of loyal but ambivalent student attitudes was one wall poster which declared, "We want Party leadership, but we are resolutely opposed to the Party alone making decisions and implementing them." Moreover, bitter criticisms of specific Party cadres were often accompanied by appeals to Chairman Mao, the Central Committee or other high Party bodies, thus indicating an abiding, if naïve, faith in the system. While Mao personally came in for denunciation as worse than Qinshihuang, respect for "the revolutionary leader who saved China" seemed a more prevalent attitude towards the Chairman. On balance, it appears that the virulence of student criticism was largely a byproduct of youthful idealism and not a rejection of Party rule.[38]

More serious than the views of youthful critics were disturbances involving students. In 1961 Mao claimed that "*big* blooming and contending" brought forth tens of thousands of "small Hungaries" including incidents at Beida, People's University and Qinghua University. Moreover, students reportedly went to factories, rural areas, and simply onto the streets to put up wall posters and argue their views among the people. This activity was in the May Fourth tradition of linking student protest to action by workers and other social groups, but it was now denounced as "setting fires" to incite opposition to the regime. Most serious were a number of incidents involving disturbances at Party buildings and attacks on officials. These incidents occurred both before and after June 8, thus indicating that student unrest was not easily checked.[39]

Probably the best known "small Hungary" involved a middle school in Hanyang county, Hubei. The incident originated on June 12 with a rumor that the enrollment quota for higher education was being sharply curtailed. This reportedly was seized upon by a "counterrevolutionary clique" led by assistant principal Wang Jianguo and several teachers to incite the students. After failing to obtain relevant documents from school authorities, some students decided to seek these documents from the county people's council. They then marched out of the school in an agitated state, allegedly shouting such counterrevolutionary slogans as "Welcome back to Chiang Kai-shek" and "Let us go to Taiwan." Once at the people's council, they stormed into the culture and education bureau and rummaged through its files, raided other offices and broke down the county magistrate's door. Later the students moved on to the county Party committee headquarters and seized two cadres who had attempted to resist them. The next morning, moreover, about 800 students went to the people's council where the magistrate tried to dissuade them from further riotous acts. Undeterred, they tied him up. Subsequently the students assaulted a number of cadres at the Party committee and were preparing to tie up the county secretary when workers and peasants reportedly intervened. According to the official version, the workers and peasants spontaneously came to the aid of Party leaders, but the students claimed the committee organized the masses to beat them up. While it is likely that the Party did rally mass support, in this and other cases statements of popular outrage such as "now you have a full belly and instead of studying at school you are creating trouble" ring true. In any case, the worker and peasant intervention marked the turning point in Hanyang county and Party authority was quickly restored. Finally, in by far the harshest known display of coercion during the anti-rightist struggle, Wang Jianguo and two others were executed for their roles in the affair.[40]

While the seriousness of student unrest cannot be doubted, it is difficult to determine its extent. Lu Dingyi declared that only 1 to 3 percent of students were blind followers of bourgeois rightists.[i] Other reports, however, indicate that 10 percent of Beida students were labeled rightists during the anti-rightist struggle, while Mao claimed 5 percent of student Party members and 10 percent of League members "collapsed" in spring 1957. In any case, Party leaders were also concerned with a larger number of students who were caught up in campus agitation. These students were viewed as basically supporting the Party but ensnared by rightist schemes. Nevertheless, it was deeply disconcerting that youths raised in the PRC had proven so vulnerable to rightist ploys.[41]

The Anti-Rightist Struggle in Education

Student unrest together with the "blooming and contending" of professors, researchers and other academic personnel opened the university community to

[i] In terms of social origins, these students were apparently representative of students generally. In 1956 Mao said 70 percent of university students were children of landlords and the bourgeoisie, while a mid-1957 report asserted three fourths of the editorial board of a "reactionary" Beida student publication came from landlord, bureaucrat and capitalist families. They may, however, have had unusually harsh personal experiences under Party rule. The same report claimed 40 percent of the editorial board had relatives imprisoned or executed by the CCP. *SXWS*, II, 65; and *RMRB*, July 24, 1957, in *SCMP*, No. 1589.

charges of rightism on a wide variety of issues. Thus a large scale struggle against rightists swept through higher educational institutions from mid-June to mid-August and then spread to primary and middle schools. At Beida, and presumably other universities, summer vacation was canceled and students, faculty and staff were required to participate in struggle meetings. Although the climax of large scale mass struggle was reached in mid-August, the unmasking of rightists continued into fall and winter while other people were criticized for wavering attitudes. Some university rightists were punished by reform through labor but most apparently continued their studies under supervision.[42]

Before rightist cases were completely disposed of, however, several measures were taken to consolidate the gains of the campaign on the educational front. One approach was to introduce formal socialist education programs. Following the climax of mass struggle in August, Politburo member Kang Sheng called for socialist ideological education classes emphasizing class struggle in place of existing political classes in higher education, and this plan was put into effect in September. Two months later the Central Committee approved a socialist education curriculum for tertiary institutions and Party schools—a one to two year program of study centering on Mao's "Contradictions" speech and including both Marxist-Leninist classics and current Party documents. Similarly, in August the Ministry of Education and Youth League Central Committee initiated "socialist ideological education classes with the anti-rightist struggle as their central theme" in place of youth training, political knowledge and similar courses in middle and normal schools.[43]

A second measure was the transfer of reliable Party cadres to leading posts in educational and cultural organizations. In a step which set a precedent for lower levels, the Central Committee sent 1,000 high ranking Party cadres including central government section chiefs, office directors, bureau heads and vice ministers to such organs. These cadres, who were chosen on the basis of cultural level and academic experience as well as political reliability, were to take charge of political work and strengthen Party leadership. In addition, Mao instructed provincial level first secretaries to take personal charge of transforming education and other specialist areas. These decisions bolstered Party control where it assertedly had been weak prior to and during the Hundred Flowers. Ironically, in view of the bitter complaints of the spring, Mao asserted that "in certain cultural and educational units the Party's leadership has not been established at all." Moreover, a refugee source described the situation before the anti-Rightist Campaign as one where Party authorities "floated on top" without penetrating very deeply the organizations they led. Now such penetration was facilitated by the dispatch of additional Party cadres. Furthermore, despite the criteria concerning cultural level and academic background, many newly transferred cadres lacked adequate professional experience. Thus another phenomenon attacked by intellectual critics—authority in the hands of technically incompetent officials—was intensified by the anti-rightist struggle. As a result, the combination of systematic political education and the transfer of Party cadres pushed Party dominance beyond what both Mao and non-Party intellectuals believed desirable in the spring, and even beyond the *status quo ante.*[44]

The Anti-Rightist Campaign in Other Urban Circles

In addition to China's universities and schools, important issues were raised during the anti-rightist struggle in other urban institutions and groups in summer 1957.[j] Here we examine some of the most prominent: not only the symbolically significant if largely powerless democratic parties, but also key segments of the propaganda sphere—the press and literary and art circles—as well as the politically important (and not solely urban) Youth League and political and legal organs.

The "Zhang-Luo Alliance" and the Democratic Parties

Because of their leading role in "blooming and contending," democratic party leaders were singled out for major attacks during the June-July phase of the anti-rightist struggle. In particular, two top democratic party figures, Zhang Bojun and Luo Longji, were severely condemned. This attack was soon extended to denunciations of a so-called "Zhang-Luo Alliance," an alleged political conspiracy aimed at the overthrow of the CCP itself. Although the actual existence of such an "alliance" is doubtful at best, various democratic party personages were linked to it in this period.

Severe criticism was directed at a number of democratic party leaders at the June–July NPC meetings.[45] When the Anti-Rightist Campaign began on June 8 it was not clear that all these people were targets for attack. Some initially responded in ways suggesting the felt they either had been honest critics or had been sufficiently careful to adjust easily to the new situation. Zhang Bojun, for example, published an article on June 12 attacking Chu Anping's "Party empire" view and demanding that democratic parties follow the socialist road. In addition, reports of casual attitudes among democratic party figures suggesting they perceived no grave threat appeared: some reportedly arrived late at criticism

[j] Besides those areas examined below, of particular significance were industrial and commercial circles (i.e., the bourgeoisie) and workers and employees in factories and mines. In both cases the movement began in late summer and involved both anti-rightist struggle and socialist education on benefits and duties under the existing system. Clearly there was greater emphasis on socialist education among workers and employees where a systematic program was adopted by the Central Committee in September and participation in anti-rightist activities was more directed at other groups than at cleansing the ranks of the working class. See Frederick C. Teiwes, "Rectification Campaigns and Purges in Communist China, 1950–61," Ph.D. dissertation, Columbia University, 1971, pp. 401–404.

forums. These reports may also indicate that CCP leaders had not yet decided on a full repudiation of these individuals. Even after the launching of the anti-rightist struggle Luo Longji was allowed to represent China on an official delegation to Ceylon. Moreover, the official treatment of Zhang Bojun in particular shows that the conspiracy theory developed gradually. On June 13, *Renmin ribao* called for "sincere" criticism of "Comrade" Zhang who, despite his contributions to socialism, had played into the hands of rightists. Several days later, however, official reports hinted broadly that Zhang, together with Luo Longji and others, was involved in planned, coordinated activities aimed at the regime. Only in the July 1 *Renmin ribao* editorial attacking *Wenhui bao* was the notion of a full-fledged "Zhang-Luo Alliance" publicized, a fact pointing to Mao's personal role in concocting the "alliance" given his authorship of the editorial. The development of this interpretation was probably influenced by the need for a coherent explanation of what went wrong with the Hundred Flowers experiment as the NPC met in the latter part of June.[46]

In the version which now emerged the ideological and political roots of the "alliance" were traced to the 1940s when Zhang, Luo and others were active in promoting a "third force" between the GMD and CCP. The "Zhang-Luo Alliance" as such assertedly became active in August 1956 under the influence of the Soviet Twentieth Party Congress and the policy of mutual supervision and long term coexistence. These developments, together with the East European events and the Hundred Flowers, reportedly reactivated the "third force" mentality of Zhang and Luo as they anticipated an increasing role for the democratic parties. At this time Zhang and Luo assertedly were able to seize control of the CDL from its legal leaders.[k] They then allegedly devised a program containing the basic views attributed to bourgeois rightists—e.g., opposition to Party leadership in scientific, cultural and educational organizations—and featuring Zhang's "political design department" and Luo's special committee to deal with *sufan* cases.[47]

Official charges against the "Zhang-Luo Alliance" went beyond advocating rightist views. Not only did Zhang and Luo assertedly usurp control of the central organizations of several democratic parties, but many provincial democratic party committees were reported in close touch with the "alliance" leaders in Peking. A picture was drawn of a nationwide conspiratorial organization opposing CCP leadership of the democratic parties. Luo in particular was charged with encouraging democratic party branches in various institutions to bypass Party and administrative authorities and contact leading democratic party personnel who could deal directly with the CCP Central Committee. This was supplemented by the demand that CCP members in leading democratic party posts be withdrawn.[48]

---

[k] From the 1940s on "third force" circles were rent with factionalism. During the Anti-Rightist Campaign CCP leaders were able to exploit those divisions and mobilize other democratic party leaders against Zhang and Luo.

This apparent effort by Zhang and Luo to obtain greater autonomy for their organizations must be understood in the context of the mutual supervision policy. According to an official analysis of this policy in fall 1956, the political freedom and organizational independence of minor parties was desirable under the new situation. The fine print of the argument, however, indicated substantial limits to political freedom since democratic parties assertedly always accepted Party leadership "voluntarily," and they were warned against behaving as opposition parties. Organizational practices, the analysis continued, had to be brought into line with political freedom. Thus CCP organs and members were not to interfere in the internal politics of democratic parties, but this did not mean that cooperation with appropriate Party committees should be terminated. On the contrary, such cooperation was necessary for the proper functioning of the democratic parties. This interpretation, then, did sanction requests for the withdrawal of Party cadres from democratic party organs. On other matters, especially the degree of consultation with CCP committees, it was more restrictive. In these circumstances, the impulse to test the limits of "political freedom" and "organizational independence" was understandable.[49]

Other "evidence" of planned anti-Party activity by Zhang and Luo was also less than clear-cut. For example, the establishment in May 1957 of four special groups within the CDL to examine the problems of mutual supervision and "blooming and contending," scientific planning, the relationship of positions and power, and the role of Party committees in institutions of higher learning was retrospectively denounced as conspiratorial activity. In fact, only the group dealing with scientific planning held meetings and its recommendations concerning limits on the leading role of the Party over scientific work was submitted to the State Council's Scientific Planning Commission, an indication that the group intended to work with existing state organs. Moreover, the so-called "emergency conference" convened by Zhang on June 6 was a similarly ambiguous development. Attended by a dozen leading professors and democratic party personalities, it reportedly was called to determine a course of action for the CDL in the light of the deteriorating situation among the students. At this meeting concern was expressed that the masses might vent their grievances against the Party and follow the students into the streets creating a Hungary. Some democratic party leaders felt the CCP could not fully cope with the situation due to its estrangement from the masses and would need their help to calm things down. This was undoubtedly the inspiration of the subsequent charge that democratic party rightists desired a Hungarian style rebellion in China so that they could come forward to "clean up the mess." The only actual measure taken at the time, however, was an abortive effort to consult with Zhou Enlai and other Party leaders on the crisis, hardly the step expected from a group of men bent on overthrowing the existing order.[50]

Another major charge against the "Zhang-Luo Alliance" dealt with organizational expansion and recruitment. Democratic party leaders reportedly sought to end the "sphere of influence" system whereby each minor party was limited to specific groups and begin recruiting among workers and youths, while Luo suggested that the CCP stop its recruitment of intellectuals. Democratic parties assertedly practiced "unrestricted expansion" since mid-1956 and sought out people hostile to the CCP including secret service agents, former GMD members, and individuals who had served terms of reform through labor. Specific appeals were also made to intellectuals who felt neglected by the Party and in need of the "warmth of an organization." Moreover, democratic parties were attacked for carelessness in recruiting; it assertedly was easier to join one party than to buy a ticket for a movie. Moreover, in their haste to expand membership, the democratic parties allegedly used questionable methods including coercion, promises of positions, assurances that participation in ideological remolding would not be required, and such blandishments as trips to Beijing, dinners and girls. As a result, the two and three fold increases made in various democratic party memberships at national and local levels from mid-1956 to mid-1957 assertedly consisted largely of undesirable elements. But notwithstanding these developments, organizational expansion *per se* was an outgrowth of the official mutual supervision policy.[51]

The above discussion indicates the official version of a nationwide "Zhang-Luo Alliance" was grossly exaggerated. While Zhang and Luo admitted various rightist opinions and cooperating with one another within the CDL, this stops far short of acknowledging an organized effort to overthrow the Party. Luo denied any secret contacts with Zhang or other rightists and attributed the similar views expressed by democratic party figures throughout the country to their bourgeois ideology and to his and Zhang's influence in intellectual circles.[52] This defense is plausible. The overall performance of Zhang and Luo in spring 1957 is that of two reasonably cautious politicians seeking to expand their influence within the framework established by the more liberal policies in effect since mid-1956, policies which explicitly if ambiguously called for greater political freedom and organizational independence on the part of the democratic parties. The denunciation of a "Zhang-Luo Alliance" can best be seen as an effort to find a scapegoat for the widespread criticism during "blooming and contending" which shattered the assumptions of the liberal policies. Since the discontent of the Hundred Flowers period could not be attributed to the system's shortcomings, blame was placed on a small group of bourgeois rightists who led well intentioned people astray. Zhang and Luo, as prominent democratic party leaders who played a major role in forums of intellectuals, were obvious candidates to symbolize this imagined conspiracy of rightists.

Although the targets of criticism began to broaden after the June–July NPC session, criticism of the "Zhang-Luo Alliance" and other leading democratic party rightists continued. Finally, in January 1958 it was announced that Zhang and Luo had adequately confessed and their "clique" had been smashed, and they were officially removed from their ministerial posts together with Zhang

Table 3

Rightists Exposed within Democratic Parties

Position	% of Rightists
China Democratic League	
Standing Committee of Central Committee	36
Central Committee members	29
Central Committee alternate members	43
Provincial and major municipal committee chairmen	46
Municipal and county committee chairmen	35.4
Total membership	6.6
Guomindang Revolutionary Committee	
Central Committee members	15.2
Central Committee alternate members	27.9
Provincial and major municipal committee members	18.9

Naiqi. In the meantime, rectification within the democratic parties was extended to local and basic level organizations. The impact of the movement is suggested by Table 3 which summarizes the exposure of rightists in the CDL, the largest democratic party, and the GMD Revolutionary Committee. Since rightists were generally removed from their party posts, this summary indicates extensive dismissals within the two parties. In addition, key leaders of other democratic parties were also removed and rightists reportedly were strongly represented in the basic level units of these parties.[53]

Democratic party members serving in government posts were also major victims of the anti-rightist struggle. A substantial portion of minor party personnel in central government ministries reportedly were labeled rightists—e.g., 20 percent of democratic party members in the Ministry of Culture and its subordinate units.[54] Moreover, seven of eight ministers and vice ministers ousted as rightists were democratic party leaders.[55] At lower levels democratic party figures and non-Party democrats removed from government posts included vice governors of three provinces and deputy mayors of seven major cities,[56] and minor party members were prominent victims in the universities, journalism, judicial organs, and state representative bodies. Thus relatively severe formal disciplinary sanctions as well as intense struggle sessions marked the Anti-Rightist Campaign in democratic party circles.

In the long run, the impact of the Anti-Rightist Campaign on the top leaders of the minor parties was considerably less significant than the effect on the overall role of democratic parties in the political system. Starting at the end of 1958, many democratic party rightists including Zhang Bojun and Luo Longji were restored to most of their minor party positions and once again placed on the major representative bodies, the NPC and CPPCC. At the April–May 1959 CPPCC National Committee session many leading rightists reported on their successful ideological remolding; they were also among the 26,000 rightists whose labels were removed as part of the amnesty granted on the PRC's tenth anniversary in October.[57] But if democratic party leaders were not consigned to political oblivion, neither did they or their organizations recover their limited prior influence. Zhang, Luo and the other rightist figures were not restored to their governmental posts. Moreover, the overall proportion of non-Party personnel of ministerial rank underwent a long term decline from 33 to 16 percent over the 1955–65 decade.[58] Thus while the Hundred Flowers experiment reflected the high tide of democratic party influence in post-1949 China, the Anti-Rightist Campaign marked both a sharp turnabout in the immediate fortunes of those parties and a general decline of the united front in Chinese politics.

The Attack on the Press

As we have seen, the press was a center of controversy both before and after the launching of the anti-rightist struggle. Initially Mao berated the Party press in particular for failing to push "blooming and contending" while praising non-Party papers which had been more active in this regard. By summer 1957 Mao again belabored the press—particularly non-Party papers but also the CCP's own newspapers—but now for indiscriminately publishing attacks on the Party. Thus the journalistic and publishing profession inevitably became a key target of attack during the Anti-Rightist Campaign. While the two papers singled out by Mao for the most extensive denunciations, Shanghai's *Wenhui bao* and Beijing's *Guangming ribao,* were official organs of democratic parties,[1] criticism of Party and Youth League publications and of Party as well as non-Party journalists also developed. Table 4 lists the leading figures of national publications and publishing houses attacked as rightists during the movement.[59] In addition, editorial personnel of lesser rank on national publications and the heads of some local newspapers were also denounced.

Although the national Party press escaped violent attacks, even *Renmin ribao* was not immune. In June Mao accused the Party daily of sharing the "bourgeois view of journalism," while in December it was criticized for overemphasis of ability and neglect of political criteria resulting in "management of the paper by scholars." Meanwhile, in July, the leadership of the paper was reorganized with

[1]The two papers were linked to the "Zhang-Luo Alliance" through the personal involvement of Zhang and Luo. Zhang was director of *Guangming ribao* and Luo, although lacking official positions, reportedly was influential in both. Although the official view implies close organizational control by Zhang and Luo, and while both apparently were consulted about the policies of the two papers, their role probably was to support the papers' bold policies rather than to direct their daily operations. See *PDA,* pp. 334, 340.

Table 4

Leading Rightists in Press and Publications Circles

Official	Position	Affiliation	Sanctions
Chu Anping	chief editor, *GMRB*	Jiu San Society	dismissed
Xu Zhucheng	president & chief editor, *WHB*	?	suspended
Pu Xixiu	deputy chief editor, *WHB*	CDL	dismissed
Zhang Liqun	director & chief editor, *ZGQNB*	?	criticism
Chen Mo	deputy chief editor, *ZGQNB*	CCP	expelled from Youth League CC; dismissed
Li Kang	ex-vice director & chief editor, Chinese Youth Press	CCP	criticism
Zeng Yanxiu	director, People's Publishing House	CCP	criticism
Yuan Youming	chief editor & Party secretary, *DGB*	CCP	criticism
Ge Yang	chief editor, *Xin guancha*	CCP	criticism
Ding Zong	deputy chief editor, *Renmin huabao*	CDL	criticism

the appointment of Wu Lengxi as chief editor replacing Deng Tuo. Deng, who had drawn Mao's ire in April for the Party daily's sluggish response to his spring initiative, now apparently received a mild slap on the wrist for his attempts to respond to the Chairman's concerns. In any case, Deng was not disgraced. He was named the paper's director and continued to perform many of his previous functions. Here, as with leading Party journalists generally, a lenient approach was adopted.[60]

The views attributed to rightists in journalistic and publishing circles naturally focused on the proper role of the press. At root, they saw their job as gathering and printing news without regard for political criteria. Thus they advocated publishing unedited news dispatches, emphasized speed in news publication, liked scoops and inside stories, and viewed uncovering contradictions within the system as a major function. Zhang Bojun's opinion that "it is our task to expose, the solution of problems is the business of the Communist Party" amply summarized the alleged rightist attitude. In addition, rightists desired to make the press more entertaining; as a result they were now denounced for appealing to low tastes. Nevertheless, some support for this approach which Mao attacked in mid-May as renouncing the class nature of the press could be found in Party policies and leaders' statements from mid-1956 to spring 1957.[61]

In holding these views, rightists assertedly were striking out on an independent path opposing Party leadership of the press. For example, Zhang Bojun reportedly advocated that *Guangming ribao* adopt a line different from that of NCNA, while Luo Longji urged *Wenhui bao* to distinguish its mode of operations from that of *Renmin ribao*. Organizational issues were basic. A number of steps had been taken since 1956 to increase the role of democratic parties in the management of the non-Party press. In Shanghai, democratic party organs were established in *Wenhui bao, Xinwen ribao* [News Daily], and *Xinmin bao* [New People's Daily] in 1956. As the Hundred Flowers experiment developed in spring 1957 further inroads on Party authority occurred: the appointment of non-Party figure Chu Anping as chief editor of *Guangming ribao,* and an April decision, taken under the authority of the Party's united front department, abolishing the CCP fraction in the paper which left complete control to the democratic parties. This apparently resulted in pressure for similar changes in *Wenhui bao.* Luo Longji assertedly advocated ignoring the Party fraction while chief editor Xu Zhucheng cited the *Guangming ribao* precedent to ask whether a Party fraction was required in his paper. Moreover, there were further reports that *Wenhui bao,* which had recently severed connections with the Ministry of Education, resisted plans for organizational links to the Ministry of Culture. In addition, in the heady days of spring 1957 intellectuals organized a wide variety of independent journals in several large cities.[62]

As with "bourgeois" attitudes towards journalism generally, these attempts at greater organizational independence had been encouraged by the views of high ranking leaders and official CCP policies. In mid-1956 Liu Shaoqi reportedly advocated that NCNA should be an "independently run" unofficial news service rather than a state agency. Moreover, in November 1956 the Writers' Union granted greater responsibility to editors of literary journals in the running of their magazines, while the increasing role of democratic party organs in the press was clearly an outgrowth of the mutual supervision policy. And rightist demands for more non-Party papers and the right to criticize the Party on minor issues while supporting it on major ones could be linked with Mao's spring 1957 advocacy of non-Party papers in every province to provide views different from those of the Party press. When the Chairman argued in June that although non-Party papers "should not be exactly the same as Party organs . . . their general orientation should be the same as other papers," he emasculated the liberal policies he and other leaders had pushed for over a year.[63]

The impulse to increase operational independence from Party organizational control was not limited to major non-Party papers; it affected important Party and Youth League publications and journalists as well. An editor of the Party daily in Lüda reportedly challenged sole CCP leadership of the Party press and advocated an equal share for non-Party people in running the paper. While such views focused on an increased democratic party role in the nation's Party newspapers, perhaps more significant were attempts by CCP press officials to maximize their independence from Party propaganda authorities. Thus the Party secretary and chief editor of *Dagong bao* was accused of ignoring Party leadership and attempting to set up an independent kingdom. Similarly, the deputy chief editor of *Zhongguo qingnian bao* [Chinese Youth Daily], a member of the Youth League Central

Committee, reportedly complained of rude interference by responsible officials of the League center in the affairs of his paper, while an editor of the local Beijing Youth League paper resisted the leadership of the municipal League committee. These strains between Party and League propaganda authorities and independent minded editors intensified during "blooming and contending." The most spectacular incident occurred in May 1957 when a bitter dispute broke out between *Anshan ribao* and the municipal Party committee over an attempt by leading members of the committee to censor a report of a journalists' forum. Leading officials of the paper including the Party branch secretary attacked the municipal committee for its bureaucratic action and refused to accept its decisions. Reflecting the heady atmosphere of the period, they claimed to be "good Party members, with strong Party character" while rejecting the authority of the local Party apparatus. As in so many other areas, the policies of the Hundred Flowers period had exacerbated the everpresent contradiction between professional journalistic interests and Party control of the press.[64]

Clearly, a major factor in the special attention the press received during the anti-rightist struggle was its key role in the developments of the spring. During the Hundred Flowers experiment Party and non-Party papers alike served as the main communications channel for critical opinions of non-Party intellectuals. The availability of this information undoubtedly contributed to "ideological confusion." Although publication of intellectuals' views was in accord with official policy at the time, during the Anti-Rightist Campaign various newspapers were attacked for having published opinions hostile to the Party without refuting them. Thus *Shishi shouce* [Current Events Handbook] was denounced for treating positive and negative views of the CCP alike, while *Zhongguo qingnian bao* was chastised for making only feeble refutations of rightists. As in other matters, *Guangming ribao* and *Wenhui bao* were the alleged prime offenders. While the leaders of the two papers claimed their errors had been due to a one-sided understanding of "blooming and contending," Mao accused them of intentionally launching a violent attack on the existing order. The two papers were judged "guilty of arson," of deliberately seeking to "set fires" by publishing "reports of a seditious nature." The "seditious effect" on students of reports on events at Beijing University was especially emphasized, conveniently overlooking the fact that *Guangming ribao* and *Wenhui bao* each published only one report on the Beida situation. These attacks further ignored the explicit policy of *not* responding to criticism which had been adopted in early May.[65]

In sum, the function performed by the press in spring 1957 left newspapers vulnerable to charges of being insufficiently alert to ideological heresy once the overall Party line changed in June. The shake-up of personnel in *Renmin ribao* indicated that even the most authoritative Party organ could not escape the dilemma inherent in implementing the Hundred Flowers although leading Party journalists generally seemed to escape with mild sanctions. For to encourage even a relatively free debate required unprecedented tolerance of unorthodox viewpoints, a tolerance which Mao subsequently interpreted as evidence of political unreliability. While the Chairman was able to execute a political reversal at minimal personal cost, the instruments of his policies could not escape responsibility so easily.

Literary and Art Circles

Rightist literary and art views reflected both opinions aired during the Hundred Flowers period and issues at the center of Communist literary disputes since the 1930s. Among the "revisionist theories" and erroneous tendencies under attack in summer 1957 were: regarding art serving workers, peasants and soldiers as "formalism" *(gongshizhuyi);* overemphasizing artistic standards at the expense of political criteria; claiming writers possessed special genius which could not be bound by arbitrary rules; insisting authors write the truth as they see it and expose the "dark side" of the socialist system; denigrating Soviet literature; and rejecting Party leadership as lacking adequate expertise to guide literary affairs.[66] Each of these issues was a constant source of tension between the Party's cultural bureaucracy and China's creative intellectuals. While the new policies of 1956 gave some cautious encouragement to such attitudes, in mid-1957 they were declared beyond the pale.

Although the campaign was aimed at deviations among both Party members and non-Party people in literary and art circles, unlike most areas greatest importance was attached to Party members. According to a September 1957 *Renmin ribao* editorial, "The writers inside the Party do more harm than those outside. The easiest way to attack a fortress is . . . from within." The major target of the movement was a group of old revolutionary writers who were mostly Party members of long standing. Dubbed the "Ding-Chen anti-Party group," it included: Ding Ling, an influential female writer who had been attacked for her sharp criticism of the Party as far back as 1942 but still held a number of important literary posts in the early 1950s; Chen Qixia, a former chief editor of *Wenyi bao* [Literary Gazette]; Vice Chairman of the Writers' Union Feng Xuefeng, an essayist and poet who had participated in the Long March; and the poet Ai Qing. Moreover, the "Ding-Chen anti-Party group" reportedly extended its influence to the artistic sphere where is members included Jiang Feng, deputy director and Party secretary of the China Association of Artists. Thus the official denunciation focused on a group which not only had considerable literary prestige but also possessed wide experience in bureaucratic posts dealing with literature and art.[67]

Despite concerted efforts to refute various "revisionist" ideas attributed to the Ding-Chen group, advocacy of these ideas does not appear to have been the main cause of the intense attack on Ding Ling and associates. Indeed, these writers had been relatively cautious in the opinions they expressed during the "blooming and contending" period; the most outspoken writers during the spring were from the generation trained by the CCP. What seems more important is that Ding Ling and Chen Qixia symbolized the recurrent tension between Party authority and artistic creativeness and had become a cause célèbre in the Hundred Flowers period. While these writers had been involved in clashes with the Party's literary watchdogs headed by Zhou Yang since the 1940s, it was events in 1954–55 which made them centers of attention in spring 1957. In 1954–55 they resisted a Party investigation of the literary journal *Wenyi bao* over the journal's handling of a dispute concerning an eighteenth century novel, *The Dream of the Red Chamber,* an issue in which Mao had taken a personal interest. As a result of this and other disputes with the cultural hierarchy, Ding and Chen were accused of resisting Party leadership and sowing discord in literary circles. Despite initial attempts to attribute the entire problem to long standing personal conflicts with Zhou Yang's group, they finally made the appropriate self-criticisms. Although the matter was not made public at the time, in January 1955 the Writers' Union convened an enlarged meeting to condemn Ding and Chen. Subsequently Chen sought to reopen the case by going over the head of the propaganda apparatus through letters to a high Party leader. This resulted in renewed attacks on Ding and Chen at meetings held in August–September 1955 and February–March 1956. Thus these figures were in official disfavor *before* "blooming and contending" as shown by Mao's January 1957 reference to Ding Ling as someone who should be publicly disgraced.[68]

During the Hundred Flowers period demands were made for reopening specific cases, most notably Hu Feng's but also that of Ding and Chen. While Ding apparently began to speak out in small gatherings, it was generally others such as Ai Qing and especially younger writers who demanded a reexamination of the case and sharply attacked the literary bureaucrats for their role. In this manner, much as Chen had done with his letters, they attempted to distinguish between Party authority *per se* and the rule of the literary apparatus headed by Zhou Yang. These writers argued that Zhou and his henchmen had distorted Central Committee policy in dealing with their old antagonists within the literary sphere. Unfortunately for Ding and Chen, while Mao had been critical of the literary bureaucracy's performance in the past he was particularly critical of *Wenyi bao*'s role in the *Red Chamber* case. During the anti-rightist struggle the Chairman revealed a special antagonism for Ding Ling and Feng Xuefeng whom he denounced as hopeless anti-Communists. It was in this context that the Party committee of the Writers' Union convened a series of meetings in early June to denounce Ding Ling. At first she resisted and apparently won some support in literary circles. Ding and Chen reportedly planned to withdraw from the Writers' Union in anticipation that others would follow suit thereby bringing pressure on the literary authorities. By July and August, however, a more intensive round of meetings was launched against Ding and Chen followed by a campaign to discredit the revolutionary writers lasting into 1958. At the same time criticism unfolded against other dissident writers.[69]

Of all the alleged deviations of Ding, Chen, *et al.,* the most vexing was their independence. They were repeatedly charged with rejecting Party leadership, refusing to carry out official policies with which they disagreed, and treating literary organizations as independent kingdoms. Especially galling was that they acted as if Party discipline did not apply to them despite their CCP membership. As in the case of Party newspapers resisting control by the propaganda apparatus, the problem was not one of non-Party opposition to CCP authority. Instead, skilled specialists holding Party membership apparently attempted to use their political status to escape strict organizational discipline as they pursued their professional bent. Their independence was further threatening because of the considerable prestige of Ding Ling and her colleagues, especially among young writers. This combination of independent inclinations and broad prestige, in a situation as fluid as that of spring 1957, created an alternative focus of leadership which could have seriously weakened the control of the literary bureaucracy. The emphasis the Anti-Rightist Campaign placed on discrediting the "Ding-Chen anti-Party group" was designed to prevent such a development and destroy the influence of the revolutionary writers.[70]

Although criticism never reached the degree of unrelenting denunciations directed at Hu Feng in 1955, the revolutionary writers were subjected to repeated struggle meetings where all made some sort of confession. In addition, punishment generally included temporary removal from literary posts and stints of labor in villages and factories. Ding Ling was expelled from the Party as well as from her literary positions, and underwent two years of reform through labor. Moreover, her works and those of Ai Qing were banned from China's schools and universities. The younger writers, however, received more lenient treatment as their problems were considered those of ideological understanding.[71]

As in other areas, the anti-rightist struggle in literary and art circles gradually shifted emphasis from attacks on leading figures to more general indoctrination in Party cultural policies, the study of documents, and criticism and self-criticism sessions. Particular emphasis was placed on breaking down barriers between mental and manual labor and learning from workers and peasants. Measures taken included the reduction of writers' fees and their systematic dispatch to the countryside and factories for extended periods. As in education, efforts were made to strengthen political controls by transferring reliable Party cadres to literary posts. Such personnel measures were regarded as especially important since the tendency of Party organs to appease writers and artists instead of exercising strict supervision was blamed for many of the problems in literature and art.[72] Ironically, this effort to restore orthodoxy in literature not only involved reaffirmation of Soviet works as models for Chinese writers, it also to some degree paralleled Khrushchev's simultaneous crackdown on unorthodox Soviet writers[73]—all at a time when China was on the verge of a dramatic break from the Soviet economic model. This was a further indication that the Anti-Rightist Campaign, with its emphasis on organizational control, was by no means inherently linked to innovative departures from Soviet practice.

The Communist Youth League

The Anti-Rightist Campaign also had a major impact on the Communist Youth League, the organization charged with preparing young people for Party membership. Attacks on rightists within the League were common in summer 1957 and involved leading personnel from branch to Central Committee levels. The importance of the Youth League as a target was probably due to two factors. One was the League's role among students. Not only did student excesses infect Youth League members as indicated by Mao's statement that perhaps 10 percent of student members at Beida "collapsed," but some League cadres reportedly incited students to commit unruly acts. Second was the large number of rightists reported in League publications which also assertedly encouraged undesirable behavior. Together these factors suggest that League officials played an important role in the excesses of the spring.[74]

Rightists within the League were often scathing about the organization's performance. They depicted the League's work as "a mess," charged it with losing youth support, and even suggested its abolition. The fundamental cause of this situation assertedly was the organizational dominance of the Party over the League. The depth of resentment over the League's subservience was reflected in descriptions of Party-League relations as those of "the oppressor and the oppressed," refusals to carry out CCP directives, and calls for discarding the role of the Party's "assistant." Further attacks claimed the Youth League Central Committee never expressed its own opinions and always deferred to the Party Central Committee, while basic level Party organizations allegedly despised League officials. In order to break the grip of Party dominance, some rightists demanded "the League's right of independent activity," proposed that the League have projects of its own, and even advocated that the League exercise supervisory powers over the CCP and function as a coequal "second Party." This situation was hardly unique in 1957. What is striking is that the desire for independence was so deeply felt in an organization closely tied to the Party in terms of function and career expectations. As the bureaucratic system crystallized in the mid-1950s, even the most favored institutions sought to carve out spheres of relative autonomy.[75]

Another major target was League cadre policy. In part, this was a further manifestation of opposition to Party control since one objection was to cadres dispatched by the CCP to the League apparatus. More basically, as in other spheres, criticism was directed at overemphasis on political reliability at the expense of technical expertise. Attacks especially focused on old cadres and officials of worker and peasant origins who had a low cultural level, assertedly were unsuited to their posts and did nothing but eat and sleep, yet were still promoted. In obvious parody of the traditional selection criteria of "both ability and virtue," one rightist claimed the League's attitude was "without ability [a cadre] is even more virtuous." Others reportedly demanded that such incompetent cadres be overthrown, and proposals were made for genuine elections of League officials from basic to central levels.[76]

League ideological and political education also received sharp criticism. The main thrust of the rightist argument was that such education was excessively restrictive and turned young people into "robots" and "yes-men." Erroneous ideas were attributed to the naturally inadequate knowledge and understanding of the young, thus implying this could be overcome by normal processes of growth without intensive ideological efforts. In seeking a reduction of political education, rightists reportedly opposed the use of class analysis in dealing with ideological problems and even opposed the study of Marxism-Leninism within the League. These views reflected a broader feeling that class struggle had ceased and political life could be safely depressurized, and thus could be linked to official analyses of the new situation following the victory of socialist transformation.[77]

Many Youth League organizations apparently were seriously infected with rightist personnel and attitudes. The presence of rightists reportedly caused League organizations to be dissolute and lax, and in some cases League branches disintegrated because of their activities. Moreover, the response of Youth League leaders to rightist attacks was often weak and uncertain. Some League personnel reportedly believed that to attack rightists would violate the spirit of the Hundred Flowers, other dismissed the problem of rightist views as minor ideological questions, and still others applauded rightists within the League and shielded them from criticism.[78] While some of this behavior could be attributed to official encouragement of "blooming and contending" before late May, manifestations continued well into the Anti-Rightist Campaign suggesting a disturbing unreliability within the organization charged with training future Party members. And although the evidence is largely impressionistic, it seems that there was far greater sympathy in the Youth League with its large student membership than within the CCP rank and file for the now disgraced bourgeois rightists.

Despite official claims that "rightists form a very small number within . . . the Youth League," it is clear that the impact of rightist views was much wider. In Bi county, Sichuan, 5 to 8 percent of Youth League cadres reportedly had "right leaning thought," while the figure for League members as a whole was 10 to 25 percent. The struggle reached the Youth League Central Committee where it not only resulted in the dismissal of Chen Mo, deputy chief editor of *Zhongguo qingnian bao,* but also of alternate member Dong Xuelong, deputy secretary of the Yunnan Youth League Provincial Committee. Rightists in other responsible positions in provincial and municipal League organizations were also reported with some frequency. Thus while the precise contours of the anti-rightist struggle in the Youth League are unclear, it appears that both a significant proportion of the membership and some middle and high ranking officials were directly affected. Although Mao called for League as well as Party rectification by "gentle breeze and mild rain" methods, it seems the anti-rightist effort had a much deeper impact on the Youth League than on the Party. The youth body apparently could not defuse the discontent of its student members and had to pay the price for its organizational failures.[79]

Political and Legal Organs

According to Mao, rightists created chaotic conditions in political and legal organs on a national scale. The Chairman apparently first drew attention to problems in the sensitive area of the courts, procuracies and judicial departments at the Qingdao conference in July 1957, although the highest ranking officials affected were not dealt with until late in the year.[80]

Those criticized and disciplined during the anti-rightist struggle in political and legal departments included a variety of types—retained personnel from GMD judicial organs, non-Party cadres, ordinary Party cadres, and responsible Party officials. As in other areas, the most serious problems concerned non-Party people; most rightists reportedly were retained personnel. Nevertheless, despite assertions that problems generally had not penetrated the most important leadership posts, leading Party cadres of courts, procuracies and judicial departments at the county, municipal and provincial levels were involved. At the national level, the main Party rightists were Jia Qian, president of the criminal section of the Supreme People's Court, Zhu Yaotang, vice president of the criminal section, Lu Mingjian, director of the research office of the Supreme People's Court, Liu Huizhi, deputy chief procurator of the railway and water transport procuracy, and Wang Lizhong, director of the first office of the transport procuracy. In addition, an unnamed Vice Minister of Justice and the entire Party fraction of the ministry were criticized for rightist ideas.[81]

A basic theme of attacks on political and legal rightists was that excessive leniency had developed in the handling of both political and criminal cases, a tendency which Mao cited as the main deviation at Qingdao.[m] This was seen in light sentences for counterrevolutionaries, premature release of convicted criminals, and emphasizing education and reform divorced from punishment. A concrete example concerned a municipal judge who assertedly failed to detect the "counterrevolutionary motives" involved in a case of writing "down with the Communist Party" in a public toilet. Criticism of rightism linked such cases to the more general view that class struggle had ended, the suppression of counterrevolutionaries was no longer a primary task, and mass mobilization methods should not be used to fight criminals. Such attitudes were clearly encouraged

[m] Anti-rightist criticism was linked to the reversal of "overly lenient" judicial decisions and a new intensification of the continuing *sufan* movement. For about a month from late July 1957 media reports emphasized armed counterrevolutionary activity which assertedly drew inspiration from rightist attacks on the CCP. New stiff penalties including capital punishment were imposed. See NCNA, Xining, July 24, 1957, in *SCMP,* No. 1585; *RMRB,* August 16, 1957, in *SCMP,* No. 1602; NCNA, Hefei, September 13, 1957, in *SCMP,* No. 1616; and *PDA,* pp. 300, 351.

both by the overall relaxation of 1956–early 1957 and by lenient measures adopted in political and legal work in this period. Moreover, the emphasis on "contradictions among the people" which had been the core of Mao's spring analysis apparently contributed to rightist tendencies. Many political and legal cadres reportedly feared confusing such contradictions with "contradictions with the enemy" and as a result didn't enforce the law.[82]

Related to these deviations was advocacy of legal concepts taken over from Western and GMD practice. Under the slogan of "the science of the law," rightists reportedly pushed such basic Western concepts as "the benefit of the doubt" and "innocent until proven guilty." Moreover, they regarded pre-1949 laws as having the "backing and experience of decades" and allegedly consulted GMD codes "to find bases for exonerating counterrevolutionaries." Attitudes derived from Western concepts also had major implications for the principle of Party leadership. Thus Jia Qian and others in the Supreme People's Court allegedly advocated "the independence of the judiciary" and "independent judgment." Party leadership was held applicable only to making laws and not in adjudication. Moreover, leading rightists assertedly regarded Party committee members as "ignorant of the law" and unsuited for judicial leadership. These views were also linked to problems of organizational discipline: rightists in the Supreme People's Court allegedly resisted both central directives and decisions of the court's Party fraction; certain high level political and legal institutes were unresponsive to central warnings about employing legal personnel from the old regime; and the deputy director and Party secretary of the Anhui judicial department joined forces with non-Party officials to oppose Party directives.[83]

Thus leading rightists in political and legal departments resemble Ding Ling *et al.* in the literary sphere: they saw themselves primarily as legal specialists rather than Party cadres. Although Party members they apparently used that status to avoid complying to authoritative CCP bodies and joined the more numerous non-Party rightists in claiming professional autonomy. In this respect, the tension between professionalism and Party control in political and legal work was yet another by-product of the effort since 1956 to encourage contributions by trained experts to national development.[n]

Developments in the Countryside

Although the Anti-Rightist Campaign focused on urban areas, CCP leaders also came to grips with rural problems in summer 1957. This was due to two factors:

[n] In another respect, rightist views had implications for the Great leap Forward, a fact which perhaps explains the handling of major cases *after* the fall 1957 plenum. This concerned reported efforts of leading rightists to impose centralized vertical leadership on the transport procuracy, thus undercutting the role of local Party committees emphasized by the Great Leap strategy. *RMRB*, December 20, 1957, in *SCMP*, No. 1687. The issue was drawn more sharply in the case of the Ministry of Supervision (see Chapter 8).

developments growing out of the general relaxation of 1956–57, and poor agricultural performance. As we saw in Chapter 6, adjustment of the new APCs was one of the items on the agenda after the success of cooperativization, and considerable criticism was directed at APC mismanagement and the crude methods of rural cadres. Mao complained in his "Contradictions" speech that this had grown into a "small typhoon," while in January 1957 he noted that some ministers and many cadres shared a bleak view of the new collective institutions. Despite Mao's February defense of the APCs, further challenges to the cooperatives appeared in the Hundred Flowers period.[84]

Equally significant was worsening economic conditions in the Chinese countryside. The poor agricultural year of 1956 was followed by an even slower growth rate in 1957. A particular cause of concern was a severe grain supply crisis resulting from the lag in food grain output behind the rate of population increase. In August Party leaders initiated several measures to cope with the situation. One step was a modest increase in total state investment in agriculture reflecting a heightened awareness of the importance of the agricultural sector for overall economic growth. Another important measure was a State Council decision to clamp down on the rural free market, thus increasing state control over the grain supply and strengthening the collective sector generally. These steps were linked to the rectification of tendencies which had appeared since 1956. At the Qingdao conference in July Mao declared his support for "a directive to be issued at once by the Central Committee to initiate a large scale socialist education movement among the entire rural population to criticize right opportunist ideas within the Party, the departmentalism of certain cadres and the capitalist and individualist ideas of well-to-do middle peasants, and to strike at the counterrevolutionary activities of landlords and rich peasants." Only with such tendencies brought under control could the state firmly reassert its command over China's grain resources.[85]

The Hundred Flowers and Rural Deviations

Peasant dissatisfaction was shown by substantial withdrawals from APCs in the winter and spring of 1956–57—e.g., 117,916 peasant households in Guangdong province alone. The Hundred Flowers experiment reportedly led to a further deterioration of the situation. Although peasants were not mobilized to "bloom and contend," rightist criticism of CCP rural policies allegedly emboldened landlords, rich peasants and counterrevolutionaries to engage in a variety of disruptive activities. These elements, "feeling their time had come," assertedly engaged in agitation against Party policies, beating up cadres, poisoning livestock and destroying seeds, threatening peasants, promoting superstitious beliefs, seeking to regain land and houses lost during land reform, and organizing counterrevolutionary groups to stage riots. A similar picture—minus the imputation of landlord culpability—was given by a refugee source: "A few of the more brutal cadres were attacked and torn to pieces by angry [peasant] mobs. Cadres who had been arrogant were driven out with pitchforks. Government granaries were forced open and the hungry peasants ate adequately for the first time in years." In the official interpretation, an alliance existed between bourgeois rightists and rural dissidents, but the only apparent connection was the encouragement these dissidents received from intellectual attacks on the regime. Generally such encouragement was derived from press and radio reports, although in some cases rightist activity at the county level was reported.[86]

Even more basic to the deteriorating rural situation was "spontaneous capitalism" *(zibenzhuyi zifa qingxiang)* and other backward tendencies among the peasants. This included further withdrawals from APCs, decentralizing cooperative responsibility to individual households, demands for more money and grain from the state, selling less surplus grain and other major agricultural products to the state, and speculative activities. Much of this behavior was ascribed to "ideologically wavering" upper middle peasants, but it was also recognized that a less narrowly defined "part of the peasantry" was guilty of "individualism and group exclusiveness which disregard national and collective interests." While agitation by landlords and rich peasants was cited as one cause of these developments, more general factors were the "inevitable" problems of new APCs and the slackening of political and ideological education following the high tide of cooperativization. Since spring 1956 efforts had focused on the economic front and official policies made many concessions to individual peasant interests. As a result the political awareness of many peasants assertedly declined and they began to feel the "two road struggle" between capitalism and socialism was over. These lax political circumstances were undoubtedly exacerbated by the new currents from urban areas during the Hundred Flowers. In this context, increasingly vigorous assertion of peasant interests was indeed inevitable.[87]

Most disturbing was the considerable involvement of rural cadres and Party members in deviant behavior. Widespread political lethargy assertedly infected cadres who were both confused by the utterances of urban intellectuals and influenced by dissatisfied peasants. In some cases they not only shared peasant views on the superiority of independent farming but also openly aired peasant grievances including the "egalitarian" *(pingjunzhuyi)* notion that peasants were getting a raw deal compared to workers.[o] Moreover, some cadres actively participated in speculation and themselves withdrew from APCs. Especially serious was cadres concealing or underestimating grain output. This practice involving

[o] Earlier, in January 1957, Mao cited a survey in Jiangsu showing that "in some places 30 percent of the cadres at the county, district and [administrative village] levels made complaints on behalf of the peasants." Mao attributed this to the fact that most of the cadres concerned were themselves well-to-do peasants with surplus grain to sell. *SW,* V, 357.

cadres from APC to county levels reflected departmentalist attitudes which placed peasant interests above state interests. In some cases it also reflected fear of peasant disturbances if demands for more grain were not met. Thus cadre rightism in the countryside involved both sympathy for peasant interests and a lack of confidence in their own ability to lead the masses. While most cadres reportedly only suffered from inadequate ideological awareness, a small number of class dissidents who seriously violated law and discipline assertedly held cadre posts at county, district and administrative village levels.[88]

The Rural Socialist Education Movement

In mid-summer 1957 socialist education was launched to combat the above tendencies in coordination with cadre rectification at the district and administrative village level. The movement centered on a "two road debate" over the comparative virtues of socialism and capitalism. This closely guided debate focused on a number of areas where "erroneous" ideas flourished: the evaluation of APCs and the planned purchase and supply system; the relations of the individual, collective and state; the relations of workers and peasants and of urban and rural areas generally; and the results of the campaign to suppress counterrevolutionaries. These issues had all figured in the urban criticism of the spring and apparently also raised substantial doubts among the peasants. In October Mao estimated that 10 percent of the peasantry opposed socialism, cooperatives, and planned purchase and supply, but that through socialist education all but 2 percent of the people could be won over to the Party's side.[89]

The guiding principles for rural socialist education were relatively mild and apparently the movement was less intense than the urban Anti-Rightist Campaign. Crude or violent methods were prohibited although excesses did occur in some areas. As a general rule, the use of anti-rightist slogans or rightist labels was prohibited among the peasantry, and only a small portion were to be subjected to criticism and self-criticism. Upper middle peasants were to be educated and united with and not treated as landlords or rich peasants. A combination of education and economic penalties was used to curb withdrawals from APCs and capitalist tendencies. However, a certain harshness appeared in handling offending landlords and rich peasants, and arrests of these elements undoubtedly instilled fear in wider circles of peasants. The combination of these approaches seemingly was successful in checking deviant tendencies and resulted in an upsurge of selling grain to the state, peasants retracting demands for increased food and clothing, and the return of peasants who had withdrawn from APCs.[90]

A major aim of socialist education was the rectification of Party members and cadres and overhaul of Party branches in conjunction with APC overhaul. By rectifying cadre work style CCP leaders attempted to improve cadre-peasant relations, thus reaffirming one of the original goals of the 1957 movement. Here, as with the treatment of ordinary peasants, Party guidelines emphasized leniency. According to a September directive on APC overhaul, cadres with minor shortcomings were not to receive disciplinary punishment and those guilty of serious mistakes were still given the chance to mend their ways. Nevertheless, a Guangdong report that APC Party organs had purged 3 percent of their members and Youth League organs 8 percent suggests a more severe process than that indicated by the guiding principles of the movement. Moreover, the stipulation that APCs should guarantee the predominance of poor and lower middle peasants in leading posts may have led to significant leadership changes—particularly in the 10 to 20 percent of cooperatives judged to be performing below par. Finally, one analyst relying heavily on interview data concluded that under the rubric of persuasive appeals considerable coercion was directed at targets selected as "negative examples" to illustrate the "two road debate." This in turn created considerable tension among cadres and peasants alike.[91]

In contrast to the anti-rightist struggle in urban units, the rural socialist education movement was implemented through work teams. While methods varied by locality, work teams generally conducted experiments in key point villages in August and early September before additional teams extended it throughout the countryside in September and October. The work teams included not only high level provincial leaders, cadres from the special district, county and district levels, as well as young intellectuals, students and recent graduates from the cities, but also administrative village cadres. These *xiang* cadres, who received special training along with cadres from higher levels at conferences convened from the special district to administrative village levels, provided an important local component to the teams conducting the movement in September and October. While still outsiders to the APCs, they undoubtedly had close links with the cooperative power structure. At Qingdao, moreover, Mao ordered that rectification was to be "conducted by the local cadres with the assistance of work teams sent from above." Yet the role of the work teams led by higher level, outside cadres was crucial. As in past rural movements such higher level leadership was necessary given the lower proportion of Party members and more lax political life in the countryside than the cities.[92]

In summer 1957 the use of work teams also reflected the seriousness of the problems involved. Despite official assertions that there were fewer opponents of socialism in rural than urban areas, the deviations which exacerbated the grain crisis could not be left to local cadres for their solution. Moreover, the central importance of cadre rectification suggests the campaign could not have been entrusted solely to the regular chain of command. Although the conduct of the movement minimized the threat to local leaders (see below), necessary leadership changes, especially in the most backward APCs, required some degree of outside intervention. While urban Party leaders could be expected to carry out anti-rightist measures directed primarily at non-Party critics, rural leaders undoubtedly were less enthusiastic about purging the ranks of cadres and Party members which formed the backbone of local political power. The general considerations raised concerning work teams in Chapter 2, despite their non-applicability in cases of non-Party urban groups, held for rural socialist education in 1957.[93]

During the implementation of the socialist education movement the three-cornered relationship among work teams, local cadres and village peasants which had played such a dynamic role in 1948 reappeared but in significantly altered form. As in 1948, upon arrival in a village work teams consulted with poor peasants in order to learn about local conditions. Moreover, when discussions were organized, at first only poor peasants were allowed to speak. But in contrast to 1948, and reflecting Mao's Qingdao emphasis on the role of local cadres, work teams also consulted leading local cadres and such cadres participated in setting up debates and selecting targets. The work teams did not assume a deep conflict of interests between cadres and the village masses. Nor were there reports of teams "kicking aside" local Party branches as had been the case in 1948 and, to a lesser extent, in 1951–54. Rather than a sharp dichotomy between local leaders and poor peasants, the official analysis guiding the work teams depicted both groups as basically sound but containing some elements which had either degenerated or wavered under the pressures of spontaneous capitalism. Thus both groups, with the prodding of the teams, could uncover both dissidents within their own ranks and more numerous dissident elements among higher peasant strata. While peasants were granted the right to criticize cadres, this does not appear to have happened except under tightly controlled conditions. Indeed, at Qingdao Mao had declared the need to reject any "bad" opinions which surfaced during criticism.[94]

The basic difference was that in 1948 rectification was aimed at cadre behavior believed fundamentally antagonistic to land reform and the majority of the rural population, while in 1957 socialist education was aimed at behavior damaging the cooperative system which was found *in varying degree* in all peasant strata. In the latter case, although cadres were also prone to deviations, they were the rural group whose interests were most closely linked to the collective sector. Thus a major aim of socialist education was to restore cadre authority *vis-à-vis* peasants generally as an integral part of the effort to bolster socialism in the countryside. The emphasis on increased cadre authority despite the use of work teams indicates not only that the lesson of 1948 concerning the need to maintain cadre morale was still recognized, but also that the implications of the new interest structure in the collectivized countryside were well understood by Party leaders. Mao and his colleagues had failed to assess properly the interests of urban cadres in the spring, but they steadfastly avoided a similar error in shaping rural rectification in the summer.

Conclusion

By mid-May 1957 the top CCP leadership embarked on a reassessment which culminated in the Anti-Rightist Campaign. Mao himself, the chief architect of "blooming and contending," again was in the forefront formulating the new line. The Chairman issued the secret inner Party circular of May 15 warning of the need to turn the CCP's attention to fighting revisionism. His remarks upholding socialism ten days later were quickly spread to China's troubled student community. And various subsequent measures—the concoction of the "Zhang-Luo Alliance," the attack on the very papers Mao had praised in April, the assault on Ding Ling, and the unfolding of rural socialist education—all showed signs of the Chairman's own hand. Mao's about-face undoubtedly smoothed over whatever differences may have existed concerning the Hundred Flowers experiment within the Politburo. Moreover, it now relieved considerable anxieties among leading and ordinary cadres at all levels who joined enthusiastically in the counterattack on the rightists.

With the anti-rightist struggle rectification increasingly took on features of "coercive persuasion." The coercive and persuasive aspects tended to focus on different targets: sharp and intense struggle was sanctioned for ideologically suspect bourgeois intellectuals, while educational measures were applied within the Party as well as to broad population groups such as workers and peasants. Within the category of bourgeois intellectuals, particularly important struggle targets were singled out on the basis of their real or imagined roles during the Hundred Flowers period. Thus leaders of democratic parties who had taken the lead in the spring forums served as convenient scapegoats around which the movement could be organized. The press, which had both demonstrated independent tendencies and had been a vehicle for spreading unorthodox views, albeit largely in accord with official policy, was once again brought under stringent control. And students, whose violent actions deeply shocked Party leaders, received harsh sanctions such as reform through labor. While severe measures focused on such groups, coercion tended to have a spill over effect on the population as a whole due to the atmosphere generated by the Anti-Rightist Campaign.

In certain respects, the situation in mid-1957 was not ripe for a more coercive approach. Apart from the mobilization accompanying the anti-rightist drive itself, China did not enter a mobilization phase. The policies outlined by Zhou Enlai in June maintained the basic moderation which had existed since mid-1956. Moreover, in mid-1957 the international situation remained basically calm; no major external threats existed to support the shift towards coercion.[p] Clearly, then, the sole factor was the internal political threat generated by the

[p] In one respect, however, the situation did change. The reaction of the GMD authorities to anti-American riots on Taiwan in May 1957 indicated a strengthening of the GMD-US alliance and therefore a failure of CCP efforts to obtain a negotiated reunion of Taiwan and the mainland. Since the CCP approach depended to a large degree on the moderate image projected by the policies of 1956 and early 1957, the failure of that approach removed a possible—though clearly very secondary—inhibiting factor to the greater use of coercion. See MacFarquhar, *Origins 1*, pp. 299–301.

events of the spring. While these events, notwithstanding student demonstrations and peasant discontent, posed no real danger to the survival of the regime, they did threaten the elaborate system of Party direction over all spheres of life. A significant degree of coercion was sanctioned to end that threat.

Coercive measures notwithstanding, throughout the Anti-Rightist Campaign the "gentle breeze and mild rain" approach Mao had advocated since late 1956 continued to be emphasized as the guiding principle of inner Party rectification. Clearly Party cadres were viewed as basically sound; moreover, as the beneficiaries of the anti-rightist struggle they were eminently persuadable of the new line. To a certain degree, furthermore, Party figures received preferential treatment when caught by the sudden policy shift. Thus leading Party journalists such as Deng Tuo received mild rebukes for promoting "blooming and contending" in contrast to the onslaught against the non-Party press. By established organizational principles they could not be held culpable for implementing Mao's wishes, but the same protection did not extend equally to non-Party newsmen.

In some cases, however, sterner measures were invoked against Party members. These cases all concerned situations where CCP cadres challenged Party organizational control. Those Party members who were labeled rightists had expressed the same doubts as bourgeois rightists outside the Party about CCP competence to lead various specialized areas, thus emphasizing their professional roles rather than their place in the vanguard of the proletariat. Moreover, in many cases they assertedly violated organizational discipline: editors of municipal papers rejected the authority of the local propaganda authorities; Party branches in universities "collapsed" in the spring and Youth League organs continued to encourage intellectual criticism *after* the anti-rightist struggle was launched; court cadres rejected Party fraction decisions in the name of judicial independence; and Ding Ling *et al.* engaged in a running battle with the Party's cultural hierarchy. Finally, in rural areas where Party rectification tended to involve a somewhat greater degree of tension and purging than suggested by official guidelines, the role of Party cadres in concealing grain and other serious deviations not only raised questions of organizational discipline, it was also a major threat to CCP control of the countryside at a time of stagnating agricultural production.

When the Third Plenum met in September–October 1957, Party leaders took a basically optimistic view of the results of rectification and the anti-rightist struggle. While Mao declared the need for regular rectification each year to avoid recurrence of the "queer arguments" of the spring, he saw the efforts of the summer as having resulted in a fundamental victory on the political and ideological front. Essentially, this was a victory restoring the leading role of the Party organization. As Mao indicated, this was still compatible with a major role for professional specialists under firm Party leadership.[95] Clearly, it was also compatible with a centralized, highly articulated Party and state bureaucracy and moderate economic policies. The Third Plenum, however, saw new currents which not only introduced a radical approach to economic development, but challenged many vested interests and existing procedures of official institutions. As these developments took hold in late 1957 and 1958, further rectification efforts were required which now brought the bureaucracy, higher ranking officials, and traditional Party norms under threat.

PART III

The Norms Under Stress: Rectification and Purging, 1957–1965

8
Rectification and the Great Leap Forward

The Third Plenum in fall 1957 marked a fundamental turning point in the history of the PRC. This meeting saw the first steps towards new economic policies which emerged as the Great Leap Forward in 1958, an unprecedented developmental strategy breaking decisively from the Soviet model.[a] The new strategy inevitably involved basic changes in organizational relationships and methods. A far-reaching administrative decentralization and a more fluid work style were decreed, measures which upset long standing interests within and without the CCP. Moreover, the departure from the Soviet model which had been the basis of the policy consensus of the previous eight years injected a new note of dissent into higher Party councils. This, in turn, resulted in rectification and purging now increasingly involving high ranking officials and their *policy views,* a development ominous for an open decision making process. Moreover, despite Mao's continued advocacy of "gentle breeze and mild rain" methods, rectification within the Party took on more coercive overtones.

While the Great Leap Forward was basically a response to China's declining economic growth rate, it also reflected a basically positive assessment of the overall situation in fall 1957. Now Mao not only declared "the success of the socialist revolution in the political and ideological fields," but by spring 1958 prophesied "there probably won't be more than a few more rounds in the strug-

[a] Although Mao called for study of the Draft Program for Agricultural Development (see the following note, below) at the July Qingdao conference, moderate economic policies were still dominant a week before the Third Plenum. At that time the Central Committee issued directives scaling down the size of APCs and emphasizing material incentives to bolster agricultural production. While there were still contradictory signals at the plenum, it did revive several key aspects of the early 1956 leap forward including the draft program. According to Mao in 1958, "The Third Plenum gave . . . a clearer direction. After[wards] we had the Great Leap Forward." *SW,* V, 482; *MMT,* I, 117; and *PDA,* pp. 16–18.

gle between the two roads." CCP leaders, moreover, now argued that political victories could be translated into a fundamental economic breakthrough. Thus at the Third Plenum, similar to his unconvincing claim that the "anti-reckless advance" of 1956 brought about the rightism of 1957, Mao advanced the equally unpersuasive view that the success of rectification and the anti-rightist struggle gave a big push to peasant enthusiasm for the now revived Draft Program for Agricultural Development.[b] More broadly, Mao soon saw the "clarification of our problems" in 1957 as unleashing unprecedented zeal for production and development, thus creating the circumstances for "permanent revolution" *(buduan geming)* where "the emphasis in the Party's work [would shift] to the technical revolution."[1]

As we argued in Chapter 7, however, the political victory of the Anti-Rightist Campaign was essentially one of Party organizational control, a victory not necessarily linked to a radical economic strategy. Indeed, the restoration of controls substantially following Soviet bureaucratic patterns was more compatible with the FFYP approach. The Great Leap, involving unprecedented economic targets, simultaneous growth of the traditional and modern sectors, "self-reliance" *(zili gengsheng)* on local resources, and massive labor mobilization accomplished by organizational and ideological measures,[2] had quite different ramifications. The leap forward necessitated organization shorn of bureaucracy that could be linked directly to the people, the motive force of the new strategy. In work methods *ad hoc* adaptation to rapidly changing circumstances was preferred to careful planning. Only leaders acting without rigid preconceived notions would be able to combine effectively with and give shape to the creativity of the masses—and this could be better provided by local Party cadres whose skills were substantially organizational than by remote planners in Beijing. The imperatives of mass mobilization, together with the leap's stress on maximum use of local resources, led to a major decentralization in late 1957 and 1958. Under the principle of "centralized policy and divided management," the leaders in Beijing retained control over both general policy and economic targets, but vast administrative powers were ceded by the central government to provincial and lower level authorities.[3] This in turn placed a premium on disciplined policy implementation by local leaders, and rectification quickly became a key method to assure that discipline. By late 1957 the movement was both attacking policy views skeptical of the Great Leap and removing individual leaders whose organizational reliability was in question. As rectification continued in 1958 its aims were inseparable from those of the Great Leap Forward.

---

[b] The draft program which set ambitious targets for rural development was originally promulgated in January 1956 but was quietly shelved a few months later as dislocations became apparent. The Third Plenum endorsed a slightly revised version of the program, and with it the mass mobilization approach which was so central to the Great Leap. See *PDA*, pp. 18, 119–26.

Although divisions existed from the outset at the highest possible level with the apparent doubts of Party Vice Chairman Chen Yun (see below), a strong majority formed within the leadership behind the new approach. Mao himself, as with the Hundred Flowers earlier, again was clearly the critical figure pushing forward an innovative program. The Chairman received vigorous support from other key Party leaders, most notably Liu Shaoqi.[c] Moreover, although skepticism remained at high levels as the leap forward unfolded, its illusionary successes in 1958 contributed to further support and optimism. This resulted in no small measure of national pride; Mao claimed China's policies were achieving a faster rate of growth than Russia and saw the CCP "enriching Lenin's mass line."[d] Despite a new concern with inner Party splits, it also reaffirmed Mao's basic confidence in his leadership colleagues and the Party as a whole. Thus in January 1958 the Chairman took another step toward an orderly succession by announcing his intention to give up the chairmanship of the state, a post which would fall to Liu.[4] Similarly, throughout the coming year Mao continued to voice support for traditional rectification principles. But a process eroding these principles was already under way.

From Rectification and Improvement to Opposing Right Conservatism

While the anti-rightist struggle continued in various units, the Third Plenum marked a shift back to the original aim of rectification—correcting shortcomings in Party and government performance. This return to the larger goals of the spring, together with the reendorsement of such measures as "blooming and contending" and wall posters, did not, however, mean a revival of the Hundred Flowers approach. The new stage of rectification and improvement *(zhenggai)* which unfolded from the central to county levels did not solicit criticisms from intellectuals *per se* but was limited to cadres within specific departments where

[c] Although some analysts have viewed Liu as a moderating force during the Great Leap, the best evidence suggests he collaborated closely with Mao in shaping the strategy and vigorously pushed its implementation in 1958. Indeed, Cultural Revolution sources basically attack Liu and other Party leaders for a " 'left' in form but right in essence" ploy of reckless implementation of leap forward principles. E.g., see *Nongye jixie jishu* [Agricultural Machinery Techniques], September 18, 1967, in *SCMM,* No. 610.

[d] *SXWS,* II, 161–62, 206. Ironically, relations with the Soviet Union *improved* following Chinese support for Soviet leadership of the socialist camp at the November 1957 Moscow meetings at the very time the Great Leap began to take shape. In spring 1958 Mao declared the camp was "firmly united" and cited Khrushchev as the kind of cadre with local experience needed for the leap. *Ibid.,* pp. 173, 198. Moreover, the Great Leap probably drew encouragement from Soviet economic decentralization measures and increased attention to agriculture, as well as from the Russian earth satellite and missile breakthroughs which led Mao to conclude "the East wind prevails over the West wind." See *PDA,* pp. 19, 390–91; and MacFarquhar, *Origins 1,* p. 317.

views were expressed in forums tightly controlled by unit leaders. Given the events of the spring, the problem was not one of preventing a repetition of unbridled criticism but of overcoming inhibitions. As both Mao and Liu Shaoqi noted, many unit leaders were unwilling to promote rectification for fear of disruption, while ordinary cadres held back due to possible reprisals.[5]

The response to these problems was cautious. Leading cadres such as Party secretaries of ministries were ordered to assume personal leadership of rectification and engage in self-criticism. While ostensibly encouraging "blooming and contending," this undoubtedly moderated the whole process by placing it firmly in the hands of the established chain of command. Moreover, in encouraging ordinary cadres to express themselves leadership control was assured by officially sanctioned practices of organizing debates around designated topics and guiding criticisms to important problems. The non-disruptive emphasis of the new stage was also seen in the pragmatic, unit orientated nature of the shortcomings examined. Specific administrative arrangements, inefficiencies in production management, problems of cadre work style, and staff grievances were the major types of issues discussed. While some redress for grievances—e.g., the reduction of individual working hours—was granted, the basic guideline of no compromise with excessive demands further served to bolster the authority of unit leaders. In addition, those found guilty of serious defects of work style apparently were only required to make public self-examinations, thereby limiting tension. Thus the conduct of rectification and improvement, which was not to affect daily work or production, conformed to the persuasive, controlled pattern of the traditional approach.[6]

Although the rectification and improvement stage initially was not tied to the implementation of the Great Leap,[e] by the end of 1957 its emphasis had shifted to one of bolstering the new economic strategy. As one official statement put it in early 1958, "Rectification ... must be adapted to the needs of production." The heart of the new emphasis was criticism of right conservatism. As early as November 1957 rectification became concerned with eliminating right conserva-

[e] One feature of this stage, however, already fit closely with the leap forward strategy: organizational retrenchment and the *xiafang* of cadres. Measures already undertaken in late 1956 and 1957 had resulted in the downward transfer of 300,000 cadres, and the Third Plenum prescribed further retrenchment on a more systematic basis. By February 1958 the total number of cadres sent to production or lower level leadership posts reached 1.3 million, and in spring 1958 another million cadres were dispatched for a year's labor. Considerable retrenchment was achieved: various reports claimed 30 to 50 percent of provincial personnel were sent down, while 10 to 20 percent was reported for the county level. The result was not only to simplify higher level organs as decentralization required, but to provide the basic level leadership capabilities and modernizing skills necessitated by self-reliance. See *ZZXX*, November 13, 1957, in *ECMM*, No. 117; *RMRB*, November 17, 1957, in *SCMP*, No. 1657; *Dazhong ribao* [Masses Daily] (Jinan), January 22, 1958, in *SCMP*, No. 1723; NCNA, Beijing, February 23, 1958, in *SCMP*, No. 1724; and Lee, *"Hsia Fang,"* pp. 43–47.

tive ideas and implanting instead leap forward thinking. As output targets rose these objectives became more pronounced. The attack was against any opinions which questioned the feasibility or desirability of Great Leap policies, any views which expressed preference for a slower and less risky pace of development. Thus as far as ordinary cadres were concerned rectification was no longer, as it had been during the anti-rightist struggle, directed against attitudes concerning Party rule *per se,* but now focused on views concerning a particular set of policies. Mao underlined the need for the new emphasis in March 1958 when he stated only a few million people out of a total population of 600 million and 12 million Party members felt the economic policies were correct compared to many more who doubted those policies.[7]

Among the ideas denounced as right conservative were: "production cannot make rapid advances in mountainous areas, low lying areas, sand and alkaline areas"; "agricultural production can only advance step by step and may not take a leap"; and "we cannot leap forward, need not leap forward, and dare not leap forward." Cadres were criticized for underestimating production potential and overestimating difficulties, believing that one is guilty of subjectivism only when running ahead of reality and not when lagging behind, and ignoring the urgent desire of the masses to change their backward conditions. Arguments that local conditions made high targets and rapid development unattainable, and officials who relied excessively on higher levels for funds and resources despite the Great Leap emphasis on self-reliance were also criticized. Another troublesome tendency was fear of chaos and mistakes if all out efforts were made. Thus the so-called "doctrine of the mean" appeared: one is better off not to strive for the top as long as one is not backward. Clearly such misgivings were due to past experiences with rapid growth policies which were subsequently reversed. As cadres in Fujian reportedly put it, "We were very vigorous in the first half of 1956 and were censured in the second half of the year. This year we're asked to be even more vigorous. Is there a bigger censure waiting?"[8]

In January 1958 the CCP officially declared opposition to waste the central feature of rectification and improvement. Shortly thereafter, conservatism was added as a major target and a movement against waste and conservatism *(fan lanfei, fan baoshou yundong),* also known as the Double Anti Campaign *(shuangfan yundong),* unfolded over the next two to three months. The linkage of rectification and the Great Leap was explicit in the characterization of the new movement as "a socialist campaign for a leap forward in production and culture, and a campaign of decisive importance to the improvement of state work and the entire people's vigor during rectification." This link was further seen in the campaign's focus on the waste of investment funds at a time when overall investment was rapidly increasing. It criticized departmentalist attitudes as manifested in overstocking materials, unplanned recruitment of temporary workers, and other measures emphasizing one's own unit at the expense of the whole. A concerted attack on such problems assertedly could save 20 to 25 percent in capital construction investment funds urgently needed for large scale socialist construction. Moreover, this attack on waste and conservatism was different from earlier production increase and austerity movements in that its aims extended beyond eliminating waste and overfulfilling quotas and involved a struggle against "all backward phenomena in the ideological, political, and economic fields." These aims too were consistent with the Great Leap strategy which called for basic changes in attitudes and behavior as well as production gains.[9]

One aspect of the Double Anti Campaign was opposition to "one sided attention to technical work." During the frantic construction of the leap forward such ideas as making technical considerations central and declaring Party activities illegal during periods of administrative work reportedly were common. In combating these tendencies the movement emphasized the primacy of politics and Party committee leadership, both essential aspects of the Great Leap approach. Another theme of the Double Anti Campaign concerned the proper attitude toward plans and regulations. According to the official view, the leap forward inevitably disturbed previous economic balances and plans and resulted in smashing established rules and regulations. Such developments were seen as positive phenomena; views stressing rigid adherence to established plans and regulations were denounced. Instead, emphasis was placed on the need to seek new balances and revise "irrational" rules and systems which shackled popular initiative and the growth of productive forces. This faithfully reflected Mao's January 1958 "Sixty Articles on Work Methods," particularly the section on revising or abolishing regulations as conditions changed—a section apparently drafted by Liu Shaoqi. Although various notes of caution were articulated—e.g., "outdated" economic rules could be broken but "necessary" ones should be preserved—the predominant theme was the need to throw off prior restraints and continually readjust to a situation of dynamic change. Thus the aims of rectification had virtually fused with those of the Great Leap Forward. As the movement entered its concluding stage,[f] not only were the themes of rectification debates consistent with Great Leap strategies, but these debates were explicitly organized with Great Leap plans and targets in mind.[10]

Despite repeated statements since the Third Plenum emphasizing unity toward

[f]The final stage of studying documents and self-examination began at central and provincial levels several months behind schedule in May-June 1958 and concluded by July-August in most central units. The close ties to the leap forward in this stage were seen in its study of the May 1958 Party Congress documents detailing the new economic policies, and in "discussions of the abstract" and debates on being both "red and expert." The former discussions emphasized a dialectical approach constantly seeking a new equilibrium on the basis of expanded production, while the "red and expert debates" asserted the primacy of politics. In addition, throughout 1958 "all people rectification" was fully realized as socialist education was now extended to virtually all groups in society. See NCNA, Beijing, January 23, May 21, 26, June 16, 1958, in *SCMP,* Nos. 1701, 1787, 1797; *RMRB,* July 4, 1958, in *SCMP,* No. 1811; and *PDA,* p. 419.

comrades and the traditional "save the patient" approach, as rectification developed in 1958 signs of increasing coercion became apparent. In part, this was a by-product of the intense mobilization accompanying the Great Leap. According to a resident of China at the time, great tension was created by drives to "weed out doubtful elements" among the population, a process affecting workers and Party members as well as those of suspect backgrounds. This effort, which led to attacks on matters derived from the still continuing anti-rightist struggle as well as on production shortcomings, reportedly involved mass trials and caused a significant number of suicides.[11]

With regard to Party rectification *per se,* there were also indications of a harsher approach. This was hinted by Mao in January 1958 when, in contrast to his statements of summer 1957, he declared CCP rectification must be stricter than that conducted within the democratic parties. More concretely, it appears there was a significant increase in the inner Party purge rate as the Great Leap unfolded. Edgar Snow "was told on what ought to be good authority . . . that as many as a million Party members were dropped or put on probation during the 1957–58 rectification campaign." While this leaves indeterminate the number actually expelled, it does indicate severe Party discipline against 8 to 9 percent of the CCP's membership.[g] Further evidence is provided by Party membership figures. From the 1956 Party Congress to the Third Plenum the CCP grew by just under 2 million members despite a virtual suspension of recruitment for at least several months in spring 1957. The large net growth—the largest recorded yearly growth in the history of the CCP—was in large measure due to a low purge rate during both the Hundred Flowers period when disciplinary measures were eschewed and the anti-rightist struggle when they focused largely on non-Party targets. Thus most purging of Party members came after the Third Plenum as the leap forward and attacks on right conservatism gained momentum. Accordingly, despite large scale Party recruitment in conjunction with the Great Leap and commune movements, CCP growth in the two years from the Third Plenum to the tenth anniversary celebrations was only 1.2 million members, or one half to one third the yearly increases since 1954. This sharp drop in CCP growth, together with Snow's statement, indicates a purge of considerable proportions in 1957–58. While the percentage involved was slightly less than the 10 percent expelled or "persuaded" to withdraw in 1951–54, it was considerably more than the roughly 2 percent of Party members identified as rightists in some localities by fall 1957,

[g] The 9 percent figure is calculated on CCP membership as of the fall 1956 Eighth Party Congress and the 8 percent figure as of the fall 1957 Third Plenum. This, however, is considerably higher than a former cadre's report that 1 to 2 percent of cadres participating in rectification received Party and administrative sanctions in Huidong county, Guangdong, in summer 1958, and also higher than the 3.6 percent of Party rightists uncovered in Yunnan in the same period. See Frederick C. Teiwes, "A Case Study of Rectification: The 1958 *Cheng-feng Cheng-kai* Campaign in Hui-tung County," *Papers on Far Eastern History,* March 1973, p. 92; and below, p. 281.

and decidedly more than what one would expect from "gentle breeze and mild rain" methods which theoretically still applied after the Third Plenum.[12]

The Downgrading of Chen Yun

While a higher purge rate among Party members generally indicated one pressure affecting traditional organizational norms, developments at higher levels also posed challenges to established procedures. Clearly, a greater degree of policy dissent than was normal during the previous eight years created conditions threatening the open policy process. At the Second Session of the Eighth Party Congress in May 1958, both Mao and Liu Shaoqi devoted an extraordinary amount of attention to Party critics of the Great Leap—the so-called "tide watches" and "accounts settlers." [13] While no systematic purge of those opposed to or skeptical of the new policies ensued, discipline was applied to a significant number of critics in high ranking posts. Although formal sanctions were avoided, one of the earliest to suffer was Party Vice Chairman Chen Yun.

Chen Yun was the PRC's fifth ranking leader in 1957. A member of the all important Politburo Standing Committee, Chen was the ranking vice premier and the Party's leading spokesman on economic affairs. While no formal disciplinary measures were taken against Chen, his power clearly began to wane as the Great Leap strategy unfolded. Although Chen made frequent ceremonial appearances in late 1957 and 1958, thus indicating continued good health, his economic functions were now minimal. Indeed, his major task of attending the Moscow meetings of the Council on Mutual Economic Assistance in May 1958 served to keep him out of China at the time of the Party Congress session which formally sanctioned the Great Leap Forward. In September 1958, moreover, he was removed *(mianzhi)* from his major operational post as Minister of Commerce. At that time Chen was appointed head of the newly formed State Capital Construction Commission, but this body never became active. While Chen continued to make infrequent appearances and was still listed in his Politburo and vice premier positions, by 1959 he was virtually silent on the economic issues he had dominated in the early and mid-1950s.[14]

No direct evidence exists indicating Chen's opposition to the emerging Great Leap in the crucial period starting with the Third Plenum.[h] There is, nevertheless,

[h] Cultural Revolution attacks on Chen ignored this question and focused on his role in the "anti-reckless advance" policies of 1956–57 and in dealing with the economic crisis in 1962 (see chapter 10). E.g., *Hongweibing* [Red Guard] (Beijing), January 27, 1967, in *SCMP-S,* No. 232. The absence of charges concerning the post-Third Plenum period is perhaps explained by the fact that Mao clearly got his way on the points at issue in contrast to the other two instances, as well as to Chen's policy advocacy being in accord with established principles. More broadly, there were relatively few Cultural Revolution accusations against Chen on *any* grounds, undoubtedly because he had not been exercising power for the previous three or four years.

considerably circumstantial evidence suggesting that differences relating to the new strategy were central to Chen's quiet downgrading. First, it is clear from both his contemporary statements and Cultural Revolution revelations that Chen was a major architect of the "anti-reckless advance" policies initiated in mid-1956. These policies, with their emphasis on gradual growth, balanced development and material incentives, were the antithesis of the Great Leap program. At the May 1958 Congress both Mao and Liu attacked the "anti-reckless advance" forces for exaggerating the defects of the early 1956 leap forward and hampering progress in production until their errors were corrected at the Third Plenum. Second, the report Chen delivered to the plenum on administrative decentralization and increasing agricultural production was never published. On agricultural production Chen probably emphasized the material incentives approach of the APC directives issued just before the Central Committee meetings. His decentralization proposals, moreover, most likely clashed with the measures implemented as the Great Leap unfolded. While Chen's views on decentralization cannot be known with certainty, Franz Schurmann has persuasively argued that they were reflected in a September 1957 article by Xue Muqiao, the head of the State Statistical Bureau. Xue's proposals called for a revamping of economic administration to enhance the powers of ministries, provincial authorities and enterprises at the expense of central planning agencies. Increasing discretionary authority at the enterprise level, moreover, meant some reliance on market mechanisms and material incentives. In contrast, the post-Third Plenum decentralization heavily favored the provinces over central ministries—particularly Chen's Ministry of Commerce—as well as central planning authorities. Furthermore, although provision was made for increased flexibility for enterprise managers, it was now in a context emphasizing social mobilization rather than market incentives. The result, then, was a clear defeat for the approach advocated by Xue Muqiao, and presumably Chen Yun.[15]

Chen Yun's downgrading marked an important development in politics at the apex of the CCP leadership. For the first time since the establishment of the PRC, or indeed since the adoption of the rectification approach in Yan'an, differences over current policy decisions apparently were the key factor in emasculating the authority of a Politburo member.[i] Prior to this Gao Gang was the only

[i] Chen's downgrading was not totally without precedent, however. Significant losses of authority were suffered by Minister of Finance Bo Yibo in 1953 over taxation policy and Central Committee rural work head Deng Zihui in 1955 over collectivization. See above, p. 90; and MacFarquhar, *Origins 1*, pp. 18–19. In addition to the fact that neither Bo nor Deng were Politburo members at the times of their career setbacks, their cases differed from Chen's in that they apparently recovered fully in about a year (although Deng also went into eclipse again with the unfolding of the Great Leap) while Chen, with the exception of a brief period during the economic crisis of the early 1960s, never again exercised major influence.

figure of Politburo rank to be affected by the rectification-purge process, but as argued in Chapter 5 policy issues were not a central aspect of Gao's demise. Where policy differences had occurred earlier within the Politburo, those in the minority continued to play active leadership roles while maintaining discipline in policy implementation. Now, however, Chen's loss of economic powers indicated a new situation. The changed ramifications of policy dissent are best understood in terms of the evolution of the policy context. With the broad consensus on the Soviet model during the earlier period, differences on such matters as rates of development did not threaten overall leadership cohesion and adequate support of official policy could reasonably be expected from those who had argued opposing views. By 1958, however, the issue was one of basic economic strategy where the new policies were not only untried, but flew in the face of the previous consensus. This implied that opposition was more fundamental than in the past, and in such circumstances the removal of key doubters from direct operational authority was a prudent step.

But if Chen Yun's case was an important development in the handling of top level differences, it was still a limited step. The fact that Chen was subjected to neither formal disciplinary punishment nor, insofar as can be determined, to internal criticism, indicates that established principles of leadership debate were still in force to a substantial degree. Chen had certainly done no more than advocate a particular policy line and perhaps retain his opinion after his views were rejected—all of which was legitimate under existing norms. By shielding Chen from direct attack these rights were partially honored, at least at the Politburo level. Moreover, there undoubtedly were many other leading officials who argued for more cautious policies in fall 1957 but stayed on to play major roles during the Leap Forward—not the least of whom apparently was Zhou Enlai.[16] That the old norms held as well as they did despite the plunge into unprecedented policies is testimony not only to the unity developed under Mao's leadership over decades of revolutionary struggle, but also the general record of success achieved in the first eight years of the PRC. Even though the Hundred Flowers experiment had resulted in failure, the damage was repaired and any leadership differences resolved relatively quickly with the onset of the antirightist struggle. It would take the accumulation of considerable evidence of severe shortcomings in the new leap forward before leadership unity would show substantial signs of cracking.

By spring 1958, then, a situation existed where the erosion of the policy consensus had affected but not subverted traditional Party norms. This was reflected in Mao's ruminations of the period concerning unity and splits within the Party. On the one hand, he continued to emphasize unity as a desirable goal and advocated "gentle breeze" methods to obtain it. The "accounts settlers" who doubted the wisdom of the Great Leap would be persuaded of the virtues of the new strategy. Criticism and struggle might be employed in their cases, but the goal was unity. The importance of unity was indicated by the Chairman's injunction to talk about it every day, and his warning of chaos if a split occurred. On the other hand, while Party splits were to be avoided, Mao referred to them as natural phenomena which contributed to overall progress.[17] Mao undoubtedly was responding to a higher level of policy controversy within the Party than had previously existed. While he sought to retain the commitment to unity which had served his leadership so well, the Chairman also seems to have anticipated that this was becoming more difficult under the changed circumstances. The ambivalence of Mao's attitude was reflected in the handling of Chen Yun. Direct attacks had been avoided in the name of unity, but the informal stripping of power in effect weakened the right to hold minority views.

The Shake-up in the Ministry of Supervision

If Chen Yun's apparent opposition to the Great Leap Forward reflected a preference for a professional approach and central ministerial authority, these attitudes were clearly widespread among central officials. A case in point was the Ministry of Supervision which became a focus of conflict in the latter half of 1957. Although the case began in the summer as part of the anti-rightist struggle,[j] the shake-up reached its climax in October and November following the Third Plenum. Then it resulted in mass meetings denouncing Wang Han, a vice minister and deputy secretary of the Party fraction. Wang, who lost his posts, was accused of forming an "anti-Party clique" together with rightists who had been exposed in August: Peng Da, deputy director of the ministry's second department and a Party member of twenty years standing, Chen Dazhi, deputy head of the research office, Liang Jianyi, head of the translation section of the research office, and An Rudao, deputy director of another department.[18]

The relevance of the Ministry of Supervision's case to the Great Leap was indicated by several accusations against Wang Han, Peng Da, *et al.* A major theme concerned alleged opposition to mass line techniques and political and ideological work, approaches which were especially emphasized by the new developmental strategy. These officials reportedly opposed the study of Marxism-Leninism by supervision cadres and argued that "administrative work itself is politics." They had little use for such practices as handling letters from the people and supervision correspondents. The preference for a technical and

---

[j] The anti-rightist aspects of the case focused on such familiar matters as advocacy of ending class struggle, objections to excesses in past campaigns, opposition to official cadre policy, and attacks on the administrative competence of the Party fraction. NCNA, Beijing, August 20, 1957, in *SCMP*, No. 1605; and *RMRB*, December 5, 1957, in *SCMP*, No. 1679.

administrative approach was also seen in charges against Wang Han for his activities before 1949. As deputy head of the political department of a New Fourth Army division, Wang assertedly advocated the primacy of military work while neglecting Party work and the relationship between soldiers and masses. Moreover, he allegedly had looked down upon cadres of worker and peasant origins and advocated intellectual cadres for positions in the army's political organs, an attitude increasingly out of tune with the revised view of the significance for national development of workers and peasants on the one hand and intellectuals on the other.[19]

The powers of the ministry was the key issue. Wang and the others apparently sought to expand as much as possible the authority of the ministry and maintain maximum independence from Party control. Specifically, they reportedly opposed a March 1956 Central Committee decision to place supervision organs under the dual leadership of local Party committees as well as the ministry and instead advocated an independent supervision system under the ministry's vertical control, an advocacy which particularly clashed with the decentralization measures of late 1957. Moreover, Wang *et al.* apparently envisioned an expanded role for the ministry *vis à-vis* other institutions besides Party committees. Rather than simply checking up on violations of law in economic enterprises after the fact, they argued for comprehensive powers including the right to examine the formulation of economic plans and directives, to investigate their implementation, and to halt expenditures by financial and economic organs. Peng Da reportedly told supervision cadres simply to disregard managers of state enterprises while Wang Han criticized the work of various ministries, characterizing economic plans as either too adventurous or too timid. What was being asked for, in effect, was that the ministry assume a major role in economic planning and policy making. Wang's tendency to bureaucratic aggrandizement was further revealed by his reported advocacy of the political and organizational independence of the political work system within the army before 1949. As summed up by *Renmin ribao,* "No matter what department [Wang] worked in, he always wanted to place the authority of the department above all others so that everything was under his command." Such empire building by a central ministry was clearly incompatible with the leap forward's administrative changes and emphasis on maximum lower level initiative.[20]

Closely linked to advocacy of expanded ministerial powers were organizational deviations. After openly opposing dual leadership at first, Wang and his colleagues assertedly feigned acceptance of the system while privately spreading rumors against it. They reportedly sought to seize leadership of the ministry by attacking the Party fraction and only implemented decisions they agreed with. Taking the attitude that "whoever is correct is the leader," they disobeyed legitimate orders from superior authorities and made arbitrary decisions without proper consultation. Thus the views of the supervision officials, as those in other cases dealt with in this period,[k] were not only incompatible with the Great Leap Forward emphasis on the mass line, Party committee leadership and decentralized management of the economy, they were also exacerbated by a lack of organizational discipline. The combination of discordant policy views and organizational unreliability could not be tolerated in a situation where unprecedented administrative demands were being made, and severe consequences resulted for the ministry. In addition to the late 1957 shake-up, the ministry saw its powers whittled away in 1958 as increasing emphasis was placed on the subordination of supervision work to local Party and government bodies. Finally, in April 1959 the Ministry of Supervision was abolished although supervision bureaus continued to exist within various ministries. This, then, was an extreme example of the attack on vested bureaucratic interests by rectification during the Great Leap Forward, an attack which contributed to the elimination of a separate, hierarchically organized supervision system.[21]

The Provincial Purges of 1957–58

The dangers posed by dissenting policy views combined with questionable organizational discipline were even more critical in China's provincial Party secretariats. The existence of serious problems at the provincial level was indicated by an 11 month series of purges and "semi-purges" in 12[l] provinces and autonomous regions beginning in December 1957. In rough chronological order, leading provincial officials in Zhejiang, Anhui, Gansu, Qinghai, Hebei, Yunnan, Guangdong, Xinjiang, Guangxi, Henan, Liaoning and Shandong were expelled from the Party and/or dismissed from their Party and government posts. With the exception of the fall 1958 Liaoning and Shandong cases, these disciplinary measures were reviewed at the May 1958 Party Congress the meeting which in-

[k] In addition to political and legal organs (see above, p. 250n), and the provincial cases discussed below, similar problems resulted in dismissals and other disciplinary measures in central and provincial trade union organizations during 1958. The central charges raised were "economism" *(jingjizhuyi),* a defense of immediate worker interests which clearly clashed with the Great Leap's mass mobilization approach, and "syndicalism" *(gongtuanzhuyi),* the separation of trade union organization from Party control which contravened the leap's emphasis on Party committee leadership. Moreover, the imperatives of the leap forward were revealed by the new December 1957 constitution of the All China Federation of Trade Unions which altered its guiding organizational principal from vertical to dual control. For detailed analysis, see Paul F. Harper, "Political Roles of Trade Unions in Communist China," Ph.D. dissertation, Cornell University, 1969, chs. 6–7.

[l] In May 1958 Mao indicated that 13 provinces and provincial level municipalities had "developed problems." SXWS, II, 223. At that time 11 provinces (all of those listed below except Liaoning and including Shandong due to the cases of special district leaders) had publicized purges and dismissals. Whether the discrepancy indicates a failure to publicize disciplinary measures or action short of such measures in other provinces is impossible to say.

veighed against opponents of the Great Leap Forward. The purge victims[m] included four alternate members of the Central Committee, one provincial first secretary, eleven additional Party secretaries, eight heads of deputy heads of Party departments, four governors and ten vice governors, plus approximately 25 officials holding other Party and/or government positions. In addition, the dismissal of two special district officials, the first secretaries of Huimin and Tai'an, Shandong, is discussed below since they were included in the cases reviewed at the May Congress. Table 5 lists the major figures involved together with the major disciplinary action taken in each case.[22]

It is important to bear in mind that the alleged errors of the disgraced officials mainly occurred from 1956 to mid-1957—i.e., before the launching of the Anti-Rightist Campaign. Like many non-Party intellectuals attacked during the anti-rightist struggle, these high ranking provincial leaders had actually advocated positions in line with central policy during the earlier period, but which now were regarded as deviant following the various policy changes since mid-1957. Indeed, many positions attributed to the provincial officials mirrored those of bourgeois rightists. In part this involved issues raised by the Hundred Flowers experiment and the general political relaxation of 1956-early 1957, but more fundamental were questions of economic strategy which were only a minor aspect of the rightist critique. With few exceptions, the purged leaders were not charged with direct opposition to the Great Leap Forward. Nevertheless, the content of the accusations against them suggests these leaders were by and large committed to the policies associated with "anti-reckless advance," policies which were the antithesis of the leap forward. But the sins of provincial officials extended beyond support for such policies. Their "anti-Party activities" were summed up as an attack with "one spearhead at the political line, another at the organizational line."[23] Similar to the case of the Ministry of Supervision, these men were suspect not only because they presumably favored cautious economic policies, but also because their organizational reliability was in question at a time when increasing administrative authority was being devolved to the provincial level. The purges of such leaders, we argue, can best be regarded as preemptive measures to remove from power officials who conceivably might have obstructed implementation of the Great Leap program.

Policy Issues

While the question of basic approach to economic policy provided a general theme, the scope of specific policy issues involved in the 1957–58 purges was quite broad, ranging from literary and artistic policy (Zhejiang) to the amount of

---

[m]Although leaders dismissed from office were technically not purged, for convenience's sake this term will be used to cover both officials receiving only this sanction as well as those expelled from the Party.

Table 5

Major Victims of the 1957-58 Provincial Purges

Official	Province	Party Posts	Other Posts	Sanction
Sha Wenhan	Zhejiang	secretary	governor	expelled
Yang Siyi	Zhejiang	dir, organization dept	vice governor	expelled
Peng Ruilin	Zhejiang	SC	chief procurator	expelled
Sun Zhanglu	Zhejiang	dir, finance & trade dept	dir, trade dept	expelled
Sun Diancai	Gansu	SC	vice governor	expelled
Liang Dajun	Gansu	1st sec, Yinchuan spec dist	vice governor	expelled
Chen Chengyi	Gansu	sec, CCP fraction in legal organs	vice governor	expelled
Li Shinong	Anhui	secretary	vice governor	expelled
Zheng Dun	Yunnan	dir, organization dept		expelled
Wang Jingru	Yunnan	dep dir, organization dept		expelled
Chen Zaili	Guangxi	SC	vice governor	expelled
Sun Zuobin	Qinghai	secretary	governor	expelled
Liu Hongdao	Hebei	dir, united front dept		expelled
Gu Dacun	Guangdong	secretary; CC alternate	vice governor	dismissed
Feng Baiju	Guangdong	secretary; CC alternate	vice governor	dismissed
Savlayev	Xinjiang	secretary	chief procurator	dismissed
Iminov	Xinjiang	SC	vice governor	dismissed
Ashad	Xinjiang	SC	vice governor	dismissed
Pan Fusheng	Henan	1st secretary; CC alternate	pol com, Henan Military Dist	dismissed
Li Feng	Shandong	1st sec, Huimin spec dist		dismissed
Zao Lijin	Shandong	1st sec, Tai'an spec dist		dismissed
Du Zheheng	Liaoning	secretary	governor	dismissed
Wang Zheng	Liaoning	secretary		dismissed
Li Dao	Liaoning	secretary	vice governor	dismissed
Zhao Jianmin	Shandong	secretary; CC alternate	governor	dismissed
Wang Chuoru	Shandong	SC	vice governor	dismissed

Key: dep dir = deputy director; sec = secretary; spec dist = special district; pol com = political commissar; SC = provincial CCP standing committee.

emphasis on large as contrasted to small industry (Liaoning). Only the most important issues, i.e., those which affected most provinces, are dealt with here.

In almost every purge rural policy was an issue. It was clearly *the* policy issue in Guangxi and Henan, and of particular importance in Yunnan, Gansu, Guangdong, Liaoning and Shandong as well. In these provinces there was sharp disagreement over the speed of economic development. After the speedup of cooperativization and the early 1956 effort to complete the FFYP a year ahead of schedule, there was considerable provincial grumbling about adventurism and "reckless advance." Such "pessimistic" views were aimed at the whole sphere of economic construction, but this "conservative" outlook was usually treated vaguely except in the case of agriculture. Apparently some provincial leaders felt the enthusiasm engendered by the policy of rapid advance had blinded their more radical comrades to the harsh realities of the countryside. They charged reports of production increases were boasts and leading officials were only interested in hearing good news. A more cautious approach was called for because, in the alleged melancholy words of Henan First Secretary Pan Fusheng, "Population is large, land area is small, land is lean and people are poor, farming is crude, famine has occurred continuously." Such sentiments assertedly overlooked the revolutionary will of the masses which was so central to the Great Leap strategy.[24]

The main object of criticism was the APC. The view that "cooperatives are a mess" was attributed to disgraced leaders in province after province. Pan was accused of exaggerating defects to the point of denying the basic superiority of APCs. He allegedly sought to reverse the socialization of the countryside and reestablish a small peasant-capitalist economy. These charges are undoubtedly distortions. The real issues can best be summarized as the size of APCs, peasant withdrawals from them, the encouragement of rural capitalist activities, the behavior of rural cadres, and the nature of class struggle in the countryside. Pan and others of like mind felt APCs were too large to be efficient units of production. He reportedly complained that peasants had to walk 15 *li* and then queue up for an interview before they could see the manager of their cooperative. In order to solve this problem, Pan split APCs into smaller units. It was reported that under his auspices in spring 1957 the number of cooperatives in Henan doubled and the average size decreased from 358 to 180 households. During the same period some peasants withdrew from APCs. Pan allegedly not only approved but even complained that not enough were leaving. Although this may be an exaggeration, the charge that he regarded withdrawals only as "contradictions among the people" suggests Pan was tolerant of this development.[25]

Life in the cooperatives and the behavior of rural cadres had been sharply criticized by purge victims. Many provincial leaders apparently believed the peasants were being driven too hard and the danger of serious disaffection existed unless measures were taken to ease conditions. Pan Fusheng supposedly painted a grim picture of socialist production in the countryside:

> The peasants . . . are the same as beasts of burden today. Yellow oxen are tied up in the house and human beings are harnessed in the field. Girls and women pull plows and harrows, with their wombs hanging down. Cooperation is transformed into the exploitation of human strength.[26]

Rural cadres who drove the peasants were bitterly criticized not only in Henan, but also in Guangdong, Guangxi and Yunnan. Commandism was a common and perhaps mild description of their activities; Pan assertedly labeled the contradiction between leader and led in the countryside antagonistic. But if the methods of cadres who "stuck up their tails" were rejected, what would replace them to raise agricultural production? The conservative answer was increased incentives which meant capitalist activities in the cooperativized countryside. In Henan, such activities reportedly thrived, including the expansion of private plots, private reclamation of wasteland, and private planting of trees.[27]

The alleged viewpoint of officials like Pan was attacked on the grounds that it represented a retreat from socialism to capitalism. The fundamental issue as articulated by the dominant leadership in 1958 was the nature of class struggle in the countryside. In over half a dozen provinces purge victims were specifically charged with inventing theories denying the existence of class struggle. They reportedly viewed political issues in the countryside as basically settled and felt attention should be given to economic matters. Furthermore, they saw a conflict between excessive emphasis on political goals and production gains, and argued that politics should not be pressed too hard. Pan assertedly said the main contradiction in rural areas was not between socialist and capitalist tendencies but between the willingness and unwillingness of the peasants to produce. Emphasis on class struggle would only cause tension and confusion harmful to production according to this view. Yang Jue, an associate of Pan, allegedly lamented over the futility of class struggle:

> The struggle against the landlord class has basically concluded, and if we have to struggle further against the landlord class, we must then treat the well-to-do middle peasants as landlords and struggle against them. At the same time we may . . . turn the middle and poor peasants into landlords.[28]

Although Mao himself saw class struggle coming to a successful conclusion, from the perspective of the post-Third Plenum period such views still seemed dangerously revisionist. First of all, there was no conflict between politics and production under the Great Leap strategy. Production would increase because of the revolutionary will of the masses and the superiority of socialist organization. Moreover, class struggle had not ended but had intensified in the first half of 1957 when "landlords, rich peasants, counterrevolutionaries and bad elements launched vicious attacks on socialism." To deny this struggle in order to increase production through the efforts of the rich bourgeoisie, said *Henan ribao* ominously, amounted to adopting the policies of Bukharin. While class struggle was achieving a fundamental victory, there was still every need to continue the attack on rural capitalism under the leap forward policies.[29]

Another frequent charge was that during "blooming and contending" provincial officials supported bourgeois rightist attacks on the Party. Although it was usually unclear precisely what this involved, the purge victims reportedly had great difficulty in distinguishing between "contradictions among the people" and "contradictions with the enemy." There apparently was a predisposition on their part to accept a wide variety of people as legitimate members of society and a broad range of criticism as tolerable discourse. As in so many other groups in spring 1957, this attitude assertedly had led to substantial opposition to the policy of suppressing counterrevolutionaries. In Anhui this was the main issue. Secretary Li Shinong and his "clique" allegedly argued the Party was "too cruel" to counterrevolutionaries and sought redress for people who had suffered wrongs during suppression campaigns. They invented the "two-faced character" theory for dealing with counterrevolutionaries: a counterrevolutionary had both good and bad points which had to be balanced against one another before taking action. What must be avoided, they argued, is indiscriminate action which creates antagonistic contradictions out of non-antagonistic ones.[30]

Li reportedly wanted to shift the object of political and legal work from counterrevolutionaries to common criminals. This, commented *Renmin ribao*, was to substitute bourgeois dictatorship for proletarian dictatorship. The issue here resembles the question of class struggle in the countryside. The condemned view was that with the basic question of political power settled there was no urgency for rapid political transformation. Therefore, further advances should be gradual and based on gentle methods of persuasion. Rapid transformation by repeated suppression and anti-rightist struggles would only divide the population and needlessly alienate the most creative elements. Although the charge that Yunnan officials had advocated "unlimited democracy" could imply opposition to the political primacy of the CCP, it is more likely the views under attack reflected a desire for the relaxation of relations between Party and society, a loosening up within the structure of a Party led nation, and a cooling off of an ideologically charged atmosphere. Such normalization was clearly out of step with the pressures of an unprecedented mass mobilization.[31]

The desire for normalized relations underlay the problem of the proper role of the Party in government work. This was a major issue of dispute in a half dozen provinces. Sun Zuobin, the purged Governor of Qinghai, was accused of saying that Party committees should only criticize and make suggestions concerning government administration. Others echoed complaints made by non-Party people during "blooming and contending" that there was "no distinction between Party and government" and "the government has no real power." Many officials with primary responsibility for government work felt overeager Party committees were unduly interfering with their jobs. Thus there was an alleged call for a "division of labor" in Yunnan.[32] The resentment at Party meddling was intensified by a feeling of special competence on the part of government specialists. This was strikingly revealed by the reported attitude of the "clique" headed by Vice Governor Wang Chuoru of Shandong:

> They openly called themselves experts, and, regarding the members of the provincial Party committee as laymen ignorant of economic and financial ad-

> ministration, they thus opposed their leadership. "Financial problems," they said, "should be handled by one man who alone should make decisions. One has no idea how expensive rice and firewood are if he does not run the household." [33]

The basic conflict was between the desire of officials everywhere to grab as much authority as politically feasible and the effort of ranking political authorities to make the government apparatus fully responsive to their leadership. But advocacy of governmental authority had a special weight in 1956–1957 when the Chinese bureaucracy was achieving its full articulation and the dominant policies favored the expertise which bureaucrats could provide. With the Great leap Forward, however, the simplification and decentralization of the administrative structure, the downgrading of expertise, and the emphasis on direct leadership by Party committees placed such advocacy in fundamental opposition to the new strategy.

All the deviant views discussed above are "conservative" or "rightist." There was one case, however, where offending officials came from the other end of the political spectrum. Li Feng and Zao Lijin, first secretaries of Huimin and Tai'an special districts, Shandong, were charged with "leftist doctrinairism." While other purge victims erred by interpreting "contradictions among the people" too liberally, they were accused of saying, "It is not right to stress contradictions to the neglect of class struggle." Many of their mistakes were almost precisely the "correct" views proclaimed in other cases. This was strikingly the case concerning rural policy:

> During the winter of 1956–57 and the spring of 1957, there was a minor disturbance caused by the belief that "the cooperative system is not superior." In some rural areas a small number of people also demanded more grain rations and made trouble in their APCs. Such incidents took place principally because after cooperativization, the masses were not yet accustomed to the new social system; because the leadership cadres lacked adequate experience in running the cooperatives well and showed shortcomings in their work. . .; and because small numbers of rich middle peasants hesitated to follow the people. . . . Comrade Li Feng, however, took the opposite view. Alarmed at the situation, he concluded that "landlords, rich peasants, counterrevolutionaries and other bad elements are on the rampage . . ." [and used] dictatorial methods in dealing with the people.[34]

This was a glaring exception to the remarkable overall consistency of policy views attacked during the 1957–58 provincial purges. Its inclusion in the cases reviewed at the May 1958 Party Congress suggests the special salience of organizational matters.

Organizational Issues

In almost every case purge victims were charged with attacking or attempting to seize control of provincial Party committees. Although occasional mistakes were admitted, the various provincial committees were always treated as essentially upholding the Party line. This was even true in Henan where Pan Fusheng was criticized for attacking the provincial committee before he became first secretary, and bullying and ignoring it afterwards. Although the views criticized at length were, with the one exception, conservative, on a number of occasions people holding those views allegedly accused provincial committees of rightist deviations. Right or left, such opposition was in retrospect considered unprincipled struggle designed to split the Party into cliques. In Liaoning, factional efforts were reportedly so intense that two provincial committees, the legitimate one and an underground competitor, existed side-by-side with the result that political and economic work suffered greatly.[35]

Even where "anti-Party cliques" were apparently less powerful than in Liaoning, their activities weakened Party unity. Cliques assertedly were often active at Party conferences where they introduced jarring notes by behind the scenes politics or "organized attacks through designated speakers." When not engaged in attacking provincial committees, they reportedly spent their energy fabricating and spreading rumors against other small groups. Some cliques, for example the Gansu group headed by deposed Vice Governor Sun Diancai, reportedly dated to revolutionary days. Others were only recently formed, as that allegedly established in 1955 by former Guangdong enemies Gu Dacun and Feng Baiju. Cliques were built on several factors. Policy, of course, was one. Another, as in Gansu, was personal relationships of long standing, particularly those based on common service in local guerrilla and underground forces. Party status also provided an important focus for small group activity. Attacks were made on those who used their status as veteran cadres as political capital to develop personal followings.[36]

Perhaps the most important element in clique building, however, was "localism" *(difangzhuyi).* The dismissed Governor of Shandong, Zhao Jianmin, reportedly built his influence by saying, "I am a native of Shandong, I am for the people of Shandong and cadres of Shandong."[37] In provinces with many outside cadres, cliques developed on a native-outsider basis. The charge of localism or local nationalism was specifically raised in eight provinces: Zhejiang, Gansu, Guangxi, Guangdong, Liaoning, Shandong, Xinjiang and Yunnan. This problem, which also affected cadres down to the basic levels, is discussed more fully below.

Cliques were viewed with particular alarm where they attained an organizational or territorial base by monopolizing key posts. In several provinces independent kingdoms allegedly appeared: territorial bases were established on Hainan Island by Feng Baiju, in Huimin special district by Li Feng, and in Yinchuan special district by Sun Diancai. Sun also reportedly had an organizational base in the Gansu People's Council. Another organizational base was the government financial and planning bodies for the Wang Chuoru group in Shandong. Leading posts were also monopolized in Anhui's political and legal departments by Li Shinong's group, and in the Yunnan organization department by the Zheng Dun-Wang Jingru clique.[38]

One of the most important misuses of organizational power concerned the assignment of cadres. One practice was to attack and dismiss loyal cadres; another was to place rightists or clique members in key posts. How such maneuvers were accomplished usually was not described; the routine business of Party secretariats undoubtedly provided ample opportunities. A few specific methods were revealed, however. In Yunnan, the organization department clique of Zheng Dun and Wang Jingru was accused of using the examination of cadres to fabricate charges against those they opposed. Opportunities were also provided by the considerable retrenchment of cadres taking place under the *xiafang* program. This retrenchment reportedly allowed several cliques to dismiss or otherwise remove loyal cadres from key posts and install instead "anti-Party elements."[39]

The extent to which any cliques were able to build an organizational following is unclear. In Yunnan, an April-September 1958 campaign exposed 1,795 Party members (3.6 percent of those participating) as "Zheng-Wang clique [members] and rightists." However, no indication was given as to how many belonged to the clique and how many were simply rightists uncovered in the broader rectification process.[40] In all other provinces where cliques assertedly operated, their membership as revealed in official accusations amounted to only a handful of people. This failure to reveal widespread alliances suggests, with the possible exceptions of Yunnan and Guangdong,[n] that clique activities were comparatively small scale. Indeed, it might even be questioned how validly the term "clique" can be used. Perhaps people who argued the same views were simply lumped together during the purge. But information concerning long associations and localist sympathies appears genuine, and it is likely that bonds of mutual interest illegitimate under Party organizational principles existed to some degree.

CCP leaders also claimed that democratic centralism was jeopardized by the activities of some officials. In a number of ways certain provincial Party and government organizations apparently were less than entirely reliable instruments of the Party Center. In several instances the Center was unable to get satisfactory information from lower levels. The Shandong group headed by Wang Chuoru allegedly had two sets of books for financial work, an accurate set and another to show higher authorities. In another case, leftist Li Feng was criticized for reporting only good news, and when higher level inspection teams arrived to check his work he reportedly cold shouldered them and prevented them from gaining a true picture of conditions. The most spectacular case of information manipulation, however, concerned Pan Fusheng. Pan allegedly not only delivered a false report to a national Party conference, he was also charged with "cheating

[n] The activities of Feng Baiju's clique on Hainan Island were reportedly large scale. *XHBYK,* No. 19, 1958, in *URS,* Vol. 13—No. 14; and below, pp. 289–90.

Chairman Mao face to face" when Mao made an inspection of Henan.[41]

While such practices clearly violated established procedures, a more ambivalent aspect of the information problem concerned the use of mass line methods. In a number of cases the purge victims were accused of the bureaucratic failure to go out to the masses, and thus being unable to present an accurate picture to higher levels. However, very bitter criticism was leveled at a number of high level cadres who did go to the people, visited APCs, and held on the spot conferences. Their activities allegedly were designed to gather material for attacks on CCP policies. Although Li Feng was denounced for claiming that the class line and mass line are contradictory, he unintentionally pointed out the danger in relying too heavily on mass line methods when they led to conclusions contrary to official policies.[42] The mass line must be tempered by a "correct" political posture if it is to be acceptable, a situation which became particularly suffocating as Great Leap pressures eroded the traditional right to muster evidence in support of dissenting views.

A more important issue than communications up the Party structure was communications down. A frequent charge was that directives from Peking simply did not get implemented. Pan Fusheng reportedly resisted central grain plans and complained that cadres had neglected local needs by being too submissive to the Center. Pan expressed the views of other provincial leaders when he allegedly said, "Henan is different from Beijing and Shanghai, and [what is] marked out by the central leadership can serve only as a guide." In Yunnan, the Zheng Dun group was accused of using individual words and phrases in directives to distort the meaning of Party policies. In other places contrary directives were reportedly forged and passed on in place of those from the Center. The normal practice, however, was simply pigeonholing, as in Anhui where Li Shinong allegedly forbade political and legal departments to relay directives to lower levels. If such practices became widespread the ability of central authorities to lead the nation would have been seriously damaged at a time when political discipline was required to counterbalance administrative decentralization.[43]

The Rationale of the Purge

What is striking about "deviant" policy views expressed in the provinces is the degree they reflected shifting central policy. As we have seen, for a good part of 1956–57 moderate views predominated in national policy. Although opposition to "reckless advance" had been official CCP policy when most provincial leaders aired such opinions, these sentiments were damned during the purges. As was the case with bourgeois intellectuals, close parallels can be demonstrated on specific issues as well. The recommended size of APCs according to the September 1956 Central Committee-State Council directive was 100 households in mountainous areas, 200 households in rough hillside regions, and 300 households in the plains. While it is difficult to estimate how far Pan Fusheng may have strayed from these guidelines when he reportedly reduced the average APC in Henan from 358 to 180 households, a policy of cutting their size was definitely called for. The same directive also warned against commandism by rural cadres and overemphasizing the collective interest at the expense of private plots and other individual endeavors, again the alleged views of Pan.[44] While Pan may have overstepped the limits of central policy, his actions clearly reflected the thrust of the official line.

Further examples abound. If unfortunate provincial leaders underestimated the strength of counterrevolutionaries, Mao Zedong himself did not think them too strong in his "Contradictions" speech. If rightist Party members in the provinces believed loosening political controls would stimulate the development of intellectual resources, they were merely concurring in early 1957 wisdom of Chairman Mao. Concerning central-local relations, the September 1956 APC directive said, "Targets fixed by government organs can only be used as guides," a statement very similar to Comrade Pan's heresy. Purge victims in Xinjiang who erred by thinking Han chauvinism a greater problem than local nationalism (to be discussed subsequently) only had to read "On the Correct Handling of Contradictions among the People" to find similar views.[45]

By the time of the 1957–58 provincial purges radical views had gained ascendancy in Beijing, views which led to the Great Leap Forward. Although opposition to the Great Leap was specifically cited only in Yunnan and Shandong, reported criticism of rapid cooperativization and the drive to fulfill the FFYP a year ahead of schedule clearly could be applied to the leap as well. In most provinces the pessimism of the purge victims was specifically contrasted to the great advances to be gained through the leap forward. In the wake of the victory of the radical line in Beijing, it is conceivable that the most outspoken provincial conservatives were purged for their opinions during the 1956–57 period in gross violation not only of minority rights, but even of organizational discipline since their positions reflected the official policies of the earlier period.

But this would seem to overstate the case. While policy issues were clearly a major factor in a purge or rectification for the first time since 1949, it is unlikely that provincial leaders were ousted *primarily* for their 1956–57 views. If the purges were designed to eliminate provincial leaders holding conservative opinions, they would have been of considerably larger scale. The continued existence of conservatives was explicitly acknowledged in most provinces. While their anonymity makes it impossible to say how high they ranked, it would be surprising if they did not include some top echelon officials. The continued functioning of conservatives suggests at least partial adherence to Party principles allowing a permissible area of debate within the bounds of organizational discipline. Yet a subtle contraction of the limits of debate apparently was occurring. Accusations frequently alleged past rightist views to purge victims dating to land reform and before, but these officials survived previous policy swings to the left. On those occasions, policy differences were apparently dealt with by criticism rather than disciplinary action. Now, with the CCP setting out on the uncharted path of the Great Leap and the policy consensus of the early 1950s under increasing strain, it is possible that policy debates became more bitter, political maneuvering less cautious, and retribution dealt by victors more harsh. Still, if policy differences were the determining factor, an unobtrusive removal from effective power as happened to Chen Yun would have been more appropriate than public purges, particularly in view of Mao's injunction that unity should be the objective in dealing with "accounts settlers." Other concerns must explain the severity of the measures against provincial leaders.

The key, then, was organizational discipline. If differences of opinion remained tolerable within limits, failure to implement policy once it had been decided was not. As indicated, one of the crucial charges raised in 1957–58 was subversion of Party policy by ignoring central directives. A brief look at three contrasting cases is instructive. Pan Fusheng's rightist crimes and Li Feng's leftist deviations allegedly occurred in the same time span, spring and early summer 1957, and both were disciplined at the May 1958 Party Congress. The nature of their policy views, as reported, were virtually the mirror images of each other. Yet in both cases Party leaders felt they had lost control of affairs in the areas concerned. Although *Henan ribao* claimed Pan's theory of the non-existence of class struggle was particularly culpable because he persisted in forbidding an all out attack on rural rightists as late as mid-July 1957—i.e., more than a month after the launching of the anti-rightist struggle—this does not appear to be the real measure of his organizational unreliability. In fact, central policy prior to the Qingdao Conference (which apparently took place after Pan issued his ban) also prohibited the extension of rectification to the countryside during the busy agricultural season. What Pan did do in violation of organizational principles was to manipulate information once he heard Mao outline the new direction of rural policy at Qingdao. He allegedly concocted data more in line with the new policy for his report at Qingdao, tried to prevent discussion of his earlier ban on anti-rightist activities in rural areas at a subsequent provincial committee meeting and finally "cheated Chairman Mao face to face" by hiding his errors from the touring Chairman.[o]

But if Pan's problems derived from an effort to avoid the appearance of lagging behind a new policy, Li Feng was attacked for acting too *soon.* Li had dealt blows to rightists even before the Anti-Rightist Campaign, but he was not rewarded for his precociousness. Instead, he was severely attacked for applying methods suitable to the "summer situation" during the "spring situation." The

---

[o] *Henan ribao* [Henan Daily], July 4, 1958, in *CB*, No. 515; and *XHBYK*, No. 15, 1958, in *CB*, No. 515. Pan's position undoubtedly was especially difficult due to the presence of a potential rival in Governor Wu Zhipu. A more secure leader might have been able to undergo self-criticism and admit past "mistakes" without fearing for his position, but it seems Pan felt any admissions would have weakened his authority *vis-à-vis* Wu. See below, pp. 285, 299.

third figure of interest is Shandong Governor Zhao Jianmin. When Zhao came under fire in August 1958, he was accused of failing to learn from the anti-Party mistakes of Li Feng. Since Zhao's views were denounced as "right opportunist," it would seem the essential lesson of Li Feng was that personal views must be subordinated to the Party line of the moment, a lesson embedded in long standing CCP organizational practices. This lesson was particularly appropriate given the Great Leap emphasis on decentralized operations. Firm organizational discipline was necessary if the new powers given provincial leaders were not to lead to the pursuit of individual preferences instead of official goals.[46]

Organizational Ramifications

One of the most puzzling charges raised was that "anti-Party elements" attempted to seize control of provincial committees. Certainly political maneuvering would inevitably accompany policy debate. Those of conservative inclination were bound to benefit to some degree from moderate policies at the center. Yet whatever political advantage might have been gained from the moderate line of 1956–57, "seizing" a provincial committee could only be done with direct help from the Party Center which held the powers of appointment and dismissal. The purged officials were not particularly well placed organizationally to gain such assistance despite their rank. In no case did they hold a position of undisputed primacy. This seems true even in Henan where Pan Fusheng was first secretary but Governor Wu Zhipu held full Central Committee membership compared to Pan's alternate status. In most cases purge victims lacked Central Committee membership of any sort, while in every province except Qinghai at least one other leader had such status. Moreover, it is striking that the purges did not touch any first secretaries except Pan even though in nearly half the provinces affected the ranking leaders had served locally without interruption since liberation.[47] In spite of the fact that ample opportunity existed for the development of local perspectives, responsiveness to the Center was apparently maintained by these people. Although there was unreliability in the provinces, it was not among those on whom Beijing counted heaviest for the implementation of its policies. Indeed, the purge victims ostensibly clashed with the most powerful local leaders as well as the Center. As China embarked on the uncharted path of the Great Leap the carefully circumscribed nature of the 1957–58 purges indicated the confidence of central leaders in provincial Party organizations as a whole.

The Center's confidence in provincial organizations was further demonstrated by the fact that in only two cases were people sent into a province to assume key posts in conjunction with the purges. Huang Huoqing, a Central Committee alternate, was transferred from Tianjin to Liaoning about August 1958 to assume the duties of first secretary. Huang Oudong, first secretary since September 1956, was designated second secretary and assumed the duties of the dismissed governor, Du Zheheng. In July 1958, several months after the purge of Qinghai

Governor Sun Zuobin, the post was given to Yuan Renyuan after his transfer from Beijing. Of the two other governors ousted, Sha Wenhan in Zhejiang was replaced by a non-Party figurehead, and Shandong's Zhao Jianmin by Tan Qilong, a Central Committee alternate who had been serving as the province's second secretary since November 1955. When Pan Fusheng was dismissed, Wu Zhipu simply took over his posts while continuing to serve as governor. It would appear, therefore, that the provincial purges were accomplished with a minimum amount of organizational upheaval.

There can be little doubt about the guiding role of the central leadership in the purges. Not only were most of the cases reviewed at the May 1958 Congress, there is also evidence of Beijing's hand at a number of the purging sessions. Zhou Enlai gave a report on rectification to the January 1958 Anhui purge meeting. Tan Zhenlin, who had emerged as the CCP's leading spokesman for the Great Leap in agriculture, was present for the July 1958 denunciation of Pan Fusheng after three previous visits to Henan in late 1957. Deng Xiaoping and Li Fuchun gave important reports at the September 1958 session which dismissed key leaders in Liaoning. The evidence is less clear, but Mao Zedong himself was reportedly in Hangzhou in December 1957, the month of initial provincial purge in Zhejiang. Mao was also reported in Nanning in January 1958, although the first indications of the Guangxi purge were not given until the May Congress.[48]

This close attention indicates the importance attached to the provincial purges in furthering the new national policies. The whole purging process, however, reflected the top leadership's ambivalent attitude. While the Party took exceptionally strong action against some individuals, Mao in particular argued for a persuasive approach in general and limited discipline in handling particular cases, and concluded that local government overall was "very good."[49] Moreover, although the centrality of organizational issues suggests fidelity to traditional norms, the extensive attacks on policy views demonstrated a significant threat to those same norms.

The Struggle against Localism and Local Nationalism

The twin problems of localism and local nationalism were not only heavily involved in the 1957–58 provincial purges, they also affected important segments of the general public, non-Party cadres, and Party officials down to the basic levels. At the provincial level, the most prominent localists were Zhejiang Governor Sha Wenhan, Shandong Governor Zhao Jianmin, Gansu Vice Governor Sun Diancai, and Guangdong Secretaries Gu Dacun and Feng Baiju, while the leading local nationalists were Secretary Savlayev and Vice Governors Iminov and Ashad of Xinjiang. Sha and Sun were expelled from the Party while the others were dismissed from office. Scattered data indicate that significant disciplinary action was taken at lower levels during major campaigns against these deviations since summer 1957, but its extent cannot be determined.

Localism

While the tensions of socialist transformation and the subsequent relaxation both contributed to centrifugal tendencies in 1956–57, the Great Leap made localism a critical problem for the CCP. How could authority be safely decentralized so lower level officials did not pursue narrow local interests? Could the rapid development sought by the central leadership be realized in China's diverse localities? These questions had to be answered satisfactorily for the leap forward strategy to succeed.

A major localist argument was that local conditions dictated adjustments in Party policy, an argument used in an effort to curb the rate of socio-economic change. Considerable bitterness was directed at the implementation of past campaigns. This was shown during a review of questions festering since land reform launched by Guangdong provincial authorities in 1956. At that time, the provincial leadership under Tao Zhu indicated a willingness to make amends for overly harsh treatment of local cadres during land reform in order to facilitate local enthusiasm for national development. In the course of the subsequent debate, however, local cadres reportedly made sweeping charges concerning the conduct of land reform, arguing that local conditions had been ignored and the attack on landlords had been too violent and too wide in scope. Once the policy line had changed in 1957, however, the proponents of such views were vulnerable to attacks which unfolded at Guangzhou and Guangdong Party Congresses in November. The provincial leaders now countered with the standard view that the rightist deviation of "peaceful land reform" had taken place in 1951 because of local cadres' familial ties to and misguided sympathy for landlord elements. They alleged, moreover, that local cadres had "reversed the verdict on localism" and attempted to replace the existing leadership with localists.[50]

Similar issues appeared in other provinces concerning such programs as agricultural cooperativization, the suppression of counterrevolutionaries, and rapid industrialization. For example, a localist group in Gansu headed by Sun Diancai allegedly advanced the "theory of Gansu's backwardness" in order to justify a slower pace of economic development. These officials emphasized the province's complex social and nationality situation and deplored central policies as too "left" and "impetuous." Objections to large scale construction also reflected fear that rapid growth would alter the local balance of power: e.g., the immigration of workers from other provinces would mean "Lanzhou is no longer the Lanzhou of the natives of Gansu." The Gansu localists further claimed that violent deviations had occurred during land reform, and significantly attributed this to the fact that none of the leading officials of the Northwest Party Bureau at the time were Gansu natives.[51] Such reservations were especially suspect at a time when CCP leaders were calling for an unprecedented rate of social and economic change.

The last complaint by Gansu localists pointed squarely at the key feature of localism—the relationship of outside *(waigan)* and local cadres *(digan)*. Throughout the early and mid-1950s Party leaders had promoted a "localization of cadres" *(ganbu difanghua)* policy emphasizing recruitment of local people to strengthen the regime's roots in areas lacking Communist activity before 1949.[p] By the Third Plenum, however, the "localization" policy was subordinated to the "Communization" of cadres as rectification turned to combating localist sentiments. In particular, friction between native cadres and those sent from outside areas came under criticism. Such strains detracted from national priorities at a time when outsiders were often required for vigorous implementation of the new economic strategy's ambitious programs.[52]

As noted previously, cliques frequently formed on native-outsider lines and localist leaders such as Zhao Jianmin assertedly built political support by appealing directly to provincial feelings. Fueling this division was the feeling of local cadres that they had been unfairly subordinated to outsiders within their own areas. In Guangdong, local cadres complained that all native officials had been removed from positions of power during land reform and replaced by outsiders. They denounced the reform of cadres accompanying land reform as "outside cadres reforming local cadres" and "northerners scrambling for spheres of influence." Feng Baiju reportedly challenged the role of outsiders with the barb that he could not find a policy of relying on outside cadres in the writings of Marx. Guangdong authorities acknowledged some validity to these complaints by reporting that 80 percent of native cadres of county level leadership rank or above lost their positions in the aftermath of land reform. The official position, however, was that obstruction of land reform by local officials had necessitated the sending in of outsiders.[53]

Unfair treatment in other regards was alleged by the localist critique. Outside cadres assertedly received faster promotions than natives. Local cadres also felt disadvantaged by various political movements. They complained of being sent to the countryside during *xiafang* because of their greater knowledge of local dialects and customs, and viewed rectification as a device for purging natives. Moreover, a consistent theme of localist dissent was that outsiders were unsuited for responsible posts because of their ignorance of local conditions, ignorance assertedly resulting in both rightist and leftist errors. Party spokesmen admitted that native cadres did have certain advantages due to their dialects, social habits and knowledge of localities, but held that the key to work was wholeheartedly serving the people. Thus outside cadres unable to speak the local dialect assertedly "have a language in common with the masses" because of their devotion to the Party's cause. In this regard, attacks were launched against distorting the "localization" policy by advocating that only local cadres fill leading posts. This, it was pointed out, focused solely on the recruitment and promotion of native

[p] Another aspect of the policy was to integrate cadres sent from the outside with the local population by encouraging them to learn local dialects and customs.

cadres while overlooking the second aspect of "localization"—the promotion of outside cadres who had familiarized themselves with local conditions.[54]

While the resentments of local cadres drew sustenance from the strong attachment to native place and distrust of outsiders in Chinese culture, more was involved in localist sentiments. The situation in Guangdong, where many key leaders were provincial natives, indicates native-outsider tensions were not the sole cause of localism. An additional cleavage was between cadres including Guangdong natives and other southerners whose pre-1949 careers were spent with the main CCP forces in North China and those who had served in local guerrilla forces or underground. These guerrilla and underground cadres had by and large operated independently with few organizational links to the main Communist forces. When such links were established with the guerrilla forces on Hainan Island, moreover, Feng Baiju allegedly sought to force out cadres dispatched by the Center.[55]

The independent operations of the revolutionary period had ramifications in post-1949 China. Former guerrillas had strong ties to the people of their former base areas and reportedly utilized their revolutionary exploits to become "local heroes." Moreover, they had a deep commitment to their fellow guerrillas based on a common revolutionary heritage:

> Localists [in Guangdong] often put up the pretext that "we must not sever history," and "we must honor history," in order to make local revolutionary work completely independent of the work of the Party as a whole, taking local revolutionary history out of the entire revolutionary history of the Party. . . . Stemming from this mistake, it is natural that they hold that certain local posts, certain local military establishments, and certain local powers are all sacred and inviolable, and must be preserved and inherited by themselves one generation after another.[56]

Similarly, former underground leaders in Gansu reportedly felt a moral obligation to place old associates behind enemy lines in important posts. But whatever posts former underground and guerrilla cadres were able to secure, the main problem grew from feelings of discrimination over their failure to attain higher Party rank. For example, Sun Diancai reportedly began revolutionary activities in the "white area" of Gansu in 1932, but after liberation he rose no higher than vice governor. In contrast, the provincial first secretarial position was filled by Zhang Zhongliang, a regular Red Army commander during the revolutionary period. The discontent generated by such thwarted ambitions is suggested by the fact that in Yunnan 122 of 158 purged Party members under the jurisdiction of the provincial committee had been active in underground work before liberation.[57]

Such grievances were also the cause of serious localist disruption on Hainan Island, the guerrilla base of Feng Baiju. Feng, although transferred to posts in the Guangdong provincial apparatus, retained a deep interest in Hainan affairs. At the time of the 1956 Party Congress he allegedly wrote a letter to the Central Committee attacking the Guangdong Provincial Committee and outside cadres for interfering in Hainan. Moreover, under Feng's reputed instigation, "the Hainan anti-Party localist group" began secret factional activities in mid-1956 which hindered implementation of Party policies. Subsequently, "all Hainan Island was swept by a wave of discrimination, attack, insult and threat against outside cadres [with the result that] everybody was plunged into a state of panic." This came to a climax in December 1956 with a "miniature Hungarian incident" in Lingao county. Officially described as armed resistance in league with class enemies to usurp Party and government leadership, the incident involved over 300 army veterans led by former guerrillas who had been replaced by new cadres. They surrounded county Party and government offices, cut telephone wires, collected weapons, and forced the county magistrate to reinstate members of Feng's guerrilla forces to their cadre positions. At about the same time a similar incident reportedly took place in neighboring Nada county, and again the issue was restoring old cadres to their previous posts. While these events took place at the end of 1956, systematic measures against localism in Guangdong only began in summer 1957 and intensified after the Third Plenum when far-reaching decentralization measures came into effect.[58]

Despite the seriousness of the Hainan incidents, localism was largely considered an ideological problem to be handled by lenient methods. In the official view localists generally responded to educational measures, and even in serious cases magnanimous organizational measures were advocated where there was a willingness to reform. Moreover, an effort was made to counter grievances of local cadres by calling attention to the significant number of native officials who had received promotions. It was also emphasized that outside cadres had shortcomings and would have to improve their knowledge of local conditions and dialects. In addition, more substantial measures were taken. In Guangdong, emphasis was given to economic development of old base areas with the October 1957 establishment of an Old Revolutionary Base Construction Committee nominally led by Gu Dacun and Feng Baiju. This was a double edged measure. Although providing needed attention to economic growth, it also involved sending large numbers of outside cadres to lead construction projects in Hainan, something which localists elsewhere had resisted. Moreover, despite the lenient official posture, as we have seen purges did take place. Finally, Cultural Revolution sources claim that in Guangdong Tao Zhu waged a brutal struggle against ordinary cadres on the pretext of opposing localism. While such allegations cannot be adequately evaluated, it would be surprising if a substantial degree of tension did not accompany an anti-localist struggle undertaken at a time of increasing demands on both cadres and general population.[59]

Local Nationalism

Due to ethnic and cultural differences between Han Chinese and national minorities, local nationalism is potentially more divisive than localism in Han areas.

Until mid-1957, CCP policy allowed considerable leeway for local customs and a slower rate of social change in minority areas. In his "Ten Great Relationships" and "Contradictions" speeches Mao viewed Han chauvinism, the excessive dominance of Han Chinese over minorities, as a greater danger than local nationalism. The tensions of socialist transformation, however, produced a substantial increase in local nationalist feeling which was vigorously expressed during the Hundred Flowers period. In summer 1957 a forum on nationalities work marked a reversal in the assessment of the main danger.[q] A basic shift in Party policy now called for fuller integration of minorities in national society and launched an extensive campaign against local nationalism.[60] The need to combat this deviation was soon intensified by the acceleration of social change in minority areas due to the Great Leap Forward.

Many aspects of local nationalism resemble problems aired in attacks on localism. For example, various movements were criticized as excessive while modernizing measures such as building railroads and reclaiming land were opposed by local nationalists. Criticisms, however, went deeper than the claim that policies had not been adjusted to local conditions. Some saw Party policies as inherently alien to nationality customs and traditions. Thus APCs were described as "only suited to the Han nationality," while socialist transformation assertedly "destroyed nationality characteristics." The greatest objection was to the influx of Han settlers which accompanied social and economic change. Local nationalists feared that even the limited local autonomy which existed would be abolished while minority peoples were culturally assimilated by Hans.[61]

Tension between Han and minority cadres was a key issue. Minority officials claimed that they held posts without real authority, argued that the CCP neither valued nor trained nationality cadres, and equated Party leadership with leadership by Hans. Some promoted the idea that only nationality Party members could

[q] Han chauvinism was still recognized as a problem, however. Not only were appeals issued for Han cadres to examine their shortcomings, but Han chauvinism was an issue in the purge of provincial leaders in Gansu and Liaoning. In Gansu, the same "localist clique" which sought to restrict the influx of Hans from other parts of China reportedly discriminated against Hui cadres within Gansu. *Gansu ribao* [Gansu Daily], August 16, 1958, in *CB*, No. 528.

Moreover, tensions existed among various minority nationalities. Jahoda, the purged Governor of the Ili Kazakh Autonomous Department, was charged with opposing Uighurs as well as Hans. He allegedly said, "The enemy near at hand (referring to the Uighur people) is more serious than the enemy at a distance (referring to the Han people)," and attempted to move 20,000 Uighur households from Yining. In a similar case, Liang Wanggui, Secretary of the Miao-Tong Autonomous Department in southeast Guizhou, was purged for assertedly provoking Tong nationality cadres, discriminating against Miao cadres, and plotting to set up a Tong autonomous area. George Moseley, *A Sino-Soviet Cultural Frontier: The Ili Kazakh Autonomous Chou* (Cambridge: Harvard East Asian Monographs, 1966), p. 65; and *Guizhou ribao* [Guizhou Daily], April 30, 1958, in *SCMP*, No. 1813.

protect the interests of minority people, while others held only the upper strata of nationalities could truly represent minority interests. Nationality cadres in Xinjiang reportedly expressed their disapproval of Han cadres openly and told them to "go home." Similarly, a local nationalist in Guangxi argued that minorities could not exercise their powers as long as Han cadres remained and advocated the evacuation of all such cadres from minority areas. Others urged the "nationalization" of the Party by means of assigning Party posts according to the ratio of nationalities in an area. In response to this agitation, the official view argued that substantial strides had been made in training minority cadres but Han leadership was both unavoidable and beneficial at the present stage. For example, minority cadres assertedly were now 35 percent of all cadres at the county and higher levels in Xinjiang. The predominance of Hans in responsible positions was attributed to the history of the Chinese revolution, and, in any case, was judged necessary for aiding nationality areas to overcome their backwardness.[62]

Local nationalist agitation centered on increasing the autonomy of minority areas. In some cases this only involved complaints that Party authorities did not attach sufficient importance to the regional autonomy proclaimed by the CCP's own policies. In others, demands were made for raising the administrative status and expanding the territory of nationality regions. More seriously, separatist ideas and activities appeared not only among non-Party intellectuals but also among Party members, including high ranking cadres. Officials of various nationalities reportedly advocated "independent republics" or "federal republics." More specifically, Uighur cadres in Xinjiang demanded a "Uighurstan," while the Kazakhs of that area asked for the reestablishment of the "East Turkestan Republic" which had existed at different times during the 1930s and 1940s. The official line rejected such pressure and argued Chinese conditions were not suited to the establishment of a federal republic due to the intermingling of populations and the overwhelming numerical preponderance of Han Chinese.[63]

As with localism, official guidelines called for discriminating handling of cases of local nationalism. But the implication of a somewhat sterner attitude was conveyed by the statement that while the latter deviation was a "contradiction among the people" in some regards, it was a "contradiction with the enemy" in others, and careful efforts were called for to distinguish proper nationality sentiments, typical nationality prejudices, and bourgeois nationalism. Moreover, as we have seen, purges of significant figures were carried out. Still, the ostensible emphasis was on persuasion and leniency. While severe criticism was called for it was to be conducted with caution, and special attention was to be devoted to winning over middle of the road elements. The overwhelming majority of cadres were judged good despite the fairly widespread presence of nationalist ideas; rectification and socialist education were generally considered adequate for dealing with their problems. Meanwhile, Great Leap policies were implemented in minority areas with fewer concessions than had previously been the case. Although the assimilation this was designed to achieve would theoretically undercut local nationalism, in the short run it undoubtedly intensified such tendencies and made countermeasures necessary.[64]

Rectification in the People's Liberation Army

Although the Chinese military participated in rectification in spring and summer 1957,[r] it was only during the Great Leap Forward that a major impact was felt. The "politics in command" emphasis of the leap was now reflected in PLA activities. In January 1958 a new training program was instituted with the basic tasks of "increasing the political consciousness of all personnel and studying Comrade Mao Zedong's writings on military affairs." The program further called for strengthening ideological leadership by Party committees and declared improved political work would increase the effectiveness of military training and aid in the mastering of modern techniques. In March, the Central Committee's Military Affairs Committee (MAC) launched a full scale campaign for the study of Mao's military writings. By mid-summer a "new upsurge" of Mao study was noted and research committees and study groups for this purpose were set up in army units. Moreover, various military academies revised their programs to increase time devoted to political studies, rewrite materials to stress Mao's writings, and install political commissars in both classes and field units. In the latter half of 1958 various programs designed to bolster the PLA's role in society and inner army democracy were implemented: increased PLA participation in productive labor, militia organization on a nationwide scale, and the system of officers serving as ordinary soldiers for one month each year.[65]

[r] In spring 1957 PLA rectification focused on contradictions between officers and men and between the army and civilians. Criticism was directed at arrogant behavior toward the public, extravagant living by officer families, indiscriminate relations with local women, and carelessness regarding people's property during maneuvers. In addition, criticism appeared of doctrinaire study of foreign [i.e., Soviet] experiences. During the anti-rightist struggle In summer 1957 there were no exposures of high ranking PLA leaders although the army newspaper did denounce "the clamor of bourgeois rightists for abrogating Party leadership in the armed forces." Deng Xiaoping's September overview of the movement reported only a few army rightists had been uncovered and the composition of the PLA was "comparatively pure." But while the political and ideological situation was judged basically healthy, concern was shown over manifestations of individualism and lack of discipline which was attributed to the peaceful environment, large numbers of new recruits in the PLA, and an "inappropriate stress on specialization to the neglect of ideological and political work." As in other spheres, these problems were dealt with by systematic socialist education as stipulated by a September GPD directive. This was to be conducted as "a gentle breeze and mild rain" through organized debates under the control of unit commanders. See NCNA, Beijing, May 12, September 5, 1957, in *SCMP,* Nos. 1547, 1611; *JFJB,* May 18, 21, 23, 1957, in *URS,* Vol. 8—No. 5; NCNA, Chongqing, May 22, 1957, in *SCMP,* No. 1539; and Teng, "Report on Rectification," pp. 357–58.

A major development in this period was an enlarged rectification meeting of the MAC from May 27 to July 22. During the Cultural Revolution this MAC session was declared the culmination of the first great post-liberation struggle within the PLA, a struggle which assertedly had been simmering since the Korean War.[66] The key issue was doctrinairism, the tendency to accept uncritically Soviet methods of military modernization. In a late June speech to the meeting Mao repeatedly criticized those who had "blind faith" in the Soviet Union and suggested such attitudes reflected an inferiority complex. In terms reminiscent of the 1942–44 rectification campaign, the Chairman called for the integration of advanced Soviet experiences with the PLA's own traditions and innovations. This need to preserve Chinese traditions—particularly the emphasis on political and ideological work and inner army democracy—had been advocated since 1956 but now, as in other areas, a distinct assertion of the *superiority* of Chinese methods was added. This did not mean that advanced military technology was ignored. Despite the 1958 stress on "man over weapons" it was precisely this area, according to Mao and Lin Biao, that the Russians had the most to offer. But such technical advances would have to be integrated with a strategic doctrine more suited to China's situation. Soviet doctrine, Mao complained, was entirely offensive in nature (and thus suited to Europe where the Soviet Union had a large conventional advantage) and made no provision for defensive war (such as would be required against a technologically superior invader of China). Throughout the entire discussion Mao invoked the themes and specific example of the Great Leap—self-reliance, combining native and foreign methods, liberating ideology, and overturning superstitions. Military affairs thus paralleled economic developments: an initial modification of the Soviet model in 1956 had given way to a vigorous assertion of an independent Chinese path in 1958.[67]

While intensified political efforts were partially an extension of the steps undertaken since 1956 to revitalize PLA traditions, the extent of the 1958 measures reflect two factors: the dynamics of the leap forward and resistance to previous political measures in 1956–57. This resistance was based on the feeling of many officers that the revolutionary traditions of the PLA were not suited to a modern army and the military theories of Mao were outdated for contemporary warfare. Such officers assertedly gave onesided emphasis to technique and military affairs while neglecting ideology and the role of the masses, as well as blindly worshipping foreign practices.[68] These attitudes were particularly disturbing because they were linked to an attack on the Party committee system:

> [P]urely military views, warlordism, and doctrinairism have revived among a part of the personnel. They assert that collective leadership of Party committees is not adapted to the requirements of modernization and regularization. Onesidedly stressing the suddenness and complexity of modern warfare, they

> assert that the system of Party committees will impede the better judgment and concentration of command. *They even openly advocate liquidation of the system of Party committee leadership.* Further, they liquidated and restricted the activities of Party committees in leadership and political work. While these views have not predominated in the whole army, they have caused certain ideological confusion and weakened the fine tradition of our army in practical work.[69]

Thus in the PLA as in other areas the question of organizational control was raised during the Great Leap Forward. The limited nature of actual purges in the army,[s] however, suggests the problem was not as serious as in some other institutions.

In terms of high level leadership differences within the PLA, the situation apparently mirrored conditions within the Party as a whole. The existence of high level divisions was suggested both by Mao's June 1958 reference to a "two line struggle" in military affairs and his sharp criticism of leading figures such as Vice Minister of Defense and head of the PLA's General Training Department, Xiao Ke.[70] Beyond this, whether Lin Biao's May 1958 promotion to the Politburo Standing Committee and his leading role at the enlarged MAC session reflected dissatisfaction with Defense Minister Peng

[s]Only one high ranking officer was publicly purged in the entire 1957–58 period. Chen Yi, the head of the cultural department of the GPD (not to be confused with the Minister of Foreign Affairs), was expelled from the Party and dishonorably discharged from the PLA as a "bogus left winger and genuine right winter" following a November 1957–February 1958 GPD conference. The charges against Chen focused on his activities during the Hundred Flowers period. During the first half of 1957 Chen, who had been regarded as a long time defender of orthodoxy, was criticized by dissident writers for doctrinairism and muzzling army literary personnel. In 1958, however, Chen was depicted as a vigorous advocate of the interests of PLA literary workers. In sharp contrast to the dissidents' 1957 view, he was now said to have argued that the Hundred Flowers movement was stifled within army organizations and the PLA had become estranged from the masses. While the contradictions between the two views of Chen cannot be resolved on the basis of available evidence, it can be hypothesized that he was caught between the conflicting pressures of his job. On the one hand, he was to assert political control over army writers and thus inevitably earned the resentment of at least some of them. On the other hand, in order to obtain results from writers under his leadership Chen would have to make some concessions to their interests, a need undoubtedly resulting in actions which could be attacked as superficially left but actually right from the anti-intellectual perspective of 1958. That Chen apparently was unable to negotiate the various shifts of line in 1957 may have been due to the most significant charge against him, that of organizational unreliability. It was alleged that Chen had treated the cultural department as an independent kingdom, resisted supervision and criticism by his superiors, appointed personnel without proper organizational approval, and opposed the merger of the cultural and propaganda departments of the GPD which would have meant the end of his independent power. See *CNA,* No. 216 (1958); and *RMRB,* March 1, 1958, in *SCMP,* No. 1729.

Dehuai must remain speculative.[t] In any case, as in other areas, Mao seemed determined to keep the struggle within bounds and aim for unity. In his June speech the Chairman declared "one need not write down the names of comrades who committed errors" in the conference resolution. As with the Great Leap in the economy, new directions in military affairs had exacerbated differences at the policy making level, but the divisions were not so deep as to invalidate traditional approaches to leadership cohesion in Mao's eyes.

Conclusion

The rectification and purge measures taken following the Third Plenum were on the whole closely linked to the Great Leap Forward. The overall course of the campaign, after initial concern with mundane improvements in bureaucratic procedures, was soon explicitly tied to the themes and goals of the new economic strategy. More broadly, there was now a closer fit between the problems attacked and alternating consolidation and mobilization phases than had been the case in the early 1950s (see Chapter 4). Much as the spring 1957 criticism of bureaucratism, secretarianism and subjectivism was suited to the consolidation emphasis on redressing imbalances, rectification after the Third Plenum—by attacking caution, doubt and preferences for established practices—fully supported a sweeping mobilization aimed at far-reaching social, economic and political change.

Meanwhile, purges and lesser disciplinary action affecting high ranking officials reflected the leap forward in a more subtle fashion. While few of the officials disciplined were directly accused of opposition to the Great Leap, they were charged with a policy orientation in 1956–57 fundamentally at odds with the leap in two respects: (1) a cautious, incentive oriented economic outlook which attached considerable weight to technical considerations; and (2) a position favoring increased autonomy for specialist organizations *vis-à-vis* Party committees. Whether the issue was the relationship of Party and government organs in daily administration, dual versus vertical rule in the supervisory system, or the independence of military commanders, the opinions under attack pointed to a dilution of Party committee authority. But policy views were not the sole consideration. They were linked to alleged breeches of organizational discipline including the formation of cliques, false reports to higher levels, failing to

[t]According to W.F. Dorrill, *Power, Policy and Ideology in the Making of China's "Cultural Revolution,"* RAND memorandum RM–5731-PR, August 1968, p. 22, Lin led the rectification conducted by the enlarged MAC session. Lin clearly was active at this meeting as his interjections in Mao's June speech indicate. Peng, however, gave the concluding speech at the conference, a sign of some authority over its proceedings. Moreover, no specific Cultural Revolution charges against Peng were found for his role at this conference, or for his military performance at this time. Cf. the discussion of the possible role of military issues in Peng's 1959 dismissal in Chapter 9.

implement central directives, and the creation of independent kingdoms. Since the leap forward placed a premium on Party committee leadership and organizational discipline in pursuit of rapid growth, officials who both held contrary policy views and had demonstrated questionable organizational reliability were a matter of considerable concern. The post-Third Plenum purges and dismissals, then, were essentially prophylactic measures designed to firm up political leadership for the heavy demands of the Great Leap.

In an important sense, rectification after the Third Plenum involved a search for a new type of Party leadership. While the initial steps toward rectification in 1956 and early 1957 sought to redefine Party leadership in terms of perceived changes in the overall situation after the victory of socialist transformation, now a further redefinition took place in accord with the needs of the Great Leap. While there were continuities with the reaffirmation of Party authority during the anti-rightist struggle, there were also important departures. In both cases Party officials reasserted their control of specialized institutions; professional autonomy *per se* would not be allowed. The anti-rightist measures, however, were compatible with not only a highly centralized bureaucracy, but one where specialists could still have a major influence by operating *through* Party officials overseeing their activities. While this approach may have imposed unwanted political burdens on experts, a working relationship with Party cadres could further a specialist orientation in official policies. The Great Leap approach, on the other hand, led to a far more radical concept of leadership with power devolved to lower level Party committees. Now the emphasis was on a less bureaucratized administration where cadres and masses working together would try to transform China at unprecedented speed. The disruption of established routines which resulted was considerable. Not only were about two million cadres sent to lower levels, but the reallocation of bureaucratic authority weakened many central units and even led to the dissolution of the Ministry of Supervision.

The Great Leap Forward, undoubtedly the most thorough mobilization in China since 1949, generated considerable social tension as millions were exhorted to pursue constantly escalating production targets. This tension inevitably spilled over into the rectification process despite continued advocacy of "gentle breeze and mild rain" methods. As anticipated, this was reflected in a more coercive disciplinary approach both in terms of purges and other sanctions directed at high ranking figures and an increasing purge rate within the Party as a whole. While the degree of coercion was still limited, it came increasingly into conflict with official pronouncements affirming the "save the patient" approach for what were regarded as largely problems of understanding. Thus, in a general context of unrealistic goals and bloated rhetoric, an estrangement between rectification theory and practice began to appear. This estrangement would grow in subsequent rectification campaigns.

While the relatively greater incidence of coercion during the intense mobilization of 1957–58 was to be expected, several other propositions advanced in

Chapters 2 and 3 were not borne out by events. First, the harsher sanctions directed at Party members after the Third Plenum were largely handled by the regular chain of command and not by work teams.[u] This is probably explained in part by the fact that although relatively severe, these sanctions still fell far short of a massive, totally disruptive purge. More importantly, unit leaders caught in the Great Leap vortex were under such pressure that overly protective attitudes toward subordinates became politically risky. Second, coercive measures were unrelated to increasing international tension. To the extent that Mao's November 1957 reassessment of the world balance of forces contributed to the optimistic assumptions underlying the Great Leap, an international factor was present. But more basically, increasing coercion was not a response to foreign threats. Although the summer 1958 Taiwan Straits crisis has been viewed by some observers as creating a tense climate where mobilization policies could be pursued,[71] the crisis only arose well after leap forward programs were in force and at the very tail end of the rectification campaign. Thus the Taiwan Straits crisis at best only amplified the internal considerations which led rectification into harsher channels.

The increasingly coercive cast of rectification was only one indication of traditional norms coming under stress. Even more significant was the fact that contemporary policy differences became a central issue in Party rectification for the first time. In 1942–44 policy questions were raised, but they had long been settled in Mao's favor. In 1947–48 and the early 1950s rectification efforts concerned questions of policy implementation and organizational purity, while disciplinary measures left the policy making levels virtually untouched. The purge of Gao Gang and Rao Shushi did reach the very apex of the decision making structure, but did not involve policy issues in any central fashion. While there was inner Party opposition to the Hundred Flowers experiment which perhaps involved the Politburo level, these did not lead to significant disciplinary sanctions. Verbal rebukes to critics such as Chen Qitong were the limit of the action taken. And while some relatively high ranking Party cadres were caught by the policy switch of mid-1957, those who received significant punishment did so largely because of their critical *attitude* towards Party leadership and organizational unreliability rather than due to any specific *policy advocacy.* Policy views became a key target of rectification only as the Soviet economic model was fundamentally rejected following the Third Plenum. Although Mao was able to build a strong majority in favor of the Great Leap in policy councils, the previous consensus was now shattered and many officials entertained severe

---

[u] Rectification in this period was conducted through existing organs down to the county level. However, its extension to the countryside in conjunction with production investigations and establishing people's communes in summer and fall 1958 involved the use of work teams primarily composed of county cadres. See Teiwes, "Case Study," pp. 92–93.

reservations as China plunged down an uncharted economic path.

As policy differences tended to become more matters of basic approach than questions of timing or degree within a commonly accepted framework, the viability of both established procedures of inner Party debate and traditional rectification measures came under increasing strain. For example, the fact that Pan Fusheng and Wu Zhipu could be seen as representing fundamentally opposed economic policies in Henan undoubtedly was a crucial factor in Pan's dismissal. Wu not only attacked Pan as a "thorough pessimist" who wanted to walk the capitalist road, he also became one of the foremost advocates of the Great Leap.[72] If the issues had been less polarized it would have been easier to treat the dispute as a legitimate expression of differing views or as a problem requiring no more than criticism and self-criticism.

Still, it must be emphasized that, at least in this early stage of the Great Leap, Mao and other Party leaders had considerable success in their efforts to retain traditional approaches and methods. In the case of the highest ranking official apparently affected, Chen Yun, neither formal discipline nor informal criticism was applied, a tacit admission of the right of Party leaders to hold minority opinions. Moreover, in the cases of provincial and other leaders where disciplinary measures were taken, dissenting policy views were insufficient justification; violation of established organizational principles apparently was crucial. In any case, the purges and dismissals at these levels are notable for their limited scope. Although vice ministers, provincial secretaries and governors were involved, no key officials of central Party organs, Party member ministers or full Central Committee members were dismissed. Thus when Mao said at the March 1958 Chengdu conference that "We have neither been carrying out struggles nor identifying rightists, but talking in gentle tones like a gentle breeze and mild rain so that everyone can say what is on his mind," he was not only affirming a long standing method of dealing with inner Party differences, but also reflecting partially if not totally the current state of affairs at the highest policy making levels. Nevertheless, Mao's growing concern in this same period with "inevitable" inner Party splits and assertions that his projected retirement from the state chairmanship did not mean political abdication imply an awareness that conditions were changing which might preclude both the Party unity required for mild rectification and the completion of his graceful withdrawal to the "second line."[73]

The rectification process after the Third Plenum had both successes and failures. In a sense, rectification was too successful.[74] Together with other political pressures, it silenced critics and energized vast numbers of cadres to work long hours in the pursuit of ambitious goals. But in so doing seeds of future crisis were sown for both the rectification process and the political system generally. The alacrity with which Party cadres as a whole took up the Great Leap program prevented moderating influences and led to excesses which hastened the collapse of the strategy. Also, with high level officials suffering career setbacks at least in part for their views, the policy process began to lose some of its former vitality.

As the deficiencies of the Great Leap Forward became increasingly clear, the already frayed leadership unity would be further shaken while cadres who inevitably were blamed for the leap's shortcomings would be progressively demoralized. From this perspective, the successes of rectification in late 1957 and 1958 were hollow victories indeed.

9
The Dismissal of Peng Dehuai

The dismissal of Defense Minister Peng Dehuai was the culmination of the second top level leadership crisis in post-1949 China. While some observers have stressed military and foreign policy issues as the underlying cause of Peng's demise,[1] most analyses—including this one—focus on differences concerning the Great Leap Forward. By late 1958 CCP leaders had become aware of shortcomings in the leap and several important policy changes were decreed at a series of high level meetings which continued until mid-1959. Although Mao formally resigned the chairmanship of the state in favor of Liu Shaoqi at this time, he did not in fact retire to the "second line" but instead took a leading role in the process of policy readjustment. Dealing with the defects of the Great Leap was still the key item on the agenda when China's top leaders met in Lushan in July and August 1959.

A major confrontation took place between Mao and Peng Dehuai at Lushan. While some scholars argue that Mao had undercut Peng's position well before Lushan and the events there merely involved administering the *coup de grace*,[a] most interpretations depict a frontal assault on Peng's part directed at Mao's programs and leadership.[2] This interpretation, in contrast, sees Peng taking the initiative not to attack the Chairman but to persuade him of the need for more far-reaching changes in the leap forward strategy than had previously been adopted. More fundamentally, this study analyzes the conflict at Lushan in terms of Mao's response to Peng's views—a response which seriously breached tradi-

[a] See especially J.D. Simmonds, "P'eng Te-huai: A Chronological Re-examination," *CQ*, No. 37 (1969). Simmonds' argument relies heavily on speculation about personnel changes in the defense establishment in early 1959 which he claims significantly weakened Peng. The personnel data, however, is fragmentary and open to other interpretations. In our analysis, Mao's surprise at developments at Lushan (see below) casts doubt on the theory that Peng had been set up for what unfolded in July-August 1959.

tional Party norms. Although organizational questions were raised against Peng and his "anti-Party clique" of PLA Chief of Staff Huang Kecheng, Vice Minister of Foreign Affairs Zhang Wentian and Hunan First Secretary Zhou Xiaozhou, basically Mao reacted in anger to Peng's critique of the Great Leap. By removing Peng and his associates from their operational posts, Mao and those leaders who supported him—most notably Liu Shaoqi and Zhou Enlai—in effect violated the right to air minority views freely in official Party forums. With divisions over the new economic strategy more intense than in late 1957 and 1958, Politburo level leaders were now ousted from their positions and subjected to harsh inner Party criticisms. While Chen Yun had been quietly downgraded for his policy dissent, Peng *et al.* received formal disciplinary sanctions.[b]

Although Mao had broken long established understandings, there was a degree of ambivalence in his actions. Not only did he stop short of expelling Peng and the others from the Party, a measure which had been invoked in defending traditional norms against Gao Gang and Rao Shushi, but the Chairman contradictorily called for boldness in expressing opinions at the same time he attacked Peng Dehuai. These efforts notwithstanding, the events at Lushan clearly had an eroding effect on the norms. Other leaders, seeing Peng's fate, were less willing to assert their rights in policy debates. Moreover, Mao's "individual style" which had already caused grumbling before Lushan was underlined by his emotional reaction to Peng's critique. In addition, rectification principles were also endangered by the subsequent campaign against "right opportunists" *(youqing jihuizhuyi fenzi)* who held similar views to those of Peng and associates. Not only were cadres at various levels attacked for their policy views, but the harshness of the movement led to bitter complaints that the discredited "ruthless struggles and merciless blows" approach to elite discipline was again in vogue.

Political Profiles of Peng, Huang, Zhang and Zhou[3]

Peng Dehuai

One of the greatest military figures in the history of the CCP, Peng was born in the same Hunan county as Mao Zedong. Peng spent his early career in warlord and GMD armies. He was also exposed to left wing and Marxist ideas, however, and in 1928 joined the Party. Shortly thereafter, Peng and others established the Fifth Red Army on the basis of ex-GMD units. By the latter part of 1928 Peng had joined forces with Mao and Zhu De at Jinggangshan. Although sometimes

[b] Although no public criticism of Peng and associates unfolded and their removals *(mianzhi)* were announced as mere administrative changes, the secret resolution of the Lushan meeting left no doubt their loss of posts was a disciplinary measure. See below, p. 325.

fighting separately and sometimes with the Mao-Zhu forces, for the remainder of the southern phase of the revolution his career was closely intertwined with that of Mao. Most significant was Peng's support of Mao during the Futian incident late in 1930. After Mao had ordered the mass arrest of opponents within the Red Army, supporters of the arrested men proclaimed support for Peng and Zhu De while demanding Mao's overthrow. Peng and Zhu, however, stood by Mao and helped him prevail.

Peng was one of the leading figures of the historic Long March and arrived in Shaanxi with Mao at the head of vanguard units. It was at this time that Peng's support of Mao was rewarded by his elevation to the Politburo. During the Sino-Japanese War and subsequent civil war, Peng was second only to Zhu De in the CCP military hierarchy. While frequently commanding forces in battlefront areas, Peng also spent considerable time in Yan'an providing overall military leadership, particularly in the 1943–47 period. After Yan'an fell to the GMD in 1947, the paths of Mao and Peng separated as Mao moved to Hebei while Peng remained in the Northwest during the final stages of the war. After liberation, although holding high central posts, Peng initially remained in the Northwest as the key regional leader until a short time before Chinese forces entered the Korean War. Peng commanded these forces for the duration of the fighting. With the reorganization of the central government in 1954, he was named head of the newly created Ministry of Defense.

A striking aspect of Peng's career is its links to Mao Zedong. Also, as one of the most senior central army leaders both before and after 1949, Peng was continually involved in discussions with Mao over military policy. This is particularly notable in view of many accusations concerning Peng's pre-1949 activities which appeared during the Cultural Revolution.[4] The theme of these charges is that Peng consistently opposed Mao on a wide variety of issues from Jinggangshan on. Leading Western analysts, furthermore, have argued that a fundamental conflict existed throughout Peng's career between the professional military ethic allegedly represented by Peng and Mao's policies emphasizing guerrilla warfare and political control.[5] While differences surely occurred and on at least one occasion in Yan'an resulted in sustained criticism of Peng by Mao,[c] assertions of a basic, unchanging divergence of views are clearly overdrawn. Moreover, in political terms, Peng stood with Mao at two critical points, the Futian incident and on the Long March. Whatever the conflicts between the two

[c] Significant differences apparently occurred over Peng's famous Hundred Regiments Offensive and other issues in the early 1940s, and Peng reportedly was struggled against for 40 days at a conference convened before the 1945 Party Congress. This incident left a residue of bitterness on Peng's part which assertedly contributed to his actions at Lushan. See *CB*, No. 851, p. 7. Peng's loss of favor at this time is further suggested by the fact that Lin Biao rather than the more senior Peng received the choice Manchurian command after the Sino-Japanese War, and also by the disparity in the two men's ranking at the 1945 Congress (see below).

men, the picture of systematic opposition to Mao must be regarded as a gross distortion.

However, other Cultural Revolution revelations that personal friction existed between the two men and Peng believed this hindered his career may be more pertinent. According to one Red Guard source, Peng complained in 1953 that "The Chairman doesn't like me. Neither does he hold me in esteem. The young men have come up. I do not want to be in authority any longer." [d] That there may have been some basis for this feeling is suggested by comparing Peng's status with that of Lin Biao. Despite Peng's military position second only to Zhu De, he was only the 35th ranking member of the Central Committee elected at the 1945 Party Congress while Lin ranked sixth. When the central government was reorganized in 1954, Lin outranked Peng on the list of vice premiers despite his lack of a ministerial post. Similarly, Lin placed seventh in the Politburo elected at the 1956 Party Congress, while Peng ranked 14th despite his greater seniority on that body. Finally, despite an apparent lack of operational responsibilities because of poor health, Lin was elevated to the Standing Committee of the Politburo and Party Vice Chairmanship in May 1958.

If Peng had cause to feel slighted by Mao, it is also possible that Mao took umbrage at Peng's legendary lack of tact. Perhaps a significant example was Peng's suggestion that the "Thought of Mao Zedong" be deleted from the 1956 Party Constitution. While such a proposal made sense in the context of developments within the international Communist movement in 1956 and all evidence points to Mao's consent, it is plausible that Mao harbored submerged resentment of Peng's boldness in raising the issue.[6] While none of these personal frictions necessarily meant a lack of respect for Peng's abilities on Mao's part, they probably had the cumulative effect of excluding Peng from the Chairman's innermost circles and maximizing the potential for conflict when differences did emerge.

Huang Kecheng

Huang, also a native of Hunan, had substantial career ties to both Peng and Mao. Huang apparently joined the CCP while fighting with Mao's forces during the 1927 Autumn Harvest Uprising and subsequently retreated to Jinggangshan with Mao. From 1929 to 1935 Huang served with Peng's Third Army and participated in the Long March as part of that army. During the Sino-Japanese and civil wars, however, Huang's career branched off from both Peng and Mao as he served with the New Fourth Army under Chen Yi and subsequently in Northeast China

[d] *Mass Criticism and Repudiation Bulletin* (Guangzhou), October 5, 1967, in *The Case of Peng Teh-huai 1959–1968* (Hong Kong: Union Research Institute, 1968), p. 123. Peng, for his part, admitted quarreling with Mao during the Kiangsi period and thereafter "harboring exceedingly wrong personal prejudice" against the Chairman. *Ibid.*, p. 33.

with Lin Biao's armies. He remained with Lin's forces as they moved south and after 1949 took up leading Party, government and military posts in Hunan. By mid-1952 Huang was transferred to Peking to become Deputy Chief of Staff of the armed forces. With the reorganization of 1954, he assumed the key posts of Vice Minister of Defense and Director of the PLA's Rear Services Department. At that point his career and that of Peng Dehuai again became closely intertwined. Huang gave up his rear services post in 1956 shortly after being named a Central Committee secretary, but during the 1958 Quemoy crisis he replaced Su Yu as PLA Chief of Staff. In sum, although he had important career ties to Peng Dehuai, Huang's position as a major figure was bolstered by significant links to other leaders including Lin Biao and Mao himself.

Zhang Wentian

Of the major figures denounced at Lushan, only Zhang Wentian had a clear record of past factional conflict with Mao. Zhang was a leader of the returned student group which struggled with Mao for control of the CCP in the early 1930s. Although the policy differences between Mao and Zhang may have been less pronounced than those between Mao and other returned student leaders, it was Zhang who replaced Mao in early 1934 as head of the Chinese Soviet Republic's cabinet when significant gains were made by the returned students in the leadership struggle. Nevertheless, when Mao gained preeminence within the CCP at the Zunyi Conference in January 1935, Zhang apparently became Party general secretary and held this post for several years. Although the position no longer had its former power, Zhang's holding of the office probably indicated both limits on Mao's authority and Zhang's ability to reconcile differences with Mao. Subsequently, Zhang remained an active figure in Yan'an with responsibilities in propaganda, theoretical work and cadre training until at least the 1942 *zhengfeng* campaign. During the post-1945 civil war he held a number of responsible posts mainly at the provincial level in the Northeast. After liberation he undertook a diplomatic career, serving as ambassador to the Soviet Union from 1951 to 1954 and then as the ranking Vice Minister of Foreign Affairs until his dismissal in 1959. During this period he participated in many important negotiations, especially with the Soviet Union. Thus despite his connection with the returned student group, Zhang played a responsible if definitely secondary role under Mao's leadership, a position symbolized by his demotion from full to alternate Politburo status in 1956. Although Zhang worked briefly with Peng during the 1950s especially regarding the creation of the Warsaw Pact, it is noteworthy that there was little connection between the two over their full careers.

Zhou Xiaozhou

Zhou, a Hunanese like Peng and Huang, is the most obscure member of the "anti-Party clique." Little is known of his pre-1949 career, but he reportedly made the Long March and served as Mao's personal secretary for a brief period in Yan'an. Scattered information reports him engaged in guerrilla activities in Hunan and other areas in subsequent years. After 1949 he held a number of Party and government posts in Hunan and by 1955 was identified as first secretary. In May 1958 he became an alternate member of the Central Committee. While the available evidence gives no indication of career ties to Peng or Zhang, Zhou clearly worked with Huang Kecheng in the Hunan Party apparatus during the early 1950s. Overall, in this case as the others, there is little to suggest close factional ties based on long standing career interests.

The Prelude to Lushan

The Lushan Party meeting was convened in late June or early July 1959 against a background of eight months of coping with the consequences of the Great Leap and people's communes. The extreme optimism which appeared following the August 1958 decision to establish rural communes on a nationwide basis was soon tempered by a growing awareness of problems of administration, distribution and cadre behavior within the communes, and also of problems in the national economy despite reports of massive production increases. Starting in November 1958 at Zhengzhou, a series of high level Party meetings was held which examined these problems. According to Mao at Lushan, during the period of these meetings "the Party Central Committee made stringent criticisms of the errors and shortcomings of various important activities under its own leadership."[7] At first there was no sense of defeat in the policy adjustments made in response to these criticisms. Rather, Mao and the majority of his associates seemed to view this as an inevitable process required to consolidate a great victory. By spring 1959, however, further knowledge of the number and scope of shortcomings created a less confident, more divided leadership. Throughout this period Mao played a leading role in attacking excesses and formulating policy changes. But while he later characterized himself as a "middle of the roader" *(zhongjian pai),* "center leftist" would have been more appropriate.[8] Mao acted as both pragmatist and visionary in this period and the uneasy marriage of the two strains contributed much to the conflict at Lushan.

Initial Policy Adjustments

The November Zhengzhou meeting decided to overhaul the newly established communes, a decision formally promulgated by the Wuhan Central Committee plenum of late November and early December. The Wuhan decision pointed out major defects in commune management, warned of exaggeration and becoming "dizzy with success," and admonished against commandist methods of leadership. It also sought to mitigate excessive egalitarianism by stressing the principle of "to each according to his work" and the primacy of wages over free supply for the time being. Peasant incentives were further recognized by allowing commune members to retain individual means of livelihood and engage in small private sideline occupations. Moreover, the decision characterized as "rashness" and a "petty bourgeois trend" attempts to accomplish the transition from socialism to Communism immediately.[9]

These steps fully reflected Mao's views. In the period of the Zhengzhou and Wuhan gatherings the Chairman singled out coercive leadership methods and false reporting of production achievements as the main problems, emphasized the need to take account of peasant needs, and called for a slowing down of the transition to Communism. He underlined his "middle of the road" position by explicitly taking issue with Anhwei First Secretary Zeng Xisheng—one of several radical provincial leaders who would face disciplinary action in 1961–62 (see Chapter 10). Zeng had castigated low targets as "opportunism"; Mao retorted he was willing to practice such "opportunism." Mao summed up his view of the requirements for leadership by criticizing himself for a subjective estimate of steel production in summer 1958: "I was enthusiastic at that time and failed to combine revolutionary fervor and a practical spirit." These qualifications notwithstanding, in the months following Wuhan Mao and his colleagues did not retreat from the objectives of the Great Leap and commune movement. Instead, the Chairman pushed for continued progress in changing forms of ownership and plans were drafted for an "even greater leap forward" in 1959.[10]

In this contradictory climate, despite the warnings of the adjusted policy line, cadre mistakes and peasant disaffection reached serious proportions in early 1959. At Lushan Mao spoke of a "wind of Communism" or "Communist style" *(gongchan feng)* which alienated the people for several months around the spring festival and was only checked in March and April. Undoubtedly much of the problem derived from continuing pressure for a leap forward and commune collectivism. As in 1947–48, cadres faced with specific caveats to a still decidedly radical overall policy felt it safer to lean to the left. Moreover, specific blame must be attached to Mao's early February conclusion that "There has been an air of cutting back for two months [since Wuhan]. Now . . . [w]e must go all out." Thus basic level cadres drove peasants for long hours in pursuit of Great Leap targets and forced them into communal mess halls, nurseries, and other collective endeavors. The injunction of the Wuhan plenum concerning the primacy of wages did not prevent the extension of the supply system in many places. Not only private property, but the property of production brigades and teams was confiscated as confusion reigned concerning the system of ownership within the communes.[11]

As the need to combat the "wind of Communism" became apparent, Party authorities further emphasized avoiding force and compulsion, going slow in extending the free supply system, and the voluntary nature of mess halls and other communal activities. Most important, an enlarged Politburo meeting held at Zhengzhou in late February and early March examined problems of administration and ownership resulting from excessive centralization within communes.

This soon led to the adoption of "three level ownership and three level accounting, with the brigade as the basic unit" at the subsequent Shanghai meetings.[e] Implementation of this system brought about a more decentralized commune management, resulted in the return of brigade and team property which had been seized earlier, and increased peasant incentives by bringing production decisions and the distribution of rewards closer to individual commune members. Even at Zhengzhou, however, ambivalence marked official actions. This was particularly clear in the words of Mao. On the one hand, the Chairman harshly criticized excessive commune appropriation of peasant production and declared his support for peasants who concealed their output from cadres. On the other hand, Mao held that the superiority of the commune "has been completely affirmed [and if] one still has problems about such a basic question, then he is entirely mistaken and must be a right opportunist." Clearly, the contradiction between the need for pragmatic policy adjustment and continued fidelity to Great Leap principles was becoming acute.[12]

Following the February–March Zhengzhou meeting, CCP leaders increasingly turned their attention to the national economy. According to a Red Guard source, Deng Xiaoping reported that "the major problem now is that there are many difficulties and confusion in production and construction work; there are serious tendencies toward exaggeration, the blind issuance of orders, and increasing [targets] as they are transmitted down the hierarchy." In addition to formalizing the three level ownership system, the enlarged Politburo meeting followed by a Central Committee plenum in Shanghai in late March and early April grappled with these problems. At Shanghai, moreover, differences surfaced within the leadership. Mao subsequently recalled that proposals were made to lower economic targets but the majority did not agree. While there is no clear indication that Peng Dehuai or any of his Lushan followers were among those calling for lower targets, Mao and Peng reportedly did clash at Shanghai over Peng's opposition to Mao "assuming command in person." Thus the *style* of policy making had become an issue in addition to the substance of policy.[13]

Further Adjustments and the Intensification of Leadership Differences

Although Mao undoubtedly stood with the "majority" at Shanghai in opposing a revision of targets, the evidence indicates that in the period between Shanghai and Lushan the Chairman fully sanctioned further pragmatic policy adjustments

[e] The issue apparently was not settled at Zhengzhou as some leaders advocated the production team as the basic unit of ownership, and others the brigade. Surprisingly, at this time Zhou Xiaozhou took a more radical position than Mao by advocating brigade level ownership while the Chairman leaned towards the team. *MMT*, I, 166–67.

which placed him at increasing odds with the left within Party councils.[f] The clearest instance of such tension concerned Mao's late April letter to cadres from the provincial to production team levels. In this letter Mao emphasized the Party's "woeful inexperience" in leading agriculture and industry and called for a realistic, step-by-step approach in overcoming problems. He criticized rigid directives from above concerning close planting which ignored local conditions and alienated experienced peasants. Mao's foremost concern was with inflated production targets which he viewed as "mere bragging." Here, as with close planting, he placed primary blame on instructions from higher levels and urged lower level cadres to "ignore them and simply concentrate on practical possibilities."[14] Mao summarized his mood in a somewhat wistful concluding paragraph:

> In comparison with the high sounding talk currently making the rounds what I am saying here is very much low key. The objective is to stir up activism and achieve the target of increased production. If [production] is not actually as low as I make it out to be, and has achieved a relatively higher target, I will then become a conservative. Thank heavens if that is so. It will be a great honor indeed.[15]

According to Cultural Revolution sources, Sichuan Party leader Li Jingquan reacted strongly to Mao's letter, declaring it was "blowing a cold wind" and "making people waver at a crucial moment." To counteract the effect of the letter, Li assertedly appended instructions that the letter was to be understood "from [its] positive aspect" and the grain output and close planting targets were not to be altered. Ironically, Li allegedly raised the same specter cited by Mao at both Zhengzhou in March and Lushan in August: "At present, *right opportunism* prevails among the leadership at all levels. . . . The source of these problems lies in the Chairman's [April letter]."[16]

If Mao faced opposition from the left at this juncture, many other Party leaders welcomed both the April letter and other moderating statements by Mao in the period leading up to Lushan. Zhang Wentian, for example, while criticizing Mao's "individual style" in issuing the letter nevertheless declared that it had "played a useful role." Chen Yun, who had spoken up against Great Leap excesses in March despite his eclipse since the Third Plenum, must have been gratified by Mao's comment on the eve of Lushan that Chen's view of the need to arrange for markets before expanding capital construction had been proven correct. Most significant was the reaction of leading economic officials who

[f]Mao had already faced disagreement from some who were to his left. For example, in 1962 he noted that at the 1958 Zhengzhou meeting some comrades "weren't happy to hear" his criticisms of the failure to implement pay according to labor. *JPRS*, No. 52029, p. 26. We have also seen that in the same period he rebuked Anhui's Zeng Xisheng for advocating excessively high targets; above p. 307. At Lushan, moreover, Mao identified Sichuan (see below), Henan and Hubei as "leftists" in contrast to his own "middle of road" position. *Case of Peng*, p. 23.

were in a position to take advantage of Mao's relative moderation. Thus Bo Yibo reportedly capitalized on Mao's warning to the Shanghai plenum that a "lack of planning will not do" to correct imbalances in the coal industry. Moreover, in June the Party Center instructed provincial officials to adjust targets despite the action taken at Shanghai. Other measures undertaken in the same period reflecting Mao's views included calls to "shorten the capital construction front," concentrate resources on high priority projects, strengthen financial and market controls, and restore elementary rural markets abolished during the commune movement.[17]

As Lushan approached a diversity of views had appeared within the Party which were increasingly difficult to reconcile. Mao seemingly had aligned himself with the forces of moderation, and Lushan was projected as a meeting where problems would be further scrutinized and additional adjustments made. Moreover, he called on officials on several occasions in the post-Shanghai period to speak out about shortcomings and not to fear retribution.[18] In this Mao was, of course, merely reasserting traditional Party principles. Yet his attitude seemingly reflected a gross underestimation of the erosion of policy consensus within the Party. In May he declared the CCP's problems were merely those of implementation:

> Everybody supports the Party's general line. The principal political objective last year was to define the general line, but we did not achieve as much as we had anticipated. This concerns our work method. Our central problem today is the work method.[19]

Thus on the eve of Lushan the political situation gave cause for two vital miscalculations. For those disenchanted with the leap forward, Lushan appeared an opportunity to move further away from Great Leap policies. For Mao, Lushan apparently was to be a forum where frank discussions among basically united comrades would solve problems and thus strengthen the unique Chinese developmental model. Expectations that the vigorous discussions guaranteed by traditional Party norms would be the order of the day were based on widely varying assumptions.

Peng's Tour and Sino-Soviet Relations

While the above developments were taking place in Chinese domestic affairs, relations with the Soviet Union reached a delicate stage. Differences on international matters which had marred Sino-Soviet relations in the second half of 1958 did not disappear and in June 1959 the Chinese media expressed skepticism about the possibilities for US-Soviet detente. Moreover, according to later CCP charges, in 1958 the Soviet Union made unacceptable demands during negotiations on joint defense arrangements. And finally, Chinese hints that Communism was not far off were apparently regarded as a challenge to Soviet preeminence in the socialist camp by the Russians who also showed concern over the wisdom of the Great Leap strategy. Nevertheless, as Donald Zagoria has concluded, in the first half of 1959 neither side seemed willing to press matters and something of a tenuous compromise emerged.[20]

It was in this context that Peng Dehuai led a military goodwill tour of East Europe, the Soviet Union and Outer Mongolia from April 24 to June 13 during which Peng undoubtedly discussed important foreign policy questions with his Soviet counterparts. Zhang Wentian was also in East Europe at the time in his capacity as Chinese observer at Warsaw Pact meetings, and it is probable he had some contact with Peng during this period. Most importantly for subsequent events, during consultations with Khrushchev Peng reportedly expressed misgivings concerning the Great Leap and commune policies. Although Khrushchev presumably was sympathetic to Peng's views, this did not lead him to bless the Chinese Defense Minister's visit with any tangible rewards. On the contrary, undoubtedly reacting to the strains in Sino-Soviet relations, on June 20 shortly after Peng's return to China the Soviet Union, according to later Chinese claims, "unilaterally tore up the agreement on new technology for national defense concluded between China and the Soviet Union on October 15, 1957, and refused to provide China with a sample of an atomic bomb and technical data concerning its manufacture." Thus whatever similarity of attitude may have existed between Peng and Soviet leaders, Soviet action on the eve of the Lushan conference made Peng's most recent assignment in his own defense sphere a failure.[21]

The Crisis at Lushan

The ambiguity of Mao's position as CCP leaders gathered in Lushan at the end of June was revealed by his statement that "Our achievements are great, problems are quite few, and the future is bright."[22] In the context of the moment, many Party officials were prepared to concentrate on the "quite a few" problems. As was generally the case preceding high level conferences, many officials had toured parts of the country to investigate actual conditions and brought their findings to Lushan. Much of the information collected was, from the perspective of the Cultural Revolution, one-sidedly focused on shortcomings in a deliberate attempt to slander the leap forward and communes.

In one case, Fujian Governor Jiang Yizhen, assertedly acting on the orders of Peng Zhen, collected materials which "put words in the mouths of the masses." These included: "If we follow the Party 100 percent we will die 100 percent"; and "If things go on like this the peasants will support the GMD." In some cases such materials were prepared for use by various leaders; economic specialists Xue Muqiao and Sun Yefang reportedly prepared a draft speech for Bo Yibo based on "seamy data." Much of this gathering of data and its use at the meeting seems to have been done on the initiative of individual leaders or small groups of officials not acting in coordination with others sharing skepticism of the Great Leap. Nevertheless, once information was tabled at Lushan others could use it to bolster their points of view. Thus Peng Dehuai, in addition to data gathered on his own investigations, also cited materials aired by others during the relatively uninhibited atmosphere before and at the outset of the Lushan conference.[23]

In this fluid context various leaders put forward opinions concerning the problems created by the leap forward strategy. Some leading officials responsible for the economy, most notably Li Xiannian, apparently aired their misgivings. The strongest critique, however, came from Peng Dehuai and his cohorts who, with the exception of Zhou Xiaozhou, had no direct authority for economic or rural matters. The views of Peng *et al.*, which were subsequently denounced as fundamental opposition to the Great Leap and communes, were expressed both orally at small group discussions and in written memoranda. The most concise statement was Peng's "letter of opinion" to Mao written on July 14 and distributed by Peng to participants at the Lushan meeting. Opposition to Peng's critique reportedly came from left-inclined local leaders Ke Qingshi and Li Jingquan, both of whom had been elevated to Politburo status during the leap forward in 1958. At the crucial Politburo Standing Committee level, Liu Shaoqi and Zhou Enlai, whatever reservations they may have had on policy grounds,[g] stood with Mao once he launched a frontal attack on Peng. Zhu De, however, assertedly spoke out in Peng's behalf while Chen Yun, apparently still under a cloud, Deng Xiaoping, who "slipped away on the pretense of ailing legs," and Lin Biao were absent for all or at least the critical portions of the conference.[24] Before discussing the reactions of some of these figures and Party leaders generally to the Mao-Peng conflict in greater detail, we will first examine the substance of the critique which was subsequently labeled "right opportunist."

The Right Opportunist Critique

The criticisms offered by those dismayed at the consequences of the Great Leap had to be presented in a politically appropriate manner. As *Renmin ribao* complained: "Of course [their] negation of everything . . . is only in substance and not in words. In words they often abstractly recognize achievements."[25] Despite official assertions that the critique represented fundamental opposition to the leap forward, the actual statements of the critics generally asked no more than

[g] While his position was not necessarily at variance with Mao's, at Lushan Liu reportedly said "shortcomings must be thoroughly and freely revealed"; *Xinwen zhanxian* [News Front] (Peking), June 30, 1967, in *SCMP-S,* No. 196. Zhou, it may be recalled (see above, p. 270), was a leading advocate of "opposing reckless advance" in 1956–57 and apparently out of step with the emerging leap forward policies at the Third Plenum. This, of course, did not necessarily mean he was out of step with Mao in July–August 1959, and the Chairman may have implied the opposite. See *Case of Peng,* p. 20.

adjustments in existing policies, adjustments which were frequently consistent with what Mao himself had said in the preceding months. Thus the analyst must speculate in the murky realm of human intent and motivation in interpreting the statements of Peng Dehuai and like-minded leaders. Moreover, he is further burdened by uncertainty over precisely what was said at Lushan, as well as by alleged right opportunists in other forums.[h]

These caveats notwithstanding, it does seem clear that many critics drew up a decidedly more negative balance sheet concerning the leap forward and communes than Mao. While Mao had declared mistakes compared to achievements were but one finger out of ten, right opportunists assertedly said "shortcomings . . . are not merely one finger, but several fingers or the thumb." These critics reportedly felt that official policies reflected left adventurist errors and had resulted in losses to the virtual exclusion of gains. While Mao himself had shown concern over leftist tendencies before Lushan, at the start of the conference his general assessment was that while judging from certain limited perspectives the Party may have suffered more losses than gains, from a total point of view this was not the case.[26] In contrast, Peng allegedly articulated far-ranging negativism about the current situation at Lushan:

> Peng Dehuai has collected . . . transient and partial shortcomings, which have either long since been or are rapidly being overcome, exaggerated them out of all proportion and painted a pitch-black picture of the present situation in the country. In essence he negates the victory of the general line and the achievements of the Great Leap Forward. . . . In his letter he brazenly slandered as "petty bourgeois fanaticism" the revolutionary zeal of the Party and of hundreds of millions of people. Time and again in his remarks he went so far as to assert that "if the Chinese workers and peasants were not as good as they are, a Hungarian incident would have occurred in China and it would have been necessary to invite Soviet troops in."[27]

Apart from the overall balance sheet, it appears that many critics challenged the essentials of the Great Leap strategy—high speed development of the economy, reliance on mass mobilization in construction and production, and the primacy of politics under Party leadership. According to right opportunists the

[h] The following is reconstructed from statements purportedly made by Peng *et al.* in 1959 but revealed only in 1967–68, from direct attacks on them during the Cultural Revolution, and from charges directed at unnamed right opportunists in 1959. Several points should be made concerning this reconstruction. First, the attacks of both 1959 and 1967–68 contain a decided element of distortion. The lack of full texts of Peng's remarks plus the total absence of important speeches by his associates further hinders accurate knowledge of their views. Moreover, as the right opportunist label was applied to others besides Peng, Huang, Zhang and Zhou, particular aspects of the right opportunist critique may well have come from people totally unconnected to the Lushan dissenters. The issues examined here, however, are all subjects which Peng assertedly had spoken on and the views included are consistent with his purported sentiments.

pace of economic growth was too rapid and resulted in imbalances and dislocations. Targets were blindly raised and no measures were taken to readjust imbalances or to control the speed of development. High speed production was compared to a game of blind man's bluff which violated the law of planned and proportionate growth of the socialist economy. As Mao himself had only recently called for ignoring unrealistic targets set by higher levels and identified comprehensiveness and balance as a critical problem, these specific criticisms by themselves do not appear particularly extreme. However, some critics assertedly went on to attribute violation of objective economic laws to "politics in command" and the mass mobilization approach. Although right opportunists acknowledged the role of mass movements in revolution, agriculture and small scale projects, they allegedly denied applicability to economic construction, modern industry and technology, and urban areas generally. In this view, mass movements in such spheres were unscientific and upset the order of production.[28] As for the primacy of politics, Peng put the case concisely in his "letter of opinion":

> In the view of some comrades, putting politics in command could be a substitute for everything. They forgot that putting politics in command was aimed at raising the consciousness of labor, insuring improvement of products in both quantity and quality, and giving full play to the enthusiasm and creativeness of the masses in order to speed our economic construction. Putting politics in command is no substitute for economic principles, still less for concrete measures in economic work.[29]

Even here Peng's position could be interpreted as merely objecting to a distortion of "politics in command," a view which Mao presumably shared. But by a different reading Peng could be seen as rejecting "politics in command" *per se,* a view definitely anathema to the Chairman.

Although the charges were overdrawn, the accusation that right opportunists did not support and guide the mass movement but instead set limits to restrict its scale and depth due to fear of destroying established rules struck close to home. Critics emphasized a number of factors which conflicted with the Great Leap strategy. First, they attached great importance to an adequate material basis for economic development and tended to downplay the creative potential of the masses. Instead, they assertedly claimed mass movements did not reflect popular self-consciousness but in fact were forced upon the people and contributed to alienation from the Party. In the name of the mass line they advocated lower targets and material incentives. Critics further stressed careful research into actual conditions and policy implementation on a steady and reliable basis to offset subjectivism resulting in premature decisions. Once again similar themes could be found in Mao's pre-Lushan comments on the need for realism, his concern for providing adequate incentives, and his singling out distortion of the mass line as one of the Party's most critical problems. But while Mao also defended relatively high wages for experts, he does not appear to have placed the same emphasis on technical and professional expertise as the critics who, assertedly regarding the common people as too ignorant to avoid blunders in enterprises of technical complexity, believed economic affairs were the business of a small number of insiders and specialists.[30]

The importance attached to expertise had major implications for the role of Party leadership. Right opportunists allegedly questioned both the principle and concrete manifestations of Party committee leadership in economic construction. In a small group forum at Lushan Peng declared: "At present collective leadership by Party committees is ignored. Only decisions by individuals count. What has been decided by the first secretary counts, but not that by the second secretary." But despite complaints of unilateral actions, critics reportedly advocated restoring one man management by experts in factories. While Mao had also raised his voice against arbitrary practices by Party secretaries, there is nothing to suggest his disenchantment with Party committee leadership *per se*. Moreover, Peng's concern with collective leadership also had implications for Mao's "individual style" which he and others had already criticized in the previous months.[31]

One of the central thrusts of the Lushan critique was that pressures built up by mass movements inevitably led to gross exaggerations which both denied the leadership necessary information for decision making and damaged the regime's credibility in the eyes of the people. According to Peng's "letter of opinion":

> The habit of exaggeration spread in various areas and departments, and some unbelievable miracles were also reported in the press. This has surely done tremendous harm to the prestige of the Party.
>
> . . . More serious, in a rather long period of time, it was not easy to get a true picture of the situation. Even up to . . . the conference of secretaries of provincial and municipal committees in January of this year, we were not able to find out the realities of the overall situation.[32]

Moreover, it was extremely hard to go against the tide in a situation where exaggeration and boastfulness were commonplace. In a discussion at Lushan, Peng reportedly said it was especially difficult to correct leftist mistakes since most people did not dare speak out during radical political campaigns. As has been indicated above, Mao's attitude in the pre-Lushan period was similar.[33]

One of the key policies of the Great Leap, the effort to achieve a breakthrough in iron and steel production, came under heavy attack. Critics charged excessive emphasis on iron and steel had deprived other sectors of needed resources creating an economic imbalance. The sharpest criticism, however, was reserved for the mass campaign to increase steel output by building small, indigenous blast furnaces. As Peng Dehuai put it in his "letter of opinion": "In the course of refining steel by the whole people, some small and indigenous blast furnaces which were not necessary were built, with the consequence that some resources (material and financial) and manpower were wasted. This of course was a relatively big loss." Yet when the Lushan conference met, Mao was already on record as having second thoughts about unrealistic steel targets and implying that the indigenous steel sector would play a relatively limited supplementary role to modern plants. Moreover, at the conference itself he emotionally referred to the "great disaster" of the mass campaign to produce iron and steel.[34]

Other economic policies also came under fire. Various measures to boost agricultural output including the double wheel plow and close planting assertedly led to decreased production. Critics also pointed to the depletion of stocks of key materials such as steel products and timber caused by rapid expansion of capital construction. In this situation, Peng called for suspending many projects started in 1958 and unnamed critics advocated a cutback in capital construction investment by ¥5 to 6 billion. Shortages of various commodities led to claims that tension existed in every corner of the market and what had been available before liberation could no longer be purchased, while some right opportunists alleged that living standards had actually declined. In addition to the above, critics attacked poor quality in production which they claimed was the price of emphasizing quantity of output. While avoiding the rhetorical excesses attributed to right opportunists, Mao had voiced concern on all these matters in the first half of 1959.[35]

People's communes were criticized on a number of grounds. Right opportunist critics reportedly charged communes had been poorly built, were not as good as APCs, and were generally a mess. In his Lushan talks Peng Dehuai claimed the communes had been set up too early before the APCs had fully played their role and without proper experimentation. Critics also challenged the official line that communes were set up in response to peasant demands and instead asserted popular desires had been violated due to the "subjective wishes of a few." Moreover, right opportunists assertedly seized upon the adjustments in commune structure since late 1958 to argue communes were retreating, were doomed to failure and eventually would be dissolved. Indeed, Peng noted that some communes had already collapsed. Others reportedly claimed that under the three level system of ownership communes were an empty form existing in name only and rural organization had in fact returned to the stage of higher APCs, thus proving communes were unnecessary in the first place. Peng, however, was careful in his "letter of opinion" to say that although there had been "a period of confusion regarding the question of the system of ownership" within the communes this had in the main been corrected by the conferences of late 1958–early 1959, a position not too removed from that of Mao.[36]

The use of the free supply system within communes came under sharp attack. It assertedly reflected ultra-egalitarianism and violated the socialist principle of remuneration according to work, a principle Mao had emphasized since the 1958 Zhengzhou meeting. Right opportunists allegedly argued the combination of free supply and wages was harmful to peasant incentives and there was no place for elements of Communism in socialist communes. Thus they demanded the abolition of the system. Peng himself apparently did not go this far and only expressed concern with the premature negation of the law of exchange of equal values, a position not unlike Mao's support for continued commodity production and exchange.[37]

Some of the harshest criticisms were directed at communal mess halls. As with the communes themselves, mess halls assertedly lacked a proper material basis and were forced on the masses. Critics charged mess halls were poorly managed, wasteful of grain, fuel and labor, hindered production and caused a decline in peasant living standards. Moreover, mess halls and other communal welfare projects restricted the masses' freedom and clashed with their living habits to the extent that the family life of commune members was destroyed. Critics further claimed that large numbers of people had withdrawn from mess halls due to these problems and Mao himself admitted some had been scrapped. Against this was the official allegation that right opportunists had undermined mess halls by advocating their reduction in size to small kitchens for a few households or their dissolution, and by actually reducing and dissolving them in a number of areas under their control.[38]

The system of ownership within the communes also came in for scrutiny. As noted above, Peng's letter referred to confusion on this matter. Moreover, critics argued "the more decentralization the better" within the communes and sought changes in the three level system of ownership. Viewing collective production as excessively rigid and detrimental to the production enthusiasm of peasants, they advocated measures promoting "small freedoms" and individual incentives. These measures included making the production team the basic unit of ownership, allocating large amounts of capital goods and public assets to teams and individual households, contracting labor, output and production costs to households, and permitting commune members to reclaim wasteland on a large scale and expand their private undertakings. In advocating such measures, right opportunists allegedly were reflecting demands of well-to-do middle peasants whom they regarded as experienced in production, and thus the rural group to be relied upon. While Mao clearly did not support most of these proposals, he had viewed the communal structure as overcentralized and, ironically, in March had taken a more favorable stance toward team accounting than Zhou Xiaozhou.[39]

On the people's commune issue generally, there apparently was a greater disparity between Mao's expressed pre-Lushan position and the right opportunist critique than on most other matters. In part this was due to Mao's silence on the question in the three months leading up to Lushan. Although Mao stressed some themes analogous to those raised by the critics in his comments of late 1958 and early 1959, from the conclusion of the Shanghai plenum in early April he apparently did not address the communes in his cataloging of problems to be dealt with. This undoubtedly reflected the shift in attention to construction matters as the leadership decided not to tinker further with the adjusted communes for the duration of spring planting. However, even when Mao had attacked defects in communal structure earlier in 1959, he asserted the superiority of the commune for the transition to higher forms of ownership, something which he saw as both an historical trend and a priority of current policy. By March he had concluded the commune was completely affirmed and attached the right opportunist label to anyone who doubted this.[40] Thus in raising the commune issue critics had less reason to anticipate Mao's concurrence than on production and construction questions where the Chairman's post-Shanghai "conservative" views provided ample grounds for hope.

To summarize, the right opportunist critique had much in common with official views in the period leading up to the Lushan conference. While qualifications are necessary concerning the people's communes, on substantive issues critics could generally find encouragement in the public media and Mao's own statements. Here there is a parallel with the intellectuals of 1957 whose comments during "blooming and contending" derived to such a substantial extent from official recitations of shortcomings. The difference, of course, was that now the major critics were high ranking Party leaders. Moreover, Mao's plea for open criticism in the months preceding Lushan and his statement that "problems are quite a few" at the very start of the conference could only have encouraged those distressed with the results of the Great Leap to assert their traditional rights in the policy making process and address themselves to those very issues. Where the critics appear to have departed company with Mao was in tone and overall evaluation. Even if, as appears likely, the views articulated at Lushan did not have the same bite as the words subsequently attributed to right opportunists, at least some of the statements made at the conference were sharp and by implication cast grave doubt on the Chairman's assertion that "the future [was] bright" under the Great Leap developmental strategy.

The Question of Mao's Leadership Style

Apart from substantive policy questions, critics also challenged the way in which policy was made with emphasis on Mao's personal role and its impact on traditional Party norms. In part, as we have seen, unfortunate tendencies in inner Party life were due to the recurrent phenomenon that "whenever something leftist comes up, it always prevails over everything [and] many people dare not speak out," a phenomenon which concerned both Peng and Mao. But the Lushan critics did not see the problem solely in the dynamics of mobilization phases. The perceived contraction of debate at the highest levels of the Party was also attributed to Mao's increasingly individualistic tendencies. This issue is difficult to assess in that there are only fleeting references in the Lushan materials and no mention was made of it during the 1959 attacks on right opportunism. Nevertheless, despite Mao's December 1958 statement that his views were only individual opinions and couldn't be considered binding conclusions, by late spring 1959 both Peng's clash with Mao at Shanghai and Zhang Wentian's observation on Mao's April letter suggest growing concern with the Chairman's "individual style." The matter again came up at Lushan in Zhang's July 20 speech when he complained that "meetings of the Politburo were only large scale briefing meetings without any collective discussion."[41] But the clearest indication of concern with Mao's leadership methods is found in the Chairman's own words at Lushan:

> [You say] I have "reached Stalin's later years," am "despotic and dictatorial," and refuse to give you "freedom" and "democracy." I am also "vain and fond of credit," "biased in view and faith." "Where someone at the top likes it, the lower echelons like it even more." I let "the errors reach the bottom before I turn the corner, and once making the turn it reaches 180 degrees." I have "deceived" you and "hooked you as big fish." Moreover, I have come to "resemble Tito" in that no one dares to speak up in front of me.[i]

The reference to Stalin is particularly striking since Mao's leadership style from the mid-1930s had been the antithesis of Stalin's. Moreover, if Mao's previous encouragement of vigorous debate within leadership circles was giving way to a more rigid and arbitrary pattern of policy formulation, then this tendency would inevitably be reflected in Party discipline. While the measures adopted fell far short of those of Stalin, this indeed was the case as the Lushan critics came in for harsh denunciation and dismissal. Unlike Chen Yun, whose apparent policy dissent in fall 1957 resulted in a *de facto* erosion of authority but no formal disciplinary action, Peng Dehuai and other right opportunists received formal sanctions. While disciplinary measures had been used in 1957–58 against conservative provincial Party leaders and other high ranking officials, the important issue of organizational reliability in carrying out approved Party policies was also involved. In this instance, not only were such charges not raised against right opportunists, but in the cases of Peng, Huang and Zhang they clearly could not be raised (except in the military sphere discussed subsequently) given their lack of operational responsibility for the economy. In these circumstances it was necessary to find an organizational issue to discredit Peng et al., and the accusation that their activities represented a conspiracy against the Party quickly emerged.

"Conspiracy" or "Legal Struggle"?

The Central Committee resolution adopted at Lushan stated the conspiracy theory succinctly:

> The mass of facts brought to light at the Lushan meeting proved that Peng Dehuai and his gang were a clique of conspirators, which had a specific objective, had made preparations, and had ready plans and an organization for usurping Party and army leadership.[42]

[i] *CLG*, Winter 1968–69, p. 70. These remarks cited by Mao undoubtedly were more directed at his unusual behavior at Lushan than at his actions in the pre-conference period.

Many of the allegations raised against Peng and associates bore striking resemblance to the "unprincipled struggle" of Gao Gang and Rao Shushi to which Peng, Huang and Zhang were now explicitly linked (see Chapter 5). Peng and the others allegedly engaged in factional activities designed to split the Party both prior to and during Lushan, and their methods included "promising official promotions, trafficking in flattery and favors, first attacking and then cajoling, creating dissension, and spreading rumors, lies and slanders." Moreover, in 1959 right opportunists had been accused of saying nothing during discussions of policy at Party meetings but instead disseminating views contrary to the official line "behind the back of the Party." In sum, this view holds that Peng and his associates operated in clear violation of Party norms with the aim of directly challenging the leadership of Mao Zedong.[43]

An alternative view can be reconstructed from official and unofficial sources. An official source early in the Cultural Revolution implied Peng's activities were well within the bounds of accepted practice by characterizing the right opportunists as having used "legal struggle" to oppose the Party.[44] It further implied that such means consisted of open dissent over established policy—i.e., exercising minority rights sanctioned by Party organizational norms. Peng, in effect, argued along these lines in various statements since his disgrace. In a self-examination during the Cultural Revolution, Peng said his actions at Lushan were those of a forthright man who spoke his mind:

> I wrote my letter with good motives. I had the roughness of Zhang Fei but not his caution.
>
> The Chairman received my letter on the 17th. On the 23rd, the Chairman delivered a speech for 40 minutes with regard to my problem, hitting my vital points. . . . The Chairman said that my letter was "rallying support" and "ambitious" and "hypocritical." I could not accept these comments.[j]

What evidence is there of planned opposition activity prior to or at Lushan? Although a Red Guard source traces Peng's opposition to the Great Leap to early

[j] *CB*, No. 851, p. 18. Zhang Fei was a warrior in the *Romance of the Three Kingdoms* known for his hot temper but who also acted with caution. In his self-examination at Lushan Peng referred to his actions as "prepared and organized," but much of his detailed discussion implied the opposite. *Case of Peng*, pp. 36–38.

While Peng's letter as well as his comments at small group meetings were offered in the "open and above board" manner demanded by Party norms, in circulating his letter before Mao received it Peng may have offended the Chairman and contributed to his sense of surprise and feeling pressured (see below). As pointed out by Linda Perkin, "The Chinese Communist Party: The Lushan Meeting and Plenum, July-August 1959," M.A. thesis, Columbia University, 1971, the Chairman's handling of Peng's letter contrasts to his handling of similar written criticisms from a lesser official which he praised and himself circulated to the conference. However, as argued below, p. 331, this incident is probably explained by Mao's attempt to limit the damage to Party principles after he had acted against Peng.

1958, this apparently involved no more than private derogatory remarks about various leap forward policies until at least early 1959. From early 1959 to April, however, Peng carried out investigations in Hunan and other areas assertedly to gather materials on leap forward defects for use in opposing the strategy. During his Hunan investigations Peng allegedly formed an alliance with Zhou Xiaozhou. But in late 1958-early 1959 many Party leaders including Mao engaged in inspections of local areas, and consultation with local Party leaders such as Zhou was quite natural under those circumstances. Moreover, as we have seen, Zhou took a more radical position than Mao on the level of accounting within the communes in spring 1959. In any case, at Lushan Mao claimed his critics had been silent at the meetings held since fall 1959 except that "they mumbled something at the Shanghai conference."[45]

As noted previously, the March–April Shanghai meeting saw differences emerge over lowering targets and Mao personally assuming control of work, although Peng was explicitly linked only to the latter issue. There are also allegations of right opportunist activities in the period between Shanghai and Lushan. In 1959 the press repeatedly attributed declining industrial and agricultural production from June to early August to such activities and the related appearance of rightist sentiments among cadres and masses. One report charged right opportunists with launching attacks on the Party in the entire April to July period. Mao, however, tacitly admitted that the leadership's own efforts to correct leftist defects in the first half of 1959 contributed to the slowdown of production. In any case, it is difficult to relate these charges directly to Peng Dehuai since he was out of the country from shortly after the Shanghai meeting until mid-June. It is likely that the accusations were directed at a broader grouping of people who had articulated criticism of the Great Leap independently of Peng.[46]

According to Peng, he had discussed internal conditions with Huang Kecheng both following the Shanghai meeting and after his return to China. While maintaining that Huang did not know of the "letter of opinion" beforehand, Peng acknowledged that they had the same rightist views and had influenced each other in their conversations. This relationship between Peng and Huang undoubtedly formed the basis of Mao's charge that a "military club" *(junshi julebu)* was the "headquarters" of organized action.[k] Similarly, after Peng's return from abroad and then at Lushan Zhang Wentian, who Mao later chided for having formed a "civilian-military alliance," visited Peng on several occasions and they

[k] Although several other PLA leaders were later attacked over military issues (see below), only GPD head Tan Zheng was linked to the economic questions raised at Lushan. *CB,* No. 851, pp. 13–14. In addition, Parris H. Chang, *Power and Policy in China* (University Park: The Pennsylvania State University Press, 1975), p. 117, cites refugee sources who claim many PLA leaders had endorsed Peng's letter to Mao, but no confirmation of this has been found in official or unofficial sources.

discussed various problems such as making steel by small, native furnaces. Peng admitted reading portions of his "letter of opinion" to Zhang during one visit, but claimed Zhang was there only "by chance." He also denied prior knowledge of Zhang's July 21 speech which apparently criticized aspects of the leap forward. Peng argued although they were in tacit agreement their criticisms at Lushan were not based on any concrete plan. While Peng's testimony might be discounted as self-serving, it gains credence from several factors. First, Cultural Revolution sources do not allege illicit contacts with leading economic officials which we would expect if Peng had been attempting to build a clique on a platform of opposition to the leap forward.[1] Second, as we shall see, many Party leaders believed Peng's actions were wholly within accepted guidelines of inner Party debate, thereby discounting any secret plotting. Nevertheless, the fact that Peng's discussions with other leaders before and at Lushan could be attacked as conspiratorial points to an important ambiguity in official norms: when do informal exchanges of views become unacceptable factional activity? Clearly, once Mao rebuffed the critics they felt uneasy and Zhang Wentian reportedly advised against further informal discussions.[47]

The manner of Peng's criticism at Lushan also bears scrutiny. In his self-examination at the plenum Peng cited using insinuations to damage Mao's prestige as his greatest mistake. The only available texts of Peng's Lushan remarks, admittedly non-verbatim notes on talks to the Northwest group from July 3 to 9 and the complete text of his "letter of opinion," provide a somewhat contradictory picture. Peng's purported comments in group discussions contained several sharp references to Mao. In one talk he in effect charged Mao had lied concerning conditions in a Hunan commune they both had visited. On another occasion, Peng reportedly said the responsibility for defects was shared by everybody including Mao.[48]

Peng's "infamous" letter was quite a different matter, however. This letter bore the imprint of a memorial to the emperor. Peng began in the tone of a supplicant: "I am a simple man . . . and indeed I am crude and have no tact at all. For this reason, whether this letter is of reference value or not is for you to decide. If what I say is wrong, please correct me." In the body of the letter, Peng attempted to circumscribe carefully his criticisms with affirmations of Great

---

[1]No Cultural Revolution charges were found directly linking economic officials and Peng *et al.* One source, however, did accuse Jia Qiyun of the State Statistical Bureau of collecting and publishing material on Great Leap defects to "provide shells for the bombardment of Chairman Mao . . . at Lushan" to an unnamed "three-anti" element. Radio Guiyang, June 16, 1967, in *NFCPRS,* No. 212. The most irregular activity alleged concerns a leading propaganda official, Hu Qiaomu, who was attacked for telling Peng's clique "many things against the Party and Chairman Mao" and "participating in 'black' sessions held under the auspices of the anti-Party clique." *Wenxue zhanbao* [Literary Combat Bulletin] (Peking), April 14, 1967, in *SCMP,* No. 3942.

Leap achievements. He wrote that shortcomings were unavoidable and many of the most serious problems had already been corrected, themes which would become part of the official defense of the leap forward after Lushan. Indeed, Peng concluded that conditions for a continued leap were present and predicted the task of overtaking Britain could be basically achieved in four years. Moreover, errors were not attributed to Mao but to the imperfect understanding and implementation of his policies by others:

> Although the Chairman last year called on the whole Party to combine skyrocketing zeal with scientific analysis and set forth the policy of walking on two legs, it appears that both the call and the policy have not been appreciated by the majority of leading comrades. I am, of course, no exception. . . .
>
> For instance, the slogans raised by the Chairman, such as "grow less, produce more and reap more" and "catch up with Britain in fifteen years" were strategic and long range policies. But we lacked research; we failed to give attention to and study the current concrete conditions, and we failed to arrange work on a positive, steady and reliable basis.

In conclusion, Peng's requests were modest. He asked only for a systematic summing up of achievements and lessons gained since the second half of 1958 so that cadres throughout the Party could be further educated, and he specifically requested that no effort be made to determine personal responsibility for errors.[49]

Although the nature of the sources necessitates caution, some propositions can be offered concerning Peng's activities. First, it appears that Peng and his fellow critics sought to win Mao over to their views rather than launch a frontal attack against him. To be sure, there was disaffection over Mao's personal role. But references to Mao as "despotic and dictatorial" appear to have been grumbling over a situation which the critics did not expect to be able to change. Particularly revealing is Peng's account of a conversation he had with Zhang Wentian. Zhang reportedly said that Mao was brilliant but also ruthless in handling people as Stalin had been in his late years. Peng replied that the first emperor of any dynasty in the past was always ruthless and brilliant.[50] This suggests the memorializing tone of Peng's letter was not a deceptive tactic; it rather reflected the political reality of Mao's ultimate authority. Remarks such as those made by Peng in the discussions of the Northwest group are best seen as the type of indiscretion for which Peng was notorious rather than as attempts to build anti-Mao support.

Second, there was ample reason for Peng to believe Mao's position was flexible in view of the Chairman's remarks of the preceding months which set him at odds with the left wing of the Party. Indeed, Peng's assertion at a mass trial during the Cultural Revolution that his letter had been directed at Liu Shaoqi rather than Mao has a certain credibility.[51] The letter did, after all, point to failure to implement properly the Chairman's policies rather than the policies themselves as the source of China's troubles. Moreover, Liu was deeply implicated in the Great Leap both as an advocate of the strategy and in his position as a key Party leader charged with its implementation. With Mao having indicated his dissatisfaction with the performance of higher level cadres before Lushan, it is not inconceivable that Peng sought to pin the excesses of the leap forward on Liu much as Cultural Revolution sources would eight years later. But given his advocacy of not fixing the blame it is unlikely that Peng's design was so specific at the time. Rather, it would appear that Peng was encouraging Mao to take a face saving way out, to retreat further from the Great Leap and commune policies without explicitly rejecting those programs, and to shift the blame to those responsible for their implementation. Given Mao's position on the eve of Lushan the calculation that Mao would opt for such a face saving solution was hardly rash. Such a course, far from being a major blow to Mao's prestige, would have served to rally moderate opinion around the Chairman much as had happened in mid-1957 when Mao discarded the Hundred Flowers experiment without openly renouncing that policy.

Finally, Peng's actions can be explained by the fact that he was a relative outsider in the decision making process. Neither he, Huang nor Zhang were functionally concerned with economic and rural policy, while Zhou Xiaozhou was too low ranking to play a major role in national policy formulation. Although Peng and Zhang were Politburo members, neither were in the inner circle. Moreover, it is likely that Mao's alleged low personal regard for Peng further reduced Peng's influence and that the same situation applied to Zhang, the former returned student. Thus, in contrast to Gao Gang and Rao Shushi, their silence at earlier Party meetings need not be seen as a sinister circumvention of Party norms.[52] It can be explained as the natural reaction of officials not immediately concerned with the issues in question and lacking access to the relevant decision making forums. As they became increasingly concerned with the excesses of the leap forward, a concern which may have been intensified by the new strategy's impact on Sino-Soviet relations and the declining morale of a largely peasant army, Peng and others of like mind quite naturally exchanged views privately. The fact of such exchanges can hardly be equated to a conspiracy in the absence of evidence of more detailed planning. Ironically, it may have been the lack of informal access to Mao that forced Peng to opt for methods of "legal struggle" and go public at Lushan.

Mao's Response

Whatever the precise intent of Peng and his associates, Mao refused to accept their criticism as legitimate dissent and instead interpreted it as a personal attack challenging his leadership. After Peng had been airing his opinions for about a week in small group meetings Mao spoke out on July 10 in terms at striking variance with his pre-Lushan assessment of basic unity:

> Because of the lack of consensus on the situation, it is impossible to have solidarity. In order to have inner Party solidarity, we must first clarify problems and achieve ideological unity.
>
> . . . .
>
> Some people say that the general line is basically wrong. The so-called general line is nothing but [achieving] greater, faster, better, and more economical results, and this cannot be basically wrong.[53]

Having both indicated serious concern with signs of dissension within leadership circles and a continuing commitment to Great Leap policies, Mao apparently retreated into silence and "listened with a stiffened scalp" until he again spoke out on July 23 to refute the critics and warn the assembled officials not to waver. In this rambling and highly emotional talk Mao, although apparently not mentioning Peng by name, clearly indicated the depth of his concern and the target of his discontent by declaring that in the event the propagation of critical views led to a national collapse, "I would go to the countryside to lead the peasants to overthrow the government. If the PLA won't follow me, I will then find the Red Army. I think the PLA will follow me." The Chairman subsequently called the Central Committee into plenary session, a move Huang Kecheng allegedly derided as "calling for reinforcements." Mao delivered a second speech to the plenum on August 2 which, in contrast to the discursive speech of July 23, sharply denounced the critics as right opportunists who had launched a "frantic attack on the Party." In addition, Mao recalled his May 1958 warning against splits in the Party and declared that while there were no clear signs of a split then one had taken place at Lushan.[54]

The plenum also heard a self-examination by Peng and passed a resolution denouncing the "anti-Party clique headed by Peng Dehuai." Actually, Peng, Huang, Zhang and Zhou were treated far more leniently than one would expect had a genuine conspiracy existed, a fact which further supports the "legal struggle" interpretation. The resolution of the plenum called for an attitude of sincerity and warmth towards them and although stripping them of operational posts allowed retention of nominal Politburo and Central Committee membership with the proviso that their future behavior would be under scrutiny. This was consistent with Mao's observation at the close of the Lushan Plenum that "up to now, they are different from the renegades Chen Duxiu, Luo Zhanglong, Zhang Guotao and Gao Gang in that [they] constitute a contradiction among the people, while [Chen, Luo, Zhang and Gao were] contradictions between the enemy and ourselves." Thus despite his denunciation of right opportunism Mao continued to advocate the traditional rectification approach for Peng and associates.[55]

Still, the question remains why Mao responded as sharply as he did? Was it really necessary to label Peng and the others as an "anti-Party clique" and remove them from positions in the military and foreign affairs field? If, as we have argued, Peng's activities were more "legal struggle" than conspiracy, would not limited inner Party criticism have been a more appropriate response, a response more in keeping with established CCP norms? There are a number of factors which help explain Mao's reaction: (1) the element of surprise; (2) the Chairman's psychological involvement with the Great Leap and commune policies; (3) the possible impact of Peng's views throughout the Party; and (4) the role of Soviet leaders.

While it is possible to interpret the sequence of events as deliberately orchestrated by Mao to draw out into the open the full range of criticism and critics, the Chairman appears to have been genuinely taken by surprise at Lushan. Although certainly aware of both the problems caused by the leap forward and differences of opinion within the Party, Mao's underlying optimism was revealed in both his May assessment that "everybody supports the Party's general line" and his remark at the outset of the conference that "the future is bright." When group discussions and subsequently written statements by Peng and others revealed an unanticipated degree of disillusionment with the leap forward, Mao seemingly was caught off balance and retreated into silence. Apparently feeling provoked by this turn of events, Mao then broke his silence to launch a counterattack.

Mao's response was also influenced by a sense of deep personal involvement in the policies of the Great Leap Forward. Despite Peng's effort to attribute defects of the Great Leap to others' misunderstanding of Mao and his own self-appraisal as a "middle of the roader," Mao clearly regarded the leap forward and people's communes as *his* policies. He brushed aside the option of a face saving retreat by declaring, "The fact is that you have all refuted me, though not by name perhaps."[56] Although his remarks at Lushan were sprinkled with criticism of others, the Chairman emotionally claimed that the major responsibility was his:

> Before August last year, I devoted myself mainly to the revolution. I am absolutely no good a construction, and do not understand industrial planning. . . . I said not to write about my wise leadership. I had not even taken charge of those things so how could it be called wise leadership? However, comrades, *in 1958 and 1959 I should take the main responsibility, you should blame me.* In the past, the responsibility was on others, Enlai and XX. Now you should blame me for I indeed have taken charge of a great many things. . . . Was it Ke Qingshi or I who invented the massive smelting of iron and steel? I say it was I. . . . In June [1958] I set the target at 10.7 million tons. . . . This created a great disaster as 90 million people went ahead to smelt steel.
>
> . . . .
>
> Next was the people's commune. I did not claim the right of inventing people's communes, but I had the right to suggest. In Shandong, a reporter asked me: "Is the commune good?" I said, "Good," and he immediately published it in the newspaper. This might be due to some petty bourgeois fanaticism. Hereafter, newspaper reporters should leave [me alone].[57]

Thus Mao associated himself with policies he admitted were "a partial failure." The intensity of his identification may, as Stuart Schram suggests, have been particularly acute with respect to the people's communes, the area of rural organization where Mao *did* feel competent. Indeed, at Lushan the Chairman seemed more resistant to changes in commune policies than elsewhere. His overall feelings may have been further sharpened by the fact that, as we shall see, he found it necessary in effect to accept many of the adjustments advocated by the right opportunists. Whatever the precise reasons, at Lushan Mao was in a frame of mind where he was unable to separate his prestige from the successes and failures of the Great Leap. In Mao's eyes, an attack on his policies was an attack on him.[58]

Another element affecting Mao's response was his overall assessment of ideological conditions within the Party and nation. Once disabused of his notion of consensus, Mao saw particular danger in the influence of Peng's views on others. Peng and company were not viewed as a major threat by themselves but because their opinions struck a responsive chord in Party members at all levels including leading economic and provincial officials. In 1959 the press distinguished between "a small number of right opportunists" and a much larger number of people with right conservative ideas or whose ardor for the leap forward had markedly cooled. Moreover, in his comments at Lushan the Chairman declared, "Though we are not afraid of the frantic attack of the rightists, nevertheless, we are afraid of the wavering of [middle of the road] comrades because this is detrimental to the . . . solidarity of the people and the Party's effort to bolster zeal, surmount difficulties, and strive for victory." While, as Mao admitted, rightist thought was due in no small part to official criticisms of defects in the entire period since November 1958, he also saw it as a chronic disease appearing in periods of rapid change. Thus particular attention was given to the parallel between the dampening effect of right opportunist activity on production to the situation in 1956–57 when rightist attacks on adventurism allegedly caused a marked slowdown in economic development. Mao apparently thought that by launching a sharp attack against right opportunism he was preventing the spread of a recurrent political malady which threatened a significant segment of the Party unless promptly checked. Although he subsequently estimated that only 1 to 5 percent of Party members actually supported Peng's views, at Lushan the Chairman observed that reactionary ideas affected large numbers of the Chinese people and could not be changed at once. This implied not only the need for a persistent effort combating the offending views in order to preserve the viability of the leap forward and commune policies, but Mao projected that in the long run 20 to 50 years of class struggle would be necessary to safeguard the socialist revolution.[59]

A final factor perhaps explaining the sharpness of Mao's response was Soviet criticism of the communes and possibly Peng's contacts with Khrushchev during his spring military tour. Cultural Revolution sources have linked Peng's Lushan behavior to the Russians. Peng assertedly expressed opposition to the Great Leap and Mao in the presence of Soviet officials and informed Khrushchev of shortcomings in CCP policies which the Russians were able to use as ammunition against China. In response, Khrushchev, who had already made known Soviet skepticism concerning China's internal direction, allegedly encouraged Peng to return to China and oppose Mao. Thus Peng's activities at Lushan were reportedly undertaken with the support and active instigation of Khrushchev. Moreover, on July 18 during the Lushan meeting Khrushchev sharply if indirectly attacked the Chinese communes in a speech in Poland. It is easy to imagine Mao's outrage at this interference in Chinese domestic affairs. At Lushan he fulminated against "Khrushchevs [who] oppose or are skeptical about ... the Hundred Flowers, people's communes, and Great Leap Forward," and attacked Peng's letter for "taking advantage of a difficult time when the Party is under a double attack both internally and externally."[60] Although it is not clear that Mao knew of Peng's alleged conversations with the Russians at the time he launched his counterattack,[m] by mid-September he was aware of the episode and expressed bitter resentment:

> One should by no means betray one's fatherland by conspiring with foreign countries.... We won't allow Chinese Party members to sabotage the Party organizations of foreign countries by encouraging one segment of the people to oppose another segment. Nor could we permit anyone to be lured by any foreign country behind the back of the Central Committee.[61]

There are two separable issues here which could help explain Mao's reaction. The first concerns Mao's nationalistic resentment that the Russians, with whom relations were already strained, had interfered in CCP affairs. Even without detailed knowledge of Peng's exchange with Khrushchev, the very fact that the Soviet leader spoke out at a time of high level inner Party discussions would have been viewed by Mao as interference and thus increased his antagonism toward internal critics. Ironically, as we have seen, Peng's Soviet "friends"[62] may have undercut his position before Lushan when they abruptly canceled the 1957 nuclear agreement in mid-June, an act which would not only fuel Mao's suspicion of anyone arguing views similar to those of the Russians, but one which also represented a failure for Peng's recent mission. While the cancellation of the agreement conceivably convinced Peng of the folly of Mao's policies, it paradoxically weakened his ability to influence those policies.

Under the above scenario Peng's specific acts while on tour are not linked to Mao's response. It was probably enough to argue a line parallel to that of the Russians to raise the Chairman's ire. But beyond this Peng was charged with violating an important Party norm, the confidentiality of Politburo discussions. While Mao, at least by mid-September, clearly was incensed that Peng had apparently discussed CCP affairs with Khrushchev, it is less obvious that Peng's

[m] His attacks on Peng at Lushan were for speaking out at the same time as the Russians; they did not allege collusion.

actions were as sinister as subsequently claimed. As we saw in the case of Gao Gang, the norms of conduct for high level discussions with leaders of fraternal parties are far from clear. Although, with reference to Gao, Mao in late 1956 had cautioned against providing information to the Russians, the Chairman subsequently dwelled on internal CCP affairs in his own conversations with Soviet leaders. According to Khrushchev, Mao was eager to draw him out on such matters as the Hundred Flowers experiment.[63] More broadly, it was normal for domestic matters to come up in high level exchanges given the close scrutiny Communist leaders give to developments in other socialist states. Thus Peng would seem to have blundered by voicing critical opinions to Khrushchev at a time of strained Sino-Soviet relations rather than by having violated any unambiguous guidelines concerning discussions with foreign Communist officials.

It would be a different matter, of course, if Peng had engaged in detailed collaboration with Khrushchev to attack on Mao. Such links, however, have not been demonstrated by Cultural Revolution sources which indicate little more than a sympathetic exchange of views between the two men. While the timing of Peng's Lushan criticism and Khrushchev's Poland speech raises unanswered questions, the lack of specifics in Cultural Revolution attacks on this incident suggests that, though not quite a coincidence, it involved less than elaborate coordination. As in other contexts, Peng seems guilty of little more than indiscretion in his dealings with Soviet leaders. Unfortunately for him, by the time of the Lushan meetings the Sino-Soviet question had become extremely sensitive, particularly in the eyes of Mao.

In sum, Mao's decision to react in dramatic fashion to the critics at Lushan probably reflected a variety of factors. The unexpected nature of the Lushan developments seemingly left Mao feeling provoked. Furthermore, his intense self-identification with the Great Leap and communes led the Chairman to view criticism of those policies as personal attacks. Mao also sensed it was necessary to act decisively to prevent the spread of views similar to those expressed at the meeting to wide segments of Party leaders, cadres and masses. And knowledge of Soviet interference in CCP affairs and possibly of Peng's conversations with the Russians undoubtedly inflamed his nationalist sentiments. These factors—together with reputed long term friction with Peng—provided the basis for Mao's response at Lushan.

The Reaction of Party Leaders

As we have seen, when Peng Dehuai began his critique a substantial number of leaders gathered at Lushan appear to have been sympathetic to his position. Not only had a number of economic officials and provincial leaders gathered data critical of the leap forward, but in addition leading propaganda cadres Hu Qiaomu and Wu Lengxi publicly or otherwise spread such information. Whatever their inclinations, as Mao made clear his dissatisfaction with Peng's criticism most leaders backed the Chairman and scrambled to disassociate themselves from any critical posture they themselves had adopted. Li Xiannian, the Minister of Finance, at a 1967 confrontation with Red Guards admitted, "On the first day I agreed with the views of Peng Dehuai but on the second day I opposed them." Moreover, Bo Yibo reportedly discarded the critical speech he had prepared and substituted a new draft supporting the Great Leap once Peng had come under attack.[64]

Others who were vulnerable assertedly survived due to the backing of high Party leaders. For example, Wu Lengxi, who in addition to voicing his own critical opinions at Lushan had also praised Peng Dehuai as a man of integrity who said what others dared not say, suddenly found himself out on a limb when Mao declared Peng's activities "anti-Party." Wu's protestations that he "had been taken in" apparently were not enough. With Peng Zhen assertedly providing guidance, Wu was counselled not to overdo his defense at the conference, a leading official guaranteed there was "no relationship" between Wu and Peng Dehuai, and after a "sham" self-examination further investigation was dropped.[65] At this point assurances that factional ties did not exist despite strong ideological affinities apparently were sufficient to avoid punishment, given strong political backing. This would not always be the case, but it did reflect the continued influence of traditional Party norms guaranteeing the right to speak one's mind even as those norms were violated regarding Peng Dehuai.

The reactions of two Politburo Standing Committee members, Liu Shaoqi and Zhu De, are of particular interest. Little is known of Liu's role at Lushan apart from the fact that he did back Mao, perhaps because there was little to criticize in his actions from a Cultural Revolution perspective. But it does appear that Liu engaged in a heated exchange with Peng during which he said, "I would rather usurp the Party myself than have you usurp it." As Peter Moody has noted, this is the kind of remark that could be said in anger, perhaps as a retort to an accusation by Peng that Liu had *already* usurped effective Party leadership.[66] Such an interpretation is bolstered not only by Peng's later claim that his letter was directed at Liu and not Mao, but even more by the logic of the situation which made Liu and the Party apparatus convenient scapegoats if Mao were to opt for a face saving solution. While any conclusion must remain speculative, Liu's support for Mao at Lushan may not have been based simply on a calculation that the course of prudence was to back the Chairman or even a sincere belief in the Great Leap policies. It can also be seen as a defense of his most vital interests.

Zhu De, however, responded very differently. Zhu, who apparently shared many of Peng's views concerning the Great Leap, spoke out in his defense saying he was hardworking and capable and should not be removed from office. In addition to defending Peng, Zhu was standing up for the traditional right to speak frankly in Party councils when he said, "Don't be afraid whether people call you leftist or rightist, [you should] say what is on your minds." Zhu apparently took it on himself to defend this tradition: "If people of our standing do not speak out who else will dare to?" While Zhu was forced to write a self-criticism for his forthright stand, he had touched an issue which struck a deep chord among those assembled at Lushan and would continue to be a major source of inner Party conflict for the next three years and beyond.[67]

Mao sought to offset the concern over decision making and disciplinary procedures in several ways. In a late July latter to Li Zhongyun, a relatively obscure planning official who had raised criticisms very similar to those of Peng Dehuai, Mao praised this cadre for his forthrightness in speaking out, thus suggesting that criticism was still welcome within the Party. Moreover, the relatively lenient treatment of Peng *et al.*, Mao's advocacy of a rectification approach, his observation that Peng's self-criticism was sincere, and his apparent acceptance of organizational rather than ideological criteria in defining Peng's "clique" all suggested that whatever arbitrariness had crept into his style, the Chairman was far from a Stalin, young or old. Whatever strain traditional Party norms had been put under, Mao still retained a strong attachment to those organizational principles.[68]

This, however, was not enough to mollify a substantial body of opinion within the Party which held that Peng had been unfairly dealt with, that he had only exercised his legitimate right to debate Party policies. What is of particular significance is that such sentiments appeared not only in 1961–62 when the correctness of Peng's views was plain for all to see, but also during the Lushan meeting itself and the subsequent campaign against right opportunism. Moreover, sympathy for Peng was voiced by those who opposed his views. Thus Li Jingquan, who not only criticized Peng in small group meetings at Lushan but who had earlier regarded Mao as too far to the right, reportedly said shortly after the meeting that "Peng Dehuai mixed up the subjective and objective, he only said a few wrong sentences. It certainly does not mean opposing us by [using] our shortcomings."[69] Here the contrast with the Gao Gang case is striking on several counts. The measures against Gao, measures taken in response to the violation of Party norms in a situation where policy was a peripheral issue at best, created little dissent in high CCP circles. Disciplinary action against Peng, where the basic issue was policy differences argued openly according to official procedures, raised apprehension even within radical sections of the leadership.

Why, then, did the CCP rally to Mao's side at Lushan? Undoubtedly various factors influenced different leaders. Liu Shaoqi, as suggested above, may have been protecting himself from Peng's criticism. Li Jingquan may have felt continued support for the Great Leap was more important than the damage done to established organizational principles. Others undoubtedly had simply learned it was safest to back Mao in political disputes. But even more fundamentally Mao had forced a stark choice upon his colleagues—discipline Peng or repudiate the Chairman of the Party.[70] Given decades of Mao's successful leadership and the close identification of his person and the Party in the minds of CCP leaders, cadres and general population, there was little doubt what the choice would be. For men such as Liu Shaoqi and Zhou Enlai, quite apart from any other considerations, repudiating Mao was unacceptable as endangering the stability of the political system.

This, in turn, emphasizes the fragility of the entire structure of Party norms. Given Mao's unchallenged—and virtually unchallengeable—leadership, the norms to a large extent depended on his forbearance. In turning on an old comrade for speaking his mind, Mao for the first time directly breached the understandings of the early 1940s as they applied to top echelon leaders. The Chairman attempted to limit the damage by insisting that minority rights still existed, but his erratic behavior at Lushan marked a major step in the erosion of traditional principles. The vitality of these principles in the coming years would also be dependent upon Mao's actions.

The Role of Military Issues

The above discussion of events at Lushan largely ignores military considerations as there is little evidence to suggest they arose. Not only do Red Guard accounts of the meetings mostly exclude any mention of military matters,[n] but the 1959 media campaign against right opportunism rarely touched on army work.[71] Undoubtedly the most conclusive evidence is Mao's 1971 statement that Peng and Huang had "organized a military club but they did not talk about military affairs."[72]

These considerations notwithstanding, various analysts have attached considerable weight to military factors in Peng's dismissal. This is based on the functional responsibilities of Peng and Huang, the political pressures within the PLA which had resulted in the major rectification effort of 1958, and textual analyses of Peng's 1957–58 statements suggesting the possibility of dissent from Mao's "politics in command" line.[73] It also gains plausibility from the significant though still limited shake-up of the military establishment which took place shortly after Lushan.[o] Ex-

[n] Only one reference to military or foreign affairs issues was found in Cultural Revolution materials dealing with Lushan and related events. This concerns the pre-Lushan activities of Fujian's Jiang Yizhen (see above, p. 311). Jiang assertedly argued at county, special district and provincial meetings that the Great Leap and communes had "caused tension in international relations and some friendly nations [had] doubts about [them]." *Xin Nongda,* December 2, 1967, in *SCMP-S,* No. 220.

[o] Besides the removal of Peng and Huang, Hong Xuezhi (who was linked to their "bourgeois military line" by the *Gongzuo tongxun*) was ousted as head of the PLA Rear Services Department, Xiao Ke and Li Da were transferred from their posts as Vice Ministers of Defense, Deng Hua was replaced as Commander of the Shenyang Military Region, and Wan Yi apparently lost his position as head of the General Staff's equipment department. The political troubles of GPD head and Central Committee Secretary Tan Zheng, who assertedly had lent his voice to the economic criticisms at Lushan (see above, p. 321n), may also have dated from this period although he apparently retained these posts until about 1961–62. While Hong, Tan, Deng and Wan were listed as Peng's "trusted men" within the PLA by a Red Guard source (*CB,* No. 851, p. 10), it is uncertain that the military shake-up following Lushan was the result of any particular military policies advocated in concert with Peng and Huang. Several of those affected continued to be active in other posts including significant military related positions. Thus this limited shake-up could be seen as a modest effort to give new Defense Minister Lin Biao a loyal team rather than as a systematic purge of representatives of a "bourgeois military line."

plicit evidence also exists in Chinese sources. There were several references in 1961 issues of the PLA's internal work bulletin, the *Gongzuo tongxun,* to the "bourgeois military line" of Peng and Huang. Moreover, during the Cultural Revolution the PLA newspaper linked the right opportunists of 1959 to an effort to undermine the political direction of the PLA, an effort which was characterized as the second great post-1949 struggle within the army following the first struggle in 1958. Subsequently both official and Red Guard sources enumerated Peng's alleged military deviations in considerable detail.[74]

The charges concerning Peng's military deviations were extremely wide ranging. Many picked up themes which had been aired during the 1958 rectification. Thus Peng assertedly negated "politics in command" and declared training and military science the key to army building. He was further accused of discarding PLA traditions—particularly participation in production and democratic relations between officers and men—and instead slavishly copying Soviet revisionist methods. Peng allegedly even sought to replace the collective leadership of Party committees with one man leadership and also to abolish political commissars. Moreover, he reportedly claimed modern warfare made "Mao Zedong's military thinking . . . out of date and no longer applicable." In an age of nuclear weapons he assertedly opposed the Chairman's 1958 program of greatly expanding the militia under the slogan "everyone a soldier."[75]

In contrast to the above charges of professionalism, Peng was also accused of grave deficiencies in the professional military sense. He assertedly failed to make adequate war preparations and was particularly lax concerning the most modern service arms—the air force and navy. This attitude was also reflected in disinterest in research and development or in "creating an independent and comprehensive network of modern national defense industries by relying on our own efforts." This last allegation was linked to accusations of depending on the Soviet Union for nuclear deterrence, a charge which draws some support from Peng's public statements in 1957–58.[76] Finally, Peng was accused of organizational unreliability. He allegedly would not carry out policies set by Mao and the Central Committee and prevented directives from reaching lower levels. Moreover, he assertedly for a long time engaged in activities to seduce the army away from Mao. To this end, Peng reportedly attempted to abolish the MAC and, without the knowledge of the Central Committee, wanted to set up another "Military Affairs Committee" as a device for monopolizing military power.[p]

How does one evaluate such charges? Although it seems plausible that Peng

[p] NCNA, July 30, August 19, 1967, in *SCMP,* Nos. 3994, 4007. While these last allegations are certainly distortions, they may reflect tension over the management of military affairs. Peng had been in charge of daily work of the MAC but Mao as its chairman provided overall policy guidance. Peng reportedly was highly dissatisfied with this arrangement which he felt curtailed his power, and he even indicated a desire to give up his posts. See *CB,* No. 851, p. 31; and *Case of Peng,* p. 176.

would be concerned with maintaining the Sino-Soviet alliance as a bulwark of China's defense, the all inclusive nature of his alleged deviations (which the *Gongzuo tongxun* summed up as "doctrinairism and empiricism [which] swung either to the right of left") creates the suspicion that Peng and other army leaders were being made scapegoats for all that was judged defective in the PLA.[q] Accusations were generally vague concerning time and specific incidents such as Peng's deletion of a reference to Mao's thought from 1953 draft regulations for Party committees in the army generally occurred well before 1959. No allegations were found concerning military issues *in 1959*. Moreover, many of the issues raised against Peng had been pervasive within the PLA since the 1956 Party Congress. The question Lin Biao raised upon replacing Peng—could politics still be in command in a modern army—had been at the center of political efforts which became particularly pronounced with the Great Leap Forward. Significantly, in raising the issue Lin spoke only of "some comrades" with erroneous ideas and did *not* link these views to right opportunism—the code term for Peng *et al.* As we have seen, furthermore, the "first big struggle with the bourgeois military line" in 1958 focused on the same questions of modernization and copying foreign practices that were later used against Peng, but there is no direct evidence that Peng was a target of this earlier struggle. Indeed, during the "first big struggle" politics truly did seize command of the PLA while the military establishment was under the operational leadership of Peng Dehuai.[77]

In retrospect, it appears many problems within the PLA during the last few years of Peng's leadership were the result not of insufficient attention to politics but of the unsystematic manner in which politics was placed in command. On the one hand, the study of Mao's theories was made a major part of the curricula of military academies, PLA soldiers were used extensively in economic construction, officers were sent in large numbers to serve as privates and rectify their defects, and a massive effort was undertaken to build an all inclusive militia under the "everyone a soldier" slogan. Together these measures severely disrupted the careful balance between politics and military technique which had been maintained since 1956 and corroded the morale of large segments of the officer corps. On the other hand, these political efforts lacked a solid organizational base; in 1960 one third of company level units in the PLA were without Party branches. The weakness of the organizational base plus the hurried implementation of the 1958 measures meant that in reality political work was often superficial. Accordingly, when Lin Biao assumed leadership of the Ministry of

[q] It is also important to emphasize the context in which Cultural Revolution criticism of Peng's military errors appeared. These attacks were first published in late July and August 1967 following the so-called Wuhan incident in which regional military commanders briefly challenged the authority of representatives dispatched by the central political leadership. The onslaught against Peng's military "line," then, can be seen more as a warning against military professionalism *in 1967* than as an explanation of events in 1959.

Defense, he adopted a two-pronged approach. Under the banner of "politics in command," one prong was aimed at building up Party organizations and placing political education on a systematic basis. The second prong was to reestablish the balance between political and military factors. Thus devoting sufficient time to military training was emphasized, army manpower allocated to civilian construction decreased, the tempo of the officers to the ranks movement slackened, and militia building was implemented on a much more modest and cautious basis. In effect, rhetoric aside, Lin's actions served to reemphasize military functions which had earlier been overwhelmed by politics.[78]

In sum, whatever military issues may have existed in 1959 it is doubtful that they played a central role in Peng Dehuai's dismissal. While Peng's indiscretions with the Russians and his opposition to the Great Leap may have reflected dismay with the costs of Sino-Soviet tensions to China's national defense—as well as a concern with the impact of rural disaffection on the largely peasant PLA—foreign policy and defense issues were not the ones raised at Lushan. Moreover, once Peng was removed from the defense portfolio army policy in fact shifted towards greater attention to the professional considerations Peng allegedly exemplified. The shake-up within the defense establishment was essentially the aftermath of a political crisis precipitated by non-military matters. While there may have been diffuse dissatisfaction with military performance in the context of the dislocations of the leap forward, it was only after Peng was in disgrace for other reasons that the occasion was used to deal with PLA problems. The subsequent notion that Peng and Huang had developed a "bourgeois military line" was most likely designed to warn army officers that despite the retreat from the extreme measures of 1958 Party leaders still insisted on traditional PLA methods, even though on a more realistic basis.

The Campaign against Right Opportunism

The struggle against right opportunism following Lushan took several forms. One was an extensive press campaign. Over the four months from late August to the end of the year the press was filled with strident denunciations of right opportunist views; then the media campaign suddenly subsided. Meanwhile meetings were convened in August and September by provincial Party committees to study the documents of the Lushan plenum, oppose rightist thinking and call for all out efforts in production. These meetings were attended by cadres from the provincial to county levels in accord with the plenum's instruction that the struggle should focus on those levels. A major aspect of the sessions was the exposure and criticism of leading cadres who were declared right opportunists or judged seriously infected with rightist ideas. While the contemporary press did not report further meetings at these levels, a Cultural Revolution source indicates that at least in Hunan the struggle against higher level right opportunists continued well into 1960. According to this report, the main item on the agenda of the March 1960 provincial Party congress "was still right opportunism [while] in August of the same year more latent rightists were detected, exposed, criticized, punished and dismissed."[79]

Various measures were adopted during and after the provincial meetings to extend the campaign to lower levels. Right opportunism and the Lushan documents became the major content of study in Party schools and regular study sessions within organs at the county level and above. Party committees of municipalities, special districts and counties held enlarged conferences to struggle against right opportunism within their own organs and also trained cadres to carry out a basic level socialist education movement. In accord with a directive of the plenum, socialist education was launched in all government organs, schools, enterprises, factories and mines, and villages. In the countryside, the movement was coordinated with the winter-spring overhaul of people's communes and Party branches and also involved study of the Lushan documents. Although the problem originated at higher levels, right opportunists representing the capitalist sentiments of well-to-do peasants reportedly existed in rural Party organizations and among non-Party cadres, and the struggle in village branches apparently continued in 1960. The scope of the movement is indicated by a report that in Hunan all Party members and 100,000 non-Party cadres participated.[80]

The Disciplinary Impact

In the absence of comprehensive statistics it is impossible to obtain a satisfactory estimate of the extent of purging or other disciplinary measures. In fact, a contradictory picture emerges from the available evidence. No statistics were issued during the movement, but general statements that the number of right opportunists were "small" or "very small" imply limited purging.[r] On the other hand, scattered figures and other evidence in Cultural Revolution sources indicate a much harsher disciplinary process. It is the specific if somewhat fragmentary information of these sources rather than the vague statements of the contemporary media which are most persuasive concerning the character of the movement.

At the higher levels, however, discipline does seem to have been relatively restricted. Although Mao stated in September 1959 that recent provincial conferences had uncovered "quite a number of senior cadres who are right opportunists," very few were actually identified. Indeed, only two relatively obscure officials were publicly attacked as right opportunists in 1959: Xi'an Secretary Chen Yuanfang and Yue Bangxun, director of the economic research institute of

[r]Overall Party membership figures also suggest a low purge rate. Official figures indicate a substantial growth from just under 14 million in October 1959 to 17 million in July 1961. Thus in less than two years covering both the drive against right opportunists and the 1960–61 rectification campaign, annual membership growth was at one of its highest recorded rates. Lewis, *Leadership,* pp. 110–11.

the Shaanxi Academy of Sciences. Chen and Yue assertedly provided a theoretical basis for right opportunism through writings emphasizing the role of production forces, contradictions within socialist society, and the inheritance of useful things from capitalist society.[81]

An examination of personnel data also suggests a limited disciplinary impact at the central and provincial levels.[82] Despite a September 1959 administrative reorganization and personnel shuffle in the State Council, particularly in economic departments, no more than a dozen people of vice ministerial level and higher or holding other key economic posts had their careers significantly disrupted at this time, while no cases involving leading central Party office holders were found. In the provinces, a similar number of Party secretaries, governors and vice governors appear to have suffered career setbacks in the period from mid-1959 to mid-1960.[s] Although some of these cases may have reflected factors unrelated to opposition to the Great Leap, in a few instances a connection is apparent. Not only were Xue Muqiao and Jiang Yizhen attacked during the Cultural Revolution for their dissent before and at Lushan, but Mao denounced Anhui's Zhang Kaifan at the plenum for having disbanded communal mess halls. Even though such clearly identifiable cases are few, the fact of career disruption due to policy orientation was again significant. Here the linkage to policy views was even more pronounced than in the 1957–58 purges which also raised organizational issues. In contrast, none of these officials were linked to Peng's "anti-Party clique" in any way. Moreover, many of them returned to public life after

[s] In central government organs those affected were: Director of the State Council's Fourth Staff Office for Light and Consumer Industries Jia Tuofu, Director of the State Statistical Bureau Xue Muqiao, Deputy Secretary-General of the State Council Tao Xijin, Deputy Director of the Fourth Staff Office Zhou Guangchun, Vice Minister of Finance Hu Lijiao, Vice Minister of Food Gao Jinchun, Vice Minister of Foreign Trade Luo Chengde, Vice Chairmen of the SPC An Zhiwen, Luo Gengmo and Ni Wei, Deputy Director of the People's Bank Cui Guang, and Deputy Director of the Central Administrative Bureau of Industry and Commerce Luo Shiyu. The provincial officials concerned were: Fujian Governor Jiang Yizhen, Anhui Secretaries Zhang Kaifan and Lu Xuebin, Hunan Secretary Zhou Hui, Gansu Secretary Huo Weide, Xinjiang Secretary Wu Kaizhang, Qinghai Secretary Zhang Guosheng, Qinghai Vice Governor Zhang Yizhen, Henan Vice Governor Peng Xiaoqian, and Jilin Vice Governor Yang Zhandao.

Another leading central official linked to Peng and Huang by Cultural Revolution sources was Xi Zhongxun, Vice Premier and Secretary-General of the State Council. However, Xi remained active after Lushan well into 1962 and was only effectively removed from his positions about the time of the Tenth Plenum. Xi's connection with Peng seems to relate to promoting historical works praising themselves, something which may have been relevant to Peng's 1962 attempt to secure a "reversal of verdicts." Xi has also been linked to Gao Gang and in 1964 Mao referred to a letter by Xi entitled "Liu Zhidan," i.e., Gao's old guerrilla colleague in North Shaanxi. Thus in both instances Xi's vulnerability seems related more to questions of Party history than to developments in 1953 or 1959. See *Jiefangjun wenyi* [Liberation Army Literature and Art], November 25, 1967, in *SCMM*, No. 609; *JPRS*, No. 52029, p. 32; and *SXWS*, II, 479. Cf. above, p. 164n.

1960 in the same period as the "reversal of verdicts" for large numbers of right opportunists. As we shall see, the basis for "verdict reversal" would be the lack of factional ties to Peng Dehuai, a rationale which had already aided some officials with high level support at Lushan. In late 1959, however, the removal of such people was another blow to established Party norms, even if its limited extent at the most visible levels reflected an effort to contain the damage.[83]

Ironically, in view of the high level origins of right opportunism, a much harsher and broader use of disciplinary sanctions against lower ranking, less visible officials apparently occurred in at least some areas. In contrast to official advocacy of the traditional "save the patient" approach during the 1959 campaign, Cultural Revolution reports reveal considerable concern over the harm done to established principles by the excesses of the drive against right opportunism. According to those reports, both important leaders and unnamed cadres expressed resentment on a number of grounds as pressure mounted for "verdict reversals" in 1960–62. One theme paralleled complaints regarding Peng Dehuai's case by arguing that many of those labeled right opportunists during the post-Lushan campaign had been subjected to personal attacks, unjustly condemned, and victimized by frame-ups. Moreover, the campaign had a dynamic of its own which, in the words of its critics, led it to degenerate into excessive struggle that negated and overthrew everything, and in at least some instances resulted in suicides. In some areas, rather than deal with cases on an individual basis, the authorities reportedly punished people in groups. Such struggle, these remarks indicated, was extended to basic level cadres and the rural masses with a negative effect on morale. A major result, according to the complaints, was that life within the CCP became abnormal as inner Party democracy was curtailed while cadres and masses outside the Party also did not dare speak their true feelings.[84] These factors were reflected in the evaluation of the Henan situation by First Secretary Liu Jianxun after he replaced the radical Wu Zhipu in 1961:

> Henan's anti-right opportunist campaign was characterized by the four operations of arithmetic: addition (magnifying mistakes); subtraction (eliminating [what is] correct); multiplication (elevating [the level of] analysis); and division. In the campaign . . . everybody was in a state of danger and mothers and fathers and husbands and wives dared not speak to each other.[85]

While Cultural Revolution sources provide some statistics concerning disciplinary measures, these not only lack comprehensiveness but are largely limited to radical provinces and thus probably overstate the degree of purging for China as a whole. In Wu Zhipu's Henan, reportedly "several hundred thousand people were criticized, repudiated and punished," but no breakdown of criticism as opposed to disciplinary punishment was indicated. Some percentage figures are available for Li Jingquan's Sichuan, however. According to one report, in February 1960 Li assertedly decided to dismiss 20 to 30 percent of the cadres (no level was mentioned) in order to keep up the pressure for increased production. A second report has Yunnan's Yan Hongyan referring approvingly to Li's "great purge of cadres" in Sichuan and claiming it had removed 80 percent of basic level cadres. Yan, who as a Party leader in Southwest China was clearly under Li's influence, then reportedly purged 30 percent of the basic level cadres in Yunnan. While such figures should probably be treated with some reservation, even the low figure of 20 percent represents a far higher purge rate than any recorded in earlier rectification movements.[86]

Li Jingquan's Sichuan purge is of interest for two additional reasons. First, Li allegedly was still criticizing Mao's April 1959 letter as too conservative in early 1960. In this context it appears that while Li had been critical of Peng's dismissal on the grounds that no inner Party norms had been violated, he was still willing to conduct a substantial purge of lower ranking officials whose rightism he felt was obstructing Great Leap goals. Second, according to this story Liu Shaoqi praised Li's plan. If true, it indicates that Liu, despite later criticisms of the campaign against right opportunism, was supporting a harsh approach to rectification at this time.[87]

It is highly ironic that one of those complaining that the campaign had resulted in abnormalities within the Party was Li Lisan, the leader blamed for the 1930 "second 'left' line" by official CCP histories. In 1961–62 the anti-right opportunist drive was explicitly compared to the "three 'left' lines" which preceded Mao's ascendancy and the development of the rectification approach. Now both the Party discipline of the late 1920s and early 1930s and the 1959–60 movement were characterized as "ruthless struggles and merciless blows." In his January 1962 speech to an enlarged cadres conference Liu Shaoqi reportedly drew this parallel, warning that such behavior could not be tolerated in the future and traditional methods of inner Party struggle would have to be restored—a position, as we shall see, similar to Mao's.[88]

The retrogression from rectification principles to "ruthless struggles" was undoubtedly linked to the eroded policy consensus dramatically revealed at Lushan. In the broadest sense, the urgency Mao placed on the need to combat right opportunist views spilled over into the disciplinary realm. More specifically, it is significant that the greatest excesses occurred in areas controlled by such leftists as Li Jingquan and Wu Zhipu. These men were apparently determined to remove any obstacles to the enthusiastic implementation of the Great Leap regardless of whether it meant substantial purging.[t] Moreover, the continuing

[t]This may also help explain how harsh discipline was largely implemented through the regular chain of command. With the Party apparatus in these cases firmly in the hands of radical leaders, relentless pressures could be brought to bear for extensive sanctions at all levels of official institutions. While the details of how the campaign was managed remain obscure, reports on the post-Lushan conferences from provincial to county levels indicate control by the regular Party authorities. In addition, no references were found to the use of work teams in the drive against right opportunism.

presence of substantial opposition meant that those wedded to the leap forward strategy had to resort to harsh methods to bolster their temporary dominance even if the traditional rectification approach was degraded in the process.

The Impact on Policy

While policy divisions contributed to the distortion of rectification, the intense struggle thus created in turn disrupted policy implementation. The actual measures approved at Lushan did not mark a dramatic swing to the left in subsequent months. Instead, a more ambivalent set of policies emerged which uneasily combined the espousal of unshaken fidelity to the principles of the leap forward and continued grappling with the problems that had come to the fore in the first half of 1959. In dealing with these problems many of the measures adopted were consistent with views expressed by right opportunist critics. National production targets for 1959 were substantially reduced in key items—by one third for steel, nearly one half for grain, and over one half for cotton—while 1958 agricultural output figures were also revised downward. In another action continuation of the much attacked mass movement for steel production was left to the discretion of local authorities and some provinces decided to terminate it. Moreover, most of the concrete measures taken following Lushan to correct Great Leap defects such as reducing capital construction and encouraging rural markets were already familiar in the pre-Lushan period. Similarly, the post-Lushan treatment of people's communes demonstrated considerable continuity with the previous period. Problems of excessive centralization, egalitarianism and waste were cited, while overall policy toward communes combined adherence to original goals and a cautious approach to concrete implementation. For example, basic ownership by the commune was to develop gradually but current emphasis was on strengthening brigade ownership; the free supply system was to be enforced, but its scope was to be strictly limited; and although mess halls were hailed as "sprouts of Communism," they still had to be overhauled while retaining their voluntary nature.[89]

Despite the relative moderation of many post-Lushan measures, the period following the plenum also was marked by efforts to stem the retreat from various Great Leap policies which had occurred in the first half of 1959 and introduce or revive specific radical programs. Even after target revisions the 1959 plan was accurately proclaimed "still a leap forward" and the call went out to continue the Great Leap in 1960. Moreover, in an atmosphere of intensified emphasis on ideology and the adulation of Mao, specific steps such as reestablishing disbanded communal mess halls and curbing the assignment of production activities to individual households were taken. Spring 1960 saw official NPC enactment of the Draft Program for Agricultural Development which had been so prominent in the early stages of the leap forward, the establishment of urban communes in major cities, and the promulgation of the "Constitution of the Anshan Iron and

Steel Company" emphasizing "politics in command," Party leadership and mass movements as guiding principles for industrial management. While Mao clearly was a driving force behind such radical programs as the "Anshan Constitution," at the same time he also apparently endorsed fully the moderate features of post-Lushan policy and still stood to the right of his more exuberant comrades such as Li Jingquan. The Chairman, in effect, adopted a posture similar to the one he had before Lushan—one which sought a continued leap forward on a more realistic basis. As he had already discovered at Lushan, such a posture was inherently unstable.[90]

While the policies adopted at Lushan and subsequently did not lurch dramatically to the left, under the impact of the campaign policy implementation did. Given a set of policies shot through with ambiguities and the pressures created by denunciations of right opportunists, leaders at all levels found it preferable to adopt a radical posture. Thus Bo Yibo, who only recently had to shift his ground at Lushan to avoid a right opportunist position, in 1960 reportedly acted in "ultra-left" fashion by pushing high targets and giving blind direction to the industrial sector. Moreover, officials at lower levels also raised targets "because everybody was afraid . . . of deviating to the right," and more generally cadres were reluctant to implement the more pragmatic aspects of Beijing's directives. As a result, critics subsequently claimed, following Lushan a new "high tide" appeared in the leap forward which gave rise to the "five winds," deviations which were to become the main target of the 1960–61 rectification campaign.[91] From the vantage point of 1961, Tao Zhu presented an overall summary of the disruptive effect of the drive against right opportunism:

> The Lushan conference originally had the purpose of summing up experiences, . . . rectifying shortcomings and mistakes. But in the course of the conference there appeared an anti-Party clique headed by Peng Dehuai, which was opposed to the Party, the Central Committee, Chairman Mao, and the general line. This could not but call for opposition to right opportunism. However, at that time the comrades in our province were not clear about it. They did not confine the opposition to right opportunism within certain limits of the Party; instead, they continued to implement the spirit of [earlier policies]. As a result, an anti-rightist movement was set in motion and past shortcomings and mistakes, instead of being corrected, were aggravated.[92]

Finally, apart from generalized pressures, excesses in policy implementation were specifically due to anti-right opportunist struggles and dismissals aimed at intermediate to basic level cadres who failed to produce rapid production increases.[93]

In sum, the movement against right opportunism in 1959–60 distorted the policy process in China. While the thrust of the campaign was consistent with some of the measures emerging from Lushan, it undercut the more moderate aspects of post-Lushan policy with drastic consequences for the Chinese economy. Mao himself subsequently attributed the failure to deal adequately with pressing economic problems to the movement, as well as to the leadership's preoccupation with Sino-Soviet tensions throughout 1960 which was itself related to the struggle against right opportunism given the significance of the Soviet factor at Lushan.[u] In this case rectification was clearly dysfunctional to the larger aims of policy.

Conclusion

By the summer of 1959 the CCP found itself divided. This was not a simple radical-conservative division, but a more complex configuration of forces where even major proponents of the Great Leap saw the need for change. Mao occupied something of a middle ground in this configuration, willing and indeed eager to make adjustments but steadfastly refusing to alter the basic thrust of the leap forward program. In effect, the Chairman tried to have it both ways—to denounce exaggerated production figures while at the same time still demanding higher rates of growth than any country had ever achieved. When mass mobilizations led to excesses previously, the Party's normal response was to call a halt and tend to the accumulated problems in a fully articulated consolidation phase. A classic example of this was the "anti-reckless advance" measures of 1956 which, with Mao's reluctant assent, marked an end to the first attempt to leap forward. In 1959, however, Mao was unwilling to opt for a full-fledged consolidation. Instead, futile attempts to redress imbalances were undertaken while mass mobilization remained the order of the day.

Mao's straddling of the issue had disastrous results. Not only did the refusal to face up fully to the inadequacies of the Great Leap lead to a severe economic and social crisis, but in the process established Party principles were further eroded. The strains which had begun with the launching of the leap forward in late 1957 now became measurably more severe. Much of this centered on the increasingly erratic role of the Chairman. By 1959, far from retiring gracefully to the "second line," Mao was playing a leading role in readjusting the Great Leap and commune policies. In the process the Chairman apparently was increasingly seen as violating collective leadership, of developing an "individual style" independent of Politburo discussions which Peng Dehuai and others had criticized in the spring. Ironically, in substantive terms Mao's individual efforts before Lushan generally had a moderating effect on the excesses of the Great Leap.

At Lushan more serious defects in Mao's leadership style appeared which led some of the assembled officials to see comparisons to the dictatorial methods of Stalin. While this was clearly overdrawn, the Chairman did react in an emotional

[u] Speaking in January 1961, Mao recognized the disorder and "Communist wind" created by the movement but still declared the campaign had been "an absolute necessity." *MMT*, II, 238, 243–45.

and extreme fashion to open policy criticisms—criticisms which at least in Peng's "letter of opinion" were offered with considerable deference and which were consistent with many of Mao's own pre-Lushan statements. By demanding Peng's disgrace Mao made both minority rights and collective leadership meaningless. The right to air dissenting views in official forums, which had come under a shadow in 1957–58 but had never been explicitly challenged, was now effectively withdrawn in Peng's case for the complex reasons discussed earlier. The immediate result was that other leaders unconnected to Peng were no longer willing to risk stating their reservations about official policies, a development which had painful consequences for the policy making process.

At the same time collective leadership was emasculated. Collective decision making had always been dependent on Mao's forbearance, but now he was presenting his colleagues with an ultimatum—Peng or me. Such a situation was conducive to a simple declaration of loyalties, not to a careful weighing of diverse views. Ultimately, the comparison with Stalin is perhaps most relevant to the considerable degree of capriciousness and suspicion which marked Mao's actions. While the Chairman could express reservations about Great Leap programs Peng could not. A long standing comrade in arms who had stood with Mao at crucial political junctures despite personal friction in the past was now treated as a disloyal opponent for responding to the Chairman's pre-Lushan appeals to speak out freely.

Similarly, the traditional rectification approach also came under increasing stress. In addition to disciplining officials solely for their views, the new campaign marked a further turn away from persuasive measures. While greater coercion had already appeared in 1957–58 with disciplinary sanctions affecting perhaps 8 to 9 percent of Party members, following Lushan in at least some areas of upwards of 20 percent of cadres were dismissed. Moreover, despite explicit calls for traditional "save the patient" methods, excesses now led to claims that in fact the discredited "ruthless struggles and merciless blows" approach had reappeared. Thus the estrangement of rectification theory and practice which was already noticeable in the early days of the Great Leap Forward became even more pronounced.

To a certain extent a relatively coercive approach was to be expected in what was still a mobilization phase.[v] The aim of the new movement was to further the Great leap by attacking pessimistic attitudes detrimental to mobilization. In mid-1959, however, the situation was complicated by the fact that many of the defects uncovered in the economic program since late 1958 required precisely

[v] While the anti-right opportunist campaign was clearly the outgrowth of internal pressures, the Sino-Indian border conflict and the Laotian civil struggle which unfolded in the same period may also have contributed marginally to the coercive environment. An undoubtedly greater foreign factor was the poor state of Sino-Soviet relations which, as we have argued, probably influenced Mao's reaction to Peng at Lushan.

those qualities of hard headed pragmatism which were under attack after Lushan, qualities which could only suffer in a coercive environment. Thus the contradictions of the policies adopted at Lushan guaranteed that the results of the anti-right opportunist drive would to some extent be counterproductive. In contrast to the rectification efforts of 1950–53 where the aims of the various campaigns were strongly supportive of the overall program of social transformation and congruent with the interests of the new elite—and even in contrast with the 1957–58 movement which bolstered the initial thrust of the leap forward but kept coercion within limits—the post-Lushan campaign both undermined major aspects of the plenum's policies and alienated large numbers of cadres who experienced its excesses.

The harshness of the 1959–60 campaign again underlines the relationship of leadership unity to disciplinary methods. The Party unity which had been forged by the early 1940s and sustained first by revolutionary success and then by consensus on the Soviet model was now severely strained. With Mao suspicious of old comrades and foreseeing another 20 to 50 years of class struggle to guarantee the victory of the correct line, some coercion was inevitable. Moreover, leaders at lower levels who strongly backed the Great Leap strategy now had both the opportunity and need to deal harshly with those who opposed their views. With such divisions deepening, rectification was becoming less a method for reform and more a tool for purging.

Clearly Mao must take a large share of the blame for the consequences of Lushan—continued pursuit of an unrealistic economic strategy, grossly inadequate implementation of the policy adjustments approved by the plenum, a less candid and effective policy making process, and growing demoralization of China's cadres. All of these consequences were directly related to the dramatic weakening of traditional Party norms which Mao had done so much to create. Throughout the period Mao remained aware of the significance of these norms for both the CCP's success and his own leadership. Even at Lushan he attempted to reassert the very right of speaking freely which he denied to his Defense Minister. As the crisis created by the Great Leap set in subsequently, Mao and his leadership colleagues became even more aware of the value of the norms. In coping with the crisis a major priority was attached to restoring the long standing principles which had been so rudely damaged by the assault on Peng Dehuai.

10
Rectification and "Verdict Reversal" during the Crisis Years, 1960–1962

As awareness of the full extent of the economic disaster resulting from the Great Leap Forward took hold in 1960, China's leaders embarked on a course which went far beyond a normal consolidation of gains and became a headlong retreat from the official policies of the previous years. Most analyses of this period have pictured a growing divergence between Mao, now allegedly shunted to the background, and a dominant group of Politburo leaders who mapped out a pragmatic program of policy adjustments.[1] This interpretation, in contrast, sees a fragile and limited consensus reestablished by 1961 on the unavoidable need for drastic measures to cope with the unprecedented crisis. While the Chairman did finally retire to the "second line," this was a voluntary move in a context where he was increasingly preoccupied with Sino-Soviet relations and had no systematic cure for China's domestic ills himself, and in any case where he specifically endorsed the major "revisionist" policy changes during the first two stages of the retreat up to January 1961.[2] However, by mid-1962 Mao felt the third stage of the retreat had gone too far and ordered a series of measures to protect the collective sector and restore orthodox controls.

If Mao largely restricted himself to the role of arbitrating differences and ratifying programs essentially drawn up by others on substantive policy issues, he took a much more positive role concerning organizational matters. He repeatedly attempted to revive the tradition of open policy debate, particularly in his June 1961 self-criticism and January 1962 talk on democratic centralism.[3] Earlier, from late 1960 through spring 1961, a rectification campaign *(zhengfeng yundong)* unfolded with particular emphasis on rural areas in an effort to curb the excesses of the Great Leap. Here, in contrast to the anti-right opportunist drive, rectification returned to its traditional function of dealing with defects in leadership style. By 1961, however, organizational requirements went beyond restoring the original focus of rectification to making amends for the excesses of the

1959–60 campaign by "reversing verdicts" *(fan'an)* and restoring to official positions many who had been ousted as right opportunists. Although Mao decided in 1962 that this process had gone too far, the Chairman himself had earlier been a key figure insisting on the necessity of righting past wrongs.

The effort to restore traditional Party norms was only partially successful, however. While the policy process did become more effective and produce the measures required for survival, the legacy of bitterness from the preceding period was heavy. Many rehabilitated right opportunists were unwilling to forget the indignities they had suffered and sought vengeance. In addition, some leading radicals at the provincial level were now dismissed or otherwise disciplined; thus they were punished at least in part for their policy advocacy. More broadly, ordinary cadres became increasingly demoralized by worsening socio-economic conditions, confusing policy changes, and the tendency of the top leadership to attribute the collapse of the leap forward to lower level implementation rather than to the developmental strategy itself. In the unavoidable process of rectifying policy implementation the leadership in effect challenged the basic principle of Leninist discipline. Cadres were now attacked for behavior which had been demanded previously. The Great Leap virtues of bold leadership, mobilizing peasant energies and subjective factors, and developing collective life were transformed into the deviations of blind leadership, commandism, exaggeration and egalitarianism. The rectification effort, moreover, apparently involved a greater degree of coercion than one would normally expect from the traditional approach.

The Retreat: Stage One, Late 1960 to mid-1961

The post-Lushan upsurge of the leap forward lasted to mid-1960, but even in the first half of the year signs of retrenchment appeared. A fundamental revision of priorities was seen in the affirmation of "agriculture as the foundation of the economy" as basic policy in early 1960, and increased investment in the agricultural sector was reported. The impetus toward retrenchment was increased substantially by several severe blows to the economy later in 1960. In July–August in apparent response to CCP criticism of various Soviet foreign policy positions, the Soviet Union abruptly withdrew its technical advisers, scrapped economic agreements and discontinued vital supplies of equipment and material causing severe dislocation in the most modern sector of an already troubled economy. Even more important, major natural calamities struck agriculture for the second successive year which worsened the already dangerous food situation, caused critical shortages of raw materials for industry, and created disaster conditions in significant areas of China. The food shortage not only resulted in declining grain rations and widespread malnutrition, it also led to a general decline of public morale manifested in growing privatism, black market activities, a weakening of social order, and the resurgence of superstitious practices. The seriousness of the situation was revealed in the *Gongzuo tongxun* which reported soldiers and peasants complaining that people were worse off than dogs and asking whether Mao was willing to let the people starve. In at least five provinces with substantial minority populations, moreover, armed rebellions apparently caused or intensified by deteriorating economic conditions had to be put down by the PLA during 1960–61.[4]

Measures to Shore Up the Situation

Starting in mid-1960, Party leaders took a series of measures to cope with the deteriorating situation. As Mao noted at the Eighth Central Committee's Tenth Plenum in fall 1962, although policies to overcome shortcomings had been initiated since the 1958 Zhengzhou meeting, it was only in the second half of 1960 that serious efforts were undertaken to put things right. A summer 1960 central work conference at Beidaihe decided on an even greater shift of resources to the agricultural sector and it apparently also discussed setting up six regional Party bureaus which were formally established by the Ninth Plenum in January 1961 to provide greater central control of the economy.[a] With these steps the leadership came to grips with serious dislocations caused by excessive investment in industry and the radical decentralization of the Great Leap strategy.[5]

Key measures for dealing with the problems of people's communes were enacted in the November 1960 Twelve Articles and March 1961 Sixty Articles. These documents, although assertedly no more than a systematic summing up of Party policies since 1959, represented a substantial retreat. While many policies in the documents—e.g., the brigade as the basic unit of ownership and voluntary participation in mess halls—were familiar, others involved important departures. A major feature was the strengthened role of production teams. Brigades were required to recognize a set amount of team autonomy in production management and provide teams with "four fixes" of labor power, land, animals and tools for permanent use. Furthermore, production targets could not be imposed by brigades but had to be based on consultation with teams. This resulted in a contract *(bao)* system whereby output quotas were guaranteed by the team.

Another change was the reduction of commune, brigade and team size. In contrast to Mao's 1958 statement that "bigness" was an essential feature of the commune, it was now stipulated communes should not be too large. The recommended brigade size was equal to a higher APC and that of a commune equal to an administrative village, thus providing for at least a three fold increase in the

---

[a] These regional Party bureaus were designed to coordinate the activities of the provinces which had often gone their own way during the Great Leap. They were not complemented by regional government or military organs such as existed in the early 1950s. See above, p. 84n.

number of communes over the 1958 figure. Major steps were also taken to increase material incentives including a system setting production norms low enough to allow teams to achieve a surplus they could keep and a requirement that brigades deduct less income for accumulation and distribute more directly to peasants. Most important were concessions to the individual economy —encouraging family sideline enterprises, allowing private plots on 5 percent of cultivated land, and promoting trade on the free market after state deliveries were met. By these stipulations concerning private plots, free markets and small scale sideline enterprises, official policy laid the basis for the *sanzi* of the *sanzi yibao* ("three extensions [of private economic activities] and one guarantee [of output quotas by individual households]") which developed widely in 1962 and was harshly denounced during the Cultural Revolution. Moreover, even in 1960–61 the system of fixing output quotas at the team level led to pressures in some areas for production contracts with peasant households. Finally, cadres were urged to seek humbly the advice of old peasants possessing rich knowledge of local conditions, a marked change from the prior emphasis on political leadership.[6]

Measures were also taken to deal with the crisis in industry. New cuts in capital construction and the closing of factories occurred in mid-1960. At the January 1961 plenum, an industrial policy of "readjustment, consolidation, filling out, and raising standards" was announced. This policy called for attention to light consumer industries to insure adequate supplies of daily necessities and involved a further reduction in capital construction and decreasing the rate of growth in heavy industry. Attention was also given to improving the quality and variety of products, economizing on materials, lowering production costs, and raising labor productivity. The emphasis of the new policy was on regularization, strict management control and expertise although the worker participation aspects of the leap forward were not totally eliminated. Rigorous rational systems, an orderly division of labor, and cost accounting by experts became the watchwords of the day as the "one-sided activism" of the Great Leap was rejected.[7]

The retreat also brought about new policies toward intellectuals. The first signs of change came shortly after the withdrawal of Soviet technicians with an August 1960 address by Party united front work chief Li Weihan indicating a new though more restricted Hundred Flowers policy. Democratic parties were again invited to exchange "advice and criticism" with the CCP, but on this occasion the six criteria of Mao's revised "Contradictions" speech were emphasized from the outset and contention was strictly limited to academic matters. Moreover, the ideological reform of intellectuals was handled by a new device which became very prominent by spring 1961, the "meetings of immortals" *(shenxianhui)*. While the aim of these meetings was the "transformation of the bourgeois world outlook," the emphasis was on self-transformation and the entire process was to be conducted as a "gentle breeze and mild rain." Although the response of intellectuals to these moves was understandably cautious, the relaxation implicit in them undoubtedly was welcomed. In addition, the Ninth Plenum called for an improvement in the quality of scientific work and this was backed up by assurances to scientists of sufficient time for personal research, greater responsibility in directing their own work, and increased material incentives.[8]

Policy Differences and Power Relationships

The question naturally arises as to what degree the above retreat reflected or led to policy conflict and how it affected power relationships within the CCP leadership. While this entire area is highly speculative, it does appear that Mao withdrew from close oversight of the economy by mid-1960. In contrast to frequent directives in 1959—the phenomenon of "personal leadership" criticized by Peng Dehuai—there was a sharp drop in Mao's known comments in 1960–61.[b] While it is undoubtedly true that this withdrawal from operational affairs reduced Mao's ability to influence developments, assertions that the Chairman's actual authority declined significantly are misleading in at least three respects. First, Mao was not the only leader to divert his attention from economic affairs in 1960. In his own words, "the central leadership comrades devoted their main energy to international [i.e., Sino-Soviet] questions" with adverse domestic effects. Although Mao's Politburo colleagues again focused on the economy in 1961 while he seemingly remained preoccupied with Sino-Soviet affairs, the circumstances of the original "withdrawal" suggest the Chairman's ability to shape the political agenda to matters closest to his concerns even at a time of obvious economic problems. Second, although various observers have noted a decrease in the references to Mao and his thought from about 1960, the study of Mao's works remained an important feature of Chinese political life and the Chairman's public prominence still far outshone that of any of his colleagues. Thus any decline in the Mao cult and the powers ascribed to Mao's ubiquitous thought—something one would expect in the transition from mobilization to retrenchment—should be seen as a response to objective conditions rather than a curbing of the Chairman's power. Indeed, the major publishing event of 1960 was Volume IV of Mao's *Selected Works*—a collection which significantly emphasized Mao's advocacy of Party discipline and his rejection of leftist excesses in the late 1940s.[9]

Most importantly, the measures taken through mid-1961 when a more sub-

---

[b] Cultural Revolution texts are available for only five or possibly eight statements by Mao, mostly very brief ones, for the mid-1960 to mid-1961 period. To compare, *SXWS* (after texts without precise dates are assigned to the most likely period) contains 327 pages on the period from the 1958 Zhengzhou conference to March 1960, and only 16 pages on mid-1960 to mid-1961.

stantial retreat began can be linked to Mao in several regards. Not only were the critical Sixty Articles on communes based on Mao's speeches and directives dating back to spring 1959,[c] but a variety of Cultural Revolution sources indicate the Chairman's approval and/or initiative of other key policies such as "readjustment, consolidation, filling out, and raising standards." And in a vein similar to the recent addition to the *Selected Works*, in early 1961 Mao emphasized the need for investigation and research and advocated the removal of officials who ignored the needs of the masses. Thus whatever the precise authorship of the still limited retrenchment measures enacted from mid-1960 to mid-1961, the basic policy direction was clearly in accord with what is known of Mao's thinking at this juncture.[10]

It seems also clear, however, that although widespread agreement existed on the necessity for a retreat, this fell short of the broad pre-Great Leap policy consensus. On the one hand, at least in the second half of 1960, some radical leaders reportedly still resisted the moderate turn.[d] But at the same time it is very likely that other leaders felt a more basic retreat was required by the steadily worsening situation than Mao who still asserted the correctness of the leap forward policies and the possible reappearance of rightism if too much stress was placed on moderation.[11] In these circumstances Mao stressed the need for unity at the Ninth Plenum:

> On the question of unity, the unity of the Central Committee is the heart of the whole Party's unity. At the Lushan Conference a small number of comrades opposed unity, but we hope to unite with them no matter how many errors they have made.[12]

Mao went on to welcome Peng Dehuai's report on his study over the past year and even to advocate uniting with the Soviet Union "no matter what charges they make against us." [13] Thus at a time of strained policy consensus the Chairman moved to reemphasize traditional Party norms by stressing unity and discipline. In this context the 1960–61 rectification campaign unfolded.

---

[c] J. Chester Cheng, ed., *The Politics of the Chinese Red Army: A Translation of the Bulletin of Activities of the People's Liberation Army* (Stanford: Hoover Institution Publications, 1966), p. 456. This claim that the Sixty Articles derive from Mao's 1959 views gains credence from a comparison of the 1961 document and the texts of Mao's earlier statements. Although other Party leaders, notably Deng Xiaoping, were involved in the actual drafting of the document and reportedly drew Mao's criticism, there are various official assertions that Mao personally authored the Sixty Articles. E.g., Radio Kunming, December 20, 1967, in *NFCPRS*, No. 239. Moreover, the basic policies concerned remained in effect both during and after the Cultural Revolution.

[d] According to Radio Chengdu, October 3, 1967, in *NFCPRS*, No. 228, following Mao's approval of "readjustment," etc., in the second half of 1960, Li Jingquan continued his leftist posture by compelling increases in the labor force engaged in iron and steel production and persisting in high iron and steel targets.

The Rectification Campaign of 1960–61

Rectification was an important part of the retrenchment process under way by mid-1960. Although there is far less information available on the 1960–61 campaign than for any other rectification movement in the 1950–65 period,[e] the communique of the Ninth Plenum indicated its significance and aims:

> [T]here are a few cadres who, although good willed and well intentioned, are inadequate in their ideological consciousness. They lack understanding of the fundamental policies of the Party and government, they lack sufficient understanding of the distinction between socialism and Communism, of the distinction between socialist ownership by the collective and socialist ownership by the people as a whole, of the three level ownership in the people's communes with the production brigade as the basic level, and of the socialist society's principle of exchange of equal values, of "to each according to his work" and of more income for those who work more—all of which the Party has repeatedly publicized. In view of all this, Party organizations in many places in accordance with the instructions of the Central Committee have carried out [and will continue to carry out] a rectification movement . . . in rural and urban areas.[14]

The communique further decreed the nationwide implementation of the campaign in order both to improve the work style of well intentioned cadres and to

---

[e] Few specific references to the movement were found in contemporary public sources, a situation reflecting the general decline in the quality and quantity of information in the official media starting about 1959–60. Moreover, Cultural Revolution references are also extremely rare. Thus a disproportionate share of the data comes from two sets of internal documents: the *Gongzuo tongxun* for January–August 1961, translated in Cheng, *Red Army;* and reports of the Bao'an County, Guangdong, CCP Committee for September–December 1961, in *URS*, Vol. 27—Nos. 7–9. Further sources include refugee interviews and Western intelligence data.

Insights into the rectification effort can be gained from a number of other developments in this period. Starting in spring and summer 1960, a new *xiafang* movement encompassing innovative systems whereby cadres could divide time between administrative and production tasks foreshadowed rectification emphasis on cadre labor and investigating actual conditions. In October–November 1960, a press campaign emphasized the need to adhere strictly to Party policies, another prominent rectification theme. At the same time as the new *zhengfeng* drive, a movement for the suppression of counterrevolutionaries in society and purge of counterrevolutionaries in the Party *(shehui zhenfan, neibu sufan)* was carried out. Moreover, the PLA launched a campaign to cleanse and reorganize the people's militia in coordination with rectification and commune overhaul, and in April–May 1961 the entire army studied documents on investigation work and people's communes. Finally, in July 1961 Liu Shaoqi called for a new study movement to help cadres understand objective laws of socialist construction, basic Marxist-Leninist principles, and current Party policies. See Lewis, *Leadership*, pp. 229–32; *CB*, No. 646; Cheng, *Red Army*, pp. 25–28, 140, 406; and *Peking Review*, July 7, 1961.

purge Party and government organizations of an "extremely few bad elements." While the movement was undertaken in basic level units in both industry[f] and agriculture, its greatest significance apparently was within the rural people's communes. It seems that the campaign coincided with the annual winter–spring rectification and commune overhaul *(zhengfeng zhengshe)* and partly involved an intensification of that process. It most likely began with a call to mobilize the masses for rectification and commune overhaul in the November 1960 Twelve Articles. This directive, together with the subsequent Sixty Articles, became key documents for study during the rectification process. When the campaign actually ended is unclear, but it certainly was still in full swing in April–May 1961.[15] It was about this time, moreover, that a number of key provincial leaders were removed from office apparently for errors linked to those under attack during the 1960–61 rectification.

The "Five Winds"

The most important aim of rectification was to correct the shortcomings of rural cadres "with good intentions." These were summarized as the "five winds" or "five styles" *(wufeng):* "The Communist wind"; "the wind of exaggeration" *(fukua feng);* "the commandist wind *(mingling feng);* "the wind of cadre privileges" *(ganbu teshu feng);* and "the wind of blindly leading production" *(xiazhihui shengchan feng).* These deviations, which together represented a serious left adventurist tendency, reportedly were found in a fairly large number of places and infected both well intentioned cadres and bad elements. Although assertedly serious in only a few cases, the elimination of these defects was clearly necessary if the new policies were to be successful. At the Ninth Plenum Mao set "resolutely doing away with *(zhengdiao)* the five winds" as a key task for the coming year.[16]

---

[f]Extremely little is known about rectification in industrial enterprises or urban areas generally. At the January 1961 plenum Mao referred to "pilot programs" in the cities, suggesting the movement may have been conducted on a restricted basis there. In any case, it appears a major aim was to correct phenomena broadly similar to the "five winds" (see below) which had appeared in industrial enterprises. Emphasis was placed on raising the policy understanding of cadres, promoting a sober and painstaking style of work, conducting careful investigations while determining and implementing policies, and adhering to mass line principles to overcome the separation of factory leaders from workers. Criticism was also directed at units which ignored state plans and displayed one-sided activism such as recklessly setting and breaking production targets without reference to the overall needs of the economy. Another major target was dictatorial tendencies of cadres who handled leadership tasks in an impetuous fashion. See *NFRB,* October 22, 1960, in *CB,* No. 645; *RMRB,* January 24, 1961, in *SCMP,* No. 2435; *HQ;* February 1, 1961, in *SCMM,* No. 250; *MMT,* II, 239; and H.F. Schurmann, "Peking's Recognition of Crisis," in Albert Feuerwerker, ed., *Modern China* (Englewood Cliffs: Prentice-Hall, 1964), pp. 98–99.

The Communist wind, which had been attacked in early 1959 but according to Mao "blew unprecedentedly hard" after the Lushan meetings, affected cadres who were unable to distinguish between the utopian vision of the people's commune trumpeted in 1958 and concrete measures subsequently adopted for commune management. These cadres viewed Communism as something which could be achieved overnight rather than through a drawn out transition and erroneously referred to long range goals when framing practical measures. A number of problems contributed to a situation known as "one equalization and two transfers," i.e., egalitarianism in all aspects of life and unrestricted transfer of brigade manpower and materials by commune authorities. Seeds, land, labor and other brigade resources were often recklessly used to prepare for the promised basic ownership at the commune level in disregard of repeated warnings that the current task was strengthening brigade ownership. Some cadres took a one-sided view of the relationship between wages and free supplies, sought to reduce wages as much as possible, and wanted to extend the supply system to meat, fish and fruit. In the distribution of goods, they gave equal treatment to men and women, the old and young, and people capable or incapable of heavy labor, thus dampening production incentives. Other examples of excessive egalitarianism included extending the scope of communal mess halls, collectivizing too much private property, and failing to implement various incentive measures. Taking an overall view, both Mao and Liu Shaoqi were particularly harsh in denouncing "the Communist wind" as exploiting and robbing the peasants, thus requiring the Party to pay back its debts to the rural masses. Indeed, in the course of rectification, one of the most effective methods of combating "the Communist wind" was restitution and compensation for goods which had been confiscated by over eager cadres.[17]

The second "wind," that of exaggeration, was a manifestation of failure to investigate painstakingly actual conditions. Undoubtedly originating in the wildly ambitious aims of the leap forward but also found in other mobilization phases, this tendency was now attacked for causing cadres to "set production targets too high, boast in high flown language of things not yet accomplished, and proceed in this way until they became entirely subjective and casual in their handling of affairs and quite isolated from the masses." By setting high targets cadres sought to demonstrate activism to higher authorities but in fact undermined production incentives by limiting the possibility of exceeding quotas. Other attempts to demonstrate accomplishments included pursuing quantity while neglecting quality and concentrating all energies and resources in experimental fields to the detriment of regular production. Most serious was reporting false output figures either in fear of punishment for lagging behind or in hope of winning praise. An example of deception occurred in Guangxi where one county Party secretary created a miraculous rice output on experimental fields by clandestinely transplanting the best rice plants of the area to these fields. Mao's displeasure with such practices was indicated not only by his 1961 emphasis on investigation and study but also by his attacks on unrealistic targets and reports since before the Lushan meeting.[18]

The "commandist wind" was found in cadres who coerced peasants into implementing unrealistic directives from higher authorities. These cadres, who purportedly believed the masses would go wherever the Party pointed, repeated the mistakes of many others going back to the 1940s by neglecting educational work. Operating under the severe demands of the Great Leap, they felt high pressure tactics brought results, that "enthusiasm in work comes under the whip, high yields come under the whip." When peasants proved unable to meet targets, cadres attacked them for "conservative ideas" and "opposition to Party leadership." As in earlier movements, concrete manifestations of this "wind" included beating and cursing, arbitrarily labeling people bad elements, corporal punishment suppressing democracy, taking revenge against those who criticized cadre misbehavior, and various economic measures such as "not permitting commune members to eat," withholding rations and arbitrarily deducting work points. Cadres, confusing the distinction between "contradictions among the people" and those with the enemy, often called on the militia to enforce orders, illegally confiscate property, and tie up, search, arrest and jail innocent people. According to Liu Shaoqi, this style of leadership resulted in many people being beaten to death.[19]

While such practices were strictly forbidden by the Sixty Articles, the leadership carefully distinguished between proper mass line methods and erroneous tendencies of "laissez faire leadership" and tailism. This was demonstrated in a report on how three production teams of the same commune handled peasant demands to divide the sweet potato crop among commune members when the plan called for sending it to the state granary. In one team cadres responded in a commandist manner, shouting peasant demands were improper and using coercion to secure compliance to the plan. Cadres of the second team simply allowed peasants to distribute the potatoes as they wished, thus abdicating leadership. The third team, however, adhered to the mass line, investigated the peasant demands, explained the significance of Party policies and organized discussions, and in this manner reportedly secured voluntary compliance to the plan.[20]

Cadre privileges also caused considerable popular alienation. Many cadres, having obtained official status, assertedly felt they were above others. Imbued with this mentality, they favored friends and relatives in assigning positions and tasks and engaged in petty corruption while performing their duties as accountants, cashiers, grain cadres, mess hall managers and storekeepers. The Sixty Articles sought to curb these deviations by prohibiting favoritism in appointments, overeating and overacquisition, recording extra work points, and establishing separate cadre kitchens. While similar abuses had been attacked in rectification movements as early as 1947–48, in the context of the severe food shortage, Party leaders recognized the particularly explosive potential of special treatment for cadres:

> At present when there is difficulty getting supplies, all cadres of the Party, government, army, and mass organizations must share weal and woe with the people. Then difficulties can be tided over. We cannot be isolated from the masses, and if our life is specially privileged, it will arouse dissatisfaction among the masses and may even lead to unpleasant incidents.[21]

Another aspect of cadre privileges was avoiding participation in productive labor. Some cadres who themselves engaged in labor failed to mobilize their families to participate. This wasted manpower desperately needed for production, isolated cadres from the living conditions of peasants thus causing neglect of popular livelihood, and increased cadre-peasant tensions. The Sixty Articles adopted a number of measures to alleviate this situation and enforce cadre labor. These included limiting the number of supplementary work points given to cadres for administrative duties, requiring commune level cadres to spend at least 60 days a year in labor, assigning brigade level cadres to specific teams for permanent labor participation, and requiring team cadres to participate in labor under the same regulations as ordinary commune members.[22] In contrast to the other "winds," the link of "the wind of cadre privileges" to Great Leap pressures is less direct. Nevertheless, the increased powers of basic level cadres necessitated by the leap forward strategy undoubtedly helps explain the apparent seriousness of the problem.

The final "wind," blindly leading production, was common among cadres who lacked experience in agriculture and carried out production measures without making necessary allowances for local conditions. These cadres rigidly implemented new cultivation methods popularized during the Great Leap in unsuited terrain and rejected as "old habits" established methods which had been proven over the years. As a result, such aberrations as wasting labor by undertaking water conservancy projects without plans, damaging grain production by planting sweet potatoes in swampy land, and issuing orders for weeding when fields were submerged in water were common. Although similar aberrations had appeared during earlier mass mobilizations, the intensity of the leap forward undoubtedly made the problem much more severe than earlier. By urging cadres to carry out investigation and research regularly and integrate production directives with concrete conditions, the rectification movement sought to prevent further losses in the future.[23]

It is impossible to gauge with any precision the extent of the "five winds." The *Gongzuo tongxun* did report, however, that about one third of all rural districts, communes and production teams suffered from poor conditions as a result of natural disasters, the "five winds," or a combination of both.[g] Whatever

[g] Other relevant statistics in the secret military papers are: (1) militia organizations in 9.2 percent of 130 communes in Henan failed to meet basic requirements *after* several months reorganization work; and (2) from a sample of 40 team cadres in 7 communes, one quarter were judged either relatively bad in ideology and work style (8) or bad elements (2). Cheng, *Red Army*, pp. 469, 567.

the actual scope of the "five winds," they caused considerable disillusionment among the rural population. Thus popular sentiments such as "the Communist style . . . upset everyone," "most rural cadres are bad," and "cadres who have the Communist style should all be killed" were reported. Given such feelings, it is hardly surprising that Party leaders concluded rectification of the "five winds" was a key to peasant support and rural recovery.[24]

Several other factors stand out in public and private analyses of the "five winds." First, attention in public discussion was focused on errors of low ranking officials, especially basic level cadres, even though Liu Shaoqi, in an inner Party remark consistent with the logic of Mao's comments since 1959, declared the primary responsibility lay higher up. Liu also declared he himself was guilty of serious bureaucratism in this regard, having been ignorant of the seriousness of the "five winds" due to relying solely on reports through normal bureaucratic channels.[25] The actual implementation of rectification, however, apparently reflected the public view despite measures taken against some provincial leaders. This, then, laid the ground for serious disenchantment on the part of basic level officials who felt unjustly singled out for criticism when they had done their best to implement the onerous policies in force since late 1957.

Moreover, Liu's comments indicated that the situation was more serious than in the past and long tested methods no longer sufficed. Thus he reportedly noted that the method of investigation meetings developed by Mao was not enough under present conditions since commune cadres would give false reports to higher level investigators. Whether this view reflected a disagreement with Mao is unclear—especially in view of ambiguity on the same question during the Socialist Education Movement—but it certainly suggests that the strength of the "five winds" reflected a serious weakening of established organizational methods for obtaining information and controlling lower levels.[26] While this clearly derived from the pressures of the Great Leap Forward and anti-right opportunist campaign, it is also apparent that the deterioration of hierarchical control was significantly exacerbated by the disaster conditions then widespread in China.

Deviant Behavior under Disaster Conditions

Deteriorating socioeconomic conditions including widespread malnutrition, declining popular morale, local disturbances and, in Liu Shaoqi's words, "deaths in excess of those caused by the building of the Great Wall" were most clearly reflected in behavior attributed to bad elements. Such elements reportedly seized leadership of Party, government, public security and militia organs at basic and higher levels in some locales. This involved both the degeneration of cadres already holding official positions and infiltration of organs of power by bad elements in society. Those usurping power in individual areas included people classified as landlords, rich peasants, counterrevolutionaries, alien class elements, rascals, hoodlums and, especially in minority areas where the democratic revolution was incomplete, feudal elements. In his talk to the Ninth Plenum Mao pointed to connections which all three levels of the communes had developed with counterrevolutionaries and "landlord restoration" as unanticipated and disturbing features of the current situation.[27]

Using their official authority, bad elements assertedly engaged in a variety of unlawful activities and counterrevolutionary sabotage which adversely affected production and created chaos. Some of their concrete acts—beating and cursing, seizing grain, arresting innocent persons, corruption—had also been committed by good willed though ideologically confused cadres, but bad elements assertedly were motivated by desire for class revenge and unrestricted pursuit of personal profit. Moreover, bad elements engaged in unambiguously evil acts such as manslaughter, "forced death," open robbery and rape. Corrupt militia units, which frequently were responsible for the most violent acts, were bitterly denounced as "mad dogs," "bandit kings," "beat up gangs," "gangsters" and "tiger bands" by the peasants.[28]

The link between problems posed by bad elements and the breakdown of order under conditions of economic disaster was demonstrated by the location of deviant behavior. Although bad elements assertedly made up only "a few percent" of all cadres and had seized control of only "a few places," scattered reports indicate severe problems in particularly hard hit areas. Not only production teams and communes but entire counties were declared corrupt and unstable. For example, the first secretary of Guangshan county in calamity stricken Henan was cited as a typical bad element, and apparently all of Xinyang special district where Guangshan is located was endangered by widespread disturbances due to the activities of alleged class enemies. In Shangcheng county, Xinyang, 84 percent of commune armed forces department heads, 73 percent of militia regiment commanders, and 74 percent of militia battalion commanders committed serious unlawful acts. At the Ninth Plenum Mao pointed to grave situations in disaster struck Shandong, Henan and Gansu, indicating about 20 percent of the localities had "broken down." The link of unlawful behavior and disaster conditions was further revealed by a report that about 10 percent of army families in certain severe disaster areas suffered "unnatural deaths," and most of these were located in "rotten to the core" places under the control of bad people.[29]

Given the above situation, the expulsion of bad elements from Party, government, commune and militia organs, particularly from production team to county levels, became a central feature of the rectification campaign. This process of purification went beyond removal of individual bad elements and involved tightening up recruitment procedures, completely revamping organizations, and replacing degenerate officials with capable new cadres.[30] Just as the retreat under way by late 1960 ultimately went further than normal consolidation periods, these measures indicated a harsher rectification process than ordinarily appeared in consolidation phases. Crisis conditions had generated unusually severe cadre deviations and popular alienation, and these problems required firm action including significant disciplinary sanctions (see below).

Restoring Party Prestige

An important aim of the rural rectification drive was to repair the prestige of the Party and its policies which had been seriously damaged by the food crisis and economic setbacks. Revelations in the *Gongzuo tongxun* indicate substantial numbers of peasants and cadres had grave doubts about the wisdom of the Great Leap and people's communes.[h] People asked the reasons behind the food shortage, what the source of the "five winds" was, and why these deviations had not been corrected despite several years of criticism. Some answers went beyond natural disasters and the inadequacies of local cadres and blamed the people's communes as such, pressure from above during the leap forward, and even central Party leaders. In an attempt to counter this challenge, official propaganda distinguished between wicked acts by evil men and mistakes committed by good people, between superior commune regulations and defects in policy implementation, and between the consistent correctness of the Party line and the "five winds" in actual work. In addition, discussions were organized comparing the current situation with conditions prior to the establishment of communes and before liberation in an effort to demonstrate the superiority of the present system.[31]

Doubts and confusion concerning Party policies extended not only to the original Great Leap and commune policies but also to the measures taken to cope with the subsequent dislocations. Some people acknowledged the new measures were fine but argued they should have been initiated earlier to avoid the current mess. Others pointed out that many individual measures had been called for earlier but were never implemented and expressed skepticism that the Sixty Articles would fare any better. Confusion and morale problems also arose among those, undoubtedly including many basic level cadres responsible for implementing the leap forward, who perceived the adjusted policies as a retreat discarding the earlier policies. They questioned how current warnings against "one-sided bigness" could be squared with the earlier claim that bigness was an essential feature of communes. These cadres viewed reduction of commune size, brigade level ownership, payment according to labor and private plots as diminishing the excellence of communes and restoring higher APCs. They expressed concern that private plots and free markets would stimulate capitalism, cause high prices

[h] Before ideological efforts undertaken in early 1961, 30 percent of PLA soldiers reportedly had confused and wrong ideas about current conditions and about 5 percent had seriously conflicting ideas concerning the Great Leap and communes. Cheng, *Red Army*, p. 412. In the following discussion, the views and attitudes analyzed were attributed to PLA cadres and soldiers by the *Gongzuo tongxun*. Since army cadres and soldiers held those views because of their rural backgrounds, our assumption is the same or similar views were held by large numbers of peasants and basic level rural cadres.

and market chaos, and retard socialist economic construction and ideological reform of the peasantry. They further feared emphasis on distribution according to labor would harm families with more people but less able bodied laborers, thus polarizing rural society into the excessively rich and excessively poor. Still others reacted in opposite fashion to the new measures and demonstrated special interest in private economic undertakings to the point of demanding more than what was officially called for. These people concluded that "politics in command" had proven unworkable and advocated the superiority of material incentives which was more than Party leaders were willing to acknowledge openly during the 1960–61 rectification drive.[32]

Thus the Great Leap and commune movements followed by two years of policy adjustments resulted in widespread confusion and demoralization among both people skeptical of the original policies and those who had faithfully sought to implement those policies. In an effort to ameliorate the resultant damage to the prestige of the Party and its central leadership, the official line reasserted the infallibility of the developmental strategy and denied that the new policies represented a retreat. This weak response, however, only underlined the difficulties facing the rectification effort. As suggested above, one obstacle was the feeling of low ranking cadres that they were being unfairly blamed for problems created by higher authorities. Added to this was the clear contradiction between official claims for the leap forward policies and the readily observable socio-economic crisis. This contradiction was further intensified by the rapidity and scope of policy changes since 1958. While policy changes in the early 1950s could be explained with some credibility as reflecting the imperatives of new situations, the very sharpness of the post-1958 changes undercut the logical coherence required for persuasion. Moreover, by virtue of being subject to coercive sanctions—as reflected in the relatively high purge rate in the 1957–58 rectification campaign and the "ruthless struggles" of the post-Lushan period—and to unprecedented administrative pressures due to the excessive demands of the Great Leap, cadres were prone to alienation and internalized dissent. Undoubtedly, as suggested by the findings of Chapter 2, a high pressure situation had continued for too long and become counterproductive. Finally, the sharp decline in tangible rewards for both cadres and the social groups (especially the peasantry) which they represented seriously unbalanced the mix of appeals required for either attitudinal or behavioral compliance. Given these considerations an effective rectification campaign was unlikely, and the actual conduct of the 1960–61 movement further exacerbated the situation.

The Implementation of Lower Level Rectification

While the fragmentary nature of the data makes it extremely difficult to determine precisely how mild or harsh the 1960–61 rectification movement was, relative leniency would normally be expected during a consolidation phase when the emphasis is on reducing tensions and redressing imbalances. Moreover, the campaign focused on questions of work style and policy implementation rather than policy itself. In contrast to the campaigns of late 1957–58 and especially 1959–60 where the question of cadre attitudes toward and support of official policy were directly at issue—and where significant purges occurred—the issues here were more like those of the mild campaigns of 1950 and 1953 where ideological understanding was found inadequate.[i] Despite these expectations, the available information indicates a more mixed picture. As in 1957–58 and 1959–60 various official statements set mild norms for the movement which seem to have been violated in practice, thus further contributing to the estrangement between rectification theory and practice.

There were ample official signals indicating a mild rectification movement. The stipulation that "meetings of immortals" for bourgeois intellectuals should be conducted as a "gentle breeze and mild rain" suggested that "well intentioned cadres" of good class origins would receive similarly understanding treatment. Mao's emphasis on unity at the Ninth Plenum—including a warning against "Stalin's mistake [of killing cadres, and] Khrushchev's more civilized mistake of dismissing the Central Committee"—also must have been reassuring. Yet Mao's remarks were ambivalent since he further spoke of the need to remove "rigid bureaucrats" from leadership positions and placed the proportion of "good or fairly good" cadres at the commune and brigade levels at the relatively low figure of 80 percent. If this left the door open for extensive dismissals, two important articles suggested an effort to avoid excesses in the unfolding movement. First, in December 1960 *Nanfang ribao* [Southern Daily] published an analysis of the 1947–48 rectification movement which described how leftist errors had been overcome during that campaign. This was particularly relevant since the sources of leftist deviations in 1947–48—Party work teams and organizations of the poorer peasantry—were also used in 1960–61.[33]

A second and more prominent article appeared in *Renmin ribao* shortly before the Ninth Plenum's call to extend rectification on a nationwide basis. Written by Deputy Secretary-General of the State Council Gong Zirong and entitled "Rectification Campaigns Are Powerful Magic Weapons," this article did not explicitly refer to the movement then underway but its discussion of past campaigns was surely meant to guide the ongoing campaign. Gong cited a number of erroneous tendencies in past rectification leadership. One was random orders due to failure to study central directives which distorted the objectives of the process. Failure to investigate carefully local conditions, moreover, resulted in overly general

[i] It should be noted, however, that similar problems also were at issue in the somewhat harsher Party rectification of 1951–54. But even in that case, as we have argued, important restraints were apparently imposed on the severity of the movement. See above, pp. 117–19, 125–26.

reports, fascination with superficial phenomena, and issuing general appeals which could not be realized. With these observations Gong applied to rectification themes stressed for dealing with the situation generally.

Subjectivism, continued Gong, caused conflicting but equally wrong conclusions: during rectification some leaders exaggerated local and temporary shortcomings while others were blinded by achievements, concealed bad phenomena and reported only good news. Parallel to these erroneous perceptions were deviant methods of handling erring cadres. "Right sentimentalism" was manifested by those who made undue allowances for mistakes and were reluctant to criticize cadres, especially "competent cadres." Gong also cited leaders who hindered rectification out of fear their own wrongdoing would be uncovered or that the process would get out of control. In contrast, others guilty of left adventurism did not distinguish between slight and grave errors, relied only on disciplinary action to the exclusion of education, and applied "the force of movements," "the pressure of the masses," and violent measures. To avoid these pitfalls, Gong urged leaders of rectification campaigns to reveal forthrightly their own shortcomings and those of activists in addition to criticizing backward elements, take seriously the criticisms of middle of the roaders, and mobilize fully the masses through free expression in debates and wall posters. Thus Gong articulated a view eschewing both rightist and leftist errors in the conduct of rectification, one which encouraged thoroughness while avoiding excessive harshness. In the context of the recent past, however, it is possible to read his advocacy of the traditional approach as a veiled attack on the "ruthless struggles" of the campaign against right opportunism, a type of struggle which would have to be avoided if further erosion of cadre morale was to be prevented.[34]

A restrained approach was also implied by special efforts made during the campaign to achieve a proper relationship between rectification and production. In the countryside the development of agricultural production was called the basic aim of rectification, while the need to coordinate rectification and production in the industrial sector was also pointed out. Although some leading cadres felt rectification and production were in conflict, with rectification taking up time normally devoted to production, the official line claimed rectification would boost production by stimulating peasant enthusiasm. To avoid any conflict, as in earlier mild campaigns authorities stipulated rectification was not to be pushed too far, the number of meetings would be limited, and rectification was an evening activity after the completion of the day's work. Moreover, work teams in charge of the effort were divided into groups responsible for rectification, for production affairs, and in some cases for peasant livelihood. It was clearly recognized that only if production and livelihood were handled well could rectification have any chance of success.[35]

As we have seen in earlier campaigns, the problem solving approach and effort to avoid conflict with production are hallmarks of persuasive rectification efforts. Here too rectification was closely tied to overall policy trends rather than being in a dysfunctional relationship as in 1959–60. Yet the legacy of the pressures of the previous years together with the sharpness of the policy shift seemingly produced tensions which could only be resolved by more coercive measures. Thus a spring 1961 radio broadcast approvingly reported that rectification had resulted in mass demands for implementing *sanzi yibao* incentives.[36] But given the attitudes of cadres who had zealously implemented the leap forward cited earlier, it is likely that significant numbers of basic level leaders resisted the new stress on material incentives and had to be dismissed if the production emphasis of the campaign and of overall policy was to be realized.[j]

If public statements and the linking of rectification and production suggest a mild rectification, the use of work teams and poor and lower middle peasant groups indicate the possibility of a harsher, more disruptive process. The available information on work teams in the 1960–61 movement is both slight and ambiguous. Apart from rectification work teams *(zhengfeng gongzuotuan)* organized by higher level Party authorities, more than 57,000 military cadres—80 percent from the provincial military district level—participated in PLA work teams mobilized during the campaign. These army cadres, some of whom served in combined teams of PLA personnel and local cadres, worked on commune rectification as well as consolidation of militia organizations. A number of problems arose concerning the performance of army work teams, problems which undoubtedly affected Party work teams as well. Despite training before undertaking their duties, some work team cadres lacked a clear understanding of the superiority of the Great Leap and communes or the aims of the Twelve Articles and thus were unable to play an effective leadership role. Others could not bear the hardships of rural life, refused to practice the "four togethers" of eating, living, working and consulting with peasants, and were impatient to return to their regular units. Some teams upon arriving in a village set themselves up in offices and waited for things to happen. Members of these teams studied Mao's works and did office work, but because they failed to establish ties with the population they could neither understand conditions they were supposed to correct nor win peasant cooperation.[37]

All of the above shortcomings amount to lax leadership of the rectification process. Another major problem, however, concerned relations between work teams and local cadres, and here there were parallels to both the 1947–48 and 1951–54 movements. Ideally, work team members and local cadres would learn from each other and team cadres would be "staff members" of local Party committees. Some work teams, however, arbitrarily "took over the whole works," disregarded the views of local cadres and forced them to do errands, with the result that peasants lost confidence in local authorities. The loss of local author-

[j] See *Peking Review,* September 13, 1974, for a report that in 1961 a brigade secretary in Shandong was dismissed from office for opposing the *sanzi yibao.*

ity, as in 1947–48 and 1951–54 but in contrast to the 1957 socialist education effort, undoubtedly intensified the decline of morale among basic level leaders which was already severe due to the sharp policy changes and deteriorating socio-economic conditions.[38]

An important task of the work teams during rural rectification was strengthening the role of poor and lower middle peasants. This was undoubtedly in part an effort to compensate for official policy on using the skills of better off peasants, a policy which encouraged an apparently widespread feeling that poor peasants were of little use and which intensified the danger of local leadership falling into the hands of people of suspect class origins.[k] Thus the need to rely on poor and lower middle peasants was a common propaganda theme during the movement, poor and lower middle peasant activists were cultivated, and work teams assertedly depended on those elements to mobilize the masses and aid in cadre rectification. The precise role of the peasants in the rectification process, and especially the severity of their criticism of cadres, is very unclear. However, one report concerning Hunan suggests a significant link among work teams, peasants and basic level purging:

> In . . . April 1961 a great number of cadres were sent to the villages to start rectification and commune readjustment by relying on the poor and lower middle peasants—relying on the masses to correct the mistakes of the cadres. Wicked people in Party and government offices were exposed and the organization was cleansed.[39]

Efforts were also made to establish the predominance of poor and lower middle peasants in the countryside on a more permanent basis. Not only were individual peasants from this group recruited for cadre positions, but in areas where bad elements had usurped leadership poorer peasants were organized into new leadership groups. Moreover, the Sixty Articles stipulated poor and lower middle peasants should predominate in commune management and supervisory organs and that militia weapons were to be in the hands of reliable elements of those strata. Finally, the rectification campaign was marked by an effort to establish separate peasant organizations which would serve as a check on cadres. These organizations, known as poor and lower middle peasant core groups *(pinnong xiazhongnong hexin xiaozu)*, were set up from commune to team levels. Although subject to Party leadership and designed to serve as a bridge between the Party and people, these groups were empowered to supervise basic level cadres and expose their mistakes. The concrete arrangements worked out in

---

[k] It might be argued that in this regard rectification was dysfunctional to the economic retrenchment policies. However, before late 1961 official policy clearly viewed retrenchment as having certain limits and poor and lower middle peasants, assuming they understood the policy correctly, could play a constructive role in keeping retrenchment within approved bounds.

some areas included poor and lower middle peasant group leaders attending production team management committee meetings and inviting cadres to attend group meetings at which peasant demands were articulated.[40]

These measures further the parallel to the 1947–48 campaign because for the first time since that rectification peasant *organizations* were given a role in the discipline of basic level leadership. As in the past, involving ordinary citizens in elite discipline most likely generated significant cadre resentment. The traditional understanding that non-Party masses should not play a leading role in rectification, a principle ignored in 1947–48 but adhered to since liberation except for the limited lapse of the Hundred Flowers experiment, was now under challenge—a challenge which would be even more forceful during the Socialist Education Movement in 1964.

Actual data on the scope and disciplinary impact of the 1960–61 rectification campaign is elusive. While perhaps somewhat under half of China's rural communes had undergone rectification by the end of March,[41] it is unclear how far the movement was extended in the countryside during the remainder of spring 1961. Although it is difficult to demonstrate the severity of discipline on a nationwide basis, several reports indicate considerable harshness in at least some areas. According to Ezra Vogel, in Guangdong the campaign resulted in the dismissal of large numbers of brigade and team cadres and peasants were easily mobilized for scathing criticism of others who were not ousted. Another source, also apparently relying on refugee interviews, refers to executions of Party village leaders in Guangdong. Moreover, the *Gongzuo tongxun* reported that after disturbances in Xinyang special district, Henan, some local leaders "indiscriminately kicked out all militia organizations and reorganized them without exception" during rectification, thus causing severe damage to cadre morale. Finally, a Cultural Revolution source claims that during rectification and commune overhaul in late 1960 Li Jingquan, in an apparent effort to avoid responsibility for his own leftist excesses, carried out "ruthless struggles and merciless blows" against the basic level cadres of Sichuan. While such harsh measures may have been largely restricted to certain local areas, especially areas where there were severe disaster conditions, their use at all in a movement emphasizing traditional methods again indicates an erosion of rectification norms.[42]

A number of reasons have already been suggested for the excesses which took place during the 1960–61 campaign. First, despite the ostensible emphasis on policy implementation and work style, the deviations under attack were in fact inextricably linked to the Great Leap policies. Since these policies had been deeply impressed upon cadres at all levels by the intense pressures of the 1957–58 and 1959–60 rectification movements, more than mildly persuasive methods would sometimes be required to enforce the new policy line. Closely related to this was the effect of undoubted policy divisions at the higher levels. While the leaders most responsible for the Great Leap strategy—notably Mao and Liu Shaoqi—formulated and/or endorsed the retrenchment measures, clearly there was a subtle shift of influence within the leadership as a whole towards those who had been most skeptical of the leap forward. At the time of the 1960–61 campaign the process of "reversal of verdicts" which was to peak in 1962 had already begun. Thus men who had suffered in 1959 and earlier for their doubts were regaining power at various levels. In at least some cases they apparently were able to exact retribution against those at whose hands they suffered earlier. For example, in early 1961 in the journalism department of the Chinese People's University, a key point for "reversing verdicts" in the cultural and education sphere, the reinstatement of officials dismissed during the campaign against right opportunism was reportedly accompanied by the banishment of 30 "revolutionary cadres."[43]

But perhaps the most important factor causing harsh measures in 1960–61 was the deteriorating socio-economic situation. Clearly some of the extreme anti-social behavior such as rape, killings and robbery which appeared in disaster areas required a coercive rather than persuasive approach. More broadly, the widespread demoralization within the elite had sapped the effectiveness of rectification techniques. In some cases this led to lax implementation of the campaign and the failure to use systematically either persuasive or coercive sanctions. In other cases where efforts were made to grapple with extensive deviations, we may hypothesize in view of the considerations outlined in Chapter 2 that the absence of adequate tangible rewards undercut the impact of persuasive appeals and as a result led to greater reliance on coercion. Thus in at least some areas a vicious cycle had been created where cadre demoralization led to relatively coercive reform efforts which could only further alienate the basic level leaders of rural China.

Despite claims that rectification brought a bright future to rural villages, there is considerable evidence that for the reasons cited above the rectification campaign in fact worsened the serious state of cadre prestige and morale. Coming on top of the thankless task of trying to implement the Great Leap, such developments as high handed work teams, poor and lower middle peasant organizations armed with supervisory powers, and an extensive purge of basic level cadres in at least some areas seemingly had a devastating impact. Following the campaign, many cadres were unwilling to resume active leadership roles:

> The problems in thought left behind by the rectification and commune overhaul have not yet been solved. The old cadres were toppled over and the new cadres feared they might meet the same fate in the future. Therefore, they dared not boldly lead production, and people generally avoid becoming a cadre. [A certain] brigade and [its] production teams have a total of 11 cadres; apart from the financial chief and the accountant, all the others are unwilling to take up their posts. They said: "The Twelve Articles provide one rectification in three years and the Sixty Articles stipulate one year per term of service. Be it good or bad, we have four months to go; why should we make others hate us?"[44]

Given the attack on the "commandist wind," cadres were in a particularly difficult position. When peasants objected to a quota as too high or refused to repair a reservoir, cadres worried about being charged with blind leadership or issuing compulsory orders and felt helpless to act. Given the widespread prevalence of such thoughts as "If the work is done well I gain nothing more personally, but if it is not done properly I have to take the blame," the effectiveness of cadre leadership was significantly undermined.[45]

In sum, although the rectification movement undoubtedly contributed to the effort to tide over the serious disaster conditions of winter 1960–61, it also left a legacy of a weakened grass roots cadre force. This situation made it necessary for Party authorities to direct that cadres be treated leniently in the annual commune overhaul of winter 1961–62. Moreover, it was probably a key factor in the 1962 effort to restore veteran basic level cadres to their native villages. Notwithstanding these measures, cadre morale was still a major problem on the eve of the September 1962 Central Committee plenum and was one factor in the decision to launch the Socialist Education Movement.[46] Ultimately, the combination of unprecedented policies, inexperienced cadres, changing signals from the Center, and a severe economic crisis was more than could be set right by traditional techniques. The rectification aim of both correcting specific deviations *and* restoring an efficient and motivated cadre force proved unattainable. In 1960–61, China lacked the socio-economic stability that even a revolutionary regime requires for effective control and adjusting tensions.

Provincial Level Dismissals

Although the rectification campaign focused on basic level cadres, as we have seen much of the responsibility for the "five winds" and other defects lay with higher level authorities. While central officials seem to have largely escaped career setbacks, a number of leading provincial officials were quietly removed in 1960–61. The most prominent were First Secretaries Zhang Zhongliang of Gansu, Gao Feng of Qinghai, Shu Tong of Shandong and Zeng Xisheng of Anhui, and Governor Liu Geping of Ningxia.[47] Moreover, First Secretary Wu Zhipu of Henan was demoted to second secretary in the same period and subsequently transferred to the Central-South Party Bureau in 1962.[l]

---

[l] Wu's position with the bureau may have been nominal. A Cultural Revolution source quotes bureau First Secretary Tao Zhu to the effect that Wu's duties involved research in Song dynasty history. "Tao Zhu Is the Khrushchev of Central-South China" (Red Guard pamphlet), January 24, 1967, in *CB*, No. 824.

In addition, two dozen additional provincial secretaries and vice governors from 13 provinces could not be traced beyond the 1960–61 period. The 13 provinces were those where top leaders were removed or demoted except Shandong, plus Fujian, Hebei, Jilin, Guangxi, Guangdong, Liaoning, Shaanxi and Sichuan.

With a possible exception,[m] no public explanations were given for the above removals and demotion. Nevertheless, a pattern emerges when the provinces in question are examined. First, these provinces and their leaders appear to have taken a leftist course during the Great Leap Forward. This was clearest in the case of Henan which had been a pacesetter in both the 1957–58 mass irrigation campaign and the establishment of people's communes, and a province Mao had identified as being to his left. In addition, Wu's personal activism was well known in high Party circles as reflected in the Chairman's Lushan remark that "whenever the name of Wu [Zhipu] is mentioned, everybody gets nervous." In other cases, Shu Tong and Zhang Zhongliang published articles of high praise for the leap forward and Mao's thought in the period following the Lushan meeting. Moreover, in 1961 Deng Xiaoping criticized Shandong for holding frequent mass meetings which only propagated empty words—the kind of verbal boasting associated with Great Leap excesses.[48] The case of Anhui's Zeng Xisheng may be more complex. Although Zeng was criticized by Mao for his leftist stance as early as December 1958 and he continued to voice radical opinions in 1960, the timing of his removal suggests he was being disciplined for such measures as assigning output quotas to individual households during the crisis atmosphere of fall 1961.[n] But even here a connection can be drawn to earlier leftist excesses since they presumably created the conditions leading to such a far-reaching retreat. Finally, as Parris Chang has noted, all of the provinces concerned were affected by the provincial purges of 1957–58, and a leading role in these events had generally been played by radical leaders removed or downgraded in 1960–61.[49]

A second and even clearer pattern is that the provinces in question were severely affected by the deteriorating conditions of 1960–61. Not only had Mao singled out the grave situations in Shandong, Henan and Gansu at the Ninth Plenum, but armed rebellions occurred in Gansu and Qinghai in addition to substantial disturbances in Henan. Moreover, Anhui suffered from widespread devastation caused by the flooding of the Yangtze. On the view articulated by

---

[m] Western news dispatches from Beijing purportedly based on *Ningxia ribao* [Ningxia Daily] linked the removal of Liu Geping to the "liquidation of local nationalism" in Ningxia. From the context it is unclear whether Liu himself was judged guilty of local nationalism or whether he was blamed for the appearance of that phenomenon. If the latter, such a situation could have developed as a result of leftist errors and the deterioration of rural conditions. See *Communist China 1960* (2 vols., Hong Kong: Union Research Institute, 1962), I, 26–27, 38.

[n] On Zeng's leftism, see Moody, *Eighth Central Committee,* pp. 146–48; and above, p. 307. In August 1962, however, Mao referred to "secretaries like Zeng Xisheng" who might represent the well off peasants; *JPRS,* No. 52029, p. 25. Since Mao was also critical at that time of how far the retreat in Anhui had gone and the assignment of output quotas to individual households took place while Zeng was still appearing, it would seem the *immediate* cause of Zeng's fate was the rightist measures of 1961–62 rather than his earlier leftist posture.

Liu Shaoqi in January 1962 that 70 percent of the disasters were man made, it follows that leading provincial officials would be held responsible for conditions in their areas. This presumably was the logic behind the self-criticisms the leaders of Henan, Gansu and Qinghai were compelled to make in 1961, and the personnel measures taken about the same time. Although no direct charges were laid against any of the affected officials with the one possible exception, several secondary sources attribute the removals of Zhang Zhongliang and Shu Tong to mishandling the grain situation in their provinces and thus contributing to famine conditions.[50]

Another factor is suggested by possible oblique criticism of Wu Zhipu in the form of articles attacking the subjectivism and bureaucratism of leading levels, arbitrary individual opinions arrived at without discussion at Party meetings, unjust criticism of those advancing contrary opinions, and the suppression of inner Party democracy.[51] By raising the issues of unjust criticism and the suppression of inner Party democracy, these articles suggest a link between the removal of leftist provincial leaders and the "reversal of verdicts" which was unfolding in the same period.

The reassertion of central control over the affected provinces involved the transfer of new leaders from the outside.[o] The most striking but hardly the only case was Henan where Liu Jianxun, the new first secretary, was transferred from Guangxi; He Wei, previously Ambassador to North Vietnam, became second secretary; Governor Wen Minsheng was transferred from Guangdong; and Secretary Liu Yangqiao was shifted from Hubei. This degree of outside transfers stands in sharp contrast to both the administrative shake-up in the Northeast following the purge of Gao Gang and that in the various provinces affected by the 1957–58 provincial purges. In both earlier cases the personnel changes which took place largely involved reassignments within the same region or province. But now more far-reaching measures were required suggesting the erosion of still another organizational practice—if not a formal Party norm. Apparently the legacy of intra-provincial strife generated by the leap forward in both 1957–58 and 1959–60, together with deteriorating socio-economic conditions in 1960–61, had substantially weakened the confidence of central leaders in the reliability and vitality of the key sub-national organs of the Party.

---

[o] In Gansu, Wang Feng was transferred from Ningxia to become first secretary and Wang Shitai was shifted from the Center to assume a secretarial post; in Qinghai, Vice Minister of Public Security Wang Zhao became acting first secretary and subsequently second secretary when Yang Zhilin was transferred from Inner Mongolia as the new first secretary; Vice Minister of Water Conservancy and Electric Power Li Baohua became Anhui's first secretary; and Vice Chairman of the Nationalities Affairs Commission Yang Jingren assumed the posts of first secretary and governor in Ningxia. Following Shu Tong's ouster in Shandong, Zeng Xisheng briefly served as acting first secretary before returning to Anhui. Outside personnel were also sent to Fujian, Hunan, Jilin and Guangxi during this period.

The Retreat: Stages Two and Three, mid-1961 to mid-1962

The 1960–61 rectification campaign took place during the initial stage of the post-Great leap retrenchment. As significant as this had been, a far more headlong retreat unfolded from mid-1961 to mid-1962. This more extensive retreat can be further divided into a second stage from roughly May 1961, when Liu Shaoqi warned that conditions were more serious than had been previously realized, to the January 1962 enlarged central work conference which endorsed with Mao's backing a series of measures to cope with the situation, and a third stage beginning shortly after the conference when new discoveries led Liu to conclude the economy was "on the verge of collapse." In the final stage even more far-reaching concessions were made before Mao intervened in summer 1962 and finally called a halt to the retreat. It was during these latter two stages that the policy of "reversing verdicts" was most extensively developed.[52]

Stage Two: Headlong Retreat with Mao's Assent

Liu's gloomy May 1961 assessment was apparently based on his rural investigations which also led him to emphasize the seriousness of the "five winds." Adding to these woes, natural disasters struck agriculture for the third successive year in 1961. The official response in rural policy was greater decentralization of the communes. In late 1961 the production team replaced the production brigade as basic unit of ownership and accounting, a policy change personally approved by Mao. Moreover, in various local areas experiments with incentive schemes which had begun earlier were extended and developed. Thus the limits laid down for private activities by the Sixty Articles were exceeded in some localities. In fall 1961 disaster struck Anhui assigned output quotas to individual households—the *yibao* of the *sanzi yibao.* Similar practices appeared elsewhere in the same period.[53]

Severe measures were also taken in industry. In December 1961 the Party issued the Seventy Articles on industrial policy which called for halting all capital construction except specially stipulated projects, closing all industrial units running a deficit except those specially designated, and returning all local state enterprises formed by amalgamating cooperatives in 1958 to producer cooperative status. Consumer production was given priority under the policy of "the market comes first." Measures were taken to boost production enthusiasm including guaranteeing sufficient rest, reducing required political activities, and instituting piecework wages and bonuses. Quality was insisted upon and substandard products were forbidden to leave the factory. The Seventy Articles also sought to strengthen further the authority of the factory manager and bolster the role of technical personnel. In this same period steps were also undertaken to concentrate financial control at the Center and to strengthen the banking system, thus further recentralizing the national economy.[54]

The adjustments in agricultural and industrial policies were matched by measures which extended the moderate line toward intellectuals and experts. These measures were formulated in a number of decisions, such as the Eight Articles on Literature and Art and the Sixty Articles on Higher Education which were drafted in the second half of 1961 after extensive investigations. These decisions embodied a united front approach to gain the support of intellectuals in troubled times by codifying the reduced emphasis on politics, greater material benefits and enhanced status, and increased professional freedom. Perhaps the boldest public statement of the new line was an August 1961 speech by Politburo member Chen Yi which drastically revised the policy of "red and expert." Chen argued it was unrealistic and unnecessary for a person to be a specialist in both politics and technical affairs. The loyalty of an intellectual, he continued, should be measured by contributions to culture, science and the economy rather than by political activity. The new policies clearly had major implications for the role of cadres. The strong cadre leadership of the Great Leap period was superseded by a division of labor leaving technical and administrative experts broad autonomy within their own spheres of competence.[55]

Other efforts in late 1961 to ameliorate social tensions and extend the united front included the revival of the democratic parties, the celebration of the 50th anniversary of the "bourgeois democratic revolution" of 1911, and a conciliatory line toward national minorities and religious groups.[56] In addition, starting in 1961 an escape valve function was performed by literary productions and historical allegories which criticized and even mocked shortcomings in official policies and behavior. Since this phenomenon intensified in 1962 when it finally drew Mao's ire, a fuller discussion is reserved for the post-January 1962 period.

The various measures discussed above were by and large the product of policy reviews in each functional area under the supervision of a high Party leader. When the enlarged central work conference—the so-called 7,000 cadres conference—met in January 1962, Liu Shaoqi gave a report on the work accomplished by these reviews and emphasized the Party's responsibility for the critical economic situation with his famous assertion that 70 percent of the disasters were man-made. Mao had apparently been aloof from the actual process of working out the new policies, but there is no evidence that the Chairman, who had after all called for the careful investigations upon which the new line was constructed, opposed them.[p] On the

---

[p] Various analysts have asserted significant differences between Mao and Liu at the 7,000 cadres conference. While it is of course conceivable that Liu was more amenable to policy changes than Mao, such a conclusion is entirely speculative and based on an abstract conceptualization of the two men rather than actual data. For Liu's report we only have scattered although lengthy extracts, extracts which were clearly selected in order to place Liu in an unfavorable light. Yet there is nothing in the extracts inconsistent with the (incomplete) text of Mao's speech, and any attempt to assert different nuances cannot be maintained given the out of context nature of the Liu extracts. This is not to say that there were no differences, but only that none are demonstrated and in such circumstances Mao's approval of both Liu's report and specific "revisionist" measures suggests any divergence was minimal. Cf. below, pp. 372n, 377n.

contrary, in his speech to the enlarged conference Mao not only spoke approvingly of Liu's report and the various policy reviews, he also explicitly sanctioned the detailed articles on industry, higher education and other areas which would be denounced as "revisionist" during the Cultural Revolution. He further endorsed the soft approach to intellectuals by stipulating "patriotism" as the only criterion for uniting with them.[57]

Beyond this, in his speech Mao admitted important inadequacies in the leap forward. While asserting, as Liu had done,[58] that the general policy line had been correct, Mao contrasted the "fully persuasive" policies of the 1950–57 period when the Soviet model was adopted to the Party's inability to "regularize a whole set of guiding principles" during the Great Leap, and concluded that "we have bungled a lot" and "the general line is not enough." Indeed, the basic tone of Mao's speech was uncertainty over what was either possible or desirable:

> [In 1960, Edgar] Snow wanted me to discuss long term planning for the construction of China. I said, 'I don't know how.' He commented, 'You are being too cautious with what you say.' I replied: 'It is not a matter of being cautious or not. I really do not know and do not have the experience.' Comrades, it is true that we do not know. We truly are short of experience and a long range plan....
>
> In socialist construction we continue to grope our way without clear vision. ... Taking myself as an example, there are many problems in the work of building up the economy which I do not understand. Industry and commerce, for instance, are things that I do not quite understand. I know a little about agriculture, but only to a certain degree by comparison and very little at that.[59]

Thus in early 1962 Mao endorsed a set of policies designed to tide China over the current crisis. But neither he nor his Politburo colleagues could have been happy about all the concessions granted by these policies, or confident about where the future would lead.[q]

Stage Three: Further Retreat and Mao's Reaction

Having given his stamp of approval to the work of his Politburo colleagues, Mao departed from Beijing following the January meeting leaving his associates on the "first line" with the task of implementing the new guidelines. When they gathered in February at yet another work conference under Liu's

[q] An additional aspect of Mao's talk to the 7,000 cadres conference is noteworthy. In contrast to his call for unity with the Soviet Union a year earlier, the Chairman now declared the Soviet Party had been usurped by revisionists. *JPRS*, No. 52029, p. 14. This evaluation implied a tougher line towards the Russians and contributed to Mao's discontent later in the year with leaders he viewed as too soft on the issue.

chairmanship,[r] Party leaders discovered a budget deficit of ¥2 billion which seems to have resulted, at least in Mao's retrospective view, in something of a panic. Liu and others reportedly concluded the previous measures were still inadequate with the economy now "on the verge of collapse." In this situation Chen Yun, whose power had eroded at the outset of the Great Leap presumably because of his reservations about the new strategy but who was again active in economic decision making in 1961, became an extremely influential figure. Recommended by Liu as head of the financial group of the Central Committee, Chen apparently played the leading role in shaping the policies of further retreat.[60]

The intensified retreat apparently involved new sharp cutbacks in construction and investment. The most dramatic development occurred in the agricultural sector, however. Now central leaders including Chen Yun, Deng Zihui, and Deng Xiaoping advocated extensive concessions to small scale farming. Deng Zihui reportedly pushed the "Anhui responsibility system"—i.e., the system of assigning production quotas to individual households which completed the *sanzi yibao* was now recommended as general policy. Even more far-reaching steps were implemented in some areas where collective lands were actually divided among peasants on a long term basis and peasants were permitted to leave communes to engage in private farming. With regard to individual farming Deng Xiaoping made his famous remark that "white or black, so long as cats catch mice they are good cats"—the philosophy that whatever increased production was acceptable regardless of its ideological implications. While the extent of such measures on a nationwide basis is unclear, in August 1962 Mao noted that "some say" 20 percent of the land was independently farmed and various local reports suggest as much as 30 or even 50 percent under private cultivation.[61]

In the political sphere, the united front effort also intensified. The democratic parties, as in 1956–57, now talked about strengthening their basic level organs and leadership bodies at intermediate levels. Moreover, the CPPCC became very active with CPPCC committees and people's congresses at the provincial level meeting in joint sessions, and CPPCC members as well as NPC deputies conducting inspection tours. In a significant concession, the fixed interest payments to the national bourgeoisie which had been due to end in 1962 were extended. Other measures designed to obtain support in society as broadly as possible included publicizing favorable evaluations of Confucius and declaring children of landlords and other ostracized elements were to be judged by their actions rather than social origins. Thus well into 1962 the emphasis continued to be on

[r] Further evidence that this meeting rather than the 7,000 cadres conference was critical in initiating Mao's discontent with Liu is suggested by Liu's Cultural Revolution self-criticism. Liu's remarks concerning the January meeting were *pro forma* and conceded nothing in terms of differences with Mao. In contrast, he went on to refer to the February conference as "a still greater event" and indicated that Mao subsequently expressed disapproval of the measures emanating from that meeting. *Collected Works of Liu Shao-ch'i, 1958–1967* (Hong Kong: Union Research Institute, 1968), pp. 360–61. Cf. below, p. 375.

low key, long term efforts to solve "contradictions among the people."[62]

Moreover, in foreign policy it appears that following the 7,000 cadres conference various leaders believed a softer line towards both the US and Soviet Union was required by the domestic crisis. While this does not seem to have evolved into an official policy, it apparently was systematically developed by Vice Minister of Foreign Affairs Wang Jiaxiang under the slogan "three reconciliations [with imperialists, reactionaries and revisionists] and one reduction [of support to national liberation movements]" *(sanhe yishao)*.[63]

Finally, the curious phenomena of satiric and allegorical criticism of Party policies and performance which was to play such a significant role in launching the Cultural Revolution continued unabated to mid-1962. While this development, all the more puzzling because of the involvement of high ranking Party figures particularly in the Beijing municipal apparatus, cannot be fully unraveled, it is still necessary to modify the dominant scholarly interpretation of such criticism as involving a clear if indirect attack on Mao Zedong.[64] The allegories can be seen as aimed at any number of potential targets—the shortcomings of low level to fairly high ranking cadres, official policies of the Great Leap period, Mao's Politburo associates, and the Chairman himself. Although various allegories surely had different targets, it can hardly be doubted that some barbs were aimed at Mao. Nevertheless, it should be stressed that many literary efforts denounced during the Cultural Revolution as slanders against Mao corresponded closely in form and substance to the contemporary views of the Chairman. Moreover, whatever the subjective intent of various authors, it is clear that their works were not widely perceived at the time as attacks on Mao,[s] and it seems the Chairman himself did not perceive their alleged intent until several years after the fact. The most famous example of asserted allegoric attack on Mao, the Hai Jui dramas purportedly protesting the fate of Peng Dehuai, illustrates these points.

Wu Han, a non-Party vice mayor of Beijing with close ties to leading members of the city's Party apparatus, published several plays and essays between June 1959 and January 1961 on the Ming official Hai Rui, works which were widely circulated in China. Briefly, Wu depicted Hai Rui as an upright provincial governor who discovered through his own investigations the suppression of peasants by corrupt officials, punished those responsible, but was dismissed by

---

[s] Edgar Snow, *The Long Revolution* (New York: Random House, 1971), p. 86, doubtless goes too far in claiming that no China specialist including those in China itself saw the alleged analogy at the time. Nevertheless, it is striking that not only foreign scholars but literate and politically aware people in Beijing failed to make the connections later presumed obvious. A 1967 Hong Kong interview of one such woman who regularly read *Beijing ribao* [Beijing Daily], the organ publishing some of the best known "attacks" on Mao, revealed that she had no inkling of any criticism of the Chairman. At a higher level, Alex B. Ikonnikov reports that a Central Committee member he knew indicated a suspicion that something was behind some of the allegories, but professed to have no idea of who the actual target(s) might be.

the emperor following the bribing of an influential eunuch at the Ming Court. During the Cultural Revolution Wu's dramas were attacked not only for advocating individual farming since Hai Rui returned land to the peasants which had been confiscated by local tyrants, but especially on the grounds that they represented an allegory attacking Mao (the emperor) for arbitrarily dismissing a just official, Peng Dehuai (Hai Rui).[65]

Several factors suggest skepticism concerning this interpretation. First is the question of timing. Hai Rui was being praised by high Party leaders in spring 1959 well *before* the Lushan meeting and Peng's dismissal. One Cultural Revolution source even has Mao approving Hai Rui at the March–April Shanghai meeting. Second, many of the themes raised by the drama were consistent with views strongly pushed by Mao both in 1959 before Lushan and in 1961–62; the need to avoid excessive confiscations of peasant property, the importance of on the spot investigations, and the encouragement of open criticism of higher by lower officials. Moreover, Mao used the *exact same device* of historical allegories by citing fearless officials who dared criticize the court and foolish rulers who rejected such advice to encourage inner Party debate at both the Lushan meetings in 1959 and the 7,000 cadres conference in 1962.[66]

It could be argued, however, that whatever the initial message of Hai Rui it became an allegorical reference to Peng Dehuai after Lushan. Indeed, Peng is accused of declaring in mid-1962 that "I want to be a Hai Rui" when seeking a "reversal of his verdict," while Jiang Qing reportedly sought a ban on the play at the same time. But it is clear that even after Lushan many highly informed and directly interested officials did not make the connection. Thus in early 1960 Zhang Pinghua, the new First Secretary of Hunan who replaced Zhou Xiaozhou and thus had no interest in defending Peng's "clique," spoke out in favor of "promoting the image of a leftist Hai Rui." And whatever Jiang Qing's view (there is no explicit reference to her seeing the Peng analogy in 1962), Mao subsequently found her opinions concerning Wu and other historians as too negative and, on the available evidence, only arrived at the conclusion that "Hai Rui is Peng Dehuai" in late 1965. That Chinese leaders had varying and changeable perceptions rather than a clear-cut understanding of the Mao-Peng analogy is not surprising since, as Peter Moody suggests, the Hai Rui story can be read as the appeal of a loyal statesman to the emperor (Mao) to do away with the corrupt officials (Liu and the Party apparatus?) who had brought about ruinous conditions. Given the evidence that the implementers of policy were under at least some form of criticism from Peng and others at Lushan, this alternative interpretation has a degree of persuasiveness. In the final analysis, however, all that can be safely concluded is that whatever Wu Han and others meant by their writings, there was no consensus interpretation among the Chinese public, politically astute cadres, or the highest ranking leaders themselves.[67]

As suggested by the Hai Rui case, Mao's reaction to developments following the 7,000 cadres conference was not immediately decisive. Ensconced on the "second line," his initial attitude apparently reflected the uncertainty he had articulated at the January meeting. According to a remark by Zhou Enlai reported during the Cultural Revolution, Mao's response to the February budget deficit was to "Give us five years as an adjustment period." Another Cultural Revolution source even indicates the Chairman was noncommittal on the question of loaning land to the peasants in mid-1962, a posture which led Liu to interpret Mao's position as one of qualified approval.[68] But by the August Beidaihe conference, when it was becoming clear that agricultural conditions were improving, Mao had concluded the retreat had gone too far. Liu Shaoqi's 1966 self-criticism suggests both the difficulties Mao's uncertainty *cum* withdrawal created for his colleagues and the nature of his eventual response:

> I recommended Chen Yun to the Center and Chairman Mao to be head of a fiscal group. At the time, however, the Chairman was not in Beijing. So I went to the Chairman's place to seek his instruction. It was later that I knew that the Chairman basically did not agree with our calculation of the situation and our practices. . . . [The policies we adopted in 1962] opposed the general line; they reflected an overestimate of the external and internal situation. In this connection, I personally heard the opinion about distribution of land to the households, and I did not refute it. This was a big mistake. At that time already I felt very tense. The situation was serious. So I urgently requested that the Chairman return to Beijing.
>
> At the Beidaihe conference, held in the summer of 1962, I was guilty of the rightist line. From the moment the Chairman returned to Beijing we began to draft a decision concerning further development and consolidation of the collective and a decision regarding commerce. At the Beidaihe conference class struggle was brought up for discussion. It was only when the Tenth Plenum in September had adopted two resolutions and a communique that I corrected my mistakes and the situation was basically altered.[69]

At Beidaihe Mao's complaints were apparently sweeping in scope, although his alternatives were relatively circumscribed. Mao's concern over the retreat in agriculture was indicated not only by criticism of Deng Zihui, but also by his reference to independent farming as a question of taking the socialist or capitalist road. On industry and economic planning generally the Chairman had barbs for the key responsible officials, Chen Yun, Bo Yibo, Li Xiannian and Li Fuchun, and he later referred to economic plans drawn up in 1962 as capitulation to the bourgeoisie. The "three reconciliations and one reduction" and Wang Jiaxiang, who soon ceased making public appearances, also drew Mao's fire. The political relaxation did not escape unscathed with Li Weihan and the united front department coming under attack for, as Mao put it in 1964, "turning the bourgeois parties into socialist parties." The Chairman also noted his disapproval of the utilization of literature for anti-Party purposes and "the recent vogue of rehabilitations." Finally, he belabored Liu Shaoqi for establishing an "independent kingdom" in an apparent expression of displeasure over Liu's guidance of policy in his absence.[70]

As Roderick MacFarquhar has suggested, for Mao the cardinal sin was a loss of nerve in the face of difficulty and danger,[71] a tendency which he apparently saw underlying the various steps enacted since February. But both Mao's indecision during the first half of 1962 and, if we are to believe Liu's story, the seeming anxiety of at least some Politburo members over the concessions they felt obliged to make, suggest far less clear-cut differences between Mao and his colleagues at the time the decisions for further retreat were actually taken than the Chairman's strictures at Beidaihe imply.

Finally, although Mao's intervention marked a key turning point in official policy, the concrete measures adopted at the Tenth Plenum comprised only a moderate and gradual shift which curbed some of the *excessively* liberal features of the crisis period. The most pronounced changes took place in the political and ideological spheres: increasing attention was given to studying Mao's thought, toleration of heterodox views in the social sciences, humanities and arts came to an end, and, as we shall see, the "reversal of verdicts" was significantly curbed although it did not end entirely. With regard to the rural economy, measures to restrict "small freedoms" including prohibiting division of land among households, cutting back excessive private plots, and tightened control over free markets and private speculative activities were adopted. On the whole, however, the rural policies emerging from the fall plenum remained moderate: priority was still given to agriculture, the production team remained the basic unit of ownership, and peasant rights to undertake private economic activities within stipulated limits were affirmed. A new phase in the PRC's development had begun, but it was still marked by the practical caution of the earlier period.[72]

"Reversing Verdicts" and Restoring Norms, 1961–62

The "reversal of verdicts" was tied not only to the shifting overall policy environment described above, but also to a broad gauged effort to restore some of the inner Party norms which had been eroded in recent years. This effort was indicated by Mao's emphasis on unity at the Ninth Plenum in January 1961, a time when initial efforts to "reverse verdicts" were already underway on a limited basis. "Reversals of verdicts" had increased significantly by January 1962 when Liu Shaoqi attacked the "ruthless struggles" of "recent years," called for a return to traditional methods of inner Party struggle, and advocated further "reversals." Mao endorsed Liu's position at the same central work conference by advocating efforts to mollify all cadres who had been mistreated. Moreover, in a wide ranging discussion of democratic centralism the Chairman raised a number of related issues concerning the reestablishment of the open policy process which had been distorted by the campaign against right opportunism. The "reversal of verdicts" was then intensified but at the Tenth Plenum, as part of the larger policy reassessment, Mao called for a curbing of the process. Mao did not, however, call for a total halt to "reversals of verdicts" as he continued to emphasize traditional principles.[73]

In his discussion of democratic centralism at the 7,000 cadres conference Mao repeatedly dealt with the interrelated issues of open debate, collective decision making and unimpeded criticism. If a more open policy process was to develop a crucial consideration would be the willingness of high level leaders to engage in self-criticism and accept the complaints of subordinates. Mao had already taken the lead in this regard with a self-criticism at a May–June 1961 central work conference, a fact he noted in January 1962 while complaining that lower level officials had tried to preserve his prestige by suppressing the criticism:

> On June 12 [1961], the last day of the Central Committee conference in Beijing, I spoke on my shortcomings and mistakes. I asked the comrades to report what I said to all provinces and areas. Subsequently, I learned that this was not disseminated in many areas. It seems that [many comrades felt] my mistakes could and should be concealed. Comrades, they cannot be concealed.[t]

The Chairman went on to defend the right of people to speak up and criticize more generally by calling for full scale democratic life inside and outside the Party, advocating that the masses be allowed to speak even if what they say "is abusive to us." Only by encouraging such openness could the truth be recognized and mistakes rectified since lower level personnel had a better understanding of actual conditions. Without such frank speaking the higher levels would be dependent upon one sided or fabricated materials. In the decision making process, Mao continued, both majority rule and minority rights must be upheld. He attacked the arbitrary practices of some leaders, particularly first secretaries from the provincial to county levels, to make decisions unilaterally rather than on the basis of collective dismissions by the Party committees. Mao further noted, in what must have seemed less than totally convincing to those who had been concerned with *his* arbitrary actions in 1959, that he often found himself in the minority within the Politburo Standing Committee and accepted the position of the majority. On the other hand, minorities were often proven correct and it was necessary to guarantee their right both to advance policy proposals without fear of discipline and to retain their opinions following a decision of which they were not persuaded. Despite his own vulnerability on such issues, no one now championed traditional Party norms more forcefully than Mao Zedong.[74]

If Mao's attempt to revive inner Party debate, an attempt which after all was similar to his efforts in the period leading up to Lushan, was to bear fruit, measures would have to be taken to deal with the cases of those who had

---

[t]*JPRS*, No. 50792, pp. 44–45. It should be noted that the oft-quoted statement by Liu Shaoqi at the same conference that "to oppose Chairman Mao is only opposing an individual" (see *CB* No. 834, p. 22), far from being a snide attack on the Chairman, was perfectly consistent with the message Mao was trying to get across in his own remarks.

manifestly been dealt with unfairly during the campaign against right opportunism. Thus the necessity for "reversals of verdicts" and by early 1961 the process was already underway. Not only were a few of the economic officials who had disappeared following Lushan now again mentioned in the official media, but the Central Committee's propaganda department was both "reversing verdicts" on individual cases and conducting ten keypoint experiments in rehabilitations in the culture and education system. In a related September 1961 decision attributed to Liu Shaoqi and Deng Xiaoping, the Party Center laid down guidelines to encourage freedom of discussion by enforcing the three noes—"no grabbing [a cadre's weak points], no labels, and no striking with a stick"—a measure advancing cadre rehabilitation by "letting right opportunists contend without worries." The next major step came in February 1962 in the context of the intensified retreat as a directive reportedly issued by Deng Xiaoping and Peng Zhen called for an "acceleration of vindication" and declared 80 to 90 percent of the verdicts of the past few years were wrong. Deng assertedly also issued a notice to disregard punishments leveled against cadres of the county and lower levels. These measures were apparently followed up by a series of Liu-Deng directives issued through the Party's Central Control Committee, the united front department, the Youth League Central Committee and the Ministry of Education to speed up and expand the "reversal" process.[75]

The intensified process seemingly continued unabated until Mao's summer 1962 intervention, an intervention which drastically slowed "reversals" but explicitly left open the possibility of rehabilitations on a case by case basis. Mao sought both to curb the sweeping "reversals of verdicts" and—by emphasizing the Party's traditional rectification approach—at the same time to reassure cadres that inner Party norms would still be maintained. Thus individual leaders continued to reappear after the Tenth Plenum including not only important right opportunists but also victims of earlier campaigns—most notably such conservative provincial leaders as Pan Fusheng and Li Shinong who were dismissed in 1957–58.[76]

Scattered reports suggest that while the "wind of verdict reversals" was at its height rehabilitations did approximate if not exceed the 80 to 90 percent laid down by the February directive. In Henan, according to a Cultural Revolution source, new First Secretary Liu Jianxun "indiscriminately" vindicated all but two of 185 cadres under the provincial Party committee, and the remaining two had either died or been transferred elsewhere. Another report states that in the Chinese People's University, one of the keypoint experiments conducted in the culture and education system, all verdicts on those "dragged out" in 1959–60 had been reversed during 1961–63. A third source asserts First Secretary Yan Hongyan "reversed verdicts" on over 90 percent of right opportunists in Yunnan. The extent to which these are typical cases is, of course, impossible to determine. But taken together with qualitative statements about "reckless" rehabilitations, they do indicate a process which went very far to undo the disciplinary measures taken in 1959–60.[77]

The process of "reversing verdicts" involved considerably more than voiding disciplinary action taken during previous campaigns. To restore the morale of those who had been victimized earlier necessitated some unusual methods. As Li Lisan allegedly noted, resentment was quite natural on the part of those who had suffered unfairly. This required not only self-criticisms on the part of those who had previously meted out punishment, but also trips to the homes of their victims to render apologies while humbly bowing and saluting. The rehabilitated cadres assertedly were also invited to "unity dinners" and "unity meetings" where they assertedly were free to vent their anger, scold and beat assembled activists, and even launch attacks on Mao for, as one report put it, behavior comparable to that of Stalin. Beyond this efforts were made to assuage right opportunists with material benefits. Not only were they restored to their former posts and paid back wages, but other concessions were reportedly granted including priority buying rights, promotions, and transfers to choice central and regional posts.[78]

Such extraordinary measures were clearly a bitter pill for those who had been responsible for carrying out the drive against right opportunism. Work teams were used to conduct the work of "verdict reversals" apparently because of or in anticipation of resistance on the part of such officials. Moreover, whether as part of the effort to mollify those who had suffered or in order to overcome resistance, at least in some areas severe disciplinary action was taken against leftist cadres at the time of the intensification of rehabilitations in 1962.[79]

The most famous case, which became a cause célèbre during the Cultural Revolution, occurred in Yibin special district, Sichuan. In this region Li Jingquan reportedly organized work teams to investigate cases from the *sufan* movement of the mid-1950s and the Anti Rightist Campaign in addition to the 1959–60 movement. In the course of "recklessly reversing verdicts" the work teams, and Li Jingquan himself, met unrelenting opposition from the husband and wife team of Liu Jieding and Zhang Xiding, respectively Party secretaries of Yibin special district and Yibin municipality. Apart from the general trend of rehabilitations, Liu and Zhang objected vehemently to "reversing the verdict" on a former leading cadre of the special district who had been ousted as a right opportunist in 1959 reportedly for asserting Peng Dehuai had acted within his rights at Lushan. As the struggle unfolded in 1962 Liu and Zhang not only resisted the work teams' rehabilitations during deliberations in Yibin, but also wrote reports attacking the whole process to Li and also the Party Center, thus going over Li's head. The work teams and Li responded with a series of measures against Liu and Zhang extending to 1965 including struggle, suspension from duties, and finally imprisonment and expulsion from the Party. They furthermore apparently conducted a "vigorous purge" of cadres who worked under Liu and Zhang during their period in power. Thus officials who had meted out "ruthless struggles" a few years earlier were now subjected to severe sanctions themselves. Although Liu and Zhang were able to turn the tables on their antagonists during the Cultural Revolution, it is worth noting Li Jingquan's "fabrication" that Mao had earlier approved the punishment of these precocious "Maoists" as a model for the whole country.[80]

An irony emerges from the above accounts of the implementation of "verdict reversals." In the effort to restore traditional methods of handling disciplinary matters, Party leaders departed in significant ways from those methods. First, the attempt to revive a persuasive approach apparently necessitated, at least in some instances, bitter and often harshly coercive sanctions against significant numbers of people—thus jeopardizing the morale of one segment of the elite in order to appease another. Perhaps more basic is that the "reversal of verdicts" was *not* a traditional rectification movement. Under rectification procedures erring officials would have to admit their mistakes and be restored to authority on the basis of ostensible reform. In the case of the "reversal of verdicts" Party leaders admitted that *they* had made serious errors both in policy and organizational discipline and asked forgiveness by those they had wronged. A Cultural Revolution accusation that a leading cadre in the Third Ministry of Machine Building expressed discontent with both Mao and Liu for their attacks on violations of democratic centralism at the 7,000 cadres conference is highly instructive in this regard. This cadre's view was that their attacks were undermining the prestige of the Party and state.[81] Since rectification doctrine is based on the assumption of the basic correctness of Party policies, an important prop supporting the rectification approach had been demolished by the "reversal of verdicts." Thus the very effort to restore Party norms, while undoubtedly successful to a significant degree, was in another sense continuing the process of erosion which had been underway since fall 1957.

The Peng Dehuai Issue

It was obviously impossible to isolate the case of Peng Dehuai and his Lushan "clique" from the broader question of "reversing verdicts." Whether *Hai Rui* and other artistic and historical works were actually intended as support for Peng,[82] the salience of his case was indicated by reports of continued grumbling over the unfair treatment he had received. Moreover, the office established following Lushan under Politburo member He Long to investigate Peng's past and recommend further action came up with a report after more than a year's deliberations which assertedly attempted to vindicate Peng. Whether or not this was strictly so the story at least suggests an unwillingness to paint Peng entirely black.[83]

Meanwhile, Peng and his Lushan associates apparently kept active under the terms of the Lushan decision which allowed them to retain their Politburo and Central Committee posts. Zhang Wentian reportedly was assigned to an economics institute as a researcher in 1960 and in the crisis period of spring 1962 traveled about the country investigating the deteriorating situation. Peng, for his part, studied in the Higher Party School and spent considerable time in 1960–61 visiting communes in various areas, assertedly writing reports on such problems as the food shortage in Hunan which could be interpreted as defending his 1959 views. Finally, in June 1962 Peng circulated an 80,000 character document seeking a "reversal of verdicts" in his case.[84]

The strategy adopted by Mao and Liu Shaoqi, both of whom for somewhat different reasons had felt threatened by Peng at Lushan, was to distinguish his case and those of the handful of leaders officially designated as members of his "clique" from the large numbers of right opportunists who were being rehabilitated. In May 1961 Liu tacitly admitted the validity of much of the Lushan criticism but asserted that the *intent* of Peng and Zhou Xiaozhou was not to correct mistakes but to oppose the Party. At the 7,000 cadres conference Liu was more explicit in admitting that many of Peng's views had been proven correct, and he stipulated that people who had shared those views could have their "verdicts reversed" provided they had not joined Peng's "clique" or conspired with foreign countries. While this may have appeared to the skeptical as merely saying, in another phrase attributed to Liu, that "others can say this but not you, Peng Dehuai," it had an underlying rationale which was based on established Party norms.[85] Peng *et al.* were now no longer being held guilty of *policy* or *ideological* sins, but solely of *organizational* deviations—i.e., of "conspiratorial" activities within the Party and illicit ties with foreigners. But given the seeming failure of these accusations to gain widespread acceptance, in this as other attempts to restore established Party practices the effort was far from totally successful.

In any case, although Peng's attempt to have his "verdict reversed" in 1962 failed, the lenient aspects of his 1959 treatment were reaffirmed by Mao at the Tenth Plenum. Apart from sanctioning continued individual "reversals" which were to affect such lesser right opportunists as Anhui Secretary Zhang Kaifan, Mao offered some solace to even the core members of Peng's "clique":

> My advice to you comrades is that although you have worked hand in glove with a foreign country and formed a secret faction against the Party, provided you make a clean breast of yourselves in a down-to-earth manner, we will welcome you and give you work.[86]

This attitude of Mao's undoubtedly explains Peng's appointment as third deputy secretary of the construction committee of the CCP Southwest Bureau in 1963 and Huang Kecheng's 1965 posting as vice governor of Shanxi.[87] These were certainly low positions for Politburo and Central Committee members, but in theory they were consistent with the reform emphasis of rectification doctrine.

Conclusion

The severe crisis of 1960–62 saw dramatic shifts in both official policies and organizational approach. As a consolidation phase began with a series of policies designed to defuse social tensions and adjust economic imbalances, rectification again focused on cadre work style instead of dissenting policy views. The targets of the 1960–61 rectification movement were closely supportive of larger policy objectives: the campaign attacked the mobilization excesses of egalitarianism, harsh leadership methods, information distortion and subjective policy implementation. With the deviations under attack reflecting the needs of consolidation, we would also expect a relatively mild campaign and official statements did point in this direction. Other factors conducive to a persuasive approach were the emphasis on coordinating rectification with production, the development of a modicum of leadership unity based on recognition of the need for a substantial retrenchment, and the absence of a major external threat before mid-1962.[u] Nevertheless, despite some success in reorienting rectification to curb Great Leap excesses, the campaign apparently invoked harsh sanctions in at least some areas and left a legacy of substantial cadre demoralization.

Undoubtedly much of the problem was that the new phase went beyond normal consolidation and became an unprecedented retreat. Rather than merely adjusting new institutions, slowing the rate of growth and relaxing pressures on social groups, the post-Great Leap retrenchment saw an abandonment of the communes as originally conceived, a massive closing down of economic and social projects, and a far-reaching united front effort involving urgent appeals to a wide variety of groups. In such circumstances persuasive measures through the normal chain of command were insufficient; instead, work teams and peasant organizations were required to enforce rectification. In part, this was due to the magnitude and suddenness of the change in the CCP's course. Cadres who had enthusiastically or otherwise implemented the leap forward were now severely castigated for pushing the masses too hard and violating objective realities, while in public the leadership refused to admit the Great Leap itself had been at fault. Thus genuine enthusiasts balked at the new policies, while other officials were bitter at the unfair blame they received. For both groups the leadership's credibility had been severely damaged, and with it the logical consistency necessary for persuasive methods.

Perhaps an even more basic factor in the inadequacy of the traditional approach was the conditions created by the crisis itself. Severe economic deprivation, widespread social malaise, and antisocial acts on a significant scale created severe demoralization within the ranks of basic level cadres. A major problem was the degeneration of grass roots leadership in many disaster areas. With cadres and militia units engaging in corruption, robbery and rape, coercive mea-

[u] In summer 1962 there were considerable though short lived fears that the GMD would take advantage of the internal crisis to launch an attack on the mainland. Earlier, the most significant aspect of China's foreign relations was the growing conflict with the Soviet Union. While this included some border clashes, at this stage it did not involve any direct threat to national security. The Laotian crisis also intensified in this period but it does not appear to have caused major anxiety within the CCP leadership which undertook diplomatic moves in early 1961 leading to a negotiated settlement in 1962.

sures were clearly called for to curb such behavior. Moreover, even where cadres were not guilty of outright criminal acts, significant tensions existed with the local population who held them responsible for Great Leap excesses and current deprivations. This popular alienation undoubtedly contributed to harsh disciplinary practices and the use of work teams and peasant organizations, with the inevitable result that the already fragile cadre morale was further shaken. In a larger sense, the effectiveness of persuasion was undercut by the reduction of tangible rewards available to the rural elite: not only were their personal incomes cut as a result of the crisis but the broader social groups from which they were drawn were suffering badly.

Thus the disparity between rectification doctrine and the practice of these years was particularly severe. Despite efforts to revive the traditional approach severe sanctions were used with some frequency, work teams sometimes kicked aside village leaders, peasants interfered in elite discipline, the material benefits of leadership declined to an all time low, and local officials suffered for having attempted to implement higher level policy as required by Party discipline. Unsurprisingly, rectification not only failed to revive basic level leadership vitality, but cadre morale reached its nadir.

The unsuccessful attempt to reassert the rectification approach was only one aspect of a broad effort to restore traditional Party norms. Mao stood at the forefront of this effort. He emphasized Party unity, the rights of minorities to air their views, and the binding nature of collective decisions. In this period he also went beyond rectification to promote a "reversal of verdicts" on right opportunists who had suffered unjustly in the preceding years. This effort promoted organizational rather than policy criteria for judging right and wrong. Factional ties to Peng Dehuai's "conspiracy" (which still remained a contentious matter) were held culpable, but holding the same views as Peng was now excused as perfectly permissible under the principle of minority rights.

Mao's efforts, however, were far from totally successful. This could be seen in the bitterness surrounding the "reversal of verdicts." The resistance of those who had passed the verdicts in the first place necessitated the use of work teams to enforce the policy and in some instances to invoke harsh sanctions. The rehabilitated cadres, for their part, still harbored resentment for past injustices and could hardly be expected to unite wholeheartedly with those of their tormentors who remained in authority. More generally, the period saw a continuation of the post-1957 pattern of a clear linkage between policy positions and political fortunes in sharp contrast to the early and mid-1950s when the losers of policy debates normally stayed in office to implement the programs they had opposed. The most dramatic case was Chen Yun who had faded from prominence in late 1957 following his apparent objections to the emerging Great Leap strategy. Chen now became a crucial economic decision maker in 1961 and particularly 1962, only to fade again from the scene following Mao's mid-1962 intervention. Similar developments happened in reverse on a significant scale at the provincial level where such leap forward activists such as Wu Zhipu were removed from their leading positions. The norms notwithstanding, too close an identification with a discredited policy could lead to political disaster.

Finally, it is also clear that despite Mao's repeated efforts to encourage free debate many leaders, eyeing the recent past, held back. A spectacular example of this was revealed during the Cultural Revolution by an attack on one of the CCP's top officials, Peng Zhen.[v] According to this accusation, in October 1961 Peng Zhen ordered his subordinates in the Beijing Party apparatus to examine all of Mao's speeches and all documents issued by the Central Committee since 1958 in an effort to uncover the reasons for the Great Leap debacle.[88] What was significant about this review was less its nature, which after all was consistent with Mao's calls for criticism, but the fact that it allegedly was conducted in secret. Thus a provincial level organ was conducting a major policy review without informing the central authorities—a clear violation of the hierarchical subordination central to the concept of democratic centralism. If a leading Politburo member was unwilling to risk complete frankness, the likelihood of restoring a truly vital policy process was indeed dim.

While Mao had withdrawn from active policy making for much of the 1960–62 period, he still occupied the pivotal position within the leadership. Not only was his assent necessary for the adoption of major policy readjustments, but other leaders had to calculate the Chairman's reactions in formulating their own positions. In a sense this had always been the case, but since Lushan it took on a new urgency. Despite his repeated emphasis on unity and traditional Party norms, it appears that the suspicion of his most prominent comrades which had burst forth concerning Peng Dehuai in 1959 still remained a significant, if muted factor. When he concluded his colleagues had lost their nerve and made excessive concessions in 1962, Mao singled out many by name for major criticism. Moreover, during the Cultural Revolution Mao harked back to the "rightist deviation" of 1962 as the first incident giving him "food for thought" concerning the unreliability of Liu Shaoqi.[89] Although this may overstate in retrospect his disenchantment with Liu at the time, it does suggest a growing dissatisfaction with the men increasingly entrusted with the day to day running of China—an attitude of enormous potential danger for established Party principles. For the time being, however, he was willing to cope with leadership problems with traditional rectification methods, most prominently by launching the Socialist Education Movement at the Tenth Plenum.

---

[v] This incident perhaps helps explain Mao's distinction between Peng and Liu Shaoqi and Deng Xiaoping. In October 1966 the Chairman declared, "Liu and Deng are open, not secret. They are different from Peng Zhen." *JPRS,* No. 49826, p. 10.

11
Socialist Education, 1962–1965

At the Tenth Plenum Mao Zedong appealed to his Central Committee colleagues to "Never forget class struggle," but he was only partially able to indicate concrete ways of translating that slogan into Party policies. As he put it at the time, work and class struggle were "two different kinds of problems" and "our work must not be jeopardized just because of class struggle." [1] Much of the succeeding period leading up to the Cultural Revolution can be seen in terms of efforts by various actors in Chinese politics to come to terms with the contradiction between work and class struggle. Most analyses of the period depict a conflict between Mao and the leaders of the Party apparatus with the Chairman vigorously pushing measures to realize class struggle, while his Politburo colleagues and the bureaucracies they represented allegedly sought to resist his measures through obstruction and non-compliance. Here a different interpretation is offered: not only were Mao's own attitudes on the question of realizing class struggle ambivalent and shifting, but for key political figures the object was less to oppose Mao than win him over. In the years up to 1966 both "radical" and "establishment" forces competed for the Chairman's blessing, and it was only relatively late in the game that he came down on the side of those challenging the prevailing system.

The plenum also saw Mao's initiative for a new rectification effort in the form of the Socialist Education Movement. During this campaign the question of the relationship of work and class struggle was again central. If rectification measures were excessively harsh as occurred in the class struggle atmosphere following the 1959 Lushan meetings, then regular work would be severely disrupted. More broadly, the basic thrust of rectification doctrine assumes that the contradictions to be resolved are largely "within the people" rather than matters of antagonistic class struggle. Throughout the period up to the Cultural Revolution Mao never rejected and often explicitly affirmed this traditional view, even while he warned of "enemies" and "capitalist roaders" within the Party. But given such ambiguity it is not surprising that contending views emerged and the established norms of elite discipline came under considerable strain.[2]

The goals and methods of the Socialist Education Movement thus became a major political issue within the leadership over the succeeding years. As in 1957 and 1959–62, rectification again was an important bone of contention, but now one clearly involving Mao and his chosen heir, Liu Shaoqi. As in the case of overall trends, most analyses of these developments reflect the official line of clearly divergent views between Mao's approach and that of the Party leadership.[3] According to such interpretations, Mao attempted to give the Socialist Education Movement an orientation of broad social reeducation emphasizing class struggle both at the outset of the campaign in early 1963 and from the start of 1965 when he reasserted his control over the movement. In contrast, different configurations of Party leaders assertedly diverted the campaign from Mao's orientation toward more practical matters ranging from cadre corruption to immediate production tasks. While various analysts acknowledge that some Party leaders were also concerned with class struggle, these leaders allegedly differed profoundly from Mao by emphasizing Party guidance rather than mass initiative in conducting the struggle. This chapter, on the contrary, argues that from 1963 to late 1964 Mao endorsed the different views which were dominant at successive stages of the movement: first a mild approach represented by Peng Zhen until the first half of 1964, and then a much harsher policy launched by Liu after mid-1964. Subsequently, at a key series of meetings in December 1964-January 1965, Mao reacted both to problems created by Liu's policies and to the issue of rural economic development which, almost by accident, had become linked to the Socialist Education Movement. As a result, he rejected much of Liu's approach and endorsed a shift to a milder campaign similar to that earlier advocated by Peng Zhen. Now, however, the Chairman added some provocative albeit poorly understood elements to the movement's guiding principles.

Similarly, the related process of rectification in literary and art circles begun in 1964 has been interpreted as an effort by the establishment—with Peng Zhen playing a leading role—to defuse Mao's calls for radical reforms by conducting a "sham rectification."[4] The analysis presented here, while not disputing that extensive efforts were made to soften the implications of Mao's initiatives, nevertheless argues that Mao's position was again ambiguous and that Peng Zhen in particular strove to convince the Chairman of the wisdom of a more restrained approach to cultural rectification. It was only sometime in the period from fall 1965 to spring 1966 that Mao definitely rejected Peng's approach and set in train the events leading to the Cultural Revolution. Then the stage was finally set for smashing the traditional Party norms which had played such a significant role throughout Mao's leadership.

The Politics of Ambiguity, 1962–65

The Socialist Education Movement unfolded in a particularly obscure period of PRC history.[a] While much remains unknown, it is clear that developments in this period led Mao to launch the Cultural Revolution. As the CCP groped for new directions following the crisis years, the Chairman brooded over tendencies in society which he saw as signs of a possibly degenerating revolution: widespread corruption and self-seeking behavior, significant social inequality, and the emergence of a privileged "new bourgeois" stratum benefiting from China's socialist system. Socialist education was an attempt to deal with these problems by using largely traditional methods. But as Mao subsequently commented, these methods had not solved the problems and new forms were necessary, forms which would administer a rude shock to the Party during the Cultural Revolution.[5]

While Mao pondered the possibility of a "restoration of capitalism" in China, he also began to reevaluate critically the performance of his Politburo colleagues. Although Mao had often criticized other leaders in the past and they had often made self-criticisms in response, such instances had generally been in the context of a broad policy consensus and an optimistic view of the prospects for revolutionary advance.[6] With the exception of Lushan and subsequent events, this was criticism and self-criticism among comrades which did not significantly endanger the careers of those who had made "errors." Now, however, with the Chairman worried about the ultimate fate of the revolution, his critical evaluations took on more ominous connotations. Clearly he had already been severely disappointed with his colleagues over the retreat of 1962, but he apparently did not draw any damaging conclusions at that time. By his own testimony, it was only at the December 1964-January 1965 meetings dealing with the Socialist Education Movement that Mao realized his trust in Liu Shaoqi and other Party leaders had been misplaced. This disenchantment, however, was not fully developed in early 1965 and only grew gradually over the next year and a half: other

[a] Severe methodological problems make analysis of 1962–65 even more tentative than for earlier periods. First, as previously indicated the early 1960s saw a sharp decline in both the quantity and quality of the official media available outside of China. Specifically, the Socialist Education Movement was only mentioned sporadically and in highly generalized fashion in contemporary sources. Second, this situation creates unusual dependence upon notoriously polemic and unreliable Cultural Revolution sources. This is further exacerbated by the extraordinarily fragmentary nature of these sources for the period in question. Thus the material available on the critical meetings of December 1964-January 1965 is far less detailed and coherent than the admittedly incomplete accounts of the 1959 Lushan meetings. Finally, the nature of the questions at issue also raises problems. Much of the alleged opposition to Mao is pictured not as articulated policy decisions but as passive resistance, the notorious ploy of "waving the red flag to oppose the red flag"—i.e., mouthing Maoist slogans while covertly opposing Mao's objectives. When the intentions and hidden actions of politicians are at issue, analysis takes on a particularly speculative cast.

important bench marks were Mao's fall 1965 warning against the possibility of revisionism in the Party Center and the subsequent attacks on Wu Han, his spring 1966 rejection of Peng Zhen for attempting to soften criticism of Wu, and his mid-summer 1966 conclusion that Liu Shaoqi and Deng Xiaoping had mismanaged the early stages of the Cultural Revolution. Throughout this period Mao's attitudes toward individual leaders and the leadership as a whole were fluid and open to alteration. Still, his mid-1965 remark that "I am alone with the masses, waiting" suggests a profound alienation from his colleagues during the latter stages of the socialist education effort.[7]

Mao's concerns were deeply influenced by his assessment of the Soviet Union. As relations between the two countries deteriorated to the state of open schism by mid-1963, Mao saw no reason to alter his early 1962 judgment that the Soviet Party had been usurped by revisionists. The perception of betrayal of the revolution in Russia clearly was a crucial factor in the Chairman's fears for the future of socialism in China. But if Mao was especially preoccupied with the question of international revisionism and the most rigidly anti-Soviet of the leadership group, other key leaders were also involved in the conduct of the dispute with Moscow and with its implications for China. Whatever differences may have existed over tactics for dealing with the Soviet Union,[b] the participation of Mao's Politburo colleagues in the polemic mitigated the growing divergence of perspectives between Mao, still on the "second line" engrossed in large theoretical questions, and Party leaders in charge of day to day administration. Liu Shaoqi and others, whatever their involvement in practical matters, also had to confront the broader issues raised under the rubric of revisionism and the restoration of capitalism.[8]

---

[b] This is a highly contentious issue, with some analysts arguing that serious divisions existed especially in 1965–66 as various leaders pushed for cooperation with Moscow in view of American escalation in Vietnam. This, these analyses claim, was a critical factor in the removal of Chief of Staff Luo Ruiqing in December 1965. See Uri Ra'anan, "Peking's Foreign Policy 'Debate,' 1965–66," in Ping-ti Ho and Tang Tsou, eds., *China in Crisis* (2 vols., Chicago: University of Chicago Press, 1968); and Donald S. Zagoria, "The Strategic Debate in Peking," in *ibid.* In our view, while a debate did occur in this period it was over a relatively narrow range of tactics. Other top leaders apparently were less inflexible than Mao with regard to Moscow, but none advocated far-reaching concessions and all seemingly viewed the Russians with considerable suspicion and hostility. Luo Ruiqing's downfall appears to have resulted from a combination of personal friction with Lin Biao and advocacy of a major military buildup for defensive reasons, but a buildup which clashed with the political role of the PLA emphasized by Mao and Lin. In any case, in this area and foreign policy generally Mao was clearly able to enforce his views whatever contrary opinions existed. For further analysis along these lines, see Harry Harding and Melvin Gurtov, *The Purge of Lo Jui-ch'ing: The Politics of Chinese Strategic Planning,* RAND Report R–549-PR, February 1971; Michael Yahuda, "Kremlinology and the Chinese Strategic Debate, 1965–66," *CQ,* No. 49 (1972); and Frederick C. Teiwes, "Chinese Politics 1949–1965: A Changing Mao," *Current Scene,* Part II, February 1974, pp. 2–3, 5.

In the course of the polemic Mao and his colleagues elaborated a sophisticated although still not fully developed analysis of capitalist restoration. By analyzing Soviet and also Yugoslav societies, CCP leaders drew attention to the danger of Communist bureaucrats misusing their positions to turn public property into *de facto* personal property, and to the tendency for various social groups to resist the elimination of inequalities which was part of the socialist transition to Communism. The key factor was the nature of the leading group of the Communist Party. If it degenerated capitalist restoration would occur. But if it remained true to Marxism-Leninism, this would be reflected above all in policies designed to further the transition to Communism rather than maintain the *status quo.*[9]

While it was one thing to analyze capitalist restoration in Yugoslavia and the Soviet Union and suggest in general terms the possibility of similar future developments in China, it was quite another to derive specific measures for the contemporary internal situation. After all, if the nature of the central Party leadership is crucial, was not the CCP led by Mao and his "closest comrades in arms"? And if the orientation of Party policies was the measure of the leadership's purity, had not Mao set the overall course at the Tenth Plenum? The difficulty of deriving lessons for actual policy is suggested by Mao's "theories and policies" for preventing restoration laid down in the most celebrated anti-Soviet polemic, "On Khrushchev's Phoney Communism." The fifteen measures discussed were largely either restatements of broad ideological principles (e.g., the continuance of class struggle in socialist society, the dictatorship of the proletariat, and the leadership of the Party), or reaffirmations of long standing CCP programs and organizational methods (the mass line, socialist education movements, cadre participation in collective labor, and Party leadership over the armed forces). Where the "theories and policies" addressed themselves to questions of change, the emphasis was on caution as seen in the call for "rationally and gradually" narrowing wage differentials.[10] Thus far from providing a dynamic program for eliminating revisionism, Mao's guidelines simply celebrated well established practices at a high level of generality. Such a definition of the problem undoubtedly secured significant support but by the same token it provided little guidance for ongoing policy decisions.

The lack of decisiveness in Mao's program for preventing Soviet style revisionism was mirrored in many CCP policies, especially concerning economic construction. In this area the groping nature of the Party's approach which Mao had noted in 1962 was underlined in Zhou Enlai's December 1964 remark to the NPC that "there are still large unknown areas and a great many unfamiliar phenomena [in our understanding of socialist construction]." Given such uncertainty and the tentative, *ad hoc* nature of many policies in the absence of an overall five year plan, bureaucrats in both central departments and lower level organs had ample room to experiment with their own programs and seek their own goals.[11]

Besides problems created by the leaders' tentativeness on major issues, uncertainty resulted from Mao's *role* in the policy process. Removed from ongoing policy implementation by his preoccupation with theoretical questions on the "second line," the Chairman's intervention in policy matters took on an erratic and provocative nature. In this period Mao was better able to define what was bothering him about Chinese society than he was to offer remedies. He placed items on the policy agenda but generally did not provide specifics for achieving his goals, often merely requesting that problems be studied. The result was frustration and misunderstanding all around. Other leaders and officials, recognizing the necessity of responding to the initiatives of the Party's leader, found their responses hindered both by limited resources to cope with Mao's sometimes sweeping demands and frequently by the very vagueness of his statements. Thus his perplexed colleagues reportedly said: [Mao's] supreme directives are not easy to understand"; "The Chairman says something today and some other things tomorrow—it is very difficult to fathom him"; and "Everybody interprets in his own way the directives of Chairman Mao." This situation clearly opened the way for those opposing Mao's goals to distort programs to their own liking, but it also left even the most convinced "Maoist" a difficult task in satisfying the Chairman.[c] Mao, for his part, became dissatisfied both with what he saw as a failure of his colleagues on the "first line" to consult him sufficiently and with the perceived inadequacy of their responses to his initiatives.[12]

Mao's role and impact varied according to issue area. In foreign policy, it appears that Mao played a critical role in shaping the overall direction of policy and that his wishes were by and large carried out. With regard to economic matters, there is little evidence suggesting that the Chairman played an innovative role. He does appear to have been consulted on general policy, and while he occasionally vetoed proposals his more common response seemingly was to accept the programs of his colleagues. In this area, perhaps Mao's most significant advocacy was of the principle of self-reliance in agriculture, a position which was to fortuitously affect his attitudes toward the Socialist Education Movement. The areas where Mao was particularly active, and where he perceived the most opposition to his views, were the cultural and educational spheres and policies concerned with reducing inequalities in Chinese society, particularly inequalities between the cities and countryside.[13]

It is in these latter areas that a case for bureaucratic resistance to Mao is most credible yet still subject to major reservations. A case in point is the educational

---

[c] The difficulty of satisfying Mao and of assessing bureaucratic performance is suggested by the case of the Ministry of Public Health. In January 1965, the Chairman formally endorsed a ministry report reflecting many of his initiatives in the public health sphere. Yet less than six months later Mao issued a scathing directive on public health which referred to the Ministry as the "Ministry of Urban Lords' Public Health." *Xin renwei* [New People's Health], June 1967, in *SCMM-S,* No. 22; and *MP,* p. 100.

sphere where the Chairman repeatedly issued directives and concluded that many people disagreed with him. But who were these people and what was the nature of their opposition? In 1964, Liu Shaoqi was personally entrusted with the task of translating Mao's demands for educational reform into a concrete program. Liu's response was to advocate a "two track" educational system, an approach he claimed would prevent the restoration of capitalism. Under this program part-time schools were vastly expanded to provide vocational training to the huge numbers of people with limited formal education, while at the same time regular academic schools continued to meet China's advanced manpower needs. Cultural Revolution sources denounced this plan as a revisionist plot to condemn the masses to inferior education while the academic schools produced a new bourgeois elite. More broadly, these sources allege consistent sabotage by the educational bureaucracy of Mao's initiatives on enrollment, curriculum, teaching methods and other matters.[14]

Contemporary data, however, suggest a far less polarized situation. Not only is there evidence of a substantial response to many of Mao's initiatives, but in 1964 the Chairman himself seemed well disposed to accepting Liu's proposals by agreeing to the need for "two kinds of middle schools" for academic and vocational purposes. Moreover, while claiming "the present state of affairs won't do," Mao still concluded, "In my opinion the line and orientation in education are correct, but [it is only] the methods [which] are wrong, and must be changed." Thus although seeing problems and opposing views, at this stage Mao did not perceive a fundamental struggle in the educational sphere. Furthermore, he seems to have been in agreement with Liu and other top leaders concerned with education on some concrete points. Undoubtedly disagreements existed at this level, but their significance is difficult to determine. Perhaps a more likely source of resistance was officials below the Politburo level whose sole responsibilities were in the educational sphere, a situation which arguably made them more fearful of the predictable disruptions that would result from significant reforms. Here too, however, the picture is blurred, particularly in view of the significant reform measures actually implemented by the bureaucracy concerning enrollment, curriculum, etc. Finally, resistance could also be found among the practitioners of education—the teachers—and among the users—students and parents. These groups were deeply imbued with not only the established approach to teaching methods and subject matter, but they also saw education as the path to elite status—an attitude at sharp variance with Mao's. In sum, the obstacles to educational reform were deeply rooted in Chinese society and cannot be simply laid at the door of a few "revisionist" leaders.[15]

Another perplexing feature of the 1962–65 period was a new ambiguity in institutional relations created by the increasing prominence of the PLA. The army was singled out as a model for emulation throughout Chinese society, it took an increasingly active role in cultural affairs, and PLA men were transferred in significant numbers to new military style political departments set up in many sections of the civilian bureaucracy. These developments, together with the hindsight of the Cultural Revolution, have led some analysts to view the army as faithfully carrying out Mao's radical mobilizational approach to cope with China's problems in conflict with a Party bureaucracy bent on incremental institutional measures, thus blunting the Chairman's attack on the *status quo*. This oversimplifies the situation. In fact, the military was subject to the same contradiction of work and class struggle as civilian institutions. While the PLA was perhaps able to conduct political indoctrination more effectively than civilian organizations given its inherent advantages,[d] as we have seen it too made extensive concessions to operational responsibilities by such measures as reducing the amount of time spent in non-military activities. Indeed, the 1965 purge of Chief of Staff Luo Ruiqing apparently for overemphasizing military tasks suggests the revolutionary rhetoric emanating from the PLA could conceivably be taken as an example of "waving the red flag to oppose the red flag." Finally, despite evidence of objections by various Party leaders to importing unsuited PLA methods and personnel into civilian units, there is little to indicate clearly perceived conflict between army and Party *per se*. In fact, Cultural Revolution sources suggest that army officers often took on the perspectives of their new bureaucratic units once transferred.[16]

What, then, explains the new prominence of the PLA? Speculative answers include Mao's search for appropriate models to revive the revolutionary spirit, a search which might have led to the instrument of armed struggle. Another plausible explanation is Mao's approval of the apparent success of political indoctrination within the army. But perhaps the key reasons are the flattering emphasis placed on the "Thought of Mao Zedong" in PLA political training and the apparently related personal trust the Chairman placed in Lin Biao. Lin seemingly was the sponsor of many of the slogans and programs glorifying Mao in the early 1960s, and this did him no harm in Mao's eyes. At the same time, ill health apparently spared Lin from the duties of overseeing the day to day management of the PLA, thus leaving the unavoidable compromises with the demands of work in the hands of others, particularly Luo Ruiqing. Fortuitously, Lin found himself in a position similar to that of Mao—removed from ongoing affairs and limited to issuing generalized vague directives while Luo would have to pay the price for any perceived deviations in military work. As Mao's disenchantment with other Party leaders grew, he turned to his ostensibly loyal friend who was unsullied by the consequences of hard decisions.[17]

Mao's growing dissatisfaction with Liu and other Party leaders together with his increasing confidence in the relatively inactive Lin Biao suggest a significant

[d] The PLA was substantially aided by the smaller size, simpler functions, and greater discipline of military as opposed to civilian organizations. In addition, the desirability of PLA status in Chinese society also contributed to the effectiveness of political work in the army.

erosion of the collective leadership of the 1950s. Moreover, Mao's advanced age and apparently questionable health[18] raised the succession question to something of more immediate concern. In these circumstances, while Mao remained a key focus of authority that other actors had to take into account, latent competition among these actors became manifest. This was a gradual development which remained muted until at least late 1965. Nevertheless, the system was moving toward a more factional type of politics than had previously existed. Lin Biao clearly represented one important force in this new setting. The key active leaders of the Party and government bureaucracies—Liu Shaoqi, Zhou Enlai, Deng Xiaoping and Peng Zhen—represent another major force, but one which must be further refined.

As of 1965, Mao's successor seemed destined to come from this group of men, each of whom had their own following. Moreover, despite his general dissatisfaction with the performance of the leadership of the Party and state, Mao apparently distinguished among the individuals in the inner core. Seemingly his greatest disappointment was with Liu, and both Liu and Deng were criticized by the Chairman at the end of 1964 for maintaining "independent kingdoms." While Zhou's survival during the Cultural Revolution suggests Mao's blessing, it should not be taken to mean total approval. Most interesting is the case of Peng Zhen whose star was on the rise in 1964 and most of 1965; by this time Peng was a *de facto* member of the Politburo Standing Committee and Deng's deputy within the Party apparatus. Moreover, in this period he was promoted to the symbolic post of First Vice Chairman of the NPC Standing Committee and appointed head of the important five man group in charge of revolution in the cultural sphere. Most significantly, in September 1964 he was accorded the honor of being one of Mao's "close comrades in arms," an accolade surely given only with the Chairman's approval. Thus while Mao turned on Peng subsequently, for much of the immediate pre-Cultural Revolution period he seemed to be in the Chairman's favor. In sum, both the impending succession and Mao's fluctuating attitudes towards his key colleagues added to the uncertainties of the period.[19]

Perhaps the most significant sign of incipient factionalism was the emergence of a group centered on Mao's wife, Jiang Qing.[e] Starting in 1960, Jiang drew around her a coterie of literary critics and students who developed radical critiques of plays, movies and other officially approved works of art. The activities of this group and their clashes with the guardians of orthodox culture led by Zhou Yang form a major part of the story of literary and art rectification. Here it

---

[e] This group excludes other leading Cultural Revolution radicals such as Chen Boda and Kang Sheng who were important officials in their own right since the revolutionary period. The distance between Jiang and such leaders is indicated by Mao's report that Jiang told him there was no need to show the draft of the original attack on *Hai Rui* to Kang or Zhou Enlai. *SXWS,* II, 664.

suffices to make several points. First, to a substantial degree tension between Jiang and the cultural bureaucracy was generated by her abrasive personality, a long history of clashes dating back to Yan'an and earlier, and bureaucratic resentment that someone with no official standing could interfere in cultural work by virtue of personal ties to Mao. Second, while officials dealing with Jiang recognized that she had special access to and some influence on Mao, they did not assume her views were identical to the Chairman's and individual leaders were able to prevail upon him to reject certain of her opinions.[20]

This leads to a final point: Jiang's actions in the 1962–65 period were to a significant degree on her own initiative and it was only in the latter part of 1965 that Mao gave support to her efforts in a manner threatening the existing political balance. Indeed, up until late 1965-early 1966 Jiang apparently conceived her efforts largely as an effort to bring political purity to the arts rather than as a challenge to the existing hierarchy. Thus it is somewhat misleading to argue, as some analysts have done, that in the immediate pre-Cultural Revolution years Mao's circle shifted from his Politburo colleagues to *ad hoc* intimates such as Jiang. To a certain extent this did happen, but Mao did meet fairly frequently with other leaders and his contacts with Jiang appear neither as constant nor close as one might assume. Politically, the Chairman stood somewhat aloof from both key officials and his wife, leaving all concerned with some signs of support but at the same time uncertainty about the extent of that support. But the very fact that Jiang Qing and the "small fry" critics she gathered around her began to play an increasingly significant political role demonstrates the weakening of the norms of collegiality which had been such an integral part of Mao's leadership.[21]

The appearance of Jing Qing's group and Mao's growing disillusionment with his long time comrades were not the only signs of stress on traditional Party norms in the period leading up to the Cultural Revolution. A few leaders reportedly lamented signs of Stalin style arbitrariness in Mao's behavior. Also, the burgeoning cult of Mao,[f] if restrained by Cultural Revolution standards, inevitably posed a tacit threat to the principle of majority rule. Unsurprisingly, the widespread propagation of Mao's thought apparently became a source of conflict in this period as many leaders questioned the utility of such a "vulgar" and "oversimplified" emphasis on the words of the Chairman. Typically, Mao himself took an ambivalent position on the issue. On several occasions he belittled the notion that he was infallible or indispensable. Yet he also encouraged the study of his works and found claims that his thoughts contributed to championship table tennis performances "full of dialectical materialism." On balance, one

[f] Mao, in a January 1965 interview with Edgar Snow, denied that there was a Mao cult in China although he suggested there might be a need for one. Snow, *Long Revolution*, p. 18. Nevertheless, the emphasis on Mao's works and other signs of personal glorification (e.g., the Chairman's picture appeared on the front page of *Renmin ribao* 58 times in 1964) suggest that at least a minicult was in operation. *CNA*, No. 545 (1964), p. 2.

should not overestimate the degree to which established organizational principles were threatened in this period. Clearly, after Lushan it was impossible to restore fully the open policy process of the 1950s; Peng Dehuai and his associates remained excluded from effective participation in key policy bodies. But Mao, as we have seen, had made real efforts to repair the damage during the crisis period of 1960–62. That vigorous, open debate continued within leadership councils is suggested by Chen Yi's Cultural Revolution assertion that there was nothing unusual or improper in other leaders opposing Mao's views. In Chen's mind, the developments of the 1962–65 period had not invalidated long established understandings about the rights of Mao's leading comrades.[22]

Significantly, rectification principles continued to function throughout 1962–65, although not without some apparent lapses. For example, Li Weihan, head of the Central Committee's united front department, was removed in 1964 apparently for advocacy of a "soft" line in this sphere. Nevertheless, as already noted, throughout this period leaders who had fallen in earlier movements were rehabilitated. This included such diverse cases as Li Shinong, expelled from the Party in 1958 for rightist errors but now restored to his old secretarial post in Anhui, Zhang Zhongliang, removed as first secretary of Gansu for leftist excesses about 1961 but now appointed a secretary in Jiangsu, and even Peng Dehuai's Lushan supporter, Huang Kecheng, who reappeared with substantially reduced status as vice governor of Shanxi. While such rehabilitations conceivably reflected a changing factional balance within the Party, the differences among the individuals affected suggested that the rectification principle of finding useful tasks for reformed cadres was still operative.[23] Still, the rectification approach came under stress during the Socialist Education Movement as harsh sanctions and a high purge rate were applied to basic level cadres while Central Committee figures were disciplined for policy advocacy and other actions quite consistent with traditional organizational norms.

Initial Moves towards Socialist Education, Fall 1962-Fall 1963

Socialist education was first raised by Mao at the summer 1962 Beidaihe meeting, and it became a major agenda item at the subsequent Tenth Plenum. Over the next four years the Socialist Education Movement touched virtually all parts of Chinese society—villages, factories, bureaucratic units, educational institutions, cultural circles, the militia, minority areas, and even labor camps. The precise contours of the campaign are difficult to determine given the paucity of information available, but clearly the rural component was crucial in the eyes of the leadership. Here the movement was carried out one area at a time so that by mid-1965 only about one third of China's villages had experienced socialist education. The development of the campaign in urban areas, which was also known as the Five Anti movement until the end of 1964,[g] is even more elusive, but it appears to have had a significant impact in bureaucratic, cultural and educational institutions while assuming a more routine form in factories.[24]

Mao's call for socialist education was closely linked to his other preoccupations of summer and fall 1962. The effort to curb excessive private production and bolster the collective economy was a central feature of the rural Socialist Education Movement from the outset. The move to restore orthodoxy on the cultural front, initially manifested by the termination of satiric writings in the press, would gain momentum through a number of interrelated campaigns linked to socialist education in the coming years. Moreover, Mao's concern with leadership performance was central in at least two senses. First, as noted in the Tenth Plenum's communique, shortcomings in cadre work style were emphasized as so often in the past, a view suggesting rectification according to traditional procedures. But Mao also indicated his anxiety over leadership in a second, less familiar sense at the plenum. Noting that class struggle would last throughout the socialist period, he saw the danger of the restoration of reactionary classes unless steps were taken: "It is necessary to heighten our vigilance as well as to educate the youth, cadres, the masses, the middle and basic level cadres, and *even veteran cadres.* Otherwise, a country like ours may head in the opposite direction."[25] By extending his concern to tested revolutionaries and also by referring to "Chinese revisionism," the Chairman alluded to problems far more unsettling than defects in work style among lower level cadres. Nevertheless, even in this regard Mao explicitly affirmed a moderate organizational approach along well established lines. He not only declared that "Every locality and every department must put work [rather than class struggle] in first place," he further stated:

> As for the problem of how to treat revisionism within the nation and Party and the problem of the bourgeoisie, I think we must still act according to our traditional policy. No matter what mistakes a comrade has made, we still use the line of the 1942–45 rectification movement. As long as he sincerely reforms, we will welcome him and unite with him.[26]

Although Peng Dehuai and several other disgraced "comrades" remained excluded from the plenum, Mao went on to welcome other leaders who had recently been targets of his wrath. He singled out Li Weihan, whose soft united front policies he earlier denounced, for having corrected his mistakes and earned the trust of the Party. As we have seen, even participation in anti-Party cliques and conspiring with foreign countries was forgivable if the parties concerned

[g] No official identification of the Five Antis was found. However, a Hong Kong publication listed them as speculation, extravagance, corruption, going from unit to unit and place to place, and promiscuity. *Yuandong guancha* [Far Eastern Observer], June 16, 1963, in *URS,* Vol. 33—No. 9. In addition, refugee sources have rendered the Five Antis as "smuggling, running away, corruption, bribery and capitalistic tendencies." *URS,* Vol. 34—No. 1, p. 7. The term was dropped with the issuing of the Twenty-three Articles in January 1965. *SC,* p. 120.

made a clean breast of their errors. Finally, the Chairman further bolstered traditional norms by emphasizing his own fallibility and warning against treating him as a "sage free of shortcomings." Thus even while warning of the possible degeneration of the revolution, Mao affirmed the adequacy of long tested approaches to elite discipline.[27]

Rural Investigations after the Tenth Plenum

Following the fall plenum, socialist education was initially put into practice through investigations conducted in selected rural areas (as well as in some cities). An illuminating set of internal Party documents is available for one such area, Lianjiang county, Fujian.[28] These documents reveal that the rural leadership structure had not recovered from the severe shocks of the crisis years. Despite the improved harvest of 1962, the legacy of economic disaster and social malaise was reflected in extensive "unhealthy tendencies" among local leaders. Of these, which apparently affected about half of all basic level cadres to some degree, the most significant were: (1) tolerance of and participation in widespread "spontaneous capitalist" activities; (2) participation in such common practices as excessive eating and drinking, speculation and black market activities, superstitions and money marriages; (3) increasing links of cadres with former landlords and rich peasants and with well-to-do middle peasants whose economic status had risen under the collective system; (4) significant corruption and other misuse of official authority; and (5) widespread demoralization and lack of effective leadership.

Clearly one of the most vexing problems was the use of official positions to obtain special privileges. As one commune member reportedly said, "the cadres control everything," and this frequently resulted in corruption. Cadre misappropriation of public funds, their use of collective materials and labor to build private houses, and the preferential treatment they (and their families) received on matters such as state loans were all cited as urgent problems in the Lianjiang documents. Yet if some cadres benefited from their positions, the documents also provided ample evidence that many others considered the burdens and tensions of office outweighed the advantages. One of the most frequently cited cadre errors was their unwillingness to continue serving in leadership roles. Many apparently felt that being a cadre involved "suffering a loss," and they reportedly said, "I am not going to do it, get someone else." According to statistics presented in the Lianjiang documents, this attitude was held by roughly 8 percent of the production brigade and team cadres in the county. One factor behind this attitude was the high standard of thought and behavior demanded of cadres which restricted their participation in private economic activities. Tensions with the masses were another major source of morale problems. Some peasants apparently felt that the decline in living standards of the early 1960s was the fault of the cadres and thus became "quite angry with them." The cadres, in turn, felt that the commune members were not easy to lead. A concrete example concerned weighing fertilizer. Peasants in one brigade apparently tried to pass off watered down fertilizer and when the cadre in charge of weighing registered his disapproval they "gave him a hard time, abused him, and even cursed him." With incidents such as this marking the daily lives of cadres it is not surprising that there were signs of widespread demoralization at the rural basic levels in late 1962 and early 1963.

This situation cast severe doubt on whether existing rural leaders could effectively implement the policies of the Tenth Plenum. Indeed, one of the problems revealed by the Lianjiang documents was the tendency of basic level cadres to carry out directives only if they agreed with them. Other directives were ignored on the grounds they were not suited to local conditions, and non-compliance was covered up by refusing to file reports with higher levels. One county leader tried to persuade lower level cadres to toe the line by reaffirming the traditional principle that cadres could express their disagreement with higher directives, but they must unconditionally carry out official orders. The aim of the winter 1962–63 investigations was not simply to uncover existing problems, but to implement on a trial basis rectification measures which would correct the situation.[29]

Despite the seriousness of the problems revealed, the Lianjiang documents claimed socialist education measures rapidly achieved positive results. Not only was the great bulk of the land returned to collective farming, but cadre morale assertedly improved markedly with only about 15 percent of those who previously wanted to quit still insisting on resigning. All this was ostensibly accomplished with traditional rectification procedures. Thus coercion was prohibited in Lianjiang and the "gentle breeze and mild rain" guideline laid down, an approach reiterated in the national press. Nevertheless, much as had happened during the 1960–61 rectification movement, coercive excesses appeared in the Chinese countryside despite the emphasis on persuasion. Not only were "enemies within the Party" purged, but in addition the movement was marred by "indiscriminate beatings [and] struggles" which sometimes resulted in "extraordinary" deaths. As before, the social tensions and disorientation created by the post-Great Leap crisis undermined to an indeterminate degree efforts at mild rectification.[30]

Whatever excesses occurred in individual areas, the still fragile conditions in the Chinese countryside dictated a course of caution. In addition to the mild guidelines for rectification, this caution was reflected in emphasis on not allowing the disruption of production by the movement and the experimental nature of socialist education. Basic features of the campaign began to take shape as a result of rural experiments in various parts of China. Investigations in Baoding special district, Hebei, made clear the need for a major attack on cadre corruption: the Four Cleanups *(siqing)* developed there would soon be declared a central task of the movement by Mao's First Ten Points. Also, the importance of cadre participation in labor was underlined by measures adopted in Zejiang and in Xiyang county, Shanxi, and publicized in the national press. It is noteworthy that Xiyang is the home of the soon to be famous Dazhai production brigade, but this initiative came from county level authorities. Finally, the need to rely on poor and lower middle peasants was repeatedly emphasized. Great importance was attached to recruiting poor and lower middle peasant cadres since their predominance was held critical for the consolidation of the collective economy. Moreover, as during the 1960–61 rectification, separate poor and lower middle peasant organizations were established in such places as Lingling special district, Hunan. These bodies, which assumed supervisory functions over local cadres, would also become a key feature of socialist education.[31]

Throughout this initial experimental period the rhetoric of class struggle was prominent. Speaking to a Central Committee work conference in February, Mao emphasized the centrality of class struggle by declaring, "Once we grasp class struggle, miracles are possible." In May, moreover, he complained that "class struggle is still imperfectly grasped" and only a few local leaders had performed well in this regard. But what was class struggle in the context of early 1963, and how did it relate to the perennial problem of work? Surely some aspects of the new socialist education program reflected class struggle: the return of land to the collective sector, the attacks on feudal and capitalist practices, and efforts to educate the peasantry by systematic comparisons of class oppression before 1949 to conditions in People's China. But did the pursuit of other tasks such as production and technological reform indicate an effort to emasculate class struggle? Despite the assertions of Cultural Revolution polemics, it would be rash to interpret events in early 1963 in this vein. For at the very time Mao lamented the slack handling of class struggle, he linked this challenge to more prosaic tasks: "Class struggle, production struggle, and scientific experiment are the three great revolutionary movements that build up a powerful socialist nation [and] guarantee . . . do[ing] away with bureaucratism, avoid[ing] revisionism and dogmatism." Thus as he set about to draft the first critical directive on the Socialist Education Movement the Chairman affirmed the anti-revisionist as well as nation building qualities of production and scientific work. Moreover, he provided no clues concerning how to resolve any contradictions between these tasks and class struggle.[32]

The First Ten Points

According to Cultural Revolution historiography, the Central Committee resolution drafted under Mao's personal guidance[h] and issued in late May firmly set

[h] The identification of this directive with Mao should not be accepted without reservation. While there is no reason to doubt that Mao oversaw the drafting and wrote some sections himself, it is likely that other subsequently disgraced leaders also took a hand in the drafting. Nevertheless, the following analysis accepts the First Ten Points as reflecting Mao's views since he did approve the final text and his speeches of the period are consistent with the document as a whole.

the Socialist Education Movement on a course of class struggle and mass mobilization, an orientation which would subsequently be distorted by the actions of his Politburo colleagues. But perhaps the most striking feature of this First Ten Points is its broad, non-specific nature. The document raised problems and suggested approaches, but generally it did not lay down detailed operational plans for implementing the movement. In The First Ten Points Mao contented himself with summing up the results of experiments conducted since the Tenth Plenum and calling for further experiments before more detailed guidelines could be provided. Mao underlined this approach with a brief introductory section on the Marxist theory of knowledge which stressed testing ideas in social practice.[33]

The resolution did speak at length of class struggle, but it did so in a manner reflecting orthodox concerns shared by Mao's Politburo colleagues. Class struggle was defined in terms of the machinations of defeated social classes seeking to regain power and the persistence of bourgeois influences and capitalist practices. Nine specific manifestations of class struggle were cited which can be grouped under three broader categories: (1) the disruptive activities of former exploiting classes—landlords, rich peasants and reactionaries—including efforts to corrupt cadres and usurp leadership positions; (2) private economic activities of the "old and new bourgeoisie" in the countryside; and (3) actual corruption within state and collective organizations. Several points should be made about this analysis. First, class struggle was seen in terms of alien classes in society rather than as a question of ideological orientation within the Party. To the extent class struggle affected the Party, it was largely through the infiltration of such alien elements who brought speculation and other anti-social acts into basic level units. Second, even with regard to such blatantly hostile groups, Mao cautioned for circumspection in handling class struggle. In a speech earlier in the month he declared himself opposed to the situation where "In the past [some communes and brigades] advanced class struggle . . . by initiating a movement to . . . 'find landlords and rich peasants [without] exception.' " Finally, dealing with major corrupt elements was viewed as "very serious class struggle," and corruption more generally was clearly a primary target of socialist education. Indeed, the resolution addressed itself to problems of official corruption while virtually ignoring the question of how to deal with the disruptive activities of alien classes in society.[34]

In response to the problems raised by corruption, the First Ten Points endorsed Baoding's Four Cleanups. This method identified four areas of widespread official corruption which required cleaning up: economic accounting, public granaries, state and collective properties, and work point assessment. Cadre corruption especially with regard to accounts and work points was held to be the greatest single cause of peasant dissatisfaction with basic level leadership. While the most serious cases fell into the category of "serious class struggle" and could be dealt with by struggle and legal sanctions, in most cases corruption was declared a non-antagonistic "contradiction among the people." Thus education rather than punishment was the objective with official discipline to be meted out to no more than 1 percent of the cadres. This approach served a dual purpose. On the one hand, by insisting that all corruption cases be dealt with thoroughly, and that graft be returned to the collective, peasant confidence in local leadership would ostensibly be restored. At the same time, mild treatment would reassure cadres and bolster their morale so they would effectively perform their duties. As the First Ten Points put it, "The cadres shed their burdens, the masses are relieved, and both cadres and masses are more closely united."[35]

This mild approach was explicitly linked to a sanguine view of rural cadres as overwhelmingly good. At the same time, however, it is difficult to avoid the conclusion that Mao and other Party leaders were advocating non-disruptive methods precisely because of the low state of cadre morale revealed by the Lianjiang documents. The appearance of widespread corruption and its serious effect on popular attitudes underlined the fragile state of rural political leadership. The approach of the First Ten Points, i.e., recognizing class struggle but not allowing it to get out of hand in dealing with cadre shortcomings, was an appropriate response to that fragility.

The elimination of corruption was linked to cadre participation in labor. According to Mao earlier in May, "The problems of corruption and enjoying more benefits can be resolved only when there is participation in labor." More broadly, basic level cadres could only be effective leaders when they forged firm links with the masses by working alongside them. Labor participation was intended not only to bring cadres into close contact with the actual production and problems encountered by peasants in their daily lives, but also to prevent cadres from becoming bureaucrats and overlords, thus avoiding a situation likely to lead to revisionism. To meet this need the First Ten Points commended the experiences of Zhejiang and Xiyang county, stipulated the implementation of 1958 Party regulations on physical labor, and called on leading basic level cadres to participate in collective productive labor "in accordance with regularized systems." Three years was set as the target period for regular participation in production by all rural Party secretaries. It would be considered a victory if one third of this group participated during the first year.[36]

Another recommendation based on experiments of the past winter and spring termed "essential" the setting up of poor and lower middle peasant organizations. In its analysis of the rural class situation, the First Ten Points emphasized the need to rely on poor and lower middle peasants even after the collectivization of agriculture. It was still necessary to unite with the middle peasants, but little attention was given to this productive strata—an oversight which would have to be corrected in the Second Ten Points. The new peasant bodies were to be established at the commune, brigade and team levels, but the directive was noticeably vague concerning their powers and duties. A dilemma was created by giving the organizations two potentially conflicting functions—to assist and supervise local cadres. Poor and lower middle peasant groups were given a broad writ to oversee the work of commune and brigade level management committees, and the right to participate in deliberations on all important matters. But they were also warned against interfering in routine, day to day administrative affairs. As is often the case with supervisory bodies, the powers of the poor and lower middle peasant organizations were left ill defined and thus a potential source of conflict.[37]

While the First Ten Points did not grant detailed powers to the new peasant organizations, its assertion of a supervisory role for these bodies together with the insistence that they be relied on in the conduct of the Four Cleanups provided a distinctly mass mobilization gloss to the document: "the first thing to be done is to set the masses in motion to conduct an all-out, thorough check of accounts, warehouses, properties, and work points." But how were the masses to be mobilized, and who was to do the mobilizing? As in other matters, the First Ten Points was extremely vague on these questions but the document as a whole is far from radical in its approach. Leadership of the movement was to be provided by the existing rural leadership structure, with overall direction in the hands of county and higher level cadres. Basic level cadres were judged generally adequate for providing leadership, with higher level work teams required to replace corrupt village leaders only in exceptional cases. Earlier in May Mao had clearly indicated the primacy of the regular Party organization: "This time [the movement] is to be conducted from within the Party to outside the Party, from top to bottom, and from the cadres to the masses."[38]

In addition, the role of the masses was to be carefully circumscribed. In accord with the emphasis on persuasion, mass criticism was not to escalate into compulsory confessions or physical punishment and struggle meetings would be largely eschewed. Serious cases were to be handled by regular legal procedures rather than *ad hoc* popular tribunals. Moreover, all activities relating to the campaign were to be coordinated with production tasks; under no circumstances was this latest form of class struggle to disrupt production. Other indications of orderly procedures were also evident: the First Ten Points stipulated implementation on a step by step basis, and Mao summed up the measures adopted with a familiar slogan, "Fight no battle unprepared." Thus the injunction to "set the masses in motion" notwithstanding, the organizational approach of the First Ten Points gave no cause for alarm to experienced Party administrators.[39]

One final aspect of the First Ten Points requires comment. In the last of the ten points the document returned to Mao's concern with the theory of knowledge and addressed itself to the need to develop proper methods of investigation and research. In the course of the discussion it praised the practice of leading officials "squatting" *(dunxialai)* at the basic levels. The discussion then linked such measures to Mao's traditional approach to investigation and research. Yet the praise of "squatting" was significant. Not only would squatting by various leaders become controversial later during the movement, but its popularization at this time was a tacit admission that the views expressed on investigation methods by

Liu Shaoqi in 1961, and repeated in 1964, might have some validity. On those occasions Liu questioned whether the investigation methods developed by Mao in the revolutionary period were adequate for changed rural conditions after the Great Leap. The favorable mention in the First Ten Points of this more intensive approach to investigation work following an earlier approving comment by the Chairman in 1962, suggests that even Mao saw the need for more thorough methods than those he had developed before 1949.[40]

The attention to class struggle and the need for new methods of investigation notwithstanding, the First Ten Points took a position that was fundamentally optimistic. After warning that the indifference of many officials to various forms of class struggle threatened the success of socialism in China, the directive nevertheless concluded that the "many problems . . . are not only not difficult to discover, [they] are also not difficult to solve." It further anticipated that the basic tasks of the movement could be accomplished within three years. Thus while Party officials were charged with developing detailed methods to deal with critically important problems, the First Ten Points expressed the confident belief that they would be equal to the task.[41]

Spot Testing, Summer 1963

Following the First Ten Points extensive spot testing was undertaken to elaborate suitable methods for rural socialist education.[i] Throughout summer 1963 leading officials from central, provincial, special district and county organs led work teams to the basic levels to carry out investigations and test socialist education measures. These officials included Peng Zhen, who appears to have played a particularly active role, and such major regional figures as Politburo members Li Jingquan and Ke Qingshi. Moderation seemed the hallmark of the activities of such figures. While there are a few indications of excess and harsh punishment of village cadres, overall political leaders seemed to have successfully pushed the movement away from extremism. Peng Zhen in particular voiced warnings against "deviations in the high tide of mass movements" and called for lenient handling of corruption cases. Reports on the activities of Li and Ke focused on production problems, thus suggesting a muting of disruptive class struggle. On

[i] The movement also unfolded in urban areas where the Five Anti drive had been under way in some factories, schools and other institutions since early in the year. From the scattered information available, it appears that following the May directive it was extended particularly to various bureaucratic units where it assumed a mild form with emphasis on propaganda to raise class sentiments. Consideration of corruption cases did occur, but struggle was generally prevented in favor of persuasion in small group meetings. *Yuandong quancha* (Hong Kong), May 1, June 16, 1963, in *URS,* Vol. 33—No. 9; Martin King White, *Small Groups and Political Rituals in China* (Berkeley: University of California Press, 1974), p. 73; and Radio Chengdu, September 12, 1967, in *NFCPRS,* No. 225.

the basis of media reports experimentation with the Four Cleanups seemed less extensive than with other socialist education programs such as cadre participation in labor and setting up peasant organizations. And the few reports of "cleaning up" activities which did appear were couched in terms of administrative readjustment rather than attacks on cadre corruption. The atmosphere of the period seems well captured in a comment attributed to Tao Zhu: "The Socialist Education Movement must persist in stressing positive teaching, pressure must be light, the core of work should be . . . promoting a new upsurge of agricultural production."[42]

Did these developments reflect, as some analysts have suggested, a conscious effort to distort the First Ten Points?[43] This seems unlikely for several reasons. First, despite little media attention to the Four Cleanups, scattered reports of mass participation in checking up on work points and accounts suggest some progress in this delicate area.[44] Second, even if cadre rectification was relatively constrained, this was consistent with those provisions of the First Ten Points concerning careful preparations, avoiding struggle, and the importance of production. Third, while it is plausible that basic and intermediate level cadres would have an interest in using the moderate provisions of the May directive to deflect the movement away from corruption due to its disruptive potential and the personal vulnerability of many, the overall lenient emphasis of cadre rectification was determined by high ranking leaders. Here there is no indication of leadership conflict over spot testing. Not only Peng Zhen, who consistently took a moderate stance throughout the various twists and turns of the Socialist Education Movement, but also Tao Zhu, one of the most sensitive politicians to changing currents, and even Ke Qingshi who supported Jiang Qing's cultural efforts in this period, all seemingly backed a cautious, low key approach in summer 1963. Most significantly, Mao's apparent silence suggests that the Chairman saw nothing untoward in the conduct of spot testing.[j] More positively, Mao apparently approved Peng Zhen's proposals which formed the basis for the Second Ten Points (see below).

The provisions of the First Ten Points concerning cadre labor were vigorously implemented beyond any doubt. Immediately following the directive a series of "talks on cadre participation in collective productive labor" was initiated in *Renmin ribao.* These talks reiterated the demand of the First Ten Points that regular cadre labor was necessary both to guarantee sound direction of production and to prevent alienation from the masses. In July 1963, moreover, an entire issue of *Hongqi* was devoted to an examination of cadre labor, and to a review of experiences gained in various localities in implementing this policy. These experiences had shown, it was argued, that the policy was the best method for helping

[j] The most extensive collection of Mao's off the record comments, *SXWS,* records no statements by the Chairman between May and December 1963. Other collections indicate only a brief comment on opera reform in September 1963; *MP,* p. 85.

cadres to rectify their work styles. Furthermore, cadre labor was advocated as a means of "smashing and rooting out all kinds of reactionary forces which are trying vainly to erode and undermine . . . the revolutionary Party of the proletariat in our country." The systematic participation in labor was thus presented as an instrument of class struggle.[45]

Steps were now taken to tighten measures used earlier during the 1960–61 rectification. To encourage cadres to spend more time in production, the total number of subsidized work points awarded for administrative tasks was generally reduced to the equivalent of 1 or 2 percent of the total annual work points of the production team or brigade as compared to the previous common practice among cadres to claim 4 percent or, in extreme cases, as much as 10 percent as their "fixed subsidy." If this was not sufficiently compelling, a second system was adopted on an experimental basis in many areas whereby a minimum quota of labor days was fixed for cadres at each level from the *xian* to the production team. These quotas varied from place to place, but a common practice was to fix the number of mandatory labor days for county cadres at 60 days per year, commune cadres at 120 days, and brigade level cadres at 180 days. The twin systems of fixing minimum labor day quotas and maximum limits on the number of subsidized work points provided strong pressure for increased cadre participation in production and were subsequently adopted on a universal basis.[46]

The program was pushed vigorously throughout summer 1963 by the widespread use of emulation campaigns. One model to achieve national prominence at this time was Chen Yonggui, Party secretary of Dazhai brigade in Xiyang county:

> Various communes and brigades [in Xiyang county] have adopted the method of publicizing "pacesetters" . . . in performing labor and leading production. . . . The county Party committee put down Chen Yonggui's experiences in a book for use at Party training classes [and] issued copies . . . to basic level Party branches throughout the entire county for study and discussion. . . . At meetings called by the county and by the communes, the experiences of Chen Yonggui are always recommended to the audience.[47]

Thus in this early stage of the Socialist Education Movement Chen Yonggui, who would play a key role later on, emerged on the national stage. For now, it suffices to note that this emergence took place with the full support of county leaders in Xiyang.

A final proposal of the First Ten Points also implemented vigorously in summer 1963 was the organization of poor and lower middle peasant bodies. Within days of the May directive Guangdong launched a drive to establish such organizations, and other provinces were soon engaged in similar measures. Media reports on this activity emphasized the organizations' function of assisting local cadres rather than their consultative and supervisory roles. This need not be seen as a distortion of the First Ten Points, however. The May directive had left unresolved the question of how to coordinate the various roles of the peasant organizations and, in any case, the supervisory function was not ignored during the 1963 spot testing.[k]

The Second Ten Points

In September 1963 a new ten point directive sought to build upon both the lessons of spot testing and the achievements of socialist education during the previous months. This Second Ten Points claimed that the movement had demonstrated "far-reaching significance in repulsing the frantic offensive of . . . feudalist forces, in consolidating the position of the rural socialist and proletarian dictatorship, in destroying the social basis of revisionism, in consolidating the collective economy, and in developing agricultural production." Clearly there had been achievements. The private economy had contracted markedly by fall 1963, thus achieving the consolidation of the collective sector. Moreover, the measures undertaken to organize poor and lower middle peasants together with extensive efforts at class education among the rural masses undoubtedly improved the political situation. Agricultural production also improved, although it is a moot point whether this was due to socialist education or to good weather. As for "destroying the social basis of revisionism," this is harder to judge. Nevertheless, in terms of the sources of revisionism identified in the First Ten Points—e.g., cadres being divorced from productive labor—progress was made in this area as well.[48]

The new directive was a systematic effort to lay down detailed guidelines for the movement. As Wang Guangmei (Mme. Liu Shaoqi) put it, the Second Ten Points were "more complete" after the more general "fundamental principles" of the First Ten Points.[49] The Second Ten Points claimed to be based on the earlier document, which it hailed as a great contribution reflecting Mao's correct analyses of class contradictions and class struggle, as well as on the results of spot testing. The following interpretation argues that the Second Ten Points did indeed express a fundamental continuity with the May directive. First, however, it is necessary to examine the available evidence concerning the authorship of the Second Ten Points and Mao's attitude towards the new guidelines for socialist education.

---

[k] Richard Baum, *Prelude to Revolution: Mao, The Party, and the Peasant Question, 1962–66* (New York: Columbia University Press, 1975) pp. 28–31, suggests that emphasis on Party leadership over the new peasant bodies reflected a conscious effort by provincial officials in particular to downgrade their supervisory role. While this cannot be excluded, in the absence of clear directives from above on the nature of the peasant organizations' powers and given the general fragility of the rural leadership structure, there was little incentive to magnify the supervisory function. Moreover, this function was acknowledged, as in the May 28, 1963, *Nanfang ribao* injunction to rural Party authorities to "rely on [peasant representative] organizations, listen to what they say in their work, win their assistance, *submit to their supervision,* and organize the poor and lower middle peasants through them" (emphasis added).

Cultural Revolution sources have universally attributed the Second Ten Points to Mao's alleged "revisionist" enemies within the central leadership. But what individuals were involved? The most explicit evidence points clearly to Peng Zhen. Not only did Wang Guangmei claim that Peng had "delimited many policies" during his spot testing, but Liu Shaoqi asserted the September directive was based on Peng's report to Mao following Peng's summer 1963 tour of six provinces.[50] Another source, somewhat ambiguously, suggests Deng Xiaoping was the author of the Second Ten Points. On balance, however, the available information indicates that Peng Zhen was the driving force behind the new directive, whatever role Deng may have played in its drafting and formal promulgation.[1]

If Peng Zhen was the main proponent of the new guidelines, what was Mao's attitude toward them? Again, the evidence is slim. There are no statements by Mao or other evidence suggesting his opposition at the time the Second Ten Points were issued. Moreover, the apparent fact that the document was based on Peng's report to the Chairman implies his consent. Finally, and more directly, as late as March-April 1964 Mao commended the dissemination of the "double ten points" *(shuang shitiao),* i.e., the First and Second Ten Points collectively.[51] Thus even though the new directive was the work of others, the available evidence on balance indicates that the Chairman also lent his approval to the Second Ten Points.

Such approval is not surprising given the basic continuity of the First and Second Ten Points. This is seen in several features of the September directive. The essential optimism of the First Ten Points was maintained with the great majority of rural cadres judged good, the peasant masses similarly regarded as likely to follow the socialist road given adequate cadre leadership, and the target for completion of the campaign slightly reduced to two to three years. The new directive also endorsed the mild disciplinary approach of the First Ten Points: emphasis was on persuasion with the traditional policy of "curing the illness to save the patient" emphasized, and punishment was only a supplementary device limited to a relatively few cadres. Moreover, much of the content of the new document simply gave more precise guidelines to matters raised in May. A clear example concerned cadre participation in labor where the Second Ten Points elaborated the requirements for an "established system" which had been raised in May by stipulating limits on subsidized work points and calling for a fixed

---

[1]The source possibly linking Deng to the Second Ten Points is *RMRB,* November 23, 1967, which identified the author as "another top capitalist roader in the Party," a designation normally but not necessarily interpreted as meaning Deng. Our reluctance to identify Deng as a major author of the document is based on the absence of explicit charges tying him to it or to rural socialist education generally in the voluminous Cultural Revolution materials dealing with this period. In contrast, fairly extensive excerpts of Peng Zhen's statements on socialist education in mid-1963 (and later) are available. See *Peng Zhen fangeming xiuzhengzhuyi yanlun zhaibian* [Excerpts from Peng Zhen's Counterrevolutionary Revisionist Speeches] (Red Guard pamphlet), May 1967, pp. 17–28.

annual number of days for labor as had been developed in spot testing.[52]

Such continuities notwithstanding, Cultural Revolution sources have claimed that the September directive sabotaged the policies of the First Ten Points by "absolving the capitalist forces in the rural areas" and "binding the masses hand and foot." Indeed, an examination of the Second Ten Points lends a surface plausibility to these allegations given its relatively tolerant policies towards private economic activity and its careful delimitation of permissible measures in cadre rectification. Also, the relatively precise and detailed nature of the document gives it a different appearance from the more general and thematic First Ten Points.[53] Nevertheless, it too asserts the themes of class struggle and mass mobilization, while at the same time facing the contradictions of the May directive in a more explicit fashion.

Once again, the attempt to set overall guidelines for socialist education faced the contradiction of class struggle and work. The document singled out class struggle as the "most basic" task of the movement and repeatedly called for "mobilizing the masses freely," but it also cited Mao's recent instruction that the campaign should "make our cadres well versed in politics *and in business operations.*"[54] The Second Ten Points, as had the First Ten Points, stated that the movement should not disrupt production but dealt with the question in more detail: "Before the Socialist Education Movement is launched, the cadres are apt to lay too much emphasis on production and to neglect class struggle. After the movement is launched, especially after the masses are mobilized, they are apt to ignore production work. These two discrepancies should both be avoided."[55] This assessment not only reflected Peng Zhen's views developed during spot testing in summer 1963, it was also in accord with Mao's Tenth Plenum discussion of the relationship between work and class struggle.

The relatively lenient prescriptions of the Second Ten Points concerning the private economy[56] also reflected continuity with past policies identified with Mao. The various guidelines concerning private plots, private trading, etc., all cited as their source the Sixty Articles on people's communes which had been attributed to Mao. The First Ten Points had cited the Sixty Articles as the basic policy for the rural economy, and now the Second Ten Points asserted the Sixty Articles "should be [taken as] a yardstick in judging the results of the Socialist Education Movement."[57] Thus while the Second Ten Points did attempt to balance the economic benefits of private production and class struggle in a way granting some concessions to "spontaneous capitalism," its stipulations were consistent with the known policy positions of the Chairman.

The September directive further faced the contradiction between mobilizing the masses and preventing deviations. This was seen in guidelines for the organization of poor and lower middle peasant bodies. While "freely mobilizing the masses" in setting up peasant organizations was declared a basic work item of the campaign, the Second Ten Points like the earlier directive was concerned about the purity of such organizations and went on to express concern about paper bodies which had been set up overnight. Thus it demanded care in establishing peasant organs and routine work schedules in their operations. Moreover, the ambiguity of the First Ten Points concerning the relationship to local Party branches was not resolved. While the overall drift of the document emphasized Party leadership, the Second Ten Points explicitly acknowledged that many questions concerning the duties and powers of the mass organs remained and hoped more comprehensive regulations could be laid down in the first half of 1964 following continued experimentation.[58]

Mass mobilization was also stressed for the conduct of the Four Cleanups. But here, as in the First Ten Points, there was concern about possible excesses. After expressing concern about undue leniency when the masses are not mobilized, the Second Ten Points continued:

> When the lid of class struggle has been completely lifted and the masses have been fully mobilized, there may appear deviations which include failure to distinguish the conflict between the enemy and ourselves and the internal conflict of the people, exaggeration of the enemy's strength, and forming a bad opinion of basic level cadres and even regarding them as the major targets for our blows. Such deviations . . . are quite harmful and should be remedied and prevented.[59]

Thus the new document reached the same conclusion as the First Ten Points: the masses had to be launched but their activities should be kept under control. While erring cadres would have to satisfy the masses by returning graft and undergoing self-criticism before peasant representatives, punishment was to be strictly controlled and cases would be handled "at the latter stage of the movement when the leadership and masses have comparatively cooled off."[60]

Closely related to the above was the conduct of Party rectification. As we have seen, the role of the masses in the rural Party rectification had generally been restricted since 1947–48, although ambiguities arose during the 1960–61 campaign. While the First Ten Points had only mentioned in passing the need for a "basic revamping of the Party's basic level rural organizations," the Second Ten Points now made it a major item on the agenda of socialist education involving a thorough examination of each Party member, weeding out degenerates, and strengthening the leading core by cultivating activists. The approach advocated by the new directive essentially took the position evolved by CCP leaders in the early 1940s: the masses would be involved in the process but subject to strict Party control. In their capacities as basic level cadres, Party members would be asked to "wash hands and take baths" before meetings attended by poor and lower middle peasant representatives. As Party members, they were required to carry out criticism and self-criticism within their local Party branches, and upon completion of such internal discussions Party branch meetings were to be opened to "positive elements from the poor and lower middle peasants" who would continue the criticism process. Party sanctions, however, would be determined in accord with Party regulations and approved by higher levels. Thus the provisions of the Second Ten Points coincided exactly with Mao's view of May: "[Rectification] is to be conducted from within the Party to outside the Party, from top to bottom, and from the cadres to the masses." By these stipulations, the Second Ten Points sought a degree of accountability to the masses, but in a context where the established Party leadership would be setting the parameters of mass activity.[m]

Perhaps the greatest innovation of the Second Ten Points was its extended discussion of leadership methods for the movement. While the First Ten Points simply called on leading cadres to engage in investigation and research and endorsed "squatting at points," the new directive went into great detail. It criticized corruption among some provincial to county level leaders of the campaign, demanding that they undergo a cleansing process by participating in the Five Anti drive before taking charge of rural investigations. Moreover, in emphasizing the need for deeply penetrating rural reality, the Second Ten Points reintroduced "striking roots and linking up" which had been used during the 1947–48 rectification. This method, which would be attacked by Mao more than a year later, aimed at overcoming superficial investigations by establishing close ties between higher level work teams and poor and lower middle peasants.[61]

Some of the most detailed discussion dealt with the role of work teams. Work teams of leading cadres and other personnel from the provincial to county level were entrusted with leading the movement at "points," i.e., at a limited number of communes and brigades where socialist education procedures were to be developed intensively over a three month period. (In the more numerous rural units on the "plane," i.e., where the methods developed at "points" would be applied, existing local leaders would guide the campaign.) In the course of delimiting the role of work teams, the Second Ten Points came to grips with some central problems of mass mobilization and rural leadership morale. As had been demonstrated as early as 1947–48, the relationship between higher level work teams, basic level cadres and rural masses is a delicate one. If the masses are to criticize actively their local leaders some reassurance against retribution is required from an outside source. But if outside work teams provide that reassurance and encouragement, a very real danger exists of excesses resulting in a demoralized cadre force. In defining the relationship between work teams and existing basic level organs, the Second Ten Points inclined toward affirming local authority in order to maintain rural stability:

---

[m] *SC,* pp. 70, 73–74, 91; and above, p. 402. Baum, *Prelude,* pp. 47–48, distinguishes between "closed door rectification" for Party members and "open door rectification" for non-Party cadres. The September directive's stipulations concerning commune, brigade and team cadres, however, do not make distinctions between Party and non-Party cadres. Moreover, as the analysis here indicates, at least some peasant representatives were allowed behind the doors of the Party.

> In the Socialist Education Movement, it would obviously be wrong for the work teams to work in circles within the basic cadres ... without making contact and taking deep root among ... the poor and lower middle peasant masses. However, it would be equally wrong for them to brush aside the basic organizations and existing cadres, instead of carrying out work by relying upon them. *This method of doing things would create an opposition between the basic level cadres on the one hand, and the work team and poor and lower middle peasants on the other,* thereby undermining the smooth development of the movement.[62]

The warning to the work teams implied here—that they must not undermine the authority of the existing power structure in the countryside—was further reflected in the description of the relationship between work team personnel and basic level cadres. The work teams were to be the "staff" of local cadres and were strictly to avoid monopolizing the functions of the latter. Yet at the same time they were instructed to draw up plans and "enlighten the basic cadres in the analysis of problems and the determination of policies and methods." Thus a note of ambiguity was present, but the thrust of the Second Ten Points was that local leaders must not be displaced by higher level work teams except in a few places whose leadership had been usurped by undesirable elements.[63]

As a result of these stipulations, the Second Ten Points tacitly recognized the importance of outside support for mass mobilization in the rectification of rural leadership. However, the guidelines for both work teams and Party rectification, consistent with the position of the First Ten Points, were unwilling to "lift the lid off class struggle" when dealing with the rural elite. This, of course, was linked to the assessment of that elite as basically good. Were that assessment to change, the way would be open for a new relationship among work teams, basic level cadres and rural masses which could lead to a much deeper and more disruptive mobilization of China's peasantry.

Implementing and Reassessing Socialist Education, Fall 1963–Fall 1964

The period following the September 1963 directive saw the intensification and extension of socialist education programs in both rural and urban areas, although once again information is fragmentary concerning the cities. According to the 1964 *Renmin ribao* New Year's editorial, the Socialist Education Movement would be carried out "in even greater depth and scope" in the coming year following significant achievements in ideological work with cadres and masses. This optimism was further manifested in efforts undertaken from winter 1963 through mid-1964 to deal with cadre shortcomings, the so-called "small Four Cleanups," which largely conformed to the projections and methods of the Second Ten Points. However, investigations carried out in this phase—most notably those of Wang Guangmei—provided a much bleaker picture of the Chinese countryside. By the middle of 1964 CCP leaders, including Mao as well as Liu Shaoqi, were engaged in a major reassessment of the situation and the policies required to deal with it, a reassessment culminating in the Revised Second Ten Points of September 1964.

This took place against the background of other significant developments. Improved economic conditions followed a relatively good agricultural performance and overfulfillment of state plans in 1963. This undoubtedly influenced Party leaders not only to step up the tempo of socialist education but also to push forward politicization of Chinese society generally. In 1964 criticism of "deviations" on the cultural front were significantly intensified (see below), concern with the political commitment of the younger generation motivated a major drive to "cultivate revolutionary successors," vilification of Soviet revisionism reached fever pitch, the study of Mao's works was carried out on a nationwide basis, and the entire county was urged to "learn from the PLA."[64]

While, as many analysts suggest, different points of view may have existed beneath the sound and fury of these undertakings, overall it appears that the definition of revisionism and other reactionary phenomena was so multifaceted that a wide spectrum of officials could pursue a variety of projects without polarizing the leadership. Indeed, Mao himself was groping for a better understanding of the nature of revisionism in China and the proper measures to combat it. Thus while he called on the nation to "learn from the PLA" and required the bureaucracy to install PLA type political departments, he did this in a surprisingly diffident manner, commenting that "some people suggested" such measures and "it seems that this is the only way." Moreover, in March 1964, Mao flatly rejected proposals that emulation of the PLA and the model Daqing oilfields replace the Four Cleanups, arguing that people advancing these views "represent a faction which does not carry out class struggle." Thus, while the Chairman may have felt the campaign to emulate the army was a useful measure under the circumstances, the evidence suggests that in 1964 he regarded it as merely one of several approaches to the still imperfectly understood problems of Chinese society.[65]

The effort to come to grips with these problems again stumbled on the difficulty of relating class struggle to work. Mao's March 1964 remarks not only indicated he regarded fighting corruption a critical task of class struggle, he further emphasized the need to be proficient at work: "Only to carry out class struggle but not the struggle for production or scientific experimentation . . . [is] meaningless." Meanwhile, the polemics against Soviet revisionism appeared to provide guidance for applying class struggle to areas of concrete work, but the overall effect was highly ambiguous. In particular, attacks on individual peasant production, priority to economic over political considerations, and material incentives in Russia and Yugoslavia superficially gave some content to revisionism. As already suggested, however, these attacks did not have much relevance for actual Chinese policies where, for example, material incentives became "the socialist principle of distribution according to work." Such broad criteria provided little guidance on the crucial question of *where to draw the line.* Thus in August 1964 Mao warned against excessive restrictions on capitalism which would create a "one-sided approach" to the economy. At that time the Chairman also advocated the combination of "principle and flexibility" which the CCP assertedly demonstrated at the 1960 Moscow conference of Communist parties, a meeting which adopted a resolution substantially affirming the position of the revisionist Soviet leadership. Moreover, when addressing himself to class struggle within China in the same year, Mao reserved some of his most bitter comments for questions of work style: "If the managerial staff do not join the workers on the shop floor . . . they will find themselves locked in acute class struggle with the working class. . . . Those persons [will then] have turned into . . . bourgeois elements sucking the blood of the workers." Thus while the policy content of revisionism remained ill defined, socialist education measures designed to improve cadre work style and root out corruption had Mao's backing as important contributions to contemporary class struggle.[66]

Socialist Education and the Small Four Cleanups

The initial socialist education measures which were implemented after the Second Ten Points closely followed the spirit and stipulations of that document. One development was the revision and codification of systems regulating cadre labor. Cadres at the county level were now instructed to devote a minimum of one third of their time, i.e., over 100 days per year, to physical labor (compared with an earlier average of 60 days); commune level cadres were also required to spend upwards of 100 days in production (compared with 120 days); and brigade level cadres were to labor for 150 to 200 days (compared with 180 days). The most significant change was the substantial increase in the labor quotas of county cadres in order to increase on the spot leadership at the grass roots by officials above the commune. This dovetailed with press emphasis on the need for leading cadres to "squat at points" to enhance both production work and socialist education. Another theme of both the First and Second Ten Points repeatedly stressed was that socialist education must be "strictly coordinated with production," and that such political activity was a powerful force for pushing forward agricultural output. Also, in at least some areas efforts were undertaken in winter 1963–64 to set up poor and lower middle peasant organizations from the commune to team levels.[67]

Following the stipulations of the Second Ten Points, the movement was implemented differently at selected "points" where work teams played a key role and on the "plane" where local Party organizations took charge. On the "plane," the September directive stipulated that cadres study the double ten points, voluntarily correct their shortcomings, and participate in labor in addition to conducting routine propaganda work. The actual implementation of socialist education on the "plane" during the following winter and spring apparently placed heavy emphasis on mass indoctrination, especially through meetings to "recall the past" of pre-1949 class exploitation, propaganda on the superiority of socialism, and emulation of advanced economic performances. In addition, units on the "plane" received touring propaganda teams and cultural troupes dispatched by higher levels to spread the gospel through stories, films, song and dance. But in the absence of outside work teams no major efforts were undertaken to root out corruption and other serious deviations.[68]

The problem of cadre corruption, however, was not ignored at the "points." There, with the work teams playing a crucial role, what came to be known as the small Four Cleanups was carried out.[69] The work teams were headed by reliable leading cadres drawn mostly from Party organs from the provincial to commune levels. These cadres received special training of several weeks to several months duration at provincial or county headquarters. In addition, the teams were filled out by lower ranking cadres from Party and government units, PLA men, students and teachers who were given less intensive training. After training, the work teams were dispatched to preselected keypoint areas which ideally reflected a cross section of rural conditions. Once located in keypoint communes and brigades, the teams which generally numbered 10 to 40 members per brigade were further divided into smaller groups which took residence in the production teams where they sought to "strike roots and link up" with local poor and lower middle peasants. As the campaign then unfolded a division of labor appeared: the local Party branch took charge of routine ideological indoctrination while the work team concentrated on carrying out the Four Cleanups among local cadres.

The perennial problem of the relationship of outside work teams to local Party authority was a matter of considerable attention in this period. The press reiterated the demand of the Second Ten Points that the teams refrain from brushing aside local leaders, and this injunction apparently was widely obeyed during the small Four Cleanups. The work team leaders worked closely with their counterparts in the local Party structure. They initially revealed the aims of the movement in closed sessions at commune and brigade headquarters, and often relied heavily on the principal local cadres for assistance in the investigation of corruption—investigations from which these cadres were generally exempt. But if this approach avoided undue tensions between work teams and local leaders, it greatly complicated the task of those work team members who sought to "link up" with the peasants and solicit their views of village cadres. As one common saying put it, "Work teams come and go but the cadres remain. Who will protect us then?" Under the circumstances, with the work team leaders looking to responsible village officials for an understanding of the local situation, it became virtually impossible to mobilize the masses boldly to attack corruption as both the First and Second Ten Points had urged.[70]

The corollary to cooperation between work teams and local Party branches was mild rectification. This again was consistent with the analysis of the May and September 1963 directives. With the vast majority of cadres presumed good, persuasive methods were the order of the day. While there were a few refugee reports of executions, suicides and wholesale arrests,[71] overall the traditional rectification approach seems to have prevailed. From the start local leaders were told that leniency would be adopted in cases where errors were freely admitted. When corruption cases were dealt with the accused cadres were first confronted behind closed doors at cadre meetings chaired by work team leaders. If these cadres confessed and promised to repay what they had taken, they were let off without further action. If, on the other hand, doubts remained or the accused denied guilt, subsequent meetings would be held to which a few peasant representatives would be invited. But even these meetings were generally low key affairs and cadres had the opportunity to defend themselves. Reflecting the restrictive estimates in the Second Ten Points, struggle sessions affected a maximum of 5 percent of local cadres, although a significantly larger group (50 to 60 percent in given brigades) received milder forms of criticism. Disciplinary measures were handled by regular Party bodies which rarely sanctioned severe punishment.

This mild approach left a great deal of rural corruption and other shortcomings untouched. This, of course, was partially due to the efforts of local leaders who were often deeply involved in corruption themselves to deflect investigations away from threatening areas. In addition, many work team leaders were undoubtedly unwilling to cause excessive disruption of the still fragile rural political structure. In this reluctance they had the support of central policy going back to the First Ten Points. Any inclination not to stir things up was reinforced not only by specific injunctions against high purge rates or "brushing aside" local leaders, but also by the fundamentally optimistic assessment of rural conditions offered by China's top leaders.

The optimistic assessment dominated the official media well into summer 1964. On the whole, the press enthusiastically reported improved cadre work style and successful mass mobilization, worrying only that the results of socialist education were so good that some people belittled the problems which remained.[72] This continued public optimism, however, masked an agonizing reappraisal then being made in the highest Party councils.

Reappraising the Rural Situation

While most work teams proceeded along the course set by the Second Ten Points, other work teams led by important central leaders adopted a more open-minded investigatory approach which finally led to a drastic reassessment of rural conditions. Clearly the driving force behind his reassessment was Liu Shaoqi. Liu not only personally "squatted" for 18 days in Henan during the first half of 1964, but his wife's rural investigations from November 1963 to April

1964 provided the crucial experiences upon which the policy reappraisal was based. Then, in July and August 1964, Liu began to propagate systematically a new pessimistic view of the situation. Finally, in September he presided over the drafting of the Revised Second Ten Points which put the official seal of approval on the new line.

The positions of other policy makers are less clear. Certainly many high regional and provincial officials—most notably Tao Zhu and Li Jingquan—were active supporters of the revised policy. In a sense, the new policy reflected a consensus view of ranking officials who had undertaken investigations, although it is likely some simply jumped on the bandwagon. The positions of some key central policy makers are particularly cloudy. Although there are some indications to the contrary, on balance it appears that Peng Zhen—the key architect of the Second Ten Points which was now being overturned—was gradually eased out of responsibility for this area.[n] Deng Xiaoping's position is especially obscure; although some generalized Cultural Revolution allegations paint him as a supporter of the new line, Deng himself claimed he "had a few different views" from the 1964 majority position. Zhou Enlai's views are completely unknown. As for Mao, the somewhat fragmentary data which will be examined below suggest on balance that he was generally persuaded by the evidence presented by Liu and backed the new orientation of the movement. The Chairman, however, apparently placed responsibility for developing the new orientation squarely on Liu Shaoqi.[73]

The earliest move in the reappraisal process was the dispatch of Wang Guangmei's work team to Taoyuan brigade, Hebei, in late November 1963. Liu's motive for sending Wang to the countryside apparently was to secure an accurate picture of rural conditions; he stressed she should not have any preconceived notions of what she would find. According to Wang, while many opposed her mission it was not simply Liu's doing: "Many people were against me going to Taoyuan, but Liu Shaoqi was in favor . . . [and] only Chairman Mao backed me up." If true, this would indicate that Mao too was concerned with obtaining

[n] A number of Cultural Revolution reports imply Peng's support for the new initiative. The most specific are claims he gave a July 1964 report on socialist education problems jointly with Liu, later helped Liu prepare the Revised Second Points, and that Shanghai officials launched harsh struggles in urban socialist education in 1964 after learning of similar measures undertaken by Peng in Beijing. *Sanfanfenzi Liu Shaoqi zui'oshi* [History of the Crimes of Three Anti Element Liu Shaoqi] (Red Guard pamphlet), May 1967, p. 47; *Gong-nong-bing* [Workers-Peasants-soldiers], September 1967, in *SCMM-S,* No. 27; and *Gongren zaofan bao* [Workers' Rebellion Journal], February 10, 1968, in *SCMP,* No. 4131. The basis for concluding that Peng was eased out of socialist education responsibilities is the extensive collection, *Peng Zhen fangeming,* May, 1967, pp. 17–28. This compendium, which contains numerous and lengthy statements on socialist education from 1963 and 1965, has only four very brief excerpts from 1964. In addition, Peng's apparent clash with Liu in late 1964 and his subsequent role in the undoing of the 1964 line (see below) further suggest substantial differences between the two men on this issue.

more information on the situation in China's countryside.[74]

The story of Wang's stay at Taoyuan may be summarized briefly.[75] After arriving at the brigade Wang and other work team members adopted the approved method of "linking up" with local peasants who had been preselected for their reported political reliability. Unlike work at other "points," however, work team cadres operated virtually in secret. They did not inform local Party leaders of their intentions or solicit cooperation. In this manner Wang and her associates were able to uncover evidence of widespread corruption and "spontaneous capitalism" in the brigade, phenomena which were laid at the door of the principal leading cadres of the unit. They found a web of corruption involving the leading Party officials from the branch secretary down and entangling ordinary cadres and commune members. The work team's concern was with the need to restrict rural capitalism—a theme then being raised in the polemics with the Soviet Union—as well as with corruption. Extremely sharp criticism was directed at even the most minor forms of private economic activity. Overall, Wang concluded that "Taoyuan brigade has changed its color to white, basically it is not red."

Wang reported her findings to Liu who then sanctioned drastic action to correct the situation in Taoyuan. Large scale efforts were undertaken to criticize the problems uncovered in the brigade and to struggle against those held responsible. As a result, 85 percent of the brigade's cadres were severely attacked while intense mass struggle rallies and various forms of physical pressure were widely applied. In addition, formal disciplinary action was taken resulting in the removal of key brigade leaders as well as some ordinary cadres at both the brigade and team levels. These officials were replaced by other local cadres who had been hand picked by the work team, and two work team leaders remained after the team departed in late April to serve as principal brigade officials until a new branch could be fully reconstructed out of local personnel.

As Wang's investigations ground to their conclusion China's top leaders including Mao himself began to be influenced by her findings. According to Wang, Mao indicated his approval of her Taoyuan efforts both by praise of her living with the masses and by borrowing two of her criteria when he laid down his six criteria for evaluating socialist education in June.[76] Whatever the truth of these specific assertions, Mao's statements from March to August 1964 took on an increasingly pessimistic tone and supported many of the conclusions which Liu and Wang drew from the Taoyuan experience. Thus as the results of Wang's investigations began to filter back to Beijing, Mao complained in March that some areas were conducting socialist education too hastily, with the result that "it will be done in a phoney manner." In the same month he called for extending the two to three years projected by the Second Ten Points for completing the movement to three to six years in the countryside, and in May he stipulated three to five years for finishing the urban Five Antis. These steps to prolong socialist education indicated that the Chairman was taking a more serious view of problems uncovered during rural investigations.[77]

Meanwhile, Mao's comments about basic level leadership became increasingly harsh. In April he observed that many Party members and cadres were "new bourgeois elements" in disguise. In July he declared that the Soviet Union was not the only place where the class enemy had been successful: "We, too, have cases in which political power is in the grip of the bourgeoisie; these are production brigades, factories, and county committees, as well as [special] district and provincial committees, in which they have their people."[78] Finally, in August, Mao was even more pessimistic:

> In our state at present approximately one third of the power is in the hands of the enemy or of the enemy's sympathizers. We have been going for [15] years and we now control two thirds of the realm. At present, you can buy a [Party] branch secretary for a few packs of cigarettes, not to mention marrying a daughter to him.[79]

Here it is important to emphasize that Mao's concern was primarily directed at problems of corruption at the basic levels. While higher levels were mentioned by the Chairman, as they would be in Liu's Revised Second Ten Points, this was generally where superior levels provided protection for corrupt lower ranking officials.[80]

While Mao was now suggesting the need for harsher measures against low level corruption, in some of the same talks in mid-1964 he continued to emphasize the importance of established norms for dealing with comrades in high Party circles. The Chairman argued on several occasions that proper inner Party democracy required that unquestioning faith should not be placed on his personal views as he was "no god," and his importance to the revolution should not be exaggerated. In shaping major policies of the Party and state, Mao stressed the importance of solidarity with comrades, urging that any misunderstandings be settled by negotiations among the concerned parties. Moreover, his overall assessment of the leading core of the Party was optimistic. In June, while arguing the need to unite with those who "erroneously opposed us in the past," Mao noted that while attention must be paid to schemers such as Gao Gang and Peng Dehuai only a very small minority were incorrigible. Given this assessment, traditional inner Party unity was the order of the day at the commanding heights of the CCP.[81]

In this context, several specific measures were taken at a June Politburo work conference under the Chairman's leadership. First, Mao laid down six criteria for the movement which Wang Guangmei claimed were at least in part based on her Taoyuan findings:

> (1) Have the poor and lower middle peasants been truly mobilized?
> (2) Has the problem of the Four Uncleans among the cadres been resolved?
> (3) Have the cadres participated in physical labor?
> (4) Has a good leadership nucleus been established?

(5) When landlords, rich peasants, counterrevolutionaries and bad elements who engage in destructive activities are discovered, is this contradiction merely turned over to the higher levels, or are the masses mobilized to supervise strictly, criticize, and even appropriately struggle against these elements, and moreover to retain them for reform on the spot?

(6) Is production increasing or decreasing?[82]

These criteria, which avoided explicit mention of class struggle,[o] reflected a combination of new and old concerns. All the criteria can be found in Party directives from the First Ten Points on. Some, however, particularly those concerned with cadre labor, establishing a good leadership nucleus, and production performance, reflect the cautious approach which dominated in 1963. The concern with peasant mobilization, the Four Uncleans and the activities of landlords *et al.*, while not absent from earlier documents, were clearly items of increasing salience since the Taoyuan investigations. Those criteria, moreover, were fully consistent with the new guidelines for the movement which Liu began to shape in July and August and which were formalized in the Revised Second Ten Points.

The June meeting also issued the Organizational Rules of Poor and Lower Middle Peasant Associations (PLMPAs), a document which had been promised in the Second Ten Points. Cultural Revolution sources have been silent concerning the authorship of these rules. But given Mao's obvious key role at the meeting, together with the above indications that his views at this stage were close to Liu's, it is reasonable to regard the rules as a consensus document (at least between the two Chairmen) with perhaps both contributing to the drafting.

In any case, the PLMPA rules reflected some of the concerns raised by the Taoyuan experience. The PLMPAs were to regard supervising leading commune organs as an important task and to assist in the Four Cleanups. The supervisory role was further bolstered by stipulations that PLMPA leaders not hold concurrent posts as commune, brigade or team leaders, or other important cadre positions, and that no "retaliatory blows" be allowed against peasants who criticized cadres. On the whole, however, the rules were unable to avoid the fundamental ambiguity inherent in the requirement both to assist and supervise cadres. In fact, despite familiar demands that cadres consult with the peasant bodies, the PLMPA rules are surprising in the degree to which they emphasize Party leadership, a principle which Mao would again stress a month later in "Khrushchev's Phoney Communism." The emphasis was clearly on complying with CCP poli-

[o]Too much should not be made of this except perhaps as a comment on the methodology frequently employed by analysts of the period. There is a widespread tendency to emphasize vague references to "class struggle" in "Maoist" documents (although not in "Liuist" documents) in order to show a distinct position on the part of the Chairman. This unfortunately avoids consideration of what "class struggle" may have meant to any of the concerned parties, as well as ignoring cases such as this where—in what presumably was a fundamental guideline—Mao did not invoke the slogan of "class struggle."

cies, actively developing support for local Party branches, and referring problems to proper Party channels. As of mid-1964, there was apparent agreement that whatever else might be called for, the leading role of the Party remained an inviolable principle.[83]

Following the June Politburo meeting, Liu Shaoqi set out to develop in greater detail a new line for the Socialist Education Movement. The initial step was Wang Guangmei's report on her Taoyuan experiences to a Shanghai meeting in mid-July. Next, Liu and Wang toured 19 provinces to propagate their views. Although there is some indication of intermediate level resistance to the new line, on the whole China's major regional leaders appear to have accepted Liu's analysis, trained new work teams on the basis of the Taoyuan findings, and established their own "Taoyuan experiences" in urban as well as rural areas. This often involved embarrassing about-faces for local leaders. A striking example occurred in Guangdong where Central-South First Secretary Tao Zhu had cited the Shengshi brigade as a model unit and in mid-1964 the entire province was "learning from Shengshi." In carrying out the new line it was discovered that Shengshi was a "fake model" led by a corrupt local clique and Tao was forced to admit earlier investigations by provincial authorities had been superficial. Such embarrassment notwithstanding, Tao and other local leaders began to push Taoyuan methods vigorously starting in August.[84]

In July and August Liu and Wang, supported by local leaders, spelled out an analysis of rural corruption as a far more widespread and complex phenomenon than had previously been acknowledged. Corruption, together with dictatorial leadership methods and unchecked capitalism, was so widespread that, Liu concluded, "There are a large number of two-faced [counterrevolutionary] regimes in the rural areas which wave Communist flags but serve the GMD." At one point Liu estimated that 30 percent of all cadres were bad and another 40 percent were mediocre. On other occasions he held that, if anything, Mao's estimate that one third of all units were in the hands of the enemy was conservative, and that in Hebei the figure reached 60 to 70 percent while in Shanxi it was almost 100 percent. The extent of cadre corruption and other malfeasances, moreover, contributed to the complexity of the rural scene: thus Liu spoke of the "intertwining *(jiaocha)* of contradictions between the enemy and ourselves and contradictions among the people." The old approach which neatly divided problems involving easily definable class enemies from those affecting basically good cadres, Liu seemed to be saying, was no longer tenable in a situation in which large numbers of local leaders, ordinary cadres and rural masses were infected by the most serious shortcomings.[85]

A major aspect of Liu's "intertwining of contradictions" concerned ties between ostracized "four elements" and local cadres. The degree to which former landlords, rich peasants, counterrevolutionaries and bad elements were able to corrupt and infiltrate official bodies in the countryside was now regarded more seriously than at anytime since the early 1950s. But probably more worrisome was the rise of "new bourgeois elements," i.e., peasants and cadres who had prospered under the socialist system. According to Liu:

> In the countryside a stratum of affluent peasants with basic level cadres as their representatives has emerged. Today the main contradiction in the countryside is the exploitation of the poor and lower middle peasants by this stratum. The struggle between their Four Uncleans and peasant opposition to these Four Uncleans is the main content of class struggle during socialist education.[86]

The various problems uncovered not only led Liu to draw a picture of the rural situation "as black as pitch," it further caused Liu to conclude that all previous socialist education efforts had gone for naught. As he put it, "In the [past] year and more the Four Cleanups have basically suffered a defeat, . . . it has not been done well in even one commune, [and] it has not made the slightest headway in rural or urban areas." This defeat, in Liu's eyes, was partially the fault of higher level cadres whose "squatting" investigations were superficial and who were often hoodwinked by false reports of basic level officials. But much of the problem stemmed from the strength and cleverness of corrupt village cadres which could withstand any but the most powerful and determined work teams. In Liu's words, "Don't belittle the grass roots cadres, for . . . the strength of our work teams is inferior to theirs. Nothing is clear to the work teams, but [the basic level cadres] have a clear knowledge of everything." In addition to their superior local knowledge cadres reportedly were also able to use the Second Ten Points to prevent mass mobilization, an apparent reference to the restrictions on struggle and punishment in that document. And as we have seen, cadre dominance of local life served as a strong inhibition against aggrieved peasants speaking out to temporary work team personnel.[87]

Clearly, in Liu's analysis, important changes would have to be made if socialist education was to yield positive results. Liu complained, with some justification, that the policy guidelines laid down by the Second Ten Points were not favorable to mass mobilization. His main proposals centered on strengthening the role and resources of the work teams. Liu flatly contradicted the Second Ten Points by stating, "It won't do for a work team merely to serve as a staff officer. It must exercise leadership as a plenipotentiary, and should serve as a representative of the Party at a higher level." Liu further stressed the importance of placing high ranking cadres at the head of work teams. Without such leaders, he argued, it would be impossible to defeat bad men who had connections at both basic and higher levels. Furthermore, when it came to handling disciplinary matters Liu declared Party control committees should not be used. Instead, all such cases were to be referred to cadres who had served on work teams and thus were familiar with the sad state of affairs in the countryside.[88]

To enhance work team effectiveness Liu also called for increasing their size and using "human sea tactics" *(renhai zhanshu)*. Hoping that problems could be fully uncovered by blanketing an area with outside personnel, Liu advocated sending work teams of more than 30 members to production teams of less than 50 peasants and sending out several million work team cadres altogether. In addition, Liu elaborated the concept of "striking roots and linking up" with the peasants. In this version Liu placed great stress on secret work lasting one to two months among the poorer peasants while excluding open meetings. Cadre meetings were of little use, he argued, since local officials would simply avoid problems or falsify information in such forums. Investigation meetings calling together the peasants also were fruitless given their fears and misgivings. As in 1961, and as hinted in the First Ten Points, Liu concluded that the investigation methods long advocated by Mao were no longer suited to the deteriorating conditions in China's countryside.[89]

The central thread through Liu's criticism of the previous implementation of the movement was its failure to mobilize the masses. He faced squarely the fact that ordinary peasants could not criticize powerful local cadres with any enthusiasm without special measures, measures which could only be taken by strong outside work teams. Thus the first of Liu's "two high standards" for the movement paralleled Mao's first criteria of June: "Whether or not the masses are genuinely and fully mobilized." But this did not mean that Liu advocated no restraints on mass mobilization. He repeatedly warned that "the masses are like wild horses and will cause trouble when mobilized," and his second "high standard" stipulated that "disturbances should not get out of control."[90] Yet this concern with control was in the context of far-reaching efforts to get ordinary peasants to assert their views in a profoundly destabilizing fashion. As we shall see, the nature of mass mobilization would soon be a major source of conflict within the CCP leadership. But it is ironic that in summer 1964 the Party's "organization man" was the main advocate of measures which would shake the regime's rural political structure to its foundations.

The Revised Second Ten Points

Given the above analysis, a substantial revision of existing socialist education guidelines was called for. This was undertaken by Liu who, according to Wang Guangmei, had been asked by Mao to alter the Second Ten Points apparently because the Chairman felt it was not sufficiently conducive to mass mobilization. The revised document clearly reflected Liu's—and Mao's—concerns, and it also included Liu's policy recommendations of July and August. Based on the Second Ten Points, it reproduced many sections of that directive without change. Continuity was particularly noticeable in sections laying down relatively permissive guidelines for private economic activity, although there was some hardening in this area. Overall, however, extensive alterations were made in the slightly longer revised version, and a fundamental change in tone had occurred. The relatively sanguine view of September 1963 was now replaced by a profoundly pessimistic outlook. This was reflected in the altered estimate, similar to Mao's in spring 1964, that completion of the movement would require five to six years or even longer.[91]

The Revised Second Ten Points went a long way to meet Liu's criticisms of earlier work methods. Although in broad terms no new methods were introduced, the elaboration of previous methods indicated greater intensity and thoroughness. Thus while the September 1963 version had called for personal spot testing by leading cadres for a period of three months, the new directive stated that such work (now as in the First Ten Points referred to as "squatting at a point") would require about six months, and even on the "plane" socialist education was to be conducted once a year regardless of previous exposure to the movement. The major change concerned strengthening the work teams. "Staunch" work teams were to be "led by politically strong and capable persons," and consist of members who were carefully screened. No one seriously questionable in ideology or behavior could participate. Moreover, the status of the work team was significantly upgraded *vis-à-vis* local Party officials. The new directive not only stated that "the entire movement should be led by the work teams," it deleted the earlier injunction against "brushing aside" basic level cadres. Instead, the Revised Second Ten Points warned against relying too heavily on local leaders: "[If] the work team concerns itself only with activity among basic level cadres . . . it will be 'much ado about nothing' for a few people. Thus the movement will end in failure or reap very negligible results and the consequences may be quite serious."[92]

These measures were necessitated by the fact that, according to the revised directive, "the enemy's methods of opposing . . . socialism are becoming even more cunning . . . [and] we are still very unfamiliar with class struggle under these new conditions." This gloomy assessment applied to both the peasant masses and cadres. The document saw the class ranks among the peasantry as hopelessly confused. This not only required purifying PLMPAs of alien elements, but for the first time since land reform a general redesignation of rural classes was called for as part of socialist education.[93] If the situation among ordinary peasants was serious, the state of rural cadres was considered critical. A year earlier the most prevalent cadre mistakes had been treated as petty corruption. The Revised Second Ten Points saw the situation in a much graver light:

> [The basic level rural cadres] have not only committed the Four Uncleans economically, but have also failed to draw the line between friend and enemy, lost their own stand, discriminated against poor and lower middle peasants, hid their backgrounds and fabricated history . . . thus committing "Four Uncleans" politically and organizationally. . . . Some had even degenerated into agents and protectors of class enemies. . . . The problem, as we can see, is indeed serious.[94]

Rooting out these more broadly defined Four Uncleans was now given top priority. Moreover, solving problems among the peasant masses was seen as dependent upon successful efforts to overcome corruption and other cadre deviations. According to the Revised Second Ten Points, only when cadre abuses were brought under control would the masses return voluntarily to the collective path.[95]

The revised directive did not stop with its scathing analysis of basic level leadership:

> Experience . . . has revealed that cadres in basic level organizations who have committed serious mistakes are usually connected with certain cadres of higher level organizations . . . and are instigated, supported and protected by them. In such cases we must go to the origin and get hold of the responsible persons. No matter to what level the cadres belong or what positions they hold . . . they should be subjected to open criticism before the people.[96]

Clearly, the September 1964 document was promising that the attack on rural corruption would not stop at the village level. While the theme of dealing with serious problems at higher levels would be developed subsequently by Mao, it was already present in Liu's Revised Second Ten Points.

The question then became what types of disciplinary measures were appropriate to the deteriorating rural situation. While the new directive retained many clauses associated with traditional rectification policy, overall it indicated a much harsher approach. Now, rather than warning against excessive struggle, struggle was called for "if necessary." Although the 2 percent limit on cadres receiving disciplinary measures was retained, Liu's October comment that the Party should "never mind the number dismissed" was closer to the spirit of the directive.[97] The need for severity was clearly indicated in the discussion of two principal deviations in this regard. While the 1963 version had seen excessive blows as more harmful than overly lenient handling of cadre mistakes, the 1964 revision reversed this order of dangerous tendencies. Anything less than stringent measures, argued the Revised Second Points, would be counterproductive:

> During the Four Cleanups movement, because of fear of "hurting cadres' feelings," or of [adversely] affecting the unity of cadres, or of cadres quitting work, work teams in some places assumed a tolerant attitude toward cadres who had committed even serious mistakes. They were afraid to criticize, to engage in struggle and especially to mobilize the masses. . . . They thought . . . they had achieved unity. Yet the result was they were . . . divorced from the masses and achieved only a superficial, temporary and false consolidation.[98]

As with Liu's remarks during the summer, the dominant theme of the document was mass mobilization. At the outset it declared "Only by freely mobilizing the masses can this movement achieve complete victory." Subsequently, it underlined this view: "Among all work items of the Socialist Education Movement, *mobilization of the masses should be put in the first place*. . . . All those who opposed the Socialist Education Movement first oppose mobilizing the masses."[99] While some passages reflected Liu's concern that the movement avoid chaos, the directive's overwhelming thrust was to argue against inhibitions on mass mobilization. Thus those who sought to curb socialist education because of alleged disruption of production were sharply rebuked; political mobilization was to take precedence over production tasks. Moreover, various policy guidelines "must not be turned . . . into taboos obstructing the mobilization of the masses and binding our hands and feet." Whatever restrictions remained in the revised version, its spirit clearly swept aside all obstacles to an aroused peasantry.[100]

Finally, successful cadre reform was declared contingent upon mass mobilization in the area of elite discipline. Errant cadres were required to engage in self-criticism before meetings including peasant representatives and accept criticism from the masses. Although the 1963 provision that Party disciplinary cases should begin with inner Party criticism was retained, the emphasis on extending mass criticism beyond a limited number of serious cases together with the determination to get to the core of rural corruption—i.e., to expose key Party leaders who dominated village affairs—meant that "closed door" rectification was no longer a realistic possibility.[101] China's rural leaders would now stand before the masses, and the coming months would see a torrent of mass abuse directed at those symbols of CCP authority.

Rural Crisis and a New Policy Shift, Fall 1964-Summer 1965

Following the Revised Second Ten Points the Socialist Education Movement entered its most intensive phase. In the countryside this became known as the "big Four Cleanups," a campaign which developed into probably the deepest rural purge in the history of the PRC and resulted in the dismissal of perhaps one million basic level cadres.[p] While the evidence is far less extensive, at the same time the movement heated up in urban areas as "Taoyuan experiences," large work teams, and harsh discipline became features of socialist education in bureaucratic units, factories and universities.[102] During the Cultural Revolution these developments were seen as stemming from a major policy error of Liu Shaoqi, a line which was " 'left' in form but right in essence" and caused extensive damage to socialism through unjustified attacks "hitting hard at the many" cadres who were the backbone of the rural political structure. Liu's policies, which were explicitly compared to the excesses of the 1947–48 rectification for which he also bore personal responsibility, did in fact create a major crisis in the countryside.

---

[p] This estimate is based upon a purge rate of 10 percent plus (see below) for the one fourth to one third of China's 25 million team, brigade and commune cadres who were probably involved in the campaign in late 1964. For a higher estimate, see Baum, *Prelude*, p. 104.

This crisis led to a major leadership debate which saw Mao in large measure reject Liu's approach despite his earlier endorsement. Instead, in January 1965 the Chairman produced a new document, the Twenty-three Articles, which gave an uncertain redefinition to the campaign. While this document was couched in the familiar rhetoric of mass mobilization, its apparent effect was to put the lid on socialist education and restore the lenient approach of 1963. Significantly, the most articulate spokesman for this approach, Peng Zhen, subsequently reassumed major authority for guiding the movement in 1965.

The Big Four Cleanups

While the intensified Four Cleanups was not announced in the official media, contemporary reports nevertheless reflected the new approach by emphasizing the need to strengthen poor and lower middle peasant supervision over basic level cadres. According to *Renmin ribao,* the new peasant associations "must dare to supervise the cadres, dare to attack the enemy, and dare to oppose all bad people and bad things."[103] While similar exhortations had appeared earlier, the pessimistic assessment of the Revised Second Ten Points set the stage for taking up with a vengeance the invitation to supervise cadres.

Financial supervisory groups of poor and lower middle peasants, acting with the express or implied consent of Party committees at the county and commune levels, soon uncovered numerous acts of misappropriated public funds, accepting bribes from better-off peasants, and personal extravagance on the part of basic level cadres. The most frequent accusation concerned methods of recording work points. In what must have been a humiliating experience, in some areas "distribution teams" of peasants seized cadres' work point handbooks and conducted detailed examinations of the records contained therein. The peasants found numerous instances of "secret subsidies," "nepotistic favoritism," and out-and-out "falsification of records." Often cadres were discovered to have appropriated for themselves or their families fixed subsidies of as much as 6 percent of the total work points of a brigade or team despite the existing policy of a 1 to 2 percent maximum. Such practices led the editors of *Nanfang ribao* to declare that cadre misappropriation of work points was anti-socialist and exploitative in nature, and should be "dug up at the roots."[104]

Many beseiged cadres lamented that "if the masses criticize cadres, cadres will not be able to lead them at all. It's all right for higher levels to criticize cadres, but if the masses do it, things will become chaotic." A similar argument held that "we are relying too much on the poor and lower middle peasants [and] it is not easy to do our work. . . . What's the use of having cadres if the peasants are going to run things?" These views were strongly rebuked. As a warning to those officials who might be tempted to "hit back" at their critics, *Renmin ribao* sternly announced that "cadres must self-consciously and uninterruptedly accept supervision by their poor and lower middle peasant brothers."[105]

In addition to corruption, rural cadres also came under fire for allowing the expansion of private sideline occupations, aiding peasant resistance to state plans for purchasing excess grain, and generally permitting capitalist tendencies to flourish.[106] Throughout fall 1964 cadres were thus attacked from all directions and their modest efforts at self-defense were summarily dismissed as attempts to "hoodwink the masses." Clearly the prestige of basic level leaders was being severely undermined.

While the above developments were covered in the public media, the unreported development of the Four Cleanups provided even more serious shocks to the rural leadership structure. From the time of Liu Shaoqi's reassessment of the rural situation and particularly following the Revised Second Ten Points, the role and tactics of higher level work teams began to change. Now extremely large work teams were sent to the countryside. In Hebei, initially 120,000 cadres were organized into such teams, i.e., one team member for every 5 to 6 households in units selected as "points," while later their size was increased to 180,000 or one member for each 3 to 4 households. In a Guangdong county, an average of 50 to 60 work team cadres per brigade or 2 to 3 per production team were dispatched to rural "points." These work teams, in contrast to both the earlier period and the Taoyuan experience, openly declared that their primary function was to clean up local cadres including the leaders of the Party branch. Moreover, the peasant masses were assigned a role in the process. They were told to begin writing *dazibao* exposing cadre mistakes and invited to criticize local leaders at evening discussion meetings. With assurances of protection against cadre revenge and the pressure of being told that criticism was a sign of support for Chairman Mao, mass mobilization soon gathered momentum.[107]

These developments again pointed to the crucial relationship among work teams, peasant masses and local cadres. As stipulated by the Revised Second Ten Points, work teams assumed a dominant role in the movement but they apparently went even farther than suggested by the document. Assuming that corruption was rampant among rural cadres, the teams entered villages with an attitude of "suspect all." Thus work teams generally forced the established leadership to stand aside, monopolized all power including oversight of day to day affairs, and reduced the role of brigade and team cadres to one of routine administration while they attempted to uncover local counterparts to the corrupt leaders of Taoyuan. Such undermining of local leadership undoubtedly was necessary if peasants were to come forward and expose major problems. Yet while in this aspect the movement mirrored developments in the 1947–48 rectification, in 1964 work team direction over mass participation apparently was much tighter. Not only were no charges of tailism subsequently made against work teams, but refugee accounts indicate that in criticism meetings and especially when passing judgment on erring cadres peasants responded to cues coming directly from the teams. Self-examinations were initially evaluated and struggle sessions conducted behind closed doors before individual cadres received formal judgment in open mass meetings. A similar lack of mass spontaneity affected handling of commune cadres who were now for the first time key targets of the campaign. Corrupt commune leaders were interrogated at commune headquarters and only the worst offenders were subsequently taken to the brigades and teams for severe public criticism.[108]

These methods were effective in uncovering many cases of large scale embezzlement, rape and extortion of sexual favors from peasant women, and beating up local peasants. The masses had been truly aroused to purge basic level cadres and undoubtedly there was satisfaction that despotic local leaders had been brought to justice. Yet despite this the overall picture is of a rural population badly shaken and fearful as a result of the big Four Cleanups. The work teams consisted of outsiders towards whom fear was always a prominent attitude, while ties to local cadres often resulted in sympathy for their plight. Moreover, despite official assurances the possibility of future retribution by criticized local leaders could not be ruled out. Finally, ordinary peasants were often criticized by work teams for "spontaneous capitalism" or other problems. Although no broad class reclassification was actually undertaken, the provisions of the Revised Second Ten Points in this regard were sufficiently well known to cause rumors of a "new land reform" *(xin tugai)*. Thus as a result of Liu Shaoqi's policies the rural masses were mobilized, but at the same time controlled and highly traumatized.[109]

The "tense and frightening atmosphere" created in the countryside was even more severe for basic level cadres. Although ordinary cadres judged guilty of minor mistakes generally were only required to make self-criticisms and return misappropriated funds, even this group was subject to a harrowing time. Reports indicate anywhere from 60 percent to all cadres at Four Cleanups "points" were subjected to public criticism, criticism which often involved varying degrees of struggle. For those judged guilty of serious offenses the consequences were even harsher. In addition to Party and administrative disciplinary measures, criminal sanctions including forced labor and arrests were also invoked while Mao's comments of December 1964 suggest approval of capital punishment on a limited scale. But perhaps most unnerving was the intensity of struggle directed at major offenders. The constant hounding and public humiliation of repeated struggle sessions was traumatic by itself, and this sometimes degenerated into threats with firearms, corporal punishment and beatings. As in the case of the 1959–60 movement, the entire process was later denounced as "ruthless struggles and merciless blows." Some terrified cadres could not stand up to the pressure, and they sought to escape their predicament by fleeing or even suicide.[110]

Harsh methods were accompanied by a high purge rate in many instances. According to scattered Cultural Revolution sources, 40 to 70 percent of local cadres had been removed from their posts in certain keypoint areas.[111] These, however, were apparently areas of unusual intensity and the overall purge rate was undoubtedly much lower. The only comprehensive report found states that during the big Four Cleanups "over 23 percent of all basic level cadres in [Henan] province were under attack; some 10 percent were either dismissed, expelled from the Party, or similarly punished." While these figures most likely applied only to cadres actually participating in movement—probably no more than one fourth to one third of the total—they indicate a purge rate as high or higher than the 10 percent Party expulsions plus withdrawals in the early 1950s. But in contrast to the relatively persuasive atmosphere in which the earlier purge was conducted, now dismissals and expulsions were combined with highly coercive struggle and legal sanctions.[112]

Such coercive pressures together with peasant supervision of cadre behavior quite clearly resulted in a major demoralization of China's rural leaders. Although downplaying the gravity of the situation, reports in the official media plus refugee accounts indicate a widespread tendency for cadres to avoid active leadership and quit their posts. Due to their past shortcomings some cadres were scared of committing more mistakes. With existing cadres unwilling to lead and resigning their positions, the problem of finding new recruits for the rural leadership structure was also aggravated.[113] This deteriorating situation in the countryside was the result of an unavoidable dilemma. As suggested in Chapter 2 and demonstrated during the 1960–61 campaign, a relatively coercive approach is necessary for dealing with serious deviant behavior but where that behavior is extensive such an approach results in counterproductive side effects. Clearly corruption and other serious problems were widespread in rural China in the post-Great Leap years and a root and branch purge was required to attack such phenomena with any hope of success. Yet the consequences of such a purge threatened severe damage to the system's capacity to secure its minimum requirements from the peasant population. As this dilemma became manifestly apparent CCP leaders were faced with critical decisions concerning the future course of socialist education.

The impact of the big Four Cleanups was not limited to the basic levels. In October 1964 Liu Shaoqi commented that "*xian* committees cannot lead the movement" and in some cases should be overthrown, thus suggesting the vulnerability of county leaders.[114] Cultural Revolution sources also indicate that some provincial leaders and top Party figures in the educational sphere were affected. In some cases, furthermore, conflict apparently developed between Politburo members over the conduct of the movement.

Major problems arose concerning the top leaders of Guizhou province. Both Mao and Liu indicated displeasure with Guizhou, Liu citing it as a province incapable of leading the Four Cleanups while Mao listed it as one of several places with "rotten" provincial committees.[115] During the big Four Cleanups in Guizhou, socialist education was not only intensified in basic level rural and urban units but a "fierce struggle" developed in bureaucratic offices of the county level and above. In this struggle First Secretary Zhou Lin and several other provincial leaders came under attack, apparently for insufficient enthusiasm for the new harsh approach to the movement. In this context the Southwest Party Bureau sent a work team headed by Sichuan Governor Li Dazhang to bypass the provincial committee and take direct control of the Four Cleanups. Under the work team's leadership, severe measures were taken against a large number of cadres. Finally, in early 1965 the Party leadership of the province was severely shaken up. Zhou Lin was removed as first secretary while Li Dazhang temporarily became acting first secretary until another leader was transferred into Guizhou to assume the position on a permanent basis. Other leaders were also removed, while at least another three high ranking figures were transferred from Beijing and other areas to become Party secretaries. Thus differences over the campaign had major personnel consequences at the provincial level.[116]

Two disputes in the nation's capital involved even more powerful actors—Peng Zhen and Liu Shaoqi. The first concerned Beijing University. In fall 1964 the approach which Liu Shaoqi had advocated for rural China was also applied to leading educational institutions. A work team apparently under the control of the Central Committee propaganda department arrived at Beida in October and immediately began harsh criticism of the existing situation. Following the model of the big Four Cleanups in the countryside, the work team "kicked aside" the Party committee and undertook vigorous efforts to find shortcomings. Meetings were held where students and teachers attacked the top officials of the university including Party Secretary Lu Ping, a man with close ties to Peng Zhen. Central Committee propaganda chief Lu Dingyi reportedly criticized Beida for having conducted the Four Cleanups incorrectly in the past while Lu Ping sought protection from Peng's municipal committee. Thus a situation arose which would hold particular ironies once the Cultural Revolution broke out. Radical students and teachers who would turn against Liu Shaoqi's work teams in 1966, including many of the same individuals, joined forces in late 1964 with a work team seemingly responsive to Liu's policies to attack university officials linked to Peng Zhen. Peng apparently was unable to act at the time, but as we shall see once Mao's position changed at the end of 1964 he was able to turn the tables on the "Liuist" work team at Beida.[117]

The second incident in Beijing during late 1964 concerned the conduct of the Four Cleanups in suburban Tong county. Here work teams dispatched by central authorities conducted the movement under the guidelines laid down by the Revised Second Ten Points with the result that they came into direct conflict with municipal leaders. Very large work teams of some 20,000 cadres in all were sent to the county where they conducted a deep purge removing 40 to 50 percent, and in some cases 60 percent, of existing personnel. Peng Zhen, reflecting the views he had advocated earlier in the movement, opposed this development. He allegedly formulated a policy to resist the work teams: "First, we should not welcome them; second, we should not cooperate with them; third, we must find faults with them; fourth, we must discredit them; and fifth, we must drive them out." Peng and other leaders of the municipal committee set out to blunt the movement by interfering in the implementation of the movement and writing critical reports. In one instance Peng assertedly wrote to Liu Shaoqi protesting the activities of the work teams and Chen Boda who was playing a leadership role with them. In another case Beijing Second Secretary Liu Ren came into conflict with Qi Benyu, another work team leader as well as literary collaborator with Jiang Qing and future Cultural Revolution activist who criticized Liu Ren's efforts to moderate the campaign. Again, the irony was that Liu Shaoqi's future enemies were at this point carrying out his radical organizational line. According to Liu, these differences led to tension between himself and Peng Zhen who "was not happy when I tried to interfere" in Beijing. While such tension should not be exaggerated in retrospect, it seems clear that two of China's most powerful leaders stood on opposing sides as the excesses of the big Four Cleanups presented the Politburo with crucial choices at the end of 1964.[118]

Leadership Conflict and a New Decision: The Twenty-three Articles

China's top leaders debated the critical rural situation in key meetings held in December 1964 and January 1965. The First Session of the Third NPC, a Supreme State Conference, and one or several central work conferences all had socialist education high on their agendas. The result of these discussions was a new directive drafted under Mao's personal direction, the Twenty-three Articles. A vague and confusing document, the Twenty-three Articles nevertheless was an effort to reorient the movement in a major way. The document, together with very incomplete excerpts from the proceedings, indicates Mao's repudication of many of the policies evolved by Liu Shaoqi since the previous summer. It is by no means clear precisely how far-reaching a repudication was intended at the time, although Mao later claimed the incident raised serious doubts in his mind concerning Liu. But it is clear that Mao both dealt Liu a significant political rebuff and changed the basic orientation of the movement.

Why did Mao suddenly reject Liu's approach? After all, the Revised Second Ten Points reflected an effort—apparently undertaken under Mao's orders—to cope with problems deeply distressing the Chairman. Moreover, there is no indication of Mao's dissent at the time the harsh approach was formulated; indeed, it was consistent with his expressed views. Thus the Chairman apparently made an abrupt about-face at the end of 1964. Undoubtedly the major reason was the need to come to terms with the objective crisis of rural leadership —a crisis which threatened to intensify if existing policies remained in force. We shall return to Mao's response to this situation shortly. In addition, however, another largely fortuitous element appears to have contributed to Mao's decision. This was the case of the Dazhai production brigade.

As indicated earlier, Mao did not play an active role in economic policy after 1962. He urged attention to some problems, occasionally vetoed specific proposals, but overall left the job of getting the economy back on the rails to others. But if there was one theme concerning economic development close to Mao's heart it was self-reliance—the need for the state and individual economic units to rely on their own efforts rather than external sources of support. In 1963–64, Dazhai brigade of Shanxi's Xiyang county became a nationally publicized model of agricultural self-reliance based on reported achievements in increasing output without state aid. These reports apparently came to Mao's attention and in early 1964 he began to praise Dazhai and brigade Secretary Chen Yonggui.[119]

During the big Four Cleanups, however, higher level work teams were suspicious not only of cadre corruption but also of false claims by basic level units. "Fake models" were uncovered in various parts of China as we have already seen in the case of Shengshi brigade to the embarrassment of Tao Zhu. This was also a concern to provincial authorities in Shanxi where Liu Shaoqi had declared almost all basic level units were "in the hands of the enemy." These authorities dispatched a large work team to Xiyang where it was broken up into smaller teams and sent to the county's communes and brigades. The team sent to Dazhai in late October included personnel selected by the Xiyang leaders who had made Chen Yonggui a model for emulation in 1963. Although apparently at first seeking to cooperate with the brigade cadres, the work team's relations with local leaders soon deteriorated and methods associated with Liu Shaoqi were adopted. The work team suspended the brigade's leadership, "struck roots" with selected informants, and launched a bitter attack upon the cadres. It reportedly claimed the brigade had falsified its achievements by underestimating its land and overestimating grain output. In fact, the team claimed, peasants in the model brigade didn't eat well, and Dazhai was reclassified from an "advanced" brigade to one with "serious problems." Whether or not deliberate fabrication was involved, the conflict called into question a highly publicized model of self-reliance.[120]

While his reputation was under attack at home, Chen Yonggui, who had been selected an NPC representative shortly before the work team arrived in Dazhai, went to Beijing in mid-December to take his place at the Congress. Shortly thereafter Chen was granted a private audience with Mao and used the opportunity to tell his side of the Dazhai story. Mao immediately initiated a series of events indicating his full support of Chen. Chen was appointed to the NPC Presidium; Zhou Enlai praised Dazhai as a shining example of self-reliance; Chen addressed the NPC on the "magic wand" of self-reliance; and *Renmin ribao* referred to the by now familiar theme, "In agriculture learn from Dazhai," as Chairman Mao's "most recent instruction." Moreover, following the Congress the work team hastily withdrew from the brigade to be replaced by another work team dispatched by the Center and guided by the Twenty-three Articles. This team vindicated all Dazhai's claims, and with it the legitimacy of the self-reliance model.[121]

Thus what had apparently begun as an attempt by local authorities to uncover wrongdoing at the basic levels had, at least in Mao's eyes, become an attack on a cherished developmental principle. Without checking into the facts of the matter, the Chairman had moved to uphold Dazhai as a symbol of self-reliance and at the same time undercut the position of the work team. This action, moreover, implicitly raised questions about the validity of Liu Shaoqi's approach to socialist education. In a situation where that approach was increasingly questionable in any case, the Dazhai case undoubtedly was a powerful stimulus affecting Mao's change of posture on rural rectification.

While Dazhai may have been the catalyst to action, the deteriorating morale of rural cadres generally was surely the basic force acting on Mao. This is strongly suggested in Cultural Revolution attacks on the leftist nature of Liu's policies which resulted in "hitting the many" cadres. In the Twenty-three Articles and excerpts of Mao's talks at the turn of the year the problem of cadre morale was treated less directly, but it was clearly a matter of critical concern. This was apparent in Mao's December observation that he was "a bit to the right" on the question of labeling people, fearing a "tide to the 'left' " would be harmful to peasants as well as cadres. Various efforts were made to narrow the scope of attack. In January Mao pointedly declared "The Four Cleanups means . . . cleaning up *a few people*." The Twenty-three Articles demanded that clear distinctions be drawn between the vast majority of cadres who could be rectified and the few who must be dealt with severely. Under the traditional policy of "curing the illness to save the patient," the large number of cadres guilty of minor corruption were to be quickly "liberated" so as to swell the ranks of the good and relatively good cadres, and intensified education was preferred to dismissals. Other measures also emphasized leniency. In contrast to Liu's policies, full restitution of graft was no longer demanded. And where Party members fell below the standard of membership, they were to be "exhorted to leave the Party" rather than summarily purged. All of this, in the words of the Twenty-three Articles, added up to a "serious, positive and affectionate" cadre policy in sharp relief to the gloomy and harsh view of the Revised Second Ten Points.[122]

Although the new orientation was towards leniency, Mao's position on this matter was not without ambiguity. The Twenty-three Articles not only called for struggle, dismissals and purges of individuals, forced labor and criminal sanctions, and the disbanding of corrupt organizations in extreme cases, they also declared good and relatively good cadres were in the majority "under general conditions"—thus implying a significant number of cases where the harsh approach was justified. The most significant indications of ambivalence came in Mao's comments in late December. While advocating that full restitution of graft no longer be required, Mao nevertheless ordered that this policy change not be announced to basic level cadres, thus leaving their anxieties on this score unabated. Similarly, although warning against excessive killing, the Chairman declared "It is impossible for us not to kill. . . . [We must] kill a few to shock [the people]."[123] Indeed, at this juncture Mao apparently envisaged the continuation of a fairly intense movement:

> Now what I fear is the pouring of cold water [on the movement]. It is still in the anti-rightist stage. Not counting December, during January, February and March next year . . . we must [continue] work. . . . The first thing is that the area to hit at must not be too wide, and secondly don't pour cold water.[124]

Thus Mao alluded to the same two issues raised by Liu's "high standards" for socialist education: the need to push the campaign forward *and* to avoid excesses. Only now the order of mention was reversed with restricting the area of attack getting pride of place. Nevertheless, Mao's continued concern with rightism suggests that his rejection of Liu's line—and his own former views—was subject to some reservations at least initially. By the time of the Twenty-three Articles, however, the Chairman appears to have moved further towards a policy of leniency. As Liu put it subsequently, the January document limited the target of the movement to a handful of bad people.[125]

Much of Mao's criticism concerned work team methods, but it was criticism which often seemed picayune, contrived or unfair. For example, the Chairman complained of "scholasticism" and excessive study of documents, and instead advocated study limited to a day and discussion to a week before work teams were dispatched. He also queried the emphasis of the Revised Second Ten Points on the purity of work team members, arguing that including people who themselves were corrupt would provide needed expertise as well as giving the individuals in question a chance to reform. More significantly, Mao attacked the practice of "striking roots." This method, the Chairman argued, gave the movement an unnatural "quiet and mysterious" aspect and could not uncover true activists. Such activists could only emerge in open, public struggle. Thus Mao rejected the tactics adopted by Wang Guangmei in Taoyuan and instead proposed that work teams convene mass meetings and clearly announce the aims of the campaign as soon as they entered a village. But the Taoyuan experience notwithstanding, this *already* appears to have been the general practice adopted during the big Four Cleanups. In any case, the Twenty-three Articles continued to endorse "squatting at points," although it now placed renewed emphasis on Mao's established investigation techniques as well. Finally, Mao sharply attacked "human sea tactics"—the practice of sending extremely large work teams to the countryside. Not only were smaller work teams purportedly more efficient in extending the movement over a wider area, but more importantly they would mean greater scope to local leaders in the management of the movement. The new emphasis on cooperation with local cadres, a step back toward the guidelines of the Second Ten Points, was reflected in the Twenty-three Articles' stipulation that a "three way alliance" *(san jiehe)* be established among masses, cadres and work teams.[126]

Underlying the attacks on "striking roots" and "human sea tactics" was an attitude that mass mobilization had been stifled by such practices, that excessive work team dominance had prevented a true mobilization of the masses from below. Thus "striking roots," Mao asserted, was "too placid" and lacked any mass movement. The large work teams were obstructionist and inhibited the necessary "free hand" for the peasants. Mao bitterly complained that despite repeated calls for democracy no democracy existed in fact. Moreover, the Twenty-three Articles emphasized the significance of initiative from below by calling for "all power to the PLMPAs" where basic level organizations had atrophied and asserting that supervision of cadres by the masses was more important than supervision by higher levels.[127] Mao's emphasis on democratic mass mobilization from below, however, was essentially disingenuous or at least self-delusionary. It not only ignored the realities of the rural crisis but it also stood in contradiction to both the overall thrust and specific features of the Twenty-three Articles.

The contradictions of Mao's position were most strikingly illustrated by his own comments. In December Mao spoke in a vein reminiscent of Liu's remark that the mobilized masses were like "wild horses":

> XX: If the masses are fully mobilized they will be understanding and reasonable.
>
> Chairman: Sometimes this isn't so. Once the masses are aroused they become blind, and we have our own blindness too.[128]

In addition to conceding the dangers created by an aroused populace, Mao also acknowledge a fundamental problem obscured by the rhetoric of "boldly mobilizing the masses":

> Wang X raised the question of switching cadres from one county to another and from one commune to another. When there is a newcomer whose background is unknown, the masses will dare to speak out. With a new commune leader and new Party secretary, [the masses] will dare to talk about their predecessors. The movement can be developed very quickly. Why should it take so long?[129]

Here Mao tacitly admitted the lesson of the early failures of the Socialist Education Movement to get to the root of rural corruption: without a strong presence of outside authority peasants simply could not be moved to expose cadre shortcomings. This further suggested that a crucial role still had to be played by the work teams, something the Chairman explicitly conceded:

> Liu XX: The poor and lower middle peasants have plenty of ideas .... One is to mobilize the masses; the other is that after the masses have been mobilized to a certain degree, the work team should control the temperature, and be adept

> at observing the situation, deciding when to attack and when to retreat.
>
> [Chairman]: It is like in a strike: when to strike and when to resume work. The same is true in battle. You must decide whether to attack or retreat.[130]

Despite bows to supervision from below, the Twenty-three Articles also placed clear responsibility for both mobilizing the masses and keeping their activities under control squarely on the shoulders of the work team:

> In the movement [the work teams] must boldly unleash the masses; we must not be like women with bound feet. . . . At the same time, we must make a deep and fine penetration, and must not make a big fuss over nothing. We must set the facts in order, explain principles, eliminate simple, crude work methods, severely prohibit beating people and other forms of physical punishment, and prevent forced confessions.[131]

In actual fact, as was borne out by subsequent developments, the emphasis of the Twenty-three Articles on a lenient cadre policy necessarily meant a slackening of mass mobilization as work teams were prohibited from whipping up peasant resentment against cadres. But Mao apparently was unwilling to accept fully the logic of the situation and explicitly acknowledge the defeat of the Four Cleanups. Instead he chose to cover the retreat with the rhetoric of continuing mass mobilization and supervision from below. The imperative of restoring rural stability was blurred by an attempt to maintain ideological consistency.

Ideological obfuscation was also manifested in theoretical reformulations of the nature of the movement. In a number of ways more orthodox concepts were introduced by the Twenty-three Articles. The Four Cleanups were now defined as referring to politics, economics, organization and ideology rather than specific forms of corruption. In what was a clear rebuff to Liu Shaoqi, the fundamental contradiction of the movement was defined as between socialism and capitalism, while Liu's "contradiction between the Four Cleans and Four Uncleans" and his "intertwining of contradictions between the enemy and us and contradictions within the people" was rejected as "not Marxist-Leninist methods of looking at things." Finally, a new concept was introduced to express the aim of the movement: "to rectify those people in positions of authority within the Party taking the capitalist road."[132] All of this ostensibly pointed to basic political issues as the aim of the movement, shifting its emphasis from corruption and other matters which might downplay class struggle. But Mao was no more able to give class struggle a precise policy content now than he had been earlier. Beneath the language of class contradictions the new guidelines grappled with the same questions as before.

The Twenty-three Articles, like all earlier socialist education directives, warned of acute class struggle and the danger of "peaceful evolution" restoring capitalism. Although citing the "consolidation and development of the socialist battlefront" as a key objective of the campaign, it was actually less specific than the earlier documents which had called for bolstering socialist ownership and restricting capitalist practices in the countryside. When elaborating on how class struggle is reflected within the Party, the Twenty-three Articles did not refer to questions of basic policy but instead pointed to "The leadership of certain communes, brigades, enterprises and units [which] has either been corrupted or usurped." That is to say, class struggle dealt with precisely the kind of basic level problems that had been the focus of Liu Shaoqi's hard line.[133]

Then what of the reference to "people in authority within the Party taking the capitalist road," the "powerholders" who were again denounced during the Cultural Revolution? According to the Twenty-three Articles:

> Of these people . . . some are out in the open and some remain concealed. Of the people who support them, some are at lower levels and some at higher levels. . . . Among those at higher levels, there are some people in the communes, districts, counties, special districts, and even in the work of provincial and Central Committee departments, who oppose socialism.[134]

This statement, which is reminiscent of the reference in the Revised Second Ten Points to higher level "protectors" and "instigators" of wayward cadres, indicates the movement was not to be limited to the lowest levels. Indeed, under Liu's direction the campaign had already affected higher ranking figures. Moreover, when discussing higher level "capitalist roaders" the Twenty-three Articles did not charge them with ideological or policy deviance. Instead, it attacked their degeneration, receipt of bribes, collusion, and violation of law and discipline. Moreover, low level cadres were still considered the most important target of socialist education. As Mao put it, "Power is held by the Four Unclean cadres. The poor and lower middle peasants won't be satisfied if you struggle against the landlords and rich peasants only. What is more urgent is what to do with the cadres." In this context the Chairman emphasized that the movement was primarily a Party rectification and the "powerholders" to be attacked most vigorously were leading local Party cadres—a priority which coincided with that of the big Four Cleanups. Moreover, the sins of such "powerholders" were also the problems Liu had identified: corruption and other forms of exploitative behavior which alienated the masses from the rural leadership structure. Although the Cultural Revolution gave the term "powerholder" a much more sweeping connotation, as of early 1965 it referred to those Party members guilty of shortcomings which had been attacked since the outset of the Socialist Education Movement.[135]

The inability to give new content to the aims of the campaign despite the theoretical reformulations was also seen in continuing deference to regular work. The Twenty-three Articles not only stressed the need to grasp production firmly, it also stated that socialist education in a county must rest solidly on construction in science, culture, education and other spheres. Moreover, in his report to the NPC, Zhou Enlai announced Mao's call "to build our country into a powerful socialist state with a modern agriculture, industry, national defense, and science and technology." Notwithstanding the ideological redefinition of the movement, Mao continued to give high priority to achievements on the production and development fronts. The contradiction between work and class struggle remained unresolved.[136]

Thus despite the crucial shift to a more moderate cadre policy, the Twenty-three Articles contained a certain amount of inherent ambiguity. Even though problems were declared "easy to discover [and] easy to resolve," the Socialist Education Movement was still—as it had been in the Revised Second Ten Points—viewed as a long term process requiring six or seven years to complete. While some work methods—e.g., "human sea tactics"—were rejected, the importance of sending work teams of higher level cadres to "squat at points" was reaffirmed with the added stipulation that leading personnel from regional Party bureaus would now participate. The new directive was to supersede all previous socialist education directives wherever conflict occurred, but the earlier documents were still to be "actively and resolutely" executed.[137] This indecisive blend of continuity with the past and subtle shifts of emphasis for the future, combined with the fact that the Twenty-three Articles were by far the most terse and obscure of all socialist education guidelines,[138] undoubtedly created considerable confusion among policy makers and lower level cadres alike. The comment subsequently attributed to Hubei's Wang Renzhong that "I have participated in the drafting of the Twenty-three Articles but I can't say I understand them" has an intrinsic credibility.[139]

Ambiguity concerning policy directions was matched by uncertainty over the leadership implications of the new line—particularly concerning the position of Liu Shaoqi. Beginning with the Cultural Revolution, a series of statements by Mao and others point to the late 1964-early 1965 debate over the Socialist Education Movement as a watershed in the relationship between the Chairman and his chosen heir. In 1966 Mao cited these events as providing his first *serious* doubts about Liu, while in 1970 the Chairman claimed it was at this juncture he decided "Liu had to go."[140] The available (incomplete) record of events, however, suggests that at least the latter statement is an exaggeration. How deep, in fact, was the rift in early 1965?

It does appear that Liu found himself out of step with Mao from the start of the discussions on socialist education. He reportedly came to the December meetings arguing the correctness of the Revised Second Ten Points and advocating their thorough implementation throughout the country. Moreover, Mao told Edgar Snow in 1970 that at the conclusion of the meetings in late January Liu "strenuously opposed" the theoretical reorientation of the campaign. Clearly Liu's position was under attack throughout December and January. Not only were various clauses of the Twenty-three Articles explicit rebukes to Liu, but he apparently came in for substantial criticism during the debate. But here Mao's attitude was tempered. Although many of his remarks attacked Liu's positions, the Chairman also objected to personal criticism of Liu. In an obvious reference to his heir, Mao declared in December: "There must be a Qinshihuang [to issue strict orders]. Who is China's Qinshihuang? It is XXX [and] I am his aide." In another apparent defense of Liu, the Chairman rebuked Li Xuefeng by declaring "I won't endorse your way of denigrating XXX." In any case, there were signs of Liu's continued prominence. In his report to the NPC Zhou Enlai called for the continuing implementation of educational reforms according to Liu's instructions. And the Congress concluded by reelecting Liu Chairman of the PRC.[141]

On balance, however, not only had Liu's position been significantly weakened but there were signs of a watershed having been reached in Mao's attitudes towards the leadership as a whole, however dimly perceived by the Chairman at the time. Notwithstanding his remarks in defense of Liu, Mao reportedly used the occasion to criticize both Liu and Deng Xiaoping for having set up "two independent kingdoms" at the Party Center. Subtle personnel shifts also suggested Mao's dissatisfaction with existing leadership arrangements. Not only was Peng Zhen—Liu's antagonist regarding socialist education policy—raised to the position of First Vice Chairman of the NPC Standing Committee, but Lin Biao was now named first vice premier despite his sporadic activity in recent years. Moreover, in his report to the NPC, Zhou attacked the "bourgeois and revisionist viewpoints" of those who advocated retreat in the economy, the international arena and united front work in 1962—issues on which Liu, Deng and many other leaders were vulnerable. At the same time Li Weihan and other officials of the Center's united front work department came under attack and were subsequently removed for their alleged errors during the crisis years. Thus despite Mao's continuing calls for inner Party democracy during the year end meetings, Party norms were again under stress as policy views—and past policy views at that—came under assault. Finally, another sign of tension with existing norms was Mao's January 1965 comment to Edgar Snow that there was no "worship of the individual" to speak of in China, but there was a need for it. Mao had not yet broken with Party traditions, nor had he provided a usable definition of "capitalist roaders," but there were ominous straws in the wind.[142]

Implementing the Twenty-three Articles

Following the January directive, the conduct of socialist education moved decisively towards moderation in order to arrest cadre demoralization.[q] Although

[q]Baum, *Prelude*, pp. 136–38, cites the war scare precipitated by the dramatic escalation of American air strikes over North Vietnam in February-March 1965 as a further reason for the shift in cadre policy. While this development conceivably intensified the new soft line, Mao was quite confident that the situation in Vietnam was under control when he formulated the new cadre policy in January. Edgar Snow, "Interview with Mao," in Franz Schurmann and Orville Schell, eds., *The China Reader: Communist China* (New York: Random House, 1967), pp. 360–61, 370–71.

there were signs of some dissent and confusion, an interpretation of the new directive as an "anti-leftist" document generally prevailed. Indeed, Wang Guangmei's view that under Liu's policies there had been "an overestimation of class struggle" was a sensible way of cutting through the obscurities of the Twenty-three Articles. The moderate interpretation was enforced by the recall of work teams in mid-January for intensive study of the latest directive before being again dispatched to the countryside. Moreover, at the leadership level control of the movement now passed from Liu Shaoqi to Peng Zhen. Despite Red Guard claims that Peng simply "grabbed" leadership of the Four Cleanups, in the circumstances it seems most likely he was entrusted with this authority by Mao on the basis of his earlier moderation.[143] But whether Peng carried out the Chairman's wishes in all respects once he was again in charge is a moot point since—at least in the available record[144]—Mao fell virtually silent on the question of socialist education. Once again Mao was leaving direction of the movement in the hands of a close colleague, but now apparently with even less ongoing scrutiny than had been the case in 1964.

Despite the predominance of the new line in practice, Cultural Revolution accounts suggest considerable differences over the change in policy. Various leaders allegedly defended Liu Shaoqi, the Taoyuan experience and the Revised Second Ten Points after the issuing of the Twenty-three Articles. For example, agricultural spokesman Tan Zhenlin reportedly argued that the 1964 document was more detailed than the new directive on the crucial question of mass mobilization. Also, Tao Zhu, who in little more than a year would be one of the prime beneficiaries of the disgrace of Liu and Deng, assertedly concluded that the Twenty-three Articles were not designed to correct deviations in the Revised Second Ten Points and that the previous period had seen great achievements. Indeed, Tao allegedly went so far as to say that while experiments based on the First Ten Points were unable to solve problems fundamentally, with Liu's intervention the Party's understanding of those problems had been raised dramatically. In other instances, regional and provincial leaders were accused of actually continuing to implement Liu's line including propagation of the Taoyuan experience, dispatching large work teams, and harsh attacks on large numbers of cadres.[145] While the implication of systematic opposition to the new cadre line is somewhat dubious,[r] it is likely that in some areas the "leftist wind" continued to blow for a short period after the issuing of the January document.

In addition, leaders who were not attempting to defend Liu or his policies spoke critically of the inadequacies of the Twenty-three Articles. Propaganda

[r] Some leaders—e.g., new Guizhou First Secretary Jia Qiyun—were charged with both easing the struggle against erring cadres *and* employing Taoyuan methods. Radio Guiyang, June 3, July 8, 1967, in *NFCPRS*, Nos. 210, 215. A possible explanation is that in exceptional cases, as stipulated in the Twenty-three Articles, harsh measures were still used.

chief Lu Dingyi allegedly attacked the policy guidelines as "incomplete, senseless and piecemeal." Peng Zhen spoke more moderately to the same effect. Peng commented on the rather haphazard way in which the document had evolved from 15 to 17 to 23 articles under Mao's stewardship, concluding that it still contained problems and whether it was completely correct would have to be tested in practice. Echoing the views of others, Peng further observed that it was quite proper for people to retain different opinions concerning matters raised by the Twenty-three Articles. Thus even the victors in the policy debate of late 1964-early 1965 felt Mao's latest directive gave only imperfect guidance for dealing with the delicate rural situation.[146]

In any case, Peng Zhen began shortly after the Twenty-three Articles to elaborate a set of policies reflecting the comprehensiveness and consistency that Mao's document lacked. In the spirit of correcting a left deviation, Peng squarely faced the problem of past socialist education excesses. Peng complained that "disorderly struggle" *(luandou)* had appeared widely in schools, factories and villages with the result that "fear had been struck in the hearts of everyone and too many good men had been harmed." Excesses, he declared, had taken a number of forms including repeated large scale struggle meetings, high purge rates, and physical beatings. To reassure the demoralized cadres, Peng called for a cessation of such practices in favor of a "gentle breeze and mild rain" approach using small scale discussion meetings. He further urged persuasive methods when dealing with "corrupt cliques," avoidance of the "powerholder" label when dealing with cadres, restricting class struggle to the conflict of social systems and excluding it from cases of individual discipline, stopping the elimination of cadres' supplementary work points, and—in accord with the Twenty-three Articles—a lenient policy on the restitution of graft. Moreover, in addition to attacking as "impermissible" deep purges such as had been imposed over his objections in Tong county, Peng called for a "reversal of verdicts" on those who had been "wrongly struggled" during the previous phase of the movement.[147]

Peng's basic approach to improving cadre morale apparently gained general acceptance. Not only have Cultural Revolution reports accused key central and local leaders of turning the movement into a quiet affair, but refugee and contemporary official sources indicate a marked drop in the intensity of socialist education. Although the official media carried attacks on corruption up to the promulgation of the Twenty-three articles, it subsequently fell largely silent on this subject. This is not to say that the press and radio no longer gave attention to cadre shortcomings or the need for peasant supervision. Indeed, exhortations to "mobilize boldly the masses" and for peasants to become "masters of their own house" continued to be heard. But the tone and emphasis had changed to one of solicitude for hard pressed cadres. Concern was shown over the fact that many cadres feared to perform their leadership functions, and peasants were reminded of both the achievements as well as shortcomings of cadres and their own need for self-criticism. The emphasis was strongly on the need for unity among cadres and masses, with peasants urged to give active support to cadres in addition to necessary supervision. Moreover, following Peng Zhen's lead, considerable attention was given to assuring cadres they would receive the subsidized work points they were entitled. In late 1964 attacks on work point corruption had apparently resulted in the cancellation of legitimate allowances as well as excessive work points, but now *Renmin ribao* told commune members that "cadres should be adequately subsidized."[148]

Still another aspect of the effort to restore cadre morale was an adjustment of relations between local cadres and work teams. Peng Zhen attacked work teams for raising even small cadre mistakes "to the level of principle" and for kicking aside local leaders when carrying out the Four Cleanups. Peng argued that socialist education was bound to fail if cadres were pushed aside since they had ties with the peasants and understanding of local conditions; without the benefit of their knowledge work team efforts to "strike roots" would be futile. Now Peng ordered the work teams—which had been bolstered by a substantial influx of PLA personnel[*]—to pay careful attention to establishing good relations with both local cadres and masses, and even with ex-cadres who had been dismissed during the movement.[149] Under the slogan of "three way alliances" among masses, cadres and work teams, the role of the higher level teams was diluted in an effort to restore the authority of the local leadership structure.

In addition to having the major voice in reshaping cadre policy, Peng Zhen was also a dominant figure in settling several major conflicts still festering from late 1964. With regard to developments in Beijing's Tong county, Peng "drove out" the central work teams which had been implementing Liu's policies and then carried out a large scale "reversal of verdicts." In Guizhou, where he had not been personally involved in the events of late 1964, Peng now played an important role behind the scenes. Regional leader Li Jingquan reportedly consulted Peng closely by phone when deciding how to handle the Guizhou situation. The approach adopted was to organize a "wind of reversing verdicts" after Li Dazhang's work team admitted its excesses. Now Li Jingquan and new Guizhou First Secretary Jia Qiyun assertedly reevaluated conditions in the province and concluded that any shortcomings were not serious. The main problem was to deal with the "mess" created by the big Four Cleanups by establishing unity in leadership offices between cadres sent in from the outside and those originally stationed in Guizhou, and between Four Cleanups activists and those who had suffered criticism. At the very top level the campaign was defused by

---

[*]According to refugee reports, army personnel serving on Four Cleanups work teams rose noticeably in spring 1965. Baum, *Prelude*, p. 138. This may have reflected Mao's dissatisfaction with the performance of earlier work teams and Lin Biao's pledge to implement the Twenty-three Articles—a document which called on communes and brigades to learn from the PLA. However, there is no indication in the available evidence that PLA members of work teams performed any differently than their civilian counterparts during the period of Peng Zhen's leadership in 1965.

narrowing the scope of attack and treating those who had been criticized with great leniency. Thus it was declared that "the problem of Guizhou is the problem of [former First Secretary] Zhou Lin," while other secretaries who had been bitterly denounced by the "masses" were appointed to secretarial posts in the newly organized provincial Party committee. As for Zhou Lin his "punishment" was to be kicked upstairs; Zhou was quietly made a secretary of the CCP's Southwest Bureau.[150]

But the most dramatic victory for Peng Zhen concerned Beijing University. While the Twenty-three Articles were designed primarily for rural areas, it explicitly extended to the cities. Peng now used the new directive as a basis for remedial action in universities where disorderly struggle had taken place—most notably Beida. He charged that the work team had taken an excessively negative attitude and denied that anything was done properly at Beida. In fact, Lu Ping was a good man despite "some mistakes" and it was necessary to affirm that Beida was a "Communist led university." In this case Peng was assisted by Deng Xiaoping, one of the few known instances of Deng taking an active role in the Socialist Education Movement. Deng reportedly argued that in assessing Lu Ping it was necessary to make an historical analysis which took into account his revolutionary activities and his past good work at the university. Instead of doing this, he charged the work team committed the three errors of misunderstanding the nature of Beida's problems, failing to create a "three way alliance," and serious excesses in struggle methods. Essentially, Deng argued the work team neglected principle and treated the struggle as one of personal gains and losses, as one of insult and opposition between contending factions.[151]

Once the Twenty-three Articles were issued, in January and February Peng convened an enlarged conference of the Beijing Municipal Committee where the work team came under harsh attack. The team, however, assertedly refused to concede its mistakes and continued to press its critical view of the Beida leadership. In March Deng intervened and convened a conference of the central secretariat. Demanding an immediate "three way alliance" of work team, university leaders, and students and teachers, this conference purged the work team of its recalcitrant leaders and restored Lu Ping and his associates to their leading posts at the university. The episode concluded with Lu Ping, in conjunction with the municipal Party committee, organizing a rectification session for Party members who had been critical of his leadership. This session lasted for seven months from July 1965 to January 1966 at a downtown Beijing hotel but assertedly was indecisive as most of those attacked stood firm. In yet another ironic aspect of this affair, these Party members would be among the leaders of opposition to both Lu Ping and "Liuist" work teams at the start of the Cultural Revolution.[152]

Apart from the conduct of socialist education itself, new moderate policies emerged in 1965 on a number of social and economic questions affected by the hard line of 1964. Peng Zhen and others called for a relaxation of policy toward suspect groups such as reformed landlords, the children of landlords, old bourgeois professors, and "democratic personages." In addition, steps were taken to curb egalitarian distribution in the countryside. The excesses of 1964 had apparently led both to attacks on questionable groups and excessive egalitarianism. The Twenty-three Articles had made only the vaguest reference to these problems, but now under Peng Zhen an attempt was made to come to grips with them more systematically.[153]

Of all the areas requiring clarification following the Twenty-three Articles, the proper relationship of the rural private and collective sectors was most vexing. Peng Zhen's Second Ten Points had dealt with those questions in detail and elaborated a relatively liberal line. Liu Shaoqi's Revised Second Ten Points had not altered those guidelines, but the general thrust of that document embodied a dim view of "spontaneous capitalist" activities. The intense attacks of the big Four Cleanups spilled over from the cadres to the masses, apparently with a severe effect on peasant incentives. But the Twenty-three Articles did not tackle this question, speaking only in general terms of the need to "consolidate and develop progressively the socialist battlefront" and to "grasp production." In the resulting confusion great numbers of letters began to pour into newspapers and magazines from readers in all parts of the country requesting guidance concerning "spontaneous capitalist tendencies." One of the topics most frequently raised was the question of differentiating between legitimate sideline occupations and those which were capitalist leaning. The official response to such questions indicated that many work teams and cadres, assuming that all private economic activity was by nature capitalist, had decided that the scope of domestic sideline occupations should be drastically reduced. This view was now denounced as "metaphysical"; those officials who had acted to restrict severely sideline occupations were criticized for "lacking any real understanding or concern for the pressing needs of the masses of peasants in their daily life." Thus while the "potentially ruinous" aspects of individual economic activities were not ignored, the net effect was to emphasize their "progressive economic function." The need to soften economic policy was another consequence of Liu's " 'left' in form but right in essence" policies.[154]

In the broadest sense, the policy revamping accomplished under Peng Zhen's leadership converted the Socialist Education Movement from an intense struggle focused on rural leadership to a mild educational campaign subordinate to the goals of production and construction. Peng argued that the work of the Four Cleanups must be manifested in production results or it would be "empty talk." "If we only give attention to class struggle and don't grasp production or scientific experiment," he continued, ". . . then our consciousness is low." Similar sentiments were attributed to other leaders who used the Four Cleanups to deal with such problems as management and planning reforms, staff retrenchment, and food and clothing shortages. Perhaps the most grandiose example of this tendency was Guangdong First Secretary Zhao Ziyang's proposal for "building the comparatively poor countryside into an affluent socialist new countryside."

Arguing that the Four Cleanups must be based on construction, Zhao aimed for high agricultural yields and increased income for commune members based on the "four changes"—mechanization, electrification, an expanded chemical industry, and a network of water conservancy works.[155] While Zhao could have cited the Twenty-three Articles[156] and Mao's "four modernizations" to support his scheme, the heavy emphasis on production and economic advancement in the evolving policies of 1965 seem at increasing variance with the Chairman's broodings over social inequality, bureaucratic insensitivity, and a still poorly defined revisionism.

In fact, Mao Zedong's views are particularly obscure for most of 1965. According to the available record, he spoke infrequently and tersely in this period.[157] While he commented bitingly on such questions as public health and education, Mao only offered sweeping suggestions which tended to be far from practicable. More generally, the Chairman brooded about the future. In an August 1965 conversation with Andre Malraux, Mao returned to a theme he raised with Edgar Snow at the time of the Twenty-three Articles: China had two possible futures, a Marxist-Leninist one and a revisionist one, and the outcome was in doubt. Having decisively intervened in the Socialist Education Movement at the turn of the year, Mao did not demonstrate close continuing interest in the progress of the campaign. The ambiguities of the Twenty-three Articles were left to others to resolve. Without the Chairman exercising a firm hand,[t] and despite the continuing prominence of "Maoist" slogans, socialist education inexorably became subordinate to other concerns. This may have reflected conscious or unconscious distortion of aspects of the Twenty-three Articles, confusion over their meaning, or simply practical constraints inhibiting efforts to deal with the political and ideological problems Mao had identified in recent years. Most likely it reflected all three. But most important was Mao's simmering dissatisfaction as he waited "alone with the masses." When he asked his Politburo colleagues in September 1965 what they would do "if revisionism appears in the Party Center," it is unlikely that the Chairman himself had any clearly worked out answers. Yet by raising the question he signaled tumultuous times ahead.[158]

Rectification and the Cultural Front, 1963–65

As the Socialist Education Movement unfolded in both rural and urban areas, developments in high level cultural and academic circles were only loosely tied

---

[t]Baum, *Prelude*, p. 139, argues that this represented a decline in Mao's personal influence. In our view, the events of late 1964-early 1965 convincingly demonstrated Mao's continuing political clout. This interpretation attributes his subsequent lack of leadership to infirm health and uncertainty over the proper response to what he increasingly viewed as fundamental problems of political orientation.

to the movement.[u] Nevertheless, important debates and campaigns took place in this sphere in the 1963–65 period which reflected the themes of socialist education. The significance of these developments can hardly be overestimated since a literary matter—the *Hai Rui* drama—was the immediate issue provoking the Cultural Revolution.

Following the Tenth Plenum a substantial degree of orthodoxy was restored in cultural circles with the termination of satirical writings which had been tolerated during the crisis years. By 1963 this was reinforced by a marked increase in revolutionary themes in various academic and creative fields. In this context debates occurred on history, aesthetics, ethics and other academic subjects in which the need for class analysis and revolutionary struggle was strongly asserted. Among the targets of criticism were Wu Han's views on the inheritability of aspects of feudal morality, the proposition that the Taiping leader Li Xiucheng who had confessed after his capture was actually a hero who deceived his captors, and the scholar Zhou Gucheng's idea that a "spirit of the times" existed in any era which encompassed all conflicting tendencies of the period. In the same period efforts were begun to reform or "revolutionize" various art forms, a process which had the most notable results with a national conference on Beijing opera in mid-1964. Moreover, from mid-1964 the criticisms of various views escalated into full fledged campaigns which also extended to new, high ranking targets. These included Yang Xianzhen, a Central Committee member and former head of the Higher Party School who was denounced for emphasizing "two combine into one" as a basic philosophic concept, Feng Ding, a leading Party philosopher who was attacked for advocating the gratification of human desires, and Shao Quanlin, a literary theorist and assistant of Zhou Yang who was sharply criticized for promoting "middle characters" who were neither heroes nor villains in creative works.[159]

The debates and attacks in these and other cases were often abstruse, but a number of themes constantly reappeared. All of the views under criticism were alleged to negate class struggle and promote shameless compromise with feudal and bourgeois ideologies. They assertedly undermined revolutionary vigilance, diluting people's perception of the need to struggle against capitalist restoration by focusing on trivial topics such as romantic love rather than stimulating class anger, or by depicting weak melancholy characters, rather than fiercely struggling peasants on stage. All of this explicitly took place in the context of sharpening struggle with the Soviet Union; the need to refute insidious peaceful

[u] Although the Five Anti movement extended to various cultural units in 1963, in early 1964 Party leaders still spoke of "the question of whether socialist education should be introduced into cultural circles." *Hongse xuanchuanbing* [Red Propaganda Soldier] (Beijing), May 19, 1967, in *SCMP-S*, No. 205. While there was a marked increase of socialist education themes in these circles in 1964, developments generally did not closely parallel shifts in the Four Cleanups even though the moderation of spring 1965 was apparently used to justify a similar relaxation in cultural and academic spheres (see below).

change assertedly promoted by Moscow was a repeated theme. Thus Yang Xianzhen's "two combine into one" doctrine was opposed by "one divides into two," a theory emphasizing the need for uncompromising sharp struggle with "modern revisionists."[160]

At the time, analysts generally interpreted these developments as a serious effort to curb revisionist ideological tendencies and reaffirm the Maoist version of Marxist-Leninist orthodoxy. The Cultural Revolution, however, produced a different version of this period which has been reflected in much scholarly writing. According to this interpretation, the cultural bureaucracy in these years distorted Mao's efforts to inject greater class struggle into the academic and literary spheres. Zhou Yang and associates, as well as higher ranking Party leaders, were charged with limiting criticism, protecting individuals, and converting the campaigns of 1964 into a "sham rectification." Undoubtedly there was resistance to the intensifying criticism of this period, but as in other cases culpability is difficult to specify.

Several considerations argue against accepting such a starkly drawn view. First, the position of Mao again was ambiguous. Although clearly concerned with dangerous ideological trends, Mao's actual statements on these matters are difficult to come by; much of the argument relies on the Chairman's brief biting criticisms of the cultural bureaucracy in December 1963 and June 1964. But these statements leave the question of methods of redress open, and it is essentially on this matter that Cultural Revolution charges focus. Second, the accusations against the cultural authorities are made with a single brush allowing no distinction between different sections of the cultural world despite Yao Wenyuan's admission that there was "bickering and friction among those people."[161] The existence of resistance—by some officials as well as many creative artists and scholars—does not prove the complicity of particular individuals or the cultural bureaucracy as a whole. Indeed, this analysis argues, the actions taken were not inconsistent with the known views of Mao. Moreover, the very real restraints which were placed on rectification in this sphere reflected, although they did not fully honor, traditional Party norms.

Developments in cultural affairs are closely related to the emergence of Jiang Qing as a political force in the early 1960s. About 1960–61 she began to gather young teachers and students from Beijing University such as Qi Benyu for the purpose of writing radical literary criticism. By 1962–63, according to her own account, she was calling Mao's attention to particular literary issues and winning his support on some points. And by 1964 she was active in efforts to reform Beijing opera and other art forms. Initially her activities seem confined to promoting political and ideological purity in the arts. Despite substantial friction with various Party leaders there is no indication she was attacking their authority. As she subsequently admitted, she only became aware of problems in literature and art gradually and at first attempted to work through the existing authorities. Only after repeated dealings with high ranking officials did Jiang begin to suspect that they might be at fault. As she put it with regard to one of the CCP's top leaders, "I understood Deng Xiaoping only in 1964. At that time I felt our Party was in danger."[162]

Jiang's increasing prominence must be analyzed in terms of her relationship with both the cultural hierarchy and with Mao. It seems that except for Shanghai[v] existing authorities viewed her with a mixture of wariness and hostility. Jiang's personal relations with Zhou Yang had been conflict ridden since the 1930s before she met Mao, and friction continued from Yan'an days on. Zhou's attitude was indicated by his purported comment in 1950, when Jiang was also active in cultural circles, that "work becomes difficult" when Jiang Qing is present. Apart from her difficult personality, Jiang apparently caused resentment because she held no official positions and was trading on her personal link to Mao to force her way into the affairs of the leadership. Indeed, Jiang's first official post in the 1960s was the purely symbolic one of NPC deputy in late 1964, while seemingly it was only in early 1966 that she gained an official role in cultural matters when Lin Biao appointed her an adviser for PLA literary and art work. But despite her lack of an official role before 1966, Jiang was able to demand and get a voice in the ongoing process of artistic reform, but only at the cost of considerable resentment by those who regarded her as an interloper. This was clearly reflected in Peng Zhen's reported outburst over Jiang's model operas: "What kind of models are these? As head of the Central Committee's group of five [set up to oversee the reform process] I have no knowledge of them at all!"[163]

If the mutual hostility between Jiang and the cultural hierarchy is fairly clear, her relationship to Mao is more problematic. By her own account, in the early 1950s her involvement in public affairs was frequently accomplished over the Chairman's strong objections. In the 1960s, while Jiang clearly had access to Mao—although not necessarily at all times—and while he evidently supported her on specific issues such as the content of individual plays, her views by no means automatically expressed the position of the Chairman nor were they necessarily seen to by other interested parties. The situation was undoubtedly tricky for those opposing Jiang. Officials recognized her influence on the Chairman as indicated by Zhou Yang's remark that Mao's criticism of the cultural bureaucracy "must be the result of something Jiang Qing said to the Chairman." But

[v] According to Jiang's own version, Shanghai First Secretary Ke Qingshi supported her efforts while propaganda officials Zhang Chunqiao and Yao Wenyuan actively collaborated with her. Roxane Witke, *Comrade Chiang Ch'ing* (Boston: Little, Brown and Co., 1977), pp. 196, 313. Cultural Revolution sources, however, suggest the actual situation in Shanghai was more complicated. Whatever support she received from Ke *et al.*, "reactionary" plays continued to appear in Shanghai and resistance to reforms allegedly appeared in the Shanghai propaganda apparatus. *Jinggangshan* [Jinggang Mountains] (Beijing), May 25, 1967, in *SCMP*, No. 3996; and NCNA, Beijing, May 31, 1967, in *SCMP*, No. 3952.

while hers was an influence to be feared, it was also an influence to be countered by appeals to Mao himself.[164]

The nature of the conflicts between Jiang and the cultural hierarchy must also be taken into consideration: were those fundamental differences of policy as asserted by Cultural Revolution sources? The best documented case, the reform of Beijing opera, casts doubt on this assertion. A comparison of Jiang Qing's talk to the 1964 opera festival, and of an earlier speech by her purported protector, Shanghai's Ke Qingshi, with the speeches of Peng Zhen and Lu Dingyi at the festival reveals remarkable consistency on major policy questions. Peng and Lu, as well as Jiang and Ke, emphasized the need to prevent peaceful evolution in the creative arts, the existence of conscious opposition to the reforms, and the need for creative artists to "go deep into the midst of the masses." Jiang and Ke, for their part, echoed the bureaucracy's view that some traditional plays could still be put on, that the fundamental artistic character of Beijing opera must be maintained, and crude stereotyped productions were to be opposed. In contrast to this far-reaching agreement on basic policy, Cultural Revolution accounts of Jiang's clashes with Zhou Yang *et al.*, despite being presented in terms of ideological conflict, nevertheless indicate much more petty sources of friction. Such questions as the degree of financial and organizational support given Jiang's ventures, the question of Jiang's organizational authority, and the credit for new revolutionary operas repeatedly appear in these accounts. Granted that such disputes might in some instances have represented conscious resistance to Jiang's "revolutionary" innovations, such resistance may have been as much a reflection of distaste over Jiang's high handed methods as an effort to sabotage reform *per se*.[165]

In any case, the 1963–65 period saw a significant "revolutionization" of Chinese art forms. The initial tightening up in academic and artistic spheres in 1963 and the first half of 1964, however, was remarkably restrained. This no doubt reflected the well reasoned caution which had marked the Tenth Plenum's approach to virtually all problems. The need to tread warily following the traumas of the Great Leap and crisis years was intensified in the case of intellectuals who also remembered the Anti-Rightist Campaign and earlier movements within cultural circles. Since Mao himself argued in May 1964 that "Intellectuals are quite important; [we] cannot do without them," policies designed to limit damage to the morale of the intelligentsia were clearly called for. Thus the first moves were directed toward spreading orthodox themes and narrowing the range of what was acceptable, but avoiding excessively harsh criticism. In spring 1963 a national conference of literary and art workers was convened to lay down the line emphasizing class struggle. Initial steps were also taken to discuss the reform of opera and other creative arts. At the same time the propaganda media started to unfold a campaign against erroneous trends in philosophy, history and culture. While such criticisms involved attacks on individual academics and works of art, these were relatively mild.[166]

The debates on Wu Han's theories concerning morality, the historical figure Li Xiucheng, Zhou Gucheng's aesthetics and other academic subjects which emerged in summer 1963 also reflected restraint. These were lively and complex debates utilizing scholarship and mental agility rather than crude slogans. They conformed to official policy laid down in early 1963: "In academic research, scholars of any subject including those of Marxism have no authority to consider their views absolutely correct and suppress views at variance to theirs." Both the propaganda apparatus and younger critics associated with Jiang Qing such as Yao Wenyuan and Qi Benyu played prominent roles. Differences between the two groups appeared with the young critics generally being more vigorous in their writings. A particular division of opinion concerned the interpretation of Li Xiucheng with Qi Benyu attacking Li as a traitor to the Taipings and, according to Cultural Revolution sources, Zhou Yang arguing he was a national hero. But as Merle Goldman's excellent analysis has shown, despite such conflict the radical critics themselves stayed well within the boundaries of academic discussion. Their tone was one of toleration rather than personal vindictiveness, their criticisms were directed at historical methods rather than political views, and their argumentation reflected the genuine give and take of scholarly discourse. Thus in this initial period there was little sign of basic differences over *how* to deal with erroneous tendencies even if substantive differences appeared in the course of debate.[167]

A consensus on approach can also be inferred from further developments in late 1963 and early 1964. First, in October 1963 Zhou Yang gave a major report before the philosophy and social sciences faculties of the Chinese Academy of Sciences. This report had three main features: (1) a strong emphasis on the need to apply class struggle to research and cultural activity; (2) a relatively flexible attitude towards non-Marxist academic and literary work; and (3) a decidedly moderate approach to dealing with individuals with erroneous ideological tendencies. Overall, Zhou called for an all out struggle against "modern revisionism" and coined the slogan "one divides into two" which came to symbolize uncompromising attacks on all retrograde ideological trends. He stressed the danger of academic revisionism as "the mouthpiece of revisionism in politics" and drew attention to such potentially explosive matters as material incentives, profit in industrial management and political content in education, albeit with Moscow as the explicit target. At the same time, Zhou was tolerant of some less than ideologically pure works. He praised progressive ancient writers and called for the assimilation of good aspects of foreign culture. In this, it must be emphasized, he was not at variance with Mao who in the same period referred to Tolstoy as a great Russian writer and in 1965 praised the superior skills of Qing Dynasty painters. Finally, and closely related, Zhou showed a respectful attitude towards individuals, calling on Communists to unite with non-Marxist scholars, learn modestly from them, and help them to come to Marxism gradually. Where mistakes were committed a persuasive approach was called for and labeling at will was rejected. In sum, Zhou called for an intensification of efforts to make class struggle the dominant theme of cultural activity, but no witch hunt of villains was to be allowed.[168]

With Zhou Yang having laid down official policy, Mao spoke critically of the Ministry of Culture's performance in the arts. In December 1963 the Chairman charged:

> Problems abound in all forms of art such as the opera, ballads, music and fine arts, the dance, the cinema, poetry and literature, and the people involved are numerous; in many departments very little has been achieved so far in socialist transformation. The "dead" still dominate in many departments. What has been achieved in the cinema, new poetry, folk songs, the fine arts and the novel should not be underestimated, but there too quite a few exist. As for such departments as the opera, the problems are even more serious. . . . Hence we should proceed with investigation and study and attend to this matter in earnest.[169]

Mao's strictures were certainly harsher than any Zhou had explicitly directed at the internal Chinese scene, and they also pointed squarely at those officials responsible for the arts. Nevertheless, as was the case in Zhou Yang's report, Mao basically asked for action to change China's artistic output and *not* for a purge of either artists or officials. This can also be seen in a November comment on the same subject where the Chairman implied a shake-up might be necessary if no changes were made, but added that if "things are righted" no drastic action would be required.[170]

The response of the cultural bureaucracy and higher ranking Party leaders to Mao's outburst was precisely to focus on the policy questions Mao had raised. While some officials may have shared the alleged view of Zhou Yang's assistant Lin Mohan that the Chairman's comments were "laughable," Mao's intervention was quickly followed by a flood of revolutionary works, stepped up efforts to reform various art forms, and the dispatch of intellectuals and cultural cadres to the countryside and factories. An immediate result was an enlarged Politburo meeting called by Liu Shaoqi in January 1964 to consider Mao's complaints. Apart from calling for a marked increase in revolutionary plays, this meeting provided an overall review of cultural work. The official view was decidedly more sanguine than that implied by Mao's remarks. Zhou Yang reported that achievements outweighed shortcomings and had to be affirmed. While Cultural Revolution sources point to this assessment as a conscious flouting of Mao's will, the actual situation seems less clear-cut. For not only was Zhou Yang, supported by Liu Shaoqi, Deng Xiaoping and Peng Zhen making such an assessment, but in the very same period Ke Qingshi declared "revolutionary art and literature have scored one success after another" in the post-1949 period. Thus even leaders close to Jiang Qing apparently took Mao's December remarks as a pointed barb designed to stimulate bureaucratic efforts in policy implementation rather than a considered overall assessment of cultural developments.[171]

The January meeting also preached moderation in handling individuals. Zhou Yang assertedly stated that while a few people basically opposed Mao's line most were only beset with problems of understanding. Liu reportedly echoed this analysis by saying the revisionist line was only a matter of unclear thinking and casual work attitudes which would be easily overcome if the revolutionary works Mao sought were fostered. Moreover, while Liu acknowledged that it was necessary to criticize and repudiate those who opposed the Party, such criticism was not to be carried out as fiercely as had occurred during the Anti-Rightist Campaign. Thus the policy of leniency was reaffirmed, a policy which did not conflict with anything Mao had said in his late 1963 complaints over the content of the arts. That this was still a consensus view is suggested by the fact that even the likes of Yao Wenyuan continued to debate in a restrained, non-vindictive manner in spring 1964.[172]

In June 1964, however, Mao commented on the propaganda department's plans for the rectification of literary and art organizations with a new, more vehement attack on officials responsible for China's cultural life:

> In the last 15 years these associations, most of their publications (it is said that a few are good), and *by and large* the people in them (that is, not everybody) have not carried out the policies of the Party. They have acted as high and mighty bureaucrats, have not gone to the workers, peasants and soldiers, and have not reflected the socialist revolution and socialist construction. *In recent years,* they slid right down to the brink of revisionism. Unless they remould themselves in real earnest, at some future date they are bound to become groups like the Hungarian Petofi club.[173]

By asserting many officials had reached the "brink of revisionism" and raising the specter of the counterrevolutionary Petofi club, Mao implicitly raised the question of whether a purge was called for. His actual words, however, by acknowledging the possibility of reform, left open the possibility that traditional rectification methods might suffice.

The response of the Party hierarchy to Mao's June comments was swift. About this time Peng Zhen assumed control of the new five man group to oversee a "cultural revolution" in the arts, thus showing the concern of the very highest leaders. Almost immediately Zhou Yang convened a conference of representatives of various cultural associations and the Ministry of Culture and called on each organization to carry out a rectification program. Zhou led the way by criticizing his own "bureaucratism" and set up a leading group for the rectification of the ministry. In accord with Mao's rebuke of "high and mighty bureaucrats," leading figures in these bodies were singled out for criticism including Zhou Yang's aides, Vice Minister of Culture Xia Yan, Yang Hansheng of the All China Federation of Literary and Art Circles, Tian Han of the Playwrights' Association, and Shao Quanlin of the Writers' Association. That significant figures were under attack was further emphasized in the unfolding campaign against Yang Xianzhen, a member of the Central Committee as was Yang Hansheng. Further evidence of the seriousness of the new moves was that academic debate, although retained to some degree, was increasingly replaced by organized assaults on the work of the people in question. While important restraints were observed, the charges now raised had important political overtones. For example, Yang Xianzhen's theories were portrayed as catering to the demands of "modern revisionism" and serving as a theoretical weapon to resist the Socialist Education Movement, while Feng Ding was accused of slandering revolutionary martyrs. Moreover, in the case of less high ranking figures such as the non-Party scholar Zhou Gucheng, a wide range of emotion laden charges such as supporting the GMD regime before 1949 were leveled. In these instances the radical critics associated with Jiang Qing played an important role, but even more important were the attacks of writers identified with the cultural hierarchy.[174]

These steps notwithstanding, the developments of the last half of 1964 were denounced during the Cultural Revolution as a "sham rectification." These were several bases for these accusations. First, after Mao's scathing June comment, Zhou Yang again made an assessment of the situation which ostensibly was far more sanguine than the Chairman's. Zhou assertedly declared that literature and art had essentially developed along the lines laid down by the Party and attributed problems to a lack of understanding. But again, as had been the case after Mao's late 1963 outbursts, this assessment was not limited to the cultural bureaucracy. Ke Qingshi's earlier speech which had pictured the post-1949 period as basically one of achievements under Mao's line was now published in August 1964 complete with "revisions and additions . . . by the speaker." Again, even those close to Jiang Qing were *not* depicting the situation in the somber tones of Mao's directive.[175]

More central to the charges of "sham rectification" were a series of limitations placed on the campaign. First, rectification was conducted strictly under the control of established Party bodies in the cultural field. These bodies were to review all self-criticisms and Zhou Yang was accused of personally coaching some officials to help them pass the test. Moreover, despite the political implications of some of the charges aired, efforts were made to keep up the academic level of the discussions, while some degree of defense and even counterattack was allowed those under criticism. Zhou and others warned against excessive criticism and personal attacks, banned polemics and *dazibao*, and called for eschewing labels. A case in point was that of Tian Han where the bureaucracy assertedly limited criticism to eight months and forbade the mention of political questions or revisionism. Moreover, propaganda chief Lu Dingyi reportedly ruled entire subjects out of bounds—e.g., the "Three Family Village" satirical essays of the crisis years which became a major issue at the start of the Cultural Revolution. During the rectification process those Party members under attack were addressed as "comrade" and no struggle sessions or abject confessions were required. In sum, the restrictions placed on rectification by the cultural hierarchy were systematic and far-reaching.[176]

There may have been various reasons for these limitations. Undoubtedly the desire to avoid excessive disruption and demoralization of the intellectual community was one. As Merle Goldman has suggested, another may have been the close personal ties which developed among Zhou Yang and his associates over the years. In political terms, however, the charge of "sham rectification" is contingent upon the bureaucracy flouting Mao's expressed will. But no clear evidence of the Chairman either seeking harsher methods or disapproving of those actually undertaken exists; throughout Mao was ambiguous on how rectification should be implemented. In the same month as his indictment of cultural officials for having reached "the brink of revisionism," Mao's 1957 propaganda speech was published for the first time. This speech advocated restraint and understanding in the criticism of intellectuals. It is difficult to imagine such a major statement published without Mao's explicit consent. Moreover, evidence exists of Mao being consulted on some of the measures taken and giving his assent—as in the case of public criticism of the film *Early Spring* which involved an attack on Xia Yan.[177]

Mao's comments from the period further suggest a degree of toleration. In June the Chairman implied a willingness to put up with creative artists by saying "Bourgeois intellectuals may be bought if necessary according to our policy." In August he indicated toleration more specifically. With regard to Zhou Gucheng and Sun Yefang, an economist under attack for his liberal theories, Mao exclaimed: "Let them go in for capitalism. Society is very complex. If one only goes in for socialism and not capitalism, isn't that too simple? Wouldn't we then lack the *unity of opposites*, and be one-sided?" Here the Chairman's comment even suggested a subtle reservation to the crescendo over "one divides into two" by acknowledging the significance of the unity of opposites.[178]

A further possible indication of Mao's approval of limited measures against individuals was the election of Zhou Gucheng (who Mao referred to as his "rightist friend" even in fall 1966) and others under attack as NPC deputies in late 1964. The list of delegates was unlikely to have escaped Mao's attention, and he certainly would not have lacked the power to veto such a lowly non-Party figure as Zhou. Moreover, if the bureaucracy were out to sabotage the rectification effort, this would seem a provocation ultimately counterproductive to its cause for very little return indeed. Finally, evidence that Mao had not laid down any clear directive for a harsh purge can be inferred from the words of Jiang Qing in early 1966. At that time, when a major struggle within the leadership was definitely under way, Jiang lambasted the cultural hierarchy for having been basically implementing an "anti-Party and anti-socialist line which is diametrically opposed to Chairman Mao's thought" since 1949. Nevertheless, she still concluded that the main task was to "reeducate the cadres in charge of ... literature and art" and that for "most people" problems were those of "ideological understanding and of raising such understanding through education." In this light, Zhou Yang's mid-1964 insistence that problems of understanding were the main ones hardly seems incontrovertible proof of deliberate resistance to Mao.[179]

Ultimately, the reasons for the moderation of the 1964 cultural rectification may be found in a commitment to traditional Party norms, a commitment shared by both the hierarchy and Mao. In one sense, even the mild measures of 1964 stretched existing norms. To a significant extent the targets of criticism were dredged up from the past as sufficiently unorthodox sentiments apparently could not be found within the more stringent post-Tenth Plenum period. Thus Shao Quanlin's advocacy of "middle characters" dated from the 1960–62 period, while criticism of Feng Ding essentially took his books of the 1950s out of context. In these cases the individuals criticized were being attacked for views which *were in accord with official policy* at the time of their expression. To attack such views clearly threatened established notions of discipline and thus mitigation of the actual criticism was clearly called for. Moreover, other dubious practices appeared even where more contemporary views were at issue. Gross distortions of the positions of those under criticism occurred, and unpublished views which had merely been presented for discussion purposes, as in the case of Yang Xianzhen, were treated as if they represented an open attack on the Party. Clearly these measures created an atmosphere that was not conducive to the traditional free wheeling debate within the Party. Such a concern was explicitly in Zhou Yang's mind when he ruled Tian Han's remarks in debates within the Writers' Association out of bounds for criticism. If such remarks were quoted, Zhou argued, "how would anyone dare to speak again in the future?" While the need to combat revisionism may have led to some bending of the rules, the desire to maintain existing understandings insofar as was possible was a strong force for curbs on the rectification process.[180]

The final stage of the cultural rectification was initiated in early 1965 following the Twenty-three Articles, and apparently drew its rationale in at least some degree from that document. In February and March Lu Dingyi and Zhou Yang, backed by Peng Zhen and Deng Xiaoping, convened several meetings to call for a crackdown on those excesses which had occurred during the 1964 rectification. Zhou once again attacked the indiscriminate use of labels as well as dogmatism, Lu intoned against the "revolutionary masses" in cultural units becoming "feverish" during socialist education, and Deng complained that cultural rectification had hindered academic development and created a situation where no one would dare to write while certain individuals sought to gain fame by unjustified criticisms of others. The implication that the literary rectification had intensified as a reflection of the radical turn in the rural Four Cleanups can be drawn from attacks on "literary sea tactics" *(wenhai zhanshu)*, a corrollary to Liu's "human sea tactics" in the countryside. These attacks, furthermore, were said to be part of a "wind of verdict reversals" concerning the 1964 criticism movement, and thus paralleled the "verdict reversals" Peng Zhen promoted at this time for socialist education as a whole.[181]

Following this high powered attack, criticism began to fade from the public media. This did not mean, however, that cultural reform or rectification were over. Mao's thought and revolutionary themes continued to permeate the creative arts and academic writings in 1965, while 60 percent of the staff of the Ministry of Culture was sent to villages and factories. Moreover, rectification now took the form of an organizational shake-up of the Ministry of Culture and other official bodies. Already in January Lu Dingyi had replaced non-Party writer Shen Yanbing as Minister of Culture, and in April three vice ministers, Xia Yan, Qi Yanming and Chen Huanmei were dismissed. Shao Quanlin and several others were also removed from their posts in literary organizations in this period. These long time cultural bureaucrats, who were judged not guilty of revisionism and therefore were not expelled from the Party, were replaced by political officials including Xiao Wangdong, the new first vice minister who came from Lin Biao's PLA, and Shi Ximin, the new second vice minister from Ke Qingshi's Shanghai. Thus some "high and mighty bureaucrats" had been ousted, and officials from organizations and locales purportedly loyal to Mao inserted in their place. Although Xiao Wangdong would be later denounced for allegedly sabotaging the revolutionary line in the Ministry of Culture, his initial moves were attempts to bolster cultural reform through such measures increasing the number of opera troupes sent to the countryside, cutting drastically the number of traditional operas performed, and calling for struggle against those who only paid lip service to Mao's thought. These efforts, however, would not save him during the Cultural Revolution when impossible criteria were applied to all who held authority.[182]

Before the Cultural Revolution, however, there was little evidence of Mao's or anyone else's displeasure with the new team in the Ministry of Culture. Moreover, there was little to indicate concrete, articulated objections by the Chairman to the conduct of cultural rectification by the established propaganda authorities in 1964. Mao may indeed have been displeased, but the Chairman's distrust of the propaganda apparatus would only come out in late 1965-early 1966 in a most unusual sequence of events.

From Socialist Education to Cultural Revolution, Fall 1965–Spring 1966

As we have seen, following the Twenty-three Articles Mao was apparently silent on major issues, his few recorded statements being largely brief barbs directed at education and public health work with nothing said to indicate dissatisfaction with either cultural rectification or the larger Socialist Education Movement. When the Politburo Standing Committee was convened in an enlarged session in late September–early October 1965, however, the Chairman indicated his general forebodings by raising the question of revisionism appearing in the Central

Committee. Unfortunately, even fewer details are available on this crucial gathering than the meetings in late 1964-early 1965. There were many issues that were ripe for discussion: apart from likely reviews of socialist education since the most recent shift in line and the general economic situation, there is evidence of high level discussions about this time concerning youth unemployment, part-labor/part-study systems, finance and trade, and cultural work. Also, foreign affairs must have been pressing given the escalation of the war in Vietnam, international Communist proposals for united action involving both China and the Soviet Union in support of Vietnam, Chinese efforts to exclude the Russians from the proposed second Afro-Asian conference, the recent Indo-Pakistan War, and the fast moving Indonesian situation which saw the abortive coup and suppression of Indonesian Communists while the Politburo presumably was in session.[183]

Given these multiple issues, the thinness of evidence concerning concrete disagreements between Mao and his colleagues at this meeting is remarkable. Only very vague assertions have appeared in Cultural Revolution sources. Deng Xiaoping allegedly "made a speech in which he declared he was against any cultural change and against changes in the schools." In meetings dealing with cultural matters at the same time, Peng Zhen assertedly declared everyone was equal before the truth and even Mao should submit to criticism when wrong, while Lu Dingyi reportedly attacked Stalin. It should be noted, of course, that similar themes had been articulated by the Chairman himself in recent years. In addition to the question of revisionism in the Central Committee, Mao, seemingly for the first time, called for criticism of Wu Han's *Hai Rui*. Here again, however, considerable ambiguity remains since it is not clear in what terms Mao raised the issue. Mao's demand was apparently made in the context of a general renewal of the struggle against bourgeois ideology, and thus may have been seen by the participants as simply requiring a new round of criticism much on the same lines as occurred in 1964. Certainly there is no direct evidence that at this juncture Mao couched Wu Han's "problem" as a basic political error. Thus a predisposition to view Wu's case as one of "understanding" did not, apparently, contravene the Chairman's actual comments. In any case, for reasons which are not totally apparent, Mao's dissatisfaction ostensibly grew as a result of what occurred at the September-October meeting. A year later the Chairman commented that at this meeting "I felt my views couldn't be accepted in Beijing." He then gave the go ahead to Jiang Qing's associates in Shanghai to launch public criticism of Wu Han.[184]

Following the Politburo conference there were signs of an official response to Mao's concerns in the conduct of socialist education. The October 1 *Renmin ribao* editorial bemoaned the tendency to ignore class struggle and relax the movement. The class struggle theme—together with the importance of studying Mao's thought—was now increasingly emphasized in discussions of socialist education. In the countryside, however, the movement apparently continued along the moderate lines initiated by the Twenty-three Articles leading to its conclusion in about one third of China's villages by summer 1966. Another trend in this period was the consolidation of political departments and study mechanisms in urban institutions. The need to establish these on a continuing basis following the conclusion of socialist education was particularly stressed. A fall 1965 national conference on political work in finance and trade departments reported that 90 percent of Party committees at the county level and above had set up political departments in this sphere, while 60 to 70 percent of basic level finance and trade units were staffed with political officers.[185] The most significant developments, however, were a campaign to "revolutionize" county Party committees and a further intensification of Mao study.

The campaign to revolutionize county Party committees began in October with the publication of a series of articles by county cadres analyzing problems in the work of leading personnel at that level. The *Renmin ribao* editor's note accompanying the first batch of materials declared revolutionizing the leadership of *xian* committees was the key to building a socialist new countryside, a task, as suggested by the Twenty-three Articles, which followed upon successful socialist education. The media campaign, as well as meetings convened by counties to consider problems, continued throughout the fall and winter, and by late February county leaders were authoring critical self-examinations of their work. About this same time and into the spring such critical self-evaluations were compared to the sterling performance of Jiao Yulu, a deceased Henan *Xian* secretary who had been close to the masses and worked hard despite serious illness. Finally, large numbers of county officials were sent to "squat" at the basic levels.[186]

The themes which emerged during this movement can be classified under three headings: (1) attacks on various bureaucratic phenomena endemic to the political-administrative system since the establishment of the PRC; (2) restrained echoes of the Great Leap insistence on daring local leadership; and (3) a more contemporary insistence on the need to combat revisionism in all its forms. Many familiar deviations now came under attack. *Xian* leaders were charged with lack of knowledge of actual conditions at the grass roots, being content with superficial information derived from documents, and when actually getting to the villages only staying a short time and not really establishing close contact with the masses. The concerns of such officials were overwhelmingly with satisfying the demands of their bureaucratic superiors, which were regarded as "hard tasks," while giving little attention to "soft tasks" requested by ordinary people. Administrative life had many of the same features as the early 1950s; as in the New Three Anti Campaign the "five too many" again came under attack. County authorities were pictured as operating in an environment of excessive meetings, documents and telephone calls in which they tried to monopolize all decisions—a situation which only resulted in a lack of initiative and confusion below. While some analysts have seen this aspect of the campaign as an attempt by Mao's "opponents" to divert it from the more volatile target of revisionism, Mao himself expressed concern with such endemic bureaucratic problems in the same general period.[187]

In addition to such endemic shortcomings, county leadership had also not recovered from the shock of the Great Leap Forward. The need to recover some of the bold leadership style of the leap emerged as another recurrent theme. The need to overcome fear of repeating Great Leap mistakes was explicitly stated, and Tao Zhu forecast a new leap forward after the conclusion of socialist education. County officials were criticized for refusing to take risks, for seeking stability rather than daring to undertake difficult tasks. Qualifications which appeared as the Great Leap floundered such as the importance of "rational" close planting and avoiding the "blind" direction of work were now criticized as restricting cadre enthusiasm. Leaders had ceased to "aim high" and settled for a safe "middle course," but such "steady leadership" was seen as actually bringing progress to a standstill. In comparison to 1958 these enjoinders were pale imitations—particularly given the absence of high production targets—but the demand for reenergized leadership was clear.[188]

If the Great Leap themes lacked a certain concreteness, contemporary themes were even more difficult to translate into reality. As one article complained, "We have many comrades who always speak of class struggle but in fact class struggle within the Party committee is not much visible and even if it is there it is a sham." A major concern was asserted overemphasis on production, a tendency to make production results the be all and end all of work while neglecting political duties. This was linked to such related concerns as emphasizing profits and seeking state aid rather than adopting the self-reliant spirit of Dazhai. Thus demands were made to step up political work—above all the study of Mao's thought which was declared the substance of *xian* revolutionization. This demand, however, had to coexist with more cautious economic policies which still, e.g., called for careful attention to profitable sideline production, while the Great Leap echoes called for major efforts to increase output. Moreover, even such a model of the flexible study and application of Mao's thought as Jiao Yulu was deeply concerned with practical production questions.[189]

In dealing with problems official statements declared "closed door" methods insufficient and representatives of the poor and lower middle peasants were invited to make suggestions to meetings convened at the county, commune and brigade levels. Nevertheless, this part of the process was firmly under the control of the established *xian* authorities. Despite the presence of peasants and basic level cadres these meetings never developed into struggle sessions, leaders who came under criticism sometimes rejected the accusations made against them, and no reports of purges appeared. Even published self-criticisms carried the implication that on the whole those in authority had done a pretty good job. To all intents and purposes the *xian* revolutionization campaign was conducted with the same moderation that had marked other aspects of socialist education since the Twenty-three Articles. Although raising the foreboding ideological themes of the broader movement, at the same time it continued the lenient organizational approach which stressed the importance of Party leadership.[190]

The campaign to revolutionize county committees was closely linked to the more inclusive effort to study Mao's thought. Mao study had begun as a large scale undertaking in 1964, and in summer 1965 it received another boost as meetings of activists were held, study was conducted among peasants and basic level cadres, and various leaders declared Mao study should assume first place in all work. Emphasis on Mao study became even more pronounced after the September–October Politburo meeting and by early 1966 it was systematized on a large scale basis. In this larger movement many of the themes we have seen in the *xian* revolutionization campaign also appeared, particularly the leading role to politics over business affairs and the need to avoid excessive emphasis on production. Again, primary importance was placed on Party leadership. In order for Mao study to be properly developed first secretaries of Party bodies at all levels were ordered to take control of the movement. Once more orthodox techniques were used to pursue elusive ideological goals.[191]

While there is little evidence of conflict over the *xian* committee campaign, Cultural Revolution sources portray differences over the relationship of Mao study to socialist education proper. At the time, many statements explicitly linked the two movements. This was particularly the case in the Central-South where Guangdong First Secretary Zhao Ziyang declared the study of Mao's thought "The most basic guarantee for the success of the Socialist Education Movement," and where the January 1966 regional directive on Mao study selected Four Cleanups work team cadres as backbone elements for the campaign. But if Tao Zhu and his subordinates were boosting Mao study as essential to socialist education, Cultural Revolution sources claim Liu Shaoqi and others were critical of the impact of the study campaign. In addition to general complaints about the oversimplification of Mao study, in February 1966 Liu reportedly objected to Mao study undermining the Four Cleanups. Apparently Liu felt the open ended nature of the study campaign weakened the focus of the Four Cleanups and directed that only the Twenty-three Articles should be studied during this work.[192] Such views, however, do not appear to be the basis of deep rifts within the leadership. Instead, they suggest the problems facing leaders charged with balancing related yet conflicting goals—combating an imperfectly defined revisionism, promoting production, eliminating deviant behavior, and maintaining cadre morale. All of these objectives had been raised by the Twenty-three Articles but a year later China's leaders were no closer to solving the contradictions among them.

The Wu Han Affair

While the inability to reconcile the divergent goals of socialist education undoubtedly played a role in precipitating the Cultural Revolution, the Wu Han case which Mao had raised at the fall 1965 Politburo meeting was the immediate cause. The details are available elsewhere of how Mao instigated an attack on Wu from Shanghai, how Peng Zhen first resisted joining in and then downplayed Wu's sins, how Peng issued the February (1966) Outline which treated Wu's mistakes as an academic matter, and finally how Mao dismissed Peng and with him much of the Beijing Municipal Committee and central propaganda apparatus.[193] Here our analysis focuses on two aspects of the affair: (1) the relationship of Mao, Peng and other political actors, particularly Jiang Qing's group; and (2) the role of Party organizational norms in the unfolding events.

Jiang Qing had discovered "political problems" in *Hai Rui* long before the 1965 Politburo meeting. In 1962 she reportedly conducted detailed investigation and research into the play and demanded it be banned. In 1963 she attempted to convince Mao that she should be allowed to criticize the play but Peng Zhen intervened and persuaded the Chairman otherwise. Peng apparently argued Jiang was trying to denigrate the whole circle of leading historians and the Chairman restrained his wife in order to protect these historians. He did, however, permit Jiang to reserve her opinion on the matter and she continued to work on the project. By spring 1965 Mao apparently came around to Jiang's view and commissioned her to prepare an article in secret with Shanghai propaganda officials. Thus when the Chairman raised the issue at the fall Politburo conference, more serious measures were in train than his leading colleagues could have imagined. Deng Xiaoping, for one, apparently saw no great moment in Mao's call for criticism of Wu Han and still saw Wu for games of bridge. Peng Zhen, moreover, continued to treat Wu's problem as an academic one—an attitude which apparently reflected Peng's view of the need for moderation in rectification as much as any personal connections.[w]

When the attack on Wu Han came in the form of Yao Wenyuan's article in Shanghai's *Wenhui bao* on November 10, it undoubtedly caught most of China's leaders by surprise. Peng Zhen's reaction was one of anger on the grounds that his organizational authority had been ignored. Not only had a writer under the jurisdiction of one municipal committee attacked a scholar under another municipal organization, but no reference had been made to either Peng's five man group overseeing cultural reform or the central propaganda authorities. Thus Peng chided Shanghai for its lack of "Party spirit" in failing to provide advance

[w] *Hongse wenyi* [Red Literature and Art] (Beijing), May 20, 1967, in *SCMP-S*, No. 190; *Jinggangshan* (Beijing), May 25, 1967, in *SCMP*, No. 3996; and Witke, *Chiang*, p. 296. While it has often been argued that Peng "had to protect" Wu because of Wu's position as vice mayor of Beijing, there is no overwhelming evidence that this was the case. Certainly provincial level leaders had seen people of Wu's rank purged previously without detriment to their careers. Moreover, as James Pusey argues, there is little to indicate that Wu was part of Peng's braintrust whatever his ties to the Beijing establishment. James R. Pusey, *Wu Han: Attacking the Present through the Past* (Cambridge: Harvard East Asian Monographs, 1969), p. 57.

notice, while others attacked Yao's bypassing of the Center. Even at this point, however, the signs were still ambiguous since Yao's article was still firmly within the bounds of academic criticism and addressed its target as "comrade." The attack was focused on the historical class standpoint of Wu Han and not on his purported representation of Peng Dehuai. As Mao commented in December, Yao's article "fails to hit where it really hurts." Nevertheless, the unusual nature of the Shanghai attack caused some forebodings in Beijing as evidenced in Deng Xiaoping's decision to terminate social relations with Wu Han.[194]

Thus the situation was far from clear during winter 1965–66. Wu Han reportedly was nervous because he knew "some powerful person" was behind the criticism, but he was unsure of who it was. Others knew of Jiang Qing's involvement but apparently were unclear about Mao's position. Speculatively, it seems Mao was deliberately keeping people in the dark—above all Peng Zhen. As Jiang Qing put it, "Peng Zhen was risking his life to protect Wu Han. While the Chairman was quite aware of this, he didn't want to say it openly." In any case, Peng apparently decided to argue his case forcefully to Mao himself. In meetings with the Chairman in December and February Peng pushed two points: (1) that Wu Han's problems were questions of ideological understanding and should be dealt with leniently; and (2) Wu's critics—the "left"—should be disciplined, apparently for overstepping the bounds of justified criticism. In these encounters Mao seemingly took an ambiguous stand. He raised the crucial question of the relationship between Wu Han and Peng Dehuai, although seemingly he did not push it. Peng's response was to argue in terms of traditional Party norms that there were no *organizational* ties between the two men. In this regard it is instructive to return to Lushan itself and recall that various leaders who had expressed views similar to those of Peng Dehuai escaped with no more than self-criticisms on the grounds that they had no organizational links, no factional ties to him. Moreover, this same principal was adopted during the "verdict reversals" of the crisis years. Now, citing the lack of direct contact between Wu Han and Peng Dehuai, Peng Zhen again sought to invoke this rationale founded on longstanding CCP norms.[195]

Mao's response seemingly was sufficiently vague to allow Peng to believe he had won the Chairman's assent or, at the very least, not provoked his opposition. Peng assertedly spread rumors that Mao agreed with him on Wu Han's lack of ties to Peng Dehuai, something he surely would not have done had Mao explicitly indicated the contrary. Peng's belief that Mao favored a relatively mild approach to Wu Han also had some positive basis. In December, while complaining that Wu was getting worse and worse, Mao nevertheless indicated he might be posted as a *xian* magistrate, and he also noted that a demotion would be fitting punishment for Yang Xianzhen.[196]

Mao apparently was even ambiguous concerning the February Outline. Discussions of these problems in early February led to sharp exchanges within the five man group, particularly between Peng Zhen and Kang Sheng over disciplinary action against the "left." Peng allegedly drew up the February Outline "behind Kang's back." He presumably presented the document, or at least an oral account of it, when he met Mao a few days later. Although Mao reportedly resisted Peng's insistence on a quick "political conclusion" against the "left" by leaving the question open for future discussion, he apparently did not reject Peng's outline out of hand. Indeed, Mao is reported as merely *asking* whether Wu Han was "opposed to the Party and socialism." Peng was apparently confident enough of Mao's support to claim it at a subsequent Politburo Standing Committee meeting under Liu Shaoqi and Deng Xiaoping which then issued the February Outline as an official document. While subsequent charges alleged improper action on Peng's part by circumventing Kang, Peng had both consulted Mao and won Standing Committee approval.[x]

Events then unfolded rapidly. Mao made his true feelings known in late March by openly attacking Wu Han, the February Outline and the entire central propaganda apparatus. He demanded the disbanding of the propaganda department, the Beijing Municipal Committee and the five man group, thus indicating Peng Zhen's days were numbered. In the following weeks various political actors scrambled for their lives. Deng Xiaoping, for one, who had put his seal of approval on the February Outline, now attacked Peng for "opposing Chairman Mao."[197] Meanwhile, Peng and his associates fruitlessly sought to escape the net amid conditions of considerable confusion. The reported response of several of these men to various documents Mao submitted in April is suggestive:

> Liu Ren . . . asked: "What does he want after all? What is he driving at?" Zhang Tianxiang [said]: "What is Chairman Mao's intention in forwarding these . . . documents with his comment for circulation among members of the municipal committee? We are not clear, and we cannot make head or tail of this."[198]

---

[x] "Counterrevolutionary Revisionist Peng Zhen's Towering Crimes of Opposing the Party, Socialism and the Thought of Mao-Tse-tung" (Red Guard pamphlet), June 10, 1967, in *SCMM*, Nos. 639–40. The question remains as to why Mao reacted so bitterly in Peng Zhen's case. Although Peng claimed he had never opposed Mao, as we have seen the Chairman explicitly distinguished between "double dealers" such as Peng and others like Liu and Deng who were "open" in their activities. Several possibilities exist. Mao may have been pointing to such events as Peng's secret 1961 review of Great Leap policies (see above, p. 384) which probably came to light once Peng was under attack. Or he may have construed Peng's frantic efforts in 1966 to save himself by coordinated action with his subordinates as violations of organizational norms. Also, such events as Peng's willingness to sign a joint communique in March 1966 with the Japanese Communist Party referring to "united action" over Vietnam, implicitly with the Soviet Union, clearly raised the Chairman's ire, but others including Zhou Enlai and Kang Sheng were also willing to go along with the communique. But perhaps most pertinent was a sense of personal betrayal. After all, Peng had been promoted in a period when Mao apparently was developing reservations about Liu Shaoqi. Speculatively, it may well be that Mao was placing considerable faith in Peng should Liu and others be shown unworthy, only to find that Peng's ideas differed considerably from his own.

Unsure of the proper response, these men were inexorably drawn into the net of the emerging Cultural Revolution.

Clearly an unprecedented situation had been created, a situation in which traditional Party norms no longer provided safety. As the Cultural Revolution began to unfold the old defenses of organizational discipline and principled discussion did not suffice. High level cadres were heard to utter such laments as "I just don't understand why I am regarded a capitalist roader," and "All I did was carry out the errors of those above me." A pervading sense of unfairness arose as leading officials and ordinary cadres alike had no firm guidelines for acceptable behavior.[199] After years of upholding established Party norms and attempting to preserve them even when his actions dealt them severe blows, Mao had finally made a decisive break with the past in his quest for ideological purity.

Conclusion

Following the ouster of Peng Zhen, despite some initial efforts to distinguish the two campaigns, the Socialist Education Movement was officially supplanted by the Cultural Revolution by the end of 1966. In early 1967 the drastically altered leadership found itself, somewhat ironically, in the position of protecting the results of socialist education. Undoubtedly using criticisms of the Four Cleanups under Liu's stewardship in 1964 which were then emerging, many victims of the work teams sought a "reversal of verdicts." The chaos this was causing was too much for the central leadership which now declared the work teams had by and large been correct in their actions, thus implicitly exonerating Liu.[200] In cultural circles, however, no such backhand exoneration came. Instead, the men and women whose work had been criticized in 1964–65 now came under the harshest personal attack, and many more were dragged into the ever expanding vortex of the Cultural Revolution storm.

Over the course of the Socialist Education Movement proper a variety of approaches were attempted but none was fully satisfactory. Not only was revisionism difficult to define, much less combat, but the assault on more tangible problems such as corruption had to be aborted due to the severe impact of the big Four Cleanups on cadre morale. Moreover, even after the milder approach introduced by the Twenty-three Articles it was still difficult to create enthusiasm among rural cadres. In fall 1966, before the disruptions of the Cultural Revolution reached the countryside, media reports confessed the inability of socialist education to refute the viewpoint that "being a cadre means suffering a loss."[201] Thus despite some successes in curbing the private sector and restoring orthodoxy, whether coercive or persuasive methods were emphasized, or whether local organs played a major role or work teams monopolized control, the results of socialist education were disappointing.

What explains the variation in approach? The alternation between consolidation and mobilization phases does not take us very far. For one thing, the customary alternation of phases was severely disrupted by the crisis years of 1960–62. As we have seen, what occurred at that time was not a consolidation of gains, it was rather a full scale retreat. The retreat generated pressures for the restoration of orthodoxy, but when Mao moved in that direction in 1962 he and his colleagues were constrained by the very depth of the crisis. Intense mobilization efforts were out of the question; any measures would have to be undertaken with considerable circumspection to avoid further alienation of both populace and elite. When Liu Shaoqi, abetted by Mao, apparently forgot these considerations in 1964, the results were disastrous. In any case, the mobilization which did occur was restricted to socialist education itself and was not part of a more inclusive phase. It was not linked to structural changes in society as during the early and mid-1950s, or to a program for rapid economic growth such as the Great Leap Forward. Thus the CCP could not effectively bolster rectification with tangible appeals, whether real social gains or illusionary promises.

The presence of an external threat is even less helpful as an explanatory factor. Both the moderate approach of 1965 and the launching of the Cultural Revolution in 1966 came in the context of an escalating war in Vietnam and worsening Sino-Soviet relations. Despite our hypothesis linking external threat and coercive discipline, it might be tempting to see the 1965 amelioration as partially due to caution created by the Vietnam War. However, the key decisions *preceded* the escalation and came at a time when Mao was downplaying the possibility of large scale American intervention. In contrast, a year later when the Chairman set out to shake the system to its roots, to weaken it as never before, he declared his belief in the inevitability of war within two years, a war likely to involve joint Russian and American military action against China.[202] Here the external threat hypothesis might explain harsh disciplinary measures, but it cannot provide rational understanding of a fundamental weakening of the capacity to resist foreign attack.

The internal unity of the leadership, or lack of it, goes further to explain the varying approaches adopted. Mao's growing dissatisfaction with his colleagues, whether ill or well founded, clearly was the prerequisite for the unprecedented measures of 1966. Moreover, in a more subtle fashion, the apparent differences between Liu Shaoqi and Peng Zhen over the proper approach to the Four Cleanups may have exacerbated the excesses of 1964. It is at least plausible that Liu's desire to get results where Peng had failed led to even harsher methods than Liu might otherwise have advocated. On balance, however, it would appear Liu's policies, as well as those adopted by Peng and others at different junctures, reflected their honest efforts to come to terms with complex reality, a reality whose appearance changed not only in response to official policy but as a result of more thorough methods of obtaining information.

Did the various shifts in line, then, reflect a fundamental conflict between different political actors? In general, the 1962–65 period was not one of notable unity. No strong consensus existed on a clearly defined course of action such as existed in the early and mid-1950s and even, to a lesser extent, during the initial phase of the Great Leap. But differences did not mean polarization. Instead, they meant uncertainty and ambiguity, many actors experimenting with different approaches while Mao gave only infrequent and often unclear guidance. Although Peng Zhen was a relatively consistent supporter of moderation, efforts to portray an undeviating struggle between Mao—the purported advocate of a normative, moral and educational approach—and Liu—the proponent of coercive, practical and remedial measures—grossly distort the actual situation. Mao certainly wished to engender a moral regeneration of the Chinese elite, but Liu too saw his efforts as part of the struggle against revisionism. Liu did advocate a harsh approach to corruption in 1964, but the evidence indicates Mao shared his concern and supported his efforts until they went astray. Similarly, while Peng Zhen and others did try to keep ideological struggle within bounds in 1964–65, there is no evidence that Mao indicated this approach was mistaken. Ultimately, when Mao turned on the Party leadership in 1966–67 he was lashing out at deep tendencies in society, tendencies summed up as revisionism and neglect of class struggle. These problems were beyond the ability of any individual leaders to prevent despite considerable efforts in the 1962–65 period, but Mao now laid responsibility for them at the door of his longtime comrades.

With the Cultural Revolution under way in October 1966, Mao remarked that "For many years I thought about how to administer [the Party] a shock, and finally conceived [this shock of the Cultural Revolution]."[203] The shock the Chairman administered thoroughly ruptured the longstanding Party norms he had played such a large role in creating. As argued in Chapter 1, the ambiguities in these norms meant they had always been a fragile structure. To a large extent this structure was dependent on Mao accepting the norms as binding on himself. In 1959, even as he violated traditional understandings, Mao continued to assert their validity. In the 1962–65 period, he bolstered the norms on several occasions by indicating that they did apply to him, that his personal position should not be magnified out of all proportion. But as Mao pursued the elusive goal of filling class struggle with concrete meaning, as his interventions in the running of state affairs became more erratic, and as his views on various issues became evermore difficult to pin down, conditions were created which weakened established Party principles. Even so, the norms remained a potent force to the end; Peng Zhen evidently believed they could still be invoked to persuade the Chairman. Once Mao decided to administer his shock, however, a long struggle was set in motion in which the shape of organizational principles guiding elite behavior would remain a central issue of conflict.

Conclusion

From the founding of the PRC up to the Cultural Revolution elite behavior in China was guided by a relatively well defined set of organizational norms. Although these norms began to erode during the Great Leap Forward and subsequent years, they still functioned however imperfectly in 1965. Mao Zedong, who made these understandings an integral part of his leadership in the early 1940s, reaffirmed them on numerous occasions in the 1950–65 period. Nevertheless, it was Mao's actions in the years preceding the Cultural Revolution which gravely weakened the norms, and his decision which shattered them in 1966.

Rectification occupied a key place in these organizational principles. This approach, with its persuasive emphasis and avoidance of excessive purges, was applied to a variety of problems and deviations, many of which constantly recurred while others grew out of specific circumstances. Within the rectification framework, however, there have been variations in method of implementation and severity of sanctions. Indeed, as the larger system of Party norms eroded, harsh disciplinary sanctions also did significant damage to the rectification concept.

Deviations, Methods, Sanctions: Relationships and Variations

Many endemic defects of the Chinese political-administrative system appeared repeatedly over the 1950–65 period. In particular, various bureaucratic phenomena —excessive red tape, the pursuit of narrow departmental interests, leadership divorced from grass roots reality—came under attack both in relaxed periods and during intense mass movements. Nevertheless, significant variations have occurred in the problems tackled by rectification campaigns. These reflect both the particular priorities of any stage of the PRC's development and pressures resulting from the alternation of mobilization and consolidation phases.

Rectification in the initial period from 1950 to 1953 reflected the overall goals of consolidating power and economic recovery. The need to create rapidly an elite capable of governing a vastly expanded territory generated several imperatives—easing tensions among diverse elements hastily thrown into official positions, phasing out those initially retained from the GMD administration, and removing or reeducating others who managed to gain cadre status without adequate training or commitment. Moreover, the continuing prestige and influence of dominant groups from the old society necessitated a frontal assault on links between the new elite and landlords and capitalists. While the major disciplinary development of the 1954–55[1]—the purge of Gao Gang and Rao Shushi—was a high level affair essentially unrelated to more systemic problems, the study campaigns conducted in conjunction with the purge focused on problems of bureaucratic aggrandizement at a time of marked governmental expansion to support planned economic growth and socialization. Following the victory of socialist transformation, overall policy in 1956–57 encouraged broad social support for economic development, a process which saw extensive efforts to rectify sectarian and bureaucratic leadership which stifled the enthusiasm of skilled groups. However, in this effort to resolve the "contradiction of leaders and led" the demarcation of professional and Party authority became an issue, and intellectual excesses during the Hundred Flowers experiment resulted in new rectification measures to restore Party supremacy in mid-1957.

With the adoption of the Great Leap Forward in late 1957, rectification efforts became subordinate to the needs of this unprecedented economic strategy. Right conservative doubts now came under heavy criticism, technical values were subordinated to politics, and attacks on provincial organizational unreliability were clearly designed to bolster discipline as greatly expanded powers were devolved to that level. The ill conceived effort to maintain enthusiasm for the Great Leap following the Lushan meetings resulted in renewed criticism of pessimistic attitudes. By 1960–61 the abandonment of the leap was reflected in attacks on the harsh, subjective methods of leadership which had been a by-product of the earlier policies. The deterioration of the post-leap period further necessitated action against widespread anti-social behavior within the elite. Such phenomena—particularly rural corruption—were still a serious problem in 1962 and became a focus of socialist education as the leadership sought to restore political and economic orthodoxy following the far-reaching concessions of the crisis years. Such efforts were linked to the much vaguer goal of combating revisionism—an objective derived from concern with both perceived degeneration in the Soviet Union and the observable malaise in Chinese society. It was unusually difficult, however, to translate this project into concrete rectification targets.

Deviations under criticism also varied according to the rhythm of consolidation and mobilization. Indeed, the problems singled out for attack in a given phase often reflected excesses in approved behavior during the previous phase. In some periods, however, the fit between alternating phases and rectification targets was closer than others. Following the initial post-liberation years when the unique features of the period and the relative decentralization of the system somewhat mitigated the relationship, it was particularly strong from the mid-1950s to the early 1960s.[a] The attack on sectarianism and other bureaucratic high handedness during 1956–57 was a classic move to adjust tensions, while the rectification themes of late 1957–58 fully supported mobilization priorities. The 1959–60 onslaught against rightist sentiments again bolstered the fundamental mobilization thrust of the period, although now they were out of tune with some halfhearted efforts to curb excesses. The 1960–61 campaign's focus on commandism, egalitarianism and blind leadership, in contrast, fit in with the retrenchment emphasis of the post-leap policy adjustment. Subsequently, however, the rhythm of phases was significantly disrupted by the crisis years. Given the weakening of the system in the 1960–62 period, a genuine mobilization did not follow the crisis until the abortive effort of 1964, while targets such as corruption and revisionism are not inherently linked to any particular phase. But over the entire 1950–65 period there was a tendency for such problems as conservative attitudes and professional priorities to come under attack during mass mobilizations, while consolidation stages generally saw criticism of subjective exaggeration, inflexible leadership and crude commandism.

In addition to deviations under attack, the implementation of rectification also saw variations. In some respects there were few to speak of. Most rectification campaigns were conducted in all regions and functional spheres, in rural and urban areas, and among Party and non-Party cadres alike. However, some movements saw particular emphases—the initial development of several early campaigns in old liberated areas, the particularly thorough follow-up to Gao Gang's purge in the Northeast, the Three Anti emphasis on economic units where corruption was rife, and the focus of both the Hundred Flowers and anti-rightist efforts on urban intellectuals. Moreover, some significant relationships can be seen. While in many instances Party and non-Party cadres received comparable treatment during rectification, in cases where non-Party groups were singled out as prime targets (the Three Anti and Anti-Rightist Campaigns) they received much harsher treatment than that normally meted out to Party members. Also, while basic and intermediate level cadres were involved in nearly all rectification efforts, it was only starting with the Great Leap that high ranking policy makers generally became vulnerable to discipline. We shall return to these themes subsequently.

---

[a]A brief exception was the Anti-Rightist Campaign which marked a significant but limited political mobilization within certain urban circles while moderate policies still prevailed in the economic sphere. Moreover, the movement's emphasis on orthodox Party leadership is not a particular feature of either mobilization or consolidation phases.

Different organizational approaches were applied to different movements. Two basic methods were used—reliance on the regular chain of command and higher level work teams. Theoretically, each approach has its strengths and weaknesses reflecting the related but conflicting objectives rooting out deviance while improving work performance and maintaining cadre morale. Rectification by established Party bodies, we hypothesize, is more suited to dealing with concrete work problems of a non-antagonistic nature but serious violations of discipline require the presence of outside work teams for their solution. A corollary to this is the expectation that work teams will conduct relatively harsh campaigns while the normal chain of command will be utilized in persuasive efforts.

To an important extent purely administrative considerations rather than the theoretically optimal methods have determined the approach used. This was particularly clear in the 1951–54 campaign when work teams were used in areas of high population density where they apparently could move about relatively easily. More broadly, after the early years there was a general tendency to use work teams in rural areas where the indigenous Party structure was relatively weak regardless of the problems involved or degree of coercion employed.[2] Nevertheless, an examination of the actual *performance* of work teams tends to bear out our assumptions. Where problems were defined in relatively non-antagonistic terms—as in 1951–54, rural socialist education in fall 1957, and the Socialist Education Movement during 1963 and 1965—an effort was made to work with local Party leaders and disciplinary methods were relatively restrained. But where problems were defined as unusually serious—as in the big Four Cleanups of 1964 and the 1947–48 campaign before liberation—then local authorities were kicked aside and harsh sanctions were employed.[3]

Despite the emphasis of rectification doctrine, coercive measures normally accompany the process to varying degrees regardless of whether work teams or regular Party bodies are used. While some coercion is required to provide a suitable backdrop to persuasive efforts, and heavy sanctions may be required for particularly serious anti-social acts, practice demonstrates that if used to excess it easily becomes counterproductive. Moreover, although much of our analysis is in terms of the relative degree of coercion and persuasion during rectification, a third factor—tangible appeals—has been a major determinant of the effectiveness of reform efforts. This is most clearly seen in the contrast between the vitality of rectification during 1950–53 compared to its failures over the 1960–65 period. In the early post-liberation years many rewards were available to the emerging elite. Official posts were opened up to groups which had been excluded from authority in the old society, and rapid promotions were available to energetic cadres. Moreover, the reforms of this period meant substantial economic and social gains to groups from which the new elite was drawn. All of this strengthened commitment to the Party's cause and made officials receptive to the themes stressed during rectification. In contrast, the severe crisis of 1960–62 and its lingering effects undermined many of the benefits of cadre status. With economic conditions deteriorating, there were fewer material rewards available to cadres as well as masses. Moreover, the widespread deprivation suffered by the peasantry from which rural basic level leaders were drawn caused a widespread social malaise which inevitably affected the cadres. Appalled at the sufferings of their friends and relatives, and often blamed by them for the disaster conditions, significant numbers of cadres not only failed to respond to rectification measures but many sought to resign their positions. This demoralization—graphically reflected in the view that being a cadre meant "suffering a loss"—was so deep that even improving economic conditions after 1962 could not fully offset the impact of the earlier period.

The absence of adequate tangible rewards partially explains the coercive aspects of the 1960–61 rectification campaign, and also the continuing widespread rural corruption which led to harsh socialist education measures in 1964. But what other factors have affected the relative stress on a coercive or persuasive approach? This study has suggested three: (1) the degree of external threat; (2) whether the system has been in a mobilization or consolidation phase; and (3) the degree of unity and consensus within the top Party leadership. To what extent do these factors explain the variations in rectification in the 1950–65 period?

Our examination of the revolutionary period led to the hypothesis that systematic educational methods may develop where a secure environment exists, but that this is not possible where there is an external threat and instead coercive disciplinary sanctions are often invoked. The relationship of external threat and rectification methods is much weaker for post-1949 China, however, due to the qualitatively greater security provided by the fact of national power. Given the greatly reduced likelihood of interference—of the enemy "breaking in"—after victory in the civil struggle, CCP leaders have been able to conduct systematic rectification at times of their own choosing regardless of external tensions. Moreover, the relative degree of coercion and persuasion in such efforts has not been consistently related to the level of foreign danger. In only one case, the severe Three Anti Campaign during the Korean War, does an external threat appear to have influenced decisions for harsh measures. In other cases—e.g., the 1958 Taiwan crisis and tension over Laos and the Indian border in fall 1959—international conflict may have heightened already coercive tendencies, but the severity of rectification in such instances was clearly derived from domestic factors. And in other cases—e.g., the 1965 Vietnam escalation—mild rectification was conducted despite rising external danger. Conversely, periods of comparative international calm have seen relatively coercive movements—e.g., the Anti-Rightist Campaign and the Socialist Education Movement in 1964.

Overall, it appears that other international factors have had a more significant influence on inner Party discipline than actual external threats. In particular, the Sino-Soviet dispute played a pervasive if subtle role. Mao's anger at Soviet criticism of the Great Leap and Peng Dehuai's exchange of views with

Khrushchev probably affected not only his treatment of Peng but also the coercive nature of the drive against right opportunism. Moreover, the Chairman's preoccupation with Soviet revisionism in the 1962–65 period clearly was a significant factor in the rejection of his leading comrades which resulted in the unprecedentedly harsh Cultural Revolution.

The alternation of mobilization and consolidation phases has been a considerably stronger factor affecting rectification methods. Similar to the types of deviations under attack, throughout the 1950s the severity of discipline closely followed the rhythm of phases. All of the mild rectification movements of this decade—the 1950 campaign, the New Three Anti Campaign, and the rectification accompanying the Hundred Flowers experiment, as well as the study movement linked to the purge of Gao and Rao—came during consolidation efforts to defuse tensions. On the other hand, the urban mobilization of 1951–52 saw the coercive Three Anti Campaign, while the stresses of the Great Leap Forward were reflected in the harsh aspects of the late 1957–58 rectification and the "ruthless struggles" of 1959–60. The Anti-Rightist Campaign of mid-1957 is again the exception to the rule: although itself involving the significant use of coercive sanctions, this movement unfolded in what was still a consolidation phase in terms of overall policy.

As was the case with shortcomings under criticism, the link between phase and severity of rectification weakened significantly in the 1960s due to the disruption of the crisis years. Thus although a wide ranging effort to adjust imbalances took place during the 1960–62 period, the 1960–61 campaign had marked coercive aspects given the need to combat extensive anti-social behavior within the elite. Moreover, as we have seen, no clear pattern of alternating phases for the polity as a whole emerged after 1962. The fluctuating emphasis on coercion and persuasion during the Socialist Education Movement did not reflect larger decisions concerning social and economic policy, it rather was a product of changing leadership perceptions of elite shortcomings themselves.

Finally, the degree of leadership unity was a crucial factor. Leadership unity involved both a broad consensus on policy and a well defined distribution of power within the top echelons based on the unchallenged position of Mao. Consensus both furthered the articulation of clear policies and minimized the intensity of any differences which did exist. As suggested by compliance theory, clear signals greatly facilitate persuasive efforts since the aims of rectification can be effectively conveyed to the targets of the process. Where the signals are unclear or suddenly reverse previous policies—as during the 1959–60 and the 1960–61 campaigns—it is correspondingly more difficult to educate cadres thus forcing greater reliance on coercion. Moreover, while consensus exists differences are restricted to relatively narrow issues rather than fundamental approach. But where fundamental approaches are involved the stakes become higher and the fortunes of individual leaders become increasingly tied to the outcome of policy disputes.

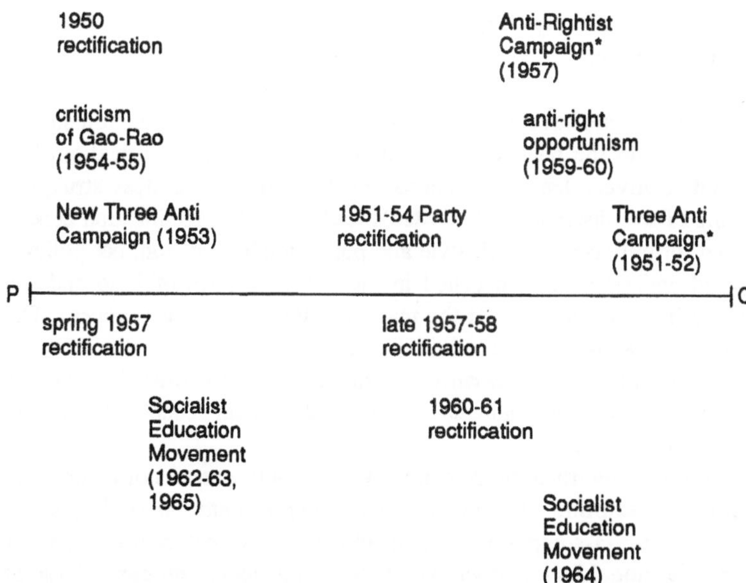

Figure 2. **Degrees of Persuasion and Coercion in Rectification, 1950–65**

Clearly, as demonstrated by our persuasive-coercive continuum in Figure 2 and discussed below, the pattern of coercive and persuasive rectification had a temporal aspect closely tied to the waning policy consensus. In the period of overall consensus through mid-1957, rectification by and large employed relatively persuasive methods. The two outstanding exceptions focused on non-Party elements drawn from suspect social groups—ex-GMD personnel during the Three Anti Campaign and bourgeois intellectuals during the anti-rightist struggle. Where the Party itself was concerned rectification never became highly coercive although the substantial purge rate of 1951–54 placed that effort somewhere in the middle of the continuum. But once the policy consensus began to break down in late 1957 rectification movements increasingly clustered at the coercive end of the continuum. The frayed unity of the 1957–65 period was further reflected in increasing vulnerability of policy making officials as purge targets and also in uncertainty and differences over rectification objectives which sapped the effectiveness of the process. In contrast to the 1950s when rectification was closely integrated with larger social programs and aimed at concrete problems, in the early 1960s it was increasingly addressed to elusive goals such as eliminating revisionism. These converging factors—divergencies over policy, high level targets, increasing uncertainty as to status with the top leadership, lessening effectiveness of reform efforts, and coercive disciplinary methods—were all tied to a larger pattern of declining Party norms.

The Decline of Party Organizational Norms, 1950–65

Important norms have guided the implementation of rectification since the early 1940s. While the need for coercion was recognized, rectification doctrine required relatively lenient sanctions and banned the "ruthless struggles" which typified Party discipline before Mao's leadership. The rectification concept further called for criticism of work style and policy implementation, not policy views. A related understanding articulated in the 1940s writings of Mao and Liu Shaoqi placed limits on the role of the masses in the disciplinary process. This understanding was violated in the initial stage of the 1947–48 rectification movement by encouraging poor peasants to struggle against cadres, but the subsequent reversal of this policy indicated the leadership again accepted the wisdom of the original principle.

Linked to rectification principles were organizational norms upholding strict Leninist discipline—the unquestioning *implementation* of higher directives based on the assumption of an ideologically correct central leadership—and principles upholding an open, vigorous *policy making process*. These principles asserted collective decisions following extensive interchange of views rather than arbitrary individual dictates, and the right of minorities to argue their points of view both before a decision is made and to retain their dissenting opinions after its adoption. But if vigorous contention over policy was encouraged, factional activities seeking to advance the power of individuals and small cliques and political maneuvering outside formal Party bodies were unacceptable.

Rectification According to the Norms, 1950–57

The norms of the 1940s held up well during the first eight years of the PRC. First, Leninist discipline continued to receive unstinting support as the Party's basic organizational principle. This was underscored by the conduct of rectification. Although shortcomings resulting from overzealous implementation of official policies were criticized, the sanctions meted out in such cases were generally mild. While lower level officials might grumble at criticism for their previous efforts once a policy had changed, the lenient nature of discipline undoubtedly attenuated whatever resentment existed and contributed to an effective cadre force. At higher levels the norms of collective leadership and minority rights operated smoothly. Operating within a broad consensus on following the Soviet model, leadership debate centered on such matters as rates of development and program modifications. Mao apparently functioned largely as a centrist balancer, warning against excesses of the left and right. Moreover, he was willing to be overruled by a majority of his colleagues as evidenced in his mid-1956 acceptance of a slowdown in the rate of economic growth. Where he did take the lead in proposing bold initiatives, as in the Hundred Flowers experiment, Mao seemingly rallied a majority within the Politburo rather than imposing his view from outside official channels,[4] while those who lost policy debates largely restricted their opposition to formal Party councils. The vitality of minority rights implicit in this collective decision making process was further demonstrated by the extremely low purge rate of officials in policy making positions.[b] Although individuals such as Bo Yibo apparently suffered career setbacks at least in part for policy advocacy, these were rare cases where those concerned quickly returned to grace.

Ironically, the strength of Party norms is suggested by the one major leadership purge of the period, that of Gao Gang and Rao Shushi. These leaders were charged with attempting to build factional support in a conspiratorial manner outside official Party channels, apparently in anticipation of the death or incapacitation of Mao. The Chairman underlined the importance of Party unity by rebuking Gao and Rao for their effort to pit group against group, declaring "The Chinese revolution was made by many factions"[5]—i.e., by groups of different backgrounds who submerged their differences to the Party's cause. In their factional efforts Gao and Rao relied on appeals based on past career links and potential future rewards, with policy issues playing only a minor role at best. Particularly striking is the apparent inability of Gao and Rao to gather significant support among key Party leaders; very few high level officials were involved in their activities even tangentially. Such leaders seemingly were unwilling to cast their lot with men whose activities threatened the relatively open political process which had contributed so heavily to CCP successes. Furthermore, the purge of Gao and Rao as violators of existing norms was widely accepted as just and proper throughout the Party.

Initially, the principle of *controlled* mass participation in elite discipline was strictly adhered to. With the lesson of 1947–48 in mind, the various rectification campaigns of the early post-1949 period were conducted under firm organizational guidance. Moreover, when the masses were mobilized during the Three Anti Campaign the target was largely non-Party personnel and not Party organizations. In 1957, however, an important departure from established practice appeared as Mao sponsored the Hundred Flowers experiment. This undertaking, which was part of a broader effort to solicit the active participation of intellectuals in the life of the country, encouraged such individuals to voice public criticisms and suggestions concerning the Party's performance. This policy led to significant opposition within the CCP, particularly among officials responsible for dealing with the intelligentsia. The notion of the Party being subjected to unstructured criticism by outsiders—particularly outsiders of bourgeois origins—was clearly difficult for many to swallow. Nevertheless, in significant respects

[b] Apart from Rao Shushi, only two of the living members of the 1945 Central Committee were not reelected to the new 1956 Central Committee.

this criticism was to be kept under control. First, it was assumed that by and large the intellectuals' views would be constructive and not, as sometimes turned out to be the case, fundamental attacks on the system. Procedurally, moreover, although Hundred Flowers criticisms were viewed as part of the concurrent Party rectification movement, the actual criticism and punishment of individual Party members was to be on the inner Party model of 1942–44. Finally, rectification was to be conducted as a "gentle breeze and mild rain," thus promising the most persuasive of disciplinary approaches. Although Mao's initiative did weaken existing understandings concerning popular intrusion into Party affairs at the cost of some dissent within the CCP, the Hundred Flowers to an important extent still respected the separation of Party and masses. Moreover, when it was felt that the process was getting out of control the experiment was quickly terminated and the Anti-Rightist Campaign was launched to underline the sanctity of the vanguard Party.

The rectification efforts of the period up to late 1957 sustained Party norms in several additional senses. These campaigns generally tended to involve persuasive methods, *at least insofar as Party members were concerned* (see Figure 2). As we have seen, in the two cases where coercive measures were widely invoked —the Three Anti and Anti-Rightist Campaigns—the major targets were, respectively, non-Party officials, particularly those left over from the GMD regime, and bourgeois intellectuals. Although individual Party members did receive the harshest of sanctions in the course of these movements, the basic thrust was not directed at the Party. The importance of the distinction was implied in Mao's subsequent approving remark that "relentless blows" were dealt out in the *sanfan* movement,[6] and it was made explicit during the anti-rightist struggle by the decree that Party rectification should continue as a "gentle breeze and mild rain." Finally, throughout the first eight years of the PRC, rectification did not single out policy views as deviations to be attacked. Not only was the Gao-Rao case treated in terms of "unprincipled" plotting, but the movements of the early 1950s all criticized shortcomings in policy implementation and work style. This began to change somewhat with the anti-rightist struggle in 1957. In essence, with this campaign the primary target of rectification shifted from leadership *style* to *attitudes* concerning Party leadership. But while these attitudes often concerned specific CCP policies, the focus of rectification had not yet fallen on *policy* as such.

The Norms under Stress, 1957–65

The launching of the Great Leap Forward in late 1957 marked a watershed in Chinese politics. It not only saw the full flowering of a distinctively Chinese path of development, in the process it inevitably weakened leadership cohesion which had been based to a significant extent on acceptance of the Soviet model. This in turn had a profound effect on Party norms. Although these organizational principles were not explicitly rejected in the period before the Cultural Revolution, they began to function in a much more uncertain fashion. To the extent that responsibility can be assigned for this development, the major share must fall to the increasingly erratic role of Mao himself. Nevertheless, at the same time as his actions began to undermine long standing norms, Mao continued to place high value on them. It was only with the Cultural Revolution that he broke decisively with traditional organizational principles.

The erosion of Party norms was initially seen in the involvement of policy making officials and policy views as targets of the disciplinary process. The quiet downgrading of Chen Yun following the adoption of the Great Leap strategy, while not a formal sanction, was apparently a response to Chen's reservations concerning the new course—and thus an infringement on minority rights. In the same period formal disciplinary measures including purges were used against a substantial number of provincial leaders, most of whom had advocated conservative economic policies out of tune with the leap forward. While these policy "deviations" were invariably coupled with more serious violations of organizational discipline, the raising of these issues was another blow to the previous practice of protecting proponents of minority views from disciplinary action. Moreover, the policy views in question were largely articulated in 1956 when they faithfully reflected official policy; thus to subject them to criticism was implicitly to take issue with Leninist discipline. The need to combat the widespread skepticism which apparently greeted the unprecedented developmental policies seemingly led to rectification measures against advocates of unsuccessful policy positions.

The dismissal of Peng Dehuai and subsequent campaign against right opportunism was an even more dramatic violation of minority rights. When the Great Leap began to run into serious problems by late 1958, a series of high level meetings were held to map policy adjustments. In order to encourage vigorous debate Mao strongly reaffirmed traditional norms by calling on Party leaders to criticize shortcomings forthrightly without fear of retribution. Mao, however, had seriously underestimated the depth of disenchantment with the leap and when Peng launched a comprehensive critique at the mid-1959 Lushan meetings the Chairman reacted sharply. Although organizational issues—Peng's alleged "conspiratorial" discussions with other leaders and his exchange of views with Khrushchev—were also cited, the core of the attack on Peng was his opposition to the leap forward. Mao was able to carry the day and secure Peng's dismissal, and also to launch a harsh rectification movement against lower level officials holding similar views. In sharp contrast to Gao and Rao, widespread sympathy for Peng existed within the Party on the grounds that he had been unjustly treated. Even strong proponents of the Great Leap reportedly argued that although Peng's views were wrong he had merely been exercising his right as a leading Party member to advocate alternative policies. Mao himself, moreover, recognized the continuing value of traditional norms and renewed his call for forthright criticism. But the lesson of Peng's fate undercut Mao's belated efforts to revive traditional practices as many senior leaders apparently muted their criticism of the economic strategy at Lushan. Political prudence had begun to sap the policy process of its vitality.

In the wake of the Great Leap's collapse a major effort was made, with Mao playing a leading role, to restore the norms which had been undermined by the Peng case and anti-right opportunist drive. In 1961–62 a large scale "reversal of verdicts" was carried out which restored to official posts leaders who had been—in terms of traditional organizational norms—unfairly dealt with in 1959–60. This effort could not fully repair the damage which had been done, however. First, Mao was unwilling to vindicate Peng Dehuai along with the lesser lights sharing his views. The criteria now used to exclude Peng were solely organizational—his "conspiratorial" activities and links to Soviet leaders. But the strength of feeling that Peng had been wronged suggests this rationale was not convincing to disgruntled officials. Moreover, the "reversal of verdicts" process was linked both to relatively harsh measures during the rectification of leap forward excesses in 1960–61 and to the removal of several leading provincial figures who had been in the forefront advocating Great Leap policies, while at the same time rehabilitating leaders who had questioned the strategy. Thus to a certain extent the rectification and "reversal of verdicts" process embodied a shift in official positions reflecting the policy changes following the leap. Unlike the early and mid-1950s when advocates of rejected policies carried on regardless and rectification ignored policy questions, now the winners and losers of policy debates were much more likely to have their political careers directly affected.

Although Mao was able to muster a majority behind his various initiatives in the 1957–65 period, it is clear that the principle of collective leadership and the general openness of the policy process was weakened. Already by the time of Lushan there was grumbling concerning Mao's "individual style," and his handling of Peng Dehuai intensified feelings that he had become arbitrary and despotic like Stalin, and that nobody dared to speak up in his presence. Despite Mao's subsequent efforts—most notably his 1961 self-criticism, his acknowledgement that he too was bound by majority opinion, and his repeated calls for airing dissenting opinions within Party bodies—fear of the Chairman's irascibility continued to erode Party norms. This is suggested by Peng Zhen's secret 1961 review of Great Leap policies, i.e., a project undertaken without informing higher Party bodies as established procedures required. In the uncertain atmosphere existing since Lushan, many Party leaders were apparently unwilling to risk their careers by being unguardedly critical of policies associated with Mao regardless of time honored traditions of openness.

In the remaining years before the Cultural Revolution the situation was further complicated by Mao's withdrawal to the "second line." Increasingly out of touch with the management of ongoing affairs, Mao's interventions in the policy process became both more unpredictable and more difficult to interpret. While he did not develop a comprehensive policy line himself, the Chairman became increasingly critical of the performance of his leadership colleagues, even to the point of seeing dangerous revisionist tendencies within high Party bodies. The assumption of a unified, correct Party leadership which was the basis of traditional organizational norms was no longer accepted unquestioningly by Mao, although he continued to assert that the norms still applied. As a result Mao's role had changed from the 1950s when he acted as the central figure of a cohesive collective to a more provocative posture of an irregular and remote critic of the top Chinese leadership.[7]

If old understandings concerning the behavior of high ranking Party leaders were starting to break down, the guiding principle of organizational discipline for lower level cadres was also under stress. Leninist discipline was never challenged theoretically, but the practice of rectification in the period following the Great Leap severely undermined that discipline. During the leap forward enormous pressures were placed on cadres to achieve the most ambitious goals. These pressures inevitably led to excesses in implementation, and these excesses were extensively criticized during the 1960–61 rectification movement. While it was nothing new for cadres to be criticized for problems generated by official policy, in the 1950s such criticism had generally been restrained and sanctions were taken in only the most extreme cases. Now, however, apparently significant numbers of cadres who had attempted to carry out the most onerous tasks were severely dealt with for errors which originated with higher Party leaders. The result was widespread demoralization and doubt about the wisdom of strictly implementing official policy.

Past norms concerning the role of mass participation in Party discipline were also eroded during the post-Great Leap period. In both the 1960–61 campaign and the Socialist Education Movement poor peasant organizations were established with supervisory powers. These bodies played a particularly dynamic role in the latter effort. While socialist education had unfolded in 1962–63 as a mild movement which left rural Party organizations largely intact, by 1964 senior Party leaders became convinced that corruption among rural Party leaders was far worse than previously believed and only a root and branch purge could resolve the problem. To accomplish this, methods similar to those used briefly in 1947–48 and then discarded were employed: poor peasants were mobilized to attack basic level cadres and to participate directly in disciplining Party members albeit under tighter work team control. The net result once again was demoralization of the rural cadre force which necessitated an end to the intervention of the peasant masses.

Finally, the basic principle of persuasion and reform was often honored in the breach thus creating a growing estrangement between rectification theory and practice. As shown by Figure 2, from late 1957 to 1965 rectification efforts increasingly tended to fall on the coercive end of the persuasive-coercive continuum. Already by 1958 the rectification campaign accompanying the leap forward, in contrast to the "gentle breeze and mild rain" methods of spring 1957, had resulted in a relatively high disciplinary rate of 8 to 9 percent of Party members. While comprehensive statistics are lacking for the 1959 anti-right opportunist drive, scattered reports indicate cadre dismissals at a rate of 20 to 30 percent or more in local areas, a rate far in excess of anything previously reported. Moreover, many Party officials regarded the conduct of this campaign as reflecting the methods of "ruthless struggles and merciless blows"—the disciplinary approach denounced by Mao in the 1940s. The available data for the 1960–61 rectification movement also indicate, at least in some instances, the use of extreme sanctions, severe struggle and indiscriminate purges. Finally, during the Socialist Education Movement in 1964 the involvement of poor peasants not only led to rough treatment of basic level cadres, but scattered reports indicate local purge rates as high as 40 to 70 percent, with the overall figure probably in excess of 10 percent. While problems of data require some caution, it is nevertheless clear that rectification in the 1957–65 period strayed far from the "save the patient" approach.

As the foregoing suggests, Mao played a pivotal role in the changing fortunes of Party norms. The norms had been forged during the consolidation of Mao's power and marked an open, tolerant style of leadership which contributed greatly to the loyalty of his colleagues. The Chairman was a source of support for the norms not only through repeated advocacy but also as a result of the stable situation created by his unchallenged authority. It is significant that the most blatant challenge to the norms was mounted by Gao Gang when it appeared Mao might be forced into inactivity by ill health. But if the norms drew sustenance from Mao, by the same token they were vulnerable to his actions. When he began to engage in individual leadership and deny the right of policy advocacy to various colleagues, there were no well charted avenues of redress. Thus in 1959 despite widespread support for Peng Dehuai, once Mao forced the issue the vast majority backed the Chairman. Moreover, while Mao continued to affirm the norms after 1959, this was on an increasingly erratic basis as his commitment to those principles frequently came into conflict with his dissatisfaction at the results achieved by established methods. Still, the norms retained some vitality given both Mao's ambivalent backing and the continued support of other leaders who valued the benefits of open policy making and lenient discipline. In addition to policy consensus and well defined power relationships at the apex of the CCP, the elite's commitment to the norms was in itself a major force affecting their strength prior to the Cultural Revolution.

The Struggle over the Norms, 1966–78

The events of the Cultural Revolution which shattered long standing Party principles are too well known to require extended discussion. Most startling was the almost free rein given to non-Party groups—student Red Guards and "revolutionary rebels" in factories and administrative offices—to attack the highest Party leaders without clear guidance from official structures.[c] The only guidance given such forces was delphic slogans in the media plus erratic intervention by a handful of individuals close to Mao; legitimate authority did not flow from either the regular Party hierarchy or *ad hoc* work teams. The distinction between Party and non-Party was not entirely eliminated, however, as the handful of leaders around Mao exercised their authority to limit attacks on specific individuals. Nevertheless, the Party as an institution and high ranking leaders had never been so exposed to spontaneous mass action.

At the same time the sanctions invoked by both non-Party groups and official authority veered toward the coercive end of the continuum. Red Guards seized senior leaders, roughly paraded them through the streets, and humiliated them in severe struggle sessions lasting days on end. In some cases officials died of heart attacks while suffering Red Guard abuse; in others leaders took their own lives in despair. In terms of formal organizational sanctions, far more sweeping dismissals and purges of leading figures took place than at any previous time in CCP history even though the overall purge rate for the CCP as a whole was low.[8] When the Ninth Party Congress met in 1969, not only were Liu Shaoqi and Deng Xiaoping gone, but about 60 percent of the previous Politburo and 70 percent of the Central Committee were removed.[9] Despite statements affirming the possibility of reform and the desirability of persuasive methods, in practice the Cultural Revolution had brutally discarded rectification principles.

The charges brought against high level leaders and the appearance of new theoretical emphases represented a frontal attack on the remaining Party norms. Many of the accusations focused on alleged opposition to Mao and his policies. Leaving aside the question of Mao's own contemporary position on the matters at issue, in many cases the culprits were in fact carrying out official CCP policies at the times in question. This, together with the exalted position assigned to Mao and his thought, clearly undermined concepts of collective leadership where Mao's vote was only equal to those of his colleagues. Attacks on various policy positions further demonstrated that mere opposition was now sufficient for punishment even if it were open and conducted strictly within formal Party bodies; assurances of minority rights became meaningless in such circumstances. Finally, Leninist discipline was challenged by the rejection of cadre defenses that they were merely implementing higher level policy. This was attacked as reflecting a "slavish mentality"; the proper attitude was to scrutinize higher directives

[c]In Mao's eyes the use of extra-Party forces achieved results where traditional methods failed. In October 1966 the Chairman stated: "In . . . the first five months [January–May 1966] of this great Cultural Revolution, there were many articles and directives from the Center which failed to attract much attention. But big character posters and the Red Guards attacked and they succeeded in attracting attention. It is impossible to ignore them."*MP*, p. 43.

in "the mirror of Mao's thought" and reject all that did not measure up. Clearly a Leninist organization could not function in this fashion.

The frontal attack on traditional norms generated widespread opposition and resentment within the Party. As in the case of Peng Dehuai, a sense of unjust treatment of high ranking leaders again appeared, but on an even deeper level. Not only did some leaders attempt to defend Liu Shaoqi against charges of opposing Mao on the grounds that all of the Chairman's colleagues had openly opposed Mao from time to time as a matter of right, but several abortive attempts were made during the Cultural Revolution to promote "reversals of verdicts" for a wide range of Party leaders. Such efforts reflected a feeling that traditional principles should again be applied, but this was not to be in the unpredictable atmosphere of the period which Chen Yi observed had put everyone in a panic. Now politics was highly personalized and factional in nature. Personal links to leaders going back decades became the basis for disgrace or survival. Zhou Enlai in particular was able to protect various leaders, but this was done in response to shifting political pressures rather than based on well defined norms. As for Mao, his increasingly personal judgments were clearly the basis for much of the flouting of organizational principle, but there were still signs of his pre-Cultural Revolution ambivalence. This was reflected not only in calls for cadres to reform themselves, but also in the Chairman's seeming reluctance to sanction a full scale attack on Liu Shaoqi until the need to focus rebellious activity on a scapegoat became imperative.[10]

Meanwhile, throughout the elite as a whole deep hostility appeared between cadres with long records of public service and young non-Party activists who both led virulent criticism of the old guard and in some cases took over leading administrative posts despite their lack of experience. This bitter legacy of the Cultural Revolution created a running sore within the leadership elite, one which has continued to plague the Chinese body politic and inhibit mild rectification down to the present day.

About mid-1968 Mao concluded the time had come to consolidate the gains of the Cultural Revolution and rebuild the political system, a process which would require a new set of Party norms as well as revived institutions. These norms would inevitably imply a greater degree of predictability and order than had been characteristic of 1966–68. Mao recognized this and endorsed a moderate cadre policy at the Ninth Congress, a policy which not only preached leniency but bolstered Leninist discipline by making cadres whose sins had merely been following higher level orders eligible for rehabilitation.[d] Such steps were

[d] Hong Yung Lee, "The Politics of Cadre Rehabilitation Since the Cultural Revolution," *Asian Survey*, September 1978, pp. 942–43. Lee's excellent analysis points out the distinction between "rehabilitation" *(pingfan)*, cases of "verdict reversal" where the Party admits a wrong decision, and "liberation" *(jiefang)*, cases where cadres have been correctly disciplined but are willing to reform. *Ibid.*, pp. 935–36. Here we use "rehabilitation" loosely to cover both processes.

necessary to cope with extensive cadre demoralization which had resulted from the Cultural Revolution. Much as in the post-Great Leap period, but now on an even more widespread basis, many officials were unwilling to play active leadership roles for fear of future punishment. Mao, nevertheless, was still insistent on an active mass role in rehabilitation, rectification and elite recruitment. Thus the first efforts in 1969 were undertaken under "open door" principles, but this floundered as non-Party activists took an extremely negative view of Party members and the factional conflicts of Red Guard and rebel groups were injected into the process. This forced a change in approach and by 1970 rectification emphasized Party leadership of the process while the initiative of non-Party masses was sharply circumscribed.[11]

While practical considerations were involved, more broadly the post-Cultural Revolution period saw the emergence of two distinct approaches to norms of inner Party life. While Mao still sporadically backed some traditional principles, the Chairman and those close to him—most notably the so-called "gang of four"[e] —were determined that the new norms would reflect the basic ideological thrust of 1966–68. At the same time, however, the rebuilding process offered an opportunity for those associated with pre-1966 political institutions—perhaps Zhou Enlai above all others—to try and restore the organizational principles adopted in the 1940s. The tensions between these two forces and approaches were considerable, and they became particularly prominent following the 1971 demise of Lin Biao who had posed a threat to both groups.

The Lin Biao affair demonstrated how severely established norms of inner Party behavior had been weakened by the Cultural Revolution. Regardless of whether official claims that Lin planned a military coup and the assassination of Mao are true, it is clear that the affair was fundamentally a factional struggle rather than a principled division over policy. Indeed, the case is reminiscent of the Gao-Rao affair in several respects. As in 1953, the question of the succession to Mao was on the minds of leading political actors. The importance of personal ties was reflected in the purge following Lin's mysterious death, a purge which focused on those working with Lin in the central military apparatus and disproportionately affected those who had served under his command during the civil war. Lin's activities, moreover, were conducted in a conspiratorial manner outside official Party bodies. Following Lin's demise Mao revived an injunction he had first issued with regard to Gao Gang: leading cadres must be "open and above board."[f]

[e] Jiang Qing, Zhang Chunqiao, Yao Wenyuan and Wang Hongwen. As we shall see, this is not to identify Mao and the "gang" or to disregard official stories of Mao's criticisms of it. We do argue, however, that on many crucial issues the "gang" spoke for the Chairman and that he viewed their role in a post-Mao China as critical to the success of his revolutionary vision.

[f] See above, p. 144. Mao's full injunction was: "Practice Marxism, and not revisionism; unite, and don't split; be open and above board, and don't intrigue and conspire." These principles—known as the "three do's and three don'ts"—were to become a major platform of those seeking to revive traditional Party norms (see below). While the first pair of do's and don'ts is vague and ideological in orientation, the latter two refer to concrete organizational norms.

Although it apparently did not affect ordinary cadres as the "criticize Lin and rectification" campaign emphasized mild study below the leadership level, the post-Lin purge cut deeply into central military organs and had a significant impact at the provincial level. When a new Central Committee was elected at the Tenth Party Congress in 1973, the purge of Lin's followers together with Cultural Revolution "ultra-leftists" resulted in the ouster of nearly one quarter of the previous Central Committee. Thus extensive purging remained a feature of post-1966 Chinese politics.[12]

Following an initial period of uncertainty after Lin's fall, Chinese politics became more polarized than at any time in the history of the PRC. This involved many policy areas with a general division between those favoring a return to political stability and the pursuit of economic modernization and others seeking to keep alive the innovations of the Cultural Revolution. Indeed, one's attitude towards the Cultural Revolution, an event which marked a dramatic change in the power of different individuals and groups, became a touchstone defining political orientation. Of course, even in this polarized setting a simple "two line struggle" did not emerge; many leaders occupied an ambiguous middle ground tailoring their actions to shifting political winds. One of the most important factors was Mao, who although significantly weakened by the betrayal of his personally chosen successor and by his own grave illness remained a key if no longer dominant force. Mao did not totally identify with either camp, but his initiatives in the 1973–76 period tended to support the radical perspective of the "gang of four." This was generally if not invariably true with regard to Party organizational norms.[13]

The conflicting organizational approaches were reflected in the new Party Constitution adopted at the Tenth Congress. This document was an uneasy amalgam of traditional norms and principles reflecting the Cultural Revolution experience. The new Constitution reaffirmed many long standing norms: Leninist discipline ("the lower level is subordinate to the higher level"), collective leadership ("the minority is subordinate to the majority"), and minority rights ("if a Party member holds different views . . . he is allowed to reserve his views"). But the Constitution, and particularly Wang Hongwen's report on it, contained elements in contradiction to these principles. The continuing role given to Mao and his thought, even if toned down from Cultural Revolution days, made true collective leadership difficult. The emphasis on the danger of capitalist restoration and the need for recurrent Cultural Revolutions bode ill for any leaders seeking to exercise their rights to articulate alternative policies. Wang Hongwen also supported another Cultural Revolution innovation, the right of non-Party masses to engage in self-directed criticism of the Party and its leaders. Thus he stressed "the right [of the masses] to exercise revolutionary supervision over cadres of all ranks" through the use of big character posters and "great debates." While Wang did acknowledge the "three do's and three don'ts," he placed the emphasis on the vague ideological injunction of opposing revisionism while downplaying the organizational requirement to be "open and above board." Finally, Wang introduced a new saying from Chairman Mao: "Going against the tide is a Marxist principle." Here the rebellious attitudes of the Cultural Revolution were reemphasized. Party members were again encouraged to test official policies against Mao's "correct line" and, by implication, reject blind obedience to organizational authority.[14]

The post-Tenth Congress period was marked by a bitter conflict between the radical forces of the "gang of four" and experienced Party officials. In this conflict organizational norms were both a key issue and a tool of struggle. Rehabilitation and rectification were key weapons in the arsenal of the old guard. While the radicals sought to apply stringent ideological criteria to rehabilitation and recruitment—both to limit the return of disgraced cadres and maximize the posts available for Cultural Revolution activists—veteran officials gained the upper hand and achieved large scale rehabilitations after the Lin Biao affair. With the great bulk of cadres at the county and lower levels rehabilitated by the end of 1972, attention increasingly turned to former high level leaders with a major breakthrough achieved in 1973 with the reappearance of Deng Xiaoping. In formal terms Deng's rehabilitation reflected rectification procedures: Deng had to undergo self-criticism, acknowledge the correctness of Cultural Revolution measures against him, and promise never to seek a "reversal of verdicts" on his case or the Cultural Revolution *per se*. Nevertheless, in political terms rehabilitations such as Deng's represented a victory of old line officials over the radical forces. Certainly many leaders viewed the return of Deng and others as a vindication, as a *de facto* "reversal of verdicts," and the restored officials pursued a relatively cohesive policy line which undermined the changes resulting from the Cultural Revolution. Unavoidably, policy orientation was again linked to the handling of disciplinary matters.[15]

With Deng Xiaoping and other veteran leaders gaining a growing hold on Party and state institutions apart from the propaganda apparatus where the "gang" remained strong, they now sought to further the linkage of policy and discipline by using the rectification process against radical elements. After the January 1975 NPC which endorsed the "four modernizations"—the concept conceived by Mao in 1964 but now pushed by Zhou Enlai while the Chairman absented himself from the Congress—Deng called for a broad rectification effort that would sweep out of official positions young Cultural Revolution activists who lacked the inclination and/or skills required for economic development.[16] While this linking of rectification and policy orientation conflicted with traditional norms in one sense, it had the virtue of both being the logical outgrowth of policies legally sanctioned by the highest organ of the state and a move obviously necessary to secure implementation of official policies.

If Deng and his allies were able to use traditional principles against the radicals, they in turn employed the nascent norms derived from the Cultural Revolution. They encouraged the mass supervision aspects of the new Constitution with the result that wall poster criticism of leaders at various levels up to the Politburo appeared on a significant scale. Moreover, they used the media to challenge obliquely both key leaders and various policies which had been endorsed by leading Party and state bodies. In this manner they were able to put pressure on policy makers in an effort to inhibit "revisionist" tendencies and to encourage many lower level officials to "go against the tide" and ignore directives which did not appear sufficiently faithful to Mao's thought. These pressures notwithstanding, the old guard continued its policy drift away from Cultural Revolution values and prevented disciplinary action against those coming under the radical attack. Something of a stalemate had been achieved with the "gang of four" invoking the innovative norms of the new Constitution to attack the reconstituted establishment, but with that establishment successfully resisting its onslaught by invoking traditional organizational discipline.[17]

The consequences of the stalemate was a highly factionalized and inefficient political system. For many cadres the conflicting signals coming from the media and official documents created confusion, fear and immobility. Not knowing which signals to respond to and fearful of being caught on the wrong side, as in the past officials at all levels eschewed active leadership and demoralization spread. Others did respond to one or another set of signals. With factional conflict dating from the Cultural Revolution still significant in all institutions, different groups engaged in an ongoing internecine struggle and responded to the opposing impulses from Beijing according to their inclinations and the needs of local combat. In these circumstances repeated calls for unity were futile. The manifestations of factional strife included the establishment of an illegal document distribution and reproduction system by the radicals, the planting of spies in the bureaucratic domains of enemy groups, and the use of public security forces to settle inner Party disputes despite the long standing practice of keeping the police out of CCP affairs. Mao was aware of and distressed by these developments, he himself issuing several plaintive calls for unity and, if we are to believe the post-Mao leadership, even rebuking the "gang" for their factional activities. Nevertheless, it was the Chairman's endorsement of the radical themes championed by the "gang" which provided both the ideological justification and political backing for their disruptive activities.[18]

The delicate political balance which served as the backdrop to these developments was altered by the death of Zhou Enlai in January 1976. Now, with Mao's backing, the "gang" launched a fierce attack on Deng Xiaoping's "right deviationist wind." Clearly many factors were involved—fundamentally conflicting policy orientations, competition for power particularly in view of the succession to both Mao and Zhou, and intense personal antagonism dating from the Cultural Revolution. Yet it is also important to examine the attack on Deng in terms of norms of elite behavior. The attack was directed at a set of measures Deng had developed through open consultation in official Party and state forums to realize the program approved by the NPC. It was based on an *ideological* rationale:

whatever legal authority had been vested in Deng through his Party and state positions and however closely his policies adhered to the officially sanctioned "four modernizations," the effect of those programs was to restore the pre-Cultural Revolution situation and therefore should be resisted. Yet from the perspective of traditional *organizational* norms Deng was blameless: he had acted in an "above board" manner to implement legal decisions. As the onslaught against Deng developed in early 1976 many senior Party leaders balked at taking disciplinary action against him, with some Politburo members reportedly leaving their posts in protest over this latest violation of long standing principles. Deng's dismissal only came when the issue was forced by the unprecedented April 1976 Tian'anmen riots, and even then Deng retained his Party membership despite allegations that his activities had represented an antagonistic struggle with Mao's political line. While their hand had been forced by events, the majority of Party leaders were unwilling to endorse fully an organizational approach which jeopardized the careers of veteran cadres and undermined the stability of the political system.[19]

Restoring the Norms after Mao

With the death of Mao the long factional conflict came to a swift, dramatic conclusion. After less than a month of intense maneuvering, the "gang of four" were arrested in a move stage managed by Premier Hua Guofeng, Defense Minister Ye Jianying and Mao's chief bodyguard, Wang Dongxing. Whatever the truth of subsequent claims that the "gang" were plotting to seize power, it is clear that Hua and company effected a coup of their own in a manner totally outside established principles: they not only ousted members of the highest Party body but apparently did so without consulting with the full Politburo.[20] In defense of Hua, Ye and Wang, conspiratorial action may have been unavoidable. In a situation where rampant factionalism had severely wounded traditional norms, they probably believed decisive action was required to restore political order.

The new post-Mao leadership quickly moved not only to restore order in society, but also to adopt a comprehensive set of policies designed to realize the "four modernizations." While there is considerable room for differences over aspects of the program, and while any efforts are complicated by the maneuvering of individual leaders reflecting both the conflicts of the previous decade and current political uncertainties, the post-Mao era has nevertheless seen the reestablishment of a substantial policy consensus based on a clear priority to economic development.[21] The new policy consensus has resulted in a further step-up of cadre rehabilitation to provide the skilled leadership required for the modernization program. Beyond this there is a widespread desire within the elite for increased predictability in political life, for a final elimination of the uncertainties and strife which have bedeviled Chinese politics since the Cultural Revolution. This desire has been reflected in Hua Guofeng's leadership style, a style emphasizing a centrist position, conciliation among different interests, and substantial delegation of authority to his colleagues—one similar in many respects to Mao's in the 1950s. It was also demonstrated by Deng Xiaoping's acknowledgement of Hua's legitimate leadership and emphasis on the crucial importance of stability at the time of his second rehabilitation in 1977.[22]

Central to the pursuit of political stability has been a major effort to restore traditional Party norms.[g] While some lip service has been given to principles derived from the Cultural Revolution, the overall emphasis has been decisively on pre-1966 understandings. This has been seen in a number of measures—the stepped up pace of rehabilitations, an attempt to invoke rectification principles even in the purge of those connected with the "gang of four," a ban on the use of the public security apparatus to handle inner Party discipline, and prohibition of "special case groups" outside regular Party bodies to examine cadres.[23] While such moves to restore long standing principles have developed progressively since Mao's death, major steps came with the August 1977 Eleventh Party Congress and the December 1978 Central Committee plenum.

The new Party Constitution adopted by the Eleventh Congress, together with the reports of Hua Guofeng and Ye Jianying, systematically reaffirmed traditional norms. First, heavy emphasis was placed on Leninist discipline. In addition to declaring centralism even more important than democracy, the Congress provided a theoretical rationale for obedience remarkably similar to that advanced in the 1940s. Then it was the correctness of the Party led by Mao, now it was the "Marxist-Leninist leading core" headed by Hua. In elaborating this rationale the new leaders gave new meaning to Cultural Revolution concepts. "Capitalist roaders" still existed, but because power was concentrated in a correct leading core they were restricted to a mere handful. If such people caused trouble there would be no reason to doubt the Party leadership, for in such a situation a new Cultural Revolution would be launched "under the leadership of the Central Committee headed by Chairman Hua," i.e., under firm Party control. Moreover, the notion of "going against the tide" was now transformed into an attack on factionalism. The new Constitution called on Party members "to go against any tide that runs counter to [the three do's and three don'ts]," while "capitalist roaders" were defined as those violating the three principles. Thus these concepts were given an organizational interpretation in direct conflict with their original ideological emphasis. CCP members were to oppose those who conspired and engaged in factional activities and not the legal decisions of higher Party bodies.[24]

[g]There may be differences of nuance within the leadership, however. As various analysts have noted, Deng Xiaoping has spoken of "restoring" *(huifu)* Party traditions while Hua Guofeng and Ye Jianying have referred to "maintaining" *(baochi)* them. *CNA*, No. 1115 (1978), p. 2. While this difference in terminology could reflect debate over the wisdom of tacitly admitting the damage caused to Party norms under Mao's leadership, this analysis sees broad agreement on the need to restore those norms in fact.

The Congress placed heavy emphasis on reviving inner Party democracy. The new Constitution encouraged debate within the Party by calling on members to "say all you know and say it without reserve," and it further guaranteed both the right to criticize Party leaders and to reserve opinions once a decision was made. Furthermore, decisions on all issues were to be made collectively and tendencies toward one man rule resisted. On handling disciplinary matters, an effort was made to restore institutionalized methods by establishing commissions for inspecting discipline (a new version of the old Party control committees). As in the norms laid down in the 1940s, the masses were to help keep the Party on its toes, but their disciplinary role would be limited. According to Ye Jianying, "we should let the masses say what is on their minds, even if they should abuse us," but his comments were far more guarded than those of Wang Hongwen four years earlier. While Wang had emphasized mass supervision over Party and state cadres and had urged arousing the masses to air their views freely, write big character posters and hold great debates, Ye avoided mention of these themes.[h] This shift in orientation was further underlined by the addition of the phrase "cadres are a decisive factor" to the Constitution, as well as by attacks on the "gang" for trying to "replace the Party with mass organizations."[25]

Finally, rectification principles were asserted in the main reports to the Congress. Hua Guofeng endorsed the "save the patient" approach for dealing with cadre shortcomings and advocated a discriminating approach to narrow the target of attack in the campaign against the "gang of four" while treating leniently those who were not deeply involved with the "gang." Ye Jianying, furthermore, invoked Mao's authority by claiming the late Chairman "was always opposed to 'finishing off' an erring comrade 'at one blow,' " and he further inveighed against "ruthless struggles and merciless blows." Clearly cadres and Party members were being promised a return to the traditional persuasive emphasis.[26]

Traditional norms were again emphasized at the December 1978 Central Committee plenum. Particularly striking was the stress on collective leadership. Not only did Hua call for less attention to individuals, but a ban on personal instructions was approved. The point was underlined by a demystification of

---

[h] *Peking Review*, No. 35–36 (1973), p. 33, No. 36 (1977), pp. 17, 30–32. The right to air views freely, etc., was carried over from the 1975 State Constitution into the 1978 version, but here too a new interpretation was put on those rights to ban their use against the Party leadership in a context emphasizing iron discipline, rules and regulations, and protecting popular rights through formal state institutions. *Ibid.*, No. 10 (1978), pp. 33, No. 11 (1978), pp. 18–20, 27. Yet such devices can in fact still have political uses as in the wall poster campaign against Politburo member Wu De, a campaign which raised issues apparently involved in Wu's 1978 removal as Beijing first secretary. See *CNA*, No. 1110 (1978), p. 3, No. 1142 (1978), pp. 4–5. Nevertheless, the leadership has sought to contain such practices and the general approach is to restore the traditional mass line of popular participation under firm Party leadership. As Hua Guofeng put it regarding the campaign against the "gang of four," "the masses have been mobilized on a very broad scale and yet in a very orderly way. . . ." *Peking Review*, No. 35 (1977), p. 43.

Mao. The plenum's communique declared that despite Mao's "indelible" achievements he was not "free of all shortcomings"—an assessment it correctly pointed out corresponded with his own. A second major feature of the plenum was its handling of historical questions, a task declared necessary to consolidate Party unity. Now there was a "reversal of verdicts" for several leading figures who had suffered under Mao—most notably the late Peng Dehuai who was declared "firm and upright, [a man] known for his honesty and integrity, never considering his personal loss or gain." Although not a formal "verdict reversal" since he had not been officially disciplined, the election of Chen Yun as Party Vice Chairman—thus restoring the position he held in the 1950s—further demonstrated the righting of past wrongs.[i]

Despite the consensus on restoring traditional norms, the effort has faced major problems. The lingering bitterness and uncertainties of the previous decade has made the application of the norms difficult. On the one hand, the animosities directed at the "gang" and Cultural Revolution radicals generally have led to coercive measures. Not only has there been a significant purge as reflected in the dropping of nearly half of the former Central Committee at the Eleventh Congress, but harsh methods including arrests and possibly capital punishment have been used in some cases. But at the same time there has been resistance to the purge and cover ups of factional activities due to the entanglement of many officials with the radical forces during the post-1966 period. Whether mild rectification or just decisions can take place in this context is uncertain. Moreover, since nearly half of all Party members joined after the Cultural Revolution, a significant part of the elite has rarely experienced strict discipline, an open policy process, or persuasive discipline. Thus a whole generation of political leaders has been socialized in circumstances at drastic variance with traditional norms.[27]

Nevertheless, the effort has been considerable at the highest levels. While significant friction between survivors and victims of the Cultural Revolution complicates the situation, it has been contained to an important degree. Thus

---

[i] *Peking Review*, No. 52 (1978), pp. 4, 7, 13–16. In addition to Peng Dehuai, "reversals of verdicts" included the cases of Xi Zhongxun, who had fallen into disgrace in 1962 (see above, p. 337n), and Cultural Revolution victims Tao Zhu and Bo Yibo. In addition, it appeared Peng Zhen had been vindicated in all but name shortly before the plenum when it was declared that the Beijing Municipal Committee had been correct before the Cultural Revolution. See *CNA*, No. 1142 (1978), p. 6. The possibility of the rehabilitation of even Liu Shaoqi was also suggested by the plenum despite Deng Xiaoping's reticence concerning Liu's case in conversations with Western newsmen in November 1978. At the December plenum repeated attacks were directed solely at Lin Biao and the "gang of four" in contrast to the NPC earlier in the year when Liu was ritualistically bracketed with Lin and the "gang." More significantly, the plenum declared that "the ... Cultural Revolution should also be viewed historically, scientifically and in a down to earth way," although there "should be no haste" in summing up its shortcomings. *Peking Review*, No. 11 (1978), p. 16, No. 52 (1978), pp. 7, 9, 15.

while Wu De was ousted as first secretary of Beijing in 1978, apparently for his role in the second fall of Deng Xiaoping, he nevertheless retained Politburo status. Whatever Wu's actual position, this approach is reminiscent of Mao's handling of erring comrades during the pre-Cultural Revolution period. While there must be winners and losers in politics, the current leaders seem intent on limiting the stakes.

In essence, the post-Mao leadership is attempting to restore predictability to political life in China. Here the experience of the Soviet Union is illuminating. After Stalin the Soviet political elite moved to eliminate terror from inner Party life. Moreover, following Khrushchev's somewhat personalized rule, the Brezhnev leadership has further regularized political life through a significant degree of personnel stability, emphasis on balanced decision making, and broad consultation within the elite. Indeed, official praise of Brezhnev stresses his "establish[ing] comradeliness, trust, and a respectful relation to people in the Party."[28]

In China, such comradeliness and trust had long been associated with Mao's leadership but it became vulnerable to the Chairman's increasingly erratic behavior since the Great Leap Forward and particularly the Cultural Revolution. While Mao had been for years a strong pillar upholding traditional norms, his enormous political strength was always a potential danger to those principles—a potential which became a reality despite a sporadic, contradictory attachment to them to the end. No elite is happy at such vulnerability, and strong pressures exist in post-Mao China as in other socialist societies to protect the rights of political leaders and provide reliable guidelines for behavior. Given the absence of truly binding constitutions in Communist systems, a degree of unpredictability will always exist. Moreover, the likelihood that no one will ever again obtain Mao's unchallenged position implies that political position will be more closely tied to policy advocacy than was the case during the unusually stable leadership of early and mid-1950s. Ultimately, however, assuming the legacy of the Cultural Revolution can be successfully defused, the norms which Mao did so much to create will be more secure in his absence.

Appendices

Notes

Introduction to the Second Edition

1. The Introduction and Chapters 1 to 10 were written by August 1976, while Chapter 11 on the Socialist Education Movement was completed in early 1978. The final editing incorporated new material published in 1977–78, most notably Volume V of Mao's *Selected Works*, but this largely served to elaborate the argument rather than result in any significant substantive alterations.

2. "Chinese Politics 1949–1965: A Changing Mao," first published in *Current Scene*, Parts I and II, January and February 1974. Republished as ch. I of *Leadership, Legitimacy, and Conflict in China* (see below, n. 3).

3. *Leadership, Legitimacy, and Conflict in China: From a Charismatic Mao to the Politics of Succession* (Armonk: M.E. Sharpe, 1984); and *Politics at Mao's Court: Gao Gang and Party Factionalism in the Early 1950s* (Armonk: M.E. Sharpe, 1990). Also relevant is my article, "Mao and His Lieutenants," *The Australian Journal of Chinese Affairs (AJCA)*, No. 19–20 (1988), which analyzes Mao's leadership style.

4. For a critical discussion of the strengths and limitations of interviews, see *Politics at Mao's Court*, pp. 12–14. For further analyses of reform period sources and historiography including comparisons to sources from earlier periods, see *ibid.*, pp. 7–12; Susanne Weigelin-Schwiedrzik, "Party Historiography in the People's Republic of China," *AJCA*, No. 17 (1987); Michael Schoenhals, "Unofficial and Official Histories of the Cultural Revolution—A Review Article," *The Journal of Asian Studies*, August 1989; and the various issues of *CCP Research Newsletter*. Cf. below, nn. 103, 168.

5. Bo Yibo, *Ruogan zhongda juece yu shijian de huigu* [Reflections on Certain Major Policy Decisions and Events] (Beijing: Zhonggong zhongyang dangxiao chubanshe, 1991). The detailed information from this source, as well as other recent sources, fully supports the analysis of *Politics at Mao's Court* and is heavily drawn upon in the following discussion.

6. While this less serious view of Mao's health basically is not contradicted by Bo Yibo's reflections, in one passage he provides some tantalizing information consistent with the premature succession struggle analysis of *Politics and Purges*. According to Bo, following a conversation with Luo Ruiqing where Mao's health was discussed, Gao told his secretary that as soon as there was news of Mao becoming seriously ill they must rush to Beijing as there was no one in the Party who could take over; *Huigu*, p. 315. Since, in

the context of the account, the conversation with Luo took place no earlier than October 1953, this incident in itself could not be a precipitating factor in Gao's activities which had been under way for at least three months. On Mao's health, see *Politics at Mao's Court*, pp. 33, 117.

7. While the evidence for these discussions relied on in *Politics at Mao's Court* (see pp. 13, 281) was limited to oral sources, a recent documentary source, Guo Simin, *Wo yanzhong de Mao Zedong* [Perceptions of Mao Zedong] (Shijiazhuang: Hebei renmin chubanshe, 1990), p. 41, provides additional indirect support. According to this account, in a February 1953 conversation with Wuhan Vice Mayor Wang Renzhong the Chairman criticized a number of Liu's policy positions. If Mao were willing to express such opinions to an official of comparatively low rank such as Wang, then the information concerning his talks on the same questions with Gao Gang gains further credibility.

8. Bo had served under Liu in the North China underground in the 1930s, and was particularly bonded to him when Liu's measures led to Bo's release from Nationalist confinement in 1936. See *Politics at Mao's Court*, p. 98.

9. Bo Yibo, *Huigu*, pp. 234–35; and *Politics at Mao's Court*, pp. 62–65.

10. Bo Yibo, *Huigu*, p. 235.

11. See *Politics at Mao's Court*, pp. 33, 41–44, 54–55, 63–64.

12. Bo Yibo, *Huigu*, pp. 235, 308–310; Lin Yunhui, Fan Shouxin and Zhang Gong, *1949–1989 nian de Zhongguo: Kaige xingjin de shiqi* [China 1949–1989: The Period of Triumphant Advance], vol.1 (Henan: Henan renmin chubanshe, 1989), pp. 326–28; Liao Gailong, ed., *Xin Zhongguo biannianshi (1949–1989)* [Chronicle of New China, 1949–1989] (Beijing: Renmin chubanshe, 1989), p. 59; and *Politics at Mao's Court*, pp. 26–30, 35–36, 180–81.

13. Bo Yibo, *Huigu*, pp. 238–42; and *Politics at Mao's Court*, pp. 65–67.

14. Bo Yibo, *Huigu*, pp. 240, 243–47, 312, 319–20; Lin Yunhui, *et al.*, *Kaige xingjin*, p. 329; and *Politics at Mao's Court*, pp. 67–70, 75–76. Mao's suggestion to Gao that he seek out Liu (Bo Yibo, p. 312) is not specifically dated, but from the context appears to have taken place at this time.

15. Here again Mao acted to ease Bo's predicament. While Bo asked Mao to send him to a key industrial project to work, the Chairman replied that he was needed at the Center. Thus although Bo was removed from his major post as Minister of Finance and was no longer first ranking Vice Chairman of the government's Financial and Economic Committee, he continued as a Vice Chairman assisting Deng Xiaoping who took over his positions under the overall leadership of Chen Yun who remained Committee Chairman. Bo Yibo, *Huigu*, pp. 249–50.

16. *Ibid.*, p. 312; Lin Yunhui, *et al.*, *Kaige xingjin*, pp. 329–30; and *Politics at Mao's Court*, pp. 75–78, 93ff.; and below, pp. xlviii–il.

17. Bo Yibo, *Hiugu*, p. 314; Lin Yunhui, *et al.*, *Kaige xingjin*, pp. 329–30; and *Politics at Mao's Court*, pp. 94ff.

18. See *Politics at Mao's Court*, pp. 102–107.

19. See *ibid.*, pp. 93–94, 108–12, where the likely timing of both the approaches to Chen and Deng and their reports to Mao is discussed. The new details from Bo Yibo's recollections do not undermine my earlier conclusions, but they add a few wrinkles. Most importantly, it is now clear that Gao approached Chen on at least two occasions. The first took place "after the financial and economic conference," i.e., probably late August or September, and involved Gao floating a proposal that he be in charge of the Politburo and Lin Biao of a new Council of Ministers, and asking Chen to take the idea to Mao. While Chen's refusal to do so is depicted by Bo as a rebuff to Gao, it clearly had the effect of avoiding an unpredictable audience with the Chairman. A second meeting, during which Gao raised a proposal that both he and Chen become Party Vice Chairmen, apparently

took place in the latter part of October or November. *Huigu*, pp. 314–15. Given this information official claims that Chen Yun immediately went to report to Mao (see *Politics at Mao's Court*, p. 111) become credible, but only with regard to this second meeting after the Chairman's attitudes had become clearer (see below).

20. See *Politics at Mao's Court*, pp. 82–87, 108–12. On the relationship between Gao and Rao, see below, p. lxvi.

21. See *ibid.*, pp. 112–13.

22. The December developments discussed in *ibid.*, pp. 116–20, are modified in one interesting respect by Bo Yibo's recollections. In Bo's account, the proposal that a system of rotating leadership be adopted rather than have Liu take over, which in all other versions was ascribed to Gao, was in fact the suggestion of Liu himself which Gao supported. What this suggests, apart from a formalistic modesty on Liu's part, is that Liu was perhaps in on a scheme to get Gao to oppose the Chairman's suggestion. *Huigu*, p. 315.

23. *Politics at Mao's Court*, pp. 60–61.

24. The degree of haste or reluctance in the retreat, as well as the manner of affecting it, was to a significant degree a function of individual personality. Chen Yun (see below) exemplified those leaders who would not pursue an argument with Mao, albeit with his own particular dignity. In contrast, the CCP's leading agricultural official in the 1950s, Deng Zihui, was an almost unique case of someone who would continue to contest issues with Mao even when the Chairman's views had been forcefully expressed; see Teiwes, "Mao and His Lieutenants," p. 14.

25. *Politics at Mao's Court*, pp. 60–61.

26. The classic statement of the opposing view, from which *Politics and Purges* benefitted greatly, is Roderick MacFarquhar, *The Origins of the Cultural Revolution, 1: Contradictions among the People 1956–1957* (New York: Columbia University Press, 1974), part III. A post-1979 version of the substantial opposition within the Politburo interpretation is Harry Harding, *Organizing China: The Problem of Bureaucracy 1949–1976* (Stanford: Stanford University Press, 1981), ch. 5. See also below, n. 27.

27. This assessment of the lack of conclusive evidence is shared by Roderick MacFarquhar in his introductory essay in the new collection of Mao speeches from 1957–58, *The Secret Speeches of Chairman Mao: From the Hundred Flowers to the Great Leap Forward*, ed. by MacFarquhar, Timothy Cheek, and Eugene Wu (Cambridge: The Council for East Asian Studies, Harvard University, 1989), p. 11. MacFarquhar, however, basically holds to his earlier view of substantial disunity within the Politburo, a view endorsed in the same volume by Benjamin I. Schwartz (p. 28).

28. *Fubuzhang*, which can mean either deputy department head or vice minister. The sources, however, cited Chen Qitong (see below) as an example of this type of official, and Chen's position was deputy head of the army's propaganda department.

29. Cf. below, pp. 200–201. In the case of post-1978 Party history materials which generally give little attention to the top level politics of the Hundred Flowers in contrast to many other cases, it could be argued that discussion of leadership differences has been suppressed for some reason, but it is at least equally logical that the absence of pronounced debate meant there was no need to treat the matter in depth. The latter appears more probable given the comparative detail on other instances arguably more embarrassing from a reform era perspective.

30. An extensive collection of these speeches appears in *Secret Speeches*, pp. 113–372. For a discussion of the Cultural Revolution compilations from which they were drawn, see Timothy Cheek's essay in *ibid.*, pp. 75–103. For Mao's description of himself as a "wandering lobbyist," see *ibid.*, p. 321.

31. *Ibid.*, p. 173. For Mao's comments on the fears, resentments and confusion of

Party officials, see pp. 195, 203, 231, 264, 299, 302, 336, 347, 354, 357.

32. *Ibid.*, p. 337. For additional references to the Center by Mao, see, e.g., pp. 169, 264, 357–58.

33. See, e.g., *ibid.*, pp. 114, 200, 208, 286, 333. Cf. the discussions of Mao's ambiguous and contradictory statements in the introductory essays to the same volume by Schwartz (pp. 27–30) and Merle Goldman (pp. 49–54), and that of *Politics and Purges*, below, p. 196.

34. *Secret Speeches*, pp. 240, 261, 267–69.

35. *Ibid.*, pp. 338, 361. Cf. below, pp. 181–84.

36. *Secret Speeches*, pp. 222, 287. The latter statement suggests the possibility that propaganda chief Lu Dingyi had been a high level opponent of the Hundred Flowers which had been raised in *Politics and Purges*, below, pp. 194–95, largely on the basis of Cultural Revolution sources, is unlikely to have been the case.

37. *Secret Speeches*, p. 268.

38. See below, p. 182.

39. *Secret Speeches*, pp. 210, 246.

40. *Ibid.*, pp. 118–19, 168–69, 252.

41. The above is based on the account skilfully pieced together in Timothy Cheek's draft manuscript, *Broken Jade: Deng Tuo and Intellectual Service in Mao's China*, (1991), ch. IV. However, Cheek takes a position between that which sees fundamental opposition to Mao's spring 1957 policies within the Politburo and my view. He interprets continuing sluggishness by the propaganda organs *after* Mao's April 10, 1957, confrontation with Deng Tuo as explicable only by the support of superiors in the "Party Center." For details of this important meeting, which we previously had not known about, see Wang Ruoshui, "Wenzhang manzhi shusheng lei—ji 1957 nian Mao Zedong de jiejian" [Articles Filling Pages, Accumulations of a Scholarly Life—Record of a Meeting with Mao Zedong in 1957], *Lianhe bao* [United Daily] (Taibei), March 10, 1989, p. 4. Cheek has interviewed other Party propagandists from Deng Tuo's circle who confirm Wang's description. The key point at issue between Cheek and myself is the degree of *Renmin ribao* "sluggishness" after April 10; see below.

For an analysis of the original text of Mao's "Contradictions" speech, see Michael Schoenhals, "Original Contradictions—On the Text of Mao Zedong's 'On the Correct Handling of Contradictions among the People,' " *AJCA*, No. 16 (1986). Schoenhals, p. 100, reports Mao's March 1 comments on not publishing the speech in its original state.

42. See Cheek, *Broken Jade*, pp. 228–29. In this account, in contrast to the rage directed at Deng Tuo, Mao made no comment on Hu's acceptance of partial responsibility for the sins of *Renmin ribao*. According to a reliable oral source, however, Hu made a self-criticism of his role.

43. See below, pp. 196–97.

44. As was argued in *Politics and Purges* in opposition to the view that Mao was reluctantly forced to change course, new evidence also points to the same pattern of Mao leading and other top officials following as the Hundred Flowers gave way to the Anti-Rightist Campaign in early June. In a recent interview one of the CCP's most senior Party historians cited the launching of the anti-rightist struggle as an example of Mao's unilateral decision making. According to his account, Mao laid down the new political orientation in his May 15 statement, "Things are Changing," and only subsequently sought the collective ratification of other leaders. Cf. below, pp. 216–19.

45. See *Hongqi* [Red Flag] *(HQ)*, No. 13 (1981), p. 66; *Women de Zhou Zongli* [Our Premier Zhou] (Beijing: Zhongyang wenxian chubanshe, 1990), p. 303; and below, pp. li–lii.

46. This is a complex story which may be briefly summarized as follows. While Mao apparently was somewhat unhappy with the *fan maojin* policies, he did not express

himself on the matter at the time and his leading colleagues were largely unaware of his dissatisfaction. At the Eighth Party Congress in September, moreover, he strongly praised Chen Yun, one of the main architects of the approach, and at the November Central Committee plenum, which he subsequently described in the "peak" of "anti-reckless advance" and an occasion on which he "compromised," Mao expressed his "complete" agreement with the policies adopted. *Dangshi yanjiu* [Research on Party History], No. 6 (1980), p. 40; *Wenxian he yanjiu* [Documents and Research], No. 7 (1984), p. 25; *Dangshi wenhui* [Party History Collection], No. 2 (1989), pp. 7–8; and oral sources. The Cultural Revolution version of a reported June 1956 statement by Mao bitterly attacking *Renmin ribao* editor Deng Tuo for the paper's editorial in support of *fan maojin* (see *Secret Speeches*, p. 395n) is surely a misdating by the Chinese editor of Mao's January 1958 statement *referring back to* June 1956.

47. *Politics and Purges*, below, p. 268, erroneously stated that Chen was kept away from the Congress session by a visit to Moscow. Chen did make the trip, but he also attended the Congress where he made a self-criticism.

48. This is suggested by the fact that when a central foreign affairs group was set up in June 1958, Zhou, the main executor of China's foreign policy, was not included; Ma Qibin, *et al.*, *Zhongguo Gongchandang zhizheng sishinian 1949–1989* [The CCP's Forty Years in Power 1949–1989] (Beijing: Zhonggong dangshi ziliao chubanshe, 1990), p. 143. It tends to support the anaylsis of MacFarquhar, *Origins 1*, pp. 312, 315, which I questioned in "Mao and His Lieutenants," p. 48n.

49. *Xinhua banyuekan* [New China Semi-Monthly] *(XHBYK)*, No. 7 (1958), pp. 109–10; Ma Qibin, *et al.*, *Zizheng sishinian*, pp. 148–49; and Cong Jin, *1949–1989 nian de Zhongguo: Quzhe fazhan de suiyue* [China 1949–1989: The Years of Circuitous Development], vol. 2 (Henan: Henan renmin chubanshe, 1989), pp. 130–31, 138. A certain amount of presumption is involved concerning the self-criticisms of Bo and Li since the available extracts are quite brief. The critical role of Li Xiannian was reflected in his appointment, along with Li Fuchun (who was *not* singled out for criticism concerning the "anti-reckless advance" policies), to the Party secretariat at the May Congress.

50. Cong Jin, *Quzhe fazhan*, pp. 123–28; and *Renwu* [Personalities], No. 1 (1986), pp. 175–76. On Zhou's excessive self-criticisms during the Yan'an rectification, see Frederick C. Teiwes with the assistance of Warren Sun, "From a Leninist to a Charismatic Party: The CCPs Changing Leadership, 1937-1945," in Tony Saich and Hans van de Ven, eds., *New Perspectives on the Chinese Communist Revolution* (Armonk: M. E. Sharpe, forthcoming). On Lin Biao's 1962 praise of Mao, see below, pp. xxxix–xl.

51 Cong Jin, *Quzhe fazhan*, pp. 128–30. This characterization of Chen's self-criticism is based on a significantly shorter excerpt than that from Zhou Enlai, but the assessment is confirmed by a well placed oral source.

52. *Selected Works of Deng Xiaoping (1975–1982)* (Beijing: Foreign Languages Press, 1984), p. 281.

53. See the discussion of Liu's role in Roderick MacFarquhar, *The Origins of the Cultural Revolution, 2: The Great Leap Forward 1958–1960* (New York: Columbia University Press, 1983), *passim*.

54. Chen's precise activities during the high tide of the Great Leap in 1958 remain somewhat obscure. While nearly all of the dozen plus Party historians questioned on the matter pictured Chen as basically inactive in this period, one well placed source recounts a more positive role at the time of the August 1958 Beidaihe conference. According to this source who was present on the occasion, Chen presided at a meeting on industrial production, stated that Mao's directive on doubling steel production had to be fulfilled, and advocated combining foreign and native (i.e., the small "backyard furnace") methods to

achieve the target. While this incident appears to contradict both the predominant opinion of Chinese scholars and the thrust of the following discussion, it is perhaps explainable as a case where Chen's status and the importance of the occasion required him to back publicly the official Party policies as a matter of discipline. On Chen's strong sense of discipline, see Mao's 1965 comments in Cong Jin, *Quzhe fazhan*, p. 580. Nevertheless, in 1958 this discipline seemingly did not extend to vigorous promotion of the leap.

With regard to eschewing contrary policy advocacy, again the situation may have been more complicated. While clearly Chen did not openly oppose the leap, a posture which can also be ascribed to his sense of discipline, he may have expressed some sceptical views privately to Mao during this period. This, at least, is the view of several Party historians, although one based on their own analyses rather than definite information.

55. Cf. David M. Bachman, *Chen Yun and the Chinese Political System* (Berkeley: China Research Monographs, 1985), p. 147, for a characterization of Chen's "rules of political action" much the same as that offered independently by my source.

56. See Cong Jin, *Quzhe fazhan*, p. 418.

57. *Ibid.*; *Chen Yun wenxuan (1956–1985 nian)* [Selected Works of Chen Yun, 1956–1985] (Beijing: Renmin chubanshe, 1986), pp. 356–57; and oral source. This financial and economic small group apparently was an enlarged version of the economic work small group which had been set up in January 1957; see Zhonggong zhongyang dangshi yanjiushi, *Zhongguo Gongchandang lishi dashiji (1919.5–1987.12)* [Chronology of CCP History, May 1919-December 1987] (Beijing: Renmin chubanshe, 1989), p. 227.

58. This is based on a discussion with a significant actor during the Great Leap period. Of course, the initiative for placing Chen in the financial and economic position could have come from someone else, but Mao surely vetted such an arrangement. In addition to the small group position, Chen also received an appointment as head of the new state body in charge of capital construction in fall 1958 which presumably reflected similiar considerations, while at the same time he was dropped from his arguably more significant position as Minister of Commerce. On the general question of status, see Teiwes, "Mao and His Lieutenants," pp. 43–44, 48n; and below, pp. lxiii–lxvi.

59. Cong Jin, *Quzhe fazhan*, pp. 163–64; *Selected Works of Deng*, p. 328; and oral sources. This is not to say that Mao was necessarily the first to perceive the problems, but simply that in the supercharged atmosphere of the time only the Chairman could openly address them. See below, pp. lii–liii and n. 143.

60. *Secret Speeches*, pp. 465, 469. The reference to Chen was fairly restrained and also included Mao's close follower, Li Fuchun, however.

61. Cong Jin, *Quzhe fazhan*, pp. 188, 256; *Chen Yun wenxuan*, pp. 96–99; Li Rui, *Lushan huiyi shilu* [True Record of the Lushan Meetings] (Beijing: Chunqiu chubanshe, 1989), p. 81; *HQ*, No. 13 (1986), p. 16; MacFarquhar, *Origins 2*, pp. 163–65; Chen Mingxian, *et al.*, eds., *Xin Zhongguo sishinian yanjiu* [Research on the New China's 40 years] (Beijing: Beijing Ligong Daxue chubanshe, 1989), p. 250; and oral sources.

62. Li Rui, *Lushan shilu*, p. 125.

63. Zhu Chengjia, ed., *Zhonggong dangshi yanjiu lunwenxuan* [Collected Essays on CCP History Research], vol. 2 (Changsha: Hunan renmin chubanshe, 1984) p. 500; and MacFarquhar, *Origins 2*, pp. 165–70.

64. Cong Jin, *Quzhe fazhan*, p. 418; and Li Rui, *Lushan shilu*, p. 80.

65. Of particular note in Western scholarship is the gloriously detailed account by Roderick MacFarquhar, *Origins 2*, ch. 10, which utilizes the first waves of PRC sources during the early post-Mao period. The most significant source of this period was Peng Dehuai's "self statement," subsequently appearing in English as Zheng Longpu, trans., *Memoirs of a Chinese Marshal—The autobiographical notes of Peng Dehuai (1898–1974)* (Beijing: Foreign Languages Press, 1984). In recent years a spate of PRC books and

articles has appeared, the most significant of which is Li Rui, *Lushan shilu*.

66. Jürgen Domes, *Peng Te-huai: The Man and the Image* (London: C. Hurst & Company, 1985), p. 91. See MacFarquhar, *Origins 2*, pp. 216, 403, for a more nuanced version of this position.

67. The following account of developments at Lushan draws on my article, "Peng Dehuai and Mao Zedong," *AJCA*, No. 16 (1986), pp. 90–91, as well as additional data which became available subsequently. The same article, pp. 87–89, also provides substantial new evidence concerning another contentious issue raised in *Politics and Purges*, the question of the impact of Peng's military views and role on his actions at Lushan. This evidence not only supports the view that Peng did not raise military issues at Lushan, but indicates that contrary to interpretations picturing Peng as the military modernizer *par excellence* his views on defense matters in 1958–59 were close to those of Mao.

68. *Women de Zhou Zongli*, pp. 303–304; Li Rui, *Huainian nianpian* [Twenty Articles in Remembrance] (Beijing: Sanlian chubanshe, 1987), pp. 258–59; Li Rui, *Lushan shilu*, pp. 184–85; and oral sources.

Chen Boda's attitude was clearly a case of someone who was out of Mao's favor for his excessively leftist stance earlier. Chen had been sharply criticised by Mao at the November 1958 Zhengzhou conference for his advocacy of abolishing commodities and money and was excluded from the key committee set up to draft an outline for the Lushan meeting. Thus he may have felt it necessary to join in the anti-left trend to repair this damage, and/or his new position may have reflected some resentment over Mao's criticism in a relatively safe fashion. Also, the fact that Chen lived together with Hu, Tian and Wu under the Lushan arrangments facilitated his participation in their discussion sessions which were also joined by two former/concurrent Mao secretaries, Zhou Xiaozhou and Li Rui. Li Rui, *Huainian nianpian*, pp. 35, 62; and oral source.

69. Mao subsequently expressed perplexity as to why Chen had made a self-criticism; Li Rui, *Lushan shilu*, p. 81. According to a well informed oral source, Chen was responding to a particularly ill-tempered period when Mao was "criticising everything to prove he was right all the time" and erroneously concluded he could be caught up in the Chairman's general dissatisfaction.

70. Cong Jin, *Quzhe fazhan*, p. 188; *Memoirs of a Chinese Marshal*, p. 502; below, pp. 310, 311–12; and oral sources.

71. *Memoirs of a Chinese Marshal*, pp. 489, 503; MacFarquhuar, *Origins 2*, p. 200; and *Liaowang* [Outlook], No. 32 (1985), p. 20. Those besides Mao urging Peng to attend were Zhang Wentian and Huang Kecheng. See Zhang Peisen, ed., *Zhang Wentian yanjiu wenji* [Collected Research on Zhang Wentian] (Beijing; Zhonggong dangshi ziliao chubanshe, 1990), p. 356; and Li Rui, *Lushan shilu*, p. 127.

72. Apart from Cultural Revolution sources claiming some sharp comments at group meetings (see below, p. 322), post-1979 data also point to one apparently testy exchange between Peng and Mao over the amount of waste caused by the steel campaign at an early to mid-July Politburo Standing Committee meeting. Three months earlier at the Shanghai conference Peng had also raised Mao's ire for reasons that are unclear but which lead the Chairman to claim that "Peng Dehuai hates me." Li Rui, *Lushan shilu*, pp. 92, 125, 128. These events point to a larger pattern which perhaps goes a long way toward explaining the eventual fury of Mao's explosion at Lushan—three decades of repeated instances of personal friction and ill temper albeit within a larger framework of political cooperation. For an overview of this pattern, see Teiwes, "Peng and Mao," pp. 83–87. After Peng's letter, Mao distorted the extent of these tensions with the conclusion that his relations with Peng had consisted of 30 percent cooperation and 70 percent conflict; Cong Jin, *Quzhe fazhan*, p. 218.

73. *Memoirs of a Chinese Marshal*, pp. 490–91, 503; and Li Rui, *Lushan shilu*, pp. 129–30.

74. *Memoirs of a Chinese Marshal*, pp. 494, 503–506.

75. *Ibid*, p. 1.

76. For the view of Peng's letter as a "memorial to the emperor," see below, pp. 322–23. I have since been persuaded by the arguments of Domes, *Peng*, pp. 91–95, and especially MacFarquhar, *Origins 2*, pp. 213–16, of the biting criticism included in the letter.

77. *Memoirs of a Chinese Marshal*, pp. 354–57; and oral source.

78. Li Rui, *Lushan shilu*, p. 281; and oral sources. In Li Rui's account, in an early August speech Lin Biao claimed that Peng had told *someone* that his letter contained stings. An authoritative oral source identified this person as Zhang Wentian, but another well informed source said Jia Tuofu was the leader in question. There are, in any case, several other versions not necessarily in contradiction with the above on the question of stings in Peng's letter. One is that Peng's friend, Huang Kecheng, said with some alarm after reading the letter that it contained stings; Cong Jin, *Quzhe fazhan*, p. 206. Another is that people unsympathetic to Peng like Ke Qingshi pointed to the stings as evidence that the letter was an attack on Mao; Peng Cheng and Wang Fang, *Lushan 1959* (Beijing: Jiefangjun chubanshe, 1988), pp. 93, 187.

79. Peng, in his 1962 letter seeking a reexamination of his case, rather than pointing to Liu indicated that the SPC, which had played the key role in economic management during the Great Leap, was a special target in his 1959 letter although he had been far from totally critical. *Dang de wenxian* [The Party's Documents], No. 5 (1990), pp. 22–23. In any case, once Mao had turned on Peng, a history of conflict between Peng and Liu may explain to some degree the severity of Liu's attacks on Peng at Lushan and subsequently. See *Politics at Mao's Court*, pp. 105–106, 140.

80. Cong Jin, *Quzhe fazhan*, p. 206; Li Rui, *Lushan shilu*, pp. 94, 135–53, 164; and oral source.

81. Li Rui, *Lushan shilu*, pp. 156–57; Zhang Peisen, *Zhang Wentian yanjiu wenji*, p. 357; *Huiyi Zhang Wentian* [Remember Zhang Wentian] (Changsha: Hunan renmin chubanshe, 1985), pp. 19–20, 314–16, 319; and oral source.

82. Li Rui, *Huainian nianpian*, p. 35; Li Rui, *Lushan shilu*, pp. 87, 181–83, 196; *Renmin ribao* [People's Daily] *(RMRB)*, October 23, 1988, p. 4; Cong Jin, *Quzhe fazhan*, p. 218; and oral source.

83. The suicide option is implied by Peng's promise to Mao at Lushan that he would not take his own life; *Memoirs of a Chinese Marshal*, p. 522. The efforts of leaders including Nie Rongzhen, Ye Jianying, Zhu De, Liu Shaoqi and Zhou Enlai to persuade Peng to give in are reported in *ibid.*, p. 507; Domes, *Peng*, p. 98; and by oral sources. The suicide option seems more a worry of other leaders, who were perhaps affected by the memory of Gao Gang taking his own life when facing political disgrace in 1954, than any serious intention on Peng's part. In any case, measures were taken to guard against any possibility of his suicide; see *Zhonggong dangshi ziliao* [CCP History Materials], No. 28 (1988), p. 96.

84. According to a 1978 letter by Huang Kecheng cited in Domes, *Peng*, p. 98.

85. The organizational arrangement of the "two lines" or "two fronts" *(zhanxian)* of leadership, whose origins can be traced back farther than suggested in the first edition to 1952–53 (see *Politics at Mao's Court*, p. 32), is conceptually distinct from "two line struggle" *(liang tiao luxian douzheng)*. The latter refers to the alleged struggle between two political orientations, while the former is simply the administrative arrangement whereby Mao (and in the post-Mao period other leaders) on the "second line" distanced himself from responsibility for daily operations which fell to his top leadership colleagues on the "first line." Similar to the analysis in the first edition, in 1978 Chen Yun pointed to

1961 as the time when in practical terms Mao actually began to retreat to the "second line"; Tian Guoliang, *et al.*, eds., *Hu Yaobang zhuan* [Biography of Hu Yaobang] (Beijing: Zhonggong dangshi ziliao chubanshe, 1989), p. 118. See below, p. li, for a discussion of the implications of this arrangement for inner Party democracy.

86. See "Resolution on Certain Questions in the History of Our Party Since the Founding of the People's Republic of China," in *Beijing Review*, No. 27 (1981), pp. 18, 19; Zhonggong zhongyang wenxian yanjiushi, *Guanyu jianguo yilai dang de ruogan lishi wenti de jueyi zhuyiben (xiuding)* [Revised Notes on the Resolution on Certain Questions in the History of Our Party since the Founding of the People's Republic of China] (Beijing: Renmin chubanshe, 1985), pp. 271ff.; and Liao Kai-lung (Liao Gailong), "Historical Experiences and Our Road of Development" (October 25, 1980), Part I, in *Issues & Studies*, October 1981, p. 86.

87. See Cong Jin, *Quzhe fazhan*, pp. 405–406; and below, pp. lvii–lviii, 377.

88. See *ibid.*, pp. 481–83, 493; and *Jiaoxue yu yanjiu* [Teaching and Research], No. 6 (1983), p. 44. Chen's contributions were particularly significant in the first half of 1962 when he was again placed in charge of the economy. While arguably favorable weather in 1962 had as much or more to do with the recovery than Chen's input, that input was significant and, importantly, it was viewed as correct by the bulk of the elite. Nevertheless, it was not enough to protect him from Mao's anger.

89. *Dangshi yanjiu*, No. 3 (1984), p. 63.

90. This account based on a well informed oral source is drawn from Teiwes, "Mao and His Lieutenants," pp. 28–29. See also Kenneth Lieberthal and Michel Oksenberg, *Policy Making in China: Leaders, Structures and Processes* (Princeton: Princeton University Press, 1988), pp. 188–90. There is another, less dramatic version of the setting up of the small planning commission, however. According to this account, with Mao's impatience over the rate of economic growth and his defense related concerns increasingly apparent, Li Fuchun and other SPC leaders in September 1964 recommended that Mao himself assume command of financial and economic work. Mao said this was not necessary (although an economic headquarters led by Mao and Liu was considered) but he should be briefed regularly, and the small planning commission was set up to put this into effect. Cong Jin, *Quzhe fazhan*, pp. 465–66; and oral source. I lean to the version given in the text on the basis of the source's access to materials concerning Li Fuchun, but both versions affirm the Chairman's authority. Moreover, they indicate a larger role for Mao in the economy during the 1962–65 period than that depicted by *Politics and Purges*; see below, p. 390. For an excellent analysis of the huge shift of resources to defense oriented construction on a so-called "third front" established in the interior in response to Mao's demands, see Barry Naughton, "The Third Front: Defence Industrialization in the Chinese Interior," *The China Quarterly (CQ)*, No. 115 (1988).

91. See below, pp. 389–91; and *Leadership, Legitimacy, and Conflict*, pp. 67–68.

92. Cf. Teiwes, "Mao and His Lieutenants," pp. 68–69. It should be emphasized that Deng's "sabotage" seemed limited to doing little or nothing, to make few or no statements in support of the leftist trends he questioned rather than any more active obstruction of Mao's wishes. Moreover, he seemingly was drawn into participation in the Socialist Education Movement during at least one crucial juncture; see below, n. 103.

93. I now believe that the analysis of a Liu Shaoqi-Peng Zhen conflict over the course of the Socialist Education Movement (see below, pp. 386, 416n, 430–31) is probably overstated. In any case, to the extent differences did exist, the suggestion in *Leadership, Legitimacy, and Conflict*, pp. 29–30, linking such differences to possible tension between Liu and Peng over the succession to Mao seems very unlikely. My current view, derived primarily from discussions with Chinese scholars, is that Liu

and Peng were much too close in the "factional" sense to be competitors and Liu's superior status meant that any succession ambitions Peng might have harbored were to succeed Liu after Liu had succeeded Mao.

94. Cf. Teiwes, "Mao and His Lieutenants," p. 19. Despite the emphasis in Cultural Revolution sources, and also the ample details in post-Mao Party history materials concerning Mao's disapproval of various measures adopted by the "first line," oral sources who addressed the issue asserted that generally the Chairman accepted the recommendations of his colleagues.

95. *Dang de wenxian*, No. 1 (1991), pp. 27–28; Cong Jin, *Quzhe fazhan*, pp. 410, 412–13; and oral sources. On this evidence the claim in *Politics and Purges*, below, p. 372, that Chen Yun played an active economic role in 1961 appears overstated.

96. Cong Jin, *Quzhe fazhan*, pp. 406–407, 410–13; Michael Schoenhals, "Edited Records: Comparing Two Versions of Deng Xiaoping's '7000 Cadres Conference Speech,' " *CCP Research Newsletter*, No. 1 (1988), pp. 5–6; and oral sources. It is worth mentioning that, apart from the timing, Deng's lauding of Mao may have reflected a more general tendency on his part to sing the Chairman's praises when required whatever his actual policy orientation. See Teiwes, "Mao and His Lieutenants," p. 69n; and *CCP Research Newsletter*, No. 5 (1990), p. 57.

97. *Dang de wenxian*, No. 1 (1991), p. 28; Cong Jin, *Quzhe fazhan*, pp. 401–404; Teiwes, "Mao and His Lieutenants," pp. 61–62; and oral sources.

98. In particular, Liu's stand against the returned student group in the 1930s when that group had Comintern backing; See Teiwes, "Mao and His Lieutenants," pp. 59–60.

99. Zhou apparently was referring more broadly to Liu's activities in the first half of 1962, but the observation may be taken to apply to Liu's remarks at the conference. A very senior Party historian observed that Zhou like Liu was "acute" in his appraisal of Great Leap shortcomings but his most telling comments were given in small group meetings where Mao was not present, and he avoided some of Liu's phraseology. As for Deng Xiaoping, this source considered his comments "not so acute" as Liu's. For Zhou's speech to the conference itself, see *Dang de wenxian*, No. 1 (1991), pp. 18–24.

100. See Cong Jin, *Quzhe fazhan*, p. 404. Here Cong Jin, as did many Party historians in discussions, follows Mao's August 1966 statement pointing to the developments of 1962 in concluding that the 7,000 cadres conference was a watershed. Indeed, some believe that this was the occasion when Mao determined that Liu had to go. This is necessarily a subjective judgment, as is my own (see below) which places the decisive moment in January 1965, and there is a danger in taking too literally Mao's *ex post facto* accounts of earlier events. Nevertheless, both the vehemence of Mao's subsequent position and such contemporary clues as his comments on Lin Biao's speech do suggest an unusual sensitivity to developments at the conference. For the argument that Mao's disenchantment concerning policy came *after* the conference, see below, pp. 371–76.

101. Cf. above, n. 93; and below, n. 103.

102. That is excluding Lin Biao who, although having ultimate authority (except for Mao) over military affairs and technically on the "first line," actually did little work because of ill health. Oral source.

103. Richard Baum and Frederick C. Teiwes, *Ssu-Ch'ing: The Socialist Education Movement of 1962–1966 (SC)* (Berkeley: China Research Monographs, 1968), p.73 (where "the key link" is rendered as "a principle"); Cong Jin, *Quzhe fazhan*, pp. 531–33; and oral sources.

The responsibility for the actual drafting of September 1963 document is in some dispute among Party historians. Cong Jin, *Quzhe fazhan*, p. 531, reflects the majority view by attributing this document to Liu Shaoqi and Peng Zhen, not Peng as distinct from Liu as was argued in *Politics and Purges*, below, p. 407. Another view taken by Pang Xianzhi in Dong Bian, *et al.*, *Mao Zedong he tade mishu Tian Jiaying* [Mao Zedong and His Secretary Tian Jiaying] (Beijing: Zhongyang wenxian chubanshe, 1990) p. 75, claims that Deng Xiaoping and Tan Zhenlin were responsible. Given Pang's direct involvement in the drafting process, his claim must be considered more credible. However, the dominant view from oral sources that whatever the precise responsibility for specific documents, overall direction of the Socialist Education Movement throughout 1963–64 was firmly in the hands of Liu Shaoqi (subject to Mao's approval), while Peng Zhen assisted Liu at various stages, is not necessarily inconsistent with Pang's. Moreover, Liu's relative "leftism" in this period is broadly accepted by oral sources. But Pang's assertion does cause some difficulty for the view that Deng Xiaoping generally steered clear of Mao's radical enthusiasms as it indicates his direct role in the key link slogan.

104. Although, as one senior Party historian put it, it is difficult to say why Mao became unhappy with the Revised Second Ten Points when he himself had approved and revised the document so recently, at least one of the policy related matters raised in *Politics and Purges* (see below, pp. 431ff.), the question of damage to basic level cadre morale caused by Liu's deep purge, clearly was relevant. There is evidence that Mao may have had second thoughts as early as August shortly after approving Liu's approach. See Cong Jin, *Quzhe fazhan*, pp. 539–40; and Dong Bian, *et al.*, *Mao Zedong he Tian Jiaying*, pp.75–76. No source has been located confirming the first edition's other suggestion that the attack on the Dazhai model brigade by a socialist education work team contributed to Mao's ire; this issue was not pursued in interviews, however.

105. My source's analysis is a logical inference from Mao's remarks made on the same occasion as the following quotation; see Cong Jin, *Quzhe fazhan*, p. 602. Cf. Teiwes, "Mao and His Lieutenants," p. 33. It should be noted, however, that one senior Party historian explicitly disagreed with the analysis that Mao was concerned with the possible loss of power, arguing instead that his dissatisfaction with the general orientation of the "first line" was the "profound cause" of the Cultural Revolution.

106. Cong Jin, *Quzhe fazhan*, p. 602. Cong Jin described both Mao's words and his attitude toward Liu as reflecting inner dissatisfaction or moodiness *(you qingxu)*. The interpretation here of Mao's use of the Qinshihuang analogy contrasts with that of the original edition, below, p. 439.

107. *Ibid.*, pp. 602–605; *Mao Zedong sixiang yanjiu* [Research on Mao Zedong Thought], No. 3 (1989), p. 23; and oral sources.

108. There are differences among Party historians concerning when Mao knew of the Shanghai writing group organized in early 1965 by his wife, Jiang Qing, to prepare criticism of Wu Han. Some believe Mao must have known from the outset, others that he only knew fairly late in the game in fall 1965, and still others that he was aware of development from about May 1965, and there are similar differences over his degree of involvement. The strongest evidence for Mao's early involvement comes from the Chairman himself and his wife. In a 1967 interview with Albanian visitors Mao asserted that he had proposed to Jiang that she organise the writing group; Jiang also claimed that she started her activities following the Chairman's approval. Cong Jin, *Quzhe fazhan*, pp. 610–11; and Roxane Witke, *Comrade Chiang Ch'ing* (Boston: Little, Brown and Company, 1977), p. 296. On the larger question of the decisive change in Mao's attitude to Liu, the view advanced here is supported by Cong Jin, *Quzhe fazhan*, p. 606. However, some scholars see an unfolding incremental change after January 1965, while others (see above, n. 100) believe the decision to dump Liu came as early as 1962.

109. Cf. the treatment of this question in Teiwes, "Mao and His Lieutentants," pp. 23–24. In this discussion, p. 24n, I note conflicting evidence that Mao adopted a tolerant view toward Liu in late 1966-early 1967, but argue that on balance Mao's determination

to achieve Liu's political demise is more credible. While I would concede that any implication in that discussion of Mao's wish for Liu's *physical* demise is perhaps overstated, nevertheless it remains the case that the Chairman did little to prevent the mistreatment of his long time colleague.

110. "Resolution on History Since the Founding," p. 20. Cf. Liao Gailong's inner Party report, "Historical Experiences," Part II, in *Issues & Studies*, November 1981, pp. 91–92.

111. See Merle Goldman's review of Tang Tsou's *The Cultural Revolution and Post-Mao Reforms*, in *CQ*, No. 109 (1987), p. 117.

112. See Lawrence R. Sullivan, "Leadership and Authority in the Chinese Communist Party: Perspectives from the 1950s," *Pacific Affairs*, Winter 1986–87.

113. See Lowell Dittmer's review article critique of *Politics and Purges*, "Rectification and Purge in Chinese Politics," *Pacific Affairs*, Fall 1980, pp. 512–14.

114. E.g., David M. Lampton with the assistance of Yeung Sai-cheung, *Paths to Power: Elite Mobility in Contemporary China* (Ann Arbor: Center for Chinese Studies, The University of Michigan, 1986), pp. 16–17, 298.

115. See below, p. 18.

116. Ch. III, especially pp. 94–99.

117. See below, pp. 56–57. For an interpretation emphasizing coercion, see Peter J. Seybolt, "Terror and Conformity: Counterespionage Campaigns, Rectification, and Mass Movements, 1942–1943," *Modern China*, January 1986. My current thinking on this issue is given in detail in Teiwes with Sun, "From a Leninist to a Charismatic Party." In brief, the argument is that while coercion was a significant factor in the cadre investigations which were integral to the rectification process and Mao bore a major responsibiltiy, the excesses involved produced substantial elite opposition, Mao lost some prestige as a result and sanctioned the termination of the worst features, and the primary official directly involved, Kang Sheng, suffered an important career setback due to his role.

For another case involving coercive measures, see Timothy Cheek, "The Fading of Wild Lilies: Wang Shiwei and Mao Zedong's 'Yan'an Talks' in the First CPC Rectification Movement," *AJCA*, No. 11 (1984), who gives a more extended and subtle evaluation of the interaction of coercion and persuasion than that provided in the brief discussion in *Politics and Purges*, below, pp. 59–60.

118. See the lengthy review of the Yan'an rectification in *HQ*, No. 23 (1983), especially pp. 6–9, which gives considerable attention to combatting liberalism, the tendency to let erroneous views pass without criticism. For a contemporary record of the struggle culture in Yan'an, see the "Diary of Struggle" concerning the Wang Shiwei case in May-June 1942 in Tony Saich, ed., with a contribution by Benjamin Yang, *The Rise to Power of the Chinese Communist Party: Documents and Analysis* (Armonk: M.E. Sharpe, forthcoming).

119. This sentiment (see below, p. 110n) was noted during the 1950 rectification campaign which followed the harsh grass roots rectification of 1947–48, but it was undoubtedly the case that any Party rectification would cause some degree of anxiety.

120. *RMRB*, October 23, 1988, p. 4; and Teiwes, "Peng and Mao," pp. 86, 95. Another leader resentful of the criticism he endured in the 1940s was Chen Yi who, over 20 years later, indicated his dissatisfaction with the Yan'an rectification. See Wang Nianyi, *1949–1989 nian de Zhongguo: Da dongluan de niandai* [China 1949–1989: The Years of Great Turmoil], vol. 3 (Henan: Henan renmin chubanshe, 1988), pp. 210, 216; and *RMRB*, June 30, 1988, p.5.

121. *RMRB*, October 23, 1988, p. 4; and Bo Yibo, *Huigu*, pp. 248–53. For examples of lower ranking figures who felt the process worked, see Cheek, *Broken Jade*, pp.

141–42; and Tony Saich's draft introduction (1991) to *Rise to Power*, pp. 54–55. See also below, p. lxi and nn. 170, 172, 178.

122. E.g., *RMRB*, August 24, 1982, p. 4, February 7, 1984, p. 5.

123. See Teiwes with Sun, "From a Leninist to a Charismatic Party."

124. According to an authoritative oral source Liu made no attempt to defend himself given his understanding that any such effort would only have made matters worse.

125. It is possible to read Mao's actions and Gao's perceptions in a variety of ways. A benign view is that Gao simply misinterpreted the Chairman's intent, while a less charitable one would suggest a failed effort on Mao's part to oust Liu and/or Zhou. For a discussion of why I favor a relatively benign interpretation, see *Politics at Mao's Court*, pp. 37–38, 149.

126. A distinction must be drawn concerning the way in which I am using the term "faction." The usage here would be rendered *shantou*, literally "mountaintop" in Chinese, and refers to inner Party constituencies formed around similar revolutionary career patterns but within the unified Maoist leadership, as opposed to *zongpai* ("factions") which indicates political groupings within the CCP leadership with their own particular programs and/or power goals which tended to bring them into conflict with other leadership groupings.

127. Discussions were underway by late 1952 concerning the organizational consequences of both the Eighth Congress and a new state constitution; see *Politics at Mao's Court*, pp. 32–33. In the event, in substantial measure due to the Gao-Rao affair, the Party Congress was delayed to 1956, while the new state apparatus was set up in fall 1954.

128. See *ibid*, pp. 95–99; and Bo Yibo, *Huigu*, p. 313. According to Bo Yibo's account and oral sources, the genesis of An's list came not from Liu but from Gao Gang who purported to transmit Mao's wishes. An was reluctant to proceed with such a delicate matter but bowed to Gao's report of the Chairman's wishes, accordingly he added those great region leaders not already on the Politburo including both Lin and Bo, but Gao then maliciously spread the rumor that Lin had not been included. Subsequently, when two new members were added to the Politburo in 1955 they were Lin Biao and Deng Xiaoping, both regional leaders in the early 1950s and figures with high military prestige. On the broader process of "factional" balancing following the Gao-Rao affair, see *Politics at Mao's Court*, pp. 134ff.

129. See *Politics at Mao's Court*, pp. 102–12; and above, n. 19.

130. See above, n. 125.

131. Bo Yibo, *Huigu*, pp. 247–48.

132. Cf. *Leadership, Legitimacy, and Conflict*, pp. 54–58.

133. *Selected Works of Deng*, p. 313. Deng dates this development from the criticism of *fan maojin* in 1958, i.e., the Nanning meeting, while Liao Kai-lung, "Historical Experiences," Part II, p. 90, although also referring to Nanning, speaks of "after 1956" as the time when Mao "began to become imperious, imprudent and divorced from the masses."

134. Liao Kai-lung, "Historical Experiences," Part II, p. 91.

135. "Resolution on History Since the Founding," pp. 25–26.

136. The view of Zhang Wentian as particularly sensitive to these issues comes primarily from an oral source specializing in Zhang, but it is convincingly documented by specific evidence. According to this source, a cause of friction between Zhang and Mao in the 1930s was the former's insistence on the forms of collective leadership, while Zhang's sensitivity to the democracy question after 1949 came in part from his experiences as Chinese ambassador to the Soviet Union both under Stalin and during the Soviet de-Stalinization campaign. In the latter period Zhang's actions were relatively limited, but he did send back to China Soviet materials criticising the cult of personality after Stalin's death. With regard to Liu Shaoqi, in his initial version of *How to be a Good Communist*

Liu endorsed Wang Ming's abnormal organizational methods against Li Lisan in the early 1930s as politically correct, while Zhang prevented publication of part of Liu's article apparently because he felt Liu's argument did not guarantee collective leadership. *Liu Shaoqi yanjiu lunwenji* [Collected Research Papers on Liu Shaoqi] (Beijing: Zhongyang wenxian chubanshe, 1989), pp. 235, 237.

137. Deng Zihui's case was only touched upon tangentially in the first edition since it did not result in a leadership purge or rectification campaign; see below, p. 269n. The case is examined in detail in double issue Nos. 3–4 (1993) of *Chinese Law and Government (CLG)* edited by Frederick C. Teiwes and Warren Sun, "Mao, Deng Zihui, and the Politics of Agricultural Cooperativization." Briefly, Mao's position on the pace of building cooperatives shifted in the first half of 1955 from one of supporting Deng's cautious position to an increasingly impatient view. Although Deng initially accommodated the Chairman's opinion, he baulked at Mao's later demands, and tried to continue arguing his case. Mao not only overrode Deng, but harshly criticised his view as a "right deviation" with the result that all contrary opinions were stifled.

138. See above, n. 46.

139. *Dangshi wenhui*, No. 2 (1989), p. 8; Cong Jin, *Quzhe fazhan*, pp. 111–12; oral sources; and the sources cited above, n. 45.

140. See below, n. 142.

141. Zhang Peisen, *Zhang Wentian wenji*, p. 351; Liao Kai-lung, "Historical Experiences," Part II, p. 90; and oral sources.

142. The view expressed here and earlier of a broad leadership consensus and relatively benign handling of differences stands in some conflict to the analysis of *Politics and Purges*, below, pp. 270–71, 273–75, which points to Mao's ruminations concerning Party splits and the dismissals of local leaders in 12 provinces at the Congress session. Based on discussions with several Party historians, I have tentatively concluded that Mao's concern with splits, and thus the disciplinary measures taken, focused on the lower levels while substantial if pressured unity and comparatively lenient rectification treatment notwithstanding some harsh criticism prevailed at the top.

143. According to an oral source specializing in Zhang, in October 1958, at about the same time as Mao, Zhang formed a more or less clear view of the left errors of the Great Leap but owing to his lesser position and status he couldn't initiate proposals to deal with them. Another well informed source reported that at the time of the August 1958 Beidaihe conference Zhu De's secretary calculated that the claims for grain yields were impossible but this was not reported to Mao.

144. Tan Zhongji, *et al.*, *Shinianhou de pingshuo—"Wenhua dageming" shilunji* [Commenatary 10 Years After—Collected History Essays on the "Cultural Revolution"] (Beijing: Zhonggong dangshi ziliao chubanshe, 1987), p. 2; *Dang de wenxian*, No. 1 (1989), p. 96; Li Rui, *Lushan shilu*, p. 162; Zhang Wentian xuanji zhuanjizu, ed., *Zhang Wentian Lushan huiyi fayan* [Zhang Wentian's Lushan Speeches] (Beijing: Beijing chubanshe, 1990), p. 33; and oral sources.

Although on the basis of Cultural Revolution sources the first edition (below, p. 308) discussed Peng Dehuai raising the democracy issue at Shanghai and there is evidence in post-1978 sources of Peng's dissatisfaction at that time with Mao's leadership style (see Li Rui, *Lushan shilu*, p. 131), overall the new material indicates the theoretically minded Zhang was the main figure in raising the issue while it is unclear to what extent Peng openly aired his concerns.

145. Li Rui, *Lushan shilu*, pp. 78, 130–31; *Huiyi Zhang Wentian*, p. 313; Zhang Peisen, *Zhang Wentian wenji*, p. 355; *Zhang Wentian fayan*, pp. 18–21; below, pp. 315, 323; and oral sources.

146. Although an authoritative oral source declared that Peng, a notoriously prickly personality, was on bad terms with all the other marshals, there is ample evidence to indicate that he was personally close to at least Zhu De. Zhu reportedly had often spent social time with Peng, and was greatly depressed over his friend's fate. See *Yanhuang zisun* [Chinese Descendants], No. 3 (1989), p. 5.

147. *Selected Works of Deng*, p. 280.

148. Li Rui, *Lushan shilu*, pp. 178, 186–87, 210.

149. See the discussion of traditional factors in *Leadership, Legitimacy, and Conflict*, pp. 59–61, 66.

150. See below, p. 331.

151. Li Rui, *Lushan shilu*, pp. 182–83.

152. *Ibid*, p. 181; Cong Jin, *Quzhe fazhan*, pp. 306–307; and *RMRB*, June 30, 1988, p. 5. In his criticism Zhu, like Tan Zhenlin, noted the positive aspect of Peng's letter.

153. The proposition that Mao's increasingly undemocratic leadership style was rarely discussed publicly or privately after Lushan is, of course, impossible to substantiate, but I am struck by lack of evidence to this effect from both published and oral sources during the reform period. Indeed, one senior Party historian stated that he not only had no evidence but considered such private criticism quite impossible in the post-Lushan atmosphere since no one could be sure that a critical comment would not be reported. A small number of Cultural Revolution sources, however, asserted that cadres and a few leaders drew parallels between Mao's behavior and that of Stalin after Lushan; see below, pp. 379, 394.

A possible exception to the apparent reluctance to criticize Mao on this question occurred in the allegorical criticisms allowed during the crisis years of 1961–62; see Cheek, *Broken Jade*, pp. 317–18. Cheek's broader discussion of these allegorical writings provides a subtle and variegated picture which is consistent with the interpretation of *Politics and Purges*, below, pp. 373–74.

154. See *Politics at Mao's Court*, pp. 140–41; and David Holm, "The Strange Case of Liu Zhidan," *AJCA*, No. 27 (1992).

155. In this analysis my source was referring to collective discussion to resolve questions among themselves before presenting their recommendations to Mao for his approval or rejection. On Deng's measured behavior in this period, see above, p. xxxviii and n. 92.

156. See below, p. 384.

157. This is the assessment of my source except for the clause I have added that the focus on leftist errors was consistent with Mao's position at the time.

158. Schoenhals, "Edited Records," p. 6.

159. See below, pp. 335–42.

160. *Dangshi tongxun*, No. 7 (1984), pp. 21–27. For an incomplete Cultural Revolution text of Mao's June 12, 1961, speech which excludes the self-critical passage, see *Xuexi wenxuan* [Selected Materials (from Mao's Speeches and Writings) for Our Study], vol. 3 (n. p.: n. pub., 1967), pp. 270–72.

161. *Dang de wenxian*, No. 1 (1991), pp. 24–25, 27–29, 32–33; *Dangshi yanjiu*, No. 5 (1981), pp. 21–22; Cong Jin, *Quzhe fazhan*, p. 413; Stuart Schram, ed., *Mao Tse-tung Unrehearsed, Talks and Letters: 1956–71 (MU)* (Harmondsworth: Penguin Books, 1974), pp. 164–67; and oral source.

162. See above, p. xxxix. Chen did, however, speak to a group meeting the day after the conclusion of the conference, ironically on the topic of abnormal inner Party life; *Dang de wenxian*, No. 1 (1991), p. 32.

163. *MU*, p. 167; Michael Schoenhals and Brewer S. Stone, "More Edited Records: Liu Shaoqi on Peng Dehuai at the 7000 Cadres Conference," *CCP Research Newsletter*, No. 5 (1990), pp. 3–5; oral sources; and above, pp. xxxix–xli. Despite Mao's reported anger,

Liu's remarks on Peng Dehuai were not at great variance with the Chairman's own more general observation a few days later that people were free to speak out as long as they obeyed Party discipline and did not form secret factions; *MU*, p. 183.

164. This was explicitly stated by one high ranking Party historian with regard to Mao's outburst aimed at Liu Shaoqi and Deng Xiaoping at the end of 1964, while it is an obvious deduction from several discussions dealing with the Chairman's attacks on various leaders at the fall 1962 Tenth Plenum.

165. *Memoirs of a Chinese Marshal*, pp. 521–23; *Dang de wenxian*, No. 5 (1990), pp. 31–32, 35; and oral source. This account alters the interpretation of the September 1965 meeting speculatively advanced in Teiwes, "Peng and Mao", pp. 91–92. In that interpretation I concluded probably erroneously that since the overall pattern of evidence suggested Mao's unbending hostility toward Peng after Lushan, Mao was trying to lull the other top leaders present in view of the coming Cultural Revolution. While the present analysis provides a less cynical view of Mao, it does not rule out deception at the September 1965 meeting and in any case confirms the Chairman's continuing antipathy to Peng. For a somewhat inaccurate reference to He Long's committee, see below, p. 380.

166. See below, pp. 460–64.

167. *Dangshi tongxun*, No. 6 (1984), pp. 18–27; Tan Zhongji, *et al.*, *Shinianhou*, pp. 8–9; and oral source. This version indicates even stronger pro-Wu Han signals from Mao than Cultural Revolution materials which claimed he said in December 1965 that Wu could be a *xian* magistrate; see below, p. 462.

168. Hu Hua, ed., *Zhonggong dangshi renwu zhuan* [Biographies of Personalities in CCP History], vol. 7 (Xi'an: Shaanxi renmin chubanshe, 1983), pp. 289–91; and oral source.

The question of Wu Han's mood in late 1965 raises an important methodological issue. While many post-1978 sources, particularly in established Party history journals, can be regarded as much more reliable than Cultural Revolution materials, this is not inevitably the case. In this instance, an article appearing in *Dangshi wenhui*, No. 4 (1988), pp. 4–28, pictured Wu Han as being much more worried months earlier than the account presented here. This article, however, was subsequently disowned by the journal following extensive scholarly criticism which was acknowledged by the author; *ibid.*, No. 6 (1988), p. 21. On the larger issue, see the perceptive discussion of various types of publications on Party history by Schoenhals, "Unofficial and Official Histories."

169. Interview by Mary G. Mazur with a relative of Wu Han. Mazur is not clear concerning the precise timing of this comment but believes it was made about January 1966. When directly questioned about this reported statement, a senior Party historian said it was "credible," and added that no one expected the serious consequences which flowed from the affair.

170. This interpretation, which I find completely credible, is drawn directly from personal communication with Mary Mazur. Carol Lee Hamrin, in her work on Yang Xianzhen including interviews with Yang, came to the similar conclusions that Yang observed official norms in his behavior and had considerable faith in Mao's own commitment to traditional understandings; personal communication. See also below, n. 172.

171. Even after the Cultural Revolution had entered uncharted waters Mao was still speaking of it as a rectification and stating that he hoped his long time colleagues and followers could "pass the test"; see Teiwes, "Mao and His Lieutenants," pp. 22n, 74.

172. Timothy Cheek, *Broken Jade*, p. 402, on the basis of an extensive study of Wu Han's colleague, Deng Tuo, including interviews with various members of Deng's circle, also concluded that "faith that the 'old man' would ultimately figure out the right

answer . . . and forgive any unjustly punished sons or daughters continued at the very least until the spring of 1966. . . ."

173. See *Leadership, Legitimacy, and Conflict*, pp. 46–49, 63–64, 67. Mao's unchallenged leadership within the CCP can be dated to 1943, if not earlier, and it had charismatic aspects from that time. The victory of 1949, however, made that charisma indelible. Cf. Teiwes, "Mao and His Lieutenants," pp. 7–10.

174. *Chen Yun wenxuan*, p. 257.

175. See "Resolution on History Since the Founding," p. 25; and Stuart R. Schram, "Party Leader or True Ruler? Foundations and Significance of Mao Zedong's Personal Power," in Schram, ed., *Foundations and Limits of State Power in China* (Hong Kong: The Chinese University Press, 1987), p. 255.

176. See Lawrence R. Sullivan, "The Analysis of 'Despotism' in the CCP: 1978–1982," *Asian Survey*, July 1987, pp. 812–15.

177. *Politics at Mao's Court*, pp. 85, 103–104, 109. Secrecy apparently based on status considerations also affected other cases examined in this introduction. According to oral sources, less than 100 top leaders knew of Mao's criticism of Zhou Enlai and Chen Yun at the 1958 Nanning Conference, while many incidents of the Chairman's arbitrary behavior towards his closest associates during the early 1960s were not known outside the highest circles.

178. Oral sources emphasize the point that criticism and self-criticism was accepted within the elite as a regular part of inner Party life, and thus in the normal course of events it was not threatening to the position of top officials. When Mao was dissatisfied, and other leaders seized on the Chairman's discontent to attack their colleagues, however, life could become very anxious for those being criticised; see, e.g., above, pp. xvii–xx.

179. Cf. the aftermath of the Gao-Rao affair when, as late as April 1956, Mao noted that lower level officials reacting to the case remained fearful of airing their thoughts; *Politics at Mao's Court*, p. 140.

180. Comparing the status of Lin and Peng is tricky. Although Peng had nearly two decades of seniority on the Politburo over Lin, Lin outranked Peng by a substantial margin in both the 1945 and 1956 Central Committees. Crucially, in terms of military reputation, Lin if anything had greater prestige than his fellow marshal, Peng. On Lin's status and the perception of same within the elite, see Teiwes, "Mao and His Lieutenants," p. 48n.

181. There are some claims that when Lin turned down Mao's offer in 1950 to lead the Chinese forces in Korea on health grounds it had more to do in fact with his disapproval of the venture; see *Politics at Mao's Court*, p. 307. However, it does appear from the testimony of various oral sources and other materials that Lin did have consistently poor health after 1949 and was frequently on sick leave.

182. *Ziyou beiwanglu—Su Xiaokang quanjing baogao wenxueji* [A Memorandum on Freedom—A Collection of Su Xiaokang's Panoramic Reportage] (Beijing: Zhongguo shehui kexueyuan chubanshe, 1988) pp. 279, 301; Huang Yao, *et al.*, *Luo Ronghuan hou shiwunian* [Luo Ronghuan's Last 15 years] (Beijing: Renmin chubanshe, 1987), pp. 94–95; Teiwes, "Mao and His Lieutenants," p. 65; and oral sources.

183. According to a high ranking oral source, the right to invoke leave is reserved for the very highest leaders. This source of ministerial level commented that if a meeting were convened that required his attendance, he would have to go no matter how sick he was.

184. Chen was officially on sick leave at the start of 1962 when he first declined to speak to the 7,000 cadres conference and subsequently initially demurred to requests that he assume leadership of the financial and economic small group although he apparently only used ill health as an excuse in the latter case. *Zhou Enlai yanjiu xueshu taolun huiyi wenji* [Collection of Essays from the Zhou Enlai Research Academic Confer-

ence] (Beijing: Zhongyang wenxian chubanshe, 1988), p. 329; oral source; and above, p. xxxix.

The more general question of Chen Yun's use of sick leave is a complex one. On the one hand, Chen does generally seem to have suffered from somewhat poor health and genuinely required sick leave from time to time; see *Politics at Mao's Court*, p. 29. Yet at the same time Chen seems to have had an uncanny facility for being ill at politically convenient times. Thus Chen was on sick leave during the 1953 financial and economic conference when the new tax system which he had approved came under fierce assault (see above, p. xix), and, perhaps for health reasons (oral source), he was not at the Nanning conference where he himself came under sharp attack. As for the crucial Lushan meetings, although under doctor's orders Chen's behavior differed from that of the also ill Lin Biao who rushed to Lushan once the Peng Dehuai affair exploded while Chen stayed away; oral source. What this pattern suggests is that even allowing for genuine poor health, it is plausible that Chen was able to utilize that factor in a discriminating manner.

185. See Zhong Kan, *Kang Sheng pingzhuan* [Critical Biography of Kang Sheng] (Beijing: Hongqi chubanshe, 1982), chs. 13–14. For other factors contributing to Kang's "sick leave," see above, n. 117.

186. See *Politics at Mao's Court*, pp. 39–40.

187. Ironically, as indicated previously both Peng Dehuai and Zhang Wentian initially intended to stay in Beijing to attend to their respective defense and foreign affairs duties, as was their privilege, before deciding to go to Lushan; see above, pp. xxxii–xxxiii.

188. See *Politics at Mao's Court*, pp. 45–46.

189. When asked to comment on the view advanced here, a ministerial level official said it was hard to answer since the top leaders were "so deep inside Zhongnanhai," but his impression was that contact among such figures had declined since 1949. An example of leaders who had little contact after 1949 is Peng Dehuai and Bo Yibo, officials with different functional responsibilities and a history of conflictual relations during the revolutionary period; *RMRB*, October 23, 1988, p. 4.

190. As of 1966 only Gao Gang, Peng Dehuai and Zhang Wentian of the 1945 Politburo had been dismissed from official positions for political reasons, and in the cases of Peng and Zhang this did not apply formally to their seats on the Politburo. In addition, all members and alternates of the Politburo elected in 1956, again with the exception of Peng and Zhang, were in place at the start of the Cultural Revolution.

191. The initial, somewhat halting effort to restore the norms in 1977–78 is discussed in the Conclusion to the first edition, below, pp. 487–91. These efforts were greatly intensified in a number of respects following the December 1978 Third Plenum with the increasing dominance of the veteran leaders headed by Deng Xiaoping. One major aspect was a deepening and broadening of the "reversal of verdicts" which now extended to large numbers of wrongly expelled Party members and virtually all past leaders who had suffered during the Cultural Revolution and earlier campaigns; see Hong Yung Lee, *From Revolutionary Cadres to Party Technocrats in Socialist China* (Berkeley: University of California Press, 1991), chapter 8. Also, traditional CCP principles were recodified in the "Guiding Principles for Inner Party Life" (see *Beijing Review*, No. 13 (1980), pp. 11–20) adopted by the February 1980 Central Committee plenum, and the inculcation of these norms was a key aim of the Party rectification carried out from 1983 to 1987. For a thoughtful overview of this rectification effort, see Bruce J. Dickson, "Conflict and Non-Compliance in Chinese Politics: Party Rectification, 1983–87," *Pacific Affairs*, Summer 1990. Finally, the push for lenient treatment of political losers predicted in the first edition (pp. 490–91) can be seen in the limited sanctions applied to Hua Guofeng, Hu Yaobang and, more ambiguously, Zhao Ziyang after their respective removals from office in the 1980s.

Introduction to the First Edition

1. For a critique of the "two line struggle" model of analysis as applied to the pre-Cultural Revolution period, see Teiwes, "Chinese Politics."

2. *Xinmingci cidian* [New Terminology Dictionary], (Shanghai: Chunming chubanshe, 1953), p. 0120.

3. For example, the 1955–57 campaign to purge hidden counterrevolutionaries *(sufan yundong)*. See Frederick C. Teiwes, "Rectification Campaigns and Purges in Communist China, 1950–61," Ph.D. dissertation, Columbia University, 1971, ch. 11.

4. Donald W. Klein, "The 'Next Generation' of Chinese Communist Leaders," in Roderick MacFarquhar, ed., *China under Mao: Politics Takes Command* (Cambridge: The M.I.T. Press, 1966), p. 82.

5. Zhonggong zhongyang zuzhibu yanjiushi, *Dang de zuzhi gongzuo wenda* [Questions and Answers on Party Organization Work] (Beijing: Renmin chubanshe, 1965), p. 68.

6. See the discussion of the suspended death sentence in Jerome Alan Cohen, *The Criminal Process in the People's Republic of China, 1949–1963: An Introduction* (Cambridge: Harvard University Press, 1968), pp. 537–39.

Chapter 1

1. For example, Ying-mao Kau, "The Organizational Line in Dispute: Editor's Introduction," *CLG*, Spring 1972; and Lowell Dittmer, *Liu Shao-ch'i and the Chinese Cultural Revolution: The Politics of Mass Criticism* (Berkeley: University of California Press, 1974), ch. 10.

2. Key writings on the subject are: Mao Tse-tung (Mao Zedong), "On Contradiction" (August 1937), in *Selected Works of Mao Tse-tung (SW)* (5 vols., Beijing: Foreign Languages Press, 1961, 1965, 1977), I, 311–37; and Mao Tse-tung, "On the Correct Handling of Contradictions among the People" (June 1957), in *Communist China 1955–1959: Policy Documents with Analysis (PDA)*, with a foreword by Robert R. Bowie and John K. Fairbank (Cambridge: Harvard University Press, 1965), pp. 275–94. The most systematic application of contradictions theory to organizational problems is Liu Shao-ch'i (Liu Shaoqi), "Self-Cultivation in Organization and Discipline" (July 1939), *CLG*, Spring 1972, pp. 24–77.

3. "On Contradiction," p. 317.

4. "Correct Handling," pp. 275–81.

5. *Ibid.*, p. 276 (emphasis added).

6. "Training the Communist Party Member" (August 1939), in Boyd Compton, trans., *Mao's China: Party Reform Documents, 1942–44* (Seattle: University of Washington Press, 1966), p. 110.

7. "In Opposition to Party Formalism" (February 1942), in Compton, *Mao's China*, p. 37.

8. "Correct Handling," p. 278.

9. For example, see the September 1963 socialist education directive in *SC*, p. 85.

10. "Self-Cultivation in Organization," p. 27.

11. *Ibid.*, pp. 38–42, 45.

12. E.g., "Reform in Learning, the Party, and Literature" (February 1942), in Compton, *Mao's China*, pp. 9, 24; and "In Opposition to Several Incorrect Tendencies Within the Party" (December 1929), in *ibid.*, pp. 239–41. The 1929 article was reissued in altered

form as a rectification document in the early 1940s.

13. *SW*, III, 44.

14. "Self-Cultivation in Organization," p. 39; Liu Shao-ch'i, "On the Party" (May 1945), in *Collected Works of Liu Shao-ch'i, 1945–1957* (Hong Kong: Union Research Institute, 1969), pp. 57–58; and "Opposition to Incorrect Tendencies," p. 241.

15. "On the Intra-Party Struggle" (July 1941), in Compton, *Mao's China*, p. 236.

16. *Ibid.*, pp. 215–18, 225; "Self-Cultivation in Organization," p. 47; and "Reform in Learning," pp. 22–24.

17. "Intra-Party Struggle," pp. 204–205, 219; "On the Party," p. 57; and Mao Tse-tung, "In Opposition to Liberalism" (September 1937), in Compton, *Mao's China*, p. 185.

18. "Self-Cultivation in Organization," pp. 30–36, 44–45, 56–57.

19. "On the Party," p. 93.

20. "Opposition to Formalism," pp. 42, 44; Liu Shao-ch'i, *How to Be a Good Communist* (Beijing: Foreign Languages Press, 1964), p. 6; "On the Party," p. 65; and *SW*, III, 121.

21. "Opposition to Incorrect Tendencies," p. 242.

22. Intra-Party Struggle," p. 203–206; and "Opposition to Liberalism," pp. 184–85.

23. "Opposition to Formalism," p. 40.

24. "Intra-Party Struggle," pp. 222–23.

25. *Ibid.*, p. 208.

26. *Ibid.*, pp. 210–11 (emphasis added).

27. *Ibid.*, p. 220.

Chapter 2

1. For a comprehensive comparison, see Frederick C. Teiwes, *Elite Discipline in China: Coercive and Persuasive Approaches to Rectification, 1950–1953* (Canberra: Contemporary China Papers, 1978), pp. 11–15.

2. Alexander Dallin and George W. Breslauer, *Political Terror in Communist Systems* (Stanford: Stanford University Press, 1970), pp. 4, 26, 31–32, 49, 57.

3. Secondary literature is rich in discussions of small groups. Among the most useful are: Martin King Whyte, *Small Groups and Political Rituals in China* (Berkeley: University of California Press, 1974); A. Doak Barnett with Ezra Vogel, *Cadres, Bureaucracy and Political Power in Communist China* (New York: Columbia University Press, 1967), pp. 25–26, 30–33, 161–65; John Wilson Lewis, *Leadership in Communist China* (Ithaca: Cornell University Press, 1963), ch. 5; James R. Townsend, *Political Participation in Communist China* (Berkeley: University of California Press, 1969), pp. 174–76; Robert Jay Lifton, *Thought Reform and the Psychology of Totalism: A Study of "Brainwashing" in China* (New York: W.W. Norton & Company, 1961); and Edgar H. Schein with Inge Schneier and Curtis H. Barker, *Coercive Persuasion: A Socio-psychological Analysis of the "Brainwashing" of American Civilian Prisoners* (New York: W.W. Norton & Company, 1961), especially pp. 290–98.

4. For detailed discussions of the specific bureaucratic control devices involved—the personnel dossier *(dang'an)*, cadre assessments *(ganbu jianding)*, and the investigation of cadres *(shencha ganbu)*—see Barnett with Vogel, *Cadres*, pp. 49–52, 165–68; *Dang zuzhi*, pp. 29–30; and *Xinhua yuebao* [New China Monthly] *(XHYB)*, February 1955, pp. 33–35.

5. Although no comprehensive comparison is possible, Barnett and Vogel concluded on the basis of interviews that in one South China county perhaps 1 percent of all Party

members were expelled and another 5 percent punished in other ways in years without major political campaigns, while these rates rose as high as 3 and 7 percent in some campaign years. See Barnett with Vogel, *Cadres,* p. 146.

6. Cohen, *Criminal Process,* pp. 20, 190–91, 193; and Barnett with Vogel, *Cadres,* p. 34.

7. Barnett with Vogel, *Cadres,* pp. 33–34, 71; Cohen, *Criminal Process,* pp. 20, 165–66, 263–64; and Chow Ching-wen, *Ten Years of Storm: The True Story of the Communist Regime in China* (New York: Holt, Rinehart and Winston, 1960), pp. 127, 131–32.

8. Cf. Cohen, *Criminal Process,* pp. 218, 265. The January 1965 directive on the Socialist Education Movement stipulates "change in work assignments" *(diaohuan gongzuo)* as a method of dealing with questionable cadres. See *SC,* p. 123.

9. *Dang zuzhi,* p. 71; and Barnett with Vogel, *Cadres,* p. 146.

10. Administrative measures listed below are from the 1957 "Provisional Regulations of the State Council of the PRC Relating to Rewards and Punishments for Personnel of State Administrative Organs," in Cohen, *Criminal Process,* p. 194, unless otherwise noted. Similar sanctions were used before 1957.

11. This sanction, also rendered *zhiming fanxing,* is not listed in the 1957 administrative regulations but was reported in my interviews and has been mentioned in the official press. See *Changjiang ribao* [Yangtze Daily] *(CJRB),* March 8, 1952.

12. Information on this sanction including an explanation distinguishing it from *kaichu* (see below) was obtained from a refugee source interviewed in Hong Kong in 1967.

13. See Cohen, *Criminal Process,* pp. 193–94, 198–99.

14. See New China News Agency (NCNA), Beijing, February 9, 1953, in *Survey of China Mainland Press (SCMP),* No. 514.

15. Party disciplinary measures listed below are from Article 13 of the 1956 Constitution of the CCP, in *Dang zuzhi,* p. 68, unless otherwise noted. Similar measures were used in the early 1950s as stipulated by the 1945 CCP Constitution.

16. Major demerit is not listed in the CCP Constitution but was reported as a Party sanction in my interviews and in Barnett with Vogel, *Cadres,* p. 146.

17. Information about this sanction including an explanation distinguishing it from *kaichu dangji* was provided by the refugee source cited in n. 12, this chapter. For an official reference, see *Renmin shouce* [People's Handbook] *(RMSC),* 1959, p. 16.

18. *Dang zuzhi,* p. 70; and Barnett with Vogel, *Cadres,* p. 146.

19. Cohen, *Criminal Process,* p. 265. Cf. below, p. 34.

20. Cohen, *Criminal Process,* pp. 191–92, 196, 199.

21. See *ibid.,* pp. 20–21.

22. See *ibid.,* pp. 261–64, 268; and Barnett with Vogel, *Cadres,* pp. 403–12.

23. For a rare official statement on the coercive nature of discipline, see Cohen, *Criminal Process,* p. 195.

24. See *ibid.,* p. 194.

25. *Current Background (CB),* No. 256; and Donald W. Klein and Anne B. Clark, *Biographic Dictionary of Chinese Communism 1921–1965* (2 vols., Cambridge: Harvard University Press, 1971), I, 45–47, II, 956–59.

26. Klein and Clark, *Biographic Dictionary,* I, 397–401.

27. *Ibid.,* II, 707–10.

28. Frederick C. Teiwes, *Provincial Party Personnel in Mainland China 1956–1966* (New York: Occasional Papers of the East Asian Institute, Columbia University, 1967), pp. 42, 86.

29. On this contradiction, see Richard H. Solomon, "On Activism and Activists: Mao-

ist Conceptions of Motivation and Political Role Linking State to Society," *(CQ)*, No. 39 (1969), pp. 103–104.

30. Lifton, *Thought Reform*, pp. 301, 400.

31. See William Hinton, *Fanshen: A Documentary of Revolution in a Chinese Village* (New York: Vintage Books, 1966), pp. 266–68, 515.

32. See Whyte, *Small Groups*, pp. 219–20.

33. This is not to state a general rule but merely to indicate one possible pattern under given circumstances. On the tendency of veteran cadres to feel immune from rectification, see *CJRB*, September 5, 1950. On the insecurity of non-Party people, note the hesitant response of non-Party intellectuals to the Hundred Flowers policy in 1956–57; Roderick MacFarquhar, ed., *The Hundred Flowers (HF)* (London: Stevens & Sons, 1960), pp. 7–9, 21–25.

34. See Lifton, *Thought Reform*, pp. 254, 319, 401; and Mu Fu-sheng, *The Wilting of the Hundred Flowers: The Chinese Intelligentsia under Mao* (New York: Frederick A Praeger, 1962), p. 228.

35. See Frederick C. Teiwes, "A Case Study of Rectification: The 1958 *Cheng-feng Cheng-kai* Campaign in Hui-tung County," *Papers on Far Eastern History*, March 1973, pp. 90–91.

36. The most graphic example of this is the low morale of PLA men due to the economic deprivations suffered by their families in the early 1960s. J. Chester Cheng, ed., *The Politics of the Chinese Red Army: A Translation of the Bulletin of Activities of the People's Liberation Army* (Stanford: Hoover Institution Publications, 1966), pp. 12–14.

37. *Coercive Persuasion*, p. 18.

38. Dallin and Breslauer, *Political Terror*, pp. 104–109.

39. See above, p. 16.

40. Schein, *et al.*, *Coercive Persuasion*, pp. 120–36, 172–73, 240, 301; and Lifton, *Thought Reform*, pp. 31, 67–73, 411.

41. Schein, *et al.*, *Coercive Persuasion*, pp. 79, 285, 297, 301; Lifton, *Thought Reform*, pp. 346, 411–12; and Dallin and Breslauer, *Political Terror*, p. 54.

42. Schein, *et al.*, *Coercive Persuasion*, pp. 79, 284, 292; and Lifton, *Thought Reform*, pp. 322, 326, 336.

43. Schein, *et al.*, *Coercive Persuasion*, pp. 136–38, 164–65; and Lifton, *Thought Reform*, p. 152.

44. Lifton, *Thought Reform*, pp. 152ff.; and Schein, *et al.*, *Coercive Persuasion*, pp. 273–74.

45. Schein, *et al.*, *Coercive Persuasion*, pp. 250–51; and Whyte, *Small Groups*, pp. 211ff.

46. Cf. Townsend, *Participation*, pp. 205–207; Solomon, "On Activism," pp. 77–79, 87–88; and Whyte, *Small Groups*, 214–15.

47. On using the established leadership, see Teiwes, "Case Study," pp. 73–79. On work teams, see below, pp. 68–70.

48. See *Jiefang ribao* [Liberation Daily] *(JFRB)*, July 27, 1950; and Chow, *Ten Years*, p. 127.

49. See Lewis, *Leadership*, p. 117; *RMRB*, April 9, 1952, in *CB*, No. 180; and *CJRB*, June 24, 1952, in *CB*, No. 200.

50. See Teiwes, "Case Study," pp. 88–89.

51. *CJRB*, August 9, 1950.

52. Whyte, *Small Groups*, p. 93; Schein, *et al.*, *Coercive Persuasion*, pp. 103–104, 259–68, Lifton, *Thought Reform*, pp. 401–402, 412, 426–27; and Teiwes, "Case Study," especially pp. 98–99.

Chapter 3

1. Mao's version of the policies at issue is given in "Resolution on Certain Questions in the History of Our Party" (April 1945), *SW,* III, 177–225. For a discussion suggesting that Mao's actual position was less at variance with that of the returned students than he later claimed, see James Pinckney Harrison, *The Long March To Power: A History of the Chinese Communist Party, 1921–72* (New York: Praeger, 1972), pp. 212–13.

2. "Resolution on Questions in History," pp. 208–209.

3. Otto Braun, a Comintern military adviser to the CCP in this period, claimed that the returned student leadership compromised with Mao and even gave in on important questions. See "Kak Mao Tse-dun shel k vlasti" [How Mao Zedong Came to Power], *Literaturnaya Gazeta,* December 5, 1973, p. 13.

4. Harrison, *Long March,* p. 217, concludes that "many thousands were purged . . . in the early 1930s, including some senior leaders. . . ."

5. See John E. Rue, *Mao Tse-tung in Opposition 1927–1935* (Stanford: Stanford University Press, 1966), pp. 171–88. The versions of the resolution published during the 1942 rectification campaign, and subsequently, underwent substantial alterations.

6. See Harrison, *Long March,* pp. 212–17.

7. *Wenge fengyun* [Cultural Revolution Storm], No. 4 (1967), in *Selections from China Mainland Magazines (SCMM),* No. 635.

8. *Ibid.*

9. "Collection of Chen Yi's speeches" (Red Guard pamphlet), in *SCMM,* No. 636.

10. See Harrison, *Long March,* pp. 320–21, 323, 326–29; and Mark Selden, *The Yenan Way in Revolutionary China* (Cambridge: Harvard University Press, 1971), pp. 191–92.

11. See Harrison, *Long March,* pp. 281–86, 288–89; *SW,* II, 61–74, 195–235; and Gregor Benton, "The 'Second Wang Ming Line' (1935–38)," *CQ,* No. 61 (1975).

12. He Ganzhi, *Zhongguo xiandai gemingshi* [A History of the Modern Chinese Revolution] (Hong Kong: Sanlian shudian, 1958), p. 230.

13. Harrison, *Long March,* pp. 326, 329; Selden, *Yenan Way,* pp. 188–90; and Conrad Brandt, Benjamin Schwartz and John K. Fairbank, *A Documentary History of Chinese Communism* (New York: Atheneum, 1966), pp. 353, 373.

14. He Ganzhi, *Gemingshi,* p. 249.

15. Harrison, *Long March,* p. 323.

16. Wang Ming himself, however, did not hold any major Party posts after about 1940. See *ibid.,* pp. 324, 587–88.

17. See *ibid.,* p. 316. For a different interpretation, see Selden, *Yenan Way,* pp. 177ff.

18. Klein and Clark, *Biographic Dictionary,* I, 621.

19. See He Ganzhi, *Gemingshi,* pp. 251–54; Selden, *Yenan Way,* p. 206; and Stuart Schram, *Mao Tse-tung* (Baltimore: Penguin Books, 1966), pp. 220–23.

20. On the development of the movement up to this point, see Zhao Han, *Tantan Zhongguo Gongchandang de zhengfeng yundong* [Talks on the CCP's Rectification Campaigns] (Beijing: Zhongguo qingnian chubanshe, 1957), pp. 19–20; Harrison, *Long March,* pp. 321, 325–26, 334, 337; Selden, *Yenan Way,* pp. 192, 199; and Tanaka Kyoko, "Mass Mobilisation: The Chinese Communist Party and the Peasants," Ph.D. dissertation, The Australian National University, 1972, pp. 125–32.

21. "Lun fayang minzhu" [On the Expansion of Democracy] (1944), in *Liu Shaoqi wenti cailiao zhuanji* [A Special Collection of Materials on the Liu Shaoqi Question] (Taibei: Institute for the Study of Chinese Communist Problems, 1970), pp. 134–42.

22. See Selden, *Yenan Way,* pp. 39–71, 200–203.

23. See *ibid.,* pp. 207–54 *passim.*

24. Zhao Han, *Tantan,* p. 21; and Harrison, *Long March,* pp. 340–42.

25. *SW,* III, 118.

26. For yearly figures (excluding 1943), see Lewis, *Leadership,* p. 110.

27. See Zhao Han, *Tantan,* pp. 21–22; *SW,* III, 163–64, 177–225 *passim;* and Harrison, *Long March,* pp. 324–25, 343–44.

28. See the comments of leading and ordinary Communists shortly after the rectification campaign to the American reporter, Jack Belden, *China Shakes the World* (New York: Monthly Review Press, 1970), pp. 67–68.

29. See Merle Goldman, *Literary Dissent in Communist China* (Cambridge: Harvard University Press, 1967), pp. 19–36.

30. *Ibid.,* pp. 37–50; and Harrison, *Long March,* pp. 339–40.

31. See Harrison, *Long March,* p. 591, for an estimate largely based on Taiwan sources of an 8 percent dismissal rate of Party and government office holders. This estimate, which is much less than recent Soviet claims, is plausible in view of both anti-subversion efforts and Mao's statement quoted above, p. 57.

32. He Ganzhi, *Gemingshi,* p. 255.

33. Red Guard source cited in Harrison, *Long March,* p. 344.

34. *Shanxi-Suiyuan ribao* [Shanxi-Suiyuan Daily], November 27, 1947 (cited in Harrison, *Long March,* pp. 347, 416).

35. See Tanaka, "Mass Mobilisation," pp. 129–31.

36. Hinton, *Fanshen,* p. 517.

37. *SW,* II, 32.

38. Land reform and Party rectification were also conducted in the Shaan-Gan-Ning Border Region but there problems required only minor readjustments. See Takeuchi Minoru, *et al.,* eds., *Mao Zedong ji* [Collected Works of Mao Zedong] (10 vols., Tokyo: Hokubosha, 1970–72), X, 125.

39. *Ibid.*

40. See the detailed account in *Qianjunbang* [The Massive Cudgel] (Tianjin), April 1967, in *Joint Publications Research Service (JPRS),* No. 41,858. Liu admitted most of his alleged mistakes in his October 1966 "self-criticism"; see *Collected Works of Liu Shao-ch'i, 1958–1967* (Hong Kong: Union Research Institute, 1968), p. 360.

41. *SW,* IV, 121.

42. Tanaka Kyoko, "The Civil War and Radicalization of Chinese Communist Agrarian Policy, 1945–1947," *Papers on Far Eastern History,* September 1973, pp. 70–114 *passim.*

43. *Ibid.,* pp. 72–108; Harrison, *Long March,* pp. 409–13; and Liu Shao-ch'i, "Report on the Question of Agrarian Reform," in *The Agrarian Reform Law of the People's Republic of China and Other Relevant Documents* (Beijing: Foreign Languages Press, 1959), pp. 73–74.

44. *SW,* IV, 231–32.

45. See Stuart R. Schram, "Introduction: The Cultural Revolution in Historical Perspective," in Schram, ed., *Authority, Participation and Cultural Change in China* (Cambridge: Cambridge University Press, 1973), p. 35n.

46. When the Party leadership divided into two groups in early 1947, Mao's group continued to be identified as the Central Committee while Liu's group took the title Working Committee of the Central Committee.

47. *SW,* IV, 147–52, 157, 234; Hinton, *Fanshen,* pp. 250, 263, 322; Harrison, *Long March,* p. 413; and Isabel and David Crook, *Revolution in a Chinese Village: Ten Mile Inn* (Routledge and Kegan Paul, 1959), p. 174.

48. Hinton, *Fanshen,* pp. 222–31, 248; and Crook, *Revolution,* pp. 156–57.

49. Hinton, *Fanshen,* p. 239.

50. Zhao Han, *Tantan,* pp. 23–24; and *SW,* IV, 166, 234.

51. Hinton, *Fanshen,* p. 264.

52. *Ibid.*, pp. 490–91.

53. *Ibid.*, pp. 269–309, 549, 618; and *SW,* IV, 183, 228–29, 232, 235–36.

54. Hinton, *Fanshen,* p. 297. See also *ibid.*, pp. 253, 265; *SW,* IV, 182–83, 197–98, 232; and *Qianjunbang,* April 1967, in *JPRS,* No. 41,858.

55. Zhao Han, *Tantan,* p. 26; *Nanfang ribao* [Southern Daily] *(NFRB),* December 22, 1960, in *SCMP,* No. 2431; and *SW,* IV, 186, 198.

56. The Long Bow gate dealt only with Party members and the movement as a whole focused on Party branches. Non-Party cadres were inevitably drawn into the process, however, as in the final restitution of graft in Long Bow. See Hinton, *Fanshen,* p. 571.

57. *Ibid.*, pp. 256–58, 311, 219ff.; and *SW,* IV, 186.

58. Hinton, *Fanshen,* pp. 326–40, 358–64, 375–76, 431, 449–53, 518–23.

59. *SW,* IV, 158–59, 232; and Liu, "Report on Agrarian Reform," pp. 74–75.

60. "P'ingshan Sets Examples in Land Reform and Party Rectification," *Collected Works of Liu 1945–57,* pp. 119–22.

61. 10 of the 11 statements appear in *SW,* IV, 157–76, 181–89, 193–210, 219–45. The three available in the original including one not in the *Selected Works,* are in *Mao Zedong ji,* X, 97–116, 125–41.

62. See especially *SW,* IV, 164. It is of note that the December 1947 Central Committee resolution on Mao's report called on the Party to "strictly apply in practice this document and, in connection with it, the documents published on October 10, 1947 [namely, 'Outline Land Law of China']. . . ." See *ibid.*, pp. 158–59.

63. *Ibid.*, p. 164 (emphasis added).

64. See Hinton, *Fanshen,* pp. 248–49, 412.

65. *SW,* IV, 166.

66. *Mao Zedong ji,* X, 126.

67. *SW,* IV, 186, 194.

68. *Ibid.*, pp. 193, 195, 230, 239; *Mao Zedong ji,* X, 125; and *NFRB,* December 22, 1960, in *SCMP,* No. 2431.

69. Liu, "P'ingshan Sets Examples," p. 120; and Hinton, *Fanshen,* pp. 272–74.

70. Hinton, *Fanshen,* pp. 273–74, 306, 319, 323.

71. Liu, "P'ingshan Sets Examples," p. 120.

72. *Ibid.*, pp. 120–22; and Hinton, *Fanshen,* p. 332.

73. Hinton, *Fanshen,* pp. 264, 272.

74. *SW,* IV, 219–20. Mao claimed, however, that "in recent months" the Party had been mainly fighting leftist deviations.

75. Hinton, *Fanshen,* pp. 376–77, 400–16, 488–93.

76. For membership figures, see Lewis, *Leadership,* p. 110.

77. Hinton, *Fanshen,* pp. 419–25, 430–31, 453, 468–72, 533–34.

78. *Ibid.*, pp. 376–77, 381–86, 412–14, 496, 499–500.

79. *Ibid.*, pp. 378–80, 496–97, 500, 504.

80. *Ibid.*, pp. 501–502 (emphasis added).

81. *Ibid.*, pp. 504–507.

82. See above, p. 46n.

83. *SW,* IV, 166.

84. Party directives pointed out that land reform and rectification could be thoroughly undertaken only when a high degree of security existed. See, e.g., *SW,* IV, 202.

Chapter 4

1. Comprehensive studies of the period include: A Doak Barnett, *Communist China: The Early Years, 1949–55* (New York: Frederick A. Praeger, 1964); S.B. Thomas, *Government and Administration in Communist China* (New York: International Secretariat,

Institute of Pacific Relations, 1953); and Ezra F. Vogel, *Canton under Communism: Programs and Policies in a Provincial Capital, 1949–1968* (Cambridge: Harvard University Press, 1969), chs. 2–4. For a brief overview, see Teiwes, *Elite Discipline,* ch. 2.

2. For greater detail on this and subsequent rectification campaigns of the 1950–53 period, see Teiwes, *Elite Discipline,* chs. 3–6.

3. On these movements, see Vogel, *Canton,* pp. 62–65; and Kenneth Lieberthal, "The Suppression of Secret Societies in Post-Liberation Tientsin," *CQ,* No. 54 (1973).

4. This designation was rarely used in official reports, but it apparently was used widely as shorthand for the campaign. See *SW,* V, 97. In addition, there were a good number of references in the first half of 1953 (e.g., *Dagong bao* [Impartial Daily] *(DGB)* (Tianjin), March 31, 1953) to an "anti-bureaucratism campaign" which clearly was the same undertaking.

5. See Kenneth R. Walker, "Collectivisation in Retrospect: The 'Socialist High Tide' of Autumn 1955-Spring 1956," *CQ,* No. 26 (1966), pp. 14–16.

6. "Talk at Expanded Central Committee Meeting" (January 1962), in *JPRS,* No. 52029, p. 13.

7. See Mao's 1950–51 statements on the need to avoid excessive killings when suppressing counterrevolutionaries. *Mao Zedong sixiang wansui* [Long Live Mao Zedong's Thought] *(SXWS)* (2 vols., Taibei: 1967, 1969), II, 5–9.

8. See, e.g., Liu Shaoqi's 1951 statement that "The victory of . . . the Chinese revolution is inseparable from the correct Marxist-Leninist leadership of Comrade Mao [Zedong]. . . ." *Collected Works 1945–57,* p. 253.

9. See Teiwes, *Elite Discipline,* p. 61n.

10. For a general discussion of Mao's intellectual outlook in the consolidation period and subsequent years through 1957, see Teiwes, "Chinese Politics," Part I, pp. 6–8.

11. Cf. Parris H. Chang, "Struggle Between Two Roads in China's Countryside," *Current Scene,* February 15, 1968, p. 3. This conclusion is based on Mao's and Liu's behavior over a longer period than 1950–53, but it tends to be borne out by fragmentary evidence on the consolidation period itself.

12. Dittmer, *Liu,* p. 311, found that 39.2 percent of criticisms of Liu made in a sample of the Red Guard and official press referred to "crimes" allegedly committed in the 1949–59 decade (compared to 49.6 percent for 1960–66). Of these, nearly twice as many accusations dealt with 1954–59 as with 1949–53.

13. See Kenneth Lieberthal, "Mao versus Liu? Policy towards Industry and Commerce: 1946–49," *CQ,* No. 47 (1971).

14. "Speech at the Chengdu Conference (March 1958)," as trans. in Stuart R. Schram, "Mao Tse-tung and the Theory of Permanent Revolution," *CQ,* No. 46 (1971), p. 237.

15. See Teiwes, *Elite Discipline,* pp. 63–64n.

16. In the first three years after liberation the number of civilian cadres increased from 720,000 to 3,310,000. *People's China,* No. 1, 1953. Meanwhile, Party membership grew from 4.5 million at the end of 1949 to 6.6 million at the end of 1953 (Lewis, *Leadership,* p. 110), while the Communist Youth League expanded from 200,000 in 1949 to 9 million in 1953 (Harrison, *Long March,* p. 467).

17. Cited in Vogel, *Canton,* p. 71.

18. *Ziliao zhuanji* [Collected Materials], November 1968, in *Survey of China Mainland Press-Supplement (SCMP-S),* No. 246.

19. *Gong-nong-bing* [Workers-Peasants-Soldiers], September 1967, in *Selections from China Mainland Magazines-Supplement (SCMM-S),* No. 27.

20. See Thomas P. Bernstein, "Problems of Village Leadership after Land Reform," *CQ,* No. 36 (1968), pp. 5, 10.

21. *SW,* V, 103–11.

22. *Ibid.*, pp. 103, 108; and Klein and Clark, *Biographic Dictionary*, II, 740–42.

23. *RMRB*, September 20, 1950.

24. *RMRB*, April 2, 1953.

25. See Bernstein, "Village Leadership," pp. 15–17; and NCNA, Beijing, February 9, 1953, in *SCMP*, No. 514.

26. Cited in *CB*, No. 46, p. 1 (original source not given).

27. E.g., *RMRB*, September 14, 1950, in *CB*, No. 46.

28. *XHYB*, November 1950, p. 26.

29. *RMRB*, September 6, 1950; and *Ganbu xuexi ziliao* [Cadre Study Materials], No. 16, September 1950.

30. *RMRB*, July 8, 1950; and Barnett, *Early Years*, p. 217.

31. *Ganbu xuexi ziliao*, No. 16, September 1950; and *RMRB*, September 14, 1950, in *CB*, No. 46.

32. *RMRB*, September 2, 14, 1950; and *JFRB*, August 14, 1950.

33. NCNA, Beijing, February 9, 1953, in *SCMP*, No. 514.

34. Bernstein, "Village Leadership," pp. 17–18; and *RMRB*, June 26, 1953, in *SCMP*, No. 602.

35. *RMRB*, December 30, 1951, January 5, 1952, in *SCMP*, Nos. 251, 257. Note also the connection between bureaucratic behavior and violations of law and discipline during the New Three Anti Campaign; see above p. 92n.

36. *Guangxi ribao* [Guangxi Daily], April 23, 1953, in *SCMP-S*, No. 598; and Bernstein, "Village Leadership," pp. 17–18.

37. *CJRB*, February 9, 1952, in *SCMP*, No. 287.

38. Documentation on this case is collected in *CB*, No. 244, and *SCMP*, No. 504.

39. *RMRB*, January 23, 1953, in *CB*, No. 244; *and JFRB*, February 19, 1953, in *CB*, No. 244.

40. *Ibid.*

41. Party membership was 1.35 million in 1946, 2.76 million in 1947, and 3.07 million in 1948. *Shishi shouce* [Current Events Handbook] *(SSSC)*, September 25, 1956, in *CB*, No. 428. Thus before victory became apparent there were between two and three million Party members. In addition, there were numerous non-Party cadres of this seniority. See Hinton, *Fanshen*, pp. 326–29.

42. NCNA, June 30, 1950.

43. *XHYB*, June 1950, p. 254, September 1950, p. 985.

44. *Xuexi* [Study] *(XX)*, January 1, 1951, in *CB*, No. 180.

45. *JFRB*, July 1, 1950; *DGB* (Hong Kong), July 2, 1950; *CJRB*, July 31, 1950; *Ganbu xuexi ziliao*, No. 16, September 1950; and *RMRB*, October 10, 1950.

46. See *RMRB*, February 12, 1953, in *CB*, No. 251; and below, pp. 107, 115–16.

47. *Xinhua ribao* [New China Daily] *(XHRB)* (Chongqing), October 23, 1952.

48. *CJRB*, September 2, 1951, in *SCMP*, No. 182; and *RMRB*, September 24, 1951, January 12, 1952, January 31, 1953.

49. *RMRB*, July 3, 1951, in *CB*, No. 163; and *Jilin ribao* [Jilin Daily], November 19, 1953.

50. *RMRB*, July 14, December 22, 1951, in *SCMP*, Nos. 157, 260; and *XHYB*, July 1951, p. 536.

51. *RMRB*, December 22, 1951, in *SCMP*, No. 260.

52. *RMRB*, June 11, September 7, 20, 1950.

53. *RMRB*, January 24, 1952, April 2, 1953; *CJRB*, April 8, 1952, in *SCMP*, No. 327; *NFRB*, August 2, 1951, in *SCMP*, No. 160; *JFRB*, December 7, 1952; and Bernstein, "Village Leadership," pp. 5–6, 8–10.

54. *NFRB*, June 14, 1952. See also *NFRB*, May 4, 1952. There were several versions

of the "five sames" which included the same native place, same surname and same nationality.

55. *RMRB*, January 12, 1952.

56. See Barnett, *Early Years*, p. 54.

57. The greatest detail on ways in which pre-1949 elite elements influenced rural cadres is provided by reports from an early 1952 regional campaign in Central-South China, the reform of rank and file land reform cadres *(zhengdun* or *zhengbian tudi gaige ganbu duiwu)* which was linked to the Three Anti Campaign. Reports on the movement in Guangdong are found in *CB*, No. 184. On ties to the Three Anti Campaign, see *NFRB*, March 15, April 18, May 17, 1952, in *CB*, No. 184.

58. *NFRB*, July 21, 24, 1952, in *CB*, No. 204.

59. *CJRB*, January 16, 1952, in *SCMP*, No. 268; *JFRB*, March 11, 1952, in *SCMP*, No. 297; and Vogel, *Canton*, pp. 106–10.

60. *RMRB*, February 16, 1952, in *SCMP*, No. 281.

61. *RMRB*, October 23, 1951.

62. *RMRB*, January 24, 1952, in *CB*, No. 163.

63. NCNA, Beijing, February 1, 1952, in *SCMP*, No. 269.

64. *Dongbei ribao* [Northeast Daily] *(DBRB)*, December 1, 1951, in *SCMP*, No. 240; NCNA, Beijing, December 15, 1951, in *SCMP*, No. 240; and *RMRB*, December 18, 1951, January 8, 1952, in *SCMP*, Nos. 245, 260.

65. *RMRB*, January 24, February 16, 1952, in *CB*, No. 163, *SCMP*, No. 281.

66. *DBRB*, December 1, 1951, in *SCMP*, No. 247.

67. *CJRB*, February 9, 1952.

68. *JFRB*, January 31, 1952; *RMRB*, February 3, 1952; and *Fujian ribao* [Fujian Daily], July 6, 1952.

69. NCNA, Beijing, August 17, 1952, in *SCMP*, No. 401.

70. *JFRB*, April 3, 1952; *XHRB* (Chongqing), April 10, 1952; and *Zhejiang ribao* [Zhejiang Daily], March 8, 1952.

71. See Teiwes, *Elite Discipline*, pp. 77–78, 89–90; and Sherwin Montell, "The San-Fan Wu-Fan Movement in Communist China," *Papers on China*, Vol. VIII (Cambridge: Harvard Committee on International and Regional Studies, February 1954), p. 139.

72. See Teiwes, *Elite Discipline*, pp. 117–18, 149, 209.

73. See *ibid.*, pp. 78–79, 152–53.

74. A comparison of the 1950 and 1951 issues of *RMSC* reveals that only 32 of over 1,000 posts listed in the 1950 *RMSC* were filled by different persons in the 1951 listings. Of these 32 only two could not be soon identified in other official positions on the basis of an examination of major biographical sources—the biographical files of Donald W. Klein; those of the U.S. Consulate General, Hong Kong; *Gendai Chūgoku Jimmei Jiten* [Modern China Biographic Dictionary] (Tokyo: Gaimushō, 1966); and *Directory of Party and Government Officials in Communist China* (Washington: U.S. Department of State, 1953).

75. Bernstein, "Village Leadership," p. 6.

76. See *SW*, V, 31; and *SSSC*, June 5, 1951, in *SCMP*, No. 120.

77. *XHYB*, September 1950, p. 989.

78. See Bernstein, "Village Leadership," pp. 20–22.

79. This conclusion is based on an examination of the organizational listings in *Directory of Officials* in conjunction with the biographical sources listed in n. 74, this chapter.

80. E.g., NCNA, Baoding, February 6, 1953, in *SCMP*, No. 514; *NFRB*, March 3, 1953; and *Fujian ribao*, April 4, 1953.

81. NCNA, Beijing, February 1, 1952, in *SCMP*, No. 268; *NFRB*, February 21, 1952, in *SCMP*, No. 283; *RMRB*, March 12, 1952, in *CB*, No. 168; and Chow, *Ten Years*, pp. 126–31.

82. These provisions are found in NCNA, Beijing, March 11, 1952, in *CB*, No. 168.

83. NCNA, Beijing, March 25, 1952, in *SCMP*, No. 307.

84. See Robert Loh as told to Humphrey Evans, *Escape from Red China* (New York: Coward-McCann, 1962), pp. 98–102. Loh discusses the Five Anti Campaign but there is every reason to believe his observations apply to the Three Anti Campaign as well.

85. *RMRB*, February 24, June 18, 1952, in *SCMP*, Nos. 289, 361; NCNA, Tianjin, June 14, 1952, in *CB*, No. 201; Montell, "San-Fan Wu-Fan," pp. 144–45; and Loh, *Escape*, pp. 105–107.

86. *RMRB*, April 9, July 1, 1952, in *CB*, Nos. 180, 191; NCNA, Beijing, September 30, 1952, in *CB*, No. 251; and *People's China*, January 1, 1953.

87. He Ganzhi, *Gemingshi*, p. 366.

88. NCNA, Beijing, February 9, 1953, in *SCMP*, No. 514. Under the GAC regulations officials found guilty of graft in the ¥1 to 10 million range were also subject to criminal sanctions but only in cases of serious circumstances or stubborn resistance to reform.

89. E.g., *RMRB*, December 11, 1951; and *JFRB*, January 23, February 1, March 26, 1952.

90. *JFRB*, December 28, 1951.

91. Chow, *Ten Years*, p. 133, estimates the number of people sent to labor as a result of the Three and Five Anti Campaigns at "about 300,000." The same author estimates that over 200,000 people committed suicide during these movements.

92. E.g., *RMRB*, December 9, 1951; *Xinjiang ribao* [Xinjiang Daily], December 30, 1951; and *Qingdao ribao* [Qingdao Daily], January 15, 1952.

93. Loh, *Escape*, pp. 82–83; Chow, *Ten Years*, pp. 127–30; and Ezra F. Vogel, "From Revolutionary to Semi-Bureaucrat: The 'Regularisation' of Cadres," *CQ*, No. 29 (1967).

94. This conclusion is based on an examination of the biographical files of Donald W. Klein and the U.S. Consulate General, Hong Kong. All relevant personnel who were removed from their posts at the approximate time of the Three Anti Campaign continued to function in comparable positions.

95. See *RMRB*, January 7, 13, 24, 1952; and Montell, "San-Fan Wu-Fan," p. 148.

96. *RMSC*, 1953, p. 432.

97. See *NFRB*, February 7, 1952; *RMRB*, March 16, 1952; and *Zhejiang ribao*, March 2, 8, 1952.

98. See *RMRB*, March 30, 1952; *NFRB*, May 9, 1952; and *CJRB*, January 9, 1952.

99. *SW*, V, 111n.

100. Zhao Han, *Tantan*, p. 31.

101. NCNA, Beijing, February 9, 1953, in *SCMP*, No. 514.

102. *RMRB*, April 2, 1953; and *People's China*, July 1, 1953.

103. *RMRB*, April 2, 1953; *Qunzhong ribao* [Masses Daily] (Xi'an), August 17, 1953, in *SCMP-S*, No. 611; and *JFRB*, May 18, 1954, in *SCMP-S*, No. 847.

104. For evidence of a purge quota during the Three Anti Campaign, see *China News Analysis (CNA)*, No. 637 (1966), p. 3.

105. *RMRB*, April 2, 1953; and *CJRB*, November 22, 1951. Such reports, however, also complained of excessive leniency during the implementation of the movement in some units.

106. See Bernstein, "Village Leadership," p. 7.

107. *SW*, V, 48.

108. See Lewis, *Leadership*, p. 110.

109. Zhao Han, *Tantan*, pp. 27–28; *XHYB*, July 1950, p. 506; and *RMRB*, September 2, 1950.

110. Zhao Han, *Tantan*, p. 28. On state supervisory organs, see Franz Schurmann, *Ideology and Organization in Communist China* (Berkeley: University of California Press, 1966), ch. 5. On Party control committees (at that time called "discipline inspection committees"), see Paul M. Cocks, "The Historical and Institutional Role of the Party Control Committee in the CCP," unpublished paper available at the East Asian Research Center, Harvard University, 1966.

111. *SW*, V, 85–86, 90–91; *RMRB*, March 13, 1953, in *SCMP*, No. 532; and Bernstein, "Village Leadership," p. 20.

112. E.g., *RMRB*, December 11, 1951, March 3, April 21, 1952; *Tianjin ribao* [Tianjin Daily], December 15, 1951; and Loh, *Escape*, pp. 85ff.

113. Zhao Han, *Tantan*, pp. 30–32; *Henan ribao* [Henan Daily], November 22, 1951; *RMRB*, December 22, 1951; *NFRB*, March 4, 1953; and He Ganzhi, *Gemingshi*, p. 373.

114. Zhao Han, *Tantan*, p. 32; *RMRB*, April 2, June 6, 1953; and *SW*, V, 48.

115. In some cases this involved officials who had received Three Anti education; see *RMRB*, June 4, 1954, in *SCMP*, No. 828.

116. For official claims that the Three and Five Anti Campaigns changed popular attitudes towards the bourgeoisie and its lifestyle, see *People's China*, March 16, 1952; and NCNA, Beijing, March 26, 1952, February 9, 1953, in *SCMP*, Nos. 308, 514.

117. See Figure 2, below, p. 473.

118. Although fear and even suicides due to harsh discipline were reported during Party rectification (see above, p. 118), no reports of struggle sessions and only vague references to "disciplinary action" were found.

Chapter 5

1. E.g., Harold C. Hinton, *The "Unprincipled Dispute" Within the Chinese Communist Top Leadership*, U.S. Information Agency IRI Intelligence Summary, No. LS–98–55, July 1955; and Schurmann, *Ideology and Organization*, ch. 4.

2. See John W. Lewis, *Chinese Communist Party Leadership and the Succession to Mao Tse-tung: An Appraisal of Tensions*, U.S. Department of State Policy Research Study, January 1964, p. 9.

3. The most comprehensive and up to date statement of this view is Mineo Nakajima, "The Kao Kang Affair and Sino-Soviet Relations," *Review* (Japan Institute of International Affairs), March 1977.

4. See *SXWS*, II, 138; and above, p. 5n.

5. See Walker, "Collectivisation," pp. 16–21.

6. The following is primarily drawn from Klein and Clark, *Biographic Dictionary*, I, 408–11, 431–35.

7. Of 12 Politburo members, apart from Gao only Peng Zhen had not been an active participant in the South China revolution.

8. *Wenhui bao* [Wenhui Daily] *(WHB)* (Shanghai), May 20, June 1, 1968, in *SCMP*, No. 4205; *Gongren zaofan bao* [Workers' Rebellion Journal], February 10, 1968, in *SCMP*, No. 4131; *Pi Tan zhanbao* [Criticize Tan Combat Bulletin], August 25, 1967 (cited in Michel Oksenberg, "Methods of Communication within the Chinese Bureaucracy," *CQ*, No. 57 (1974), pp. 6–7); and *SW*, V, 161. Cf. Philip Bridgham, "Factionalism in the Central Committee," in John Wilson Lewis, ed., *Party Leadership and Revolutionary Power in China* (London: Cambridge University Press, 1970), p. 206.

9. See above, p. 90.

10. "Speech at Expanded Meeting of CCP Political Bureau" (April 1956) in *Miscellany of Mao Tse-tung Thought (MMT)* (2 vols.: *JPRS*, No. 61269, February 1974), I, 31.

11. *SW*, V, 161–62, 165.

12. *Ibid.*, pp. 162, 165; and NCNA, Beijing, February 18, 1954, in *SCMP*, No. 751.

13. The above is based on the biographical files of the U.S. Consulate General, Hong Kong, and those of Donald Klein.

14. Data on the plenum are from its communique, NCNA, Beijing, February 18, 1954, in *SCMP*, No. 751, unless otherwise noted.

15. *Zhengfa gongshe* [Political and Legal Commune] (Beijing), June 9, 1967, in *SCMP-S*, No. 192. In addition, Zhu De assertedly said "Gao Gang and Rao Shushi are good men" *after* they had been "dragged out"; *Dongfanghong* [The East Is Red] (Beijing), February 11, 1967, in *SCMP-S*, No. 172. This, however, is suspect since Zhu spoke at the Fourth Plenum undoubtedly in support of its decisions. In general, as shown below, once Gao and Rao had been ousted the reaction of leading cadres was to disassociate themselves from their activities rather than to offer any defense for them.

16. *NFRB*, April 15, 1954, in *SCMP-S*, No. 818; and *RMRB*, July 1, 1954.

17. *RMRB*, April 23, 1954, in *SCMP*, No. 800; and *Shanxi ribao* [Shanxi Daily], December 19, 1954.

18. *RMRB*, March 11, April 23, December 13, 1954, in *SCMP*, Nos. 772, 800, 959.

19. *RMRB*, March 11, April 4, July 1, 1954, in *SCMP*, Nos. 772, 787, 847.

20. *NFRB*, April 15, 1954, in *SCMP-S*, No. 818; *RMRB*, May 7, 1954, in *SCMP*, No. 811; and *Jiangxi ribao* [Jiangxi Daily], December 26, 1954.

21. *CJRB*, April 6, 1954, in *SCMP-S*, No. 812.

22. *RMRB*, April 4, July 1, 1954, in *SCMP*, Nos. 787, 847.

23. *RMRB*, April 4, 1954, in *SCMP*, No. 787.

24. *RMRB*, March 22, April 4, 13, 1954, in *SCMP*, Nos. 779, 787, 793.

25. E.g., NCNA, Xi'an, April 9, July 21, 1954, in *SCMP*, Nos. 787, 857; *RMRB*, May 14, 1954; and *JFRB*, May 23, 1954.

26. E.g., *RMRB*, April 7, 1954; NCNA, Guangzhou, April 15, 1954, in *SCMP*, No. 796; and NCNA, Wuhan, April 18, 1954, in *SCMP*, No. 815.

27. NCNA, Shanghai, April 18, 1954, in *SCMP*, No. 793; and *JFRB*, May 23, June 10, 1954.

28. *WHB* (Shanghai), May 20, 1968, in *SCMP*, No. 4205. It is possible that a self-examination by Tao Zhu before the Guangdong Provincial Committee also took place in this period, but the report of this self-examination was vague concerning timing. See *Pi Tao zhanbao* [Criticize Tao Combat Bulletin] (Beijing), April 10, 1967, in *SCMP*, No. 3962.

29. NCNA, Shenyang, April 27, 1954, in *SCMP*, No. 799.

30. See below, p. 147, for this development in the Northeast. Another possible case is Fujian's Zeng Jingbing, an alternate member of the Central Committee. Zeng dropped from public view after mid-1954; although elected to some provincial posts in early 1955 he was not reelected to the Central Committee in 1956. Klein and Clark, *Biographic Dictionary*, II, 860. Other evidence, however, indicates Zeng's downfall resulted from "localist" activities apparently unrelated to the Gao-Rao case. See Victor C. Falkenheim, "Provincial Leadership in Fukien 1949–66," in Robert A. Scalapino, ed., *Elites in the People's Republic of China* (Seattle: University of Washington Press, 1972), pp. 235–36.

31. *SW*, V, 162–65.

32. See the biographical files of the U.S. Consulate General, Hong Kong.

33. NCNA, Shanghai, April 19, 1954, in *SCMP*, No. 793. Xiang was also still listed as vice governor of Shandong in *RMSC*, 1955.

34. *Xin Nongda* [New University of Agriculture], March 24, 1967, in *SCMP-S*, No. 238. Cf. n. 43, this chapter.

35. Trans. in *CB*, No. 891. See also *SW*, V, 163.

36. NCNA, Beijing, April 4, 1955, in *CB*, No. 324; and *SW*, V, 158, 168.

37. Chow, *Ten Years*, pp. 68–69, says Rao was sentenced to life imprisonment. According to a Red Guard pamphlet, "Down with Liu Shaoqi—Life of Counterrevolutionary

Liu Shaoqi," May 1967, in *CB*, No. 834, Gao was "put to death" not long after the conference.

38. NCNA, Beijing, April 4, 1955, in *CB*, No. 324.

39. *Ibid.*

40. *SW*, V, 156 (emphasis added).

41. NCNA, Beijing, April 4, 1955, in *CB*, No. 324.

42. *Zhongguo qingnian* [Chinese Youth] *(ZGQN)*, April 16, 1955, in *SCMP*, No. 1036; and *XX*, August 2, 1955, in *Extracts from China Mainland Magazines (ECMM)*, No. 14.

43. NCNA, Beijing, April 4, 1955, in *CB*, No. 324. While this group was defined by the documents of the 1955 conference, a degree of ambiguity concerning its composition appeared in Mao's concluding speech. In one reference, Mao did not include Chen Bocun but added Shanghai public security chief Yang Fan to the clique. In another place he did not mention Chen, Yang or Xiang Ming when naming the "lieutenants" of Gao and Rao. *SW*, V, 162, 168. On links among Rao, Yang and Pan Hannian as alleged during the *sufan* campaign, see Teiwes, "Rectification Campaigns," pp. 262–64. Cf. above, pp. 140–41.

44. Apart from Rao, Xiang Ming, Yang Fan, Pan Hannian and perhaps Zeng Jingbing (see n. 30, this chapter) no leading East China officials at the regional or provincial levels suffered career setbacks in this period. In addition, only a small number of lower ranking regional government officials could not be traced to comparable posts after 1955, a fact easily attributable to gaps in the data. This was determined by an examination of the sources listed above, n. 74, ch. 4. See, however, the report of a refugee purportedly present at a Shanghai meeting dealing with the Gao-Rao affair which claims that Chen Yi conducted an intensive personal investigation of provincial governments in the area and removed many officials. Albert Ravenholt, "Feud Among the Red Mandarins," *American Universities Field Staff Reports Service*, East Asia Series, Vol. XI, No. 2 (Communist China), 1964.

45. *SSSC*, April 25, 1955, in *SCMP*, No. 1052.

46. *RMRB*, April 14, 1955, in *SCMP*, No. 1034.

47. NCNA, Beijing, April 4, 1955, in *CB*, No. 324. The basic difference between the new and old systems was a strengthened vertical chain of command under control committees to prevent total dominance by Party committees. Nevertheless, control committees were still instructed to "work under the direction of Party committees of [the same] level"; thus the basic problem was far from resolved. Cf. Cocks, "Party Control Committee," especially pp. 6–12.

48. On the Northeast as a model region, see Frederick C. Teiwes, "Kao Kang's 'Independent Kingdom' in the Northeast: A Re-evaluation," paper presented at the 1972 annual meeting of the Association for Asian Studies, pp. 2–3.

49. Li Zhuoran, Liu Zhiming and Liu Zizai. See *Directory of Officials*, p. 218.

50. This was determined by an examination of the sources listed above, n. 74, ch. 4.

51. The procedure adopted was to consult *CB*, No. 368, pp. 15–16, and data provided by Donald W. Klein to identify the military personnel, and then to trace their careers in *Gendai Chūgoku* and the biographical files of the U.S. Consulate General, Hong Kong.

52. Zhang Xiushan, Guo Feng and He Jinnian. Zhang can be traced to the Shaan-Gan-Ning Border Region; Guo entered the Northeast after the Sino-Japanese War; and He was active in both pre-1935 North Shaanxi and Shaan-Gan-Ning. Thus all three had pre-1949 links to Gao Gang.

53. The procedure adopted was to trace the careers of all officials listed in *Directory of Officials* as serving in the Northeast by consulting *Gendai Chūgoku;* Klein and Clark, *Biographic Dictionary; Who's Who in Communist China* (Hong Kong: Union Research Institute, 1966); *Hongqi piaopiao* [The Red Flag Waves] (10 vols., Beijing: 1957–59), V,

108–18; *Shaan-Gan-Ning bianqu canyihui wenxian* [Documents of Shaan-Gan-Ning Border Region Congresses] (Beijing: 1958), pp. 168, 268; and Mark Selden, "The Guerrilla Movement in Northwest China," *CQ*, Nos. 28–29 (1966–67). The last three sources focus on the old North Shaanxi base and Shaan-Gan-Ning, thus maximizing chances that old associates of Gao would be included in this sample of important Northeast leaders.

54. Klein and Clark, *Biographic Dictionary*, I, 553–58; and "Down with Liu," in *CB*, No. 834.

55. Lewis, *Leadership and Succession*, p. 9.

56. Donald W. Klein, "The State Council and the Cultural Revolution," *CQ*, No. 35 (1968), p. 88.

57. Teiwes, *Provincial Personnel*, p. 19.

58. The post-1954 military leaders were identified in a U.S. government listing provided by Donald W. Klein.

59. *SW*, V, 340.

60. "Talks at the Chengdu Conference" (March 1958), in *MU*, p. 100.

61. O.B. Borisov and B.T. Koloskov, *Sino-Soviet Relations 1945–1973: A Brief History* (Moscow: Progress Publishers, 1975), p. 116.

62. *Khrushchev Remembers: The Last Testament*, trans. and ed. by Strobe Talbott (Boston: Little, Brown and Company, 1974), pp. 243–44.

63. *Ibid.*, pp. 242, 252–53; *SW*, V, 155–56, 340–42; and personal communication from Alex B. Ikonnikov.

64. *ZGQN*, April 16, 1955, in *SCMP*, No. 1036.

65. *RMRB*, April 5, 1955, in *CB*, No. 324; and NCNA, Beijing, April 10, 1955, in *SCMP*, No. 1052.

66. *SSSC*, April 25, 1955, in *SCMP*, No. 1052.

67. See Schurmann, *Ideology and Organization*, ch. 4; and Roy Franklin Grow, "The Politics of Industrial Development in China and the Soviet Union: Organizational Strategy as a Linkage between National and World Politics," Ph.D. dissertation, University of Michigan, 1973.

68. *RMRB*, June 5, 1950, in *CB*, No. 163.

69. *DGB* (Tianjin), May 13, 1954, summarized in Schurmann, *Ideology and Organization*, pp. 257–62. Positive press references to the system continued in 1954–55.

70. E.g., see *RMRB*, October 1, 1952, September 21, 1956.

71. E.g., see Li Fuchun's comments in NCNA, Beijing, September 29, 1952, in *CB*, No. 219.

72. Cited in Walker, "Collectivisation," p. 30.

73. *SXWS*, II, 276. "[Liu]" has been inserted where "X" appeared in the text since only Liu Shaoqi had the status to be listed ahead of Zhou Enlai, and because this deduction is confirmed by other evidence (see below).

74. NCNA, Beijing, April 4, 1955, in *CB*, No. 324.

75. Chen Yun, Zhang Wentian and Peng Zhen. Peng, of course, had a clear "white area" identification.

76. For Hong Kong sources asserting that Lin was heavily involved in the Gao-Rao affair, see Thomas W. Robinson, "Lin Piao as an Elite Type," in Scalapino, *Elites*, pp. 155, 159, 186.

77. See n. 15, this chapter; and below, p. 161n.

78. NCNA, Beijing, August 15, 1967, in *SCMP*, No. 4004.

79. See "Selected Edition on Liu Shaoqi's Counterrevolutionary Revisionist Crimes" (Red Guard pamphlet), April 1967, in *SCMM*, No. 652; and *Da pipan tongxun* [Big Criticism Bulletin] (Guangzhou), October 5, 1967, in *SCMP*, No. 4124.

80. Support for this possibility is suggested by Mao's remark, "Peng . . . colluded with [Gao and Rao], but I did not know it." "Talk at the Report Meeting" (October 1966), in *MU*, p. 267.

81. *Pi Tao zhanbao* (Beijing), April 10, 1967, in *SCMP*, No. 3962. Interestingly in view of Gao's apparent criticism of Liu's work (see above, p. 155), Tao admitted having held critical views of Liu's performance during land reform.

82. NCNA, Beijing, April 10, 1955, in *SCMP*, No. 1026. Cf. *SW*, V, 165.

83. Klein, "Next Generation," pp. 70–74.

84. See Roderick MacFarquhar, "On Photographs," *CQ*, No. 46 (1971), p. 292.

85. Minister of Public Security Luo Ruiqing was a "base area and army" cadre despite a year's service in 1946–47 on a CCP delegation engaging in negotiations with the GMD. Interestingly, Luo was accused of participation in Gao-Rao activities by Cultural Revolution sources although only in the most generalized terms. See "Thirty-three Leading Counterrevolutionary Revisionists" (Red Guard pamphlet), in *CB*, No. 874; and *Gong-nong-bing*, September 1967, in *SCMM-S*, No. 27. Kang Sheng probably provided overall leadership in the security sphere, however, and his career included important "white area" work in the late 1920s and early 1930s although his later work in base areas appears more significant overall; see above, p. 156n.

86. Radio Shanghai, February 9, March 20, 1968, in *Foreign Broadcast Information Service: Communist China (FBIS)*, Nos. 33, 58 (1968); and *WHB* (Shanghai), May 20, June 1, 1968, in *SCMP*, No. 4205.

87. See NCNA, Shenyang, July 1, 1955, in *SCMP*, No. 1087; and above, p. 141.

88. Although significant international tension resulted from the intensification of fighting in Indochina in late 1953-early 1954 and the Taiwan straits crisis of late 1954-early 1955, the PRC was able to mitigate the dangers involved by diplomatic means and the larger trend of the period was towards a relaxation of tension. See A. Doak Barnett, *Communist China and Asia: A Challenge to American Policy* (New York: Vintage Books,1960), pp. 95–105.

89. The closest thing to an accusation of an explicit deal was a report that Tao supported Gao for vice chairman of the government [sic] while Gao promised Tao a vice premiership, a version which goes further than that discussed above, p. 158. *Gong-nong-bing*, September 1967, in *SCMM-S*, No. 27. Moreover, Mao also implied that few elaborate arrangements had been made; *SW*, V, 161–62.

90. The only possible exceptions are Cultural Revolution sources implying a residue of support for Gao's reputation as a leader of the North Shaanxi base area. See Radio Beijing, April 14, 1968, in *FBIS*, No. 79 (1968); *Guangming ribao* [Guangming Daily] *(GMRB)*, April 15, 1968, in *SCMP*, No. 4176; and *RMRB*, April 18, 1968, in *SCMP*, No. 4176. In these instances, however, Gao's prestige seems limited to past local accomplishments and there is no indication that sympathy extended to his 1953 activities.

Chapter 6

1. See especially the exhaustive analysis in MacFarquhar, *Origins 1*. For another interpretation emphasizing leadership divisions, see Richard H. Solomon, *Mao's Revolution and the Chinese Political Culture* (Berkeley: University of California Press, 1971), ch. 17.

2. "Speech to Supreme State Conference" (January 1956), trans. in Hélène Carrère d'Encausse and Stuart R. Schram, *Marxism and Asia* (London: The Penguin Press, 1969), p. 292; and *SW*, V, 242–44, 249–50.

3. "Speech to Supreme State Conference" (January 1956), p. 293.

4. See MacFarquhar, *Origins 1*, pp. 101–102, 105–107, 152–56.

5. "Correct Handling," p. 281.

6. For greater detail, see Michel C. Oksenberg, "Policy Formulation in Communist China: The Case of the Mass Irrigation Campaign, 1957–58," Ph.D. dissertation, Columbia University, 1969, ch. 8; *PDA*, pp. 7–8; and K.C. Yeh, "Soviet and Communist Chinese Industrialization Strategies," in Donald W. Treadgold, ed., *Soviet and Chinese Communism: Similarities and Differences* (Seattle: University of Washington Press, 1967), pp. 340ff.

7. *RMRB*, June 20, 27, November 28, 1956, in *SCMP*, Nos. 1321, 1326, 1428; and Teng Hsiao-p'ing (Deng Xiaoping), "Report on the Revision of the Constitution of the Communist Party of China," *Eighth National Congress of the Communist Party of China* (3 vols., Beijing: Foreign Languages Press, 1956), I, 184.

8. MacFarquhar, *Origins 1*, pp. 36–37; Jerome Ch'en, ed., *Mao* (Englewood Cliffs: Prentice-Hall, Inc., 1969), pp. 76–78; and "Correct Handling," pp. 281–83.

9. Ch'en, *Mao*, p. 74; "Correct Handling," p. 287; and Liu Shao-ch'i, "The Political Report of the Central Committee of the Communist Party of China to the Eighth National Congress of the Party," *Eighth Congress*, I, 78–81.

10. Ch'en, *Mao*, pp. 71–73, 75; Liu, "Political Report," pp. 77–78; Teng, "Report on Revision," pp. 182–83, 190–92; Chou En-lai (Zhou Enlai), "Report on the Proposals for the Second Five-Year Plan for Development of the National Economy," *Eighth Congress*, I, 310–12; *Sichuan ribao* [Sichuan Daily], October 18, 1956; and *RMRB*, April 5, 1956, in *PDA*, p. 149.

11. Chou En-lai, "On the Question of Intellectuals" (January 1956), in *PDA*, pp. 130–31; and *SXWS*, II, 29, 34.

12. D.W. Fokkema, *Literary Doctrine in China and Soviet Influence 1956–1960* (The Hague: Mouton & Co., 1965), especially pp. 77–81, 91–92, 95–96, 109ff.

13. See *MU*, p. 103; and *Khrushchev Remembers*, pp. 271–72.

14. Chou, "Question of Intellectuals," pp. 132–43.

15. Lu Ting-i (Lu Dingyi), "Let a Hundred Flowers Blossom, a Hundred Schools of Thought Contend!," in *PDA*, pp. 152–60.

16. Goldman, *Literary Dissent*, pp. 161–64, 166; MacFarquhar, *Origins 1*, pp. 75–77; and Loh, *Escape*, pp. 211–12.

17. Ch'en, *Mao*, pp. 74–76; NCNA, Beijing, July 4, 1956, in *SCMP*, No. 1324; Liu, "Political Report," pp. 72–73; and Lyman P. Van Slyke, *Enemies and Friends: The United Front in Chinese Communist History* (Stanford: Stanford University Press, 1967), pp. 241–43.

18. See Goldman, *Literary Dissent*, pp. 162–65.

19. See *ibid.*, pp. 165ff.; Solomon, *Mao's Revolution*, pp. 283–84; and Theodore H.E. Chen, *Thought Reform of the Chinese Intellectuals* (Hong Kong: Hong Kong University Press, 1960), pp. 122–24.

20. See Goldman, *Literary Dissent*, pp. 180–81; and NCNA, Beijing, April 29, 1957, in *SCMP*, No. 1526.

21. Benjamin I. Schwartz, *Communism and China: Ideology in Flux* (Cambridge: Harvard University Press, 1968), p. 111.

22. *SSSC*, August 10, 1956, in *ECMM*, No. 54; and *Gongren ribao* [Workers' Daily] *(GRRB)*, September 11, 1956, in *SCMP*, No. 1413.

23. *ZGQN*, January 16, 1957, in *ECMM*, No. 70. Cf. MacFarquhar, *Origins 1*, pp. 177–78.

24. For evidence of Mao's total endorsement of the April editorial, see MacFarquhar, *Origins 1*, pp. 43, 333.

25. Liu, "Political Report," pp. 101–102; Zhao Han, *Tantan*, p. 65; and Ellis Joffe, *Party and Army: Professionalism and Political Control in the Chinese Officer Corps,*

1949–1964 (Cambridge: Harvard East Asian Monographs, 1965), p. 117.

26. *RMRB*, September 11, 16, October 10, 1956; NCNA, Jinan, September 9, 1956, in *SCMP*, No. 1382; and NCNA, Baoding, September 11, 1956; in *SCMP*, No. 1384.

27. *Eighth Congress*, I, 9–10. See also Teng, "Report on Revision," pp. 174, 185–86.

28. MacFarquhar, *Origins 1*, pp. 112–18; and Teng, "Report on Revision," p. 175.

29. *Eighth Congress*, I, 132; and above, p. 173. Even after the Congress, *RMRB*, November 19, 1956, in discussing mutual supervision referred to "Mao's directive" that the Party should "listen to" outsiders while at the same time correcting those with mistakes.

30. MacFarquhar, *Origins 1*, p. 177; Zhao Han, *Tantan*, p. 65; *RMRB*, October 12, 1956; NCNA, Beijing, October 25, 1956, in *SCMP*, No. 1416; and *Zhengzhi xuexi* [Political Study] *(ZZXX)*, November 13, 1956, in *ECMM*, No. 62.

31. "Correct Handling," p. 277.

32. *SXWS*, II, 66–67, 135; and János Rádvanyi, *Hungary and the Superpowers: The 1956 Revolution and Realpolitik* (Stanford: Hoover Institution Press, 1972), p. 28.

33. NCNA, Beijing, November 15, 1956, in *SCMP*, No. 1414; and *SW*, V, 342–47.

34. *SW*, V, 348.

35. See MacFarquhar, *Origins 1*, p. 333.

36. *PDA*, p. 266.

37. *SXWS*, II, 73–77, 84–86; and *SW*, V, 353, 358–59, 370.

38. *SXWS*, II, 86; and *SW*, V, 362, 375, 380.

39. *RMRB*, January 7, 1957, in *CB*, No. 452; Goldman, *Literary Dissent*, pp. 179–86; and MacFarquhar, *Origins 1*, p. 179.

40. *ZGQN*, January 16, 1957, in *ECMM*, No. 73; and *RMRB*, January 31, 1957, in *SCMP*, No. 1472.

41. *ZGQN*, February 1, 1957, in *ECMM*, No. 75; *SW*, V, 344–45, 373–74; and *SXWS*, II, 74–75.

42. *RMRB*, February 17, May 20, 1957.

43. *Speech at the Chinese Communist Party's National Conference on Propaganda Work* (Beijing: Foreign Languages Press, 1966), pp. 12–13.

44. *Ibid.*, pp. 1–2; and "Correct Handling," pp. 275–81.

45. *Speech on Propaganda*, pp. 3–4, 15–16; "Correct Handling," p. 286; *SXWS*, II, 98, 103, 107; and Mu, *Wilting*, p. 167.

46. *Speech on Propaganda*, pp. 4–6, 8; "Correct Handling," p. 286; and *SXWS*, II, 91, 98, 102, 104, 107.

47. "Correct Handling," pp. 291, 293; *SXWS*, II, 93, 96; Loh, *Escape*, 289–91; *RMRB*, April 13, 1957, in *SCMP*, No. 1512; and MacFarquhar, *Origins 1*, p. 210.

48. *Speech on Propaganda*, pp. 13–14.

49. Loh, *Escape*, pp. 290–92; and *SXWS*, II, 93–94, 99–100.

50. *Speech on Propaganda*, pp. 15–16.

51. Loh, *Escape*, p. 292; Mu, *Wilting*, p. 167; *SXWS*, II, 90, 92, 106; and MacFarquhar, *Origins 1*, pp. 209, 262–66, 268, 393.

52. *Speech on Propaganda*, p. 22.

53. *SXWS*, II, 96, 102, 133; *New York Times*, June 13, 1957, p. 8; Loh, *Escape*, p. 292; *Speech on Propaganda*, pp. 24–25; and "Correct Handling," pp. 288–89.

54. *Speech on Propaganda*, pp. 25–26.

55. *Ibid.*, pp. 13–14; "Correct Handling," p. 278; and *SXWS*, II, 92–93, 101, 105.

56. *SXWS*, II, 105; NCNA, Beijing, April 18, 29, May 19, 1957, in *SCMP*, Nos. 1521, 1526, 1548; and *Xin guancha* [New Observer], May 16, 1957, in *ECMM*, No. 97.

57. Selected speeches from the CPPCC meetings are collected in *CB*, Nos. 439, 441–50. For commentary, see *CB*, No. 450, pp. i-ii; and *HF*, pp. 19–23.

58. *RMRB*, April 13, 1957, in *SCMP*, No. 1516. See also *CB*, Nos. 472–73, for a

chronology of the period including many of the conferences and forums held.

59. E.g., NCNA, Taiyuan, April 13, 1957, in *SCMP*, No. 1526; NCNA, Tianjin, April 18, 1957, in *SCMP*, No. 1523; and NCNA, Changsha, May 2, 1957, in *SCMP*, No. 1529.

60. NCNA, Beijing, May 8, 1957, in *SCMP*, No. 1543.

61. *RMRB*, April 22, 26, 1957; *GMRB*, May 7, 20, 1957; NCNA, Beijing, May 8–16, May 21-June 1, 1957, in *SCMP*, Nos. 1543, 1550; *Xin guancha*, May 16, 1957, in *ECMM*, No. 97; and *HF*, pp. 60, 64–66, 226–30.

62. NCNA, Beijing, April 30, 1957, in *SCMP*, No. 1523; and MacFarquhar, *Origins 1*, pp. 207–10.

63. NCNA, Beijing, May 6, 8, 9, 1957, in *SCMP*, No. 1537; and *RMRB*, May 27, 1957, in *SCMP*, No. 1547. Cf. MacFarquhar, *Origins 1*, pp. 231–40.

64. For summaries of provincial plans, see *SCMP*, Nos. 1527, 1537.

65. NCNA, Beijing, May 5, 30, 1957, in *SCMP*, Nos. 1525, 1532; and *RMRB*, June 4, 1957, in *SCMP*, No. 1551.

66. From a self-examination by an alleged rightist in *RMRB*, July 18, 1957 (cited in Solomon, *Mao's Revolution*, p. 305).

67. Goldman, *Literary Dissent*, pp. 186, 189–91; and MacFarquhar, *Origins 1*, pp. 193, 201, 219, 376, 379.

68. *CB*, No. 897, p. 48.

69. See MacFarquhar, *Origins 1*, p. 194.

70. *Dou-pi-gai* [Struggle-Criticism-Transformation], May 15, 1967, in *SCMM-S*, No. 19; and *Wenxue zhanbao* [Literary Combat Bulletin] (Beijing), April 4, 1967, in *SCMP*, No. 3942. In view of Mao's own comment (*SXWS*, II, 100) that his speeches to the Supreme State Conference would have to be supplemented and revised before publication, charges concerning the non-publication of these talks seem somewhat unfair.

71. *SXWS*, II, 105–106; and MacFarquhar, *Origins 1*, pp. 200–202, 207, 219.

72. E.g., *RMRB*, April 13, 26, May 17, 1957, in *SCMP*, Nos. 1512, 1524, 1538; *RMRB*, April 26, 1957, in *HF*, p. 31; and NCNA, Beijing, April 22, 1957, in *SCMP*, No. 1517.

73. E.g., NCNA, Beijing, April 18, 1957, in *SCMP*, No. 1521; *Zhongguo qingnian bao* [Chinese Youth Daily] *(ZGQNB)*, April 27, 1957, in *SCMP*, No. 1533; and *RMRB*, May 2, 1957, in *SCMP*, Nos. 1525, 1527.

74. *RMRB*, August 3, 1957 (cited in Solomon, *Mao's Revolution*, p. 304). An earlier version of this quote (*RMRB*, July 29, 1957) went on to say "Liu Shaoqi and Peng Zhen are pressuring Chairman Mao."

75. *RMRB*, July 17, 1957 (cited in MacFarquhar, *Origins 1*, p. 285).

76. For a different interpretation, see MacFarquhar, "Photographs," p. 303.

77. *RMRB*, April 22, May 10, 1957.

78. See MacFarquhar, *Origins 1*, pp. 196–99, 226–29, 375, 381, 386, 388–89. Partial texts of Liu's addresses to cadres in Shanghai on April 27 and to leaders of the Higher Party School on May 7 are available in *SCMM-S*, No. 35, and isolated excerpts from other talks on his provincial tour are found in various Red Guard sources.

79. *SCMM-S*, No. 35.

80. "Record of Deng Xiaoping's Reactionary Utterances" (Red Guard pamphlet), April 1967, in *SCMP-S*, No. 208; MacFarquhar, *Origins 1*, pp. 178, 369; and above, pp. 181, 192n.

81. MacFarquhar, *Origins 1*, p. 178; and *SXWS*, II, 74–75, 93–94.

82. Cited in MacFarquhar, *Origins 1*, p. 311.

83. See Oksenberg, "Policy Formulation," ch. 9.

84. *RMRB*, March 19, 1957, in *HF*, p. 21; NCNA, Beijing, May 21, 1957, in *SCMP*, No. 1550; and *GMRB*, April 21, 1957, in *HF*, p. 29.

85. *RMRB*, April 20, 1957, in *HF*, pp. 27–28.

86. NCNA, Beijing, April 18, May 16, 30, 1957, in *SCMP*, Nos. 1521, 1543, *HF*, p. 49; *Shaanxi ribao* [Shaanxi Daily], June 6, 1957; *GMRB*, May 16, 1957, in *HF*, p. 121; *Tuanjie bao* [Unity Bulletin], May 15, 1957, in *SCMP*, No. 1600; and *SXWS*, II, 105.

87. NCNA, Beijing, May 11, 1957, in *SCMP*, No. 1543; and *GMRB*, May 11, 1957, in *HF*, p. 65.

88. *DGB*, May 12, 1957, in *HF*, p. 62; *GMRB*, May 18, 21, 1957, in *HF*, pp. 215, 204; and NCNA, Beijing, May 25, 1957, in *HF*, p. 206.

89. *RMRB*, March 23, 1957, in *HF*, p. 20; NCNA, Beijing, May 11, 1957, in *HF*, p. 44; *GMRB*, May 19, 23, June 5, 1957, in *HF*, pp. 93, 222, 68; and *Anhui ribao* [Anhui Daily], June 6, 1957.

90. NCNA, Beijing, May 30, 1957, in *SCMP*, No. 1550.

91. *RMRB*, March 23, 1957, in *HF*, p. 20; NCNA, Beijing, May 15, 1957, in *HF*, p. 45; and *GMRB*, June 9, 1957, in *HF*, pp. 112–13.

92. NCNA, Beijing, May 17, 1957, in *HF*, p. 63; *Wenyi bao* [Literary Gazette], June 2, 1957, in *HF*, p. 183; and above, p. 172.

93. *RMRB*, April 21, 1957, in *HF*, p. 26; *GMRB*, May 1, 15, 19, 1957, in *HF*, pp. 90, 80, 111; and *Jingji yanjiu* [Economic Research], October 17, 1957, in *HF*, pp. 118–19.

94. *RMRB*, May 25, 1957, in *SCMP*, No. 1549.

95. *RMRB*, June 2, 1957, in *HF*, pp. 51–52.

96. *Wenyi bao*, June 16, 1957, in *HF*, p. 178.

97. Liu, "Political Report," pp. 73–74; *GMRB*, May 4, 1957, in *HF*, p. 79; and NCNA, Beijing, May 8, June 3, 1957, in *SCMP*, No. 1529, *HF*, p. 226.

98. NCNA, Beijing, June 5, 1957, in *HF*, pp. 226–27.

99. NCNA, Beijing, May 8, 10, 21, 30, June 5, 1957, in *HF*, pp. 40–41, *SCMP*, No. 1543, *HF*, pp. 48, 51, 227; Liu, "Political Report," p. 96; and Teng, "Report on Revision," pp. 202–203.

100. NCNA, Beijing, May 9, 10, 16, June 3, 1957, in *HF*, pp. 41–42, 42–43, 46–47, 226; and above, p. 173.

101. *RMRB*, March 19, 1957, in *HF*, pp. 21–22; NCNA, Beijing, May 21, 1957, in *HF*, pp. 47–48; Liu, "Political Report," p. 76; and MacFarquhar, *Origins 1*, pp. 23, 115, 275–76.

102. NCNA, Beijing, May 8, 16, 22, 1957, in *SCMP*, Nos. 1529, 1545, 1550; and NCNA, Shanghai, May 19, 1957, in *SCMP*, No. 1539.

103. Lu, "Hundred Flowers," p. 162; *RMRB*, October 27, 1966, August 29, 1967, in *SCMP*, Nos. 3818, 4019; *Wanshan hongpian* [All Mountains are Red], April 1967, in *SCMM-S*, No. 33; *SXWS*, II, 108, 158; and MacFarquhar, *Origins 1*, pp. 277–78.

104. *GMRB*, May 11, 16, 1957, in *HF*, pp. 66, 121; NCNA, Beijing, May 22, 1957, in *HF*, p. 48; *Shenyang ribao* [Shenyang Daily], in *HF*, p. 105; and René Goldman, "The Rectification Campaign at Peking University: May-June 1957," *CQ*, No. 12 (1962), p. 143.

105. *GMRB*, May 8, 11, June 3, 5, 1957, in *HF*, pp. 94, 104, 223, 68; NCNA, Beijing, May 8, 16, 1957, in *SCMP*, No. 1543, *HF*, p. 47; and Chow, *Ten Years*, p. 162.

106. E.g., *GMRB*, May 16, 1957, in *HF*, p. 203; and NCNA, Beijing, May 22, June 4, 1957, in *HF*, pp. 49, 212–13.

107. NCNA, Beijing, May 16, 22, 1957, in *HF*, p. 47, *SCMP*, No. 1550; *GMRB*, May 16, 1957, in *HF*, pp. 202–203; and *RMRB;* May 31, 1957, in *HF*, p. 87.

108. *RMRB*, May 31, 1957, in *HF*, pp. 87–88.

109. NCNA, Beijing, May 29, 1957, in *SCMP*, No. 1549; and *RMRB*, June 2, 1957, in *HF*, p. 52.

110. See Loh, *Escape*, pp. 292–93.

Chapter 7

1. See MacFarquhar, *Origins 1*, pp. 220–23; and below, pp. 230–33.

2. "Things are Changing," in *CB*, No. 891, p. 24; and *SW*, V, 440–44, 461.

3. *CB*, No. 891, p. 24; NCNA, Beijing, May 29, 1957, in *SCMP*, Nos. 1548, 1549; *HF*, p. 60; and above, pp. 188, 195–96.

4. NCNA, Shanghai, May 20, 1957, in *HF*, pp. 200–201; and NCNA, Guangzhou, May 23, 1957, in *HF*, p. 201.

5. NCNA, Beijing, May 25, 1957, in SCMP, Nos. 1540, 1548; and MacFarquhar, *Origins 1*, pp. 219–21, 262, 396.

6. NCNA, Beijing, June 1, 1957, in *HF*, pp. 53–54.

7. *RMRB*, June 9, 12, 1957, in *SCMP*, No. 1553.

8. "Correct Handling," p. 290. On the evolution of these criteria, see MacFarquhar, *Origins 1*, pp. 262–66.

9. Teng Hsiao-p'ing, "Report on the Rectification Campaign" (September 1957), in *PDA*, p. 343.

10. *SXWS*, II, 105, 144, 207; MacFarquhar, *Origins 1*, pp. 200–201, 224–25, 279; above, pp. 189, 195, 210–11; and below, pp. 240–42.

11. *RMRB*, June 22, 1957, in *SCMP*, No. 1559; NCNA, Beijing, July 12, 23, 1957, in *SCMP*, Nos. 1580, 1589; Teng, "Report on Rectification," pp. 343–47; and *SXWS*, II, 133.

12. Teng, "Report on Rectification," pp. 344–48; *XX*, July 3, 1957, in *ECMM*, No. 103; and NCNA, Beijing, July 11, August 16, 1957, in *SCMP*, Nos. 1572, 1598.

13. Chou En-lai, "Report on the Work of the Government" (June 1957), in *PDA*, p. 327; Mao, "The Situation in the Summer of 1957 (excerpts)" (July 1957), in *SCMP-S*, No. 191; Teng, "Report on Rectification," pp. 343, 347; *SXWS*, II, 114; *SW*, V, 473, 495–96, 503; and *RMRB*, July 1, 8, 16, August 16, September 15, 18, 1957, in *SCMP*, Nos. 1567, 1574, 1578, 1604, 1615, 1616.

14. Teng, "Report on Rectification," p. 348; *RMRB*, June 12, 1957, in *SCMP*, No. 1553; and *SW*, V, 443, 505–506.

15. *XHBYK*, No. 18, 1957, as trans. in MacFarquhar, *Origins 1*, p. 291 (emphasis added).

16. See Oksenberg, "Policy Formulation," chs. 10–11.

17. "Situation in the Summer," in *SCMP-S*, No. 191, *SCMP*, No. 4000; and *SXWS*, II, 119, 121.

18. Chou, "Report on Work," pp. 303–26, 328; and *RMRB*, June 18, 1957.

19. *SXWS*, II, 111.

20. *Ibid.*, pp. 114, 117–18. Cf. *SW*, V, 462, 466–67, 474.

21. *SW*, V, 443, 447, 459, 477.

22. NCNA, Beijing, July 12, 23, August 7, 1957, in *SCMP*, Nos. 1579, 1584, 1594; and *RMRB*, July 20, 28, 1957, in *SCMP*, Nos. 1583, 1590.

23. *SW*, V, 459–60; and *SXWS*, II, 223.

24. Teng, "Report on Rectification," pp. 344–45; NCNA, Anshan, June 9, 1957, in *SCMP*, No. 1553; *RMRB*, June 13, 19, August 5, 1957, in *SCMP*, Nos. 1560, 1561, 1595; and NCNA, Beijing, July 3, 16, 1957, in *SCMP*, Nos. 1566, 1575.

25. This discussion draws heavily on Oksenberg, "Policy Formulation," ch. 10. Accounts of the NPC meetings appear in *CB*, Nos. 463–471.

26. Teng, "Report on Rectification," p. 343; *RMRB*, July 26, August 16, 1957, in *SCMP*, Nos. 1590, 1604; NCNA, Beijing, July 26, 1957, in *SCMP*, No. 1581; and *SXWS*, II, 114.

27. Teng, "Report on Rectification," pp. 345, 347; *RMRB*, August 27, 1957, in *SCMP*, No. 1609; and NCNA, Beijing, August 9, September 12, 1957, in *SCMP*, Nos. 1590, 1611.

28. *SW*, V, 474; *Communist China 1957* (Hong Kong: Union Research Institute, 1958), pp. 11, 13; and below, p. 233.

29. *SW*, V, 457–58, 471, 496, 503, 510; *SXWS*, II, 109–10, 125, 171; *MMT*, I, 75, 86; Vogel, *Canton*, p. 202; Loh, *Escape*, p. 362; Mu, *Wilting*, p. 150; Martin King Whyte, "Corrective Labor Camps in China," *Asian Survey*, March 1973, pp. 255–56; and below, pp. 239–40.

30. Teiwes, "Case Study," pp. 77–78.

31. *SW*, V, 449.

32. *Ibid.*, p. 481.

33. Dallin and Breslauer, *Political Terror*, p. 109; and above, p. 37.

34. See *Collected Works of Liu 1945–57*, p. 420.

35. *WHB* (Shanghai), May 27, 1957, in *SCMP*, No. 1575; NCNA, Beijing, July 12, 1957, in *SCMP*, No. 1577; and Goldman, "Peking University," pp. 141–42, 152.

36. NCNA, Tianjin, June 29, 1957, in *HF*, pp. 141–42; *RMRB*, July 12, 24, 1957, in *HF*, pp. 153–54, 139; NCNA, Lanzhou, July 15, 1957, in *SCMP*, No. 1575; Goldman, "Peking University," p. 152; and MacFarquhar, *Origins 1*, p. 221.

37. *WHB* (Shanghai), May 27, 1957, in *SCMP*, No. 1575; *RMRB*, August 17, 1957, in *HF*, p. 144; and Goldman, "Peking University," pp. 142–48, 152.

38. NCNA, Tianjin, June 29, 1957, in *HF*, p. 142; NCNA, Beijing, July 12, 1957, in *HF*, p. 135; *Guangxi ribao*, October 3, 1957, in *HF*, pp. 162–64; Goldman, "Peking University," pp. 143, 145, 149; and Dennis J. Doolin, trans., *Communist China: The Politics of Student Opposition* (Stanford: The Hoover Institution, 1964), pp. 28, 44, 50, 55, 59–60, 70.

39. *SXWS*, I, 259; *Chengdu ribao* [Chengdu Daily], July 9, 1957, in *HF*, p. 156; and *RMRB*, July 12, August 17, 1957, in *HF*, pp. 154, 144–45.

40. NCNA, Wuhan, August 5, 1957, in *SCMP*, No. 1589; *RMRB*, August 8, 1957, in *HF*, pp. 145–53; and *Jiaoshi bao* [Teachers' Daily] (Beijing), September 13, 1957, in *SCMP*, No. 1624.

41. NCNA, Beijing, July 11, 1957, in *SCMP*, No. 1572; *SXWS*, II, 113; and Goldman, "Peking University," pp. 150, 153.

42. NCNA, Beijing, July 16, August 1, 18, 1957, in *SCMP*, Nos. 1575, 1593, 1599; *RMRB*, August 16, 1957, in *SCMP*, No. 1604; and Goldman, "Peking University," pp. 150, 153.

43. NCNA, Beijing, August 18, 28, September 3, 1957, in *SCMP*, Nos. 1599, 1610; and *XX*, November 18, 1957, in *Union Research Service (URS)*, Vol. 10—No. 10.

44. NCNA, Beijing, October 22, 1957, in *SCMP*, No. 1641; *SW*, V, 78; interview with former staff member of Shanghai's *Wenhui bao*, Hong Kong, November 1966; and Goldman, *Literary Dissent*, pp. 241–42.

45. For a complete list together with official posts and Party affiliations, see Teiwes, "Rectification Campaigns," p. 375.

46. *GMRB*, June 12, 1957, in *SCMP*, No. 1561; *RMRB*, June 13, 16, 18, 1957, in *SCMP*, Nos. 1560, 1561, 1570; NCNA, Beijing, June 17, 1957, in *SCMP*, No. 1558; and MacFarquhar, *Origins 1*, p. 280.

47. NCNA, Beijing, May 10, June 30, July 3, 15, 1957, January 15, 1958, in *HF*, p. 43, *SCMP*, Nos. 1571, 1572, 1699; Lo Lung-chi (Luo Longji), "My Preliminary Examination," in *PDA*, pp. 333–34; Chang Po-chün (Zhang Bojun), "I Bow My Head and Admit My Guilt Before the People," in *PDA*, p. 339; *RMRB*, June 16, 1957, in *SCMP*, No. 1560; and *HF*, pp. 263–65.

48. NCNA, Beijing, June 30, December 24, 1957, in *SCMP*, Nos. 1571, 1694; *RMRB*, July 20, 1957; and *GMRB*, July 29, 1957, in *SCMP*, No. 1590.

49. *RMRB*, November 20, 21, 1956.

50. Lo, "Preliminary Examination," p. 336; Chang, "I Bow My Head," pp. 339–40;

NCNA, Beijing, July 3, 18, 23, 1957, in *SCMP*, Nos. 1571, 1594; and *RMRB*, July 4, 1957, in *SCMP*, No. 1571.

51. NCNA, Beijing, June 20, 25, August 15, 16, 28, 1957, in *SCMP*, Nos. 1569, 1571, 1606, 1611; *GMRB*, August 9, 29, November 16, 1957, in *SCMP*, Nos. 1600, 1623, 1663; Lo, "Preliminary Examination," p. 332; and *RMRB*, August 20, 1957.

52. Lo, "Preliminary Examination," pp. 331–37; and Chang, "I Bow My Head," pp. 337–41.

53. NCNA, Beijing, August 27, December 24, 1957, January 19, 31, 1958, in *SCMP*, Nos. 1611, 1694, 1699, 1706; *Tuanjie bao* (Beijing), September 12, 1957, in *SCMP*, No. 1689; *GMRB*, October 21, 1957, in *SCMP*, No. 1663; and *RMSC*, 1957, pp. 250–57, 1958, pp. 303–304.

54. NCNA, Beijing, September 12, 1957, in *SCMP*, No. 1623.

55. In addition to Ministers Zhang Bojun, Luo Longji and Zhang Naiqi, these were Vice Ministers Lin Handa (Education), Zeng Zhaolun (Higher Education), Fei Xiaotong (Nationalities Affairs), and Huang Qixiang (Physical Education and Sports). *XHBYK*, No. 15, 1958, p. 187.

56. *Guizhou ribao* [Guizhou Daily], November 15, 1957, in *SCMP*, No. 1740; NCNA, Changsha, January 2, 1958, in *SCMP*, No. 1689; NCNA, Beijing, February 1, 1958, in *SCMP*, No. 1706; *CJRB*, February 28, 1958, in *SCMP*, No. 1784; *Guangzhou ribao* [Guangzhou Daily], March 11, 1958, in *SCMP*, No. 1788; *NCNA*, Kunming, March 20, 1958, in *SCMP*, No. 1742; *Xiamen ribao* [Amoy Daily], April 14, 1958, in *SCMP*, No. 1779; and *Fujian ribao*, April 21, 1958, in *SCMP*, No. 1803.

57. *CB*, No. 583; and *HF*, p. 265. Additional rightists had their labels removed in 1960, 1961 and 1962.

58. Michel Oksenberg, "Paths to Leadership in Communist China," *Current Scene*, August 1, 1965, p. 3.

59. NCNA, Beijing, July 17, 26, September 14, 18, 1957, in *SCMP*, Nos. 1591, 1590, 1635; *GMRB*, July 15, 1957, in *SCMP*, No. 1585; *ZGQNB*, September 21, 1957, in *SCMP*, No. 1635; *XHBYK*, No. 20, 1957 (cited in James R. Townsend, *The Revolutionization of Chinese Youth: A Study of "Chung-kuo Ch'ing-nien"* (Berkeley: Center for Chinese Studies, 1967), pp. 33–34); and *WHB* (Shanghai), March 13, 1958, in *SCMP*, No. 1739.

60. "The Bourgeois Orientation of *Wenhui bao* for a Period of Time" (June 1957), in Jerome Ch'en, ed., *Mao Papers: Anthology and Bibliography (MP)* (London: Oxford University Press, 1970), pp. 55–56; *Xinwen yu chuban* [News and Publishing] (Beijing), December 10, 1957, in *SCMP*, No. 1687; and MacFarquhar, *Origins 1*, pp. 194, 282, 397.

61. NCNA, Beijing, July 10, 1957, in *SCMP*, No. 1576; *GMRB*, July 15, 1957, in *SCMP*, No. 1585; *CB*, No. 891, p. 24; and above, p. 173.

62. NCNA, Beijing, June 28, July 3, 1957, in *SCMP*, Nos. 1566, 1571; NCNA, Shanghai, July 2, August 3, 1957, in *SCMP*, Nos. 1567, 1600; *GMRB*, July 15, 1957, in *SCMP*, No. 1585; Lo, "Preliminary Examination," p. 334; and Goldman, *Literary Dissent*, p. 219.

63. NCNA, Beijing, September 1, 1968, in *SCMP*, No. 4253; Goldman, *Literary Dissent*, p. 164; MacFarquhar, *Origins 1*, pp. 75–76; and *MP*, p. 55.

64. NCNA, Lüda, August 7, 1957, in *HF*, p. 74; NCNA, Beijing, September 14, 1957, in *SCMP*, No. 1635; *ZGQNB*, September 21, December 16, 1957; and NCNA, Anshan, July 28, 1957, in *HF*, pp. 68–71.

65. NCNA, Beijing, June 14, July 10, 1957, in *SCMP*, Nos. 1567, 1576; *RMRB*, July 1, 9, 1957, in *SCMP*, Nos. 1567, 1576; *GMRB*, July 15, 1957, in *SCMP*, No. 1585; and *HF*, pp. 59–60.

66. *RMRB*, September 1, 27, 1957, in *SCMP*, Nos. 1607, 1629; *Zhongguo dianying*

[Chinese Movies], January 8, 1958, in *HF*, p. 194; Goldman, *Literary Dissent*, pp. 218, 224–225; and Chou Yang (Zhou Yang), *A Great Debate on the Literary Front* (Beijing: Foreign Languages Press, 1965), pp. 27ff.

67. NCNA, Beijing, July 28, August 14, 1957, in *HF*, pp. 192, 193; and *RMRB*, September 11, 1957.

68. NCNA, Beijing, August 6, 1957, in *SCMP*, No. 1590; Goldman, *Literary Dissent*, pp. 115–19, 194, 208–10; and *MMT*, I, 48.

69. Goldman, *Literary Dissent*, pp. 211–23, 230–38; and *SXWS*, II, 136, 218.

70. Goldman, *Literary Dissent*, pp. 224–29; NCNA, Beijing, August 6, 7, 1957, in *SCMP*, Nos. 1590, 1588; and Chou, *Great Debate*, p. 23.

71. Goldman, *Literary Dissent*, pp. 223, 231.

72. *Ibid.*, pp. 238–42; and *RMRB*, September 1, 1957, in *SCMP*, No. 1607.

73. Chou, *Great Debate*, pp. 31–32; and Fokkema, *Literary Doctrine*, pp. 123, 185ff.

74. *ZGQNB*, July 17, 1957, in *SCMP*, No. 1582; *Jilin ribao*, August 24, 1957; *ZGQNB*, August 26, September 6, 10, December 18, 1957; and above, p. 233.

75. *ZGQNB*, August 2, September 21, 1957, in *SCMP*, Nos. 1593, 1635; and NCNA, Kunming, August 26, 1957, in *SCMP*, No. 1615.

76. *Xi'an ribao* [Xi'an Daily], August 6, 1957; *Liaoning ribao* [Liaoning Daily], October 27, 1957; and Teng, "Report on Rectification," p. 360.

77. *ZGQNB*, August 2, 1957, in *SCMP*, No. 1593; NCNA, Kunming, August 27, 1957, in *SCMP*, No. 1615; and Teng, "Report on Rectification," p. 360.

78. *ZGQNB*, June 21, August 2, September 21, 1957, in *SCMP*, Nos. 1565, 1593, 1635.

79. *ZGQNB*, August 2, 24, September 21, December 18, 1957; NCNA, Kunming, August 26, 1957, in *SCMP*, No. 1615; *Kansu ribao* [Gansu Daily], September 10, 1957; and above, p. 225.

80. *SXWS*, II, 223; and *Zhengfa gongshe*, June 9, 1967, in *SCMP-S*, No. 192. No reports were found alleging rightism in the public security apparatus.

81. NCNA, Beijing, September 18, December 6, 1957, in *SCMP*, Nos. 1621, 1678; and *RMRB*, December 20, 1957, in *SCMP*, No. 1687.

82. *RMRB*, August 19, October 14, 1957, in *SCMP*, Nos. 1598, 1638; and NCNA, Beijing, December 11, 1957, in *SCMP*, No. 1691.

83. NCNA, Beijing, September 18, December 6, 11, 1957, in *SCMP*, Nos. 1621, 1678, 1691; and *RMRB*, December 20, 1957, in *SCMP*, No. 1687.

84. "Correct Handling," p. 283; *SW*, V, 351–52; and above, pp. 169–70.

85. *SW*, V, 475; MacFarquhar, *Origins 1*, pp. 293–97; and Vogel, *Canton*, p. 205.

86. NCNA, Guangzhou, May 14, July 25, 1957, in *HF*, pp. 233–34, *SCMP*, No. 1584; NCNA, Xi'an, July 25, 1957, in *SCMP*, No. 1584; NCNA, Zhengzhou, August 4, 1957, in *HF*, p. 238; Teng, "Report on Rectification," pp. 349–50; and Loh, *Escape*, p. 209.

87. NCNA, Lanzhou, July 25, 1957, in *HF*, p. 236; *RMRB*, August 10, 15, October 11, 1957, in *SCMP*, Nos. 1592, 1608, 1638; *ZGQNB*, August 12, 1957; Teng, "Report on Rectification," p. 349; and Vogel, *Canton*, p. 204.

88. NCNA, Guangzhou, July 28, September 14, 1957, in *SCMP*, Nos. 1584, 1616; *RMRB*, August 10, 1957, in *SCMP*, No. 1592; *Hubei ribao* [Hubei Daily], September 18, 1957; Teng, "Report on Rectification," p. 350; and Vogel, *Canton*, p. 205.

89. NCNA, Taiyuan, July 28, 1957, in *SCMP*, No. 1589; NCNA, Beijing, August 9, September 25, 1957, in *SCMP*, Nos. 1590, 1624; and *SXWS*, II, 129–31.

90. NCNA, Changchun, August 1, 1957, in *SCMP*, No. 1589; NCNA, Lanzhou, October 2, 1957, in *SCMP*, No. 1633; Teng, "Report on Rectification," pp. 345, 350–53; and Vogel, *Canton*, p. 208.

91. NCNA, Beijing, September 15, 1957, in *SCMP*, No. 1618; Teng, "Report on Rectification," p. 350; Vogel, *Canton*, p. 209; *NFRB*, December 8, 1957; and Oksenberg, "Policy Formulation," ch. 11.

92. Vogel, *Canton*, pp. 205–206; Teng, "Report on Rectification," p. 350; NCNA, Beijing, September 25, 1957, in *SCMP*, No. 1624; and *SW*, V, 475.

93. Vogel, *Canton*, p. 206; *ZZXX*, September 13, 1957, in *ECMM*, No. 112; and above, pp. 41–42, 126–27.

94. See Vogel, *Canton*, pp. 206–208; Oksenberg, "Policy Formulation," ch. 11; *SW*, V, 475; and above, pp. 68–70, 121–22.

95. *SW*, 478–79, 489, 501, 506, 511. Cf. *CB*, No. 891, p. 26.

Chapter 8

1. *SW*, 506, 511; *MMT*, I, 85, 88; *MP*, pp. 63–64; Mao, "Talk at Reception for Our Country's Students and Trainees in Moscow" (November 1957), in *CB* No. 891, p. 26; and Mao, "Speech at Supreme State Conference" (January 1958), in *CLG*, Winter 1968–69, p. 12.

2. For a comprehensive analysis of the Great Leap strategy, see Yeh, "Industrialization Strategies," pp. 350–57.

3. See Teiwes, "Chinese Politics," Part I, pp. 8–10; Vogel, *Canton*, pp. 224–27; and Nicholas R. Lardy, "Centralization and Decentralization in China's Fiscal Management," in *CQ*, No. 61 (1975), pp. 28–29, 49ff.

4. See MacFarquhar, *Origins 1*, pp. 311–15, 405.

5. Teng, "Report on Rectification," pp. 348–49; *RMRB*, September 5, 23, October 30, 1957, in *SCMP*, Nos. 1613, 1626, 1656; *DGB* (Beijing), September 26, 1957; *SW*, V, 508; and Liu Shao-ch'i, "The Significance of the October Revolution" (November 1957), in *PDA*, p. 398.

6. *RMRB*, September 23, 1957, in *SCMP*, No. 1626; NCNA, Beijing, September 10, 23, November 14, 16, December 6, 9, 1957, in *SCMP*, Nos. 1614, 1626, 1671, 1678; and *Liaoning ribao*, December 1, 1957, in *SCMP*, No. 1708.

7. *NFRB*, February 6, 1958; and *SXWS*, II, 170–71.

8. NCNA, Zhengzhou, December 4, 1957, in *SCMP*, No. 1671; *Xin Hunan bao* [New Hunan Daily], December 15, 1957, in *SCMP*, No. 1712; *RMRB*, December 18, 28, 1957, May 14, 22, 1958, in *SCMP*, No. 1685, *CB*, No. 487, *URS*, Vol. 11—No. 17, *PDA*, p. 9; and Vogel, *Canton*, p. 222.

9. *RMRB*, January 8, February 2, 18, May 14, 1958, in *SCMP*, Nos. 1691, 1721, 1724, *URS* Vol. 11—No. 17; *JFRB*, April 25, 1958; NCNA, Beijing, January 8, 1958, in *SCMP*, No. 1691; and Vogel, *Canton*, p. 223.

10. *RMRB*, January 14, 15, February 18, March 6, 29, 1958, in *SCMP*, Nos. 1702, 1724, 1734, 1755; NCNA, Beijing, March 3, 23, 1958, in *SCMP*, Nos. 1727, 1741; Liu Shao-ch'i, "The Present Situation, The Party's General Line for Socialist Construction and its Future Tasks" (May 1958), in *PDA*, p. 435; and *MP*, pp. 57, 66–67.

11. *SW*, V, 514; *MMT*, I, 107, 113; and Stanley Karnow, *Mao and China: From Revolution to Revolution* (New York: The Viking Press, 1972), pp. 97–99.

12. *SXWS*, II, 158; Edgar Snow, *The Other Side of the River* (London: Victor Gollancz Ltd., 1963), p. 344; Lewis, *Leadership*, pp. 110–11, 117–19; *Gongren shenghuo* [Workers' Life] (Wuxi), March 21, 1957, in *SCMP*, No. 1521; *SW*, V, 483–85; and above, pp. 117–118, 224–25, 228–29.

13. *MMT*, II, 102ff.; and Liu, "Present Situation," pp. 427ff.

14. Klein and Clark, *Biographic Dictionary*, I, 149–53; and biographical files of the U.S. Consulate General, Hong Kong.

15. *Caimao hongqi* [Finance and Trade Red Flag] (Beijing), February 8, 1967, in *SCMP-S*, No. 172; Liu, "Present Situation," pp. 426–27; *MMT*, I, 101; Peter R. Moody, Jr., *The Politics of the Eighth Central Committee of the Communist Party of China* (Hamden: Shoe String Press, 1973), p. 126; and Schurmann, *Ideology and Organization*, pp. 76, 195–208.

16. See MacFarquhar, *Origins 1*, pp. 88, 122–26, 312, 315.

17. *SXWS*, II, 168, 179, 204–205, 208–209, 214–15.

18. *RMRB*, December 5, 1957, in *SCMP*, No. 1679; and NCNA, Beijing, August 20, 1957, in *SCMP*, No. 1605.

19. *Ibid.*; and *RMRB*, December 8, 1957, in *URS*, Vol. 9—No. 24.

20. *Ibid.*; and Schurmann, *Ideology and Organization*, pp. 354ff.

21. NCNA, Beijing, August 20, 1957, in *SCMP*, No. 1605; *RMRB*, December 5, 1957, in *SCMP*, No. 1679; and Schurmann, *Ideology and Organization*, pp. 361–63.

22. *Second Session of the Eighth National Congress of the Communist Party of China* (Beijing: Foreign Languages Press, 1958), pp. 12–14; *Yunnan ribao* [Yunnan Daily], May 3, 1958, in *SCMP*, No. 1850; *Liaoning ribao*, October 31, 1958, in *SCMP*, No. 1925; and *Qingdao ribao*, November 4, 1958, in *SCMP*, No. 1924.

23. This phrase was used concerning the activities of Gu Dacun and Feng Baiju in Guangdong, but it could be applied to virtually all victims of the provincial purges. *XHBYK*, No. 19, 1958, in *URS*, Vol. 13—No. 14.

24. *Qinghai ribao* [Qinghai Daily], March 11, 1958, in *SCMP*, No. 1755; *RMRB*, May 26, July 15, 1958, in *SCMP*, Nos. 1797, 1819; and *Henan ribao*, July 4, 1958, in *CB*, No. 515.

25. *Henan ribao*, July 4, 1958, in *CB*, No. 515; and *People's Communes in China* (Beijing: Foreign Languages Press, 1958), p. 32.

26. *Henan ribao*, July 4, 1958, in *CB*, No. 515.

27. *Yunnan ribao*, May 3, 1958, in *SCMP*, No. 1850; *Henan ribao*, July 4, 15, 1958, in *CB*, No. 515; *RMRB*, July 15, 1958, in *SCMP*, No. 1819; and *XHBYK*, No. 19, 1958, in *URS*, Vol. 13—No. 14.

28. *Henan ribao*, July 15, 1958, in *CB*, No. 515.

29. *MMT*, I, 88; and *Henan ribao*, July 4, 15, 1958, in *CB*, No. 515.

30. *RMRB*, March 10, 1958, in *SCMP*, No. 1736. Cf. the anti-rightist struggle in Anhui political and legal organs; above, p. 250.

31. *RMRB*, March 10, 1958, in *SCMP*, No. 1736; *Henan ribao*, July 4, 1958, in *CB*, No. 515; and *Yunnan ribao*, May 3, 1958, in *SCMP*, No. 1850.

32. *Yunnan ribao*, May 3, 1958, in *SCMP*, No. 1850; *Qinghai ribao*, July 4, 1958, in *SCMP*, No. 1864; and *Gansu ribao*, August 16, 1958, in *CB*, No. 528.

33. *Dazhong ribao* [Masses Daily] *(DZRB)* (Jinan), November 3, 1958, in *JPRS*, No. 1723-N.

34. *DZRB* (Jinan), June 24, 1958, in *SCMP*, No. 1850.

35. *RMRB*, December 28, 1957, in *CB*, No. 487; *Henan ribao*, July 4, 1958, in *CB*, No. 515; *Gansu ribao*, August 16, 1958, in *CB*, No. 528; and *Liaoning ribao*, October 31, 1958, in *SCMP*, No. 1925.

36. NCNA, Beijing, December 26, 1957, in *CB*, No. 487; *Zhejiang ribao*, December 27, 1957, in *CB*, No. 487; *DZRB* (Jinan), June 24, 1958, in *SCMP*, No. 1850; *Gansu ribao*, August 16, 1958, in *CB*, No. 528; and *XHBYK*, No. 19, 1958, in *URS*, Vol. 13—No. 14

37. *Qingdao ribao*, November 4, 1958, in *SCMP*, No. 1924.

38. *RMRB*, March 10, 1958, in *SCMP*, No. 1736; *Yunnan ribao*, May 3, 1958, in *SCMP*, No. 1850; *DZRB* (Jinan), June 24, November 3, 1958, in *SCMP*, No. 1850, *JPRS*, No. 1723-N; *Gansu ribao*, August 16, 1958, in *CB*, No. 528; and *XHBYK*, No. 19, 1958, in *URS*, Vol. 13—No. 14.

39. *Yunnan ribao*, May 3, 1958, in *SCMP*, No. 1850; *RMRB*, May 26, 1958, in *SCMP*, No. 1797; and *Liaoning ribao*, October 31, 1958, in *SCMP*, No. 1925.

40. *Yunnan ribao*, October 11, 1958, in *URS*, Vol. 13—No. 26.

41. *DZRB* (Jinan), June 24, 1958, in *SCMP*, No. 1850; *Henan ribao*, July 4, 1958, in *CB*, No. 515; and *Qingdao ribao*, October 29, 1958, in *SCMP*, No. 1924.

42. *DZRB* (Jinan), June 24, 1958, in *SCMP*, No. 1850.

43. *RMRB*, March 10, 1958, in *SCMP*, No. 1736; *Henan ribao*, July 4, 1948, in *CB*, No. 515; *Gansu ribao*, August 16, 1958, in *CB*, No. 528; and *Yunnan ribao*, October 11, 1958, in *URS*, Vol. 13—No. 26.

44. NCNA, Beijing, September 12, 1956, in *SCMP*, No. 1382; *Henan ribao*, July 4, 1958, in *CB*, No. 515; and *People's Communes*, p. 32.

45. NCNA, Beijing, September 12, 1956, in *SCMP*, No. 1382; and "Correct Handling," pp. 282–83, 286–87.

46. *DZRB* (Jinan), June 24, November 3, 1958, in *SCMP*, No. 1850, *JPRS*, No. 1723-N.

47. Jiang Hua of Zhejiang, Zeng Xisheng of Anhui, Huang Oudong of Liaoning, Lin Tie of Hebei, and Wang Enmao of Xinjiang. Huang Oudong was demoted to Liaoning's second secretary in summer 1958, but his was not a disciplinary measure as Huang had been locked in conflict with the purge victims in that province. See *Hongweibing* [Red Guard], July 12, 1967. Huang's decline in rank was apparently due to the need to make room for a more powerful official sent in to take charge of the situation (see below).

48. NCNA, Hefei, January 7, 1958, in *SCMP*, No. 1689; *Liaoning ribao*, October 31, 1958, in *SCMP*, No. 1925; Roy Hofheinz, "Rural Administration in Communist China," *CQ*, No. 11 (1962), pp. 152, 154; and *Communist China 1958* (Hong Kong: Union Research Institute, 1959), p. 1.

49. *MMT*, I, 115, 121.

50. *RMRB*, December 14, 1957, in *SCMP*, No. 1676; *XHBYK*, No. 19, 1958, in *URS*, Vol. 13—No. 14; *Fandui difangzhuyi* [Oppose Localism] (Guangzhou: Guangdong renmin chubanshe, 1958); and *San-san-san zhanbao* [3–3–3 Combat Bulletin] (Guangzhou), June 28, 1967, in *SCMP*, No. 4016.

51. *Gansu ribao*, August 16, 1958, in *CB*, No. 528.

52. Teng, "Report on Rectification," p. 360.

53. Vogel, *Canton*, p. 121; *XX*, February 3, 1958, in *ECMM*, No. 129; and *XHBYK*, No. 19, 1958, in *URS*, Vol. 13—No. 14.

54. *RMRB*, December 14, 28, 1957, in *SCMP*, No. 1676, *CB*, No. 487; *Zhejiang ribao*, January 7, 1958, in *URS*, Vol. 10—No. 7; *XX*, February 3, 1958, in *ECMM*, No. 129; *Gansu ribao*, August 16, 1958, in *CB*, No. 528; *XHBYK*, No. 7, 1959, in *ECMM*, No. 169; and Vogel, *Canton*, p. 213.

55. *Zhejiang ribao*, January 7, 1958, in *URS*, Vol. 10—No. 7; *XHBYK*, No. 19, 1958, in *URS*, Vol. 13—No. 14; and Teiwes, *Provincial Personnel*, pp. 20–22.

56. *XX*, February 3, 1958, in *ECMM*, No. 129.

57. *Gansu ribao*, August 16, 1958, in *CB*, No. 528; *Yunnan ribao*, October 22, 1958, in *URS*, Vol. 13—No. 26; and Klein and Clark, *Biographic Dictionary*, I, 26.

58. Vogel, *Canton*, pp. 211–16; *Fandui*, especially pp. 2–6; and *XHBYK*, No. 19, 1958, in *URS*, Vol. 13—No. 14.

59. *Zhejiang ribao*, January 7, 1958, in *URS*, Vol. 10—No. 7; *XX*, February 3, 1958, in *ECMM*, No. 129; *Fandui*, p. 4; Vogel, *Canton*, pp. 215–16; and *San-san-san zhanbao* (Guangzhou), June 28, 1967, in *SCMP*, No. 4016.

60. NCNA, Beijing, February 28, 1958, in *CB*, No. 495.

61. *RMRB*, November 6, December 15, 26, 1957, January 17, 1958, in *SCMP*, Nos. 1656, 1689, *CB*, No. 512, *SCMP*, No. 1699; NCNA, Urumchi, June 26, 1958, in *CB*, No.

512; George Moseley, *A Sino-Soviet Cultural Frontier: The Ili Kazakh Autonomous Chou* (Cambridge: Harvard East Asian Monographs, 1966), pp. 64–65; and *Fandui*, p. 20.

62. *RMRB*, November 23, December 26, 1957, January 11, 1958, in *SCMP*, No. 1672, *CB*, No. 512, *HF*, p. 255; NCNA, Beijing, January 17, February 28, 1958, in *SCMP*, No. 1699, *CB*, No. 495; NCNA, Urumchi, June 26, 1958, in *CB*, No. 512; and Moseley, *Cultural Frontier*, pp. 64–65.

63. NCNA, Urumchi, November 30, 1957, June 26, 1958, in *SCMP*, No. 1672, *CB*, No. 512; *RMRB*, December 26, 1957, January 11, July 15, 1958, in *CB*, No. 512, *HF*, pp. 255–57, *SCMP*, No. 1819; and NCNA, Beijing, February 28, 1958, in *CB*, No. 495.

64. *RMRB*, December 15, 1957, in *SCMP*, No. 1689; NCNA, Beijing, February 28, 1958, in *CB*, No. 495; *Fandui*, pp. 22, 27; and Henry G. Schwarz, "The Treatment of Minorities," in Michel Oksenberg, ed., *China's Developmental Experience* (New York: Praeger Publishers, 1973), pp. 203–205.

65. *Jiefangjun bao* [Liberation Army Daily] *(JFJB)*, January 16, 1958, in *SCMP*, No. 1786; Joffe, *Party and Army*, pp. 122–26, 133–36; and John Gittings, *The Role of the Chinese Army* (London: Oxford University Press, 1967), pp. 182–83, 209ff.

66. *JFJB*, August 1, 1966. The other major struggles allegedly involved Peng Dehuai in 1959 (see Chapter 9) and "recent" opponents of Lin Biao's emphasis on politics—i.e., Luo Ruiqing who was ousted as PLA Chief of Staff at the end of 1965.

67. Mao, "Speech at the Group Leaders Forum of the Enlarged Conference of the Military Affairs Commission (excerpts)," in *CLG*, Winter 1968–69, pp. 16–21; *SXWS*, II, 265–66; and *CNA*, No. 626 (1966), pp. 4–5.

68. *JFJB*, May 23, August 17, 1958, in *SCMP*, No. 1900, *JPRS*, No. 10,240; and Gittings, *Role*, chs. 8, 11 *passim*.

69. *JFJB*, July 1, 1958, in *SCMP*, No. 1881 (emphasis added).

70. "Speech at Enlarged MAC," pp. 16–19. Mao criticized several other leaders but their names were excised from the Cultural Revolution text of this speech. Xiao may have lost this training post as a result of Mao's attack since he was no longer identified in that role after spring 1958, but he apparently continued to serve as Vice Minister of Defense. Klein and Clark, *Biographic Dictionary*, I, 336.

71. See Solomon, *Mao's Revolution*, pp. 363–66; and Vogel, *Canton*, pp. 245–47.

72. See below, pp. 366–67.

73. *SXWS*, II, 179, 268–69; and *MP*, p. 75.

74. Cf. Vogel, *Canton*, p. 224.

Chapter 9

1. See Gittings, *Role*, pp. 225–34; Ellis Joffe, *Between Two Plenums: China's Intraleadership Conflict, 1959–1962* (Ann Arbor: Michigan Papers in Chinese Studies, 1975), pp. 12ff.; and Gregory J. Terry, "The 'Debate' on Military Affairs in China: 1957–1959," *Asian Survey*, August 1976.

2. E.g., Bridgham, "Factionalism," pp. 212–20.

3. The following is primarily drawn from Klein and Clark, *Biographic Dictionary*, I, 61–67, 219–20, 397–401, II, 727–37.

4. For a detailed Red Guard compilation, see *CB*, No. 851, pp. 1–8.

5. See William W. Whitson with Chen-hsia Huang, *The Chinese High Command: A History of Communist Military Politics, 1927–71* (New York: Praeger Publishers, 1973), pp. 98–99 and *passim*.

6. See MacFarquhar, *Origins 1*, pp. 100–102.

7. *CLG*, Winter 1968–69, p. 49.

8. Mao described himself as a "middle of the roader" at Lushan; *The Case of Peng*

Teh-huai 1959–1968 (Hong Kong: Union Research Institute, 1968), p. 23. In 1970, Mao did use the appellation "center leftist" to describe himself in an interview with Couve de Murville. See Ross Terrill, *800,000,000: The Real China* (Boston: Little Brown, 1972), p. 68.

9. Trans. in *PDA*, pp. 490–503.

10. *MMT*, I, 130–31, 133–34, 138, 142; and Parris H. Chang, *Power and Policy in China* (University Park: The Pennsylvania State University Press, 1975), pp. 100, 237–38.

11. *CLG*, Winter 1968–69, pp. 30–32; *MMT*, I, 151; Frederick C. Teiwes, "Government and Politics in the Provinces of China," paper presented at the Conference on Government in China, Cuernavaca, Mexico, August 1969, pp. 71–72; and above, pp. 71–73.

12. Teiwes, "Government," pp. 71–72; *SXWS*, I, 8–9; and *CLG*, Winter 1968–69, p. 23.

13. *CLG*, Winter 1968–69, pp. 60, 81; *CB*, No. 851, pp. 13, 30–31; *Case of Peng*, p. 37; and Kenneth Lieberthal, *A Research Guide to Central Party and Government Meetings in China 1949–1975* (White Plains: International Arts and Sciences Press, 1976), pp. 135–38.

14. *MMT*, I, 170–72.

15. *Ibid.*, p. 172.

16. Radio Guiyang, June 17, December 23, 1967, in *News from Chinese Provincial Radio Stations (NFCPRS)*, Nos. 212, 239 (emphasis added).

17. *Case of Peng*, p. 36; *CNA*, No. 638 (1966), p. 7; *MMT*, I, 175, 182–84; *Dongfanghong*, February 15, 1967, in *CB*, No. 878; *HQ*, November 16, 1959, in *JPRS*, No. 1168-D.

18. *MMT*, I, 176, 180–81.

19. *Ibid.*, p. 178.

20. Donald S. Zagoria, *The Sino-Soviet Conflict 1956–1961* (New York: Atheneum, 1969), pp. 109–16, 125–34, 240–41; and Gittings, *Role*, pp. 229–30.

21. David A. Charles, "The Dismissal of Marshall Peng Teh-huai," in MacFarquhar, *China under Mao*, pp. 21–24; *Case of Peng*, pp. 387–89; and *Peking Review*, September 13, 1963.

22. *CLG*, Winter 1968–69, p. 63.

23. *Xin Nongda*, December 2, 1967, in *SCMP-S*, No. 220; *Weidong* (Tianjin), June 15, 1967, in *SCMP-S*, No. 207; *Xinwen zhanxian* [News Front] (Beijing), June 30, 1967, in *SCMP-S*, No. 196; and *Guangyin hongqi* [Broadcasting and Publishing Red Flag] (Guangzhou), March 1968, in *SCMP*, No. 4162.

24. *Caimao hongqi*, February 15, 1967; Radio Chengdu, September 23, 1967, in *NFCPRS*, No. 226; MacFarquhar, "Photographs," pp. 298–99; *Case of Peng*, p. 205; and below, pp. 320–31. Concerning Lin, although various Cultural Revolution sources claim his support for Mao, no source was found which actually places Lin at the conference and he was not clearly visible in the official picture which focused on Mao, Liu and Zhou.

25. *RMRB*, August 30, 1959, in *SCMP*, No. 2093.

26. *RMRB*, September 17, 23, October 2, 10, 1959; *CB*, No. 851, p. 22; *CLG*, Winter 1968–69, pp. 47–48; and *SXWS*, I, 66.

27. NCNA, Beijing, August 15, 1967, in *SCMP*, No. 4004.

28. *RMRB*, September 22, 1959; NCNA, Beijing, October 27, 1959, in *CB*, No. 602; *DGB* (Beijing), October 29, 1959, in *SCMP*, No. 2142; and *MMT*, I, 170, 182.

29. *CB*, No. 851, p. 22.

30. *RMRB*, October 31, November 11, 1959, in *SCMP*, Nos. 2141, 2152; *HQ*, November 1, 1959, in *JPRS*, No. 1098-D; *Xin jianshe* [New Construction], November 7,

1959, in *ECMM*, No. 206; *Peking Review*, August 18, 1967; *SXWS*, I, 44; and *MMT*, I, 182–84.

31. *RMRB*, December 5, 1959, in *SCMP*, No. 2160; *HQ*, December 16, 1959, in *ECMM*, No. 196; *Case of Peng*, p. 5; *CB*, No. 851, p. 26; *MMT*, I, 175–76; and above, p. 308.

32. *CB*, No. 851, p. 21.

33. *Ibid*., pp. 25–26; and above, pp. 309–10.

34. *ZGQNB*, September 1, 1959; *Anhui ribao*, November 29, 1959, in *SCMP*, No. 2170; *CB*, No. 851, p. 20; *Case of Peng*, p. 9; *MMT*, I, 144–45; and below, p. 326.

35. *RMRB*, August 30, November 11, 1959, in *URS*, Vol. 16—No. 24, *SCMP*, No. 2154; *RMRB*, September 9, 20, 23, 1959; *Case of Peng*, p. 8; *CB*, No. 851, pp. 19–21; and *MMT*, I, 157, 170, 182.

36. *RMRB*, August 29, 1959; *Case of Peng*, pp. 3–4, 8; and above, pp. 307–308.

37. *Peking Review*, October 16, 1959; *Case of Peng*, p. 12; and *MMT*, I, 130–31.

38. *RMRB*, September 20, 21, 22, November 30, 1959; and *CLG*, Winter 1968–69, pp. 36–37, 64, 67–68.

39. *Dongfeng* [East Wind] (Tianjin), November 10, December 10, 1959, in *URS*, Vol. 18—No. 6, *JPRS*, No. 2754; *Xin Hunan bao*, November 19, 1959, in *URS*, Vol. 18—No. 4; and above, p. 308n.

40. *MMT*, I, 130–32; and above, p. 308.

41. *Case of Peng*, pp. 3, 36; and *MMT*, I, 140.

42. NCNA, Beijing, August 15, 1967, in *SCMP*, No. 4004.

43. NCNA, Beijing, July 31, August 15, 1967, in *SCMP*, Nos. 3994, 4004; and *HQ*, December 16, 1959, in *ECMM*, No. 196.

44. *JFRB*, May 26, 1966.

45. *Case of Peng*, pp. 12–13; *CLG*, Winter 1968–69, p. 81; and above, p. 308n.

46. *Gansu ribao*, August 30, 1959, in *SCMP*, No. 2151; *HQ*, November 1, 1959, in *JPRS*, No. 1098-D; *Jiangxi ribao*, January 2, 1960, in *SCMP*, No. 2226; *CLG*, Winter 1968–69, p. 49; and above, p. 308.

47. *CLG*, Winter 1968–69, pp. 54–55, 67; *CB*, No. 851, pp. 28, 30–31; and below, p. 331.

48. *CB*, No. 851, pp. 24–25, 29.

49. *Ibid*., pp. 19–23.

50. *Ibid*., p. 30.

51. *Jinggangshan* and *Guangdong wenyi zhanbao* [Jinggang Mountains and Guangdong Literary Combat Bulletin] (Guangzhou), August 26, 1967, in *SCMP*, No. 4032. Cf. below, p. 330.

52. See Mao's Lushan complaint about their failure to voice opinions at these meetings. *CLG*, Winter 1968–69, pp. 45–56.

53. *Ibid*., p. 44.

54. *Ibid*., pp. 35, 61–63.

55. *Ibid*., p. 75; *CB*, No. 851, pp. 27–31; and NCNA, Beijing, August 15, 1967, in *SCMP*, No. 4004.

56. *CLG*, Winter 1968–69, p. 40.

57. *Ibid*., pp. 38–39, 41 (emphasis added).

58. Schram, "Historical Perspective," p. 61; *CLG*, Winter 1968–69, p. 37; and below, p. 340.

59. *RMRB*, August 30, 1959, in *SCMP*, No. 2108; *ZGQN*, November 16, 1959, in *ECMM*, No. 197; and *CLG*, Winter 1968–69, pp. 44–45, 49–50, 73–74, 81.

60. *Jinggangshan* and *Guangdong wenyi zhanbao* (Guangzhou), September 5, 1967, in *SCMP*, No. 4047; *CB*, No. 851, p. 14; Zagoria, *Sino-Soviet Conflict*, pp. 134–35; and *CLG*, Winter 1968–69, pp. 25, 53.

61. *CLG,* Winter 1968–69, p. 84.

62. On his visit to China in early October, Khrushchev assertedly praised Peng as "correct," "brave," and his "best friend." *CB,* No. 851, p. 14.

63. *Khrushchev Remembers,* pp. 271–72; and above, pp. 150–51.

64. *Xinwen zhanxian* (Beijing), June 30, 1967, in *SCMP-S,* No. 196; *CNA,* No. 761 (1969), p. 4; *Weidong* (Tianjin), June 15, 1967, in *SCMP-S,* No. 207; and above, pp. 311–12.

65. *Xinwen zhanxian* (Beijing), June 30, 1967, in *SCMP-S,* No. 196. In a similar case Hu Qiaomu reportedly "slipped through" on the strength of an assurance given by Tao Zhu. *Wenxue zhanbao,* April 14, 1967, in *SCMP,* No. 3942.

66. Moody, *Eighth Central Committee,* pp. 142–43.

67. *Dongfanghong,* February 11, 1967, in *SCMP-S,* No. 172; "The Towering Crimes of Zhu De" (Red Guard poster), January 25, 1967, in *URS,* Vol. 47—No. 2; and "Exposing the Towering Crimes of Counterrevolutionary Revisionist Li Qi" (Red Guard pamphlet), April 1, 1967, in *SCMM-S,* No. 23. According to British intelligence sources another Politburo member, Lin Boqu, was also required to make a self-criticism for his support of Peng at Lushan. Charles, "Dismissal," pp. 21, 24–25.

68. *CLG,* Winter 1968–69, pp. 47–49; and *MMT,* I, 187.

69. Radio Chengdu, August 31, 1967, in *NFCPRS,* No. 223.

70. Cf. Lowell Dittmer, " 'Line Struggle' in Theory and Practice: The Origins of the Cultural Revolution Reconsidered," *CQ,* No. 72 (1977), p. 689.

71. The only references found were *RMRB,* September 27, 1959, in *CB,* No. 596; and *Xin Hunan bao,* November 22, 1959, in *SCMP,* No. 2155.

72. *Issues & Studies,* September 1972, p. 66.

73. See Terry, "Debate," pp. 793ff.

74. Cheng, *Red Army,* p. 66; *JFJB,* August 1, 1966, in *SCMP,* No. 3754; and *Case of Peng,* pp. 145ff. Cf. above, pp. 293–96.

75. NCNA, Beijing, July 31, August 16, 20, 1967, in *JPRS,* No. 42977, *SCMP,* Nos. 4005, 4007; and *CB,* No. 851, pp. 10–11.

76. NCNA, Beijing, August 20, 1967, in *SCMP,* No. 4007; *Jinggangshan* and *Guangdong wenyi zhanbao* (Guangzhou), September 5, 1967, in *SCMP,* No. 4047; and Terry, "Debate," pp. 796–97, 802, 805–806.

77. Cheng, *Red Army,* pp. 66ff., 217, 617; *Case of Peng,* p. 164; *Peking Review,* October 6, 1959; and above, p. 296n.

78. See Gittings, *Role,* chs. 8–10, 12.

79. *RMRB,* September 18, 1959, in *SCMP,* No. 2106; *Jiangxi ribao,* January 2, 1960, in *SCMP,* No. 2226; and *CNA,* No. 632 (1966), p. 3.

80. *Hubei ribao,* November 17, 1959, in *SCMP,* No. 2156; *Xinjiang ribao,* November 26, 1959, in *SCMP,* No. 2167; *Qinghai ribao,* November 26, 1959, in *SCMP,* No. 2188; *RMRB,* December 23, 1959, in *SCMP,* No. 2170; and *CNA,* No. 632 (1966), p. 3.

81. *CLG,* Winter 1968–69, p. 81; and *Shaanxi ribao,* November 21, 23, December 2, 12, 1959, in *SCMP,* No. 2176.

82. For State Council personnel the procedure was to compare the 1958, 1959 and 1960 *RMSC,* and then consult standard biographical sources in cases where officials were apparently removed from their posts during the 1959–60 campaign. Since the 1960 edition was published in October 1960 it should include any dismissals due to the 1959–60 campaign. The same procedure was followed for provincial government posts but for Party posts (both central and provincial) a wider range of sources was consulted to determine the 1959 officeholders. See Teiwes, *Provincial Personnel,* pp. 69, 111–12. The listing below does not include several officials cited in Charles, "Dismissal," p. 30, and Moody, *Eighth Central Committee,* p. 141, where a close check of biographical data does not point to the 1959–60 campaign as a career watershed.

83. *CLG*, Winter 1968–69, p. 67; above, p. 311; and below, pp. 377–80.

84. *GRRB*, December 10, 1966, in *SCMP*, No. 3854; *Dou-pi-gai*, May 15, 1967, in *SCMM-S*, No. 19; "Liu Shaoqi's Reactionary Speeches" (Red Guard pamphlet), April 1967, in *SCMM-S*, No. 25; "Record of Deng's Reactionary Utterances," April 1967, in *SCMP-S*, No. 208; "Counterrevolutionary Revisionist Peng Zhen's Towering Crimes of Opposing the Party, Socialism and the Thought of Mao Zedong" (Red Guard pamphlet), June 10, 1967, in *SCMM*, No. 640; *Xiju zhanbao* [Drama Combat Bulletin] (Beijing), June 24, 1967, in *SCMP-S*, No. 203; and *Dongfanghong bao* [The East is Red Bulletin], June 27, 1967, in *SCMP-S*, No. 196.

85. "Facts about Liu Jianxun's Crimes" (Red Guard pamphlet), March 12, 1967, in *SCMM-S*, No. 32.

86. "Record of Deng's Reactionary Utterances," April 1967, in *SCMP-S*, No. 208; and Radio Guiyang, October 19, December 23, 1967, in *NFCPRS*, Nos. 230, 239.

87. Radio Guiyang, December 23, 1967, in *NFCPRS*, No. 239.

88. *Dongfanghong bao*, June 27, 1967, in *SCMP-S*, No. 196; "Liu Shaoqi's Reactionary Speeches," April 1967, in *SCMM-S*, No. 25; and below, pp. 376–77.

89. NCNA, Beijing, August 26, 28, September 24, 1959, in *CB*, Nos. 589, 590, *SCMP*, No. 2108; *HQ*, August 16, 1959, in *ECMM*, No. 183; *RMRB*, August 27, 1959, in *CB*, No. 589; *JFRB*, September 5, 1959, in *SCMP*, No. 2157; *ZGQNB*, September 6, 1959, in *SCMP*, No. 2104; and Teiwes, "Government," pp. 81–85.

90. Byung-joon Ahn, "Ideology, Policy and Power in Chinese Politics and the Evolution of the Cultural Revolution, 1959–1965," Ph.D. dissertation, Columbia University, 1972, pp. 97–100; Teiwes, "Government," pp. 80–84; Vogel, *Canton*, pp. 266–75; *MMT*, I, 229–30; and Radio Chengdu, December 8, 1967, in *NFCPRS*, No. 239.

91. *Dongfanghong*, February 15, 1967, in *CB*, No. 878, "Peng Zhen's Towering Crimes," June 10, 1967, in *SCMM*, No. 640; *GMRB*, August 9, 1967, in *SCMP*, No. 4014; and *Xiju zhanbao*, June 24, 1967, in *SCMP-S*, No. 203.

92. "Look at Tao Zhu's Ugly Face" (Red Guard pamphlet), January 22, 1967, in *SCMP*, No. 3937.

93. E.g., Radio Chengdu, October 3, 1967, in *NFCPRS*, No. 228; and Radio Guiyang, December 23, 1967, in *NFCPRS*, No. 239.

Chapter 10

1. E.g., Joffe, *Between Plenums;* and Ahn, "Ideology," pp. 456ff.

2. Cf. Teiwes, "Chinese Politics," Part II, pp. 13–15; and Dittmer, "Line Struggle," pp. 690–96.

3. See Teiwes, "Chinese Politics," Part II, pp. 3, 14–15.

4. Teiwes, "Government," pp. 80–84, 87; Zagoria, *Sino-Soviet Conflict*, p. 344; Vogel, *Canton*, pp. 271ff.; and Cheng, *Red Army*, pp. 13, 190–91. The provinces experiencing armed rebellions were Gansu, Qinghai, Sichuan, Tibet and Yunnan.

5. *MU*, p. 190; Chang, *Power*, p. 126; Ahn, "Ideology," pp. 102–103; and *JPRS*, No. 52029, p. 20.

6. "Urgent Directive and Letter from the Central Authorities of the CCP Regarding the Problems of Present Policy toward Rural People's Communes" (November 1960), in *URS*, Vol. 28—No. 12, pp. 200–201; *Nongcun renmin gongshe gongzuo tiaoli cao'an* [Draft Regulations for Work in Rural People's Communes] ("Sixty Articles") (March 1961), document available at the East Asian Institute, Columbia University, *passim;* Cheng, *Red Army*, pp. 350, 455ff., 525ff.; *RMRB*, January 14, 1961, in *SCMP*, No. 2426; Ahn, "Ideology," pp. 103–106; Chang, *Power*, pp. 126–28; and H.F. Schurmann, "Peking's Recognition of Crisis," in Albert Feuerwerker, ed., *Modern China* (Englewood Cliffs: Prentice-Hall, 1964), pp. 94–96.

7. Schurmann, "Peking's Recognition," pp. 97–99; Vogel, *Canton*, pp. 271–72; and Stephen Andors, "Factory Management and Political Ambiguity, 1961–63," *CQ*, No. 59 (1974), pp. 438ff.

8. Dennis Doolin, "The Revival of the 'Hundred Flowers' Campaign: 1961," *CQ*, No. 8 (1961), pp. 35–39; "Peking Weeds the Intellectual Garden," *Current Scene*, May 31, 1961, pp. 2–6; Merle Goldman, "The Unique 'Blooming and Contending' of 1961–62," *CQ*, No. 37 (1969), p. 61; and *CNA*, No. 639 (1966), p. 4.

9. See Schram, "Historical Perspective," p. 68; W.F. Dorrill, *Power, Policy and Ideology in the Making of China's "Cultural Revolution,"* RAND memorandum RM-5731-PR, August 1968, p. 47; Teiwes, "Government," p. 87; Solomon, *Mao's Revolution*, pp. 395–400; Doolin, "Revival," p. 40; and Dittmer, *Liu*, p. 53.

10. Joffe, *Between Plenums*, p. 28; Moody, *Eighth Central Committee*, pp. 238, 241; "Long Live the Invincible Thought of Mao Zedong!" (Red Guard pamphlet), in *CB*, No. 884; and *MMT*, II, 242–43, 246.

11. *MMT*, II, 240.

12. *Ibid.*

13. *Ibid.*, pp. 240–41.

14. NCNA, Beijing, January 20, 1961, in *CB*, No. 644.

15. See *CNA*, No. 632 (1966), p. 4; and Oksenberg, "Methods of Communication," p. 24.

16. *SXWS*, I, 260; Cheng, *Red Army*, pp. 15, 458, 525; and *URS*, Vol. 28-No. 12, pp. 198–200.

17. *URS*, Vol. 28—No. 12, pp. 198–99; Cheng, *Red Army*, pp. 286, 456, 528; *NFRB*, September 2, November 9, 1960, in *CB*, Nos. 645, 646; *RMRB*, October 31, 1960, in *SCMP*, No. 2379; *MMT*, II, 243–45; *Liu Shaoqi zuixinglu* [Record of Liu Shaoqi's Crimes], September 1967, in *SCMM-S*, No. 26; and Vogel, *Canton*, pp. 277–78.

18. *URS*, Vol. 28—No. 12, pp. 199–200; Cheng, *Red Army*, pp. 457–58; *NFRB*, October 5, November 9, 1960, in *CB*, Nos. 645, 646; and *RMRB*, February 2, 1961; and above, pp. 170, 309.

19. *URS*, Vol. 28—No. 12, p. 199; "Sixty Articles," Articles 40, 47; Cheng, *Red Army*, pp. 142–43; *NFRB*, November 3, 1960; *Liu Shaoqi zuixinglu*, September 1967, in *SCMM-S*, No. 26; *RMRB*, February 7, March 24, 1961; and above, pp. 53–54, 65–66, 91–92, 170.

20. *NFRB*, February 8, 1961.

21. Cheng, *Red Army*, p. 166.

22. *URS*, Vol. 28—No. 12, p. 200; *NFRB*, September 16, November 23, 1960; *RMRB*, November 16, 1960, March 14, 1961; and "Sixty Articles," Articles 34, 43, 44, 48, 50, 52, 53.

23. *URS*, Vol. 28—No. 12, p. 199; Cheng, *Red Army*, p. 457; *NFRB*, November 3, 1960, in *SCMP*, No. 2400; "Sixty Articles," Article 45; and above, pp. 92, 169–70.

24. Cheng, *Red Army*, pp. 137–38, 497, 525.

25. *Liu Shaoqi zuixinglu*, September 1967, in *SCMM-S*, No. 26; and "Selected Edition on Liu Shaoqi's Crimes," in *SCMM*, No. 651.

26. *Liu Shaoqi zuixinglu*, September 1967, in *SCMM-S*, No. 26; and below, pp. 402–403, 421–22.

27. Cheng, *Red Army*, pp. 119, 141; "Liu Shaoqi's Reactionary Speeches," April 1967, in *SCMM-S*, No. 25; Vogel, *Canton*, p. 284; and *MMT*, II, 237–38.

28. Cheng, *Red Army*, pp. 15–16, 119, 138, 141–42, 163; and *NFRB*, December 22, 1960, in *SCMP*, No. 2431.

29. Cheng, *Red Army*, pp. 16, 119, 138, 164, 459; and *MMT*, II, 240.

30. Cheng, *Red Army*, pp. 119, 138–39, 385, 470; and "Sixty Articles," Article 59.

31. Cheng, *Red Army*, pp. 287, 466–69, 493, 518, 522–23.

32. *Ibid.*, pp. 467, 492–93, 497, 515, 528.

33. *MMT*, II, 240–41, 243; and *NFRB*, December 22, 1960, in *SCMP*, No. 2431.

34. *RMRB*, January 5, 1961, in *SCMP*, No. 2424.

35. *NFRB*, February 7, 1961; and *HQ*, February 1, 1961, in *SCMM*, No. 250.

36. Radio Shanxi, March 14, 1961, in the Taiwan collection, *Zhonggong difang guangbo* [Chinese Communist Local Broadcasts].

37. *NFRB*, February 7, June 24, 1961; and Cheng, *Red Army*, pp. 378ff.

38. Cheng, *Red Army*, pp. 379–81; and above, pp. 69–70, 121–22, 255.

39. Radio Changsha, September 27, 1966, in *CNA*, No. 632 (1966), p. 4.

40. *NFRB*, February 7, April 28, May 10, June 24, 1961; *RMRB*, March 20, April 7, 13, 1961; and "Sixty Articles," Articles 6, 57, 58.

41. Cheng, *Red Army*, p. 440, reported over 11,000 communes (93 percent of all communes rectified) had carried out militia reorganization. Therefore, the total number of communes rectified was over 11,800 or about 46 percent of the 25,450 communes existing in December 1959. The March 1961 Sixty Articles called for a substantial increase in the number of communes but this may have already begun. Thus it is possible that considerably less than half the communes had undergone rectification.

42. Vogel, *Canton*, p. 278; *CNA*, No. 399 (1961), p. 3; Cheng, *Red Army*, p. 566; and Radio Chengdu, August 31, 1967, in *NFCPRS*, No. 223.

43. *Dou-pi-gai*, May 15, 1967, in *SCMM-S*, No. 19.

44. *Bao'an tongxin* [Bao'an Bulletin], September 23, 1961, in *URS*, Vol. 27—No. 7.

45. *Bao'an tongxin*, October 6, 1961, in *URS*, Vol. 27—No. 8. See also Vogel, *Canton*, pp. 278–79; and Schurmann, *Ideology and Organization*, pp. 401–402.

46. Vogel, *Canton*, p. 284; John Wilson Lewis, "The Leadership Doctrine of the Chinese Communist Party: The Lesson of the People's Commune," *Asian Survey*, October 1963, pp. 457–58; *CNA*, No. 632 (1966), p. 4; and Richard Baum and Frederick C. Teiwes, "Liu Shao-ch'i and the Cadre Question," *Asian Survey*, April 1968, pp. 325–26.

47. Teiwes, *Provincial Personnel*, pp. 29–30.

48. *Case of Peng*, pp. 23, 410; Moody, *Eighth Central Committee*, pp. 148–49; "Record of Deng's Reactionary Utterances," in *SCMP-S*, No. 208; and above, p. 309n.

49. Chang, *Power*, p. 130. Ningxia was only reestablished as an autonomous region in 1958, but the purge in Gansu explicitly involved areas which subsequently became part of Ningxia.

50. Ahn, "Ideology," p. 121; "Selected Edition on Liu Shaoqi's Crimes," April 1967, in *SCMM*, No. 652; *JPRS*, No. 50792, p. 42; *Communist China 1960* (2 vols., Hong Kong: Union Research Institute, 1962), I, 29; *China Notes*, No. 158 (1966); Chang, *Power*, p. 130; and n. 4, this chapter.

51. *RMRB*, September 2, 1961, July 3, 1962. The first article was a Henan editorial published about the time of Wu's demotion. The second was authored by the director of the Central-South Bureau's organization department about the time of Wu's transfer to the bureau.

52. Chang, *Power*, p. 134; "Selected Edition on Liu Shaoqi's Crimes," April 1967, in *SCMM*, No. 652; and "Liu Shaoqi's Reactionary Speeches," April 1967, in *SCMM-S*, No. 25.

53. Valuable insights into rural conditions and policy responses in late 1961 are given in internal documents of the Bao'an County, Guangdong, Party Committee from September to December 1961, in *URS*, Vol. 27—Nos. 7–9. See especially *Bao'an tongxin*, November 18, December 8, 1961. See also *RMRB*, January 1, 1962; and Ahn, "Ideology," pp. 120–23.

54. See the Chinese Nationalist intelligence report, *Gongfei gongye zhengce qishitiao zhuyao neirong* [Important Contents of Communist Bandits' Seventy Article Industrial

Policy], available at the East Asian Institute, Columbia University; and Ahn, "Ideology," pp. 125–27.

55. *ZGQNB*, September 2, 1961, in *SCMP*, No. 2581; Goldman, "Unique 'Blooming and Contending,' " p. 56; and Ahn, "Ideology," pp. 128–37.

56. A.M. Halpern, "Between Plenums: A Second Look at the 1962 National People's Congress in China," *Asian Survey*, November 1962, p. 7, and NCNA, Beijing, November 9, 1961, in *SCMP*, No. 2622.

57. Ahn, "Ideology," pp. 138–39; and *JPRS*, No. 52029, pp. 1, 7, 12.

58. See *JPRS*, No. 52029, p. 9; and *Collected Works of Liu 1958–67*, pp. 131–46.

59. *JPRS*, No. 50792, pp. 49–50.

60. *Collected Works of Liu 1958–67*, p. 361; "Liu Shaoqi's Reactionary Speeches," April 1967, in *SCMM-S*, No. 25; and "Selected Edition on Liu Shaoqi's Crimes," April 1967, in *SCMM*, No. 652.

61. *Collected Works of Liu 1958–67*, p. 361; "Selected Edition on Liu Shaoqi's Crimes," April 1967, in *SCMM*, No. 652; NCNA, December 9, 1967, in *SCMP*, No. 4079; *SXWS*, II, 479; *JPRS*, No. 52029, p. 29; Radio Kunming, August 23, 1967, in *NFCPRS*, No. 222; and Pi-chao Chen, "Individual Farming after the Great Leap: As Revealed by the Lien Kiang Documents," *Asian Survey*, September 1968, p. 781.

62. Halpern, "Between Plenums," p. 8; George T. Yu, "The 1962 and 1963 Sessions of the National People's Congress of Communist China," *Asian Survey*, August 1964; *RMRB*, May 10, 1962, in *SCMP*, No. 2745; and *ZGQNB*, July 3, 1962, in *SCMP*, No. 2785.

63. "Long Live the Invincible Thought of Mao!" in *CB*, No. 884; *SXWS*, II, 479; and Solomon, *Mao's Revolution*, pp. 419–20.

64. E.g., Goldman, "Unique 'Blooming and Contending'," pp. 68ff.; and Joffe, *Between Plenums*, pp. 29ff.

65. The most detailed and sophisticated analysis of Wu Han's work is James R. Pusey, *Wu Han: Attacking the Present Through the Past* (Cambridge: Harvard East Asian Monographs, 1969). Pusey argues that conscious political satire was involved in Wu Han's works and Peng's case was being alluded to, but also that the identification of Peng with Hai Rui was not essential to Wu's satire.

66. "Peng Zhen's Towering Crimes," June 10, 1967, in *SCMM*, No. 640; *CLG*, Winter 1968–69, pp. 56–59; *JPRS*, No. 52029, p. 5; and above, pp. 308, 310.

67. Dittmer, *Liu*, pp. 69, 72, 110; "Comrade Jiang Qing on Literature and Art" (Red Guard pamphlet), May 1968, in *Issues & Studies*, October 1975, p. 92; *RMRB*, January 12, 1960, in *CNA*, No. 631 (1966), p. 3; Moody, *Eighth Central Committee*, p. 143; above, pp. 323–24, 330; and below, pp. 460ff.

68. See Edward E. Rice, *Mao's Way* (Berkeley: University of California Press, 1972), p. 290; and J.D. Simmonds, *China: The Evolution of a Revolution, 1959–66* (Canberra: A.N.U. Department of International Relations, 1968), pp. 33–34.

69. "Selected Edition on Liu Shaoqi's Crimes," April 1967, in *SCMM*, No. 652.

70. Joffe, *Between Plenums*, p. 48; *JPRS*, No. 52029, p. 20; *SXWS*, II, 479; "Thirty-three Leading Revisionists," in *CB*, No. 874; "Long Live the Invincible Thought of Mao!" in *CB*, No. 884; *CLG*, Winter 1968–69, pp. 91–92; and Klein and Clark, *Biographic Dictionary*, II, 900.

71. Personal communication, April 1973. Another key example of this cited by MacFarquhar is Mao's contempt for Khrushchev based on the latter's perceived loss of nerve in dealings with the US.

72. See Ahn, "Ideology," pp. 166–69; *JPRS*, No. 52029, p. 20; and *Nongcun renmin gongshe gongzuo tiaoli xiuzheng cao'an* [Revised Draft Regulations for Work in Rural People's Communes] ("Revised Sixty Articles") (September 1962), document available at the East Asian Institute, Columbia University, *passim*.

73. "Liu Shaoqi's Reactionary Speeches," April 1967, in *SCMM-S*, No. 25; *JPRS*, No. 52029, p. 3; and above, pp. 350, 365.

74. *JPRS*, No. 52029, pp. 2ff. These themes were also emphasized in the public media in this period. See Charles Neuhauser, "The Chinese Communist Party in the 1960s: Prelude to the Cultural Revolution," *CQ* No. 32 (1967), p. 15.

75. *Dou-pi-gai*, May 15, 1967, in *SCMM-S*, No. 19; "Record of Deng's Reactionary Utterances," April 1967, in *SCMP-S*, No. 208; *Liu Shaoqi zuixinglu*, September 1967, in *SCMM-S*, No. 28; "Selected Edition on Liu Shaoqi's Crimes," April 1967, in *SCMM*, No. 651; *Jinggangshan* (Beijing), March 8, 1967, in *SCMP*, No. 3933; and above, p. 310.

76. *CLG*, Winter 1968–69, pp. 90–92; and above, p. 34.

77. "Facts about Liu Jianxun's Crimes," March 12, 1967, in *SCMM-S*, No. 32; *Dou-pi-gai*, May 15, 1967, in *SCMM-S*, No. 19; and Radio Guiyang, July 13, 1967, in *NFCPRS*, No. 216.

78. "Facts about Liu Jianxun's Crimes," March 12, 1967, in *SCMM-S*, No. 32; "Exposing the Towering Crimes of Counterrevolutionary Revisionist Li Qi" (Red Guard pamphlet), April 1, 1967, in *SCMM-S*, No. 23; *Dongfanghong bao*, June 27, 1967, in *SCMP-S*, No. 196; *Hongse zaofan bao* [Red Rebel Paper] (Lhasa), September 9, 1967, in *SCMP-S*, No. 231; and "Selected Edition on Liu Shaoqi's Crimes," April 1967, in *SCMM*, No. 651.

79. See Chang, *Power*, p. 140; and *Nongcun qingnian* [Rural Youth], December 10, 1967, in *SCMM*, No. 626.

80. Radio Guiyang, June 17, 23, July 7, November 29, 1967, in *NFCPRS*, Nos. 212, 213, 215, 236.

81. *Hongqi bao* [Red Flag Paper] (Beijing), May 22, 1967, in *SCMP-S*, No. 210.

82. Other works appearing in this period allegedly in support of Peng were histories of the revolution in Jiangxi and the Pingjiang uprising, and the film "Wave of Anger" which also dealt with the Pingjiang uprising. See *CNA*, No. 685 (1967), p. 6; *Jiefangjun wenyi* [Liberation Army Literature and Art], September 10, 1967, in *SCMM*, No. 608; and *Xin huagong bao*, January 13, 1968, in *SCMP*, No. 4112.

83. Radio Chengdu, September 6, 1967, in *NFCPRS*, No. 224; and Rice, *Mao's Way*, pp. 185–86.

84. *Jinjun bao* [Forward March Bulletin] (Beijing), May 31, 1967, in *SCMP-S*, No. 194; *CB*, No. 851, pp. 14–15; and *Peking Review*, August 18, 1967.

85. "Liu Shaoqi's Reactionary Speeches," April 1967, in *SCMM-S*, No. 25; and *Gedi tongxun* [Correspondence from All Parts of the Country] (Dalian), September 13, 1967, in *SCMP*, No. 4081.

86. As trans. in Solomon, *Mao's Revolution*, p. 429.

87. Radio Chengdu, September 23, 1967, in *NFCPRS*, No. 226; and above, p. 33–34.

88. *GMRB*, August 9, 1967, in *SCMP*, No. 4014; and *Tiyu zhanxian* [Physical Culture Front], May 18, 1967, in *SCMP*, No. 4001.

89. *MP*, p. 117.

Chapter 11

1. "Speech at the Tenth Plenum," in *CLG*, Winter 1968–69, pp. 90, 92.

2. See *SXWS*, II, 435; and above, p. 15n.

3. See especially the sophisticated study by Richard Baum, *Prelude to Revolution: Mao, the Party, and the Peasant Question, 1962–66* (New York: Columbia University Press, 1975).

4. The best examples of this interpretation are Ahn, "Ideology," pp. 372–429; and Merle Goldman, "The Chinese Communist Party's 'Cultural Revolution' of 1962–64," in

Chalmers Johnson, ed., *Ideology and Politics in Contemporary China* (Seattle: University of Washington Press, 1973).

5. See Teiwes, "Chinese Politics," Part I, pp. 10–12; and *SXWS*, II, 660, 664.

6. See Walker, "Collectivisation," pp. 32–33; and above, pp. 90, 269n.

7. *MP*, p. 117; Ch'en, *Mao*, p. 96; Edgar Snow, *The Long Revolution* (New York: Random House, 1971), p. 17; and Joffe, *Between Plenums*, p. 58.

8. See *MMT*, II, 349; and "Three Trials of Pickpocket Wang Guangmei" (Red Guard pamphlet), in *CB*, No. 848.

9. For an extended analysis, see Graham Young and Dennis Woodward, "Chinese Conceptions of the Nature of Class Struggle within the Socialist Transition," in Marian Sawer, ed., *Socialism and the New Class: Towards the Analysis of Structural Inequality within Socialist Societies* (Adelaide: APSA Monograph Series, 1978), pp. 35–38.

10. "On Khrushchov's Phoney Communism and Its Historical Lessons for the World" (July 1964), in A. Doak Barnett, *China after Mao* (Princeton: Princeton University Press, 1967), pp. 184–91.

11. *Main Documents of the First Session of the Third National People's Congress of the People's Republic of China* (Beijing: Foreign Languages Press, 1965), p. 15; and Teiwes, "Chinese Politics," Part II, p. 7.

12. See Teiwes, "Chinese Politics," Part II, pp. 5–6, 14–15; Ahn, "Ideology," pp. 371–72, 393, 424–25; and *CNA*, No. 618 (1966), p. 2.

13. See Ahn, "Ideology," pp. 332–72, 480–81; Teiwes, "Chinese Politics," Part II, pp. 9–11; *MMT*, II, 351–55; and above, p. 388n.

14. E.g., *RMRB*, July 19, 1967, in *SCMP*, No. 3996.

15. See *MU*, pp. 201, 209; Donald J. Munro, "Maxims and Realities in China's Educational Policy: The Half-Work, Half-study Model," *Asian Survey*, April 1967, pp. 258–64; Teiwes, "Chinese Politics," Part II, p. 15; and Ahn, "Ideology," pp. 354–65.

16. See Ahn, "Ideology," pp. 243ff., 300ff.; Gittings, Role, 195–97; CNA, No. 661 (1967), pp. 3–5; RMRB, August 13, 1967, in *SCMP*, No. 4015; and above, pp. 334–35, 388n.

17. See Teiwes, "Chinese Politics," Part II, pp. 4, 6.

18. For possible indications of ill health, see Solomon, *Mao's Revolution*, p. 457; and Moody, *Eighth Central Committee*, p. 179.

19. "Selected Edition on Liu Shaoqi's Crimes," April 1967, in *SCMM*, No. 653; Chang, *Power*, p. 174; and *Geming gongren bao* [Revolutionary Workers' News] (Beijing), January 12, 1967, in *SCMP-S*, No. 167.

20. *Jinggangshan* (Beijing), May 25, 1967, in *SCMP*, No. 3996; *Hongse wenyi* [Red Literature and Art] (Beijing), May 20, 1967, in *SCMP-S*, No. 190; "A Collection of Zhou Yang's Counterrevolutionary Revisionist Speeches" (Red Guard pamphlet), in *SCMM*, No. 648; Ahn, "Ideology," p. 393; and below, p. 461.

21. See Chiang Ch'ing (Jiang Qing), "Speech at the Enlarged Meeting of the MAC," April 12, 1967, in *Issues & Studies*, July 1970; *SCMP-S*, No. 192, p. 8; and Dittmer, *Liu*, pp. 49, 60–66. Jiang Qing's own account of her career, as told in Witke, *Chiang*, clearly suggests that she often acted on her own. Unfortunately, Jiang was not very forthcoming about events in the crucial period just before the Cultural Revolution.

22. *Zhanbao* [Battle News] (Beijing), February 24, 1967, in *SCMP-S*, No. 175; *MMT*, II, 359–60, 403; *MP*, p. 99; and Teiwes, "Chinese Politics," Part II, pp. 3–4.

23. *MMT*, II, 412; *SXWS*, II, 479; *China Notes*, No. 158 (1966); and above, p. 33–34.

24. Lieberthal, *Research Guide*, pp. 189, 191; Baum, *Prelude*, p. 205; and Whyte, *Small Groups*, pp. 73–76, 174–76.

25. *Peking Review*, No. 39 (1962); and *SXWS*, II, 431 (emphasis added).

26. *SXWS*, II, 434.

27. *Ibid.*, pp. 434–36; and above, p. 381.

28. Trans. in C.S. Chen, ed., *Rural People's Communes in Lien-chiang* (Stanford: Hoover Institution Press, 1969).

29. For accounts of conditions in Lianjiang, see Baum and Teiwes, "Cadre Question," pp. 325–26; Ahn, "Ideology," pp. 244–47; Chen, "Individual Farming"; and Harry Harding Jr., "The Organizational Issue in Chinese Politics, 1959–72," Ph.D. dissertation, Stanford University, 1974, pp. 123–25.

30. Chen, "Individual Farming," pp. 787–88; Neuhauser, "Party in the 1960s," pp. 10–11; *CNA*, No. 632 (1966), p. 4; and *HQ*, January 23, 1963, in *SCMM*, No. 353. The references to beatings and deaths in the Lianjiang documents (Chen, *Rural Communes*, pp. 167–68) are ambiguous and may apply only to ordinary peasants. It is likely, however, that some cadres were also subjected to such treatment.

31. *SC*, pp. 13–14, 65; Vogel, *Canton*, p. 306; *RMRB*, December 10, 1962, January 11, March 26, 1963; *NFRB*, January 25, May 1, 1963; *CNA*, No. 632 (1966), p. 4; and above, pp. 363–64.

32. See Baum, *Prelude*, pp. 17, 20; and *SC*, p. 70.

33. *SC*, pp. 58–59.

34. *SC*, pp. 60–61, 66; and *MMT*, II, 314.

35. *SC*, pp. 65–67; and *MMT*, II, 315, 322.

36. *MMT*, II, 322; and *SC*, pp. 67–69.

37. *SC*, pp. 62, 64–65.

38. *SC*, pp. 66–67; and *MMT*, II, 314, 316.

39. *SC*, pp. 67, 70; and *MMT*, II, 314, 317.

40. *SC*, p. 69; Dittmer, "Line Struggle," p. 700n; above, p. 356; and below, pp. 421–22.

41. *SC*, pp. 61, 69–70.

42. *CNA*, No. 487 (1963), p. 5; *Peng Zhen fangeming xiuzhengzhuyi yanlun zhaibian* [Excerpts from Peng Zhen's Counterrevolutionary Revisionist Speeches] (Red Guard pamphlet), May 1967, pp. 19–20; Radio Chengdu, October 26, 1967, in *NFCPRS*, No. 231; Baum, *Prelude*, pp. 35–37, 41; and Radio Guangzhou, October 26, 1967, in *NFCPRS*, No. 231.

43. See Baum, *Prelude*, pp. 28–42.

44. *Ibid.*, p. 36.

45. *RMRB*, May 20, 25, June 2, 4, 18, 1963; and *HQ*, No. 13–14 (1963).

46. *HQ*, No. 13–14 (1963); and above, p. 355.

47. *RMRB*, June 2, 1963 (cited in Baum, *Prelude*, p. 34).

48. *SC*, p. 72; Whyte, *Small Groups*, pp. 144–45; and Baum, *Prelude*, pp. 37–38.

49. *Dongfanghong*, May 7, 1967.

50. "Three Trials of Wang," in *CB*, No. 848; and *Collected Works of Liu 1958–67*, p. 362.

51. *MMT*, II, 340, 348. Cf. Baum, *Prelude*, p. 63.

52. *SC*, pp. 67–69, 75, 80, 85–90. The projection for disciplinary action was slightly higher at 2 percent compared to 1 percent in May.

53. See Baum, *Prelude*, pp. 57–58.

54. *SC*, p. 73 (emphasis added).

55. *SC*, pp. 77.

56. For a detailed discussion, see Baum, *Prelude*, pp. 48–52.

57. *SC*, pp. 59–60, 76–77.

58. *SC*, pp. 64–65, 81–82.

59. *SC*, p. 85.

60. *SC*, pp. 67, 74, 86–87.

61. *SC*, pp. 75–76; and above, pp. 68–69.

62. *SC*, p. 76 (emphasis added).

63. *Ibid.*

64. See Richard Baum, "Ideology Redivivus," *Problems of Communism*, May–June 1967.

65. *MP*, p. 98; *MMT*, II, 337–38, 356.

66. *MMT*, II, 342, 386–87, 404; and Tang Tsou, "Mao Tse-tung Thought, the Last Struggle for Succession, and the Post-Mao Era," *CQ*, No. 71 (1977), p. 520.

67. *SC*, pp. 23–25; and *NFRB*, December 14, 28, 1963, August 12, 1964.

68. *SC*, pp. 77–78; Baum, *Prelude*, pp. 67–68; Frederick Yu, "With Banners and Drums: The Mass Campaign in China's Drive for Development," *Current Scene*, May 1, 1966, pp. 7–9; Radio Changsha, December 27–28, 1963, in *NFCPRS*, No. 39; and Radio Xi'an, January 11, 13, 1964, in *NFCPRS*, No. 41.

69. For references to this designation, see Baum, *Prelude*, p. 76; and Radio Guangzhou, December 6, 1967, in *NFCPRS*, No. 237. The following discussion is primarily drawn from accounts relying on refugee sources: Baum, *Prelude*, pp. 68–76, 185–87; Ahn, "Ideology," pp. 259–62; and Whyte, *Small Groups*, pp. 147–50.

70. See Baum, *Prelude*, pp. 62, 72.

71. See *URS*, Vol. 34—No. 1, p. 7; *CNA*, No. 506 (1964), p. 1; and *China News Summary (CNS)*, January 23, 1964.

72. *SC*, p. 28; Radio Xi'an, June 29, 1964, in *NFCPRS*, No. 63; *ZGQN*, August 6, 1964; and Radio Guangzhou, September 3, 1964, in *NFCPRS*, No. 73.

73. See, e.g., Radio Guangzhou, October 26, 1967, in *NFCPRS*, No. 231; Radio Chengdu, December 8, 1967, in *NFCPRS*, No. 237; Teng Hsiao-p'ing, "Self-Criticism at the Central Work Conference on October 23, 1966," in *CLG*, Winter 1970–71; and below, pp. 416ff.

74. Ahn, "Ideology," p. 271; and "Three Trials of Wang," in *CB*, No. 848. A refugee source supports Wang's claim; Baum, *Prelude*, p. 190.

75. For extensive Chinese accounts, see *RMRB*, September 6, 1967, in *SCMP*, No. 4024; and *Zhengfa gongshe* (Beijing), No. 17 (1967), in *SCMP*, No. 3958. For an interpretative summary, see Baum, *Prelude*, pp. 84–89.

76. "Three Trials of Wang," in *CB*, No. 848; and Chang, *Power*, p. 249.

77. *MMT*, II, 337, 342, 351.

78. *SXWS*, II, 488; and *MU*, pp. 243–44.

79. *MU*, p. 217.

80. See "Krushchov's Phoney Communism," p. 183. For a case where Mao was more concerned with policy and ideological deviations, see *MU*, p. 216.

81. *MMT*, II, 358–60, 403–404; and *CB*, No. 888, p. 12.

82. As cited in the Revised Second Ten Points. *SC*, p. 104.

83. For another interpretation, see Baum, *Prelude*, pp. 78–81.

84. *Ibid.*, pp. 83–84, 89–90, 112–16; Ahn, "Ideology," pp. 264–65; *Sanfanfenzi Liu Shaoqi zui'oshi* [History of the Crimes of Three Anti Element Liu Shaoqi] (Red Guard pamphlet), May 1967, p. 46; "Selected Edition on Liu Shaoqi's Crimes," April 1967, in *SCMM*, No. 652; Radio Chengdu, October 3, 1967, in *NFCPRS*, No. 228; and Radio Guangzhou, October 26, 1967, in *NFCPRS*, No. 231.

85. Radio Guangzhou, October 26, 1967, in *NFCPRS*, No. 231; *8.13 Hongweibing* [August 13 Red Guards], May 13, 1967, in *SCMM*, No. 588; "Liu Shaoqi's Reactionary Speeches," April 1967, in *SCMM-S*, No. 25; "Selected Edition on Liu Shaoqi's Crimes," April 1967, in *SCMM*, No. 652; and "Down with Liu Shaoqi," May 1967, in *CB*, No. 834. Cf. Harding, "Organizational Issue," pp. 144–45; and Ahn, "Ideology," pp. 274–75.

86. Radio Guangzhou, October 26, 1967, in *FBIS*, No. 212 (1967).

87. "Liu Shaoqi's Reactionary Speeches," April 1967, in *SCMM-S*, No. 25; *8.13*

Hongweibing, May 13, 1967, in *SCMM,* No. 588; "Selected Edition on Liu Shaoqi's Crimes," April 1967, in *SCMM,* No. 652; Baum, *Prelude,* p. 91; and above, pp. 408–10.

88. "Selected Edition on Liu Shaoqi's Crimes," April 1967, in *SCMM,* No. 652; "Liu Shaoqi's Reactionary Speeches," April 1967, in *SCMM-S,* No. 25; and *8.13 Hongweibing,* May 13, 1967, in *SCMM,* No. 588.

89. "Selected Edition on Liu Shaoqi's Crimes," April 1967, in *SCMM,* No. 652; "Down with Liu Shaoqi," May 1967, in *CB,* No. 834; and above, p. 356.

90. *Sanfanfenzi Liu,* May 1967, p. 47; and NCNA, Beijing, August 30, 1967, in *SCMP,* No. 4014.

91. "Three Trials of Wang," in *CB,* No. 848, Baum, *Prelude,* pp. 98–99; *SC,* p. 104; and above, p. 417.

92. *SC,* pp. 104–107.

93. *SC,* pp. 109–110.

94. *SC,* p. 112.

95. *SC,* pp. 103, 108.

96. *SC,* p. 115.

97. *SC,* pp. 86, 112–14; and Baum, *Prelude,* p. 92. Actually, the disciplinary impact of the 1964 document was implicitly harsher since its 2 percent limit referred to "punishment such as expulsion from the Party or dismissal from administrative positions" while the 1963 version simply spoke of "punishment," presumably including lesser sanctions.

98. *SC,* p. 112.

99. *SC,* p.106 (emphasis added).

100. *SC,* pp. 106–107, 111.

101. *SC,* pp. 91, 103, 112–13, 116.

102. See *Dou-pi-gai,* May 15, 1967, in *SCMM-S,* No. 19; "Down with Du Zhengxiang, Top Party Powerholder and Capitalist Roader in the Guangzhou Municipal Finance and Trade System" (Red Guard pamphlet), May 15, 1967, in *SCMM,* No. 628; Radio Chengdu, October 3, 1967, in *NFCPRS,* No. 228, and Whyte, *Small Groups,* pp. 74–76.

103. *RMRB,* October 29, 1964.

104. *NFRB,* October 14, December 23, 26, 1964.

105. Radio Tianjin, December 19, 1964, in *NFCPRS,* No. 88; Radio Nanchang, December 18, 1964, in *CNS,* No. 48; and *RMRB,* December 4, 1964.

106. E.g., *NFRB,* November 9, 1964; and Radio Wuhan, November 10, 11, 23, 1964, in *CNS,* No. 47.

107. *8.13 Hongweibing,* May 13, 1967, in *SCMM,* No. 588; "Tao Zhu Is the Khrushchev of Central-South China" (Red Guard pamphlet), Guangzhou, January 14, 1967, in *CB,* No. 824; and Baum, *Prelude,* pp. 107–108.

108. "Tao Is Khrushchev," January 14, 1967, in *CB,* No. 824; Radio Guangzhou, October 26, November 21, 1967, in *NFCPRS,* Nos. 231, 235; and Baum, *Prelude,* pp. 108–110.

109. Radio Guangzhou, November 21, 1967, in *NFCPRS,* No. 235; *RMRB,* November 20, December 25, 1964; Baum, *Prelude,* pp. 108–109; Whyte, *Small Groups,* pp. 159–160; Vogel, *Canton,* p. 317; and Richard Curt Kraus, "Class Conflict and the Vocabulary of Social Analysis in China," *CQ,* No. 69 (1977), pp. 60–61.

110. "Tao Is Khrushchev," January 14, 1967, in *CB,* No. 824; Radio Guangzhou, November 21, 1967, in *NFCPRS,* No. 235; Radio Wuhan, March 10, 1968, in *FBIS,* No. 50 (1968); Baum, *Prelude,* pp. 109–11, 195; and Whyte, *Small Groups,* pp. 159–60.

111. NCNA, Beijing, April 18, 1967, in *SCMP,* No. 3924; "Peng Zhen's Towering Crimes," June 10, 1967, in *SCMM,* No. 639; Radio Wuhan, March 10, 1968, in *FBIS,* No. 50 (1968); and *Dongfanghong,* May 7, 1967.

112. Radio Zhengzhou, December 12, 1967 (cited in Baum, *Prelude*, p. 194). Cf. *ibid.*, pp. 103–104, 205; and above, pp. 117–19.

113. Radio Xi'an, February 24, 1965, in *NFCPRS*, No. 96; *NFRB*, October 14, 1964, June 4, 1965; and Whyte, *Small Groups*, p. 160.

114. *8.13 Hongweibing*, May 13, 1967, in *SCMM*, Nos. 583, 588.

115. *8.13 Hongweibing*, May 13, 1967, in *SCMM*, No. 583; and *MMT*, II, 412. Mao also listed Anhui, Qinghai and Gansu as "rotten," while noting serious problems in Yunnan.

116. Radio Guiyang, June 3, 4, 1967, in *NFCPRS*, No. 210; Radio Chengdu, August 31, 1967, in *NFCPRS*, No. 223; and Teiwes, *Provincial Personnel*, p. 35. The evidence is less clear concerning the other provinces cited by Mao (see n. 115, this chapter), but there is some indication of limited personnel movement in each case.

117. *Dou-pi-gai*, May 15, 1967, in *SCMM-S*, No. 19; "Record of Deng's Reactionary Utterances," April 1967, in *SCMP-S*, No. 208; and Victor Nee with Don Layman, *The Cultural Revolution at Peking University* (New York: Monthly Review Press, 1969), pp. 42–44.

118. "Peng Zhen's Towering Crimes," June 10, 1967, in *SCMM*, No. 639; *Zhanbao* (Beijing), February 24, 1967, in *SCMP-S*, No. 175; *Xin Beida* [New Beijing University], June 14, 1967; and "Liu Shaoqi's Reactionary Speeches," April 1967, in *SCMM-S*, No. 25.

119. *MMT*, I, 351, 354; and Baum, *Prelude*, pp. 117, 196.

120. Baum, *Prelude*, pp. 117–19; *HQ*, No. 12 (1967), in *SCMM*, No. 589; and Mitch Meisner, "Dazhai: the Mass Line in Practice," *Modern China*, January 1978, pp. 50–54.

121. Baum, *Prelude*, pp. 120–22; and *HQ*, No. 5 (1967), in *SCMM*, No. 572.

122. *MMT*, II, 414–17, 440 (emphasis added); and *SC*, pp. 121, 123–24.

123. *SC*, pp. 123–24; and *MMT*, II, 417, 426.

124. *MMT*, II, 417.

125. *Collected Works of Liu 1958–67*, pp. 362–63.

126. *MMT*, II, 437–39, 441–44; *SC*, pp. 121–22, 125–26; and above, p. 427.

127. *MMT*, II, 430, 442–43; and *SC*, pp. 124–25.

128. *MMT*, II, 417. See also *ibid.*, p. 414.

129. *Ibid.*, p. 444.

130. *Ibid.*, p. 441.

131. *SC*, p. 121.

132. *SC*, pp. 119–120.

133. *Ibid.*

134. *SC*, p. 120.

135. *Ibid.*; and *MMT*, II, 411–12, 418–19.

136. *SC*, pp. 121, 125; and *Documents of Third NPC*, p. 19.

137. *SC*, pp. 118–19, 122, 124.

138. The Chinese text of the Twenty-three Articles has approximately 5,600 characters compared to approximately 10,000 characters in the First Ten Points, 19,000 in the Second Ten Points, and 20,000 in the Revised Second Ten Points.

139. Radio Wuhan, April 24, 1968, in *FBIS*, Nos. 82–83 (1968).

140. See Snow, *Long Revolution*, p. 17; and Chang, *Power*, p. 250. Cf. above, p. 384.

141. *MMT*, II, 415, 422; *Sanfanfenzi Liu*, May 1967, p. 48; Snow, *Long Revolution*, p. 17; and *Documents of Third NPC*, pp. 31, 68.

142. *Geming gongren bao* [Revolutionary Workers' News] (Beijing), January 12, 1967, in *SCMP-S*, No. 167; *Documents of Third NPC*, pp. 26–27, 69, 76; *MMT*, II, 412, 430–32; Klein and Clark, *Biographic Dictionary*, I, 539–40; and above, p. 394n.

143. "Peng Zhen's Towering Crimes," June 10, 1967, in *SCMM*, No. 639; and "Three Trials of Wang," in *CB*, No. 848.

144. Only one comment by Mao concerning socialist education in 1965 following the Twenty-three Articles has been located, a passing reference in June. *MP*, p. 101.

145. *Keji hongqi* [Science and Technology Red Flag] (Beijing), March 26, 1967, in *SCMP-S*, No. 181; Radio Guangzhou, October 26, 1967, in *NFCPRS*, No. 231; *Wenge pinglun* [Cultural Revolution Comment], January 1968, in *SCMP*, No. 4126; Radio Huhehot, June 26, 1968, in *FBIS*, No. 137 (1968); and *Peng Zhen fangeming*, p. 24.

146. *Wanshan hongpian*, April 1967, in *SCMM-S*, No. 33; and *Peng Zhen fangeming*, pp. 17–18.

147. *Peng Zhen fangeming*, pp. 18, 20–22, 24–26; "Peng Zhen's Towering Crimes," June 10, 1967, in *SCMM*, No. 639; and *WHB* (Shanghai), May 15, 1968, in *SCMP*, No. 4203.

148. *Dongfanghong*, February 15, 1967, in *CB*, No. 878; Whyte, *Small Groups*, p. 76; *CNA*, No. 561 (1965), p. 6; *NFRB*, February 19, April 16, June 4, 1965; Radio Xi'an, February 24, 1965, in *NFCPRS*, No. 96; Radio Nanning, March 10, 1965, in *NFCPRS*, No. 98; and *RMRB*, May 21, 1965.

149. *Peng Zhen fangeming*, pp. 19, 25.

150. "Peng Zhen's Towering Crimes," June 10, 1967, in *SCMM*, No. 639; Radio Guiyang, June 3, 4, 25, 29, 1967, in *NFCPRS*, Nos. 210, 213, 214; and Radio Chengdu, August 31, 1967, in *NFCPRS*, No. 223.

151. *SC*, p. 126; *Peng Zhen fangeming*, p. 23; *Sanfanfenzi Liu*, p. 66; and *Gong-nong-bing*, September 1967, in *SCMM-S*, No. 27.

152. Nee with Layman, *Peking University*, pp. 42–44; *Hongqi zhanbao* [Red Flag Combat Bulletin] (Beijing), December 1, 1966, in *SCMP-S*, No. 162; and *Deng Xiaoping fandang fan shehuizhuyi fan Mao Zedong sixiang de yanlun zhaibian* [Excerpts from Deng Xiaoping's Anti-Party, Anti-Socialist, Anti-Mao Zedong's Thought Speeches] (Red Guard pamphlet), April 1967, p. 32.

153. *Peng Zhen fangeming*, pp. 20, 23–24; *Hongweibing zhanbao* [Red Guard Combat Bulletin], February 16, 1967; Radio Guangzhou, December 6, 1967, in *NFCPRS*, No. 237; Radio Kunming, April 28, 1965, in *NFCPRS*, No. 105; and *SC*, pp. 121, 125.

154. *SC*, pp. 120–21; and *RMRB*, May 21, October 10, 1965.

155. *Peng Zhen fangeming*, p. 27; Radio Chengdu, September 12, 1967, in *NFCPRS*, No. 225; "Down with Du Zhengxiang," May 15, 1967, in *SCMM*, No. 628; *CNA*, No. 637 (1966), p. 6; *NFRB*, March 22, 1965, in *SCMP*, No. 3447; and *Xiaobing* [Young Fighters] (Guangzhou), February 25, 1967, in *SCMM*, No. 575.

156. Article XVI, "The Four Cleanups Must Rest Firmly on Construction," *SC*, p. 125.

157. The most complete collection, *SXWS*, II, 614–24, contains only three short statements from the Chairman for the period from February through November 1965. A few other brief comments are available in other sources.

158. *MP*, pp. 100–102; *SXWS*, II, 621; Edgar Snow, "Interview with Mao," in Franz Schurmann and Orville Schell, eds., *The China Reader: Communist China* (New York: Random House, 1967), pp. 374–75; and Joffe, *Between Plenums*, p. 58.

159. For detailed accounts of these developments, see Joseph Simon, "Ferment among the Intellectuals," *Problems of Communism*, September-October 1964; Stephen Uhalley, Jr., "The Controversy over Li Hsiu-cheng: An Ill Timed Centenary," *Journal of Asian Studies*, February 1966; Guy Alitto, "Thought Reform in Communist China: The Case of Chou Ku-ch'eng," M.A. thesis, University of Chicago, 1966; Byung-joon Ahn, "The Politics of Peking Opera, 1962–1965," *Asian Survey*, December 1972; Donald J. Munro, "The Yang Hsien-chen Affair," *CQ*, No. 22 (1965); Adam Oliver, "Rectification of Mainland China Intellectuals, 1964–1965," *Asian Survey*, October 1965; and "Chairman Mao and the Heretics: Peking's 'Great Debate,' " *Current Scene*, February 15, 1965.

160. See especially Chou Yang, *The Fighting Task Confronting Workers in Philosophy and the Social Sciences* (Beijing: Foreign Languages Press, 1963).

161. *HQ*, No. 1 (1967), in *SCMM*, No. 559.

162. Witke, *Chiang*, pp. 297ff.; Dittmer, *Liu*, p. 60; *Issues & Studies*, 1970, pp. 87–88; and "Selected Edition on Liu Shaoqi's Crimes," April 1967, in *SCMM*, No. 651.

163. Witke, *Chiang*, pp. 7, 158–59, 232–44, 311, 318; Dittmer, *Liu*, p. 60; and *Jinggangshan* (Beijing), May 25, 1967, in *SCMP*, No. 3996.

164. Witke, *Chiang*, pp. 224, 226, 240, 301; "A Collection of Zhou Yang's Counter-revolutionary Revisionist Speeches" (Red Guard pamphlet), in *SCMM*, No. 648; and below, p. 461.

165. *A Great Revolution on the Cultural Front* (Beijing: Foreign Languages Press, 1965), pp. 3–5, 8–9, 11, 15–19, 30, 34, 56, 59, 81–82; NCNA, Beijing, May 9, 1967, in *SCMP*, No. 3938; Witke, *Chiang*, pp. 311, 313–14; Ahn, "Ideology," pp. 388–90; and *Jinggangshan* (Beijing), May 25, 1967, in *SCMP*, No. 3996.

166. *MMT*, I, 349; Vogel, *Canton*, pp. 308–310; and *CNA*, No. 464 (1963).

167. See Goldman, "Cultural Revolution," pp. 221–32.

168. Chou, *Fighting Task*, especially pp. 1–4, 8, 24, 45–46, 56, 59–61, 67; *MP*, p. 89; and *SCMP-S*, No. 191, p. 23.

169. *MP*, p. 286.

170. *Wenyi hongqi* [Literature and Art Red Flag] (Beijing), May 30, 1967, in *SCMP*, No. 4000. For a different interpretation, see Goldman, "Cultural Revolution," pp. 235–37.

171. Ahn, "Ideology," pp. 383–84; Simmonds, *Evolution*, p. 53; Goldman, "Cultural Revolution," p. 237; and *Great Revolution*, p. 53.

172. NCNA, Beijing, May 4, 1967, in *SCMP*, No. 3935; *GMRB*, May 10, 1967, in *SCMP*, No. 3952; and Goldman, "Cultural Revolution," p. 232.

173. *MP*, p. 97 (emphasis in the original).

174. See Chang, *Power*, p. 251; Ahn, "Ideology," pp. 397–404; Alitto, "Thought Reform," p. 101; Goldman, "Cultural Revolution," pp. 242–48; and *GMRB*, November 7, 1964, in *CB*, No. 750.

175. *RMRB*, October 27, 1966, in *SCMP*, No. 3818; and *Great Revolution*, pp. 21, 53.

176. See Ahn, "Ideology," pp. 397–99; Goldman, "Cultural Revolution," pp. 249–52; *RMRB*, September 22, October 27, 1966, in *CB*, No. 812, *SCMP*, No. 3818; and *Wanshan hongpian*, April 1967, in *SCMM-S*, No. 33.

177. Goldman, "Cultural Revolution," pp. 220, 249; and *GMRB*, June 2, 1967, in *SCMP*, No. 3959.

178. *MMT*, II, 354; and *MU*, p. 216 (emphasis added).

179. *CNA*, No. 561 (1965), p. 3; *JPRS*, No. 49826, p. 11; and *Summary of the Forum on the Work in Literature and Art in the Armed Forces with Which Comrade Lin Piao Entrusted Comrade Chiang Ching* (Beijing: Foreign Languages Press, 1968), pp. 7, 21–22.

180. See Goldman, "Cultural Revolution," pp. 243–46; Alitto, "Thought Reform," pp. 99–100, 115; and *GMRB*, December 18, 1966, in *SCMP*, No. 3853.

181. *HQ*, No. 1 (1967), in *SCMM*, No. 559; *Wanshan hongpian*, April 1967, in *SCMM-S*, No. 33; *Hongqi zhanbao* (Beijing), December 1, 1966, in *SCMP-S*, No. 162; and *Sanfanfenzi Liu*, p. 48.

182. *CNA*, No. 635 (1966), p. 6; *CNS*, No. 110 (1966); Ahn, "Ideology," pp. 406–409; and Goldman, "Cultural Revolution," pp. 250–53.

183. See Simmonds, *Evolution*, pp. 76–79; and Lieberthal, *Research Guide*, pp. 228–31.

184. Rice, *Mao's Way*, p. 228; Dorrill, *Power*, pp. 81–84; and Ch'en, *Mao*, pp. 96–97.

185. "A Letter from Comrade Tao Zhu to Members of Four Cleanups Work Teams"

(Red Guard pamphlet), in *CB*, No. 830; *CNA*, No. 608 (1966), pp. 4–6; and *RMRB*, October 17, 1965, in *SCMP*, No. 3572.

186. *RMRB*, October 12, 1965, in *CB*, No. 779; and *CNA*, No. 605 (1966).

187. *RMRB*, November 17, 1965, January 17, February 1, 1966, in *SCMP*, Nos. 3596, 3628, 3640; *CB*, No. 779, pp. 4–6, 10, 25; and Harding, "Organizational Issue," pp. 182, 193, 220.

188. "Letter from Tao," in *CB*, No. 830; *CB*, No. 779, pp. 15, 24, 27, 41; and Harding, "Organizational Issue," p. 178.

189. *CNA*, No. 605 (1966), p. 3; *RMRB*, October 10, December 14, 1965, February 7, 1966, in *CNS*, No. 90, *SCMP*, No. 3609, and *URS*, Vol. 42—No. 18; *Yangcheng wanbao* [Yangcheng Evening Paper] *(YCWB)* (Guangzhou), December 2, 1965, in *SCMP*, No. 3600; *CB*, No. 779, pp. 30, 47–48, 53; and Harding, "Organizational Issue," p. 194.

190. *CNA*, No. 605 (1966), p. 5; *CB*, No. 779, pp. 44–45; and Harding, "Organizational Issue," pp. 193–94.

191. *RMRB*, March 26, 1964; *SC*, pp. 43–44; Radio Changsha, February 1, 1966, in *URS*, vol. 42—No. 12; and Harding, "Organizational Issue," pp. 195–98.

192. *YCWB*, September 8, 1965, in *SCMP*, No. 3540; Radio Changsha, February 1, 1966, in *URS*, Vol. 42—No. 12; and *Sanfanfenzi Liu*, pp. 49–50.

193. E.g., Rice, *Mao's Way*, ch. 15.

194. *RMRB*, November 30, 1965, in *Case of Peng*, pp. 235–61; "Peng Zhen's Towering Crimes," in *SCMM*, No. 640; Rice, *Mao's Way*, p. 232; Ch'en, *Mao*, p. 106; and *Dongfanghong* (Beijing), February 18, 1967, in *SCMP*, No. 3903.

195. "Peng Zhen's Towering Crimes," in *SCMM*, Nos. 639–40; *Issues & Studies*, July 1970, p. 88; and above, pp. 330, 381.

196. "Peng Zhen's Towering Crimes," in *SCMM*, Nos. 639–40; and Ch'en, *Mao*, p. 109.

197. "Peng Zhen's Towering Crimes," in *SCMM*, No. 640; and Rice, *Mao's Way*, p. 239.

198. "Peng Zhen's Towering Crimes," in *SCMM*, No. 640.

199. See Radio Zhengzhou, April 9, 1968, in *FBIS*, No. 71 (1968); and Whyte, *Small Groups*, pp. 79–80.

200. For a detailed discussion, see Baum, *Prelude*, pp. 149ff.

201. See *ibid.*, p. 203.

202. Rice, *Mao's Way*, p. 237.

203. As trans. in Solomon, *Mao's Revolution*, p. 476.

Conclusion

1. Apart from the *sufan* campaign; see above, n. 3, Introduction to the First Edition.

2. On the other hand, in the more easily controlled urban areas even the harsh Three Anti and Anti-Rightist Campaigns were implemented through the regular chain of command. This, however, was probably due to the suspect nature of their major targets (see below). For other instances of implementing severe sanctions through the regular chain of command, see above, pp. 297–98, 339n.

3. While the 1951–54 movement involved instances of kicking aside village leaders and a comparatively high purge rate, official policy sought both to prevent the undermining of local cadres and to avoid severe struggle during the weeding out process. Similar phenomena also appeared during the 1960–61 campaign, but their extent is unclear. See above, pp. 117–19, 121–22, 361–64.

4. See MacFarquhar, *Origins 1*, pp. 241–49.

5. *SXWS*, II, 479.

6. *SW*, V, 343.

7. Cf. Michel C. Oksenberg, "Policy Making Under Mao, 1949–68: An Overview,"

in John M.H. Lindbeck, ed., *China: Management of a Revolutionary Society* (Seattle: University of Washington Press, 1971), p. 107.

8. According to Zhou Enlai, the purge rate for all Party members was less than 1 percent. Snow, *Long Revolution,* p. 157. Nevertheless, many more Party members suffered other sanctions and personal humiliation in 1966–68.

9. Gordon A. Bennett, "China's Continuing Revolution: Will it be Permanent?" *Asian Survey,* January 1970, p. 4.

10. See Thomas W. Robinson, "Chou En-lai and the Cultural Revolution," in Robinson, ed., *The Cultural Revolution in China* (Berkeley: University of California Press, 1971); Donald W. Klein and Lois B. Hager, "The Ninth Central committee," *CQ,* No. 45 (1971), pp. 39, 46; Dittmer, *Liu,* ch. 5; and above, pp. 27n, 395.

11. Graham Young, "Conceptions of Party Leadership in China: The Cultural Revolution and Party Building 1968–1971," Ph.D. dissertation, Flinders University of South Australia, 1978, pp. 385, 395–403, 454–63, 497–99.

12. See Michael Y.M. Kau, "Introduction," in Kau, ed., *The Lin Piao Affair* (White Plains: International Arts and Sciences Press, 1975); and Frederick C. Teiwes, *Provincial Leadership in China: The Cultural Revolution and Its Aftermath* (Ithaca: Cornell University East Asia Papers, 1974), pp. 76–78, 115–18, 121, 126–27.

13. For a summary of developments, see John Bryan Starr, "From the 10th Party Congress to the Premiership of Hua Kuo-feng: The Significance of the Colour of the Cat," *CQ,* No. 67 (1976), pp. 457–79.

14. *Peking Review,* No. 35–36 (1973), pp. 26–33.

15. Hong Yung Lee, "The Politics of Cadre Rehabilitation Since the Cultural Revolution," *Asian Survey,* September 1978, pp. 937, 945–48.

16. *Ibid.,* p. 951.

17. See Starr, "Colour of the Cat," pp. 462ff.; and Harry Harding, Jr., "China After Mao," *Problems of Communism,* March-April 1977, pp. 5–6.

18. See Harding, "After Mao," p. 5; Kenneth Lieberthal, "The Politics of Modernization in the PRC," *Problems of Communism,* May-June 1978, p. 4; and Lee, "Cadre Rehabilitation," pp. 949–50.

19. See Starr, "Colour of the Cat," pp. 475–79; Harding, "After Mao," p. 6; Jürgen Domes, "The 'Gang of Four' and Hua Kuo-feng: Analysis of Political Events in 1975–76," *CQ,* No. 71 (1977), pp. 482ff.; and Parris H. Chang, "Mao's Last Stand?" *Problems of Communism,* July-August 1976, pp. 11–12.

20. Andres D. Onate, "Hua Kuo-feng and the Arrest of the 'Gang of Four,' " *CQ,* No. 75 (1978), especially p. 564.

21. For interpretations placing somewhat greater weight on policy differences and maneuvering among top leaders, see Lieberthal, "Politics of Modernization"; and Earl A. Wayne, "The Politics of Restaffing China's Provinces: 1976–77," *Contemporary China,* Spring 1978.

22. Cf. Harry Harding, "China: The First Year without Mao," *Contemporary China,* Spring 1978, p. 96; and Lieberthal, "Politics of Modernization," pp. 9–10, 16.

23. See Lee, "Cadre Rehabilitation," pp. 951–52; Lieberthal, "Politics of Modernization," p. 4; and *Peking Review,* No. 52 (1978), p. 14.

24. *Peking Review,* No. 35 (1977), pp. 33–34, No. 36 (1977), pp. 17, 24–25, 28–29, 31.

25. *Ibid.,* No. 35 (1977), pp. 36, 55, No. 36 (1977), pp. 27, 33.

26. *Ibid.,* No. 35 (1977), pp. 33, 44–45, No. 36 (1977), pp. 31, 34.

27. See *ibid.,* No. 36 (1977), p. 36; Lee, "Cadre Rehabilitation," p. 952; and *CNA,* Nos. 1110, 1116, 1123, 1137–38 (1978).

28. See Jerry F. Hough, "The Brezhnev Era: The Man and the System," *Problems of Communism,* March–April 1976, pp. 3–6, 13.

Selected Bibliography

Extensively Consulted Collections of CCP Newspapers, Journals and Radio Broadcasts

The following collections include major national and regional publications (see Abbreviations, above, pp. xi–xii, for a listing of the most important), as well as leading provincial newspapers and lesser official publications. Dates refer to the periods for which the collections were consulted.

China News Analysis. Hong Kong: 1953–78.

China News Summary. Hong Kong: U.K. Regional Information Office, 1964–76.

Chinese Law and Government. White Plains: International Arts and Sciences Press, 1968–78.

Current Background. Hong Kong: U.S. Consulate General, 1950–72.

Extracts from China Mainland Magazines. Hong Kong: U.S. Consulate General, 1955–60.

Foreign Broadcast Information Service: Communist China. Washington: 1966–72.

Joint Publications Research Service. Washington: 1957–74.

News from Chinese Provincial Radio Stations. Hong Kong: U.K. Regional Information Office, 1963–67.

Selections from China Mainland Magazines. Hong Kong: U.S. Consulate General, 1960–72.

Selections from China Mainland Magazines—Supplement. Hong Kong: U.S. Consulate General, 1965–1968.

Survey of China Mainland Press. Hong Kong: U.S. Consulate General, 1950–1972.

Survey of China Mainland Press—Supplement. Hong Kong: U.S. Consulate General, 1954–1955, 1960–1969.

Union Research Institute classified files. Press clippings from mainland newspapers and journals, 1949–67.

Union Research Service. Hong Kong: Union Research Institute, 1955–69.

Documentary Collections

A Great Revolution on the Cultural Front. 1964 documents on drama and opera reform. Beijing: Foreign Languages Press, 1965.

Collected Works of Liu Shao-ch'i. 3 vols., Hong Kong: Union Research Institute, 1968, 1969.

Communist China 1955–1959: Policy Documents with Analysis, with a foreword by Robert R. Bowie and John K. Fairbank. Cambridge: Harvard University Press, 1965.

Communist China: The Politics of Student Opposition, translated by Dennis J. Doolin. Student speeches and wall posters during the Hundred Flowers period. Stanford: The Hoover Institution, 1964.

Eighth National Congress of the Communist Party of China. 3 vols., Beijing: Foreign Languages Press, 1956.

Renmin shouce [People's Handbook]. Shanghai, Tianjin, Beijing: Dagong bao, 1950–53, 1955–65.

Mao, edited by Jerome Ch'en. Englewood Cliffs: Prentice-Hall, Inc., 1969.

Mao Papers: Anthology and Bibliography, edited by Jerome Ch'en. London: Oxford University Press, 1970.

Mao Tse-tung Unrehearsed, Talks and Letters: 1956–71, edited by Stuart Schram. Harmondsworth: Penguin Books, 1974.

Mao Zedong ji [Collected Works of Mao Zedong], edited by Takeuchi Minoru, *et al.* 10 vols., Tokyo: Hokubosha, 1970–72.

Mao Zedong sixiang wansui [Long Live Mao Zedong's Thought]. 2 vols., Taibei, 1967, 1969.

Mao's China: Party Reform Documents, 1942–44, translated by Boyd Compton. Seattle: University of Washington Press, 1966.

Miscellany of Mao Tse-tung Thought. 2 vols., *Joint Publications Research Service*, No. 61269, February 1974.

Bao'an tongxin [Bao'an Bulletin]. Internal documents of the Bao'an County, Guangdong, CCP Committee, September–December 1961. *Union Research Service*, Vol. 27—Nos. 7–9.

Rural People's Communes in Lien-chiang, edited by C.S. Chen. Internal documents of the Lianjiang County, Fujian, CCP Committee, February 1962–April 1963. Stanford: Hoover Institution Press, 1969.

Second Session of the Eighth National Congress of the Communist Party of China. Beijing: Foreign Languages Press, 1958.

Selected Works of Mao Tse-tung. 5 vols., Beijing: Foreign Languages Press, 1961, 1965, 1977.

Ssu-Ch'ing: The Socialist Education Movement of 1962–1966, by Richard Baum and Frederick C. Teiwes. Appendix documents on rural socialist education, 1962–65. Berkeley: China Research Monographs, 1968.

Summary of the Forum on the Work in Literature and Art in the Armed Forces with Which Comrade Lin Piao Entrusted Comrade Chiang Ching, February 1966. Beijing: Foreign Languages Press, 1968.

The Case of Peng Teh-huai 1959–1968. Hong Kong: Union Research Institute, 1968.

The Hundred Flowers, edited by Roderick MacFarquhar. London: Stevens & Sons, 1960.

The Politics of the Chinese Red Army: A Translation of the Bulletin of Activities of the People's Liberation Army, edited by J. Chester Cheng. Issues of the *Gongzuo tongxun*, January–August 1961. Stanford: Hoover Institution Publications, 1966.

Major CCP Documents and Speeches

Where more than one translation exists the most complete version is cited. Where the most complete version has been subsequently edited, both the (presumably) contemporary text and the more complete edited text are listed.

An Tzu-wen (An Ziwen). "Nationwide Struggle Against Bureaucratism, Commandism, and Violations of Law and Discipline." New China News Agency, Beijing, February 9, 1953. In *Survey of China Mainland Press*, No. 514.

Chang Po-chün (Zhang Bojun). "I Bow My Head and Admit My Guilt Before the People," July 1957. In *Communist China 1955–1959: Policy Documents with Analysis*, with a foreword by Robert R. Bowie and John K. Fairbank. Cambridge: Harvard University Press, 1965.

Chou En-lai (Zhou Enlai). "On the Question of Intellectuals," January 1956. In *Communist China 1955–1959: Policy Documents with Analysis*, with a foreword by Robert R. Bowie and John K. Fairbank. Cambridge: Harvard University Press, 1965.

———. "Report on the Work of the Government," June 1957. In *Communist China 1955–1959: Policy Documents with Analysis*, with a foreword by Robert R. Bowie and John K. Fairbank. Cambridge: Harvard University Press, 1965.

Chou Yang (Zhou Yang). *A Great Debate on the Literary Front*, March 1958. Beijing: Foreign Languages Press, 1965.

———. *The Fighting Task Confronting Workers in Philosophy and the Social Sciences*, October 1963. Beijing: Foreign Languages Press, 1963.

"Communique of the Third Plenary Session of the 11th Central Committee of The Communist Party of China," December 1978. In *Peking Review*, No. 52, 1978.

"Draft Directive on Some Problems in Current Rural Work" (First Ten Points), May 1963. In *Ssu-Ch'ing: The Socialist Education Movement of 1962–1966*, by Richard Baum and Frederick C. Teiwes. Berkeley: China Research Monographs, 1968.

"Fourth Plenary Session of the Seventh Central Committee of the CCP Issues Communique." New China News Agency, February 18, 1954. In *Survey of China Mainland Press*, No. 751.

Kung Tzu-jung (Gong Zirong). "Rectification Campaigns Are Powerful Magic Weapons." *Renmin ribao* article, January 5, 1961. In *Survey of China Mainland Press*, No. 2424.

Liu Shao-ch'i (Liu Shaoqi). "On the Intra-Party Struggle," July 1941. In *Mao's China: Party Reform Documents, 1942–44*, translated by Boyd Compton. Seattle: University of Washington Press, 1966.

———. "On the Party," May 1945. In *Collected Works of Liu Shao-ch'i, 1945–1957*. Hong Kong: Union Research Institute, 1969.

———. "P'ingshan Sets Examples in Land Reform and Party Rectification," February 1948. In *Collected Works of Liu Shao-ch'i, 1945–1957*. Hong Kong: Union Research Institute, 1969.

———. "Self-Criticism," October 1966. In *Collected Works of Liu Shao-ch'i, 1958–1967*. Hong Kong: Union Research Institute, 1968.

———. "Self-Cultivation in Organization and Discipline," July 1939. In *Chinese Law and Government*, Spring 1972.

———. "Speech at Meeting of Party Members and Cadres in Shanghai," April 1957. In *Selections from China Mainland Magazines—Supplement*, No. 35.

———. "Talk on the Question of Rectification among Trainees of the Higher Party

School," May 1957. In *Selections from China Mainland Magazines—Supplement*, No. 35.

———. "The Political Report of the Central Committee of the Communist Party of China to the Eighth National Congress of the Party," September 1956. In *Eighth National Congress of the Communist Party of China*, vol. I. Beijing: Foreign Languages Press, 1956.

———. "The Present Situation, the Party's General Line for Socialist Construction and Its Future Tasks," May 1958. In *Communist China 1955–1959: Policy Documents with Analysis*, with a foreword by Robert R. Bowie and John K. Fairbank. Cambridge: Harvard University Press, 1965.

———. "Training the Communist Party Member," August 1939. In *Mao's China: Party Reform Documents, 1942–44*, translated by Boyd Compton. Seattle: University of Washington Press, 1966. Also published as *How to Be a Good Communist*. Beijing: Foreign Languages Press, 1964.

Lo Lung-chi (Luo Longji). "My Preliminary Examination," July 1957. In *Communist China 1955–1959: Policy Documents with Analysis*, with a foreword by Robert R. Bowie and John K. Fairbank. Cambridge: Harvard University Press, 1965.

Lu Ting-i (Lu Dingyi). "Let a Hundred Flowers Blossom, a Hundred Schools of Thought Contend!" May 1956. In *Communist China 1955–1959: Policy Documents with Analysis*, with a foreword by Robert R. Bowie and John K. Fairbank. Cambridge: Harvard University Press, 1965.

Mao Tse-tung (Mao Zedong). "In Opposition to Party Formalism," February 1942. In *Mao's China: Party Reform Documents, 1942–44*, translated by Boyd Compton. Seattle: University of Washington Press, 1966.

———. "In Opposition to Several Incorrect Tendencies Within the Party," December 1929. In *Mao's China: Party Reform Documents, 1942–44*, translated by Boyd Compton. Seattle: University of Washington Press, 1966.

———. "On Contradiction," August 1937. In *Selected Works of Mao Tse-tung*, vol. I. Beijing: Foreign Languages Press, 1965.

———. "On the Correct Handling of Contradictions among the People," June 1957. In *Communist China 1955–1959: Policy Documents with Analysis*, with a foreword by Robert R. Bowie and John K. Fairbank. Cambridge: Harvard University Press, 1965.

———. "On the Ten Great Relationships," April 1956. In *Mao*, edited by Jerome Ch'en. Englewood Cliffs: Prentice-Hall, 1969.

———. "Reform in Learning, the Party, and Literature," February 1942. In *Mao's China: Party Reform Documents, 1942–44*, translated by Boyd Compton. Seattle: University of Washington Press, 1966.

———. *Speech at the Chinese Communist Party's National Conference on Propaganda Work*, March 1957. Beijing: Foreign Languages Press, 1966.

———. "Speech at the Enlarged Session of the Military Affairs Committee and the External Affairs Conference," September 1959. In *Chinese Law and Government*, Winter 1968–69.

———. "Speech at the Group Leaders Forum of the Enlarged Conference of the Military Affairs Commission (excerpts)," June 1958. In *Chinese Law and Government*, Winter 1968–69.

———. "Speech at the Lushan Conference," July 1959. In *Chinese Law and Government*, Winter 1968–69.

———. "Speech at the Ninth Plenum of the Eighth CCP Central Committee," January 1961. In *Miscellany of Mao Tse-tung Thought*, vol. II. *Joint Publications Research Service*, No. 61269, February 1974.

———. "Speech at the Second Plenary Session of the Eighth Central Committee of the

Communist Party of China," November 1956. In *Selected Works of Mao Tsetung,* vol. V. Beijing: Foreign Languages Press, 1977.

———. "Speech at the Tenth Plenum of the Eighth Central Committee," September 1962. In *Chinese Law and Government,* Winter 1968–69.

———. "Speeches at the National Conference of the Communist Party of China," March 1955. In *Selected Works of Mao Tsetung,* vol. V. Beijing: Foreign Languages Press, 1977.

———. "Speeches at the Second Session of the Eighth Party Congress," May 1958. In *Miscellany of Mao Tse-tung Thought,* vol. I. *Joint Publications Research Service,* No. 61269, February 1974.

———. "Talk at Expanded Central Committee Meeting," January 1962. In *Joint Publications Research Service,* No. 52029.

———. "Talk on the Four Cleanups Movement," January 1965. In *Miscellany of Mao Tse-tung Thought,* vol. II. *Joint Publications Research Service,* No. 61269, February 1974.

———. "Talks at a Conference of Secretaries of Provincial, Municipal and Autonomous Region Party Committees," January 1957. In *Miscellany of Mao Tse-tung Thought,* vol. I. *Joint Publications Research Service,* No. 61269, February 1974. Also in *Selected Works of Mao Tsetung,* vol. V. Beijing: Foreign Languages Press, 1977.

———. "The Situation in the Summer of 1957 (excerpts)," July 1957. In *Survey of China Mainland Press—Supplement,* No. 191. Also in *Selected Works of Mao Tsetung,* vol. V. Beijing: Foreign Languages Press, 1977.

———. "Things are Changing," May 1957. In *Current Background,* No. 891. Also in *Selected Works of Mao Tsetung,* vol. V. Beijing: Foreign Languages Press, 1977.

"More on the Historical Experience of the Dictatorship of the Proletariat." *Renmin ribao* editorial, December 29, 1956. In *Communist China: Policy Documents with Analysis,* with a foreword by Robert R. Bowie and John K. Fairbank. Cambridge: Harvard University Press, 1965.

"On Khrushchov's Phoney Communism and Its Historical Lessons for the World." *Renmin ribao* and *Hongqi* joint editorial, July 14, 1963. In *China after Mao,* by A. Doak Barnett. Princeton: Princeton University Press, 1967.

"On the Historical Experience of the Dictatorship of the Proletariat." *Renmin ribao* editorial, April 5, 1956. In *Communist China 1955–1959: Policy Documents with Analysis,* with a foreword by Robert R. Bowie and John K. Fairbank. Cambridge: Harvard University Press, 1965.

"Organizational Rules of Poor and Lower Middle Peasants Associations," June 1964. In *Ssu-Ch'ing: The Socialist Education Movement of 1962–1966,* by Richard Baum and Frederick C. Teiwes. Berkeley: China Research Monographs, 1968.

"Party Directive on Rectification Campaign," April 1957. New China News Agency, Beijing, April 30, 1957. In *Survey of China Mainland Press,* No. 1523.

P'eng Te-huai (Peng Dehuai). "Letter of Opinion," July 1959. In *Current Background,* No. 851.

———. "Talks at the Meetings of the Northwest Group of the Lushan Meeting," July 1959. In *Current Background,* No. 851.

"Premier Chou En-lai's Report on the Work of the Government to the First Session of the Third National People's Congress of the People's Republic of China (Summary)," December 1964. In *Main Documents of the First Session of the Third National People's Congress of the People's Republic of China.* Beijing: Foreign Languages Press, 1965.

"Remoulding the Party's Style of Work and Improving Its State of Organization." *Renmin ribao* editorial, July 1, 1950. In *Mao's China: Party Reform Documents, 1942–44,* translated by Boyd Compton. Seattle: University of Washington Press, 1966.

"Resolution of the CCP Central Committee Concerning the Anti-Party Clique Headed by Peng Dehuai (excerpts)," August 1959. New China News Agency, Beijing, August 15, 1967. In *Survey of China Mainland Press,* No. 4004.

"Resolution on Certain Questions in the History of Our Party," April 1945. In *Selected Works of Mao Tse-tung,* vol. III. Beijing: Foreign Languages Press, 1965.

"Resolution on the Gao Gang-Rao Shushi Anti-Party Alliance," March 1955. New China News Agency, April 4, 1955. In *Current Background,* No. 324.

"Some Concrete Policy Formulations of the Central Committee of the CCP in the Rural Socialist Education Movement (draft)" (Second Ten Points), September 1963. In *Ssu-Ch'ing: The Socialist Education Movement of 1962–1966,* by Richard Baum and Frederick C. Teiwes. Berkeley: China Research Monographs, 1968.

"Some Concrete Policy Formulations of the Central Committee of the CCP in the Rural Socialist Education Movement (revised draft)" (Revised Second Ten Points), September 1964. In *Ssu-Ch'ing: The Socialist Education Movement of 1962–1966*, by Richard Baum and Frederick C. Teiwes. Berkeley: China Research Monographs, 1968.

"Some Problems Concurrently Arising in the Course of the Rural Socialist Education Movement" (Twenty-three Articles), January 1965. In *Ssu-Ch'ing: The Socialist Education Movement of 1962–1966,* by Richard Baum and Frederick C. Teiwes. Berkeley: China Research Monographs, 1968.

Teng Hsiao-p'ing (Deng Xiaoping). "Report on the Rectification Campaign," September 1957. In *Communist China 1955–1959: Policy Documents with Analysis,* with a foreword by Robert R. Bowie and John K. Fairbank. Cambridge: Harvard University Press, 1965.

———. "Report on the Revision of the Constitution of the Communist Party of China," September 1956. In *Eighth National Congress of the Communist Party of China,* vol. I. Beijing: Foreign Languages Press, 1956.

Wang Hung-wen (Wang Hongwen). "Report on the Revision of the Party Constitution," August 1973. In *Peking Review,* No. 35 and 36, 1973.

Yeh Chien-ying (Ye Jianying). "Report on the Revision of the Party Constitution," August 1977. In *Peking Review,* No. 36, 1977.

Red Guard Materials: Newspapers and Pamphlets

"A Collection of Zhou Yang's Counterrevolutionary Revisionist Speeches." Red Guard pamphlet. In *Selections from China Mainland Magazines,* Nos. 646, 648.

"A Letter from Comrade Tao Zhu to Members of Four Cleanups Work Teams." Red Guard pamphlet. In *Current Background,* No. 830.

Caimao hongqi [Finance and Trade Red Flag]. Beijing.

"Chairman Mao's Successor—Deputy Supreme Commander Lin Biao." Red Guard pamphlet, June 1969. In *Current Background,* No. 894.

"Collection of Chen Yi's Speeches." In *Selections from China Mainland Magazines,* No. 636.

"Comrade Jiang Qing on Literature and Art." Red Guard pamphlet, May 1968. In *Issues & Studies,* October 1975.

"Counterrevolutionary Revisionist Peng Zhen's Towering Crimes of Opposing the Party, Socialism and the Thought of Mao Zedong." Red Guard pamphlet, June 10, 1967. In *Selections from China Mainland Magazines,* Nos. 639–40.

Da pipan tongxun [Big Criticism Bulletin]. Guangzhou.

Deng Xiaoping fandang fan shehuizhuyi fan Mao Zedong sixiang de yanlun zhaibian [Excerpts from Deng Xiaoping's Anti-Party, Anti-Socialist, Anti-Mao Zedong's Thought Speeches]. Red Guard pamphlet, April 1967.

Dongfanghong [The East is Red]. Beijing.

Dou-pi-gai [Struggle-Criticism-Transformation].

"Down with Du Zhengxiang, Top Party Powerholder and Capitalist Roader in the Guangzhou Municipal Finance and Trade System." Red Guard pamphlet, May 15, 1967. In *Selections from China Mainland Magazines,* No. 628.

"Down with Liu Shaoqi—Life of Counterrevolutionary Liu Shaoqi." Red Guard pamphlet, May 1967. In *Current Background,* No. 834.

8.13 Hongweibing [August 13 Red Guards].

"Exposing the Towering Crimes of Counterrevolutionary Revisionist Li Qi." Red Guard pamphlet, April 1, 1967. In *Selections from China Mainland Magazines—Supplement,* No. 23.

"Facts about Liu Jianxun's Crimes." Red Guard pamphlet, March 12, 1967. In *Selections from China Mainland Magazines—Supplement,* No. 32.

Gedi tongxun [Correspondence from All Parts of the Country]. Dalian.

Geming gongren bao [Revolutionary Workers' News]. Beijing.

Gong-nong-bing [Workers-Peasants-Soldiers].

Gongren zaofan bao [Workers' Rebellion Journal].

Guangyin hongqi [Broadcasting and Publishing Red Flag]. Guangzhou.

Hongqi [Red Flag]. Beijing Red Guard newspaper.

Hongqi bao [Red Flag Paper]. Beijing.

Hongqi zhanbao [Red Flag Combat Bulletin]. Beijing.

Hongse wenyi [Red Literature and Art]. Beijing.

Hongse xuanchuanbing [Red Propaganda Soldier]. Beijing.

Hongse zaofan bao [Red Rebel Paper]. Lhasa.

Hongweibing [Red Guard]. Beijing.

Hongweibing zhanbao [Red Guard Combat Bulletin].

"Important Speeches Made by Responsible Comrades of the Center on the Question of Tao Zhu," Red Guard pamphlet, January 12, 1967. In *Survey of China Mainland Press—Supplement,* No. 232.

Jinggangshan [Jinggang Mountains]. Beijing.

Jinggangshan and *Guangdong wenyi zhanbao* [Jinggang Mountains and Guangdong Literary Combat Bulletin]. Guangzhou.

Jinjun bao [Forward March Bulletin]. Beijing.

Keji hongqi [Science and Technology Red Flag]. Beijing.

Liu Shaoqi zuixinglu [Record of Liu Shaoqi's Crimes].

"Liu Shaoqi's Reactionary Speeches." Red Guard pamphlet, April 1967. In *Selections from China Mainland Magazines—Supplement,* No. 25.

"Long Live the Invincible Thought of Mao Zedong!" Red Guard pamphlet. In *Current Background,* No. 884.

"Look at Tao Zhu's Ugly Face." Red Guard pamphlet, January 22, 1967. In *Survey of China Mainland Press,* No. 3937.

Nongcun qingnian [Rural Youth].

Peng Zhen fangeming xiuzhengzhuyi yanlun zhaibian [Excerpts from Peng Zhen's Counterrevolutionary Revisionist Speeches]. Red Guard pamphlet, May 1967.

Pi Tan zhanbao [Criticize Tan Combat Bulletin].

Pi Tao zhanbao [Criticize Tao Combat Bulletin]. Beijing.

Qianzhunbang [The Massive Cudgel]. Tianjin.

"Record of Deng Xiaoping's Reactionary Utterances." Red Guard pamphlet, April 1967. In *Survey of China Mainland Press—Supplement*, No. 208.
Sanfanfenzi Liu Shaoqi zui'oshi [History of the Crimes of Three Anti Element Liu Shaoqi]. Red Guard pamphlet, May 1967.
San-san-san zhanbao [3–3–3 Combat Bulletin]. Guangzhou.
"Selected Edition on Liu Shaoqi's Counterrevolutionary Revisionist Crimes." Red Guard pamphlet, April 1967. In *Selections from China Mainland Magazines*, Nos. 651–53.
"Tao Zhu Is the Khrushchev of Central-South China." Red Guard pamphlet, January 24, 1967. In *Current Background*, No. 824.
"The Towering Crimes of Zhu De." Red Guard poster, January 25, 1967. In *Union Research Service*, Vol. 47—No. 2.
"Thirty-three Leading Counterrevolutionary Revisionists." Red Guard pamphlet. In *Current Background*, No. 874.
"Three Trials of Pickpocket Wang Guangmei." Red Guard pamphlet. In *Current Background*, No. 848.
Tiyu zhanxian [Physical Culture Front].
Wanshan hongpian [All Mountains are Red].
Weidong. Tianjin.
Wenge fengyun [Cultural Revolution Storm].
Wenge pinglun [Cultural Revolution Comment]. Guangzhou.
Wenxue zhanbao [Literary Combat Bulletin]. Beijing.
Wenyi hongqi [Literature and Art Red Flag]. Beijing.
Xiaobing [Young Fighters]. Guangzhou.
Xiju zhanbao [Drama Combat Bulletin]. Beijing.
Xin Beida [New Beijing University].
Xin Nongda [New University of Agriculture].
Xin renwei [New People's Health].
Xinwen zhanxian [News Front]. Beijing.
Zhanbao [Battle News]. Beijing.
Zhengfa gongshe [Political and Legal Commune]. Beijing.
Ziliao zhuanji [Collected Materials].

Books, Monographs and Articles

Ahn, Byung-joon. "The Politics of Beijing Opera, 1962–1965." *Asian Survey*, December 1972.
Barnett, A. Doak. *Communist China: The Early Years, 1949–55*. New York: Frederick A. Praeger, 1964.
Barnett, A. Doak, with Ezra Vogel. *Cadres, Bureaucracy and Political Power in Communist China*. New York: Columbia University Press, 1967.
Baum, Richard. *Prelude to Revolution: Mao, the Party, and the Peasant Question, 1962–66*. New York: Columbia University Press, 1975.
Baum, Richard, and Frederick C. Teiwes, "Liu Shao-ch'i and the Cadre Question." *Asian Survey*, April 1968.
———. *Ssu-Ch'ing: The Socialist Education Movement of 1962–1966*. Berkeley: China Research Monographs, 1968.
Bernstein, Thomas P. "Problems of Village Leadership after Land Reform." *The China Quarterly*, No. 36, 1968.
Bridgham, Philip. "Factionalism in the Central Committee." In *Party Leadership and Revolutionary Power in China*, edited by John Wilson Lewis. London: Cambridge University Press, 1970.

Brzezinski, Zbigniew K. *The Permanent Purge: Politics in Soviet Totalitarianism*. Cambridge: Harvard University Press, 1956.

Chang, Parris H. *Power and Policy in China*. University Park: The Pennsylvania State University Press, 1975.

Charles, David A. "The Dismissal of Marshall P'eng Teh-huai." In *China Under Mao: Politics Takes Command,* edited by Roderick MacFarquhar. Cambridge: The M.I.T. Press, 1966.

Chen, Pi-chao. "Individual Farming after the Great Leap: As Revealed by the Lien Kiang Documents." *Asian Survey*, September 1968.

Chow Ching-wen, *Ten Years of Storm: The True Story of the Communist Regime in China*. New York: Holt, Rinehart and Winston, 1960.

Cohen, Jerome Alan. *The Criminal Process in the People's Republic of China, 1949–1963: An Introduction*. Cambridge: Harvard University Press, 1968.

Crook, Isabel and David. *Revolution In a Chinese Village: Ten Mile Inn*. London: Routledge and Kegan Paul, 1959.

Dallin, Alexander, and George W. Breslauer. *Political Terror in Communist Systems*. Stanford: Stanford University Press, 1970.

Daniels, Robert V. *Conscience of the Revolution*. Cambridge: Harvard University Press, 1960.

Dittmer, Lowell. " 'Line Struggle' in Theory and Practice: The Origins of the Cultural Revolution Reconsidered." *The China Quarterly*, No. 72, 1977.

———. *Liu Shao-ch'i and the Chinese Cultural Revolution: The Politics of Mass Criticism*. Berkeley: University of California Press, 1974.

Dorrill, W.F. *Power, Policy and Ideology in the Making of China's "Cultural Revolution."* RAND memorandum RM–5731-PR, August 1968.

Etzioni, Amitai. *The Active Society: A Theory of Societal and Political Processes*. New York: The Free Press, 1968.

Fandui difangzhuyi [Oppose Localism]. Guangzhou: Guangdong remin chubanshe, 1958.

Fokkema, D.W. *Literary Doctrine in China and Soviet Influence 1956–1960*. The Hague: Mouton & Co., 1965.

Gittings, John. *The Role of the Chinese Army*. London: Oxford University Press, 1967.

Goldman, Merle. *Literary Dissent in Communist China*. Cambridge: Harvard University Press, 1967.

———. "The Chinese Communist Party's 'Cultural Revolution' of 1962–64." In *Ideology and Politics in Contemporary China,* edited by Chalmers Johnson. Seattle: University of Washington Press, 1973.

———. "The Unique 'Blooming and Contending' of 1961–62." *The China Quarterly,* No. 37, 1969.

Goldman, René. "The Rectification Campaign at Peking University: May-June 1957." *The China Quarterly,* No. 12, 1962.

Harding, Harry, and Melvin Gurtov. *The Purge of Lo Jui-ch'ing: The Politics of Chinese Strategic Planning*. RAND Report R–548-PR, February 1971.

Harrison, James Pinckney. *The Long March to Power: A History of the Chinese Communist Party, 1921–72*. New York: Praeger, 1972.

Hinton, William. *Fanshen: A Documentary of Revolution in a Chinese Village*. New York: Vintage Books, 1966.

He Ganzhi. *Zhongguo xiandai gemingshi* [A History of the Modern Chinese Revolution]. Hong Kong: Sanlian shudian, 1958.

Hough, Jerry F. "The Brezhnev Era: The Man and the System." *Problems of Communism,* March–April 1976.

Joffe, Ellis. *Between Two Plenums: China's Intraleadership Conflict, 1959–1962*. Ann Arbor: Center for Chinese Studies, 1975.

———. *Party and Army: Professionalism and Political Control in the Chinese Officer Corps, 1949–1964*. Cambridge: Harvard East Asian Monographs, 1965.

Kau, Michael Y.M. "Introduction." In *The Lin Piao Affair*, edited by Michael Y.M. Kau. White Plains: International Arts and Sciences Press, 1975.

———. "The Organizational Line in Dispute: Editor's Introduction." *Chinese Law and Government*, Spring 1972.

Khrushchev Remembers: The Last Testament, translated and edited by Strobe Talbott. Boston: Little, Brown and Company, 1974.

Klein, Donald W. "The 'Next Generation' of Chinese Communist Leaders." In *China Under Mao: Politics Takes Command*, edited by Roderick MacFarquhar. Cambridge: The M.I.T. Press, 1966.

Lee, Hong Yung. "The Politics of Cadre Rehabilitation Since the Cultural Revolution." *Asian Survey*, September 1978.

Lee, Rensselaer W. III, "The *Hsia Fang* System: Marxism and Modernisation." *The China Quarterly*, No. 28, 1966.

Lewis, John Wilson. *Leadership in Communist China*. Ithaca: Cornell University Press, 1963.

Lieberthal, Kenneth. *A Research Guide to Central Party and Government Meetings in China 1949–1975*. White Plains: International Arts and Sciences Press, 1976.

Lifton, Robert Jay. *Thought Reform and the Psychology of Totalism: A Study of "Brainwashing" in China*. New York: W.W. Norton & Company, 1961.

Loh, Robert, with Humphrey Evans. *Escape from Red China*. New York: Coward-McCann, 1962.

MacFarquhar, Roderick. *The Origins of the Cultural Revolution, 1: Contradictions among the People 1956–1957*. New York: Columbia University Press, 1974.

Meisner, Mitch. "Dazhai: the Mass Line in Practice." *Modern China*, January 1978.

Montell, Sherwin. "The San-Fan Wu-Fan Movement in Communist China." *Papers on China*, Vol. VIII. Cambridge: Harvard Committee on International and Regional Studies, February 1954.

Moody, Peter R., Jr. *The Politics of the Eighth Central Committee of the Communist Party of China*. Hamden: Shoe String Press, 1973.

Moseley, George. *A Sino-Soviet Cultural Frontier: The Ili Kazakh Autonomous Chou*. Cambridge: Harvard East Asian Monographs, 1966.

Mu Fu-sheng. *The Wilting of the Hundred Flowers: The Chinese Intelligentsia under Mao*. New York: Frederick A. Praeger, 1962.

Munro, Donald J. "The Yang Hsien-chen Affair." *The China Quarterly*, No. 22, 1965.

Nakajima, Mineo. "The Kao Kang Affair and Sino-Soviet Relations." *Review* (Japan Institute of International Affairs), March 1977.

Nee, Victor, with Don Layman. *The Cultural Revolution at Peking University*. New York: Monthly Review Press, 1969.

Neuhauser, Charles. "The Chinese Communist Party in the 1960s: Prelude to the Cultural Revolution." *The China Quarterly*, No. 32, 1967.

Nivison, David S. "Communist Ethics and Chinese Tradition." *Journal of Asian Studies*, November 1956.

Oksenberg, Michel C. "Policy Making Under Mao, 1949–68: An Overview." In *China: Management of a Revolutionary Society*, edited by John M.H. Lindbeck. Seattle: University of Washington Press, 1971.

Oliver, Adam. "Rectification of Mainland China Intellectuals, 1964–1965." *Asian Survey*, October 1965.

Pusey, James R. *Wu Han: Attacking the Present Through the Past*. Cambridge: Harvard East Asian Monographs, 1969.

Rádvanyi, János. *Hungary and the Superpowers: The 1956 Revolution and Realpolitik.* Stanford: Hoover Institution Press, 1972.

Rice, Edward E. *Mao's Way*. Berkeley: University of California Press, 1972.

Robinson, Thomas W. "Chou En-lai and the Cultural Revolution." In *The Cultural Revolution in China,* edited by Thomas W. Robinson. Berkeley: University of California Press, 1971.

Rue, John E. *Mao Tse-tung in Opposition 1927–1935*. Stanford: Stanford University Press, 1966.

Schein, Edgar H., with Inge Schneier and Curtis H. Barker. *Coercive Persuasion: A Socio-psychological Analysis of the "Brainwashing" of American Civilian Prisoners.* New York: W.W. Norton & Company, 1961.

Schram, Stuart R. "Introduction: The Cultural Revolution in Historical Perspective." In *Authority, Participation and Cultural Change in China,* edited by Stuart R. Schram. Cambridge: Cambridge University Press, 1973.

———. "The Party in Chinese Communist Ideology." *The China Quarterly,* No. 38, 1969.

Schurmann, Franz. *Ideology and Organization in Communist China*. Berkeley: University of California Press, 1966.

Schwartz, Benjamin I. *Communism and China: Ideology in Flux*. Cambridge: Harvard University Press, 1968.

Selden, Mark. *The Yenan Way in Revolutionary China.* Cambridge: Harvard University Press, 1971.

Simmonds, J.D. *China: The Evolution of a Revolution, 1959–66*. Canberra: A.N.U. Department of International Relations, 1968.

———. "P'eng Teh-huai: A Chronological Re-examination." *The China Quarterly,* No. 37, 1969.

Simon, Joseph. "Ferment among the Intellectuals." *Problems of Communism,* September–October 1964.

Skinner, G. William, and Edwin A. Winckler. "Compliance Succession in Rural Communist China: A Cyclical Theory." In *Complex Organizations, A Sociological Reader,* edited by Amitai Etzioni. 2nd edition, New York: Holt, Rinehart and Winston, 1969.

Snow, Edgar. *The Long Revolution*. New York: Random House, 1971.

Solomon, Richard H. *Mao's Revolution and the Chinese Political Culture*. Berkeley: University of California Press, 1971.

———. "On Activism and Activists: Maoist Conceptions of Motivation and Political Role Linking State to Society." *The China Quarterly,* No. 39, 1969.

Teiwes, Frederick C. "A Case Study of Rectification: The 1958 *Cheng-feng Cheng-kai* Campaign in Hui-tung County." *Papers on Far Eastern History,* March 1973.

———. "Chinese Politics 1949–1965: A Changing Mao." *Current Scene,* Parts I and II, January and February 1974.

———. *Elite Discipline in China: Coercive and Persuasive Approaches to Rectification, 1950–1953*. Canberra: Contemporary China Papers, 1978.

———. *Provincial Party Personnel in Mainland China 1956–1966*. New York: Occasional Papers of the East Asian Institute, Columbia University, 1967.

———. "The Evolution of Leadership Purges in Communist China." *The China Quarterly,* No. 41, 1970.

Terry, Gregory J. "The 'Debate' on Military Affairs in China: 1957–1959." *Asian Survey,* August 1976.

Townsend, James R. *Political Participation In Communist China.* Berkeley: University of California Press, 1969.

———. *The Revolutionization of Chinese Youth: A Study of "Chung-kuo Ch'ing-nien."* Berkeley: Center for Chinese Studies, 1967.

Uhalley, Stephen Jr. "The Controversy over Li Hsiu-ch'eng; An Ill Timed Centenary." *Journal of Asian Studies*, February 1966.

Vogel, Ezra F. *Canton under Communism: Programs and Policies in a Provincial Capital, 1949–1968*. Cambridge: Harvard University Press, 1969.

———. "From Revolutionary to Semi-Bureaucrat: The 'Regularisation' of Cadres." *The China Quarterly*, No. 29, 1967.

Whyte, Martin King. *Small Groups and Political Rituals in China*. Berkeley: University of California Press, 1974.

Witke, Roxane. *Comrade Chiang Ch'ing*. Boston: Little, Brown and Co., 1977.

Young, Graham, and Dennis Woodward. "Chinese Conceptions of the Nature of Class Struggle within the Socialist Transition." In *Socialism and the New Class: Towards the Analysis of Structural Inequality Within Socialist Societies*, edited by Marian Sawer. Adelaide: APSA Monographs, 1978.

Yu, Frederick. "With Banners and Drums: The Mass Campaign in China's Drive for Development." *Current Scene*, May 1, 1966.

Zagoria, Donald S. *The Sino-Soviet Conflict 1956–1961*. New York: Atheneum, 1969.

Zhao Han. *Tantan Zhongguo gongchandang de zhengfeng yundong* [Talks on the CCP's Rectification Campaigns]. Beijing: Zhongguo qingnian chubanshe, 1957.

Zhonggong zhongyang zuzhibu yanjiushi. *Dang de zuzhi gongzuo wenda* [Questions and Answers on Party Organization Work]. Beijing: Renmin chubanshe, 1965.

Unpublished and Limited Circulation Studies

Ahn, Byung-joon. "Ideology, Policy and Power in Chinese Politics and the Evolution of the Cultural Revolution, 1959–1965." Ph.D. dissertation, Columbia University, 1972.

Alitto, Guy. "Thought Reform in Communist China: The Case of Chou Ku-ch'eng." M.A. thesis, University of Chicago, 1966.

Cocks, Paul M. "The Historical and Institutional Role of the Party Control Committee in the CCP." Unpublished paper available at the East Asian Research Center, Harvard University, 1966.

Grow, Roy Franklin. "The Politics of Industrial Development in China and the Soviet Union: Organizational Strategy as a Linkage between National and World Politics." Ph.D. dissertation, University of Michigan, 1973.

Harding, Harry Jr. "The Organizational Issue in Chinese Politics, 1959–72." Ph.D. dissertation, Stanford University 1974.

Harper, Paul F. "Political Roles of Trade Unions in Communist China." Ph.D. dissertation, Cornell University, 1969.

Hinton, Harold C. *The "Unprincipled Dispute" Within the Chinese Communist Top Leadership*. U.S. Information Agency IRI Intelligence Summary, No. LS–98–55, July 1955.

Oksenberg, Michel C. "Policy Formulation in Communist China: The Case of the Mass Irrigation Campaign, 1957–58." Ph.D. dissertation, Columbia University, 1969.

Perkin, Linda. "The Chinese Communist Party: The Lushan Meeting and Plenum, July-August 1959." M.A. thesis, Columbia University, 1971.

Ravenholt, Albert. "Feud Among the Red Mandarins." *American Universities Field Staff Reports Service*, East Asia Series, Vol. XI, No. 2, 1964.

Tanaka Kyoko. "Mass Mobilisation: The Chinese Communist Party and the Peasants." Ph.D. dissertation, The Australian National University, 1972.

Teiwes, Frederick C. "Kao Kang's 'Independent Kingdom' in the Northeast: A Re-evaluation." Paper presented at the 1972 annual meeting of the Association for Asian Studies.

———. "Rectification Campaigns and Purges in Communist China, 1950–61." Ph.D. dissertation, Columbia University, 1971.

Young, Graham. "Conceptions of Party Leadership in China: The Cultural Revolution and Party Building 1968–1971." Ph.D. dissertation, Flinders University of South Australia, 1978.

Biographical and Personnel Data

Biographical Dictionary of Chinese Communism 1921–1965, by Donald W. Klein and Anne B. Clark. 2 vols., Cambridge: Harvard University Press, 1971.

Biographical Files of Donald W. Klein.

Biographical Files of U.S. Consulate General, Hong Kong.

Directory of Party and Government Officials in Communist China. Washington: U.S. Department of State, 1953.

Gendai Chūgoku Jimmei Jiten [Modern China Biographic Dictionary]. Tokyo: Gaimushō, 1966.

Who's Who in Communist China. Hong Kong: Union Research Institute, 1966.

Post-1978 Sources

i) Extensively Consulted Party History Journals

CCP Research Newsletter. Colorado Springs: Chinese Communism Research Group, 1988–90.

Dang de wenxian [The Party's Documents]. Beijing: Zhongyang wenxian chubanshe, 1988–91.

Dangshi tongxun [Party History Newsletter]. Beijing: Zhongyang dangshi yanjiushi, 1983–87.

Dangshi wenhui [Party History Collection]. Taiyuan: Zhonggong Shanxi shengwei dangshi yanjiushi, 1985–91.

Dangshi yanjiu [Research on Party History]. Beijing: Zhonggong zhongyang dangxiao chubanshe, 1980–87.

Renwu [Personalities]. Beijing: Renmin chubanshe, 1980–89.

Wenxian he yanjiu [Documents and Research]. Beijing: Renmin chubanshe, 1982–87.

Zhonggong dangshi yanjiu [Research on CCP History]. Beijing: Zhonggong dangshi chubanshe, 1988–91.

Zhonggong dangshi ziliao [CCP History Materials]. Beijing: Zhonggong dangshi ziliao chubanshe, 1982–89.

ii) Chronologies, Documents and Documentary Collections

Chen Yun wenxuan (1956–85 nian) [Selected Works of Chen Yun, 1956–1985]. Beijing: Renmin chubanshe, 1986.

Guanyu jianguo yilai dang de ruogan lishi wenti de jueyi zhuyiben (xiuding) [Revised Notes on the Resolution on Certain Questions in the History of Our Party since the Founding of the People's Republic of China], compiled by Zhonggong zhongyang wenxian yanjiush. Beijing: Renmin chubanshe, 1985.

"Guiding Principles for Inner Party Life," adopted at the Fifth Plenum of the Eleventh Central Committee, February 1980. In *Beijing Review*, No. 14 (1980), pp. 11–20.

Liao Kai-lung (Liao Gailong). "Historical Experiences and Our Road of Development,"

Parts I and II. In *Issues & Studies,* October and November 1981.
"Mao, Deng Zihui, and the Politics of Agricultural Cooperativization," edited by Frederick C. Teiwes and Warren Sun. *Chinese Law and Government,* Nos. 3–4, 1993.
Memoirs of a Chinese Marshal—The autobiographical notes of Peng Dehuai (1898–1974), translated by Zheng Longpu. Beijing: Foreign Languages Press, 1984.
"Resolution on Certain Questions in the History of Our Party Since the Founding of the People's Republic of China." In *Beijing Review,* No. 27, 1981.
Selected Works of Deng Xiaoping (1975–1982). Beijing: Foreign Languages Press, 1984.
The Rise to Power of the Chinese Communist Party: Documents and Analysis, edited by Tony Saich, with a contribution by Benjamin Yang. Armonk: M.E. Sharpe, forthcoming.
The Secret Speeches of Chairman Mao: From the Hundred Flowers to the Great Leap Forward, edited by Roderick MacFarquhar, Timothy Cheek, and Eugene Wu. Cambridge: The Council for East Asian Studies, Harvard University, 1989.
Xin Zhongguo biannianshi (1949–1989) [Chronicle of New China, 1949–1989], edited by Liao Gailong. Beijing: Renmin chubanshe, 1989.
Zhang Wentian Lushan huiyi fayan [Zhang Wentian's Lushan Speeches], edited by Zhang Wentian xuanji zhuanjizu. Beijing: Beijing chubanshe, 1990.
Zhongguo Gongchandang lishi dashiji (1919.5–1987.12) [Chronology of CCP History, May 1919-December 1987], compiled by Zhonggong zhongyang dangshi yanjiushi. Beijing: Renmin chubanshe, 1989.
Zhongguo Gongchandang zhizheng sishinian 1949–1989 [The CCP's Forty Years in Power 1949–1989], edited by Ma Qibin, et al. Beijing: Zhonggong dangshi ziliao chubanshe, 1990.

iii) Books, Monographs, Articles, and Unpublished Manuscripts

Bachman, David M. *Chen Yun and the Chinese Political System.* Berkeley: China Research Monographs, 1985.
Bo Yibo. *Ruogan zhongda juece yu shijian de huigu* [Reflections on Certain Major Policy Decisions and Events]. Beijing: Zhonggong zhongyang dangxiao chubanshe, 1991.
Cheek, Timothy. *Broken Jade: Deng Tuo and Intellectual Service in Mao's China.* Unpublished draft manuscript, 1991.
———. "The Fading of Wild Lillies: Weng Shiwei and Mao Zedong's 'Yan'an Talks' in the First CPC Rectification Movement." *The Australian Journal of Chinese Affairs,* No. 11, 1984.
———. "Textually Speaking: An Assortment of Newly Available Mao Texts." In *The Secret Speeches of Chairman Mao: From the Hundred Flowers to the Great Leap Forward,* edited by Roderick MacFarquhar, Timothy Cheek, and Eugene Wu. Cambridge: The Council for East Asian Studies, Harvard University, 1989.
Chen Mingxian, *et al.,* eds. *Xin Zhongguo sishinian yanjiu* [Research on New China's 40 years]. Beijing: Beijing Ligong Daxue chubanshe, 1989.
Cong Jin. *1949–1989 nian de Zhongguo: Quzhe fazhan de suiyue* [China 1949–1989: The Years of Circuitous Development]. Vol. 2, Henan: Henan renmin chubanshe, 1989.
Dickson, Bruce J. "Conflict and Non-Compliance in Chinese Politics: Party Rectification, 1983–87." *Pacific Affairs,* Summer 1990.
Dittmer, Lowell. "Rectification and Purge in Chinese Politics." *Pacific Affairs,* Fall 1980.
Domes, Jürgen. *Peng Te-huai: The Man and the Image.* London: C. Hurst & Company, 1985.
Dong Bian, *et al. Mao Zedong he tade mishu Tian Jiaying* [Mao Zedong and His Secretary Tian Jiaying]. Beijing: Zhongyang wenxian chubanshe, 1990.

Goldman, Merle. "Mao's Obsession with the Political Role of Literature and the Intellectuals." In *The Secret Speeches of Chairman Mao: From the Hundred Flowers to the Great Leap Forward,* edited by Roderick MacFarquhar, Timothy Cheek, and Eugene Wu. Cambridge: The Council for East Asian Studies, Harvard University, 1989.

Guo Simin. *Wo yanzhong de Mao Zedong* [Perceptions of Mao Zedong]. Shijiazhuang: Hebei renmin chubanshe, 1990.

Harding, Harry. *Organizing China: The Problem of Bureaucracy 1949–1976.* Stanford: Stanford University Press, 1981.

Holm, David, "The Strange Case of Liu Zhidan." *The Australian Journal of Chinese Affairs,* No. 27, 1992.

Huang Yao, *et al. Luo Ronghuan hou shiwunian* [Luo Ronghuan's Last 15 Years], Beijing: Renmin chubanshe, 1987.

Huiyi Zhang Wentian [Remember Zhang Wentian]. Changsha: Hunan renmin chubanshe, 1985.

Lampton, David M., with the assistance of Yeung Sai-cheung. *Paths to Power: Elite Mobility in Contemporary China.* Ann Arbor: Center for Chinese Studies, The University of Michigan, 1986.

Lee, Hong Yung. *From Revolutionary Cadres to Party Technocrats in Socialist China.* Berkeley: University of California Press, 1991.

Li Rui. *Huainian nianpian* [Twenty Articles in Remembrance]. Beijing: Sanlian chubanshe, 1987.

———. *Lushan huiyi shilu* [True Record of the Lushan Meetings]. Beijing: Chunqiu chubanshe, 1989.

Lieberthal, Kenneth, and Michel Oksenberg. *Policy Making in China: Leaders, Structures and Processes.* Princeton: University Press, 1988.

Lin Yunhui, Fan Shouxin and Zhang Gong. *1949–1989 nian de Zhongguo: Kaige xingjin de shiqi* [China 1949–1989: The Period of Triumphant Advance]. Vol. 1, Henan: Henan renmin chubanshe, 1989.

Liu Shaoqi yanjiu lunwenji [Collected Research Papers on Liu Shaoqi]. Beijing: Zhongyang wenxian chubanshe, 1989.

MacFarquhar, Roderick, *The Origins of the Cultural Revolution, 2: The Great Leap Forward 1958–60.* New York: Columbia University Press, 1983.

———. "The Secret Speeches of Chairman Mao." In *The Secret Speeches of Chairman Mao: From the Hundred Flowers to the Great Leap Forward.* Edited by Roderick MacFarquhar, Timothy Cheek, and Eugene Wu. Cambridge: The Council for East Asian Studies, Harvard University, 1989.

Naughton, Barry. "The Third Front: Defence Industrialization in the Chinese Interior." *The China Quarterly,* No. 115, 1988.

Peng Cheng and Wang Fang. *Lushan 1959.* Beijing: Jiefangjun chubanshe, 1988.

Schoenhals, Michael. "Edited Records: Comparing Two Versions of Deng Xiaoping's '7000 Cadres Conference Speech.' " *CCP Research Newsletter,* No. 1, 1988.

———. "Original Contradictions—On the Text of Mao Zedong's 'On the Correct Handling of Contradictions among the People.' " *The Australian Journal of Chinese Affairs,* No. 16, 1986.

———. "Unofficial and Official Histories of the Cultural Revolution—A Review Article." *The Journal of Asian Studies,* August 1989.

Schoenhals, Michael, and Brewer S. Stone, "More Edited Records: Liu Shaoqi on Peng Dehuai at the 7000 Cadres Conference." *CCP Research Newsletter,* No. 5, 1990.

Schram, Stuart R. "Party Leader or True Ruler? Foundations and Significance of Mao Zedong's Personal Power." In *Foundations and Limits of State Power in China,* edited by Stuart R. Schram. Hong Kong: The Chinese University Press, 1987.

Schwartz, Benjamin I. "Thoughts on the Late Mao—Between Total Redemption and Utter Frustration." In *The Secret Speeches of Chairman Mao: From the Hundred Flowers to the Great Leap Forward,* edited by Roderick MacFarquhar, Timothy Cheek, and Eugene Wu. Cambridge: The Council for East Asian Studies, Harvard University, 1989.

Seybolt, Peter J. "Terror and Conformity: Counterespionage Campaigns, Rectification, and Mass Movements, 1942–43." *Modern China,*January 1986.

Sullivan, Lawrence R. "Leadership and Authority in the Chinese Communist Party: Perspectives from the 1950s." *Pacific Affairs,* Winter 1986–87.

———. "The Analysis of 'Despotism' in the CCP: 1978–1872." *Asian Survey,* July 1987.

Tan Zhongji, *et al.,* eds. *Shinianhou de pingshuo—"Wenhua dageming" shilunji* [Commentary 10 Years After—Collected History Essays on the "Cultural Revolution"]. Beijing: Zhonggong dangshi ziliao chubanshe, 1987.

Teiwes, Frederick C. *Leadership, Legitimacy, and Conflict in China: From a Charismatic Mao to the Politics of Succession.* Armonk: M.E. Sharpe, 1984.

———. "Mao and His Lieutenants." *The Australian Journal of Chinese Affairs,* No. 19–20, 1988.

———. "Peng Dehuai and Mao Zedong." *The Australian Journal of Chinese Affairs,* No. 16, 1986.

———. *Politics at Mao's Court: Gao Gang and Party Factionalism in the Early 1950s.* Armonk: M.E. Sharpe, 1990.

Teiwes, Frederick C., with Warren Sun. "From a Leninist to a Charismatic Party: The CCP's Changing Leadership, 1937–1945." In *New Perspectives on the Chinese Communist Revolution,* edited by Tony Saich and Hans van de Ven. Armonk: M.E. Sharpe, forthcoming.

Tian Guoliang, *et al.,* eds. *Hu Yaobang zhuan* [Biography of Hu Yaobang]. Beijing: Zhonggong dangshi ziliao chubanshe, 1989.

Wang Nianyi. *1949–1989 nian de Zhongguo: Da dongluan de niandai* [China 1949–1989: The Years of Great Turmoil]. Vol. 3, Henan: Henan renmin chubanshe, 1988.

Weigelin-Schwiedrzik, Susanne. "Party Historiography in the People's Republic of China." *The Australian Journal of Chinese Affairs,* No. 17, 1987.

Women de Zhou Zongli [Our Premier Zhou]. Beijing: Zhongyang wenxian chubanshe, 1990.

Zhang Peisen, ed. *Zhang Wentian yanjiu wenji* [Collected Research on Zhang Wentian], Beijing: Zhonggong dangshi ziliao chubanshe, 1990.

Zhong Kan. *Kang Sheng pingzhuan* [Critical biography of Kang Sheng]. Beijing: Hongqi chubanshe, 1982.

Zhou Enlai yanjiu xueshu taolun huiyi wenji [Collection of Essays from the Zhou Enlai Academic Research Conference]. Beijing: Zhongyang wenxian chubanshe, 1988.

Zhu Chengjia, ed. *Zhonggong dangshi yanjiu lunwenxuan* [Collected Essays on CCP History Research]. Vol. 2, Changsha: Hunan renmin chubanshe, 1984.

Ziyou beiwanglu—Su Xiaokang quanjing baogao wenxueji [A Memorandum on Freedom —A Collection of Su Xiaokang's Panoramic Reportage]. Beijing: Zhongguo shehui kexueyuan chubanshe, 1988.

iv) Biographical Data

Zhonggong dangshi renwu zhuan [Biographies of Personalities in CCP History], edited by Hu Hua. Vols. 1–44, Xi'an: Shaanxi renmin chubanshe, 1980–89.

Index

A graduate of Amherst College, Frederick C. Teiwes received his Ph.D. in political science from Columbia University. From 1969 to 1976 he first taught at Cornell University and then held a research appointment at The Australian National University. Since 1976 he has been on the faculty of the University of Sydney where he currently holds a Personal Chair in Chinese Politics as well as a five-year research appointment as an Australian Senior Research Fellow.

Since the publication of the first edition of *Politics and Purges in China* in 1979, Professor Teiwes has been widely recognized as a leading analyst of Chinese elite politics. His subsequent major works include *Leadership, Legitimacy, and Conflict in China* (1984), and *Politics at Mao's Court* (1990). He is currently working on a number of projects concerning CCP elite politics, most notably a reinterpretation of the rise and fall of Lin Biao (with Warren Sun).

#0148 - 040716 - C0 - 229/152/35 - PB - 9781563242274